Badiou and Politics

POST-CONTEMPORARY INTERVENTIONS
Series Editors: Stanley Fish and Fredric Jameson

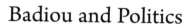

Badiou and Politics

BRUNO BOSTEELS

Duke University Press DURHAM & LONDON 2011

© 2011 Duke University Press
All rights reserved
Printed in the United States of America on acid-free paper ∞
Designed by Jennifer Hill
Typeset in Arno Pro by Keystone Typesetting, Inc.

Library of Congress Cataloging-in-Publication Data
appear on the last printed page of this book.

for Simone, Lucas, and Manu

CONTENTS

This book has been in the making for a long time. "Too long," my friends and family say, while others are perhaps whispering quietly to themselves: "Not long enough." At least some of the circumstances behind the book's conception and eventual production, however, exceed the usual domain of personal anecdotes, and they might actually shed some light on the nature and goals of the project itself. For this reason perhaps I may be allowed to recall those circumstances in the prefatory remarks that follow. Besides, do we not all secretly turn to a book's preface and acknowledgments—or, in their absence, to the endnotes—in the perverse hope of catching a glimpse of the anecdotal and the autobiographical as well?

Two encounters, one personal and the other bookish in nature, could be said to have given birth to the idea for this work. My first meeting with Alain Badiou happened in the summer of 1998, in his country house in Saint Gaudens, just south of Toulouse. For several months prior to this meeting we had been writing back and forth in preparation for Badiou's visit to Harvard, his first solo trip to the United States, which was sched- uled to take place in the winter of that same year. Unable to meet up with me in Madrid, as he had originally proposed, Badiou enthusiastically ap- proved of the idea, suggested by my partner, Simone, that the two of us cross the Pyrenees for a short visit. The parking lot in front of the small railway station of Saint Gaudens would be the place for our rendezvous.

It was hard to understand how this tall man could fit in the small Volkswagen Golf that was waiting for us at the station when we arrived after, I should add, considerable delay. Badiou, pretending to show more surprise than genuine irritation at his latecomers, drove out in front of us and led the way as we went winding down the small country road to his home, where we would spend the rest of the day talking, eating, drinking, and laughing. With Françoise we made fun of the ponderous tone that Badiou adopted when it came to defining a series of possible titles for his talks at Harvard: "Being and Event," "Being and *the* Event," and so on. After all, Badiou retorted by way of justification, is this not implicitly the title for all works of philosophy? Once the organizational matters were taken care of and put aside, our conversation drifted to more entertaining topics, such as the latest Jackie Chan movie and even the awful *Armageddon*, which had just been released. This gave Simone pause, much to the delight of Badiou, who saw an occasion to take revenge for our chuckling at the pedantry of his titles, to mock the elitism of my taste in films and showcase my complete ignorance of popular culture. Later, when the three of us retreated into the smoke-filled backroom, the discussion turned once more academic. Badiou, showing a great sense of curiosity that I would come to appreciate many times over in subsequent years as he would rummage through my personal library in Manhattan or Ithaca, asked us about the exact meaning of the field of "cultural studies" in the United States, about the place of "French theory," about our own ongoing scholarly projects, and, of course, about the reception of his work. This reception, it must be said, at the time was still nearly inexistent. Thus, when, back in the United States I would ask people if they had read Badiou, quite a few would answer with a mixture of indifference and reassurance: "Oh sure, Bourdieu"!

In fact, even though Badiou's major work, *Being and Event*, had been published in French a decade earlier, by the mid to late 1990s few people outside of his home country were familiar with the portentous ambition of its main theses—to give philosophy a new beginning by grounding ontology in mathematics over and against Heidegger's poeticizing hermeneutics —while still fewer bothered to return to the intensely militant political writings from the 1970s and early 1980s, which culminate in the famously obscure, Lacanian-style seminar called *Theory of the Subject*. Even in France it would not be until a major conference in Bordeaux, held in the fall of 1999, that Badiou was to receive official and widespread recognition from fellow philosophers, mathematicians, and literary critics—after having been ostracized for many years not only by his obvious ideological adversaries but by many of his peers as well, in large part because of the strident and polemical style of his Maoism.

There were, of course, a few isolated exceptions: the Collège International de Philosophie devoted a workshop to *Being and Event*, which included brief responses from the likes of Jean-Luc Nancy and Jacques Rancière; and the book also received a brief commentary, which ended on a harshly critical note, in Gilles Deleuze's and Félix Guattari's *What Is Philosophy?* In Saint Gaudens I even found out that a major study of all of Badiou's philosophy was already in the making. Indeed, shortly after our arrival at his country house, Badiou had pulled out a massive, 250-page, fully bound manuscript, then still titled "Generic Sovereignty," which he proceeded proudly to put on the table with the recommendation that I get in touch with the author, Peter Hallward—whom I would in fact have the pleasure of meeting and befriending a year later, at the conference in Bordeaux. By that time, though, I had already begun to notice a strange trend in the reception and interpretation of Badiou's work, a trend that would only become stronger over the years and that finds its sharpest and most eloquent formulation not only in a polished and much-revised version of Hallward's manuscript, published in 2003 as *Badiou: A Subject to Truth*, but also in the chapter on Badiou's reading of Saint Paul in Slavoj Žižek's *The Ticklish Subject: The Absent Centre of Political Ontology*, which in 1999 offered one of the first widely accessible—though in my eyes also somewhat problematic—accounts of Badiou's philosophy.

Both Hallward and Žižek, each in his own inimitable style, proceed to follow up their praise with a strong critique, to the effect that Badiou's philosophy would fall in the traps of a dogmatic, sovereign, or absolutist understanding of the event and of militant, not to say blind, fidelity to it, without giving due consideration either to the question of relationality and historical mediation (Hallward) or to that of negativity, repetition, and the death drive (Žižek). What these authors could not have foreseen, however, is the extraordinary echo that their criticisms, often without even as much as a hint of the praise that originally framed them, would find in the English-speaking world. Indeed, it is no exaggeration to say that this reading of the event as a dogmatic or downright mystical notion, diametrically opposed to the banal normality of the order of being, has now become tiresomely and overbearingly dominant in the reception of Badiou's philosophy. Above all, a similar reading was adopted overnight by a growing army of opponents, akin to those whispering voices mentioned earlier, many of whom undoubtedly feel relieved at the prospect of not actually having to read any of Badiou's books, even though they cannot resist the opportunity to lambast their author either.

My own trajectory is quite different, in fact almost the opposite. This is no doubt due to the second, strictly bookish encounter, which chronologically came long before I personally met Badiou. Indeed, it was around 1994, when I was finishing my PhD, that I first stumbled upon the French original of Badiou's *Manifesto for Philosophy* in a bookstore in Brussels. Leafing through the book, I was immediately struck by the possibility of a convergence between Badiou's proposal of a "Platonism of the multiple" centered on the concept of the "generic," which is the title of the *Manifesto*'s last section, and my work as a Latin Americanist who was writing a dissertation on Jorge Luis Borges, puzzled as I had been for some time by a remarkable footnote in "History of Eternity" in which Borges all of a sudden asserts that he does "not wish to take leave of Platonism, which may seem glacial, without affirming that the generic may, sometimes, be more intense than the particular." However, from this shared interest in Plato and the generic, not to mention the strange question of immortality (another enigmatic one-liner from Borges, after all, says that "life is too impoverished not to be immortal"), my attention was soon drawn not to the magnum opus *Being and Event*, for which the brief and didactic accompanying piece of *Manifesto for Philosophy* should have prepared me, but rather to Badiou's Maoist writings from the mid-1970s, most notably *Theory of Contradiction* and *Of Ideology*, both of which I put to work in the rather unorthodox construction of a Borgesian "theory of ideology," before deciding to take on *Theory of the Subject*.

More than anything else, it was the experience of making my way through this last book, an experience that was as exhilarating as it was labor intensive, that left me dumbfounded and as though struck by lightning. For many years my theoretical and philosophical interests had hovered around figures whose work offered some kind of alternative to the dominant tradition of Heidegger and Derrida, without being blind to the conceptual accomplishments in the deconstruction of metaphysics. Jean-François Lyotard and Gianni Vattimo, back in my days as an undergraduate at the University of Leuven, had been important guides along this tenuous path, and after my arrival in the States I continued to read pretty much everything they had ever published, together with a great deal of Foucault, Nietzsche, and American thinkers from William James to Richard Rorty to Judith Butler. But now along came a philosopher who, in *Theory of the Subject*, mapped out what I perceived to be a complete overview of the contemporary theoretical and philosophical conjuncture, from Althusser to Deleuze to Lacan, and, at first only implicitly but later also explicitly in *Being and Event* and *Ethics*, from Heidegger to Derrida to Levinas. The fact that this map or, to use the language of *Theory of the Subject*, this topology included a long section devoted to Mallarmé's poetry and another to Greek tragedy between Aeschylus and Sophocles only heightened my interest as a literary critic, just as Badiou's Maoism dovetailed with—or revealed for the first time—a whole Maoist undercurrent that previously had gone unnoticed in many of the most original political and literary experiments that I was studying at the time in Latin America, most notably in the writings of the Argentine novelist and literary critic Ricardo Piglia, who, it turned out, in the early 1970s had been a fervent Maoist and one of the first to publish Badiou (specifically his 1966 text "The Autonomy of the Aesthetic Process") in Spanish.

The Argentine connection, incidentally, did not end there. Already in the summer of 1996, as I was browsing through the section of current periodicals in Widener Library at Harvard, near the Italian journal *aut aut*, which I was actually consulting in connection with "weak thinking" or *pensiero debole*, I happened to come across another journal, *Acontecimiento: Revista para pensar la política*, which from the title alone sounded as though there might be a link with Badiou's theory of the "event" (*événement* in French, *acontecimiento* in Spanish). After picking up a current issue, I found that this journal, printed in a small in-house venture that eventually would culminate in a political collective under the name "Grupo Acontecimiento," for more than two years had been investigating the politico-philosophical situation from an angle deeply marked by Badiou's work, including sharp analyses of the significance of the Zapatista uprising in 1994 in Chiapas as well as of the originality of organizations such as the Mothers of the Plaza de Mayo in Argentina. What is more, later that same summer, or winter in Buenos Aires, in a lengthy discussion with the journal's editor, Raúl Cerdeiras, I was also able to confirm several of the working hypotheses that would eventually form the basis for the present book.

First, a historical and geographical hypothesis, namely, that Badiou's work, which was barely beginning to be "discovered" by English-language readers, had been a familiar reference for many radical intellectuals and militants in Latin America and Spain—from the Basque country, where *Theory of Contradiction* was commonly used in the 1970s, all the way to

Mexico and the Southern Cone, where Badiou's review of Althusser's canonical work, together with Althusser's own "Historical Materialism and
Dialectical Materialism," had been widely distributed as part of the popular
"Pasado y presente" series of Marxist divulgation edited by the Argentine
exile José Aricó. This familiarity, moreover, was not limited to Badiou's
early works: *Being and Event*, for example, was translated into Spanish, in a
giant collective endeavor spearheaded by Cerdeiras, long before it would
appear in English; and several talks, seminars, and even whole books have
appeared in Spanish, Galician, and Brazilian Portuguese that are as yet
inexistent in any other language, including Badiou's native French.

Second, the political hypothesis that the formative experience behind
the underlying continuity between Badiou's Althusserian work and the
grand synthesis of *Being and Event* is to be found in what I would call a
generic Maoism. To use the words of Cerdeiras's "Political Manifesto" that
would reappear as the opening statement in the first dozen or so issues of
Acontecimiento: "Mao Zedong constitutes the last practical attempt that
fails to break with Marxism-Leninism. Its major guideline was to make the
revolution after the seizure of power. It was pointless. Marxism-Leninism
was exhausted." This leaves open the task of formulating the principles of a
post-Maoism, which would effectively break with the so-called metaphysical, class-based presuppositions behind Marxism-Leninism-Maoism.

Third, and finally, the more strictly theoretical, not to say merely exegetical, hypothesis that *Being and Event* or for that matter *Logics of Worlds*,
which at the time of my conversation with Cerdeiras was already in the
making, cannot be understood without also considering *Theory of the
Subject*. Indeed, for Cerdeiras, too, this earlier book's redefinition of the
materialist dialectic, as a way of drawing up a systematic balance sheet of
the militant accomplishments and dead ends of the 1970s, had been what
originally brought him to establish contact with Badiou and start a long
collaboration that continues until this day.

Several of the personal meetings that motivated me to begin writing the
present book are thus still a distant result of that singular encounter, more
than a decade ago, with *Theory of the Subject*. Indeed, no sooner did I put
down that book than I wrote a personal letter to Badiou, telling him about
the impact his work had had on my way of understanding the current
theoretical conjuncture, proposing to do some translation of his writings
into English, and inquiring about the possibility of his visiting Harvard. It

was in answer to this letter that Badiou sent me a handwritten note of appreciation, the beginning of a long correspondence, in which he also explained that while *Manifesto for Philosophy* had already been translated by Norman Madarasz, and Louise Burchill was preparing *Deleuze: The Clamor of Being*, his short book on *Ethics* seemed to him to be the next logical candidate for translation into English. As for a visit to the States, this was something that we could discuss further down the line, as indeed we did, on that long summer day in Saint Gaudens.

In the meantime, by the end of 1999 Slavoj Žižek came to Harvard to participate in a public debate with Cornell West on the subject, among other topics, of Saint Paul. To an audience so packed that firefighters came in and threatened to cancel the lecture, Žižek spoke for almost an hour about the nature of the Pauline act. Not once was Alain Badiou's name mentioned. And yet I could not help thinking that, despite numerous insuperable differences to which we will have occasion to return below, everything that was said that evening about the "act" was, to say the least, strongly reminiscent of the way in which Badiou develops the notion of the "event" in his own book on Saint Paul. When I asked Žižek about this strange confluence during the Q & A session, he quickly added that, of course, he implicitly had been referring to Badiou's book all along and that he probably should have prefaced his long intervention in the debate with Cornell West by saying that he was going to pay homage to Badiou, whom he promptly labeled the greatest philosopher of our time. Then, in private, we went on to talk about the urgent need for a translation of Badiou's *Ethics*, which Žižek promised to endorse with the already considerable weight of his personal name and ever-growing fame.

Žižek certainly kept his promise and two years later did in fact publish Peter Hallward's excellent translation, with a long introduction, of *Ethics: An Essay on the Understanding of Evil* in his "Wo es war" series for Verso. Badiou, however, for health reasons, had to cancel his planned 1999 visit to the States, but he made up for this last-minute cancelation with a double visit the following year to both Harvard and Columbia. At Columbia, incidentally, Badiou's visit coincided with that of Ernesto Laclau, who was participating in a major international conference in honor of Cornelius Castoriadis. We chose instead to attend an individual lecture by Laclau on the rhetoric of hegemony and the role of empty signifiers, with Badiou being forced—owing to his poor English at the time—to follow from my

instantly translated handwritten notes while a homeless person was causing a ruckus over the fact that her personal couch in the lounge of Philosophy Hall was being taken over by students for the entire duration of
Laclau's talk, which in retaliation she continued to dub with a shrieking
voice worthy of Antonin Artaud. The next day, the three of us got together
for lunch, joined by Simone, to discuss plans for a major seminar on the
concept of politics, to be held behind closed doors so as to avoid the
sinister effects of the public eye, with a dozen or so political theorists and
philosophers who would vouch to submit themselves to an open and
honest discussion, as polemical as needed be, on the basis of a fixed number of pages from their published work. Regrettably, this seminar, which
otherwise could have included the likes of Gayatri Chakravorty Spivak,
who came to say hello to Badiou after Laclau's talk and who already then
proposed a public eye-to-eye debate, did not take place and nowadays is
less likely to occur than ever before, as Badiou and Laclau seem to have
parted ways almost as much as Laclau and Žižek. Spivak, however, made
good on her part of the offer by addressing "Badiou and Other Asias" many
years later in a talk on postcolonial studies at New York University. Except
indirectly, through Hallward's comparison of Badiou and Spivak in the
translator's introduction to *Ethics*, however, this debate too has remained
one-sided.

Still in New York City, Josefina Ayerza from *Lacanian Ink* contacted me
in that same fall of 2000 to organize the first in what would become a long
series of annual talks by Badiou in distinguished art galleries in SoHo
and the Upper East Side. The instant success of Badiou's performance at
Deitch Gallery, however, did not mean that his work at this point had
already gained a solid foothold in the Anglophone market. On the contrary, when around this time I sent out proposals for the translation of
Handbook of Inaesthetics and *Metapolitics* to several American university
presses—some of the same presses that would later scramble to obtain the
rights for these very same books or any other by the same author, for that
matter—they either rejected the project, on the grounds of its questionable
financial feasibility, or did not bother to answer at all.

In sum, by the time of Badiou's first visit to the States in 2000, something was clearly in the making that stirred up great intellectual excitement
and already some controversy, even though nobody could quite foresee
exactly what was going to happen. I, for one, was becoming increasingly

baffled by the way in which Badiou's work was now starting to be received in English. Indeed, everything in this reception, regardless of whether it was purely dismissive or expressed an underlying sympathy, seemed to contradict the conclusions I had drawn a few years earlier from my own interpretation of *Theory of the Subject*. Above all, Badiou was now being charged with defending an authoritarian, if not doctrinaire, allegiance to the fleeting upsurge of a purely self-sustaining event, which is precisely what he himself seemed to be arguing against in the historical dialectic propounded in that earlier book. I began to suspect that perhaps this divergence was due to the fact that English-speaking readers almost by default had to limit themselves for quite some time to the later and shorter books, starting with *Manifesto for Philosophy* all the way to the deceptively simple and perhaps overly polemical *Ethics*, while others tended to come to Badiou's philosophy only from neighboring traditions, for instance, by focusing on his *Deleuze* or on the "event" of Christianity as addressed in *Saint Paul*. Until recently, in other words, extremely few interpreters turned to Badiou's works from before *Being and Event*, which meant that most readers continued to ignore twenty years of solitary philosophical labor. In my eyes this was not just a chronological imbalance at the level of the exegesis, but it actually produced a lopsided interpretation of Badiou's entire philosophical project as well. Part of my aim in the pages that follow consists precisely in shedding some light on this conceptual imbalance in the dominant interpretations of Badiou's work.

In conjunction with the working hypotheses enumerated above, then, the basic presuppositions behind my reading of Badiou's philosophy are the following:

1. The openly dialectical writings from the 1970s and early 1980s, steeped in the experience of French Maoism, only seem to have been abandoned after 1988 with the so-called mathematical turn introduced in *Being and Event*. In reality, while much of Badiou's work in the 1990s is indeed phrased in the dangerously ultraleftist terminology, borrowed from Deleuze, of nondialectical or even antidialectical "disjunctive syntheses," I argue for an underlying continuity behind this work and the earlier arguments in favor of dialectical materialism —a continuity that reemerges and becomes explicit later on, especially with the defense of the materialist dialectic in *Logics of Worlds*.

In my introduction this choice is further explained in my answer to the question "Which Badiou?"

2. Of the four types of "truth procedure" that operate as "conditions" for philosophy according to Badiou, politics is by far the most consistent and elaborate. Even though Badiou has written extensively on art and literature, as well as on psychoanalysis as an immanent reflection on love as a truth procedure, there is no match for the depth and complexity of Badiou's interventions in the field of politics. But then the next question to be answered in the introduction is "Whose politics?"

3. This still leaves us with a third question: "Whither mathematics?" In fact, many readers will argue that this is precisely the most distinctive feature of Badiou's work, so that mathematics would actually meet, if not exceed, the importance of politics as the principal condition for his philosophy. However, as soon as we exit the domains of strict ontology and logic in the way Badiou defines them, namely, as the discourses, respectively, of being and of appearing, then the role of mathematics becomes heuristic at best and analogical at worst. This justifies, in my eyes, the modest role attributed to mathematics in my reading of Badiou and politics.

After laying out my answers to these three questions in the introduction, I proceed by way of a spiraling periodization to situate Badiou's work in the theoretical conjuncture that followed in the wake of May '68. Chapter 1 opens with a discussion of Badiou's debts to Althusser and to the latter's collective project for the outline of a renewed dialectical materialism, or a new materialist dialectic. Chapter 2, after briefly discussing Althusser's later work in relation to his failure to perceive any truth in the events of 1968 in France, turns to Badiou's settling of accounts with Jacques Lacan and with the latter's psychoanalytical contribution to the theory of the subject. Chapter 3, which constitutes the core of the book's political proposal, presents a detailed investigation into the role of Badiou's Maoism for his overall philosophy, both earlier and later. Chapter 4 proposes a dialectical reading of *Being and Event*, paying special attention to the categories and operations that cut across the binary opposition of the book's title. Chapter 5, in a partial return to the discussion with Lacan, expands on the polemical effects of *Being and Event* by tackling the question of Badiou's relation to the tradition of French Heideggerianism. Chapter 6 offers an account of *Logics of Worlds* that targets the continuities and discontinuities of this last major work in relation to *Theory of the Subject* and *Being and Event*. Finally, chapters 7 and 8 attempt to begin thinking "with" Badiou—as he invites his readers to do in *Being and Event* by offering his philosophy as a conceptual toolbox—about the relation between politics and philosophy, specifically through the categories of "potentiality" and of "radical democracy." In the conclusion I return to the question of Badiou's debts to Marxism, following the hypothesis that perhaps he is a communist before being, or perhaps without also being, a Marxist in any orthodox sense of the term. Finally, the book closes with the inclusion, in the appendices, of two interviews, which together present a coherent intellectual portrait of Badiou in the context both of his own trajectory as a philosopher and of that of his generation.

The present book, then, offers both less and more than a general introduction to Badiou's philosophy. It is *less*, insofar as I lay no claims on being exhaustive, in the way that Hallward's book, for example, manages to be a complete introduction: my take is definitely partial, in the double sense of focusing on only part of Badiou's work, namely, the part that has to do with emancipatory politics, and of doing so from the bias of a single unifying hypothesis, based on the persistence of the dialectic. However, this book is also *more* than an introduction, insofar as each chapter goes well beyond exegetical commentary on Badiou's individual writings. Thus, in almost every chapter the reader will be able to find personal interventions in the contemporary theoretical conjuncture: the introduction includes a comparison between Badiou's and Rancière's respective definitions of *metapolitics*; chapter 1 outlines what I consider one of the dominant doctrines of the subject, the real, and the critique of ideology today, a common "doctrine of science" (in the Fichtean sense of a *Wissenschaftslehre*), which can be found from Jacques-Alain Miller to Slavoj Žižek; chapter 2 discusses the role of tragedy, the law, and the force of "nonlaw," in an expanded polemic with Judith Butler and Jacques Derrida; chapter 3 includes a systematic account of the "leftist" and "rightist" deviations both in the organizational history of French Maoism and in some of its philosophical counterparts, from Deleuze to the New Philosophers André Glucksmann, Christian Jambet, and Guy Lardreau; chapter 5 highlights the polemical current underlying chapter 4 by contrasting Badiou's so-called strong thought to the "radical thinking" that philosophers such as Lacoue-Labarthe oppose to Italian "weak thought" (Vattimo and Pier Aldo Rovatti's *pensiero debole*); chapter 6 ends by discussing the possibility of doing work in "historical materialism" through a comparison of Badiou and Rancière on the role of history and philosophy in relation to art and politics; chapter 7 draws some general principles from this historical-materialist approach with regard to the idea that political change is somehow carried by the potential inherent in history, an idea variously subverted, displaced, or reinvented from Marx to Deleuze to Giorgio Agamben; chapter 8, though directly inspired by my reading of Badiou, represents an original intervention in the political philosophy of "radical democracy" shared—at least for a while—by many of the thinkers discussed in the previous chapters; and, finally, the conclusion contrasts Badiou's view of the "communist hypothesis" with similar affirmations from the likes of Jean-Luc Nancy and Antonio Negri.

ACKNOWLEDGMENTS

I am deeply indebted and wish to express my thanks to all the friends and colleagues who over the years have supported my work or who have helped me in ways that luckily had nothing to do with work at all: to Emily Apter, Étienne Balibar, Michela Baraldi, Oscar Barrau, Daniel Bensaïd, John Beverley, Susan Buck-Morss, Sebastian Budgen, Tim Campbell, Lourdes Casas, Gabriel Catren, Raúl Cerdeiras, Alejandro Cerletti, Luis Cifuentes, Tom Conley, Verena Conley, Alexandre Costanzo, David Cruz, Jonathan Culler, Laurent Dubreuil, Irene Fenoglio, Laurent Ferri, Renate Ferro, Jean Franco, Mary Gaylord, Carlos Gómez Camarena, Mitchell Greenberg, Peter Hallward, Eric Hazan, Elisabeth Hodges, Luz Horne, Stephen Jacobson, Fredric Jameson, Adrian Johnston, Patty Keller, Richard Klein, John Kraniauskas, Dominick LaCapra, Phil Lewis, Stella Magliani-Belkacem, Oscar Martín, Christie McDonald, Rodrigo Mier, Alberto Moreiras, Cristina Moreiras, Tim Murray, Edmundo Paz-Soldán, Bruno Peixe, Jorge Perednik, Gustavo Pérez-Firmat, Piero Pucci, Jacques Rancière, Ken Reinhard, Jaime Rodríguez-Matos, Jeannine Routier, León Rozitchner, Sandro Russo, Doris Sommer, Alberto Toscano, Marie-Claire Valois, Isabelle Vodoz, Geoff Waite, Gareth Williams, Cécile Winter, and Slavoj Žižek.

To my parents, Trees Cloostermans and Raf Bosteels; to my brothers Ivo, Wouter, and Maarten and their families.

To Reynolds Smith at Duke University Press, for believing in this project from day one and until the complete and revised manuscript finally hit his desk.

To Alain Badiou, a special word of thanks for his friendship, his generosity, and his willingness to engage in endless rounds of argument.

And, above all, to Simone Pinet, for being the love of my life, and to our two sons, Lucas and Manu, for being the funniest and sharpest critics of the

"blah blah" that we call work, and for being who they are—to them I
dedicate this book.

Previous versions of parts of this book have been published as follows:
segments of the preface and introduction as "On the Subject of the Dialectic," in *Think Again: Alain Badiou and the Future of Philosophy*, edited by
Peter Hallward (London: Continuum, 2004), reproduced by kind permission of Continuum International Publishing Group; parts of chapters 1, 2,
and 4 as "Alain Badiou's Theory of the Subject," *PLI: The Warwick Journal
of Philosophy* 12 and 13 (2001–2), and, in abridged version, in *Lacan: His
Silent Partners*, edited by Slavoj Žižek (London: Verso, 2006), reproduced
by kind permission of Verso; parts of chapter 2 as "Force of Nonlaw: Alain
Badiou's Theory of Justice," in "Law and Event," special issue of *Cardozo
Law Review* 29, no. 5 (2008), reproduced by kind permission of the editors;
chapter 3 as "Post-Maoism: Badiou and Politics," *positions: east asia cultures
critique* 13, no. 3 (2005); chapter 5 as "Vérité et forçage: Badiou avec Lacan
et Heidegger," in *Alain Badiou: Penser le multiple*, edited by Charles Ramond (Paris: L'Harmattan, 2002); segments from the end of chapter 6 as
"Art, Politics, History: Notes on Badiou and Rancière," in "Theses on
Contemporary Art," special inaugural issue of *Inaesthetik* 0 (2008); chapter
8 as "For Lack of Politics: Theses on the Political Philosophy of Radical
Democracy," *theory@buffalo* 10 (2005), and, in Spanish translation, in
Acontecimiento: Revista para pensar la política 17 (1999) and *Metapolítica* 18
(2001); the conclusion as "The Speculative Left," in "Thinking Politically,"
edited by Alberto Moreiras, special issue of the *South Atlantic Quarterly*
104, no. 4 (2005); in Spanish as "Más allá del izquierdismo especulativo,"
Acontecimiento: Revista para pensar la política 29–30 (2005), and segments
in Dutch both as "Een kwestie van kommunisme: Filosofie en politiek bij
Alain Badiou," in *Dossier "Alain Badiou,"* Yang 1 (2004) and as "Kritiek van
de zuivere linkse rede," in "Politieke concepten herdenken / Het politieke
herdacht," edited by Tammy Lynn Castelein and Bram Ieven, special issue
of *Ethiek en Maatschappij* 8, no. 1 (2005); the first appendix as "Can Change
Be Thought? In Dialogue with Alain Badiou," in *Alain Badiou: Philosophy
and Its Conditions*, edited by Gabriel Riera (Albany: State University of
New York Press, 2005), reproduced by kind permission of SUNY Press;
also published in Spanish as "Posmaoísmo: Un diálogo con Alain Badiou,"
Acontecimiento: Revista para pensar la política 24–25 (2003); and, partially,

as "Fidelidad, militancia y verdad: Un diálogo con Alain Badiou," *Extremoccidente* 2 (2003), reproduced by kind permission of the coeditor, Federico Galende; in French as "Peut-on penser le nouveau en situation?" in "Situations de la philosophie," special issue of *Failles* 2 (2006); and in German as "Kann man das Neue denken? Bruno Bosteels im Gespräch mit Alain Badiou," in "Theses on Contemporary Art," special inaugural issue of *Inaesthetik* 0 (2008), reproduced by kind permission of the coeditor, Tobias Huber; and the second appendix as "Beyond Formalisation: An Interview," in "The One or the Other: French Philosophy Today," edited by Peter Hallward, special issue of *Angelaki* 8, no. 2 (2003), reproduced by kind permission of the editors, Pelagia Goulimari and Peter Hallward. Finally, chapters 1, 2, 4, and 6 and the conclusion were published in Spanish as *Badiou o el recomienzo del materialismo dialéctico* (Santiago de Chile: Palinodia, 2007) and in French as *Alain Badiou, une trajectoire polémique* (Paris: La Fabrique, 2009), reproduced by kind permission of the publishers Alejandra Castillo, Miguel Valderrama, and Eric Hazan.

Introduction

ELEMENTS OF DIALECTICAL MATERIALISM

←————————————————→

WHICH BADIOU?

The true dialectical question is never in the first place: what happens
that is important? The true question is always: what happens that is
new?—BADIOU, *Théorie de la contradiction*

Two fundamental approaches dominate the now quickly expanding worldwide reception of Badiou's thought. The first, drawing mainly on the ontological meditations in *Being and Event*, studies the renewed possibility of
thinking of *being* not as oneness but as pure multiplicity. The second, by
contrast, seeks to define the truth of an *event* by turning to one or more of
the so-called truth procedures that serve as the conditions of philosophy,
namely science, politics, art, and love. Badiou himself draws attention to
the difference between these two options in his closing argument at the
first international conference devoted to his work that took place several
years ago in Bordeaux: "One takes as its point of departure the formal
theory of being, mathematics as ontology, and the difficult concept of the
situation; the other sets out primarily from the event and its consequences
in the order of a generic truth."[1] Each of these approaches in turn entails a
specific set of references, not only in Badiou's own body of work but also in
relation to other major thinkers, in France and abroad. The first approach
thus finds its most daunting interlocutors among the likes of Deleuze and
Heidegger, if not more directly in the contributions to mathematical set
theory made by Cantor, Gödel, and Cohen, while the second is more likely
to seek out the company of Lacan, Althusser, Mallarmé, or Beckett—not to
omit Marx, Lenin, and Mao: "Again, the first finds critical support in logic,
in set theory, or in the delicate relation between inconsistent multiplicity
and its thinkable presentation as consistent multiplicity. The other points
to the Lacanian subject, or to emancipatory politics, or to the theory of

artistic procedures."[2] Fundamentally, whereas the first approach remains within the bounds of ontological reason alone, the second calls on an account of truth as part of a formal theory of the subject.

The contemporary reader of Badiou's work, in other words, is confronted with a fundamental alternative between ontology as first or even as higher philosophy and philosophy practiced from the bottom up, so to speak, as theory of the subject. However, as Badiou himself in recent years has become increasingly aware, this division of labor concerning the two dominant approaches to his work—like two halves of a mystical shell—may well lose sight of the most important contribution—perhaps even the rational kernel—of his entire philosophy, that is, the way in which he forces us to think of the emergence of a new and profoundly transformed situation as a result of the articulation of a singular truth onto an existing state of things. This articulation, which I will argue throughout this book can be seen as dialectical in a sense that is today perhaps more controversial and untimely than ever before, is precisely what any reader will miss who concentrates *either* on the ontological theses *or* on the theory of the subject, so as to put being (order, situations, worlds, knowledge, nature, individuals) firmly on the one hand and the event (chance, novelty, change, truth, history, subjects) firmly on the other. Many critics argue that this is precisely what Badiou himself ends up doing, when especially in his later work following *Being and Event*, after abandoning a more traditional dialectical view, he is seen as setting up a rigid divide along Kantian (perhaps even pre-Kantian) lines between the world of phenomena and the realm of things in themselves or, along a more Sartrean lineage, between being and consciousness qua pure nothingness. As Peter Hallward writes: "From a neo-Hegelian perspective, Badiou's philosophy must figure as a return to broadly Kantian dualisms, reworked in terms of the dichotomy of truth and knowledge or subject and object."[3] Slavoj Žižek is even more radical in this accusation, concluding that Badiou's refusal to come to terms with the topic of finitude, which all modern philosophy according to Heidegger inherits from Kant, "involves a 'regression' to 'non-thought,' to a naïve traditional (pre-critical, pre-Kantian) opposition of two orders (the finitude of positive Being; the immortality of the Truth-Event) that remains blind to how the very space for the specific 'immortality' in which human beings can participate in the Truth-Event is opened up by man's unique relationship to his finitude and the possibility of death."[4] Surely, then, we

ELEMENTS OF DIALECTICAL MATERIALISM

would be on the wrong track if we sought to find a foothold in Badiou's work so as to reach a theory of the dialectic along broadly understood Hegelian lines.

Now, there are certainly numerous moments in Badiou's oeuvre where such oppositions do seem to operate. Consider, for example, the following list taken from the concluding page of *The Century*, a list meant to reinvigorate the age-old war of Plato against Aristotle: "This is a war that possesses numerous less esoteric names: The Idea against reality. Freedom against nature. The event against the state of affairs. Truth against opinions. The intensity of life against the insignificance of survival. Equality against equity. Rebellion against tolerance. Eternity against History. Science against technics. Art against culture. Politics against management. Love against the family."[5] If similar lists can be culled from other parts of Badiou's work, though, there are also many elements that resist the dualist interpretation, and this is so not only in earlier books such as *Theory of the Subject* but also after the so-called antidialectical, mathematical, or subtractive turn introduced by *Being and Event*. Not the least indicative among these elements is the fact that one of Badiou's most openly declared philosophical enemies has always been, and continues to be, for example, in *Logics of Worlds*, the little professorial figure that he identifies with the philosopher from Königsberg: "Kant is exemplarily an author with whom I cannot attain familiarity. Everything in him exasperates me, above all his legalism—always asking *Quid juris?* or 'Haven't you crossed the limit?'—combined, as in today's United States, with a religiosity that is all the more dismal in that it is both omnipresent and vague."[6] From a political standpoint, moreover, we will see that Badiou also repeatedly argues against all types of external opposition, whether they are considered "leftist" or "statist," that would leave being and event utterly and completely unrelated, or absolutely disjoined.

One of my underlying aims in the pages that follow is to investigate what is to be gained if we call the logic behind this argument for a renewed articulation of being, event, truth, and subject not just "materialist," as I will discuss in chapter 1, following in the footsteps of Badiou's teacher Althusser, but also "dialectical," in a sense that I would argue is still in keeping with a long-standing tradition of post-Hegelian thought. In any case the term itself is, to some extent, inessential: what matters are the conceptual argument and the specific operations it calls for.

On the most basic and general level, what this argument for a dialectical reading of Badiou's work involves is precisely a mode of thinking that does not seek to distinguish being on the one hand from the event on the other but rather to articulate them together within one and the same plane— even if this means passing through the paradoxes of an impasse that would seem to signal the end or undoing of all normal relations and mediations. As Lenin reminds us, incidentally right after reading Hegel's *Science of Logic*: " 'On the one hand, and on the other,' 'the one and the other.' That is eclecticism. Dialectics requires an all-round consideration of relationships in their concrete development but not a patchwork of bits and pieces."[7] Even the effort by way of an uncompromising contrast to juxtapose the two approaches mentioned above, that is, one restricted to the austere formal science of being as pure multiple of multiples and the other almost mystically enthralled by the pristine truth of an event belonging only to itself, is unable to catch hold of what I have tentatively called the rational kernel of Badiou's thinking. This kernel, to be sure, is never fully self-present but rather always happens to be split from within. As Badiou himself writes half-jokingly at the beginning of *Theory of the Subject*: "There are two dialectical matrices in Hegel. This is what turns the famous story of the shell and the kernel into such a dubious enigma. It is the kernel itself that is cracked, as in those peaches that are furthermore so irritating to eat whose hard internal object quickly cracks between one's teeth into two pivoting halves."[8] Similarly, if we seek to understand the rational kernel of Badiou's dialectic, what is needed is a full-blown account of the divided articulation —rather than the mere exteriority—between the normal order of being and the truth of an event. This is the notion of the dialectic as a logic of scission, which I will lay out beginning in chapters 2 and 3, with Lacan and Mao, respectively, adding new and unexpected twists to the materialist dialectic inherited from Althusser.

If Badiou were to propose a simple external opposition—let us say (if I may be allowed to trade an organicist for a technological metaphor) following the model of two parallel train tracks that never meet except at an illusory and ever-retreating point on the horizon that, if realized, at once would signal the fact of their disastrous coincidence—between the dispersed inconsistency of pure multiples and the emergence of truth as tied to the secularized miracle of some grand event, then the objection that he remains profoundly Kantian or even falls back into pre-Kantian dualisms would be entirely to the point. In fact, this objection was first raised against Badiou by none other than Deleuze in their unpublished correspondence, many years after Badiou himself, then still an outspoken Maoist, had leveled this same objection even more aggressively against Deleuze and Guattari.[9] But, I repeat, this objection minimizes the importance of several key moments in Badiou's theory. Between a given situation and the various figures of subjectivity that actually make a truth happen, the real issue is to account for where one can impact the other, for how long, and to what effect. Ultimately, this is nothing more and nothing less than the question of structural change, of how a given situation can be thoroughly transformed in the event of a new and unpredictable truth.

As Badiou says in the interview reproduced below in appendix 1: "My unique philosophical question, I would say, is the following: Can we think that there is something new in the situation, not the new outside the situation nor the new somewhere else, but can we really think of novelty and treat it in the situation? The system of philosophical answers that I elaborate, whatever its complexity may be, is subordinated to that question and to no other."[10] Against Ecclesiastes, we should say, there *can* be something new under the sun, even if such occurrences are rare and often short-lived, namely whenever there happens to be an excess in the situation at hand; but this excess, which on rare occasions adds something discontinuous to the situation, must nevertheless be conceived from within this situation itself, not from some unfathomable beyond or in light of some prior and long-lost origin. To think of the transformative capacity of a truth from within a given situation, furthermore, requires an account of the givenness of this given, and thus the new must be thought together with the old, in a unified logic of radical change.

Even many years after the alleged end of his Maoist period this articulation of the old and the new remains the pivotal question for Badiou: "Even when there is event, structure, formalization, mathematics, multiplicity, and so on, this is exclusively destined, in my eyes, to think through the new in terms of the situation. But, of course, to think the new in situation, we also have to think the situation, and thus we have to think what is repetition, what is the old, what is not new, and after that we have to think the new."[11] In fact, with this question of the sudden changeover between the old and the new, we are once again close not just to the Maoist definition of ideological struggle but also to one of Lenin's key concerns in his notebooks on Hegel's *Science of Logic*. Change develops "not only as decrease and increase, as repetition," Lenin writes, but also "as a unity of opposites," and it is this second conception alone that defines the dialectic insofar as it "furnishes the key to the 'leaps,' to the 'break in continuity,' to the 'transformation into the opposite,' to the destruction of the old and the emergence of the new."[12] Or, in Mao's words: "The supersession of the old by the new is a general, eternal and inviolable law of the universe. The transformation of one thing into another, through leaps of different forms in accordance with its essence and external conditions—this is the process of the new superseding the old."[13]

If we consider the title of Badiou's most encompassing and ambitious work, *Being and Event*, it is therefore the "and" that really matters as the peculiar articulation between the two orders. The fact that this articulation, as we will see in chapters 4 and 5, actually amounts to a nonrelation should not lead us immediately to conclude that for this reason it has no dialectical bearing. As Badiou says in the same interview: "I would like to insist that, even in the title *Being and Event*, the 'and' is fundamental," but this conjunction should not be seen too quickly as hiding an underlying opposition or disjunction. "Because, in my eyes, the principal contribution of my work does not consist in opposing the situation to the event. In a certain sense, that is something that everybody does these days. The principal contribution consists in posing the following question: What can we derive or infer from this from the point of view of the situation itself?"[14] Badiou's follow-up to *Being and Event* in *Logics of Worlds*, in fact, continues to map out the logic of change in an ever more nuanced way that explicitly seeks to bypass the rigid, external, if not miraculous dichotomy of being and event, or of situation and event. Along a much broader spectrum in the typology of change, the new book furthermore develops a series of intercalated concepts between situation and event: concepts such as the body, points, or the inexistent, through which a truth not only is firmly anchored in a given situation or world but also is made to appear, as a historical fragment of eternity, within the givenness of such a concrete world. As we will see in chapter 6, this is one of the many ways in which *Logics of Worlds* actually hearkens back to the dialectical framework of *Theory of the Subject*.

Unlike what happens in the programmatic titles of Heidegger's *Being and Time* or Sartre's *Being and Nothingness*, despite numerous family resemblances and conceptual ties especially to the latter, the value of the

pivotal conjunction in the title of *Being and Event* consists neither in retrieving a deeper hermeneutic proximity or overlap (the idea that being
qua being always already "is" or "gives itself" as event, as the event of
originary temporalization, which at once amounts to an ontologization of
the event), nor in rendering a primordial dualism (whereby being and
event would remain forever separate as two dimensions or realms completely isolated from one another in an inoperative externality), but of
formalizing the mechanisms by which the two are articulated through a
gap or deadlock (through the "impasse of being" itself as that which a
subject, in the event of a truth that induces it, retroactively enables to
"pass" into existence).

At this point, any reader familiar with Badiou's earlier work certainly
would expect a full account of this formalization to include some reference
or other to dialectical modes of thinking. Even as late as *Can Politics Be
Thought?*, when he is already supposed to have broken with the dialectical
framework of *Theory of the Subject*, Badiou suggests the possibility that the
keywords of his philosophy lay the groundwork for a renewal of the dialectic: "I hold that the concepts of event, structure, intervention, and fidelity
are the very concepts of the dialectic, insofar as the latter is not reduced to
the flat image, which was already inadequate for Hegel himself, of totalization and the labor of the negative."[15] These four fundamental concepts—
event, structure, intervention, and fidelity—continue to form the back-
bone of Badiou's current work, not only in *Being and Event* but also in
Logics of Worlds. In fact, this last work opens with an unabashed defense
not just of any dialectic but of a materialist one to boot: "After much
hesitation, I have decided to name *materialist dialectic* the ideological atmosphere in which my philosophical undertaking gives vent to its most
extreme tension."[16] So then, what is exactly the fate of the dialectic for
Badiou? What are the consequences, for anyone bent not just on understanding but on working with this philosopher's thought, of a sustained
confrontation with the history and theory of dialectical thinking?

The overarching question that I want to pose in this book is not only
whether Badiou can help us think dialectically but also to what extent a
dialectical interpretation might help us avoid, or at least reconsider, some
of the misconceptions surrounding his work. For most readers the answer
to both sides of this question typically involves the notion of a radical break
away from the dialectic—a break that would occur sometime in the mid to

late 1980s and that, not surprisingly, would be in tune with the larger crisis and ultimate demise of Marxism-Leninism and the collapse of the Soviet Union. Badiou was a staunch defender of the materialist dialectic—which he then still called by the orthodox name of dialectical materialism—up until and including *Theory of the Subject*, a most obscure and often misunderstood seminar written under the influence of French Maoism as much as of Mallarmé and Lacan. However, after *Can Politics Be Thought?* and most definitely starting with *Being and Event*, or so the argument goes, he is supposed to have destroyed the last metaphysical and essentialist remnants of this belief in the dialectic, including its reformulation by the most fervent followers of Mao Zedong's thought: "For a more conventionally materialist ontology, Badiou has substituted the mathematical manipulation of the void, which has become the exclusive basis for his articulation of a be-ing without substance, without constituent relation to material existence; for a historical eschatology, he has substituted a 'politics of the impossible,' a politics purged of dialectical *liens*."[17] This is why Badiou, in his later work's refusal of all dialectical mediation, can be accused of having become almost dogmatically absolutist—an accusation that his detractors are only all too happy to adopt from some of his most ardent admirers.

Mathematics, briefly put, is thought to have replaced dialectics in the more recent and more widely read works by Badiou. Now, there are certainly good reasons to accept this reading. In *Metapolitics*, to give but one recent example, Badiou does indeed seem to reject all forms of dialectical thinking as being inherently misguided—unable as they are to think politics *from within*, as would be the true task of the "metapolitics" he calls for, rather than to think merely *about* the essence of "the political," which for him has been the principal occupation of all hitherto existing political philosophies. The dialectical mode of thinking politics would thus appear to be the first victim of Badiou's proposal for a metapolitical orientation in philosophy, despite the fact that little more than a decade earlier, and while using the same keywords of *situation, event, intervention*, and so on, he had posited that politics could best be thought through such concepts as providing the main elements for a renewed dialectic.

In *Metapolitics* Badiou seems to have been especially influenced in this regard by his cohort Sylvain Lazarus, whose *Anthropology of the Name* receives an extensive, though not entirely uncritical, review in a key chapter of the book. Together with Natacha Michel, Lazarus is also one of Badiou's closest collaborators, both in terms of political militancy and in terms of their theoretical inquiries into the nature of politics in the contemporary moment. Throughout much of the 1990s, in particular, Lazarus and Badiou refused to tie the possibility of thinking contemporary politics to a dialectical articulation between objective and subjective conditions, or between the socioeconomical sphere and its concentration as the political act proper.

Consider, as an orthodox point of reference, the ambiguous sense in which Lenin describes the "ABC of Marxism": "I said again in my speech that politics is a concentrated expression of economics, because I had earlier heard my 'political' approach rebuked in a manner which is inconsistent and inadmissible for a Marxist. Politics must take precedence over economics. To argue otherwise is to forget the ABC of Marxism. Am I wrong in my political appraisal? If you think so, say it and prove it. But you forget the ABC of Marxism when you say (or imply) that the political approach is equivalent to the 'economic,' and that you can take 'the one and the other.' "[18] While on two occasions in *Theory of the Subject* Badiou approvingly cites the first part of Lenin's definition, according to which "politics is a concentrated expression of economics," we could say that in the period between *Being and Event* and *The Century*, by contrast, he opts for a reading that privileges the antidialectical consequences of the second formulation, according to which, as Mao would also insist later on, "politics must take precedence over economics."[19] If this reading can be labeled antidialectical, as Badiou repeatedly does with regard to the work of Lazarus, it is because *dialectical* in this context is seen as belonging to the same set of terms—the same episteme of historico-political knowledge—as *historicist*, *classist*, and *positivist*, all of which would designate a dominant yet obsolete figure of political intelligibility, that is, to use the terms coined by Lazarus, a "historical mode of politics" that now has become "saturated."[20]

The suspicion is that an attempt such as the dialectical one to name the entity *in relation to which* the possibility of a political sequence emerges, whether this is done in terms of history, society, and economics or in terms of time and totality, runs the risk of dispersing the singularity of such a sequence onto two or more heterogeneous fields.[21] Consequently, the outcome of such attempts typically involves the need for some type of mediation between subjective and objective factors—with Lenin's vanguard party as the organizational form brought in to close the gap between the two.[22] Even in sociological descriptions of the current state of affairs in politics, descriptions for which the party vanguard evidently no longer is an option, time almost magically comes in as a circulating term or vanishing mediator to provide an articulation, whether in terms of "progress," "delay," or the "promise" of some future reconciliation, between social being and rationality. "Time then, in a headlong flight, becomes the substance of the last utopia," as Jacques Rancière also writes: "All we need is time, give us time, clamour all our governments."[23] However, for Badiou, who on this point fully agrees with Lazarus, politics must be thought "in interiority," or from within what they term a "homogeneous multiplicity," through the categories, places, and prescriptions that mark the material index of its momentum, without making the nature of the political process transitive to any fixed combination of data, be they social being and consciousness, the mental and the material, or even discursive and nondiscursive practices in the Foucauldian sense. Completely subtracted from the realm of social objectivity, then, politics would also no longer be subordinated to the overarching sense or meaningful direction of time and history: "Such is the principal gain of the disjunction between politics and history, and of the abolition of the category of time: the seizure in thought of a political sequence remains an homogeneous operation, whether it involves an 'ongoing' politics or a bygone politics, even if the protocols to be followed in each case are distinct from one another."[24] It would seem that very little, if anything, can be said in this context in favor of a dialectical understanding of Badiou's recent thought.

Yet Badiou and Lazarus also suggest that this notion of the dialectic, which at least in this part of their work they define as a heterogeneous articulation of distinct realms in the name of circulating terms such as time, history, class, or social movement, can be found mainly in the field of the social sciences, among historians and political scientists. Their diagnosis thus leaves room for another understanding of the dialectic, one capable of thinking through the material rupture produced by a political intervention without having recourse to the organizational form of the party or to the idealist circulating terms of time and social movement, the copresence of which is typically called on to overcome an underlying heterogeneity of social being and consciousness. Badiou quotes Lazarus himself in *The Anthropology of the Name* as allowing for a strange margin of uncertainty in evaluating the exact status of the dialectic and negativity in Hegel's own formulation, to the extent that Lazarus "takes great care, for example, not to confuse what he declares as being terminated or lapsed (i.e. the historicist dialectic in the social sciences, which works on composite and heterogeneous multiplicities) with Hegelian negativity, which seems to him, on the contrary, to rely on a thought of the homogeneous."[25]

Hegel's shoes, supposing that he himself has indeed long been put back on his feet, are apparently still waiting for someone to fill them. Or perhaps it would be more accurate to suggest that the poor man's footwear, after having been so amply filled for more than two centuries with everything from the most profane to the sublime, desperately needs to be emptied out—voided in favor of a new understanding of the dialectic precisely in terms of void and excess rather than of totalization; of scission and the symptomal torsion of split identities, instead of as negation and the negation of negation; and of the breakdown of representation rather than the elusive self-presentation of the concept.

Hegel must be split rather than merely put upside down or discarded and spit on. "So at the heart of the Hegelian dialectic we must disentangle two processes, two concepts of movement, and not just one proper view of becoming that would have been corrupted by a subjective system of knowing," Badiou posits in *Theory of the Subject*, namely:

a. A dialectical matrix covered by the term of alienation; the idea of a simple term which unfolds itself in its becoming-other, in order to come back to itself as an achieved concept.

b. A dialectical matrix whose operator is scission, and whose theme is that there is no unity that is not split. There is not the least bit of return into itself, nor any connection between the final and the inaugural. Not even "integral communism" as the return, after the exteriorization into the State, to the concept of which "primitive communism" would be the simple immediacy.[26]

The question, then, is not *whether* Hegel should be revived at all but rather *which* Hegel. Or else, but this question is no doubt related to the first: *which* of his shoes should we try to fit, the left one or the right one? The one from the *Science of Logic* or the one from *Phenomenology of Spirit*?

Badiou, as we will see, first aligned himself with French Maoism via Hegel, by retrieving Hegel's *Science of Logic* together with Lenin's *Philosophical Notebooks*, against both Althusser's ferocious anti-Hegelianism and the vogue for Hegel's *Phenomenology of Spirit* that Alexandre Kojève had inspired in the likes of Bataille, Sartre, and Lacan.[27] More recently, in personal interviews, he compares *Being and Event* to Hegel's *Science of Logic*, while considering *Theory of the Subject* more akin to the *Phenomenology of Spirit* in the sense of sticking as closely as possible to the experiential content of all concepts. This is neither trivial nor purely immodest: a full understanding of a possible role for the dialectic in Badiou's thought certainly stands or falls with an adequate articulation of the differences and relations between these two major books, *Being and Event* and *Theory of the Subject*, along the lines of what happens with Hegel's *Science of Logic* and *Phenomenology of Spirit*. Each of these by itself, however, is still one-sided. Perhaps, then, to return to the earlier question, we should say that both of Hegel's shoes, like Van Gogh's ill-fated peasant boots, are left ones and that the painful task ahead of us is to put them on at the same time. This would also explain, finally, why *Logics of Worlds* can claim to be a "logic" while at other times it is called an objective "phenomenology."

Even *Metapolitics* is perhaps closer than would first appear to the dialectical premise behind an earlier work such as *Can Politics Be Thought?* To bring out this proximity, we need a mode of thinking that allows us to reflect on how the situation of what is, interrupted by an event as a break that prescribes what will have been—not in some bold messianic future but in the sober immediacy of a wager on the here and now—nonetheless continues to be a homogeneous situation. At the same time, this homogeneity should not come to designate an ever so slightly transfigured and exalted perpetuation of the status quo. The fundamental problem is thus the following: How can such a simple yet paradoxical situation be thought as a multiple that is both new and homogeneous? Or, to use a slightly different formulation, how can we think of an excess or supplement to the situation that in truth is still immanent to this situation itself? How does a truth emerge within an existing situation?

In spite of the declared obsolescence of the dialectic between subjective and objective factors, between consciousness and social being, or even between theory and practice, I will argue that the logic of emergent truths calls for a new set of dialectical categories. As Badiou adds in the interview quoted earlier: "At least in this regard I remain more profoundly Hegelian. That is, I am convinced that the new can only be thought as process. There certainly is novelty in the event's upsurge, but this novelty is always evanescent. That is not where we can pinpoint the new in its materiality. But that is precisely the point that interests me: the materiality of the new."[28] We might even say that it is precisely in order to grasp the materiality of the new that we need a renewal of the materialist dialectic, if not of the old dialectical materialism.

Ever since the fall of the USSR, many philosophers and ideologues have been quick to redeem a certain Marx—and even a certain idea of communism—from the stuffy archives of vulgar or orthodox Marxism. The time has come, though, when the stakes should be shifted in a different direction, and philosophy should come to the rescue of dialectical materialism as well. In fact, if the practice of theory or philosophy is defined by working through and against received opinions, then nothing can be more urgent than to resist the consensus that is only all too happy to sacrifice the slightest hint of materialist and especially dialectical thinking, if this is the price to be paid in order to present oneself as the proud rediscoverer of the truth of a certain Marx.

Before I turn to the place of politics in this framework, there is still another way to approach the legacy of dialectical thinking in Badiou. This would involve a closer reading of *The Century*, the book mentioned above that is based on a lecture series between 1998 and 2001 at the Collège International de Philosophie. Here, Badiou seems to want to come to terms once more with the possibility, or even the desirability, of a new figure of the dialectic. In fact, he argues that this has been a task that the past century very much imposed on itself: "The century is a figure of the nondialectical juxtaposition of the Two and the One. Our question here concerns the century's assessment of dialectical thinking."[29] But then in many ways this assessment also involves a reassessment of Badiou's own relation to the dialectic.

Instead of the more familiar schemas for the sublation of contradiction, these "lessons," as Badiou calls his lectures, insist that much of the twentieth century was dominated by what Deleuze would have described as so many cases of "disjunctive synthesis," that is, nondialectical or even antidialectical solutions to the problem of articulating not only the old and the new, the end and the beginning, the instantaneous act and the creative duration but also truth and semblance, life and the will, determinism and voluntarism, historicism and vanguardism. The highest aim of some of the most innovative political, artistic, and even scientific experiments of the past century is to come face to face with the real in an instantaneous act or ecstatic break, rather than in an internal overcoming of contradictions: "The question of the face-to-face is the heroic question of the century."[30] In fact, it is precisely the absence of any dialectical sublation that seems to have been compensated for by sheer violence, by the "passion of the real" that characterizes so many of these artistic and political sequences. "The century is haunted by a non-dialectical relation between necessity and will," for example. "Violence comes in at the point of the disjunction; it substitutes itself for a missing conjunction, like a dialectical link forced into being in the place of the antidialectic."[31] Only on a few occasions in these lessons are we given a glimpse into what might constitute a more properly dialectical understanding of truth as the articulation of an ongoing process, over and against the primacy of the violent act per se. For the most part, even as he methodically refrains from any obvious judgment with regard to either the dialectical or the nondialectical paths, Badiou clearly prefers to dwell on the century's radical experiments in disjunction and delinking.

A first conclusion after reading *The Century*, then, could be that the predominance of the act as a violent antidialectical figure proves the complete exhaustion and outright obsolescence of the whole dialectical tradition that runs from Hegel's *Science of Logic*, via Lukács's *History and Class Consciousness* and Sartre's *Critique of Dialectical Reason*, to Adorno's *Negative Dialectics*. Badiou himself, of course, is part of this tradition, and he readily identified himself with the theory of the dialectic for a long time, starting with his two early booklets *Theory of Contradiction* and *Of Ideology* (the latter coauthored by François Balmès), through the running commentary on a Maoist text by Zhang Shiying in *The Rational Kernel of the Hegelian Dialectic*, all the way to the above-mentioned statement in *Can Politics Be Thought?* Another reading of this legacy, however, could come to the reverse conclusion: instead of drawing the melancholy inference from practical endgames to a sense of theoretical exhaustion, the notion that the dialectical mode has reached a moment of closure could be attributed to the fact that the practices and experiments from the past century, be they political or artistic, failed to realize this tradition of thought. This tradition, then, would still be worth revisiting as a way of opening up concrete alternatives to the predominance of those tragically unresolved, and most often extremely violent, cases of disjunctive synthesis diagnosed in *The Century*.

Rather than consigning all forms of dialectical thinking to the dustbin of history, perhaps we should pause to consider that even Badiou's most important work, notwithstanding the overwhelming predominance of mathematics, opens with a clear tipping of the hat to the dialectical system and method. *Being and Event*, as we will see in greater detail in chapter 4, is meant, after all, to provide the ontological substructure that would be missing, or that in any case would remain insufficiently articulated, in the earlier attempt at a grand synthesis of his thinking in *Theory of the Subject*. Whereas this earlier work merely seems to *presuppose* that the subject is always already given, the later one seeks to make this supposition compatible with the thesis that mathematics *is* ontology as the science of being qua being. Recourse to the mathematics of set theory, from Cantor to Cohen, more specifically, would provide a formal alternative to the poetic ontologies of Heideggerian origin, at the same time laying out a theory of the subject compatible with the interventionist (political and clinical) doctrines of Marx and Freud, of Lenin and Lacan. Badiou immediately foresees that this ambitious plan to render the discourse of being compatible with a theory of the subject will remind certain readers of the worst outgrowths of those state-sponsored efforts under Stalin that sought to forge "diamat" into the official philosophy of Marxism.

Speaking in retrospect of the thesis about subjectivization outlined in *Theory of the Subject*, Badiou notes in the introduction to *Being and Event*: "The compatibility of this thesis with a possible ontology worried me, because the force—and absolute weakness—of the 'old Marxism,' of dialectical materialism, had consisted in postulating just such a compatibility in the guise of the generality of the laws of the dialectic, which is to say, in the end, the isomorphy between the dialectic of nature and the dialectic of history. For sure, this (Hegelian) isomorphy was still-born."[32] The isomorphy, or the simple homology, between nature and history, as well as that between society and politics, cancels out the possibility of thinking of the truth of an event from within a homogeneous multiplicity or according to an immanent excess. To avoid this risk and remain strictly within the realm of thought, which for Badiou means the realm of the subject without an object, many readers have concluded that after *Theory of the Subject* dialectics was to have been replaced by mathematics in *Being and Event*— whereby the baby was perhaps thrown out with the bathwater. By contrast, I will argue not only that the principal theses in this last book continue to be strongly reminiscent of the laws of the dialectic, provided of course that these laws or axioms are properly reformulated, but also, and perhaps even more importantly, that a failure to grasp the exact nature of the dialectic contained in these theses will continue to lead to the kind of misunderstandings and ill-conceived objections that already haunt the reception of Badiou's philosophy as a whole.

Nevertheless, even if we accept the need to articulate being, event, site, subject, intervention, and truth into a coherent philosophical doctrine, the reader may still be reluctant to call this articulation a materialist dialectic. Why give a stale blood transfusion to a horse that may have been beaten to death several decades ago? "The point is to be clear about the subject of the dialectic," as Badiou also writes in *Can Politics Be Thought?* And he adds: "The dialecticity of the dialectic consists precisely in having a conceptual history and in dividing the Hegelian matrix to the point where it turns out to be essentially a doctrine of the event, and not the guided adventure of the spirit. A politics, rather than a history."[33] Thus, dialectics ultimately means a form of thinking that grasps the truth of a situation not by way of mediation but through an interruption, a scission, or a cut in representation. The outline of the dialectic in *Can Politics Be Thought?* remains, in this sense, valid for the arguments that have come out of *Being and Event*: "Dialectical thinking will be recognized first of all by its conflict with representation. Such thinking tracks down the unrepresentable point in its field, from which it turns out that one touches upon the real."[34] Tracking down the immanent point of excess in representation, however, is still insufficient, unless this point of the real is taken up as the paradoxical leverage for a subject's emerging capacity for truth: "A dialectical form of thinking thus makes a *hole* in the disposition of knowledge (of representations), on the occasion of a symptomatic breakdown, which it *interprets* according to the *hypothesis of a capacity* in which the aftermath or *après-coup* of a subject will have asserted itself."[35] For Badiou this is the unique strength of Marx, who listened to the popular uprisings of the 1840s all over Europe and responded in the future anterior with the communist hypothesis of a proletarian political capacity, just as Freud in fin de siècle Vienna began to listen to the hysterical interruptions of the familiar discourse on sexuality and love in order to respond with the intervening doctrine of psychoanalysis.

But today, can we still hold that there exists a dialectical matrix with which to think that one divides into two? "This question of the thought of the Two has as its horizon the destiny of dialectical thought: in the end, is the category of contradiction in the Hegelian, Marxist and Sartrean heritage still pertinent or not to the conceptualization of difference?" Badiou himself asks this question in another public forum, to which he responds: "I think the question is still open."[36] This means that the question of dialectics today is ultimately a question of politics; that is, it is a question of an active and organized invention of new modes of dealing with the Two. As Badiou also writes in *Manifesto for Philosophy*: "What is being sought after today is a thinking of politics which, while dealing with strife and thus having the structural Two in its field of intervention, does not take this Two to be an objective essence. Or rather, to the objectivist doctrine of the Two (classes are transitive to the process of production), the political innovation under way attempts to oppose a vision of the Two 'in terms of historicity,' which means that the real Two is an evental *production*, a political production, and not an objective or 'scientific' presupposition."[37] Thus, if every way of thinking politics is conditioned by a specific mode of doing politics, then we first have to ask which political interventions have produced or currently are producing a new vision of the Two. Which politics, in other words, condition Badiou's renewal of the materialist dialectic? And what are some of the ideas and prescriptions, as captured in philosophy, that are inherent in these instances of politics?

WHOSE POLITICS?

> What is at stake is nothing less than the possibility, for philosophy, to contribute to maintaining politics in the realm of the thinkable and to save the figure of being that politics detains, against the automatisms of the indifferent.— BADIOU, *Peut-on penser la politique?*

A useful point of departure in the quest to understand the place of politics in Badiou's philosophy comes to us in the form of a near-axiomatic statement that runs through all of his work, both before and after the Maoist red years: "People think," or, to use the older and less euphemistic phrasing of the same principle: "The masses think." Little has changed at least with regard to this conviction, which is best summed up in Badiou and Balmès's *Of Ideology*: "Our conviction, anchored in the complete history of great popular revolts, is concentrated in this difficult evidence: The masses think, and, what is more, in the general historical movement of their uninterrupted resistance to exploitation and oppression, the masses think justly."[38] All of

Badiou's later work can, in a sense, still be grasped as an attempt to further elaborate the consequences of this principle, according to which an event in politics is one that puts people to think and, moreover, one that produces collective forms of thought that are essentially just. If film, for Jean-Luc Godard, produces just images, then politics, for Badiou, produces just thoughts.

As a first consequence of this principle, thinking and acting can no more be separated than theory and practice. Politics is in and of itself a form of thinking. "Politics is a thought," Badiou writes in *Metapolitics*: "Doing politics cannot be distinguished from thinking politics."[39] Any politics worthy of its name involves ideas, guidelines, watchwords, and so on that always give much food for thought, but it also inevitably involves an active and material form of organization: "Must we argue that organization alone can make an event into an origin? Yes, insofar as a political subject requires the historical underpinning of an apparatus and insofar as there is no origin except for a determinate politics."[40] By no means can we reduce the political process to the typical image of a previously established theory that subsequently is, or ought to be, put into practice. Badiou always rejects such programmatic images of politics, even in his most radical period when he still openly swears by the thought of Chairman Mao.

The link between thought and politics can only be understood from within a militant process, without creating a distance between that which actually occurs and the critical power to form an opinion or judgment about this very occurrence. Badiou therefore rejects the way in which Kant, in his short posthumous writings that for some interpreters amount to a kind of *Critique of Political Reason*, declares his enthusiasm for the spectacle—but not the actors—of the French Revolution. According to Badiou, who in this regard strongly opposes the orientation of many modern and postmodern Kantians such as Hannah Arendt and Jean-François Lyotard, politics has nothing to do with the faculty of judgment, let alone with the molding of public opinion, which nowadays, in any case, tends to be crushed under the weight of mindless opinion polls: "It is through Saint Just and Robespierre that you enter into this singular truth unleashed by the French Revolution, and on the basis of which you form a knowledge, and not through Kant or François Furet."[41] What is more, political events have no need for the philosopher to transmit from the outside what they themselves, as events, produce in terms of thinking or truth, or to judge which of them qualify as properly political events. In the opening chapter of his *Metapolitics* Badiou invokes this principle in a bold plea against all political philosophy: "One of the fundamental requirements of contemporary thought is to have done with 'political philosophy.' "[42] What should we understand by "political philosophy" in this context, and why is there an urgent need to make place for a "metapolitics"?

According to Badiou, who in this regard agrees with Rancière's argument in *On the Shores of Politics* and *Disagreement* in spite of their very different understanding of metapolitics, political philosophy relies on the idea that it can form a clear and distinct idea—or, better yet, a judgment—about what constitutes the essence of politics, or, at the very least, about what should constitute the essence of politics, properly speaking. From Aristotle to Kant to contemporary thinkers such as Claude Lefort, political philosophers seek to define "the political" as a specific domain or invariable instance of the social order, as distinct from the economical or the moral, for example. Rancière in this regard speaks of "political philosophy" as "the politics of the philosophers," which typically tends to obscure, displace, or supplant instances of "real politics."[43] At the same time, political philosophers generally attempt to gauge the advantages and disadvantages of various state forms or regimes of power that give order to this domain or instance of the political. Thus, it has always been a typical exercise of classical political philosophy to compare the democratic and aristocratic state forms, or anarchy, monarchy, and tyranny, whereas in modern and postmodern times the alternative usually comes down to the alternative of democracy and totalitarianism, or nowadays, democracy and fundamentalism. Democracy, in this last view, does not have to be taken as a blunt matter of fact, but it can also appear as an irreplaceable ideal, sometimes reconceptualized as a "radical democracy" that is still to come, as I will discuss in chapter 8. In any case one of the tacit presuppositions of political philosophy thereby still holds, namely that politics can be thought only after the facts and apart from the events themselves, so that the task of the philosopher always consists in debating the essence of the political act from the position of an outside observer or belated spectator: "Overall, philosophy would be a formal apprehension of States and instances of politics by exposing and pre-elaborating the types in question in accordance with possible norms."[44]

Instead of continuing this reputable tradition of "political philosophy,"

Badiou proposes to give philosophy a "metapolitical" orientation. This means that philosophy must cease to evaluate, in the way of an onlooker at a public spectacle or a judge in the tribunal of historical reason, the essence of the political (*le politique*) and instead ought to put itself under the condition of politics (*la politique*) or rather of *a* politics (*une politique*) so as to investigate which conceptual tools it should develop in order to be able to register in its midst the consequences of a political event. As Badiou writes in the guideline that serves as an epigraph to his *Metapolitics*: "By 'metapolitics' I understand the consequences that a philosophy can draw out in and for itself from the fact that true forms of politics are forms of thinking. Metapolitics is opposed to political philosophy, which claims that it belongs to the philosopher to think 'the political,' insofar as politics would not be a form of thinking in itself."[45] Ultimately, a metapolitical orientation is based on the broad materialist principle that puts philosophy under specific conditions, in this case political ones, instead of raising itself up to the lofty heights of a timeless, self-reliant and unconditioned act of speculative reason, capable of giving itself an object in the shape of a definition of the political, or of internally differentiating itself in terms of a faculty of reason such as the faculty of judgment that would discern good politics from bad politics so as to fend off the impending threat of radical evil.

Badiou's peculiar use of the term *metapolitics* for his undertaking certainly runs counter to what has become customary ever since the enlightened German liberals Gottlieb Hufeland, August Ludwig von Schlözer, and Carl von Rotteck started using the term shortly after the French Revolution. For them metapolitics refers either to the theoretical study of the principles of right derived from the state of nature or, alternatively, to the theory of the state as such, independent both of politics in the narrow empirical sense and of statistics as the theory of constitutional right and the history of individual constitutions (*Statistik* in German). The term thus acquires the meaning of a metaphysical study into the principles of politics. This is also how the antirevolutionary thinker Joseph de Maistre, albeit from the opposite end of the ideological spectrum, introduced the expression into French: "I hear that German philosophers have invented the word *Metapolitics* to be to *Politics* what the word *Metaphysics* is to *Physics*. It seems that this new expression is an apt invention to designate the *Metaphysics of Politics*."[46] In fact, de Maistre's reactionary perspective, in which politics is meant to be a matter of transcendent if not God-given values, will dominate much of the history of metapolitics until the close of the twentieth century.

Metapolitics in this first broad sense, which should not be confused with Badiou's use of the term, is the study of the ultimate founding ideas, myths, and values behind all concrete forms of political practice. It signals both a movement by which modern political science becomes increasingly self-reflexive and, more important, the possibility of rooting the empirical and mundane in transcendent or transcendental—frequently divine or eschatological—principles. Finally, this understanding of metapolitics for more than a century has been steeped in reactionary ideology and right-wing propaganda.

Starting in 1968, with the international seminar "What Is Metapolitics?," organized by the conservative think tank GRÉCE (*Groupement de Recherche et d'Étude pour la Civilisation Européenne*), *metapolitics* indeed becomes an official watchword of the European New Right, led by the French writer Alain de Benoist. Paradoxically borrowing many insights from the New Left, most notably the Gramscian idea of a cultural "war of positions" and the struggle for "hegemony," de Benoist and his followers in Belgium (Louis Pauwels, Robert Steuckers), the United Kingdom (Michael Walker), Germany (Pierre Krebs), Italy (Marco Tarchi, Carlo Gambescia), and Russia (Alexander Dugin, Eduard Limonov) give primacy to the struggle for cultural power over and above any concrete policy making, or before all politics as usual. Part of this struggle involves a will to return to the pagan Indo-European roots and the so-called originary values of Europe, as opposed to the false universality of Christian-American hegemony. Others, following the work of Silvano Panunzio, also use the term *metapolitics* as a call to recuperate the fundamental roots of politics, but for them these would be precisely Christian through and through, as opposed to the neopagan orientation of de Benoist's New Right.[47]

It would seem, therefore, that Badiou could not have picked a worse term to designate his own proposal for a mode of thinking militant politics, since for him this entails the exact opposite of a modern-day version of the "metaphysics of politics" bent on defining "the political" or even "the nonpolitical ground of politics."[48] A second use of the notion of metapolitics, however, already comes closer to Badiou's understanding of the term. From Benedetto Croce to Antonio Negri and from Manfred Riedel to

Giacomo Marramao, indeed, metapolitics refers to the strictly intraphilosophical study of concepts such as "liberty," or conceptual oppositions
such as "system/action" or "structure/social movement," in the way they
have been deployed in political philosophy from the ancients to the mod-
erns. Marramao, for example, defines *metapolitics* as follows:

> With this term we mean not so much a neo-synthesis of the political—a
> kind of "suprapolitics"—as much as the need to conceptualize a seman-
> tic field with an ambiguous profile, which emphasizes and translates to a
> level of greater complexity the intrinsic "duality" of the modern concept
> of "the political." The problematic that undergirds the category of meta-
> politics implies, in the first place, that the hermeneutic setup for grasp-
> ing the current conditions of practicability of politics must aim for
> *oblique data*, toward areas that, according to the classical topology,
> present themselves as remote or excentric with regard to the classical
> political nomenclatures; and, in the second place, that in order to deci-
> pher the potential political relevance of these zones we must try to give
> form to *symbolic networks* produced by new conflictive relations. This
> second aspect has a precise further implication: the possibility of as-
> suming the hypothesis of reading these interrelations in "systemic"
> terms, that is, of admitting the hypothesis that in the areas of postpoli-
> tics, there are not only *forces* but also *logics* that intersect and overlap.[49]

This type of analysis closely resembles the study of concepts such as
"justice" or "democracy" as names with which philosophy, according to
Badiou, proposes to turn actually existing instances of politics toward the
face of their eternity: "For every word it seizes, however recent, philosophy
seeks an in-temporal consonance."[50] This has nothing to do with setting up
a founding ideal above and beyond the muddy realm of empirical politics.
"Justice," for example, "is simply one of the words through which a philosophy attempts to *seize* the egalitarian axiom inherent in a genuine political
sequence," Badiou writes in *Metapolitics*: "Justice is not a concept for which
we would have to track down more or less approximate realisations in the
empirical world."[51] What is more, as the empty name for the operations
with which philosophy seizes egalitarian ideas and practices, metapolitics
also disentangles itself from the long history of its conservative, if not
outright reactionary, ideological usage.

Finally, perhaps the most intriguing alternative use of *metapolitics* from an emancipatory angle can be found in Rancière's *Disagreement*, where the term designates one of the three dominant figures of "political philosophy," or of "the politics of the philosophers," namely, the figure that refers to Marx, with the other two respectively being called "archipolitics" (from Plato to Bourdieu) and "parapolitics" (from Aristotle to Hobbes to Tocqueville). Through each of these three figures, political philosophers typically attempt to criticize or replace really existing instances of emancipatory politics: "Political philosophies, at least those worthy of the name, the name of this particular paradox, are philosophies that offer a solution to the paradox of the part of those who have no part, either by substituting an equivalent for it, or by creating a simulacrum of it, by performing an imitation of politics in negating it."[52] In the case of Marx, emblematized in "On the Jewish Question," the metapolitical answer to the scandalous paradox that is proper to politics as such typically oscillates between two contradictory extremes. All existing forms of politics, even revolutionary ones, on one hand, can be unmasked on the basis of the underlying truth of the social content which these forms cannot fail to cover up. On the other hand, all merely political emancipation can always be found wanting and subjected to criticism as well from the vantage point of a true, properly human emancipation yet to come, which would take us beyond politics.

For Rancière, in other words, metapolitics submits real political practices to a double verdict, either of being mere "appearances" that hide the infrapolitical "truth" of the class struggle beneath them or else of falling short of the realization of a "genuine" suprapolitics "beyond" politics, in which society would reach its true fulfillment, which would also be its end. This double verdict applies in an exemplary manner to the Marxist concept of class, which socially can be seen as the true content of all political formations while politically class has no positive content whatsoever, being merely the empty operator of the withering away of all classes in the name of the proletarian nonclass:

> As the *truth* of the lie of politics, the concept of class thus becomes the central figure of a metapolitics conceived as a *beyond* of politics, in keeping with one of the two senses of the prefix. But metapolitics can be understood at the same time according to the other sense of the prefix, which indicates *a complement, an accompaniment.* So metapolitics becomes the scientific accompaniment of politics, in which the reduction of political forms to the forces of the class struggle is initially equivalent

to the *truth of the lie* or the truth of illusion. But it also becomes a
"political" accompaniment of all forms of subjectification, which posits
as its hidden "political" truth the class struggle it underestimates and
cannot not underestimate. Metapolitics can *seize* on any phenomenon
as a demonstration of the truth of its falseness.[53]

The obvious question, then, is whether Badiou's understanding of metapolitics corresponds to what Rancière ascribes under this same name to
Marx's treatment of politics. The answer to this question, it seems to me, is
negative for at least two reasons. Badiou, first of all, has no intention
whatsoever to institute a recurrent set of operations with which to criticize
the falseness of existing forms of political emancipation as falling short of
true revolutionary politics. His aim is quite the opposite of anything resembling a Marxian (or, as we saw above, Kantian) critique, whether of
ideology or transcendental illusions. Instead, philosophy seeks to define a
conceptual space in which the thought-practice of emancipatory politics
actually becomes thinkable in the present. In this sense, and this is the
second reason why the answer to the question above must be negative,
Badiou's aim is really no different from Rancière's, since both seek to
extricate the thinking of politics from the operations with which political
philosophy attempts to obscure, displace, or deny politics as such. Thus,
ironically, while these two thinkers share a similar understanding of emancipatory politics as both egalitarian and universalist, one sees metapolitics
as an obstacle that covers up the play of liberty and equality inherent in
such politics, which the other, with the very same concept—despite the
fact that its history is steeped in right-wing ideology—proposes to think
through and set free.

According to Badiou's view, then, a metapolitical understanding presupposes that philosophy produces no truths of its own, political or otherwise.
The possibility of philosophy instead depends on the joint interplay of
multiple truths that take place outside of philosophy, or behind the philosopher's back. Politics is only one out of four such conditions of philosophy, next to art, science, and love. Philosophy, moreover, cannot in turn
subordinate the truths produced in these conditions to the norms and
concepts that would be its privilege as a crowning or higher science. Instead, philosophy opens a space of compossibility in which each of the
conditions finds its place, not so much to violently seize them but rather so
as to let itself be seized by that which takes place in them in terms of events.

Politics, understood in this sense, is no doubt the clearest and most powerful condition of Badiou's philosophy. From the late 1960s until the mid-1980s, after he abandons the idea, borrowed from his teachers Georges Canguilhem and Jean Hyppolite, that only the sciences are capable of producing truths, politics even stands as the only possible truth procedure within Badiou's system of thinking. Thus, while as late as in March 1965 he still approvingly conducts his televised interview with Canguilhem, Hyppolite, Michel Foucault, Paul Ricoeur, and Dina Dreyfus under the banners "There is no philosophical truth" and "There is only scientific truth," in *Theory of the Subject*, on the other hand, Badiou writes: "Every subject is political. This is why there are few subjects and rarely any politics."[54] The notion of a subject in this context is not to be taken as an autonomous instance that would somehow precede the event in the way of an ultimate anthropological or existential ground. The subject is rather a fragment of the sustained enquiry into the consequences of an event for a possible universal truth. Badiou's thesis that every subject is political thus entails that there are events only in politics. This claim from *Theory of the Subject* admittedly will be moderated in the collection of essays and conferences titled *Conditions*, which builds on the systematic outline presented in *Being and Event*: "Today, I should no longer say 'every subject is political,' which is still a maxim of suture. I should rather say: 'Every subject is induced through a generic procedure, and therefore depends upon an event. This is why a subject is rare.'"[55] Henceforth, philosophy should no longer abdicate its own powers by subordinating both itself and the four truth procedures to a single one of them, as Badiou himself claims to have done with politics under the influence of Marxism. "Everything is political," the recurrent slogan of the 1960s and 1970s, signals precisely such a subordination of philosophy to one of its conditions of existence—a process that Badiou now rejects as a "suture" of philosophy. Thus, a corrected version of the claim made in *Theory of the Subject* can be found in *Manifesto for Philosophy*, which together with *Ethics* is still Badiou's most accessible work: "Every subject is artistic, scientific, political or amorous. Besides, this is something that everyone knows from experience because outside of these registers there is only existence, or individuality, but no subject."[56] However, even with this opening onto the other three conditions, it is not always equally clear how art and love function as generic procedures for Badiou. In the end, and despite an uninterrupted passion for the science of mathematics that in many ways provides the formal model—what is also called the numericity or numericality—with which the other truth procedures can be deciphered, we can nevertheless argue with good reason that it is politics that receives a privileged treatment in the hands of Badiou.

Let us consider, for example, how Badiou's *Metapolitics* opens with a tribute to two French mathematicians, Jean Cavaillès and Albert Lautman, whose commitment to the Resistance during the Second World War, which would eventually cost them their lives, could not be deduced from any objective standard, not even from a moral conviction, but instead depended, as it were, purely on the internal coherence of their thinking. From this observation Badiou draws a conclusion that is valid for his concept of truth in general and of political truths in particular: "It is not the moral concern or, as people say nowadays, the ethical discourse that seem to have produced the greatest figures of philosophy as resistance. The concept seems to have been a better guide on this matter than conscience or even spirituality."[57] Here, the model of axiomatic thinking in mathematics indicates that a decision in politics does not depend on the positive study of the circumstances in which it takes place (even when these circumstances include the history of the class struggle), nor can politics be made to depend on the moral elucubrations of our (good or bad) conscience— no matter whether this is subsequently given some color and substance through the ideas of Kant, Sartre, or Levinas: "The intelligibility of the choice lies in the choice itself, in the consistent process of the ensuing action, just as an axiom can be understood only from within the theoretical developments that are supported by this axiom itself."[58] Mathematics, in other words, provides an insightful model for clarifying the way in which philosophy should come to seize politics from within, without referring the process to any explanatory data that would serve as its external guarantee.

We thus are beginning to grasp the far-reaching consequences of the apparently simple point of departure according to which in politics people are capable of just collective thought. "People think" (*les gens pensent*) is also, not coincidentally, the founding idea behind Lazarus's *Anthropology of the Name*. I have already indicated how this idea is meant to signal, first, that politics is in and of itself a form of thinking and, second, that this thinking cannot be remitted to economics, sociology, or history as disciplines that provide the data in relation to which we would have to define the nature of politics, with the task of this definition typically befalling the party or, all else failing, social movement as such, in case there is no immediate or spontaneous link between history and politics or between the socioeconomical determination of classes and the political class struggle, properly speaking. Instead, the imperative that runs like a mantra through Lazarus's *Anthropology of the Name* and Badiou's *Metapolitics* is that politics must be thought from within: "The problem is not the being of this thought, but its thinkability. Can politics be thought *as* thought? That is the question."[59] It would be an act of bad faith, therefore, to disregard the imperative to think politics in interiority while interrogating Badiou's own work.

Generally, let us say that with regard to the link between philosophy and politics, as with the interpretation of this thinker's work as a whole, we could distinguish two fundamental approaches based on the line of demarcation between practice and theory. The first approach would consist in studying the history of Badiou's own political militancy, beginning in the Maoist (Groupe pour la fondation de l') Union des Communistes de France marxiste-léniniste (UCFML) and subsequently in Organisation Politique (OP), both of which he helped cofound together with Lazarus and Natacha Michel. With the sole exception of Peter Hallward's study of Organisation Politique, this is by far the least developed approach in the study of Badiou's political work.[60] In the following pages I try to make up for this lack, especially in respect of the Maoist period, by relying on rare and hard-to-find documents, ranging from dozens of pamphlets and brochures, sometimes written under the pseudonyms of Georges Peyrol (for Badiou) and Paul Sandevince (for Lazarus), or newsletters and journals such as *Le Marxiste-Léniniste* or *Le Perroquet* (for UCFML) and *La Distance Politique* (for OP). The second approach, by contrast, would consist in studying Badiou's works that deal with politics from a more strictly theoretical perspective, starting with the early *Contribution to the Problem of the Construction of a Marxist-Leninist Party of a New Type*, when he was still a member of the Parti Socialiste Unifié (PSU), through his Maoist *Theory of Contradiction* and *Of Ideology*, until *Of an Obscure Disaster: The End of the Truth of the State*, about the "fall" of communism, and the already cited *Metapolitics*, in order to draw out the possible connections with, and points of divergence from, classical or contemporary political thinkers, including Rousseau, Marx, Lenin, and Mao, as well as Althusser, Balibar, Rancière, Derrida, Agamben, Negri, Butler, and Žižek.[61]

For Badiou, however, the whole point of metapolitics lies in the intrinsic link between these two aspects of militancy and theory. To adopt a metapolitical orientation thus includes tightening the joint between the two approaches to the relation of philosophy to politics in his work. Between Badiou's militant tracts and his philosophical treatises there may very well be a sharp difference in tone and conceptual depth, but the basic principle behind the metapolitical orientation remains unchanged, namely, that we cannot separate thinking and acting even when, or especially when, philosophy puts itself under condition of a specific mode of doing politics. Nor should we revert to some older dialectical understanding, according to which a political sequence becomes thinkable only after the fact, as when the owl of Minerva, according to Hegel, takes flight only at dusk, in the belated intelligibility of this sequence's closure—regardless of whether this closure is then conceived of as a success or, more commonly in the case of revolutionary politics, as a failure. "This would be to regress to the logic of the dialectical result, to the dialectic of synthesis and the idea that the truth of a political sequence is embodied in its future," whereas a metapolitical orientation holds that "a sequence should be identified and thought on its own terms, as a homogeneous singularity, and not in terms of the heterogeneous nature of its empirical future."[62]

We must therefore always begin by asking which events and which modes of doing politics are ultimately determining for Badiou's political thinking. This is not the same as putting forth a fixed notion of the event in order then to ponder whether there are, indeed, examples of such an event to be found amid the confusion of our current actuality. To put philosophy under the condition of politics is even the exact opposite of looking for empirical examples of the philosophical concept of politics. Of course, there are minimal conditions that must be fulfilled in order for us to be able to speak of a political event, and such conditions are regularly systematized, for example, in *Conditions* and *Metapolitics*. But we should resist the temptation of putting the cart before the horse. It is surely a concrete politics that allows Badiou to raise the general question such as the one with which he begins "Politics as Truth Procedure," in *Metapolitics*: "When, and under what conditions, can an event be said to be political? What is the 'what happens' insofar as it happens politically?"[63] For many years, to be more precise, this question continues to depend on the events of May '68 and, even more so (because we should not blow up the importance of May '68 beyond proportions as some ultraleftist "grand" event), on its prolonged aftermath in the 1970s under the banner of French Maoism, while Badiou's more recent activism since the 1980s revolves around the mobili-

zation of "illegal immigrants" or *sans-papiers* in France. In fact, part of the
investigation into this recent political history must be able to account
precisely for the ways in which the shift from the name "worker" to the
names "immigrant" or "fundamentalist" has led to a complete obliteration
of the earlier sequence of militantism, no matter how obscure or tentative
the latter's conceptualization may well have been and perhaps continues to
be. Thus, the real question depends on the way in which philosophy
registers the effects of these sequences in its very midst. Even when the
treatment appears to be narrowly philosophical, the reader should always
bear in mind the events that condition the series of concepts that constitute the true subject matter of Badiou's metapolitics.

Keeping in mind this important caveat, let me put forward a few of the
major principles in this metapolitical orientation:

1. Politics, or a (mode of doing) politics, is first of all a process or a
   procedure, that is, an active form of militant practice, and not a form
   of the state. It is precisely with regard to this first principle that most
   hitherto existing political philosophies run aground, insofar as they
   subordinate the sequence of a given political process to the structural question about the (good) form of power.
2. As a process or procedure, a politics starts out from that point in the
   social order that signals the excessive power of the state. This point is
   the place, or site, of the political event. Every political event is anchored in a specific situation through such a symptomatic site, which
   otherwise appears to be near the edges of the void, or inexistent.
3. The state is the instance that doubly controls the situation, for
   example, by first counting all the inhabitants who have the right to
   be legal citizens, residents or nonresidents, and then, as in a census,
   by counting these members a second time in terms of various sub-
   categories, or subsets: male and female, immigrant and indigenous,
   adults and minors, etc.
4. The difference between these two counting operations, first the
   elements of a set and then the subsets, corresponds to the difference
   between the simple presentation of a given situation and its redoubling or re-presentation in the state of this situation. Here as elsewhere, in an ambiguity on which I will have occasion to comment
   below, Badiou plays with the double sense of the "state": both the
   normal state of affairs (*état*) and the political state (*État*).

5. The example of the census already intuitively indicates that there is always an excess of the power with which the state of a situation exceeds this situation itself, signaled by the "etcetera" or "other" that cannot fail to appear at the end of every list of categories. The number of ways in which we can order the subsets of a given census is in principle always larger than the number of members that figure in this census to begin with. What is more, in an infinite situation, this excess can be shown to be properly immeasurable. It is this simple and fundamental axiom of contemporary set theory that marks the onset, so to speak, of a political intervention. The state's excessive power in fact becomes visible only as the result of an emergent political subject. When everything runs its course as usual, this excess remains invisible even as the errancy of the state's super-power secretly continues to serve an intimidating function. It is necessary to put a limit on the excess that otherwise remains hidden behind the semblance of communal bonds and cultural identities.

6. A political process, thus, does not start out from a previously given bond or group, not even when this social bond is defined in terms of the class struggle, but precisely from a local unbinding of the common bond. It is also not the case that the state rejects the formation of new social bonds but rather what it seeks to avoid at all cost, even if this means allowing all kinds of separations and subversions, is the coming apart of the ideological glue that holds together our particular identities. There is a primacy of struggle over the classes, a primacy that subsequent attempts at classification may actually seek to pacify or stabilize.

7. Politics is not the art of the possible but the art of the impossible. To be more precise, a political process must make the impossible possible. This means in the first place to give visibility to the excess of power in the normal state of affairs. During the revolt of May '68, no less than during the still obscure sequence of later events—from the protests of Solidarity in Poland to the uprising in Chiapas to the second Intifada—this process involves a certain gamble, or wager, through which the state is forced to lay bare its inherently repressive nature as a violent excrescence, typically shielded in a military and police apparatus used both inside and outside its own borders.

8. Politics as a procedure of truth, however, cannot be reduced to the

typically youthful protest against the eternally oppressive and corrupt nature of the state apparatus. From the symptomatic site of the event, bordering the void that lurks everywhere in between the cracks of a census even if it cannot find a place in the images of representational politics, a militant subject emerges only when the particular terms of the various memberships that define society are put down and abolished in favor of a generic concept of truth as universally the same for all.

9. Politics, in other words, has nothing to do with respect for difference or for the other, not even the absolutely other, and everything with equality and sameness. This conclusion runs counter to the moral or moralizing consensus of contemporary politicians and political philosophers alike, which holds that a true (democratic) politics can contain the dangers of totalitarianism and fundamentalism only when a place is reserved for difference in the name of freedom. But the market, too, works with differences, or at least with semblances of difference. This is even the way in which the general equivalence of the underlying order is capable of reproducing itself. There is thus nothing inherently subversive, let alone revolutionary, about the affirmation of difference, becoming, or flux within the coordinates of contemporary capitalism. Only a strict egalitarian affirmation can break through this general equivalence of capital disguised as difference.

10. By traversing and deposing the different representations of identity with which the excess of state power maintains itself in its very errancy, a political procedure gradually begins to revolve around the notion of a generic set, that is, a set without determining attributes or qualities. Ultimately, politics is nothing if it is not the active organization of a generic equality, one possible name of which continues to be communism.

11. Indeed, with the notion of the generic, which according to Badiou is the most important conceptual contribution of *Being and Event*, we finally come back to Marx. It is, after all, he who, in the posthumous *Manuscripts of 1844* and the *Grundrisse*, speaks of the possibility of the human as a generic species-being. Even more pertinently, it is Marx who in "On the Jewish Question," speaking on the subject of complete human emancipation as opposed to purely moral or politi-

cal emancipation, invokes the authority of *The Social Contract* where Jean-Jacques Rousseau—for Badiou one of the four great French dialecticians next to Pascal, Mallarmé, and Lacan—had written: "Whoever dares to undertake the founding of a nation must feel himself capable of *changing*, so to speak, *human nature* and of *transforming* each individual who is in himself a complete but isolated whole into a *part* of something greater than himself from which he somehow derives his life and existence, substituting a *limited* and *moral* existence for physical and independent existence."[64] Perhaps there is no better description of the fundamental idea behind communism than to have confidence in this capacity of *changing* human nature itself—that is, above all, of transforming the human being from an egotistic independent individual, whose self-interest is so often invoked as an ideological legitimation for the natural superiority of capitalism, into a generic species-being. This means not only that politics cannot be referred back to any ontology as first philosophy but also, and perhaps primarily, that all emancipatory thought must likewise refuse to rely on an anthropological preunderstanding of what constitutes human nature. There is no more political ontology than there would exist a political anthropology. Both expressions are equally oxymoronic.

Badiou's plea for the generic nature of all truths, in this sense, can be considered a contemporary actualization of the fundamental idea behind communism. The question that I will try to tackle throughout the following pages, before coming back to meet its demand head-on in the book's conclusion, is whether and to what extent this idea of communist emancipation also continues to presuppose the tradition of Marxism, or whether we have now, in the age of terror, entered the terrain of a resolutely postMarxist, or non-Marxist, communism. Whence the question with which I will end: Communism without Marxism?

In the contemporary renewal of the communist hypothesis, however, we should not overlook the fact that the concept of the generic also undergoes a decisive shift. For Badiou, in effect, this concept defines the nature of truth and not, as it once did for Marx, the human subject as a speciesbeing. It is the being of truth that is generic, not the communist subject. What is more, in spite of numerous allusions to the work of the young Marx, whose humanism Badiou would have learned how to rebuke from his teacher Althusser, the principal source of reference for the notion of the generic in *Being and Event* is not political but mathematical, insofar as it is a basic philosophical concept conditioned by the idea of a generic set, the existence of which in turn is demonstrated in an important scientific event in its own right by the mathematician Paul J. Cohen. For Badiou, indeed, set theory serves no more noble cause than to formalize how humanity can become a *part* greater than the sum of its *elements*. This leads me, in a last series of introductory remarks, to raise the thorny issue of the place of mathematics in relation to my reading of Badiou's philosophy in general and his thinking of politics in particular.

WHITHER MATHEMATICS?

> Only in mathematics can one unequivocally maintain that if thought can formulate a problem, it can and will solve it, regardless of how long it takes.—BADIOU, *Theoretical Writings*

> Except to add that what we did not know *before* was determined as a remainder of what has come to be known, at the crossover between the nameless movement through which the real appears as a problem and the retroaction, named knowledge, which provides the solution.
> —BADIOU, *Theory of the Subject*

The reader may well wonder at this point why mathematics does not figure more prominently in the preceding outline of my interpretation of Badiou's work. Is not the matheme what sets this work apart from any and all hermeneutic, phenomenological, textualist-deconstructive, or neoreligious vagaries? Sam Gillespie raises this objection in *The Mathematics of Novelty*: "For, however open Badiou's theory of truth may be to non-mathematical interpretations (such as found in Žižek, Critchley, Bruno Bosteels), it is in fact only through a thorough exposition of Paul Cohen's generic set-theory that we can adequately grasp what Badiou is doing with the classical category of truth."[65] In minimizing the importance of the mathematical framework, then, am I not disabling a proper understanding of this thinker's singularity, or worse, falling into the traps of a vulgar cultural bias for which mathematics is either too hermetic and coldly abstract or else, in a politically correct inversion of the same bias, too masculine, falsely universalist but actually elitist, and at bottom Eurocentric?

It is important to be precise, however, about the function of mathematics in Badiou's thought. In *Being and Event*, in particular, this function is actually twofold, in a way that has not yet received all the attention it deserves. On the one hand, mathematics *is* ontology, that is, the discourse of being qua being: "All that we know, and can ever know of being qua being, is set out, through the mediation of a theory of the pure multiple, by the historical discursivity of mathematics."[66] On the other hand, this historical discursivity is in turn punctuated by powerful axiomatic decisions, conceptual inventions, and mind-boggling demonstrations, which ought to be considered events in their own right. Cohen's 1963 proof of the existence of generic or indiscernible sets marks such an event, one that furthermore is absolutely crucial for Badiou's own overall philosophical project: "Now, we know that ever since the event in the matheme constituted by Paul Cohen's operators, it is precisely possible to produce a concept of the indiscernible and to establish under certain conditions the existence of multiplicities that fall within this concept: 'generic' multiplicities."[67] Mathematics, thus, is doubly inscribed: both as the ontological discourse of being qua being and as one truth procedure among others in which interventions can take place that as events exceed the purview of being qua being.[68] In short, if we return to the title of Badiou's major work, mathematics is operative both on the side of being and on the side of the event. This double inscription is what gives mathematics a unique status, completely distinct from politics, art, or love, which operate only at the level of truth procedures as conditions for philosophy.

Although these two uses of mathematics are not opposed to one another, the nature of their imbrication must be articulated with care. New inventions that result from events in the realm of mathematics such as the development of set theory from Cantor to Cohen, for example, will certainly impact the discourse of ontology so that when Badiou discusses the nature of truth or of the event itself in ontological terms, mathematical concepts such as "genericity" or "forcing" are bound to make their appearance. But these concepts function differently in philosophy from their original use in the daily activity of the working mathematician. In philosophy, to be precise, such concepts acquire a metamathematical or metaontological status. As Badiou writes: "In this instance, as in Plato or in my own work, philosophy's role consists in informing mathematics of its own speculative grandeur," especially with an eye on setting free what otherwise remains bound and obscure in the break with opinion that mathematics introduces on its own: "Mathematics belongs to truth, but to a constrained form of it. Above and beyond this constrained figure of truth stands its free figure which elucidates discontinuity: philosophy.["69] Finally, the issue becomes still more complicated if we consider that, once philosophy extracts and elucidates the conceptual operators with which to think the ontological grandeur of the inventions of the working mathematician, these concepts also become available for use in domains that are not strictly speaking ontological.

Now, I would argue that the exact nature of the transfer of metaontological concepts into the domain of the historico-political, which is the one that will most concern me in what follows, has not yet been rendered fully explicit. Indeed, we do well to insist that all such exportations and importations, depending on our original vantage point, can only ever have an analogical, symptomatic, or heuristic value. Even die-hard fans of Badiou's otherwise undeniable mathematical propensity are rarely clear about this. As in the case of the philosophers of the French Resistance mentioned above, mathematical operators of thought may be useful to grasp the way in which politics functions according to its own logic, regardless of morality or the state, but terms such as the "state" of a situation remain by and large analogous in comparison to concepts such as the "power set" in mathematical set theory. Put differently, metamathematical concepts are rigorously formal, and they hold true according to an intrinsic rationality only within the ontological situation; anywhere else, they are just helpful tools that by analogy, through a symptomatic reading of mathematical names such as *forcing* or *torsion*, or in a metaphorical transposition, may help us formalize situations that are not in and of themselves ontological in the strict sense.

Insofar as Badiou's idea of mathematics is resolutely opposed to any analogical or intuitive capture of its immanent powers, however, the transfer of mathematical concepts into the historico-political domain, and vice versa, will frequently turn out to be strained by an effort to erase all traces of this transfer itself, so as not to leave the impression of analogical thinking. Let me illustrate this with a brief and punctual anticipatory reading of *Being and Event*, more specifically of Meditations 8 and 9, in which Badiou seeks to define the nature of the historico-political situation and the metastructure of this same situation, called the state or State.

Before coming to this crossroads, the reader of the preceding meditations in *Being and Event* has been given a philosophical analysis of the ideas of the multiple, the situation, the void, and the excess. In each case the exposition of this analysis tends to take the form of a layered combination of conceptual, intuitive, and strictly mathematical presentations. This is true not only in the sense that the book as a whole contains three different kinds of meditation, from the conceptual to the mathematical to the historico-philosophical, but a similar threefold presentation also recurs within almost every type of meditation in *Being and Event*, as well as, later on, in the various books of *Logics of Worlds*. Badiou in fact constantly warns readers against the temptations of ordinary language, which allows mathematics to be captured by the deceptive force of intuition. We risk falling prey to spatializing intuitions, for example, when we say that a set is "larger" than a part of this set or that an element is located "inside" the set of which it is an element. Even *part* and *element* are potentially misleading terms, since they seem to unify and render compact what at bottom remains strictly multiple. If Badiou nonetheless allows intuitive language to smuggle itself into his exposition, indeed actively relies on it as an illustrative counterweight, it is because he knows that the struggle of mathematics against mere opinions and intuitions is a battle that must be started over and over again: "One must begin again, because mathematics is always beginning again and transforming its abstract panoply of concepts," but also "because the philosophical struggle against the alliance of finitude and obscurantism will only be rekindled through this recommencement."[70] We could also say that, even though mathematics presents a purely intrinsic truth that, moreover, can be immediately and universally shared, the philosophical exposition of this concrete universalism cannot fail to run up against the doxa of common beliefs, habits, and prejudices that firmly anchor us in the human condition of our finitude. In this sense, far from presenting once and for all a fully accomplished rationality, as Badiou and some of his most admiring readers at times seem to suggest, even mathematics struggles constantly against its immanent ideological tendencies.

Thus, in Badiou's exposition the concepts of philosophy serve as the in-between of absolute mathematical rigor and mere intuitive approximation, opening up a space in which the first through hard methodic labor arms itself to undo the seductive force of the second. Within the embattled domain of conceptual language, in effect, the mathematical paradigm offers a weapon that is uniquely capable of staving off the power and laziness of intuitive language, which spontaneously tends to feed into the romantic ideology of human finitude or, but this is only the other side of the same coin, merely potential or religious infinity, as opposed to actual or atheist infinity: "Mathematics provides philosophy with a weapon, a fearsome machine of thought, a catapult at the bastions of ignorance, superstition and mental servitude."[71] Even so, this use of mathematics as a weapon against finitude should not be allowed to confound the specific protocols needed to guarantee the double inscription of mathematics in Badiou's philosophy.

Let us consider the key moment when, in Meditation 8 of *Being and Event*, Badiou unexpectedly proposes to call "state" or "state of the situation" what in set-theoretical terms is called the "power set," that is, the set of all the parts or subsets of a given set. Here is how he justifies this nominal decision: "Due to a metaphorical affinity with politics that will be explained in Meditation 9, I will hereinafter term *state of the situation* that by means of which the structure of a situation—of any structured presentation whatsoever—is counted as one, which is to say the one of the one-effect itself, or what Hegel calls the One-One."[72] *Par une convenance métaphorique*, the sentence reads in the original French. In other words, the name of the "state" of a situation, which has a universal metaontological value insofar as it designates the power set for the purposes of philosophy, stems from a sheer metaphorical affinity or agreement, if not from a mere convenience. Thus, instead of conditioning philosophy as two autonomous procedures of truth, mathematics and politics are put in a relation of metaphorical cross-referencing amongst themselves. To be more precise, philosophy here circulates between three levels or domains: mathematics, politics, and the history of philosophy—with the reference to Hegel. Since what concerns me for the time being is limited to the relation between mathematics and politics, I will not address the question of knowing whether this last domain, that is, the discursive historicity of philosophy itself, might constitute a fifth condition of sorts, as Badiou suggests at least once elsewhere, namely, when he writes at the very beginning of *Being and Event* that philosophy "*circulates* between this ontology (thus, mathematics), the modern theories of the subject, and its own history" so that "the contemporary complex of the conditions of philosophy includes . . . the history of 'Western' thought, post-Cantorian mathematics, psychoanalysis, contemporary art and politics."[73]

Now, no sooner do we turn to Meditation 9 than we immediately come across another surprising gesture that further compounds the problem of formalization outside of the strict realm of mathematics. At the start of this meditation Badiou indeed proposes to give us "an example" of one such "state" in particular, namely "that of historico-social situations," with the following justification: "Besides the verification of the concept of the state of the situation, this illustrative meditation will also provide us with an opportunity to employ three categories of presented-being: normality, singularity, and excrescence."[74] In a strange torsion, what is now presented as the illustrative verification of a metamathematical concept in the historico-political domain was said earlier to have been imported into metamathematics, by reason of a metaphorical affinity, from the realm of politics!

Such a relation of torsion between the metamathematical (ontology) and the historico-political (politics), with *torsion* itself being a mathematical term with a symptomatic value outside of strict mathematics, raises the suspicion that what actually is taking place before our eyes is a process of an altogether different nature than what the exposition claims to transmit in its apparently neutral language as a purely mathematical issue:

1. The reader first of all cannot be blamed for thinking that the introduction of "state of the situation" as the metamathematical name for the power set is actively conditioned by politics as one of the four truth procedures. In *Theory of the Subject*, speaking of the use of algebra and topology, Badiou acknowledges that such an impression is both real and justified. "Regarding my examples," he says, "some could voice the suspicion that all these dialectical algorithms and theorems stand in a relation of absolute dependence to the contents which they organize—the proletariat, imperialist society, revisionism, and so on—and that this is a syntax of little interest from the moment that the semantics of it is forced," to which Badiou replies that "this is a matter of indifference to me. Because as a Marxist, I in fact posit that the contents drain the forms, and not the other way around. What is certain is that the dialectical formulations are rooted in an explicit political practice."[75] Conversely, *Theory of the Subject* also approaches certain mathematical concepts such as "forcing," "torsion," and the "power" of a set's cardinality from a symptomatic angle rather than in terms of their intrinsic rationality within mathematics. "The postulate is that no signifier finds a place in a mathematical text by random chance, and that even if it is true that its mathematical

character derives from its role within the formal texture of the demonstration, this texture should also be considered, in its overdetermination, as the retroactive analysis of this very non-random character," Badiou explains. "That is, we take the mathematical text to be in
the position of the analyst for some of its own words—as being
symptomatic of itself."[76] But then of course I would add that the
mathematical signifiers can be interpreted as symptoms only if and
when we otherwise have access to that which—most often though
not only politically—overdetermines their role as symptoms. That is,
we must already understand why these signifiers are symptoms in the
first place, and such an understanding in this instance is political
rather than mathematical. Between mathematics and politics there
would thus be a relation of active conditioning or overdetermination
and not purely one of metaphorical affinity. Nowhere in Badiou's
philosophical system, however, do we find an explicit treatment of
this type of conditioning *among* different truth procedures rather
than *between* the four truth procedures and philosophy in general.[77]

2. Anyone familiar with the classics in the Marxist-Leninist tradition also
   will have noticed that, while seemingly phrased in strictly mathematical language, the typology of the state of the situation in terms of normality, singularity, and excrescence, too, is imported from the realm of
   militant politics. Thus, in *The State and Revolution* Lenin repeatedly
   quotes expressions from Marx's assessment of the Paris Commune in
   The Civil War in France, in which the power of the state is defined
   precisely in terms of a certain excrescence: "The Communal Constitution would have restored to the social body all the forces hitherto
   absorbed by that parasitic excrescence, the 'state,' feeding upon and
   hampering the free movement of society."[78] In other words, when
   Badiou affirms that the power of the state is intrinsically excessive
   and, furthermore, that set theory demonstrates the errancy proper to
   the size of this excess, he is actually formalizing a well-established
   principle of militant political practices. Once he has formalized this
   principle, he can even pretend to look back and criticize the political
   use of the term for which he has just claimed to provide a strictly
   mathematical account: "The ambivalence in the classic Marxist analysis is concentrated in one point: thinking—since it is solely from the
   standpoint of the State that there are excrescences—that the State

itself is an excrescence."[79] But, I repeat, this is not the same as arguing for the intrinsic rationality of set theory as the ontology of political situations, as those readers seem to argue who insist on the fundamental role of mathematical set theory for all of Badiou's philosophy. Not only are we placed in a non-ontological domain where the equation "mathematics = ontology" no longer really applies, but to understand this other domain, we should always come back to the principle that "ontology ≠ politics" since politics, like the events that punctuate the historicity of mathematics as a truth procedure, involves that which is not being qua being. In other words, there is no such thing as a political ontology. This expression only hides the tensions between politics and ontology, which are best understood by clarifying the double inscription of mathematics in Badiou's philosophy.

3. As one among the four procedures of truth, politics in yet a different way can be said to overdetermine the metaontological use of mathematics, namely insofar as the pure multiplicity of being qua being, which can be described in the historical discursivity of mathematics, nonetheless becomes visible as such only on the occasion of rare and contingent events, including those of politics. This is something to which we will have to return in detail during the discussion of *Being and Event*. Suffice it here to say that the linear order of the meditations in this book—from being as pure multiple to the theory of the intervening subject—should be read as the exact inverse of the actual sequence in which the truth of a situation comes about so as to reveal the genericity of this situation's very being. In other words, what may be transmitted from the start in a strictly formal exposition as the metamathematical doctrine of inconsistent multiplicity really cannot be accessed in concrete historical circumstances unless a subject has already intervened in response to the contingency of an actually occurring event. Unlike what we will see happen in *Logics of Worlds*, which begins by positing a metaphysical theory of the subject from the start, there is a principle of retroactive clarification at work in the discursive presentation of *Being and Event*, insofar as the realities formalized in the earlier meditations become effectively thinkable only under the condition of specific events as described in the later ones. The possibility of thinking the sheer inconsistency of being qua being, which may appear to be the autonomous task of mathematics

as elucidated in philosophy, thus arrives in actual fact only if and when there happens to be a subject at work who is faithful to an event, for instance, in politics.

4. There is yet another unspoken determinant that seems to have been at work in the transferences between mathematics and politics, namely, the assumption that any concrete politico-historical situation is actually infinite. Without this assumption the transfer of the theorem of excess and the demonstration of the errancy of this excess, to which we will return in due course below, quite simply would not hold any water. For in the case of finite sets mathematics has no problem measuring the excess of the cardinality of the power set over the cardinality of the original set. So in order for this excess to be truly beyond measure, the ordinary social situations we live in must be infinite. But, in reality, this turns out to be a strictly axiomatic assumption, a matter of conviction, if not a question of personal preference pure and simple. "When I say that all situations are infinite, it's an axiom. It is impossible to deduce this point. It is an axiomatic conviction, a modern conviction," Badiou admits in an interview on the topic "Ontology and Politics" included in *Infinite Thought*. He continues: "It is better for thinking to say that situations are infinite. Because we come after a long philosophical period in which the theme of finitude and the conviction that all situations are finite was dominant, and we are suffering the effects of that sort of conviction."[80] In the end, then, the issue becomes one of ethics as a guide for measuring the consequences of a decision—namely, the decision in favor of actual infinity over and against finitude— comparable to the assumption of an axiom for which no deductions or outside legitimations are available.

These four factors, which encapsulate the difficult question of the relevance and applicability of ontological categories beyond the realm of ontology properly speaking, justify in my eyes the limited use made of mathematics in the following interpretation of Badiou's philosophy and politics. This is not meant as a belated and embellished excuse for an otherwise undeniable degree of personal ignorance on my part in all matters pertaining to the sciences. The situation is rather such that any disingenuous reliance on the supposed autonomy of the mathematical paradigm will cause us to lose sight of the true relations that operate not only between mathematics and politics but also between politics and philosophy in Badiou's work. What is more, to anyone who cries foul play when I confess to my being mathematically challenged, I could argue not only that this confession is at least more modest than if I were to lay claims to a knowledge that I actually do not possess but also that similar demands apply to those die-hard mathematical readers of Badiou who often completely ignore the links of his thought to literature, to psychoanalysis, or to politics. And in this book I am, after all, concerned only with this last condition.

From my point of view, ultimately, the question about the status of formalization should be seen as part of the larger issue, which can be brought back to another much-maligned principle of the dialectical method, one that, moreover, is already implicit in what precedes, namely the identity or at the very least the cobelonging between concept and experience, or between the logical (or ontological) and the historical (or phenomenological). Against common textbook variations on the tautology of the real and the rational, Lenin was, after all, fond of underscoring the importance of this principle for his reading of Hegel's *Science of Logic*, writing in shorthand notation in his *Philosophical Notebooks*: "Hegel as a genius *guessed* the dialectics of things, phenomena, the world (nature), in the dialectic of notions."[81] Far from merely confirming a static homology of nature and spirit according to the good old reflection theory of knowledge, the "genius" of this approach actually lies in the possibility of reading history off logic and vice versa. The reason why this can never be more than a "guess," however, depends on the presence of a constitutive gap or deadlock between concept and experience, which keeps them from ever coinciding with one another—except asymptotically. But even this gap or deadlock, at a higher level, can be read as the conjectural formalization of a historical limit. Indeed, it is only out of a strict fidelity to the thinking of historicity in the present time that one must posit a gap between concepts and things or between history and logic. Adorno, many years later, would reiterate this basic principle in his own *Hegel: Three Studies* by arguing painstakingly for the need to recapture the concrete experiential content, particularly in terms of human labor, behind Hegel's most abstract logical formalism: "Hegel has to be read against the grain, and in such a way that every logical operation, however formal it seems to be, is reduced to its experiential core."[82] This is also how I propose that we strain to read Badiou's work. Every logical and ontological operation, however formal it may well seem to be, must thus be related against the grain to the experiential core that conditions it. For the purposes of what follows, this means above all to size up the iceberg of emancipatory politics that is all but hidden—if it has not already suffered a complete meltdown as a result of global warming—below the arctic waters of mathematical formalization.

THE ABSENT CAUSE

←⋯⋯⋯⋯⋯⋯⋯⋯⋯⋯⋯⋯⋯⋯⋯⋯→

BEHIND THE PHILOSOPHER'S BACK

In the present ideological conjuncture, our main task is to constitute
the kernel of an authentic materialist philosophy and of a just philosophical strategy in order to facilitate the emergence of a progressive
ideology.—ALTHUSSER, *Filosofía y marxismo*

All philosophers, by some kind of professional deformation, have a tendency of wanting to begin with the beginning. Whether in the name of
"first causes," "originary principles," or "fundamental concepts," it is what
stands at the origin or beginning that interests them first and foremost.
From Hegel to Heidegger, and from Nietzsche to Foucault, there even
exists a long and well-established tradition that consists in differentiating
between the good and the bad uses of the beginning as principle, start,
initiation, genesis, emergence, origin, or provenance.[1] A philosophy seeking to be worthy of the name materialism, however, must begin by recalling
that philosophy itself never begins anything. Instead, insofar as philosophy
is preceded by different practices that are not themselves philosophical, this
beginning has always already happened elsewhere. It is not something that
philosophical thought can muster simply from within its own resources but
something that faces it, confronts it, and sometimes even affronts it, from
the outside. For example, in the case of so-called political philosophy since
at least Plato, this effort of the philosopher has never been anything other
than the belated response to the scandal of democracy. "It is first in relation
to politics that philosophy, from the very beginning, 'comes too late,' " as
Jacques Rancière writes in *Disagreement*: "In the form of democracy, politics is already in place, without waiting for its theoretical underpinnings or
its *arkhè*, without waiting for the proper beginning that will give birth to it
as performance of its own principle."[2] It is only the formless multitude of

the democratic masses that begins by provoking the response of the philosopher, as in the figure of the ideal republic proposed by Socrates.

This principle of the antecedence of nonphilosophical practices with
regard to philosophy proper, or if we look at the question from the opposite
end, this principle of the belated effect of philosophy with regard to that
which is not philosophical, remains entirely valid for the modern era. This
is why Badiou in *Can Politics Be Thought?* will postulate the following:
"The canonical statement (from Rousseau to Mao), which holds that the
masses make history, designates precisely in the masses this vanishing
irruption of which political philosophy only tells the always belated and
always torn story."[3] The massive eruption of *a* (mode of doing) politics,
even if its experience is often extremely short-lived and appears only in
order to disappear immediately afterward, occurs well before the arrival on
the scene of those professional philosophers who take it on themselves to
define its essence as *the* political. This is why the theme of the beginning,
seen purely and simply from within the realm of philosophy, provides us
with a false window. Not only is there no strictly philosophical beginning,
except precisely from an idealist viewpoint, but a materialist philosophy
must also accept the fact that its beginning has already occurred elsewhere,
in practices that lie outside of it.

A materialist philosophy is incapable of beginning anything for another
reason as well, namely, because all materialisms depend on the premise of a
simultaneous tradition of idealism, the dominance of which they openly
seek to attack, ridicule, or destroy. Built into the essence of materialism
there is thus a dimension of praise and blame, of villainy and debasement,
witnessed by the endless attacks and rebuttals that make up most of the
history of its struggle against idealism. This is not merely an issue of
judgment or taste, whether good or bad, added onto the ideas of materialism and idealism as a moral or political afterthought. Instead, the tactical
and strategic value of each term is inseparable from the definition of the
concepts themselves, just as the use made out of both terms belongs to the
intrinsic core of their meaning. There is thus something irreducibly practical and impure about the debate concerning materialism, a messiness that
from the start defeats the purpose of a strictly speculative or philosophical
elaboration. This is why in *Theory of the Subject* Badiou calls materialism
the "black sheep" of philosophy: "The history of materialism finds the
principle of its periodization in its adversary. Making a system out of

nothing else than what it seeks to bring down and destroy, puffed up in latent fits of rage, this aim is barely philosophical. It gives colour, with often barbarous inflections, to the impatience of destruction."[4] We should never forget, in other words, how the concept of materialism is part of a fierce polemical apparatus. Or at least such has been the case in modern times, most clearly after Marx. It is indeed above all the latter's unfinished conception of materialism that has given the term its strong cutting edge, even retrospectively with regard to the history of materialisms from before the nineteenth century, as one of the most effective arms of criticism in any scientific, ideological, or philosophical battle—including its use *within* philosophy as a weapon *against* ideology *in the name of* science.

Louis Althusser, for one, repeatedly insists on this throughout his work on the polemical function of all philosophy, as when he defines the latter as "politics in theory" or when he states that "philosophy is, in the final instance, the class struggle in theory."[5] Marxism, he explains in his lecture "Lenin and Philosophy," from February 1968, has not founded a new philosophy so much as a new practice of philosophy, conditioned by politics. "In fact, I believe that what we owe to Lenin, something which is perhaps not completely unprecedented, but certainly invaluable, is the beginnings of the ability to talk a kind of discourse which anticipates what will one day perhaps be a non-philosophical theory of philosophy," which is something that holds true for Marxism in general as well: "What is new in Marxism's contribution to philosophy is a new *practice of philosophy. Marxism is not a (new) philosophy of praxis, but a (new) practice of philosophy.*"[6] To practice philosophy, then, is a matter not just of inventing concepts with demonstrative rigor but of drawing lines of demarcation and taking a stand, particularly by means of theses. A thesis, as position, can be just or deviated, but it is never exactly true or false. There are no real mistakes in philosophy because its propositions are never strictly theoretical but theoretical *and* practical at the same time. Between Althusser's *Essays in Self-Criticism* and his final interviews with the Mexican philosopher Fernanda Navarro in *Philosophy and Marxism*, moreover, it becomes increasingly evident how every thesis is in some way already an antithesis and every proposition already an opposition. The very nature of the philosophical art of war obliges its practitioners to include preemptive strikes against likely objections, to interiorize the conflict to better master it, or directly to occupy the enemy's own territory. As a result no position ever appears in pure form; no opposition is ever absolute but only tendential—with each tendency, or arrangement of theses, being present at the heart of its opposite.

Clearly no less indebted to Machiavelli than to Marx, this view of philosophical practice holds sway particularly in the age-old battle between idealism and materialism itself, elements of which can therefore be found tendentially in any philosophical system. "In every 'philosophy,' even when it represents as explicitly and 'coherently' as possible one of the two great antagonistic tendencies, there exist manifest or latent elements of the *other* tendency," Althusser observes in *Essays in Self-Criticism*; and in *Philosophy and Marxism* he makes the same point again with minor variations: "In reality, every philosophy is only the—more or less accomplished—realization of one of the two antagonistic tendencies, the idealist one and the materialist one. And in every philosophy it is not one but the antagonistic contradiction of both tendencies that is realized."[7] Materialism and idealism are thus caught in a specular and antagonistic relation in which each one bears the other within itself, like enemy troops lying in wait inside the empty entrails of the Trojan Horse.

The opposition of materialism and idealism is not only tendential but also decisively asymmetrical. This is because only the materialist tendency in philosophy is capable of recognizing the logic of internalized conflict itself. While for idealism the history of thought offers the lofty spectacle of an uninterrupted chain of solutions to a closed set of seemingly eternal and immanent problems, only the materialist view affirms that philosophy, being articulated onto other theoretical and nontheoretical practices, has a certain outside. Here Althusser recalls how François Mauriac once confessed that as a child he believed that famous people had no behind—a confession he relates to Hegel's reference, in his *Phenomenology of Spirit*, to the "back," "rear," or "hidden backside" of self-consciousness. For Althusser, then, materialism shows that philosophy too has a hidden backside: "The irruption of practice attacks philosophy from behind," he tells his Mexican interviewer: "To have an outside is the same thing, it will be objected, as to have a behind. But having a 'behind' means having an outside that one doesn't expect to. And philosophy doesn't expect to."[8] Far from constituting a self-enclosed totality, as idealism is wont to believe, philosophy is an apparatus with which to register conflicts and to act back, albeit indirectly by way of ideology, on the very same conflicts that condition it.

To the question "What does philosophy do?" Althusser answers in conversation with Navarro: "Philosophy produces a general problematic: that is, a manner of posing, and therefore resolving, any problem that may arise. Lastly, philosophy produces theoretical schemas or figures that serve as a means of overcoming contradictions, and as links for connecting and bolstering the various elements of ideology," for example, by acting at a distance "on cultural practices such as the sciences, politics, the arts, and even psychoanalysis."[9] In a paradoxical torsion these practices constitute the outside that seizes philosophy while at the same time being seized from within by philosophy. What is more, in Althusser's examples of the kind of practices with which philosophy interacts in this way, the reader can already perceive anticipations of what will become the four procedures of truth that define the conditions of philosophy for Badiou: art, science, politics, and love (especially as treated in psychoanalysis). In fact, far from abdicating the role of philosophy in the name of these other domains of practice, Althusser will be praised years later by Badiou for having maintained the idea of philosophy together with a tentative definition of its rapport to those practices or conditions. "There are at least two such conditions: the politics of emancipation, and the sciences. Thinking that relationship is something that can only be done within philosophy, as the philosophical act is, ultimately, *that very torsion*," writes Badiou about his former teacher: "In that sense, he was, unlike Lacan, Foucault or Derrida, who were all anti-philosophers, a philosopher."[10] This then raises the serious problem, to which I will return below, of defining the specific difference between Althusser's understanding of the relation of philosophy to ideology and science, on one hand, and Badiou's own concept of a materialist philosophy, on the other.

In any case, from this brief outline we can already infer not only that the materialist tendency in philosophy stands in an uneven and asymmetrical relation to idealism but also that, precisely because of this asymmetry, the impure definition of theoretical practices and their relations of internal exclusion to other practices together constitute the very substance of any materialist philosophy. Althusser, in fact, starts out in his canonical works *For Marx* and *Reading Capital*, both published in 1965, by assigning this double task to the philosophy of dialectical materialism. Though apparently out of fashion if not long-forgotten today, this discussion remains vital against all odds, especially if we seek to grasp the originality of Badiou's contribution as one of Althusser's most engaging and original stu-

dents to the renewal of the materialist dialectic. On a more anecdotal level
this continuity was rendered official and institutionalized when Badiou in
1999—after spending thirty years at the University of Paris at Vincennes-
Saint Denis, which was founded in the wake of May '68—was invited to
occupy his old mentor's post at the helm of the Philosophy Department at
the École Normale Supérieure in rue d'Ulm, a position from which Badiou
has since retired even though he continues to hold his seminar in the same
lecture halls where he once was a student.

We thus begin to understand why the importance of Althusser's legacy
for Badiou's own philosophical project remains unsurpassed perhaps even
by the influence of Sartre, Lacan, or Heidegger. As though to anticipate this
point, one of Badiou's first publications—part of his own contingent beginning as a philosopher that thus also marks a rebeginning—is an extensive
review of Althusser's two canonical works, *For Marx* and *Reading Capital*,
titled "The (Re)commencement of Dialectical Materialism."[11] In the remainder of this chapter I will rely on this quite astonishing book review as a
reader's guide, first, to a brief account of Althusser's view on the matter as
seen through the eyes of Badiou and, then, to Badiou's own philosophy and
theory of the subject as anticipated in this same review of the canonical
Althusser.

SCIENCE AND IDEOLOGY REVISITED

> Every truly contemporary philosophy must set out from the
> singular theses with which Althusser identifies philosophy.
> —BADIOU, *Metapolitics*

Althusser's polemical aim in *For Marx* and the collective *Reading Capital*—
at least this much is unlikely to have been forgotten—is to defend the
specificity and scientificity of Marx's dialectic against the threatening return of Hegel's idealism. He does so in collaboration with his students
Pierre Macherey, Roger Establet, Jacques Rancière, and Étienne Balibar
(not Badiou, who, as he explains ironically in the interview reproduced
below, is slightly older than the rest of his generation and as a result never
was "in" with the Althusserians of the first hour), by jointly arguing for a
radical epistemological break in Marx's work, a rupture made evident in the
Theses on Feuerbach and *The German Ideology*, which supposedly liquidate
not only the entire Hegelian legacy but also its famous inversion after
Feuerbach. Marx thus changes terrains, abandoning the empiricist and

anthropological mystifications in which even this so-called reversal of Hegelianism remains caught, as he installs himself in an entirely new problematic, forsaking the humanism of the *Manuscripts of 1844* in favor of a full-
blown scientific theory of history as seen in *Capital*. Marx's doctrine,
however, not only lays the groundwork for a new science; it also contains
the elements for a new philosophy, or at least for a new practice of philosophy. His discovery thus entails a double theoretical foundation in a single
epistemological break, or two ruptures in a unique inaugural act: "By
founding the theory of history (historical materialism), Marx in one and
the same movement broke with his erstwhile ideological philosophical consciousness and established a new philosophy (dialectical materialism)."[12]
Althusser's own positive aim, then, seeks in a formidable group effort to
reconstruct this new philosophy, which, though never fully formulated as
such by Marx, nor even by Engels or Lenin, would nevertheless already be
at work, in practice, in the scientific theory of Marx himself.

Even if we were to join the complacent trend of our times by condemn-
ing the orthodox terminology to oblivion, it is not too much to say that the
difference between these two disciplines—historical materialism and dialectical materialism—continues to be a real enigma today, albeit under
different names and in different guises. Badiou explains, first of all, how this
difference is obliterated in the various types of so-called vulgar Marxism.
Althusser's comprehensive return to the distinction between historical and
dialectical materialism in fact allows us to classify these very types, insofar
as they either reduce one of the two disciplines to the other (with "metaphysical" readings of the young Marx collapsing the two into a truncated
historical materialism, and "totalitarian" Marxism, conversely, privileging
an abstraction of dialectical materialism and its laws, following Stalin), or
else merely juxtapose them without any serious consideration for their
structural asymmetry (leading to an "analogical" Marxism of the kind
found in flatfooted correspondences between literature and economy).
The struggle to pull Marx from under Hegel's prolonged shadow is only the
dramatic form of appearance of this wider debate within Marxism. Everything seems to revolve around the complex difference between historical
and dialectical materialism: how are we to articulate the intricate unity of
this difference?

A first articulation implies the response to a question raised by Althusser himself: "By what necessity of principle should the foundation of
the scientific theory of history *ipso facto* imply and include a theoretical

revolution in philosophy?"[13] The principle in question holds that after every major scientific breakthrough that produces new forms of rationality, there occurs a revolutionary transformation in philosophy. The classical example of this effect of science on philosophy, of course, refers to the discovery of mathematical science with the mythic figure of Thales as the very condition of the beginning of philosophy in ancient Greece, but according to Althusser similar encounters take place in the cases of Descartes, Leibniz, or Kant. In his later work Badiou himself always subscribes to this principle, too, but with two caveats: first, not every scientific break is always registered in philosophy; sometimes its impact goes unnoticed or for a long time is driven underground, as in the case of set theory; and, more important, the formation of a philosophy is always conditioned not just by scientific discoveries but also by emancipatory politics, by artistic experiments, and by the encounter of a truth in love, as theorized in Plato's *Symposium* or in Freudian and Lacanian psychoanalysis. These clarifications allow Badiou to postulate that Marxism, defined as a doctrine that intervenes politically in a history of singular sequences, can still be a condition for modern philosophy, even if historical materialism does not achieve the status of a science, as is indeed no longer the case—if ever it was—for the later Badiou.

Althusser's dilemma, by contrast, as he seems to admit in numerous retrospective self-criticisms, is to have mistaken a political condition for a scientific one. To be more precise, there is an unarticulated tension between politics as the fundamental practice conditioning philosophy from the outside, on one hand, and, on the other, the invocation of science as the only safeguard, within philosophy, against the ideological reinscription of this political invention, the importance of which consequently turns out to be obscured. The result is a mixture of "scientism" and "theoreticism," overcome only by the opposite trend of "politicism," that we somewhat lazily have come to identify, following among others the melancholy views of the author himself, with so-called Althusserianism. In his *Manifesto for Philosophy* Badiou describes this situation as the outcome of a misguided yet heroic attempt to relay a first "suture" of philosophy, that is, the reduction and delegation of its four generic conditions onto politics alone, with a second one, this time onto science. Without becoming the servant of a third condition—poetry or art—as happens so often after Nietzsche and Heidegger, if not of the condition of love after Lacan or Levinas, philosophy today must undo this double suture, which is in fact a belated inheritance from the nineteenth century's struggle with positivism, so as to disentangle the strict compossibility of all four generic procedures of truth.[14] Even this clarifying extension, though, remains in a way faithful to the first articulation of Althusser's materialist view of philosophy as a theoretical practice conditioned by truths that are produced elsewhere or on another scene: a scene that is not in itself philosophical but that binds philosophy to its constitutive outside.

The second and third articulations no longer invoke a general principle about science and philosophy but concern the specific nature of historical and dialectical materialism themselves. The object of historical materialism, as the theory of history, includes the various modes of production, their structure and development, and the forms of transition from one mode to another. In principle the scientific nature of this theory cannot be established by historical materialism itself but only by a philosophical theory designed for the express purpose of defining the scientificity of the sciences and other theoretical practices in their specific difference from ideological practices. This general epistemological theory of the history of the theoretical offers a first definition of dialectical materialism. As Badiou writes: "The object proper to dialectical materialism is the system of pertinent differences that both and at the same time disjoins and joins science and ideology."[15] This is the cardinal object of the discipline that Althusser in his essay "On the Materialist Dialectic" in *For Marx* distinguishes from traditional philosophy by calling it Theory: "I shall call Theory (with a capital T) the general theory, that is, the Theory of practice in general, itself elaborated on the basis of the Theory of existing theoretical practices (the sciences), which transform into 'knowledges' (scientific truths) the ideological product of existing 'empirical' practices (the concrete activity of human beings). This Theory is the *materialist dialectic*, which is none other than dialectical materialism."[16] The reconstruction of this general theory would thus seem to take an extremely perilous turn, since few distinctions have provoked more polemical outbursts than the infamous break between science and ideology, the ineffectiveness of which is often equated with the perceived failure of the entire endeavor of so-called Althusserianism.

It seems to me essential, however, that we traverse once again the very problematic nature of the difference between science and ideology if we want to understand not only Althusser's enterprise but also the systematic foundation of Badiou's philosophy, for the latter hinges on a similar Bachelardian, if not already Platonic, distinction between truth and knowledge, or between truth and opinion. In fact, this is exactly the point where a frequent misunderstanding needs to be addressed that affects the reception of both Althusser and Badiou.

In his review Badiou himself insists on the primitive impurity of the difference in question: "The fact that the *pair* comes first, and not each one of its terms, means—and this is crucial—that the opposition science/ideology is not distributive. It does not allow us immediately to classify the different practices and discourses, even less to 'valorize' them abstractly as science 'against' ideology."[17] Similarly, in a key chapter from his *Essays in Self-Criticism* Althusser admits to having reduced the theory of science and ideology, despite the injection of a recurrent dialectical struggle, to a speculative-idealist opposition of truth "against" error or of knowledge "against" ignorance. The relation of these two forms of the theoretical, however, cannot be equated with oppositions such as the one between truth and error, which do little more than stage the old illusory struggle of good and evil as recast by modern rationalism. Instead of serving as a simple point of departure or normative guarantee, the opposition must be endlessly processed and divided from within. "In reality," writes Badiou, "the opposition science/ideology, as the opening of the domain of a new discipline (dialectical materialism), is itself developed therein not as a simple contradiction but as a process."[18] Not only is every science dependent on the ideology that serves merely to designate its possible existence, but there is also no discourse known as ideological except through the retroaction of a science.

Of this further thesis regarding the difference of science/ideology, the importance of which can hardly be overestimated, the following statement from *For Marx* offers a paradigmatic rundown:

> There exists no *pure* theoretical practice, no perfectly transparent science which throughout its history as a science would be safeguarded, by I know not what grace, from the threats and taints of idealism, that is, of the ideologies which besiege it; we know that there exists a "pure" science only on condition that it endlessly purifies itself, a free science in the necessity of its history only on condition that it endlessly frees itself from the ideology that occupies it, haunts it or lies in wait for it. The inevitable price of this purification and liberation is a never-ending struggle against ideology itself, that is, against idealism, a struggle whose

reasons and aims can be clarified by Theory (dialectical materialism) and guided by it as by no other method in the world today.[19]

Always marked by the possibility of false departures and sudden relapses,
this contradictory processing of the difference between science and ideology, as much as that between materialism and idealism, is absolutely key to
a proper reconstruction of Althusser's philosophy. I would argue, moreover,
that this is likewise the case for the difference between truth and knowledge, or between fidelity to the event and its obscure or reactive counterparts, and even between the event and being as such, in the later philosophy
and theory of the subject of Badiou: "It is not exaggerated to say that
dialectical materialism is at its highest point in this problem: How to think
the articulation of science onto that which it is not, all the while preserving
the impure radicality of the difference?"[20] From this point of view the
general theory being sought after can be redefined as the theory of impure
breaks, using the same principle of unity-in-difference to articulate not only
science and ideology, or truth and opinion, but also theory and practice, as
well as the very distinction between dialectical and historical materialism.

A third and final articulation of these two disciplines in effect depends
on the peculiar unity that ties together the different instances and practices
of a determinate social formation. While historical materialism approaches
this unity from the point of view of its actual existence, mainly under
capitalism's highest stages of development, its use of a series of concepts
and their order of deployment in the course of analysis simultaneously
point to a paradigmatic exposition that, though absent as such from the
study of history itself, defines in a new way the object of dialectical materialism. The latter is no longer only the theory of the complex difference
between science and ideology but also the linked system of concepts and
their laws of combination that define the specific unity, or type of causality,
structuring the whole of any given society.

STRUCTURAL CAUSALITY

If any understanding of *Capital* depends on the construction of the
concept of this new object, those who can read *Capital* without looking for this concept in it and without relating everything to this
concept, are in serious danger of being tripped up by misunderstandings or riddles: living merely in the "effects" of invisible causes.
—LOUIS ALTHUSSER, *Reading Capital*

Althusser elaborates his theory of causality above all in "Contradiction and Overdetermination" and "On the Materialist Dialectic" from *For Marx* and in "The Object of *Capital*" from *Reading Capital*. Two concepts in particular, namely, dominance and overdetermination, define the essence of Marx's discovery of a new, structural causality, radically different from its more traditional, linear or expressive, definitions. In terms of the first of these two concepts, a society always possesses the complex unity of a structure dominated by one of its instances or articulated practices. Here Althusser relies heavily on Mao's "On Contradiction," which likewise insists that in every society there are many contradictions and yet, among these, one that is principal, just as within each contradiction there is a principal aspect and a secondary one. This means that a society constitutes a complex unity that develops unequally and hierarchically under the dominance of one contradiction or instance in particular. Depending on the conjuncture at a given moment in the history of a society, the dominant can be economical, political, scientific, religious, and so on. If a conjuncture is thus defined by the attribution of dominance to one instance or another in the social whole, we can affirm with Badiou: "The first great thesis of dialectical materialism—here considered to be the epistemology of historical materialism—posits that the set of instances defines *always* a conjunctural kind of existence."[21] Far from staying at the level of a static understanding of the structure, in other words, the concept of dominance already pushes the analysis in the direction of the concrete study of a given conjuncture.

As for overdetermination, this concept is imported from psychoanalysis to account for the causality of conjunctural change, that is, the displacement of the dominant from one instance or practice to another, as well as the condensation of contradictions into an explosive antagonism. Althusser's notoriously controversial argument holds, then, that such conjunctural variations are themselves the effect of an invariant cause, which is the finally determining instance of the economy. "Such is, brutally schematized, the second great thesis of dialectical materialism: There exists a determining practice, and this practice is *the 'economical' practice*."[22] In a peculiar decentering the latter thus fulfills two unequal functions at once, since as determining force the economical practice is absent from the structured whole, in which it nonetheless also finds a place as one articulated instance among others.

The theory of structural causality is certainly no less susceptible to attacks and misunderstandings than the break between science and ideology. Althusser's alleged structuralism, or so a common objection goes, would be incompatible with the profoundly historical insights of Western Marxism, and, as such, it would be unable to fend off the dogmatic threats of Stalinism.[23] These defects are furthermore seen as being merely two sides of the same coin. It is because the structural point of view excludes history that it cannot but lead to dogmatism and terror.

The grand battle over history and structure, however, remains blind to what is without a doubt the core aspect of the theory of overdetermination, which reemerges in Badiou's theory of historical situations, in Meditation 9 of *Being and Event*, as well as in the final scholium of *Logics of Worlds*, on Mao's rise to power from 1927 to 1929 and the gradual constitution of a victorious red force in China. This core aspect of overdetermination becomes especially clear when Althusser rereads Lenin's analysis, through his famous concept of the weakest link, of the specific conditions that enabled the success of the revolution of 1917 in Russia. In Lenin's eyes this unique historical event is made possible in the most backward of imperialist countries by the sharp accumulation and condensation of multiple contradictions and heterogeneous tendencies. Once they fuse and become antagonistic, the latter constitute the objective conditions that retrospectively can be shown to have precipitated the revolution. The resulting impasse or dead end is then the site where the party, as a chain without weak links, can subjectively force its way into history. To be more precise, the fact that such a structural impasse becomes visible is already the retroactive effect of a subjective passage.

The revolutionary situation, in any case, cannot be deduced from a simple contradiction such as that between capital and labor or that between forces and relations of production. Such a general contradiction never actually exists apart from the specific currents and tendencies that are overdetermined in the historical direction of either explosive change or blockage. As both Althusser and Badiou are fond of repeating: "The universal exists only in the specific."[24] What may appear to be an exception is in fact the rule, namely, the principle that a historical event is conditioned by a complex play of multiple contradictions and not by the realization pure and simple of a general contradiction that, as its radical origin, would be previously given.

Methodologically speaking, the whole point of Althusser's reading is not simply to reiterate Lenin's well-known analysis but rather to ask how a structure actually *seizes upon* and *becomes* history or, to put it the other way around, how history *eventalizes* and *periodizes* the structure of a given situation at the site of a subjective intervention. Technically foreign to Lenin no less than to Marx yet supposedly already at work and implied in their analyses, Freud's concept of overdetermination is thus imported into Marxism by Althusser in order to articulate history and structure without separating them, for example, in terms of concrete empirical fact and abstract transcendental or ontological principle:

> Overdetermination designates the following essential quality of contradiction: the reflection, within the contradiction itself, of its own conditions of existence, that is, of its situation in the structure in dominance of the complex whole. This "situation" is not univocal. It is not only its situation *de iure* or "in principle" (the one it occupies in the hierarchy of instances in relation to the determinant instance: in society, the economy) nor just its situation *de facto* or "in fact" (whether, in the stage under consideration, it is dominant or subordinate) but *the relation of this situation in principle to this situation in fact*, that is, the very relation which makes of this factual situation a *"variation" of the—"invariant"—structure, in dominance, of the totality.*[25]

This "situation," which transversally crosses the opposition of principle and fact, *de iure* and *de facto*, is perhaps best understood in the everyday sense in which we say that "we have a situation" when something happens that no longer fits the natural order of things. If Althusser adds the quotation marks surrounding the "situation," it is no doubt to distance himself from an overly Sartrean term, which in contrast will be pivotal to all of the later work of Badiou, until its tendential abandonment and replacement by *world* in *Logics of Worlds*. Using Badiou's terms from *Being and Event*, we could say that what Althusser describes in the passage just quoted is indeed the point where the structure of a situation suddenly becomes indiscernible, or newly discernible only through an intervention faithful to the event—in this case a political event—that will have changed the very parameters of what counts as discernible in the language of the situation. An otherwise normal or natural situation will have become historical, in other words, as the result of an event, the unpredictable possibility of which is triggered, in Althusser's terms, by specific phenomena of overdetermination and underdetermination.

To say metaphorically that the gap between history and structure is then bridged would still leave the two in a relation of externality. We would still fail to grasp the fact that, through the theory of structural causality, it is not just that dialectical materialism serves as the abstract systematization of the concrete science of historical materialism, but the latter is also present, as if immanently withdrawn, in the former. Nor is one discipline meant to provide only the empty places, structures, or necessary forms that would then have to be applied to, or filled by, the concrete forces, contents, and contingent circumstances studied by the other. Rather, what is most striking in the theory of the weakest link as developed in the concept of overdetermination is to see how a structure takes hold of the actual moment, how isolated facts are literally thrown together to form a specific conjuncture and, thus, how necessity, far from realizing or expressing itself in history, actually emerges out of sheer contingency.

Finally, to speak of the determining instance of the economy as the cause of conjunctural change does not mean letting traditional determinism reenter through the back window: "Neither at the first nor at the last instant does the solitary hour of the 'last instance' ever sound."[26] The last instance is an absent cause given only in its possible effects, which at the same time are its conditions of existence. Any change produced by overdetermination, therefore, exceeds the realm of scientific objectivity and at once, in spite of Althusser's equation of subject and ideology, becomes the site of a subjective wager, irreducible to the way individuals function ideologically in the normal state of the situation. As Badiou recalls many years later in *Metapolitics*: "Overdetermination puts the *possible* on the agenda, whereas the economical place (objectivity) is that of well-ordered stability, and the statist place (ideological subjectivity) makes individuals 'function.' Overdetermination is in truth the place of politics."[27] Historical materialism could thus still be said to be implicated, or contained, in the hollow spaces of dialectical materialism: not as the objective science of history, with its underlying meaning or direction in a traditional sense, but as the theory and concrete analysis of historical possibility.

Traversing the polemic over history and structure, then, there is the fundamental question of what truly constitutes a historical event. For instance, the version of this question that I quoted in my introduction, with regard to politics: "When, and under what conditions, can an event be said to be political?," as Badiou asks in *Metapolitics*, or again: "What is 'that which happens' insofar as it happens politically?"[28] For Althusser, at least in his two canonical works, the answer to this question requires the passage through dialectical materialism as the theory of structural causality between the economy, ideology, and politics. "What makes *such and such* an event *historical* is not the fact that it is an *event*, but precisely *its insertion into forms which are themselves historical*, into the forms of the historical as such (the forms of base and superstructure)," he writes in *For Marx*, obviously still struggling with the difficult relation between dialectical and historical materialism, somewhat ill-conceived as a relation between form and content: "An event falling within one of these forms, which has the wherewithal to fall within one of these forms, *which is a possible content for one of these forms*, which affects them, concerns them, reinforces or disturbs them, which provokes them or which they provoke, or even choose and select, *that* is a *historical event*."[29] The theory of structural causality, in this sense, is already an attempt to think through the problem of how the structure of a given situation, in the effective process of becoming historical, will have been transformed as the result of an unforeseeable event. Together with the impure difference between science and ideology, this is the other half of the unfinished task of the materialist dialectic that Badiou draws early on from the canonical works of Althusser: "In any case, it is on the solution, or at least on the posing of the problem of structural causality that the ulterior progress of dialectical materialism depends."[30]

Althusser's dialectical materialism, or his materialist dialectic, thus in at least two ways anticipates and prepares the ground for the philosophy of the event in Badiou: first, insofar as the continuous task of processing the line of demarcation between science and ideology obliges us to conceive of these two types of discourse, like truth and knowledge, as tendencies in an ongoing battle and not as two domains or orders that can be separated once and for all; and, second, insofar as the theory of structural causality and overdetermination, when properly understood, reveals itself against all odds to be a theory of historical possibility, that is, a theory of the event, and not a theory of determinism.

As an Althusserian of the first hour, Étienne Balibar, writes in the preface to a recent French pocket edition of *For Marx*, speaking of the most loyal theoretical applications of Althusserianism:

On the one hand, the idea of overdetermination has been applied to the intelligibility of the *event* (to that which, in this very book, Althusser calls the "conjuncture," the "current moment" of Lenin, based on the privileged example of revolutionary or counterrevolutionary situations), with the paradoxical combination of unpredictability and irreversibility that this carries with it. On the other, it has been applied to the transhistorical comparison of modes of production, and thus to the historical *tendency* of the class struggle and the social formations themselves, which had to be snatched away from the ideologies of progress, from economist evolutionism, and from the eschatology of the "end of history."[31]

Except that for Balibar, as is likewise the case for Badiou, rather than choosing either one of these approaches, both must be closely articulated so as to understand historicity itself as a reciprocal tension between the points of view of structure and tendency, of conjuncture and event.

GOING THROUGH THE FANTASY

> Lacan appointed himself as the educator of all future philosophers.
> A contemporary philosopher, for me, is indeed someone who has
> the unfaltering courage to work through Lacan's antiphilosophy.
> —BADIOU, *Conditions*

One of the most intriguing chapters in the ulterior development of the general theory of structural causality and of the difference between science and ideology refers to the unpublished notes for a new collective project, initiated under the guidance of Althusser less than a year after the publication of *Reading Capital*. Indeed, in the fall of 1966 Althusser sends a series of confidential letters and typewritten drafts to his former students Badiou, Balibar, Macherey, and Yves Duroux, in which he proposes to form a "group of theoretical reflection" in preparation for what is to become an ambitious work of philosophy, announced under the title *Elements of Dialectical Materialism*, which would be nothing short of their systematic *Ethics* (in an explicit reference to Spinoza).

Although this joint effort will never go beyond the exchange of personal research notes, published only in the case of Althusser and even then only posthumously in his *Ecrits sur la psychanalyse* (in a series of notes not included in the English version of *Writings on Psychoanalysis* but recently made available in *The Humanist Controversy and Other Writings*), in retrospect we might say that this collective project, fostered by the encounter with Lacan's thought, constitutes one of the major sources for Badiou's *Theory of the Subject*, together with the poetry of Mallarmé, Greek tragedy, and the still obscure political sequence after May '68 marked by French Maoism. In this sense the project certainly meets the ambitious projections of its principal animator. By contrast, what Althusser could not foresee is the extent to which this extraordinary project would lead him, if not also the other members of the group, into a theoretical deadlock that in the eyes of some commentators sums up the ultimate demise of the entire historical endeavor of Althusserianism.

The fundamental thesis of Althusser's draft, "Three Notes on the Theory of Discourses," is that the philosophy of dialectical materialism in its contemporary conjuncture must come to terms with the theoretical impact of psychoanalysis, especially through the work of Lacan. To develop this thesis entails a double task: a reflection on the status of the object of psychoanalysis, that is, the unconscious and its formations, in its relation to ideology; and the elaboration of a theory not of language or discourse as such but of discourses in the plural. Althusser's notes thus start out by distinguishing four discourses, each marked by a certain subject-effect, a particular type of structure, and the use of certain signifiers as its material:

1. the *discourse of ideology*, in which the subject is present "in person," possesses a specular structure that appears to be centered owing to an essential effect of misrecognition and operates with a variety of materials not limited to concepts but including gestures, habits, prohibitions, and so on;

2. the *aesthetic discourse*, in which the subject is present by the "interposition" of more than one person, relies on an equivocal structure of mutually exclusive centers, and likewise operates with a diversity of materials, to produce an effect of recognition and perception;

3. the *discourse of science*, from which the subject is absent "in person," proposes a decentered structure, and operates with concepts and theorems to produce an effect of knowledge or cognition; and

4. the *discourse of the unconscious*, in which the subject is "represented" in the chain of signifiers by one signifier that is its "place-holder," is supported by a structure of lack, or fading, and operates with fantasies to produce a circulation of libido, or drive.

Here I should add that Badiou's very first scholarly publication after his narrative beginnings in the novels (or antinovels) *Almagestes* and *Portulans*, and before his review article devoted to Althusser, is an article titled "The Autonomy of the Aesthetic Process," in which Badiou studies the subjectivity that is specific to the discourse of art, in particular the novel, and thus seeks to contribute to the theory of four discourses as proposed by Althusser.[32] Though essentially mixed and equivocal, as we will see, this Althusserian theory of discourses can be considered an important touchstone not only for Badiou's *Theory of the Subject* but also for some of his recent unpublished seminars on the same topic that have been reworked into the first book of *Logics of Worlds*, not to forget Lacan's own theory of the four discourses, which Lacan begins to elaborate in his seminars right after May '68, from *The Other Side of Psychoanalysis* until its last version in *Encore*, namely: the master's discourse, the hysteric's discourse, the university discourse, and the analyst's discourse.[33] In fact, the mixed nature of these theories in the case of Lacan and Althusser can be explained using Badiou's own later terms by seeing how, in the name of various discourses, they conflate two questions of an entirely different nature: the question of the different *figures* of the subject (faithful, reactive, and so on) within a given truth procedure and the question of the various *types* of truth procedure (art, science, and so on) in which these figures appear.

Althusser's description of scientific discourse, for instance, involves aspects of what Badiou calls the subjective figure of fidelity that pertains to every condition of truth, but at the same time and on another level it pretends to define science differentially in relation to other procedures such as art or love as seen in psychoanalysis. Althusser's ideological discourse does not belong on this same level since it is not an alternative procedure but rather designates a mixture, in Badiou's terms, of the act of subjectivization and the obscure and reactive figures of the subject that for any procedure conceal or deny that a truth actually took place. Lacan's hysterical and masterly discourses, similarly, describe subjective figures that in one sense are universal while in another sense are strictly internal to the clinical discourse of psychoanalysis itself, but they cannot be put on a par with the analyst's discourse in an otherwise understandable attempt to differentiate its status from university discourse—the latter being little more than a code word for revisionist ideology. Despite the obvious family resemblances, not to mention the recurrent number of four, any attempt to transpose Badiou's theory of the subject directly onto Lacan or onto Althusser's theory of discourses is thus doomed to fail from the start.

Althusser himself, however, quickly abandons the idea that there could be such a thing as a subject of the unconscious, let alone a subject of science, and instead reduces the subject-effect to a purely ideological function —a view of which he is later to provide a systematic account, through the theory of interpellation, in what is no doubt his last canonical text, "Ideology and Ideological State Apparatuses."[34] In the third and final of his research notes, as well as in the letter of presentation accompanying all three, he thus warns the other members of the group that to him the notion of the subject seems more and more to belong only to the ideological discourse, being a category inseparable from the latter's structure of misrecognition and specular redoubling. Individuals are interpellated into subjects and at the same time are given the reasons necessary for their identification with those symbolic or imaginary mandates for which, as a result, they believe themselves to have been predisposed in advance.

Without ideology a social formation would distribute the various instances and practices of its structure, including all the phenomena of dominance and determination studied in the general theory of structural causality, while designating empty places for the function of the bearers of this structure. By interpellating individuals into subjects, ideology provides the structure with the indispensable figures who will fill the blank spaces of this function. Althusser often describes this mechanism of ideology formation by using expressions from everyday life, which clearly have a didactic purpose. Ideology is indeed what allows a structure to gain a firm grasp on lived experience: it is the mechanism by which a social formation "takes hold" of individuals, as when we say that the mayonnaise "takes" or "holds," at least in French. Finally, this mechanism of ideological interpellation does not come about without an unconscious effect of misrecognition and transferential illusion, an effect that is therefore constitutive of the subject. Again speaking in everyday language, Althusser suggests that the unconscious and ideology are articulated as a machine and its combustible: the unconscious "runs on" ideology just as an engine "runs on" fuel. Ideological formations such as the structures of kinship or the religious and moral constructions of the family allow the unconscious, through repetition, to seize on the lived experience of concrete individuals.

Here, I would argue, we arrive at the unsolved problem of Althusser's encounter with Lacan and the proposed combination of the latter's return to Freud with the former's plea for Marx. To understand the historical effectivity of an event, between its blockage and its irruption, dialectical materialism had to explain how a structural cause could take hold of a specific situation, which was to be "eventalized" by the effects of conjunctural change. Similarly, to understand the individual effectivity of the practice of the cure, psychoanalysis must explain how the unconscious functions only when "repeated" in a variety of situations, between the normal and the pathological, which make up the lived experience of an individual. In both cases, though, Althusser ultimately cannot conceive of these "situations" otherwise than as a function of ideology, which further justifies the use of the quotation marks surrounding this concept. Hence, even if Freud and Marx each in his own way contribute to the new logic, or materialist dialectic, best summed up in the concept of overdetermination by the unconscious and by the mode of production, respectively—something Althusser demonstrates as early as 1964–65 in "Freud and Lacan" and as late as in his 1977 text "On Freud and Marx," both published in his *Writings on Psychoanalysis*—he can no longer explain, except by way of ideology, how this dialectic somehow already implies the concepts of history, in the guise of a materialist understanding of historical possibility.

Because the efficacy of overdetermination in producing situations for a subject is now perceived to be profoundly ideological, Althusser's philosophy can no longer register any true historical event, not even in principle let alone in actual fact, as will become painfully evident during and after the events of May '68 in France. Conversely, we can surmise what will be needed to think through the possibility of a situation's becoming historicized by virtue of an event, namely, a theory of the subject that is no longer reduced to a strictly ideological function but accounts for the specificity of various subjective figures and different types of truth procedure. This is exactly the double task that Badiou ascribes to a formal theory of the subject in all his later philosophy. *Ideology*, if the term must be maintained at all, could then be said to describe a certain configuration of the subjective space, which besets each and every condition of truth as part of its ongoing process, but it is no longer a symmetrical rival to and on a par with science, or truth, as such.

With the articulation of ideology and the unconscious, in any case, Althusser hits upon an exception to Marx's rule that humanity only poses itself those problems that it is capable of solving. "I said that there had to be some links but at the same time I forbade myself to invent them— considering that provisorily this was for me a problem without solution, for me or perhaps not only for me," he admits in a personal letter: "Not every question always implies its answer."[35]

Althusser's project thus seems to run aground when faced with the question of structure and subject. What is more, insofar as this deadlock is a result of Althusser's dialogue with the discourse of psychoanalysis, there seems to be no easy escape from this impasse by way of a return to Lacan. As Badiou writes in his *Metapolitics*: "The very frequent attempt, anchored in the few Althusserian texts on psychoanalysis, on this point to complete Althusser with Lacan is in my view impracticable. In Lacan's work there is a theoretical concept of the subject, which even has an ontological status. For the being of the subject in Lacan consists of the coupling of the void and the 'objet petit a.' There is no such thing in Althusser, for whom the object exists even less than the subject."[36] The impossible, though, can sometimes happen, and the impracticable, become real.

Back in 1959 and 1960, as he also recently recalled, Badiou himself was after all the first student to bear witness to the published work of Lacan during Althusser's course at the École Normale Supérieure: "A personal testimony: In 1960, I was a student at the École Normale Supérieure and had just discovered, with extreme enthusiasm, Lacan's published texts, when Althusser, at the time in charge of philosophy at the École, asked me to prepare a synthetic presentation for my fellow students on what was then a completely ignored author. I did this in two talks which to this very day serve me as internal guides."[37] And a few years later, after making psychoanalysis the topic of a seminar of his own in 1963 and 1964, Althusser would send another student of his to visit the ongoing seminar of Lacan. The latter, on hearing how he is interrogated about his ontology, promptly sends his colleague a word of praise for the student responsible for this intervention, the same student who is later to become Lacan's son-in-law and official editor, Jacques-Alain Miller. "Rather good, your guy. Thanks," was all Lacan's note said, but this was sufficient for Miller: "Here, a spark fixated something for me."[38]

Anecdotes, however, no matter how many, do not amount to a theory. Nor do I wish to rehearse in a nutshell the well-documented history of the encounter between Althusser and Lacan.[39] However, what I do want to signal is how, through these and other personal stories, the logic of over-determination, even when it is no longer mentioned explicitly, has become the cornerstone for a unified theoretical discourse, which today constitutes one of the most powerful doctrines in all theory and philosophy. Miller lays the foundation for this combined doctrine most clearly in "Action of the Structure," published in *Cahiers pour l'analyse*. In the conclusion to this text, Miller writes programmatically: "We know two discourses of over-determination: the Marxist one and the Freudian one. Because Louis Althusser today liberates the first from the dangerous burden that conceives of society as the subject of history, and because Jacques Lacan has liberated the second from the interpretation of the individual as the subject of psychology—it now seems to us possible to join the two. We hold that the discourses of Marx and Freud are susceptible of communicating by means of principled transformations and of reflecting themselves into a unitary theoretical discourse."[40]

Miller adds that the principal injunction behind this ambitious project could be Freud's own *Wo es war, soll ich werden* ("Where it was, I shall come into being")—a succinct condensation if there ever was one of the way substance ("it") and subject ("I") are to be articulated in the new unified theory. Two other articles by Miller, finally, remain essential references for anyone seeking to reconstruct the genealogy of what will become the common doctrine of structural causality, namely, "Suture" and "Matrix."[41] This is precisely the doctrine, however, with which Badiou seeks to come to terms most emphatically and polemically in his *Theory of the Subject* as well as, more subtly, in *Being and Event* and *Logics of Worlds*.

THE NEW DOCTRINE OF SCIENCE

> I believe you will agree with the very general principle that *absence* possesses a certain efficacy on the condition, to be sure, that it be not absence in general, nothingness, or any other Heideggerian "clearing" but a *determinate* absence playing a role in the very space of its absence. This is undoubtedly important for the problem of the irruption of the unconscious.—ALTHUSSER, "Letters to D."

While urging on a more coherent account of Miller's overall thought, which in any case is barely available in English, I will summarize this doctrine by referring to the work of a famous onetime student and analysand of his, Slavoj Žižek, whose doctoral thesis, directed by Miller and published in French in two volumes, *Le plus sublime des hystériques: Hegel passe* and *Ils ne savent pas ce qu'ils font: Le Sinthome idéologique*, provides the basic materials for his provocative entry onto the theoretical scene in the English language, above all, in *The Sublime Object of Ideology* and *For They Know Not What They Do*.[42] To this very day, Žižek's work remains quite loyal, in spite of personal discrepancies, to Miller's original synthesis of the two discourses of overdetermination—the one articulated by Freud and Lacan, the other by Marx and Althusser. This loyalty can be gauged by the following passage from *In Defense of Lost Causes*, a book dedicated to Badiou that represents Žižek's most recent attempt at an overarching systematization of the notion of a politics of militant truth, on a par with *The Ticklish Subject* and *The Parallax View*:

> There are still only two theories which imply and practice such an engaged notion of truth: Marxism and psychoanalysis. They are both struggling theories, not only theories about struggle, but theories which are themselves engaged in a struggle: their histories do not consist in an accumulation of neutral knowledge, for they are marked by schisms, heresies, expulsions. This is why, in both of them, the relationship between theory and practice is properly dialectical, in other words, that of an irreducible tension: theory is not just the conceptual grounding of practice, it simultaneously accounts for why practice is ultimately doomed to failure—or, as Freud put it concisely, psychoanalysis would only be fully possible in a society that would no longer need it.[43]

Furthermore, "*Wo es war*," Miller's watchword for the new doctrine of science borrowed from Freud, is also the name of the series that Žižek edited for Verso and in which he published not only his critical introduction to Badiou's philosophy, as part of *The Ticklish Subject*, but also Badiou's very own *Ethics: An Essay on the Understanding of Evil*.[44]

For many readers Žižek's work thus will have provided the inevitable filter through which they first read Badiou in English. This makes it all the more urgent to understand the fundamental differences between the two in terms of Lacan's legacy. As for the lineage of Marxism, or post-Marxism, the first ones to elaborate Lacan's and Miller's views on suture and structure, together with Gramsci's thought on the historical bloc, into a programmatic statement of political philosophy are Ernesto Laclau and Chantal Mouffe, in *Hegemony and Socialist Strategy: Towards a Radical Democratic*

Politics, a text that furthermore links the logic of structural causality to a critique of essentialism that is much indebted to Derrida.[45]

Three points can be made respectively regarding the real, the subject, and ideology, which together sum up the basic elements of the new doctrine of structural causality.

First, just as the symbolic order is structured around the traumatic kernel of the real, a social field is articulated around the real of antagonism that absolutely resists symbolization. Like the theory of relativity, the special theory of foreclosure needs to be generalized. To become consistent, not just a psychotic order but any symbolic order needs to foreclose a key element that paradoxically incompletes the structure by being included out. The structure is not all: there is always a gap, a leftover, a remainder or, if we slightly change the perspective, an excess, a surplus, something that sticks out. A social formation is not only overdetermined, in the Althusserian sense, but for post-Marxists such as Laclau and Mouffe it is also constitutively incomplete, fissured, or barred because of the very impossibility of society that embodies itself in its symptomatic exclusions. "There is no such thing as a sexual relationship," Lacan declared in *Encore* in a formula that Laclau and Mouffe restate, or translate, in *Hegemony and Socialist Strategy* as the impossibility of society as an essential totality: "The incomplete character of every totality necessarily leads us to abandon, as a terrain of analysis, the premise of 'society' as a sutured and self-defined totality. 'Society' is not a valid object of discourse."[46] The absence, or lack, of any organic society is then the point of the real of politics, but precisely by opening up the field of the political, this impossible identity is also the condition of possibility of any hegemonic identification: "Hegemonic practices are suturing insofar as their field of operation is determined by the openness of the social, by the ultimately unfixed character of every signifier. This original lack is precisely what the hegemonic practices try to fill in."[47]

All this may very well seem to be a supplement to the common textbook idea of structuralism, but in fact the logic of structural causality never reduces the effects of overdetermination to a closed economy of gridlike places and their differential relations. The aim is rather always to detect and encircle the uncanny element that, in the efficacy of its very absence, determines the whole structure of assigned places as such. "The fundamental problem of *all* structuralism is that of the term with the double function, inasmuch as it determines the belonging of all other terms to the structure, while itself being excluded from it by the specific operation through which it figures in the structure only in the guise of its *representative* (its *lieu-tenant*, or place-holder, to use a concept from Lacan)," Badiou writes in his early review of Althusser, describing what even today remains the principal task of a critique of ideology for someone like Žižek; to wit: "Pinpoint the place occupied by the term indicating the specific exclusion, the pertinent lack, that is to say, the *determination* or 'structurality' of the structure."[48] As an absent or decentered cause, the determining instance may well have shifted, in keeping with the increased attention for Lacan's later works, so that the real is now to the symbolic what the symbolic was to the imaginary before, but we remain firmly within the framework of the common doctrine of structural causality. As Žižek himself concludes in *The Sublime Object of Ideology*: "The paradox of the Lacanian Real, then, is that it is an entity which, although it does not exist (in the sense of 'really existing,' taking place in reality), has a series of properties—it exercises a certain structural causality, it can produce a series of effects in the symbolic reality of subjects."[49] For Althusser, of course, the finally determining instance of the economy also does not "exist"; nobody ever encounters such a cause "in person" but only through the effects that are its conditions of existence. This then raises the important question of the ontological priority attributed to the economy—or at least to the class struggle—in Marxism and refused in post-Marxism. Even when Žižek addresses this question in the introduction to *The Sublime Object of Ideology*, he himself as always ends up relying on an ontologically prior antagonism—the traumatic kernel of the real whose correlate "is" the subject. In fact, as we will see in a moment, it is precisely such a priority that guarantees the irrefutable radicality of Žižek's antiphilosophical gesture.

Second, the subject indeed "is" nothing but this gap in the structure, the fissure between the real and its impossible symbolization. The new doctrine thus avoids the metaphysical understanding of both substance and consciousness. In fact, insofar as metaphysics, in one of its more famous Heideggerian delimitations, culminates in the epoch of the image of the world as the representation and manipulation of the object by the subject, the new doctrine can also be said to entail a wholesale deconstruction of metaphysics. This means that the polemic between structuralism and humanism can be sidestepped, since the doctrine of structural causality already implies a new notion of the subject as well, one that, moreover, ceases to be merely ideological. Subject and substance are then articulated through the lack at the very center of the structure. In other words, if there is always a leftover in the process of symbolization, a stubborn remainder that signals the failure of substance fully to constitute itself, then the subject coincides with this very impossibility that causes the inner decentering of the structure as substance. "The leftover which resists 'subjectivation' embodies the impossibility which 'is' the subject; in other words, the subject is strictly correlative to its own impossibility; its limit is its positive condition," Žižek writes in a rare deconstructive move in *The Sublime Object of Ideology*, which Laclau further explains in his preface to the same book: "The traditional debate as to the relationship between agent and structure thus appears fundamentally displaced: the issue is no longer a problem of *autonomy*, of determinism versus free will, in which two entities fully constituted as 'objectivities' mutually limit each other. On the contrary, the subject emerges as a result of the failure of substance in the process of its self-constitution."[50] Before adopting any particular position, identity, or mandate, in a logical primacy that will guarantee the radical status of the new doctrine, the subject is thus the subject of lack. If to be radical means to go to the root of things, and if the root of all things is the human subject, as the young Marx was fond of recalling, what can be more radical than to show the constitutive uprootedness of the very notion of the subject, prior to any essence of the human being as invoked by Marx?

Third, and finally, ideology is a fantasy construct aimed at concealing the essential inconsistency of the sociopolitical field. The fundamental ideological fantasy, therefore, is always some version or other of the idea that society constitutes an organic, cohesive, and undivided whole. By defining society as impossible, strangely enough, the new doctrine thus gives itself an unfailing measuring stick to redefine ideology in terms of a structural misrecognition—this time not of some concrete reality hidden behind the veil of false consciousness but rather of the fact that ideology conceals nothing at all, the "nothing" of the structure which "is" the subject. As Laclau writes in his *New Reflections on the Revolution of Our Time*: "The ideological would not consist of the misrecognition of a positive essence, but exactly the opposite: it would consist of the non-recognition of the precarious character of any positivity, of the impossibility of any ultimate suture."[51] Totalitarian ideologies, for instance, are defined by their failure to

acknowledge the empty place of power, which in democracy would constitute the paradoxical object-cause of all political desires and struggles.

The critique of ideology, therefore, can no longer consist only in unmask-
ing the particular vested interests hidden behind the false appearances of
universality, as in the metapolitics that Rancière ascribes to Marx. Instead,
two rather different tasks impose themselves, which can be compared to
the ends of the psychoanalytical cure as discussed by Žižek. The aim is,
first, a traversing of the fantasy, so as to acknowledge how an ideology
merely fills out a traumatic void in the midst of the social field and, second,
in order to avoid that the symbolic order disintegrate altogether, the identification with the symptom, or what Lacan names *sinthome*, that is, the
piece of surplus enjoyment that continues to resist even after the disman-
tling of the fundamental fantasy and that thus somehow gives body to the
radical inconsistency of society itself. This obscene enjoyment, which at-
taches itself to the symptom and is ultimately nothing else but pure death
drive pulsating around the central emptiness in the midst of the symbolic
order, cannot be overcome by means of an old-style symptomal reading of
ideology nor even by a revolutionary social change. Žižek writes about the
drive to enjoyment, which, as our human condition, is the ultimate pre-
ideological support of all ideology: "The thing to do is not to 'overcome,' to
'abolish' it, but to come to terms with it, to learn to recognize it in its
terrifying dimension and then, on the basis of this fundamental recognition, to try to articulate a *modus vivendi* with it."[52] What Žižek thus adds to
Laclau's cleaner or cooler deconstructive version of structural causality is
the obscene passionate enjoyment that is the dark underside, or the nightly
obverse, of the lack in the symbolic order.

ENJOYMENT BEYOND INTERPELLATION

The (psychoanalytic) subject is nothing but the failure to become an
(Althusserian) subject.—ALENKA ZUPANČIČ, *Ethics of the Real*

Finally, in a last ironic twist, the doctrine of structural causality is turned
against Althusser—himself one of the first to use the terms of structure,
overdetermination, and absent cause in order to bring together Marx,
Freud, and Lacan! Žižek thus claims that to reduce the subject to an effect
of interpellation, as the specular assumption of imaginary and symbolic

mandates, misses the traumatic kernel of enjoyment that is the real object-cause of this process of subjectivization itself. Althusser, in other words, would fail to understand how the last support of ideology, its ultimate stronghold, is the subject of lack who remains forever trapped in a structure of fantasy, like an unbearable truth that presents itself only in the structure of a fiction: "This is the dimension overlooked in the Althusserian account of interpellation: before being caught in the identification, in the symbolic recognition/misrecognition, the subject ($) is trapped by the Other through a paradoxical object-cause of desire in the midst of it (*a*), through this secret supposed to be hidden in the Other: $◊*a*—the Lacanian formula of fantasy."[53]

Žižek then briefly feigns to retrieve Althusser's original formulation of four discourses or four subject-effects—in science, art, ideology, and the unconscious—only in his turn to reduce their variety to a single one of them as their underlying figure: "There are two candidates for the role of the subject *par excellence*—either the ideological subject, present *en personne*, or the subject of the unconscious, a gap in the structure ($) that is merely represented by a signifier. Althusser opted for the first choice (ideological status of the subject), whereas from the Lacanian standpoint the second choice seems far more productive: it allows us to conceive of the remaining three 'effects-of-subject' as the derivations-occultations of $, as the three modes of coming to terms with the gap in the structure that 'is' the subject."[54] This is a typical antiphilosophical move of radicalization in which the lack in the structure, a gap that coincides with the subject as such, is turned against the question of this subject's empirical ideological positions—a question that as a result of this move appears secondary or derivatory. Unless this absolutely prior gap is acknowledged, every philosophy and every theory of the subject will thus always stumble upon the obstacle of the real that remains unthought by them.

Žižek, who will often repeat this move in his critical rejoinders to Badiou, interprets the deadlock of the entire Althusserian enterprise as a failure to come to terms with the subject of lack, caused by an impossible enjoyment before and beyond interpellation. At issue are thus the obscure prior scenarios of guilt, complicity, or desire that predispose an individual to become the subject of interpellation to begin with and that will continue to resist its hold ever after. "In short, the 'unthought' of Althusser is that there is already an uncanny subject that *precedes* the gesture of subjectivization," Žižek writes: " 'Beyond interpellation' is the square of desire, fantasy, lack in the Other and drive pulsating around some unbearable surplus-enjoyment."[55] We would thus have to conclude with Badiou that Althusser's thought indeed cannot be completed by a return to Lacan, whose psychoanalysis rather shows that whereof one cannot speak in Althusserian Marxism. Except that this revelation from beginning to end keeps relying on the unified doctrine of structural causality—from the real of enjoyment, which is the absent cause of the symbolic law, to the subject as lack, which is strictly correlative to the object of desire itself—with ideological fantasy merely being an occultation of its perverse and uncanny efficacy.

WHY THE IDIOCY OF DIALECTICAL MATERIALISM IS STILL WORTH FIGHTING FOR

> That, philosophically speaking, Stalinist "dialectical materialism" is imbecility incarnate, is not so much beyond the point as, rather, *the point itself.*—SLAVOJ ŽIŽEK, *The Parallax View*

At this point we might well ask ourselves whether we have not left the domain of dialectical materialism altogether? If the social field is by definition barred, then the very ambition to produce a universal ontology and epistemology of which the study of history and society would be a regional application might well seem to be the quintessential idiocy. For Žižek, however, this is precisely the reason why we should remain committed to its cause. " 'Dialectical materialism' stands for its own impossibility; it is no longer the universal ontology: its 'object' is the very gap that forever, constitutively, renders impossible the placement of the symbolic universe within the wider horizon of reality, as its special region," he writes in *The Metastases of Enjoyment*: "In short, 'dialectical materialism' is a negative reminder that the horizon of historical-symbolic practice is 'not-all,' that it is inherently 'decentred,' founded upon the abyss of a radical fissure—in short, that the Real as its Cause is forever absent."[56] Years later, Žižek still returns to this same paradigm as his defining framework in books such as *In Defense of Lost Causes*: "In this sense, a cause is for Lacan, by definition, a distant cause (an 'absent cause,' as one used to put it in the jargon of the happy 'structuralist' of the 1960s and 1970s): it acts in the interstices of the direct causal network," much in the same sense as overdetermination works for Althusser. "And, perhaps, this is also how one should understand the infamous Marxist formula of 'determination in the last instance': the overdetermining instance of the 'economy' is also a distant cause, never a direct one, that is, it intervenes in the gaps of direct social causality."[57]

Althusser himself, for his part, concludes his research notes for the unfinished *Elements of Dialectical Materialism* by stating that psychoanalysis, in order to be more than a practice or a technique, requires not one but two general theories: the first, already known, namely historical materialism, which would define the specificity of psychoanalysis in comparison with other discourses and account for the conditions of its emergence and use in capitalist society; and the second, still to be constructed, a general theory of the signifier capable of explaining its function in the case of the unconscious. In letters from the same period sent to his analyst with copies to the members of his theory group, however, the author of *For Marx* shows more interest in understanding how something as radically new as language and the unconscious, for instance, emerges in the life of an infant. For Althusser this sudden irruption of novelty, which is neither generated nor developed from a previously given origin but instead introduces another structure into the existing order of things, is the essential object of what he now calls a logic of emergence, which is still no other, he adds, than the materialist dialectic as understood by Marx and Freud.

Badiou's *Theory of the Subject*, to which I turn in the next chapter, will consist entirely in confronting these two orientations of dialectical materialism: one, for which the act of subjectivization remains irredeemably anchored in the structural causality of lack, and the other, which seeks to map a subjective process onto the rare emergence of a new consistency—that is, onto the appearance of a new structure in which a subject not only occupies but exceeds the empty place in the old structure, which as a result becomes obsolete. Written several years before the key works of Laclau, Mouffe, and Žižek, this remarkable yet strangely ignored text thus strikes in advance at a basic shortcoming of what would soon—for a brief while at least—become their common doctrine, namely, its difficulty to register the making of a new consistent truth beyond the exposure and acknowledgment of the structural lack, or void, that is only its absent vanishing cause, no matter how sublime or obscene.

In fact, taking up a task already announced in "Le (Re)commencement du matérialisme dialectique," all of Badiou's subsequent work can be read as a giant polemical effort to untie the eclectic doctrinal knot that even today binds together the works of Marx, Freud, Nietzsche, and Heidegger

as read by Althusser, Lacan, and Derrida: "Can we think 'at the same time'
the reading of Marx by Althusser, that of Freud by Lacan and that of
Nietzsche and Heidegger by Derrida? Headline, in our conjuncture, of the
most profound question. If we take these three discourses in their integral
actuality, I think the answer can only be negative. Better yet: to approach
indefinitely that which keeps all three *at the greatest distance* from one
another is the very condition of progress for each one of them. Unfortunately, in our instantaneous world in which concepts immediately become
commercialized, eclecticism is the rule."[58] Thus, Badiou's small Maoist
booklets, *Theory of Contradiction* and *Of Ideology*, which otherwise correspond to the double object of dialectical materialism as defined above,
also include a staunch polemic against Althusser and, incidentally, against
Deleuze's and Lyotard's philosophy of desire; *Theory of the Subject*, as I
have already mentioned, raises to new heights the stakes for the dispute
between Marxism and Lacanian psychoanalysis; and *Being and Event* gives
ontology a mathematical foundation in a systematic alternative to the
dominant poetic suture of philosophy in the wake of Nietzsche, Heidegger,
and Derrida.

Badiou's philosophy, unlike Deleuze's affirmative style, is indeed polemical through and through. "I have never tempered my polemics: *consensus* is
not one of my strong points," he admits in his book on Deleuze, still in
keeping with a difficult but useful guideline for the materialist understanding of philosophy, first formulated in *Theory of the Subject*: "It is no doubt
more instructive to write with respect to what one does not want to be at
any price than under the suspicious image of what one wishes to become."[59] As we will now see, this principle is perhaps nowhere more evident than in Badiou's responses to Althusser and Lacan.

2

LACK AND DESTRUCTION

←————————————————→

THE ROAD TO DAMASCUS

May '68 is really only a beginning, and continuing the combat is a directive for the long run.—BADIOU, *Theory of the Subject*

There is a sort of temporary lack of distinction between what is beginning and what is coming to an end, and it is this that gives May '68 its mysterious intensity.—BADIOU, *The Communist Hypothesis*

The sharp tone of Badiou's polemic against Althusser and Lacan no doubt comes as a response to the inability, or unwillingness, of either thinker to find any significant political truth in the events of May '68. In contrast, to draw further consequences from these events for the relation between philosophy and politics remains one of the principal aims of Badiou's work in the 1970s and early 1980s. His still relatively unknown *Theory of the Subject*, presented as a Lacanian-style seminar from 1975 until 1979, with a preface written in 1981 at the time of Mitterrand's clamorous arrival to power, offers the first massive summary of this ongoing effort, which in more muted ways will continue to resonate in *Being and Event* before reemerging with full force in *Logics of Worlds*.

In the case of Althusser, "Ideology and Ideological State Apparatuses" contains perhaps his only positive theoretical attempt to register some of the effects of the revolt of 1968, including predictable examples drawn from the world of education, as well as the obligatory scene of a police officer hailing a passerby in the street. In contrast, after his much publicized *Essays in Self-Criticism*, most of Althusser's subsequent work can be read as a double effort—not unlike the two parts in Badiou's later *Can Politics Be Thought?*—in the destruction and recomposition of Marxism, respectively, in "Marx in His Limits" and "The Underground Current of the Materialism of the Encounter."[1] These final notes, published posthumously like so much

of Althusser's late work, change the terrain once more, this time from
dialectical to so-called aleatory materialism, in order to grasp the essence of
political events in their purely contingent occurrence, regardless of the so-
called laws of historical necessity. One could therefore have expected that
this extremely lyrical enquiry into the materialism of chance encounters,
falling raindrops, deviating atoms, and aleatory conjunctures would have
attuned its author in retrospect to give new meaning to explosive events
such as those of 1968 in France. At the end of a long list of examples,
however, the greatest manifestation of this watershed year still appears as a
nonevent: "the 13th of May, when the workers and students, who ought to
have 'joined up' (what a result would have resulted from that!), saw their
long parallel processions cross, but *without joining up*, avoiding, at all cost,
joining up, conjoining, uniting in a unity that is, no doubt, still for ever unprecedented (the rain in its *avoided* effects)."[2] In the language of ancient
atomism, students and workers continued to fall as the rain of atoms shoot-
ing by each other in the void, without undergoing any deviation or swerve
that might have opened up a whole new world for their coalescence. This
Althusserian interpretation leaves open the question of deciding whether
this signals a missed encounter of students and workers or, rather, the
paradoxical failure, on the philosopher's part, to come to grips with the
event of their reciprocal transformation. For Badiou, in any event, the latter
is the case.

Indeed, if Badiou's early Maoist writings are unforgiving in their attack
against Althusser, the point is above all to counter those among the latter's
theses on structure and ideology that after the events continue to facilitate
the retrospective betrayal of students, workers, and intellectuals alike. His
Theory of Contradiction thus opens on a statement of principle: "I admit
without reticence that May '68 has been for me, in the order of philosophy
as well as in all the rest, an authentic road to Damascus," and the impact of
this experience is further registered and investigated in *Of Ideology*: "The
issue of ideology is the most striking example of a theoretical question put
to the test and divided by the real movement."[3] The first booklet, thus,
seeks didactically to redefine the fundamental principles of dialectical materialism in a return to Mao's "On Contradiction," which, as we saw in the
previous chapter, already served Althusser in *For Marx*, while the second
takes aim not only at Althusser's one-sided views of ideology and the
subject in "Ideology and Ideological State Apparatuses" but also at their

alleged rectification in *Essays in Self-Criticism*: "We have to put an end to
the 'theory' of ideology 'in general' as the imaginary representation and
interpellation of individuals into subjects."[4] The question of historicity
cannot be reduced to the objective inspection of a structure of dominant
or subordinate instances, even if left incomplete by an empty place of
which the subject is invariably the inert and imaginary placeholder. The
transformative impact of an event can be grasped only if the combinatory
of places and their ideological mirroring play in the subject is anchored,
supplemented, and divided by a dialectic of forces in their active processing. This double articulation of places and forces, in a nutshell, serves as a
first attempt to theorize the abyss between Badiou's road to Damascus and
Althusser's missed encounter with May '68.

   While Althusser's failed encounter in a sense remains foreign to the
events themselves, Lacan's open indictment of May '68 by contrast is far
more inherently damaging. Before tackling the university discourse as a
whole, starting with his seminar *The Other Side of Psychoanalysis* between
1968 and 1969, Lacan clearly hits a central nerve in the student-popular
movement insofar as his accusation of its being a hysterical outburst in
search of a master anticipates in a painful irony the subsequent arguments
and apostasies of so many an ex-Maoist turned New Philosopher or Thermidorean, from André Glucksmann to the duo of Christian Jambet and
Guy Lardreau all the way to Jacques-Claude Milner's recent remorseful
indictment of the arrogance of his Maoist years.[5] At an improvised meeting on December 3, 1969, at the newly established campus of the University
of Paris VIII-Vincennes, in a speech reproduced in the official edition of
The Other Side of Psychoanalysis, Lacan thus mockingly provokes his students: "If you had a bit of patience, and if you really wanted our impromptus to continue, I would tell you that, always, the revolutionary
aspiration has only a single possible outcome—of ending up as the master's
discourse."[6] This criticism of the discourses of hysteria and mastery in their
fitting codependence, which restages much of the political battle at the
time between anarchist utopians and party hardliners, if not the ancient
philosophical struggle between skeptics and dogmatists, is clearly the unspoken impetus for Badiou's systematic reply to Lacan in *Theory of the
Subject*. To understand this situation is all the more urgent today insofar as
Žižek, in *The Ticklish Subject* and elsewhere, will throw the same Lacanian
criticism —of deriving a dogmatic masterly philosophy from a politics of

short-lived hysterical outbursts—back at the feet of ex-Althusserians, including not only Rancière but also Badiou himself.[7]

> We ask materialism to include that which is needed today and which
> Marxism has always made into its guiding thread, even without know-
> ing it: a theory of the subject.—BADIOU, *Theory of the Subject*

After the basic didactic insights from *Theory of Contradiction* and *Of Ideology*, what is the principal lesson to be drawn, according to Badiou's first
philosophical summa in *Theory of the Subject*, from the political sequence
initiated by the events of May '68?

The full effect of these events is first of all registered in philosophy as a
humbling lesson in dialectics. Even the double articulation of places and
forces, of the combinatory and the dialectic, or the negation of one by the
other, is not quite enough. The dialectic is first and foremost a process not
of negation and the negation of negation but of internal division. Every
force must thus be split into itself and that part of it that is placed, or
determined, by the structure of assigned places. "There is A, and there is A_p
(read: 'A as such' and 'A in an other place,' the place distributed by the
space of placement, or P)," Badiou writes in his reading of Hegel: "We thus
have to posit a constitutive scission: $A = (AA_p)$."[8] Every force stands in a
relation of internal exclusion to its determining place. The famous contradiction of the proletariat and the bourgeoisie, or of labor and capital, for
example, is only an abstract structural scheme, A vs. P, that is never given in
actual fact. Althusser's argument for overdetermination already rejected
the purity of these contradictions, of course, but his solution was only to
move from a simple origin to a complex structure or totality that is always
already given. Badiou's dialectic, by contrast, aims at the actual division of
this complex whole. As the history of the nineteenth century and much of
the twentieth shows in excruciating detail, what happens actually is the
constant struggle of the working masses against their determination by the
capitalist order, an order that in this process divides the proletariat from
within. There are, after all, notorious contradictions among the people, as
Mao would say. "In concrete, militant philosophy, it is thus indispensable
to announce that there is only one law of the dialectic: One divides into
two," Badiou summarizes, referring to a major debate in Maoism during

the Cultural Revolution: "Dialectics states that there is the Two, and intends to infer the One from it as a moving division. Metaphysics posits the One, and forever gets tangled up in deriving from it the Two."[9]

If determination describes the dialectical placement of a force and its resulting division, then the whole purpose of the theory of the subject is to affirm the rare possibility that such a force, though always placed, at times may come to determine the determination by reapplying itself to the very place that marks its split identity. From the slightly static point of departure that is the factual given of scission, $A = (AA_p)$, in which p is the index of the determination by P within A, so that A_p controls the divided essence of A, or $A_p(AA_p)$, we thus get the actual process that both limits and exceeds the effects of determination: $A_p(AA_p) \rightarrow A(AA_p)$, or $A(A_p)$. This is without a doubt the single most important moment in all of Badiou's *Theory of the Subject*: a symptomatic twist, or torsion, of the subject back upon the impasses of its own structural placement—a process that we will find again, but in a more succinct and potentially misleading formulation, in *Being and Event*. "It is a process of torsion, by which a force reapplies itself to that from which it conflictingly emerges," Badiou explains: "Everything that is of a place comes back to that part of itself that is determined by it in order to displace the place, to determine the determination, and to cross the limit."[10] Only by thus turning upon itself in an ongoing scission can a rare new truth emerge out of the old established order of things—a process of which the subject is neither the (humanist) pregiven origin nor the (structuralist) empty bearer so much as a material fragment or a local configuration.

Following a fairly orthodox Leninist principle that was to be revived in Maoist China, Badiou finally suggests that the dialectical process in a typical backlash risks provoking two extreme types of "relapse," or *Rückfall* in Hegel's terms: the first, drawn to the "right" of the political spectrum, remits us to the established order and thus obscures the torsion in which something new actually took place: $A_p(AA_p) \rightarrow A_p(A_p) = P$; the second, pulling to the "left" instead, vindicates the untouched purity of the original force and thus denies the persistence of the old in the new: $A(AA_p) \rightarrow A(A) = A$. These extremes correspond to the twin "deviations" of opportunism ("rightism") and adventurism ("leftism") as diagnosed in the Chinese Cultural Revolution or in Lenin's pamphlet from 1920, *Left-Wing Communism, an Infantile Disorder*. What is thus blocked or denied is either the power of determination or the process of its torsion in which there occurs a conjunctural change: "But the true terms of all historical life are rather $A_p(A)$, determination, and $A(A_p)$, the limit, terms by which the Whole affirms itself without closure, and the element includes itself therein without abolishing itself."[11] These distinctions allow Badiou to propose an extraordinary rereading of Hegel's dialectic—itself in need of a division into its idealist and materialist tendencies, and not just the resented victim of a wholesale rejection, as in the canonical case of Althusser.

The complete deployment of this dialectic with its twin deviations also provides us with a key to understanding the perceptions of failure and success that put such a heavy stamp on the assessments of May '68 and its aftermath. In fact, both the provocative accusations by astute observers standing at the sideline, such as Lacan, and the contrite about-faces by ex-Maoist renegades, such as Glucksmann, remain caught as if spellbound in the inert duel between the established order of places and the radical force of untainted adventurism. The world-famous picture of Daniel Cohn-Bendit during one of the manifestations of May '68, with the student leader smiling defiantly in the face of an anonymous member of the special riot police who remains hidden behind his helmet—a picture that eventually will come to decorate the cover of Lacan's seminar *The Other Side of Psychoanalysis* from the following year—might serve to illustrate this point. Indeed, the contagious appeal and extreme mobilizing force of this image depends on a limited structural scheme in which there appears no scission in the camp of the free-spirited students nor any torsion of the existing order of things beyond a necessary yet one-sided protest against the repressive state: "CRS = SS," as the slogan went about the "fascism" of the French riot police in May '68. The underlying structure of this schema, which is typical of a certain leftism in general, could thus be said to reduce politics to the opposition of the masses and the state, or the plebes and the state. Althusser's much-discussed example of the police officer interpellating a passerby in the street remains overly bound to this dual structure, as might likewise be the case of the definition of politics in opposition to the police, in some of the later work of Rancière.[12] For Badiou, however, this view hardly captures any specific political sequence in its actual unfolding. "There is not just the law of Capital, or the cops. To miss this point is to stop seeing the unity of the order of the splace, its consistency. It is to fall back into objectivism, whose inverted ransom, by the way, is to make the State into the only subject—whence the anti-repressive logorrhea," the author warns: "It is the idea that in this world only the necessary rightist relapse and the impotent suicidal leftism exist. It is $A_p(A_p)$ or $A(A)$ inter-mittently, that is, P and A in their inoperative exteriority."[13] Lacan's accusa-tion that the students remained caught in a hysteric's discourse that could not but lead to the discourse of a new master thus merely reproduces a face-off between the extreme outcomes of the dialectical process, without acknowledging the true torsion of what takes place in between the two.

In view of this acute diagnosis and the elaboration of an alternative materialist dialectic in the remainder of *Theory of the Subject*, there is something more than just awkward in the criticism according to which Badiou's *Being and Event* would later get trapped in a naive undialectical, or even precritical separation of two spheres—being and event, knowledge and truth, the finite animal and the immortal subject—as clear-cut and as pure as place and force still are in the earlier books *Theory of Contradiction* and *Of Ideology*, when an important polemical thrust of Badiou's work from *Theory of the Subject* to *Logics of Worlds* consists very much in de-bunking the presuppositions of such critical postures as they emerge after May '68. The almost cynical irony is that Badiou's theory of the subject arrives at this turning point in a rigorous dialogue and confrontation with Lacanian psychoanalysis, which then becomes one of the most authorita-tive points of reference for the criticisms along these same lines to be raised against Badiou.

With the need to divide the subject in relation to the order in which it receives its place, we nonetheless may still seem to find ourselves on the familiar grounds of the doctrine of structural causality, which for Badiou can be summed up in a single statement from Lacan's *Écrits*: "The subject stands, as it were, in external inclusion to its object."[14] This object can then be read as either the symbolic order itself, following the earlier Lacanian views, or else as the uncanny element of the real that has to be foreclosed if such an order is to gain any coherence at all, according to the later teach-ings of Lacan. In the first instance the subject's decentered cause would be the unconscious that is structured as a language; in the second the subject is the strict correlate of the gap in this structure, the place of which is then held by the piece of the real that is included out and as such embodies the impossible object-cause of desire. Regardless of which reading applies to the object in Lacan's statement, however, Badiou's theory of the subject hinges on how exactly we understand their dialectical relation of external inclusion—whether as a structural given or as a divided process.

For Badiou, most of Lacan's work stays within the bounds of what he calls a structural dialectic, which is strikingly similar, as far as its basic operations are concerned, to Mallarmé's poetry. These operations consist, first, in setting up a scene marked by the traces of a disappearance, say a sunken ship or a drowned siren, whose vanishing sustains the whole scene itself. This is the operation of the absent or vanishing cause, which determines the established order of things: "Nowhere placed, the vanished force sustains the consistency of all the places."[15] This vanishing cause then produces a chain effect by leaving behind a series of metonymical terms, such as a white hair or the foam on the surface of the sea, the division of which is the mark of the lack that caused them: "Thus, the absent cause is always reintroduced into the whole of its effect. This is a major theorem of the structural dialectic: *in order to exert the causality of lack, all terms must be split*."[16] Prescribed by the lack of its object, finally, a subject appears only as the unspeakable vacillation eclipsed in the flickering intermittence between two such markings. "The subject follows throughout the fate of the vanishing term, having the status of an interval between the two signifiers, S_1 and S_2, which represent it one to the other," Badiou concludes: "Whoever wants to declare its substance is a swindler."[17]

Mallarmé's poetry thus anticipates in an illuminating exposition much of the doctrine of structural causality as developed in the Lacanian-Althusserian school. For Badiou, however, the problem with this doctrine is precisely that, while never ceasing to be dialectical in pinpointing the absent cause and its divisive effects on the whole, it nevertheless remains tied to the structure of this totality itself and is thus unable to account for the latter's possible transformation. "A consequential thinking of the vanishing term is the realistic apogee of the structural dialectic," which means that there is no temporal advent of novelty: "The logic of places, even when handled by an absolute virtuoso, would be hard put to deliver anything other than the regular, virtually infinite iteration of that which vanishes and that which is annulled."[18] For Mallarmé, in the end, "nothing will have taken place but the place itself," just as Lacan indicates the unsurpassable law that forbids the emergence of the new out of a division of the old: "When one makes two, there is never any return. It never amounts to making one anew, not even a new one. *Aufhebung* is one of those pretty little dreams of philosophy."[19] Mallarmé's and Lacan's structural dialectic, in this sense, ends up being profoundly idealist according to Badiou. Let me add immediately that this is not the usual objection against the idealism of the signifier or of discourse in the name of some hard referent or concrete human practice. Badiou's argument is rather that idealism consists in denying the divisibility of the existing law of things, regardless of whether these things are ideal or material: "The indivisibility of the law of the place excepts it from the real. To link up this exception in the domain of theory amounts to stipulating the radical anteriority of the rule," he writes: "The position of this antecedence is elaborated in philosophy as idealism."[20]

After the lesson in dialectics, there thus appears to be an even more urgent need to return to the definition of materialism. The latter, as we saw at the start of chapter 1, is always marked from within by its opponent: "Materialism stands in internal division to its targets. It is not inexact to see in it a pile of polemical scorn," which is why "materialism most often *disgusts* the subtle mind."[21] The first historical target of modern materialist scorn, in its eighteenth-century enlightened form, is the idealism of religion, followed by a second onslaught, starting at the end of the nineteenth century, against the very humanism of Man with which the first materialists had tried to displace God. Nowadays, however, this antihumanist materialism, which in the wake of the so-called linguistic turn delegates the constituent power to the symbolic structure of language, risks in turn becoming idealist, insofar as it blocks the production of a new truth of the subject. This is, then, the idealism to be targeted by a third, contemporary form of materialism: "Today it is idealinguistery that the materialist assault makes into its cause. It is exactly for this reason that the essence of active materialism, by a Copernican reversal, demands the production of a theory of the subject, which previously it had the function of foreclosing."[22]

If, for Badiou, Mallarmé and Lacan are the two great modern French dialecticians, with Pascal and Rousseau being their classical counterparts, then it is also true that their legacy must be divided into its idealist and its materialist tendencies, as happened before with Hegel. In Lacan's case the dividing line may well seem to fall between his earlier and his later work. The determining role of the symbolic order tends to be idealist, while the persistence of the real guarantees a materialist outlook. "Like Hegel for Marx, Lacan for us is essential and divisible," Badiou observes: "The primacy of the structure, which makes of the symbolic the general algebra of the subject, and of *lalangue*, its transcendental horizon, is countered ever more clearly with a topological obsession in which what moves

and progresses pertains to the primacy of the real."[23] Lacan's inquiries into
the real would thus have the greatest political resonance for a materialist
philosophy.

Several years before Laclau and Mouffe would consolidate this reading
in *Hegemony and Socialist Strategy*, the Lacanian real is in fact already
understood in a political key in Badiou's *Theory of the Subject*, so that "if the
real of psychoanalysis is the impossibility of the sexual *qua* relation, the
real of Marxism can be stated as follows: 'There are no such things as
class relations.' What does it mean to say that there are no class relations?
This can be stated differently: antagonism."[24] Lacan's materialism, from
a politico-philosophical perspective, would thus lie in an undaunted insistence on some traumatic kernel of antagonism that always already fis-
sures every social order, causing society to remain impossible and forever
incomplete.

On closer inspection, however, the shift from the symbolic to the real
turns out to be a necessary but insufficient condition for a materialist
theory of the subject. To recognize in antagonism the real that is the
constitutive outside of any society, while a fundamental strategy of the
structural dialectic, at best gives us only half of the process by which a
political subject is produced, and at worst can actually keep this process
from ever acquiring the coherence of a new truth. From the point of the
real as absent cause, indeed, any ordered consistency must necessarily
appear to be imaginary—the work of a swindler—insofar as it conceals this
fundamental lack itself. For a materialist understanding of the dialectic, by
contrast, the decisive question is rather whether the real cannot also on
rare occasions become the site for a newly consistent truth.

In addition to the real as an evanescent cause, we ought therefore to
conceive of the real as a novel consistency. Badiou calls the first conception
"algebraic," insofar as the real is considered in terms of its relations of
belonging and foreclosure, while the second is called "topological," in
terms of adherence and proximity. "We must therefore advance that in
Lacan there are, adequate to the division of the One, two concepts of the
real: the real of the vanishing, which is in a position of cause for the algebra
of the subject; and the real of the knot, which is in a position of consistency
for its topology," with both being required for a materialist theory of the
subject: "From the real as cause to the real as consistency we can read a
trajectory of integral materialism."[25] Lacan's obscure topological investiga-

tions, however, are limited by the fact that they remain bound to the constraints of the structural dialectic. For this reason even his uncompromising insistence on the real, which otherwise would seem to hold the greatest political potential, threatens to become contemplative and idealist —as though the end of analysis were the mere recognition or exposure of a structural impasse, eventually accompanied by an identification with the remaining symptom of enjoyment but without the actual process of a subject conditioned by truth. Besides, it is not at all certain that, beyond the passing knowledge of a point of the real, we can speak of a truth of the real in Lacanian psychoanalysis.

The line of demarcation between idealism and materialism in Lacan's thought must therefore be drawn through the very concept of the real, splitting its core in order to mark off those aspects that remain tied to a structural lack and those that point at a torsion, or destruction, of the structure itself. "Our entire dispute with Lacan lies in the division, which he restricts, of the process of lack from that of destruction," Badiou concludes: "Destruction means torsion. Internal to the space, it ravages its places, in a laborious duration."[26] This violent language in fact only restates the rare possibility, discussed above, of overdetermining the determination, and displacing the existing space of assigned places, while the price to be paid if one seeks at all cost to avoid such violence, whether it is called symbolic or metaphysical, is the droning perpetuation of the status quo.

True change, which simultaneously means a change in what counts as true, comes about not merely by occupying but by exceeding the empty place of the existing structure—including the empty place of power under democracy that, following the work of Claude Lefort, seemed to be all the rage among so many political philosophers in the 1980s and 1990s. Can we actually register any political sequence, though, in the wearying reiterations that democracy is the only regime capable of acknowledging the inherent impossibility that is its absent center? Or, consider the condition of love: Can any new truth actually emerge in a couple from the sole recognition of the real that is its constitutive impasse? For Badiou, the truth of love or of politics is neither this impasse itself nor its symptomatic outbreaks in situations of crisis and upheaval. The formal impossibility of the sexual or social bond, which certainly reveals itself in such situations, is at best the site of a possible event, but the truth of a love encounter or a political meeting consists only in whatever a dual or collective subject makes happen afterward, on the basis of this event, as being generically applicable to the entire situation.

For a truth to take place, therefore, something has to pass through the impasse. "If, as Lacan says, the real is the impasse of formalization," then, Badiou suggests, "we must venture that formalization is the im-passe of the real," which breaches the existing state of things and its immanent dead-locks: "We need a theory of the pass of the real, in the breach opened up by formalization. Here, the real is no longer only what can be lacking from its place, but what *passes through by force*."[27] Surely anchored in the real as a lack of being, a truth procedure is that which gives being to this very lack. Exposing the absent cause or constitutive outside of a given situation, in other words, remains a dialectical yet idealist answer, unless this evanescent point of the real is forced, distorted, and extended in order to give consistency to the real as a new generic truth.

For Badiou, in sum, there are two parts to the theory of the subject in the long aftermath of May '68. The first, dialectical or algebraic, half holds that every force is divided by the law of its structural placement: "Everything that is relates to itself at a distance from itself owing to the place where it is," while the second, materialist or topological, half accounts for the emergence of a subject out of the forced torsion of its determining law: "It happens, let us say, that '*it* makes a *subject.*'"[28] This double articulation is, finally, Badiou's way of explicating the old Freudian maxim, *Wo es war, soll Ich werden*, in such a way that the subject can no longer be reduced purely and simply to the impasse of the structure itself, as seems to have become the idealist trend after Lacan.

THE FOUR FUNDAMENTAL CONCEPTS
OF THE THEORY OF THE SUBJECT

Yet even in Lacanian psychoanalysis two subjective figures seem to point toward an excess of the real beyond its placement in the existing law of things: anxiety and the superego. The first signals a radical breakdown, due to the irruption of an overwhelming part of the real, in the whole symbolic apparatus. In this sense anxiety is an infallible guide for a possible new truth, the site of which is indicated precisely by such failure. "Anxiety is that form of interruption that, invaded by the real as too-muchness, lets this order be as dead order," Badiou summarizes: "We might say that anxiety designates the moment when the real *kills* the symbolical, rather than splitting it."[29] In this way anxiety is only the revealing counterpart of a violent superego injunction, which constitutes the obscene and unlawful underside of the public law. "The superego is related to the law, and at the same time it is a senseless law," Lacan himself says: "The superego is simultaneously the law and its destruction. In this regard, it is the word itself, the commandment of the law, inasmuch as only its root is left."[30] The figure of the superego gives access to that part of nonlaw that is the destructive foundation of the law itself but only to recompose more forcefully the structural space of assigned places. In conjunction with the barbaric ferocity that serves as its native soil, the superego is a terrorizing call to order that seems almost automatically to fill out the void revealed by anxiety.

Thus, between anxiety and the superego a subject only oscillates in painful alternation, without the event of true novelty, just as the insufferable experience of formlessness without a law provokes in turn the reinforcement of the law's excessive form. At best, these two subjective figures of anxiety and superego thus indicate the point where the existing order of things becomes open to a fatal division. At worst, they can be counted on never to allow for a new order to come into being.

As early as his first seminar, however, Lacan himself raises the question whether this analysis should not be extended to include two other figures of the subject: "Where could this adjournment come to a stop? Do we have to extend the analytical intervention to the point of becoming one of those fundamental dialogues on justice and courage, in the great dialectical tradition?"[31] For Badiou, who from this point onward further elaborates what is only a suggestion in Lacan, courage and justice are indeed outmoded names for the process whereby an existing order not only breaks down, gets blocked, or is reinforced in its old ways but actually expands, changes, and lends coherence to a new truth. Like anxiety, courage stands under the dissolving pressure of the real, but this time it is in order to twist the structure at the point of its impasse. "Courage positively carries out the disorder of the symbolic, the breakdown of communication, whereas anxiety calls for its death," Badiou writes: "All courage amounts to passing through there where previously it was not visible that anyone could find a passage."[32] The part of destruction in the figure of courage, then, no longer provokes the restoration of a senseless law of terror but instead puts the old order to the test so as to produce an unforeseeable alternative. "Anxiety is lack of place, and courage, the assumption of the real by which the place is divided," so that now the old nonlaw of the law gives way to a new law, one that no longer recomposes the archaic fierceness of the superego injunction but rather produces a figure of unheard-of justice. "Justice is that by which the subject's nodal link to the place, to the law, takes on the divisible figure of its transformation," Badiou concludes: "More radically, justice names the possibility—from the standpoint of what it brings into being as subject-effect—that what is nonlaw may serve as law."[33]

Thus, Badiou's theory of the subject ties four subjective figures into a single knot. The first two figures—anxiety and courage—divide the act of subjectivization that marks a flickering moment of destruction, while the other two—superego and justice—split the moment of recomposition that is the enduring work of a subjective process. Any subject thus combines a destruction with a recomposition, following two possible trajectories, or strands, which an integral materialist theory of the subject needs to combine. The first strand—from anxiety to the superego—is subordinate to the law of the existing order of places and its founding lack; the second—from courage to justice—actively divides the consistency of the existing order so as to produce a new truth. According to the first strand, which can be called algebraic, a subject fundamentally occupies a position of internal exclusion with regard to the objective structure in which it finds its empty place; according to the second, a subject stands in a topological excess over and above its assigned placement, the law of which is then transformed.

In short, a subject insists on being caused by that which lacks at its place, but it consists in the coherence of a forced lack. As Badiou concludes: "The theory of the subject is complete when it manages to think the structural law of the empty place as the punctual anchoring of the excess over the place."[34] Lacan's psychoanalysis gives us only half of this theory—that is, the structural and algebraic strand that remains caught in an endless vacillation between the twin figures of anxiety and the superego, or between the vanishing object-cause of desire and the violent restoration of the archaic law—to which a supplementary strand of courage and justice, of a transformative process and a consistent new truth, ought to be added in Badiou's theory of the subject.

PSYCHOANALYSIS AND TRAGEDY

Already implicit in the preceding lines is a last way of measuring the distance that separates Lacan and Badiou, which involves a return to ancient tragedy as an ethical source of inspiration behind psychoanalysis. In

Freud and Lacan this source has always been Sophoclean, particularly, of course, through the figure of Oedipus. In recent years, though, there has been a push to move away from the whole Oedipus complex in order to ask what it would mean for psychoanalysis to take into account the figure of Antigone. As Judith Butler reminds us in her lectures titled *Antigone's Claim*: "In George Steiner's study of the historical appropriations of *Antigone*, he poses a controversial question he does not pursue: What would happen if psychoanalysis were to have taken Antigone rather than Oedipus as its point of departure?"[35] Today, this question clearly no longer appears to be controversial at all. On the contrary, reversing the hierarchy implicit in Steiner's and Butler's counterfactual hypothesis, I would venture to say that a theoretical shift from Oedipus to Antigone defines the ethical and political—if we can speak of politics at this level—dominant of our post-Oedipal times. Today, it is Antigone's death-driven fidelity to a principle of justice beyond Creon's terrorizing law—"a sort of justice without law, a justice beyond the law," as Jacques Derrida also might put it[36]—that sets the criteria for the authentic ethical or political act. Indeed, the very notions of ethics and politics in this line of arguing often seem to become indistinguishable, if the latter does not collapse into the former altogether. As such, though, we still remain by and large within the bounds of the Sophoclean model of tragedy.

Badiou's aim in *Theory of the Subject*, by contrast, could well be summed up in an even broader and more controversial question than the one Butler adopts from George Steiner, namely: Why is it that psychoanalysis—and today I would add critical theory and philosophy in general—has set its eye so completely and exclusively on Sophocles? Why not step back for a moment from *both* Oedipus *and* the mirroring relationship between Antigone and Creon so as to put them into a dialectical tension with the twin figures of Orestes and Athena in the *Oresteia*? In short, why not supplement Sophocles with his predecessor, Aeschylus? Badiou writes: "The whole purpose of our critical delimitation with regard to the psychoanalytic contribution to the theory of the subject can be evaluated by asking the following question: Why is its theory of the subject essentially based on Sophocles, that is, predicated on the Oedipus complex?"[37] If, in the world of Sophocles, Antigone and Creon name the respective figures of anxiety and the superego, that is, the formlessness of what persists without legal place and the surfeit of form that restores the law as terror, then Badiou's aim in turning to the alternative model of Aeschylus is to find examples of courage and justice in the twin figures of Orestes and Athena, that is, the interruption of the vengeful law of things and the recomposition of a new legal order. "Thus we see that there exist indeed two Greek tragic modes," he suggests: "The Aeschylean one, the direction of which is the contradictory advent of justice by the courage of the new; and the Sophoclean one, the anguished sense of which is the quest, through a reversal, for the superegoic origin."[38] Lacan firmly establishes himself in the world of Sophocles while merely pointing toward its extension by Aeschylus, which is precisely where the theory of the subject must come according to Badiou.

Badiou first of all reads Sophoclean tragedy in terms of the above-mentioned duel between anxiety and the superego as figured by Antigone and Creon. Through these two figures the space circumscribed by the order of the law is disrupted—first, by way of a lack in the law, or rather a lack of lack, unmistakably exposed in anxiety, and, second, by the law's inner excess over itself, laid bare in superegoic fury: " 'Creon' is the name of the superego: the law deregulated—destroyed—by its very own native essence as it returns in excess of the place that it circumscribes. 'Antigone' is the name of anxiety, that is, the principle of the infinity of the real, unplaceable within the regulated finitude of the place. From this point of view, Antigone and Creon, although they are antagonists in the play, in my eyes accomplish the same process, which defines the Sophoclean tragic subject."[39] Badiou, like many after him, thus underscores the mutual dependence of the Sophoclean heroes. Not only does Antigone's anxiety-ridden decision not to give up on her desire seem to provoke in return the destructive rage inherent in the law, that is, the element of violent nonlaw parading in the guise of the law of the city-state; but, what is more, her rebellion is already nothing more than a reaction to the excessive form of Creon's law. It comes after and completely depends on the latter for its force. As Butler also insists in her reading of the play, Antigone cannot voice her desire except in the very language of the rule of law: "Although Hegel claims that her deed is opposed to Creon's, the two acts mirror rather than oppose one another." Later Butler adds, still speaking of Antigone: "Her words, understood as deeds, are chiasmically related to the vernacular of sovereign power, speaking in and against it, delivering and defying imperatives at the same time, inhabiting the language of sovereignty at the very moment in which she opposes sovereign power and is excluded from its terms."[40] Unlike Butler, however, Badiou finds several of the terms to define this relation of chiasmic implication already at work in the published teachings of Lacan.

The superego, to begin with, should not be confused with the law, since it opens onto the latter's destructive root. What it uncovers is thus the pure force of injunction that sustains the senseless excess of linguistic tautology. "The superego gives access to the source of the force of law, to that which is no longer of the order of language but which lies at the core of the imperative character of the law," writes Badiou, commenting on the passage from Lacan's *Seminar* quoted above. "If the law can bear the advent of destruction—the excess over the repetition that the law itself dictates—it is because the very order of the law, grasped as pure commandment, is in itself essentially excess and destruction."[41] This element of excess and destruction is the nonlaw in the law, which as such lies revealed in the ferocity of the superego injunction, reduced to a pure *You must* or to redundancies of the type *The law is the law*: "The nonlaw is what manifests itself as the affirmative side of the law; for this reason the superego can be simultaneously the sign of the law and of its destruction."[42] Through the notion of the superego the law itself paradoxically lays bare its potential for subversion from within.

Badiou also borrows a Lacanian (clearly much more so than a Sartrean) understanding of anxiety to approach the figure of Antigone. What produces anxiety in this understanding is not the loss of a specific object, but neither is it the case that anxiety is devoid of all relations to the object, as is often argued even in Lacanian circles. Instead, signaling an encounter with the real, anxiety can be defined as the lack of lack, owing to the appearance of something—anything whatsoever really—in the empty place supposed to mark the lack in the structure. Already from anxiety as lack of lack, though, the attention then begins to shift toward the question of a certain mastery of the effects of such a redoubling of the logic of lack. "Lacan says superbly, anxiety is nothing but the lack of lack," Badiou writes, referring to *Seminar XI: The Four Fundamental Concepts of Psycho-analysis*: "But when the lack comes to lack, its metonymic effect is interrupted and a mastery of real loss begins, paid for by the ravaging of all symbolic points of reference. Hence anxiety never deceives. Destruction must reach the law of lack in order for the lure of deception, semblance, and the oblivion of oblivion to be swept away."[43] There is thus something in anxiety, in the rapport to the real for which the affect of anxiety serves as an unmistakable index, which already puts us in touch with a dimension beyond a purely structural account of subjectivity based on its constitutive lack.

Through Creon's superegoic ferocity and Antigone's anxiety, in sum, the excessive form of the law and the formlessness of nonlaw come head to head, without providing any way out of the impasse—at least not in the Sophoclean model—other than death and sacrifice in the ongoing cycle of revenge and counterrevenge. Even if they are not the only terms available in this reading of ancient tragedy, however, anxiety and the superego are not for this reason any less necessary for a coherent theory of the subject and possibly even for a theory of justice as well. Badiou thus concludes his analysis of Sophocles: "Anxiety and the superego are therefore two fundamental concepts of the subject (there are two others), if by this we mean to designate that which lies at the crossing of the inert and civilized law of lack and the barbaric interruption of destruction," but he is quick to add: "There is, however, another truth and another tragedy: that of Orestes and of Aeschylus. Here, destruction assures the subject of a certain mastery of loss. . . . What does this mean, if not that in this way we come out of the radical impasse to which the unity of the place, that is, the insurmountable fixity of the symbolic confines us?"[44] Specifically, courage and justice, as hinted by Lacan in the comment from *Seminar I* quoted above, are the two fundamental concepts of the subject that allow Badiou to move beyond the dominant influence of the Sophoclean paradigm.

Aeschylus opens up the possibility of discussing these themes of courage and justice, respectively, in the figures of Orestes and Athena: "If Aeschylus excels in anything, it is rather in grasping, on the superego's firm ground, the moment of the *institutive disruption*. There is never a return to order in his theater, but rather the recomposition of a different order."[45] This also means that, instead of remaining caught in a chiasmic relation to the cycle of violence and revenge, the possibility of a new law emerges at the precise point where the old law is found wanting. Anxiety, thus, retains its indispensable diagnostic value as that which never fails to put us on track toward the real—except that courage now breaks anxiety's death-driven nature by inverting its orientation: "As a result, it is no longer the formal excess that serves as the engine, but rather the courageous refusal. Although devoured by anxiety, and in fact *precisely because* he is devoured by anxiety, Orestes does not internalize the law of the debt of blood with its endless allocations, nor does he turn against it in a blind fury. Instead, he demands a discussion based on facts; he resists and does not give in to the murderous seduction of the Erinyes. 'Orestes,' who is first the name of anxiety, is the name of courage. 'Athena' is the name of justice."[46] With the intervention of Athena in the tribunal at the end of the *Oresteia* trilogy, the chain of murders is interrupted and a new law, a new right, or a new type of consistency is instituted. This is, finally, the task of recomposition, attributed to the concept of justice as distinct from, yet necessarily instructed by, anxiety and the superegoic injunction: "Justice makes no sense as a constitutive category of the subject if the symbolic operates on indivisibility whose kernel of terror founds the consistency of the subjective process, in the obsessive fabric of repetition. Justice requires a dialectical precariousness of the law, susceptible of being shaken up in the process of its scission. This is not the precariousness of this or that particular law, but of the very principle of commandment itself."[47]

Badiou's reading of Greek tragedy thus brings into play the four fundamental concepts of the subject: "The courage of the scission of the laws, the anxiety of an opaque persecution, the superego of the blood-thirsty Erinyes, and finally justice according to the consistency of the new: these are the four concepts that articulate the subject."[48] Through the proposed shift from Sophocles to Aeschylus, in particular, the overall reason for adding a subjective strand that runs from courageous refusal to the recomposition of justice consists in avoiding the disastrous consequences of desubjectivization, which derive from the conviction that, beyond the truths that lie revealed in anxiety and superegoic fury, all action would be illusory, if not impossible.

FORCE OF NONLAW

Under the pretence of defending the legal apparatus and parliamentary democracy, the State is essentially the illegal being of all legality, of the violence of right, and of the law as nonlaw. On the other hand, the communist theme is justice, for it claims that, under the withering away of classes and of the State, nonlaw can become the last law of proletarian politics.—BADIOU, *Theory of the Subject*

One of the most intriguing aspects of the discussion of law and justice in *Theory of the Subject* is how this work can be said to anticipate certain themes in Derrida's famous "Force of Law: The 'Mystical Foundation of Authority,' " itself in large part a painstaking analysis of Walter Benjamin's classical, but for this reason no less cryptic, essay "Critique of Violence."[49] Both Badiou and Derrida, in fact, seek to bring the law to the limit-point where it capsizes so as to uncover a dimension of "nonlaw" internal to the law itself. In French, to be exact, they respectively write of *non-loi* and *non-droit*. We can thus initiate an unexpected rapprochement between Badiou and Derrida through the notion of the nonlaw—even if what they end up doing with this notion may well take us again in two widely diverging directions.

For Badiou as for Benjamin, despite Derrida's reluctance to follow the latter along this perilous path, the possibility of justice would require that we supplement and extend the iterability of law and nonlaw with a principle of interruption, or even with destruction. In the absence of destruction as a mastering of lack, by contrast, what remains today—both in historical terms and at the level of theory and philosophy—seems to be reduced once again to the alternative of either boldly embracing the anxiety produced by the lack of lack or else anticipating the impossible possibility of an absolute beyond of the law's terrorizing ubiquity—a beyond that, precisely because it does not entail an effective interruption, may very well leave intact the regime of terror except to point up its obscene underside, its groundless foundation, or its rootedness in pure nonlaw. In fact, the courage of thought today, if we can still call it this, seems increasingly to depend precisely on such a sinister exposure alone. Put differently, I would argue that the Sophoclean dominant of our times can be seen as a symptom of the fact that once courage and justice are dismissed as so many blinding illusions of dogmatic voluntarism, what we are left with are precisely only the twin dispositions of anxiety and terror, that is to say, an excessive dimension of the real as too-much that at the same time exposes the fragility and precariousness of the law qua nonlaw. Badiou uncannily seems to have predicted this when in *Theory of the Subject* he writes: "I believe that this subjective figure, whose dialectical edge is limited to that of anxiety and the superego, always prevails in times of decadence and disarray, both in history and in life."[50] If this is the case in history and in life, then we must also ask ourselves what happens when, in the current disarray, theory and philosophy in turn appear increasingly unable to propose anything significantly different.

We can retrace some of the steps along the trajectory that has brought us to this point by taking a closer look at two series of criticism, one actual and the other virtual, aimed against Badiou's philosophy. The result of these criticisms, or an unwanted side-effect of their underlying principles, is that just as historically anxiety and terror seem to spread as wildfire throughout the world, so too in theory the suspicion now prevalent is that there can be no new law beyond the nonlaw except at the risk of falling prey to a transcendental illusion, blind dogmatism, or the mystifications of good (bad) conscience. What this suspicion confirms is that ultimately there is no other of the Other. Or, rather, as the surest sign of a prohibition, the consensus seems to be that there *cannot* be an other of the Other because their *ought not* to be one.

One of Žižek's often-repeated moves in his ongoing polemical rejoinders to Badiou, as we saw in chapter 1, amounts to reducing all false pretenses of novelty to being little more than death-driven repetition in disguise. Thus, with reference to the proposition that Orestes's courage and Athena's justice would exceed the anxiety/superego dyad of Antigone and Creon, our Slovenian friend wonders out loud: "Convincing as this example is, we cannot avoid the obvious question: is not this new Law imposed by Athena the patriarchal Law based on the exclusion/repression of what then returns as the obscene superego fury?"[51] More generally, this objection targets a supposed blind spot in Badiou's thinking in relation to psychoanalysis, that is, his inability to think of the death drive and hence of repetition itself other than as a dimension wholly outside of the domain of truth and fidelity to the event. "Perhaps, the reason Badiou neglects this dimension is his all too crude opposition between repetition and the cut of the Event, his dismissal of repetition as an obstacle to the rise of the New, ultimately as the death drive itself, the morbid attachment to some obscure *jouissance* which entraps the subject in the self-destructive vicious cycle," Žižek still writes more recently, adding the paradoxical lesson that the event can emerge only out of repetition, not against it. This would be a lesson drawn not only from Freud or Lacan but also from Deleuze—with a bonus illustration taken from Benjamin:

> The proper Deleuzian paradox is that something truly New can ONLY emerge through repetition. What repetition repeats is not the way the past "effectively was," but the virtuality inherent to the past and betrayed by its past actualization. In this precise sense, the emergence of the New changes the past itself, that is, it retroactively changes (not the actual past—we are not in science fiction—but) the balance be-

tween actuality and virtuality in the past. Recall the old example provided by Walter Benjamin: the October Revolution repeated the French
Revolution, redeeming its failure, unearthing and repeating the same
impulse.[52]

It should be clear, though, that the cut of the event is here merely
displaced onto the balance between actuality and virtuality. Without some
split between the past as mere pastness and that portion of the past that is
as yet purely virtual, no redemption of failure—and hence no revolution—
would ever be possible. And yet it is precisely this split between repetition
and that within repetition that is not yet actualized which defines the locus
of the work of destruction for *Theory of the Subject*. The whole purpose of
adding the fundamental dialogues on courage and justice, in the great
dialectical tradition, consists precisely in disentangling the element of
repetition and the nonrepeatable—whether as an interruption or as a mastering of loss, as a refusal or as a torsion. Conversely, the zeal with which
the figures of repetition and the death drive are wielded about today in
psychoanalytically inflected arguments runs the risk of an equally crude
dismissal of all novelty in the name of the irrefutable radicality in which
these very same figures always seem to be cloaked.

Derrida, for his part, also relies on repetition—on the law of iterability—
in his reading of Benjamin in "Force of Law," many arguments of which can
be read in a virtual dialogue, including a polemical one, with *Theory of the
Subject*. Derrida thus takes as his point of departure an unavoidable "contamination" between the two types of "mythic" violence, one law-founding
and the other law-preserving, that Benjamin in his original essay tries in
vain to keep separate:

> For beyond Benjamin's explicit purpose, I shall propose the interpreta-
> tion according to which the very violence of the foundation or *positing
> of law* (*Rechtssetzende Gewalt*) must envelop the violence of the *preser-
> vation of law* (*Rechtserhaltende Gewalt*) and cannot break with it. It
> belongs to the structure of fundamental violence in that it calls for the
> repetition of itself and founds what ought to be preserved, preservable,
> promised to heritage and to tradition, to partaking [*partage*]. . . . And
> even if a promise is not kept in fact, iterability inscribes the promise as
> guard in the most irruptive instant of foundation. Thus it inscribes the
> possibility of repetition at the heart of the originary. Better, or worse, it

is inscribed in this law [*loi*] of iterability; it stands under its law or before its law [*sous sa loi ou devant sa loi*]. Consequently [*du coup*], there is no more pure foundation or pure position of law, and so a pure founding violence, than there is a purely preserving violence. Positing is already iterability, a call for self-preserving repetition.[53]

Both forms of mythic violence, as Derrida abruptly suggests, may also be called Greek. In light of Badiou's reading in *Theory of the Subject* we might even say that they are more specifically Sophoclean (in the case of law-preserving violence) and Aeschylean (law-founding violence). If this is the case, though, then iterability once again destroys the illusion that there could ever be a pure foundation or a pure position of law without or beyond the anxiety over the law's preservation. This means that once again, the theory of justice and courage according to Aeschylus would be contaminated through and through by the theory of superegoic terror and anxiety according to Sophocles. The latter, by subjecting us to a law of all laws—the law of iterability—also puts an insurmountable obstacle on the path of any disingenuous belief in the existence of an other of the Other. Instead, what we are left with literally comes down to a combination of anxious responsibility—anxiety *as* responsibility—and a sense of the law's rootedness in the—superegoic—ferocity of its inherent force.

While justice and even courage are constantly invoked in Derrida's text, therefore, they take on a role that runs completely counter to the significance the two concepts have for Badiou. In fact, the structural presence of anxiety or anguish (*angoisse* in French) here actually blocks justice as a new law from ever coming into being in the first place. Unless anxiety is that which keeps justice from being anything other than the exposure of the element of nonlaw within the law:

> It is a moment of suspense, this period of *epokhè*, without which there is, in fact, no possible deconstruction. It is not a simple moment: its possibility must remain structurally present to the exercise of all responsibility if such responsibility is never to abandon itself to dogmatic slumber, and therefore to deny itself. From then on, this moment overflows itself. It becomes all the more anguishing. But who will claim to be just by economizing on anguish? This anguishing moment of suspense also opens the interval of spacing in which transformations, even juridicopolitical revolutions, take place. It cannot be motivated, it cannot find

its movement and its impulse (an impulse that, however, cannot itself be suspended) except in the demand for an increase or a supplement of justice, and so in the experience of an inadequation or an incalculable disproportion. For in the end, where would deconstruction find its force, its movement or its motivation if not in this always unsatisfied appeal, beyond the given determinations of what one names, in determined contexts, justice, the possibility of justice?[54]

Derrida admittedly seems to be arguing here for a diagonal passage from anguish to justice, even anticipating the necessary conditions for the possibility of juridicopolitical revolutions. He also, though somewhat more ambiguously, points out that such revolutions in principle presuppose the founding of a new law and a new state, which is why they inevitably revert back to the necessary contamination between law-preserving and law-founding violence that he finds in Benjamin: "All revolutionary situations, all revolutionary discourses, on the left or on the right (and from 1921, in Germany, there were many of these that resembled each other in a troubling way, Benjamin often finding himself between the two), justify the recourse to violence by alleging the founding, in progress or to come, of a new law, of a new state."[55] Derrida's never-ending vigilance and his reluctance to embrace this violence as a necessary component of revolutionary situations, though, seem to cause him to remain on guard so as not to indulge in the good conscience of ever affirming the existence of justice in the present: "Is it ever possible to say, 'I know that I am just?' I would want to show that such confidence is essentially impossible, other than in the figure of good conscience and mystification."[56] To avoid all mystification, then, justice seems to exhaust itself in the exposure of the excessive force that is the foundation of the law, as the very opening of a dimension that is in law more than law itself.

We might even say that what Derrida calls "the mystical" precisely works from within against mystification insofar as "it is, in law, what suspends law. It interrupts the established law to found another. This moment of suspense, this *epokhè*, this founding or revolutionary moment of law is, in law, an instance of nonlaw [*dans le droit une instance de non-droit*]. But it is also the whole history of law."[57] Perhaps in the end, then, this is not altogether different from the anxious-compulsive return to the obscene underside of the public law, its surplus enjoyment, or its perverse fantasy dimension, that we see so often laid bare in the case of Žižek.

AN OTHER OF THE OTHER

Badiou's argument in his reconfiguration of Greek tragedy ultimately is not so much with Aeschylus or Sophocles as historical events, not even with Hegel or Hölderlin's partial reappropriations of Sophocles and the concomitant displacements of Aeschylus that set the tone for all subsequent romantic and postromantic theorizing, so much as with Lacanian psychoanalysis. More specifically, the aim is to supplement and extend Lacan's doctrine on two unshakable presuppositions: first, the presupposition that the truth of the subject, psychoanalytically speaking, is of a structural order, rather than resulting from the rare and contingent occurrence of an event, and, second, the presupposition that there is no other of the Other. In both cases, taking a step beyond psychoanalysis requires a passage from lack to destruction in order for a subject of justice to come into being. "In this sense, we must say that, historically, there where a subject arises at the crossroads of lack and destruction, and at the point of anxiety but in the inversion of its truth, there is truly found something the existence of which Lacan denies—an other of the Other, from which it follows that what functions as the first Other is no longer a disguised modality of the Same."[58] This also implies that a given impasse or contradiction, if we can still speak in these terms, appears to be no longer structural but historical: "If the *structural* concept of contradiction (the splitting) points to the lack as its mainspring and to the law as its horizon, the *historical* concept of contradiction is forged on the basis of destruction whose sphere of action lies in the *nonlaw*."[59] Consequently, far from merely signaling a structural deadlock, the appearance of an impasse actually subjects the structure as a whole to the possibility of transformation.

What we might call therefore "the force of nonlaw," following the thrust of destruction beyond the law of lack and its redoubling, consists precisely in the capacity to bring into being the nonrepeatable within repetition: "The conservative term can be identified with the law of lack and subordinates the other to itself as repeatable. Force is nothing but that which, by concentrating in itself, out-of-place, a term that was assigned to repetition, jams up the mechanism of repetition and thus triggers the possibility for the destruction of its law. There where the old coherence prescribed a mere sliding displacement, an interruption arises through a purification that exceeds the place. This is the history of force."[60] This is also, I might add, how the history or prehistory of the concept of the event, so central in this philosopher's better-known later work, is anticipated in the force of nonlaw: "From this point of view, just as there is only *one* subject, there is also only *one* force whose existence always surfaces as an event. This event, the trace of the subject, cuts across both lack and destruction."[61] An event, then, is not just the sudden apparition of the empty place at the heart of a given situation; it also requires an excess over the gaping void revealed in the latter's structure. Something else has to happen, beyond the mere occupation of an empty place. Otherwise, the structure of what is given would merely open itself up to a flickering alternation between the false appearance of plenitude and the vanishing act of the real of lack.

Badiou's theory of justice, in other words, seeks to break with the law qua law. This polemic, which is specifically but not exclusively aimed at Lacanian psychoanalysis, actually is a constant throughout his work—bringing forth an argument that reappears in different guises from *Theory of the Subject* all the way to *Logics of Worlds*. What requires interruption is not this or that law as a particular or empirical injunction, whether written or not, but rather the very lawlike status of the law as a structural or transcendental bedrock. This bedrock must be broken so as to open up the possibility for another law and for an other of the Other.

This plea for an other of the Other is not unlike Butler's ongoing argument, including in *Antigone's Claim*, against a tendency of following what she calls "a theological impulse within the theory of psychoanalysis that seeks to put out of play any criticism of the symbolic father, the law of psychoanalysis itself," which as a result appears to be an incontestable limit: "The theory exposes its own tautological defense. The law beyond laws will finally put an end to the anxiety produced by a critical relation to final authority that clearly does not know when to stop: a limit to the social, the subversive, the possibility of agency and change, a limit that we cling to, symptomatically, as the final defeat of our own power. Its defenders claim that to be without such a law is pure voluntarism or radical anarchy!"[62] What Butler does not seem to consider, though, is the extent to which the possibility of such a limit, posited as intractable, may well be an imposition of the Sophoclean model with which she otherwise seems incapable of breaking. It is Sophocles, if not historically then at the very least in his reappropriations by romantics and postromantics alike, who may have set this limit—another, ontologically dignified name for which would be finitude. This is why today it may seem increasingly unlikely, not to say undesirable, to want to supplement the anxiety of Antigone vis-à-vis the law, which Butler invokes, as well, as a final safeguard—if not the only one—against the closure of Antigone's relation to Creon's authority, with the courage and justice of Orestes and Athena.

I do not wish to take leave of the theme of justice as the law of nonlaw in *Theory of the Subject*, however, without at least hinting at a wildly speculative last possibility. Even Derrida, after all, does not stop at the necessary contamination between the two types of "mythic violence" that he so boldly redefines as being both essentially Greek; he also opposes the latter to Benjamin's "divine violence," which breaks with the violence of myth and which, by contrast with the latter's typically Greek nature, would be characteristically Judaic. We could compare this to Hölderlin's opposition, in his remarks on Antigone, between the "native form" and the "formless," whose struggle takes to the stage precisely as tragedy and that later on, for Nietzsche, will be the basis for the opposition between the Apollonian and the Dionysian. For Hölderlin this opposition corresponds to the struggle between what is properly Greek and the background against which all Greek form seeks to define itself, that is, its multiple and orgiastic soil, which in this peculiar romantic flight of geopolitical fancy is considered Asiatic.

Extending this fantasy with another speculative move, then, could we not argue that, in addition to the Greek myth and the Judaic God that Derrida locates in Benjamin, there lies a vanishing mediator in what Hölderlin names the Asiatic? What this mediator proposes, right before vanishing into the obscure backdrop of an Orientalist bias from which it never completely frees itself, is a justice that would be neither mythic nor divine but rather—what? perhaps secular and communist? Is this not what Marx himself, and after him many of the boldest thinkers of the Third World, intuited as a primitive communism to be retrieved in superior conditions, through the infamous and much maligned notion of an Asiatic mode of production? The formlessness of the form, then, would serve not as the exoticized other of civilized law and order but as the bottomless ground for a truly generic type of justice, another name for which would be communism: the force of nonlaw as law. "The communist hypothesis as such is generic, it is the 'basis' of any emancipatory orientation, it names the sole thing that is worthwhile if we are interested in politics and history," Badiou writes: "Indeed, there is no other hypothesis, or at least I am not aware of one."[63] This is the hypothesis to which I will return in my conclusion.

ELEMENTS OF SELF-CRITICISM

In retrospect Badiou's *Theory of the Subject* can still be said to suffer the effects of several shortcomings, or possible misgivings:

First, philosophy, in *Theory of the Subject*, still appears to be sutured onto the sole condition of politics. The procedures of art, science, and love—as well as the eternal shadow condition of religion—are already present throughout the book, but they may seem to be mere illustrations or analogues, rather than conditions in the strict sense, given that the subject of truth is defined exclusively in terms of politics. Instead, beginning with *Manifesto for Philosophy*, Badiou will insist that an important precondition for the possibility of taking another step in the modern configuration of philosophy requires a strict unsuturing or desuturing of philosophy from the four truth procedures. "The gesture I propose is purely and simply that of philosophy, of de-saturation," Badiou writes, only to add that today, in the wake of Heidegger, the principal suture is poetic rather than political as in Marxism: "It so happens that the main stake, the supreme difficulty, is to de-suture philosophy from its poetic condition. Positivism and dogmatic Marxism now constitute but ossified positions. As sutures, they are purely institutional or academic."[64] The need for desuturation could even be considered a fifth condition, albeit in a slightly different sense from what Badiou understands by the four truth procedures as conditions of philosophy: "One could thus say that there is also a fifth condition of philosophy: philosophy has to pull itself away from the immediate grip of its own conditions, while nevertheless remaining under the effect of these conditions."[65] Yet even if philosophy should refuse to be the servant of politics alone in order equally to define a space of compossibility for the other truth procedures as well, does not the striking force of *Theory of the Subject* lie precisely in the fact that, as in the case of the events of May '68 themselves, the book bears witness to the impossibility of drawing a clear and distinct line of demarcation between the political revolt, the liberation of love, graphic art, and the experiments in film and street theater? Does not Badiou himself, toward the end of the first interview reproduced below, call for the articulation of a network or series of connections among the four conditions? In a manner prescient of some of the goals set out yet not quite realized in *Logics of Worlds,* this would make a virtue out of what otherwise can be considered a shortcoming of *Theory of the Subject.*

A second limitation has to do with the fact that within the condition of politics, *Theory of the Subject* still considers the party the only effective organizational structure, albeit in a constant dialectic of masses, classes, and party: "Without the mass line, the party is null and void. Not to include the party disarms the masses in questions of politics"; "Let us recall that the political subject is the class party."[66] As I anticipated in my introduction, Badiou has since then abandoned this strict identification of the political subject with the party, which in all its incarnations over the past century—whether as single party or in the parliamentary-electoral multiparty system—has remained overly bound to the form of the state. In practice, after years of seeking to found a Leninist party of a new type, this crisis of the party-form of politics led Badiou and his cohorts Lazarus and Michel to split with the Maoist UCFML and create a new group simply called Political Organization. In a recent issue of this group's newsletter, *Political Distance,* we read: "The balance of the nineteenth century is the withering away of the category of class as the sole bearer of politics, and the balance of the twentieth century is the withering away of the party-form, which knows only the form of the party-State."[67] Philosophically, moreover, this search for a new figure of militantism without a party will bring Badiou back to an old acquaintance, in *Saint Paul: The Foundation of Universalism,* as though almost thirty years had to pass before Badiou could finally come to terms with his personal road to Damascus: "For me, Paul is the poet-thinker of the event, and at the same time the one who practices and voices the invariant features of what we might call the militant figure."[68] Even this return to Paul as the militant thinker of a politics without the party, however, should not overshadow the fact that for Badiou politics will always require a form of organization. If for *Theory of the Subject,* the party is this body of politics, then the withering-away of the party-form merely puts on the agenda the need for a different discipline for the embodiment of collective thought. "The point at which a thought subtracts itself from the State, inscribing itself into being, makes the entire real of a politics," Badiou writes in the final lines of *Of an Obscure Disaster*: "And a political organization has no other end but that of 'holding the step that was won'—that is, of giving a body to the thought which, collectively re-membered, was capable of finding the public gesture of the insubordination that founds it."[69] This will lead, in *Logics of Worlds*, to a theory of what constitutes the body of a truth, whether political or otherwise.

As late as in *Metapolitics*, as a matter of fact, Badiou retrieves even a general notion of the party from Marx and Lenin as a mobile and precarious form of organizing consciousness. "It is crucial to emphasise that for Marx and Lenin, who are both in agreement on this point, the real characteristic of the party is not its firmness, but rather its porosity to the event, its dispersive flexibility in the face of unforeseeable circumstances," he writes, before referring specifically to *The Communist Manifesto*. "Thus, the communists embody the unbound multiplicity of consciousness, its anticipatory aspect, and therefore the precariousness of the bond, rather than its firmness."[70] We do well to remember that Marx himself, in a letter from 1860, went so far as to assert that after the dissolution of the communist Ligue in 1852, he "*never* belonged to any society again, whether *secret* or *public*," adding that "the party, in this totally ephemeral sense, has ceased to exist for me eight years ago," whereas there is perhaps another, more grandiose sense: "In talking about the party, I understood the party in the grand historical sense of the word."[71] In this sense we might say, the party also remains a major concern to this date for Badiou.

Third, *Theory of the Subject* seems to presuppose from the start that there is such a thing as subjectivity, without giving this thought much ontological support. It is certainly true, even though this is often forgotten, that the book in the end already introduces the whole question of Cantorian set theory, and pinpoints the location of the subject in the immeasurable excess of inclusion over belonging. Nevertheless, only later will the underpinnings of this thesis become systematically elaborated from a metaontological, that is to say metamathematical, point of view. In the preface to *Being and Event* Badiou writes in retrospect: "The (philosophical) statement that mathematics *is* ontology—the science of being qua being—is the stroke of light that illuminates the speculative scene which, in my *Theory of the Subject*, I had limited by presupposing purely and simply that 'there was' some subjectivation."[72] The new task in *Being and Event* will consist in articulating a coherent ontology together with a theory of the subject—a task that an older version of dialectical materialism would have accomplished by means of a homology between the dialectics of nature and the dialectics of spirit but that today requires a careful reformulation—

this time above all in a polemic with Heidegger and not only, as in the case of *Theory of the Subject*, with Lacan.

Fourth, and finally, much ink has been spilled, including on the part of Badiou himself, to correct the violent language of destruction with which *Theory of the Subject* seeks to displace the structural dialectic of lack in Mallarmé or Lacan. The tone of this language at times reaches chilling heights indeed, especially toward the mid-1970s, when it comes to affirming the part of loss and death that inheres in any new truth. "Every truth affirms itself in the destruction of nonsense. Every truth is thus essentially destruction," Badiou already writes in one of his early Maoist books, *Theory of Contradiction*: "In order for the new totality, the different process, or the scission of a different unity to come into being, it so happens that a fragment of the real, waste of the movement, drops out. This is the rationale behind the militant expression: the dustbins of history. History has worked all the better when its dustbins were better filled."[73] Toward the end of *Being and Event*, however, the author admits: "I went a bit astray, I must admit, in *Theory of the Subject* concerning the theme of destruction. Back then, I still supported the idea of an essential link between destruction and novelty."[74] In a strict ontological view the part of loss in novelty must be rephrased in terms not of destruction but of subtraction and disqualification. A new truth cannot suppress any existence, but by extending a given situation from the point of its supplementation that is an event, an enquiry into the truthfulness of this event can disqualify, or subtract, certain terms or multiples—namely, those inegalitarian ones that are incompatible with the generic nature of all truth. Destruction is then only a reactive name for the fate of that part of knowledge that no longer will have qualified as truthful in the extended situation.

The distinction between these two paths of destruction and subtraction is moreover a key topic of the author's ongoing inquiries. Much of Badiou's *Ethics*, for instance, deals with the specific restraints that must apply to any process of truth in order to avoid the disastrous catastrophe of forcing an entire situation. There is thus a limit, or halting point, which cannot be forced from the point of the situation's extension by a new truth. "Let us say that this term is not susceptible of being made eternal," Badiou writes: "In this sense, it is the symbol of the pure real of the situation, of its life without truth."[75] To force this limit, which marks the unnameable or neutral that is specific to each generic procedure, is a major cause of what Badiou defines as evil. Examples of this would include Nietzsche's mad act of breaking the history of humankind in two, or the disastrous suppression of all self-interest, in the guise of total reeducation, as proclaimed by certain Red Guards at the height of the Chinese Cultural Revolution. Badiou himself, in fact, tends to read his earlier doctrine of lack and destruction as such a disastrous forcing of the unnameable. Everything thus seems to point toward the notion of destruction as the principal misgiving in Badiou's early thought, which was very much sutured onto politics under the influence of Maoism.

In view of this last crucial objection, I only want to recall how Marx himself defines the scandalous nature of dialectical thinking, in his famous postface to the second edition of *Capital*: "In its mystified form, the dialectic became the fashion in Germany, because it seemed to transfigure and glorify what exists. In its rational figure, it is a scandal and an object of horror to the bourgeoisie and its doctrinaire spokesmen, because it includes in its understanding of what exists at the same time that of its negation and its necessary destruction."[76] What is happening today, however, is a new transfiguration of the given that may well cast itself as radical but that, precisely by trying to ward off the horrifying scandal of thinking not so much in terms of negation as much as through scission and destruction, merely ends up confirming the status quo in the name of an ethical principle of respect devoid of all truth. The mandatory limit of the unnameable, then, far from restraining an ongoing process of truth from within, actually blocks such process in advance and thus keeps a truth from ever taking hold to begin with. Even when it is transfigured by an acknowledgment of the real as its inevitable kernel of idiotic nonknowledge, a mortal life without truth is the radically mystified figure of today's revamping of the structural dialectic. By criticizing the ferocity of destruction in his own earlier work, Badiou perhaps unwittingly allows his thought to participate in this trend, which, guided by the undeniable authority of Lacan or Levinas and their doctrinaire spokesmen, is only all too quick to abandon the idea that, in addition to respect for the other or recognition of the real, a truth implies a symptomatic torsion of the existing order of things.

Destruction, in *Theory of the Subject*, means such a torsion whereby a subject is neither chained onto the automatism of repetition nor fascinated by the haphazard breaking in two of history (as in Nietzsche's figure of the overman) or by the sudden death of the whole symbolic order as such (as in the figures of anxiety and the superego in Lacan or Žižek). For Badiou, at least in *Theory of the Subject*, destruction was not to be confused with death pure and simple or with a total wipeout of the existing law of things. Since *Being and Event*, however, he himself seems to have forgotten that destruction—even as an exaggerated figure of resentment for which the past always remains the heaviest weight—names part of the process of torsion by which a new subject comes into being and as a result of which something drops out of the old picture.

Much of Badiou's *The Century*, finally, is also devoted to this alternative between destruction and subtraction, especially in art, as answers to the question of the end and the beginning that haunts the entire century—or rather Badiou's "brief" twentieth century, from the Revolution of 1917 until the period of what he calls the Restoration in the 1980s. However, the reader will have to wait for the discussion of *Logics of Worlds* to find ways in which Badiou currently tries to strike a balance between the theme of destruction, central to his *Theory of the Subject*, and that of subtraction, which is key to *Being and Event*. A truth, then, involves *both* a disqualification or subtraction (of being) *and* a destruction or loss (of appearing).[77] The example discussed at some length along these lines in *Logics of Worlds* refers to a lasting consequence, despite its ultimate failure, of the Paris Commune. "Though crushed and convulsive, the absolutization of the workers' political existence—the existence of the inexistent—nonetheless destroyed an essential form of subjection, that of proletarian political possibility to bourgeois political manoeuvring," Badiou writes, immediately before concluding: "We can draw from this a transcendental maxim: if what was worth nothing comes, in the guise of an eventual consequence, to be worth everything, then an established given of appearing is destroyed."[78] Significantly and, in my eyes at least, symptomatically, this reformulation of the question of destruction happens in a book that to a large extent is framed by a renewed appreciation of the legacy of Maoism. Thus, when Badiou talks in *Logics of Worlds* of "the inevitable death of some element" as a last consequence of an event in the strong sense of the term, he is in part retrieving a principle from his early Maoist pamphlet *Theory of Contradiction*, where he wrote: "There is no true revolutionary thought except one that leads the recognition of the new all the way to its unavoidable reverse side: something of the old must die."[79] Aside perhaps from Nietzsche, Badiou indeed echoes no one more than Mao when he writes: "The opening of a space of creation requires destruction."[80] This gives us all the more reason to devote the next chapter entirely to the question of Badiou's Maoism.

ONE DIVIDES INTO TWO

←——————————————→

THE RED YEARS

In "So Near! So Far!," the first section in his polemical *Deleuze: The Clamor of Being*, Badiou briefly recalls the tense ideological situation in the late 1960s and early 1970s in which he once went so far as to boycott his older colleague's course at the recently created University of Paris-VIII at Vincennes: "Then came the red years, 1968, the University of Vincennes. For the Maoist that I was, Deleuze, as the philosophical inspiration for what we called the 'anarcho-desirers,' was an enemy all the more formidable for being internal to the 'movement' and for the fact that his course was one of the focal points of the university."[1] In the original French version this passage—like the remainder of the brief introduction in which it appears—is actually not written in the past tense but in the present. *Pour le maoïste que je suis*, Badiou writes, literally: "For the Maoist that I am."[2] Of course, the French usage merely represents a sudden shift to the narrative present; technically speaking, we are still in the past, and, in this sense, the English translation is by no means incorrect. Nevertheless, something of the heightened ambiguity attached to the use of the narrative present is lost in the passage from one language to the other, as the overall image of a potentially discomforting past replaces the suggestion of an ongoing loyalty, or at the very least a lingering debt, to Maoism.

In this chapter I want to argue that Badiou's relation to Maoism, which I will suggest amounts to a form of post-Maoism, can in fact be summarized in the ambiguous use of the narrative present. If we were to spell out this ambiguity, we could say that Badiou was and still is a Maoist, even though he no longer is the same Maoist that he once was. There is no real mistake, therefore, in reading the line quoted above as if it applied to the present. As Badiou himself also says at the beginning of a recent talk on the Cultural Revolution, quoting Rimbaud to refer to his red years: "J'y suis, j'y suis toujours" (translated as "I am there, I am still there" [or "I am here, I am still here"]).[3] Yet we also sense that an impression of pastness undeniably overshadows the past's continuing presence in the present. What seems so near is also exceedingly far; and what is there is perhaps not quite here. By the same token, we should not overlook the possibility that a certain inner distancing may already define the original rapport of Maoism to itself. In fact, Mao's role for Badiou will largely have consisted in introducing an interior divide into the legacy of Marxism-Leninism, including therefore a division of Maoism. "From the Jinggang Mountains to the Cultural Revolution, Mao Zedong's thought is formulated against the current, as the work of division," Badiou summarizes in *Theory of Contradiction*, before identifying Mao's logic of scission as a prime example of such dialectical thinking: "Rebel thinking if there ever was one, revolted thinking of the revolt: dialectical thinking."[4] Maoism, then, in more strictly philosophical terms will come to mark an understanding of the dialectic as precisely such a thinking of revolt, the logic of scission, which proceeds without end through inner splits and divided recompositions. As Badiou would write several years later in an article for *Le Perroquet*, one of the periodicals of his Maoist group: "At stake are the criteria of dialectical thinking—general thinking of scission, of rupture, of the event, and of recomposition."[5]

THE TWO SOURCES OF FRENCH MAOISM

One of the unfortunate side-effects of the belated reception of Badiou's work in the English-speaking world, with most readings, as I mentioned in my introduction, typically limiting themselves to texts from after *Being and Event*, is a strong disregard precisely for Badiou's long-standing debts to Maoism and to the political sequence of the Cultural Revolution. Badiou explains in his *Ethics* that this Maoist period actually involved a double allegiance, that is, a fidelity not to one but to two events, referring to "the politics of the French Maoists between 1966 and 1976, which tried to think and practise a fidelity to two entangled events: the Cultural Revolution in

China, and May '68 in France."[6] By now many readers are of course familiar with the fact that during those tumultuous years, while never being strictly speaking "pro-China," Badiou was a staunch defender of the ideas of Chairman Mao. The author himself makes enough references throughout his work to suggest how formative this experience was, and still continues to be, for his thinking.

Furthermore, as I also mentioned above, part of the commonly accepted wisdom among Badiou's readers now holds that, by the mid-to-late 1980s, we witness a clean break from all dialectical forms of thinking—including a break away from the thought of Mao Zedong. Thus, after devoting the first chapter of his introductory guide to Badiou's "Maoist Beginnings," Jason Barker seems to reduce the lasting impact of Maoism to little more than a form of "militant vitality" now long gone: "Today the legacy of Maoism has all but disappeared."[7] Peter Hallward has the virtue of outlining the possibility of a much more painstaking investigation into the continuing legacy of Badiou's Maoism. This legacy involves not just an unflinching fidelity to forms of political commitment but also a whole series of theoretical and philosophical invariants. "What should be stressed is that Badiou's properly decisive concepts—concepts of the pure, the singular, and the generic—are themselves at least relatively constant," Hallward writes. "Certainly, for every disclaimer of 'early excesses' there have been many suggestive symptoms of a global continuity, at least from May 68 to the present."[8] If this is indeed the case, however, should we not beware of drawing too quick a line in the sand between the "early" and the "later" Badiou?

THE MAOIST INVESTIGATION

Even today Badiou's concept of politics as a procedure of truth remains to a large extent inseparable, despite the apparent self-criticisms, from the theory and practice of his vision of Maoism. In fact, to give but one symptomatic indication of this continuity, all procedures of truth, and not just the political one, involve a sustained "enquiry" or "investigation" into the possible connection or disconnection between the various aspects of a given situation and that which will have taken place in this situation under the sign of an event. Badiou writes in *Being and Event*: "In the end, therefore, we can legitimately treat the enquiry, a finite series of minimal reports [*constats*], as the truly basic unit of the procedure of fidelity" and, thus, through "the subtle dialectic between knowledges and post-evental fidelity" that is at stake in such procedures, as part of "the very kernel of the dialectic between knowledge and truth."[9] Badiou certainly has not forgotten that the task of undertaking such "enquiries" or "investigations" (*enquêtes* in French) in many parts of the world was one of the most important lessons drawn from Maoism.

A whole chapter in Mao's *Little Red Book* is dedicated to this very question under the title "Investigation and Study,"[10] proposing a method of which one of the earliest concrete examples can be found in Mao's own 1927 *Report on an Investigation of the Peasant Movement in Hunan*, the main topic of which—the revolutionary role of the peasantry that already sounded a strong note of dissonance in comparison with orthodox Marxism and Leninism—he would later revisit among other places in his 1941 *Rural Surveys* (again, in French editions of these texts, the same term, *enquête*, is used to translate the concepts that appear as "investigation" and "survey" in English). In the preface to this last text Mao reiterates the principle of the investigation as a form of concrete analysis of a concrete situation, so to speak, going against the abstraction of pure and unconditioned theory: "Everyone engaged in practical work must investigate conditions at the lower levels. Such investigation is especially necessary for those who know theory but do not know the actual conditions, for otherwise they will not be able to link theory with practice. Although my assertion, 'No investigation, no right to speak,' has been ridiculed as 'narrow empiricism,' to this day I do not regret having made it; far from regretting it, I still insist that without investigation there cannot be any right to speak."[11] Among French Maoists, furthermore, interest in the investigation is both systematic and widespread. In April 1967 *Garde Rouge*, the central journal of the Maoist UJC(ML), or Union of Communist Youths (Marxist-Leninist), publishes its fifth issue with a cover that reproduces the original assertion, "No investigation, no right to speak," first made in a 1930 text by Mao, "Against the Cult of the Book."

Serge July, a leading member of the soon to become ex-Gauche Prolétarienne, by far the most famous French Maoist group, and a subsequent cofounder of the communist daily *Libération*, would later go on to observe that "the investigation is the theoretical key to French Maoism."[12] In fact, the principle of the investigation, or *enquête*, together with the so-called assessment of experience, or *bilan d'expérience*, is one of the fundamental features behind Badiou's own Maoist organization, the UCFML, or Union of Communists of France Marxist-Leninist. The investigation is precisely that which enables any given militant process to continue moving along in the spiral between the various political experiences and their effective theoretical concentration. Thus, in a collection of texts summarizing the achievements of the UCFML's first year of existence, we read: "The Maoist investigation is not a simple observation of facts [*un simple constat*], not even the enthusiastic observation of the consequences of our interventions. It solves a problem. Which problem? That of the takeover of the effects of the intervention by the workers," and later on, in another document from the same collection: "The investigation must not only bear on the search for a new objective in the struggle, it must propose the putting into place of lasting practices, set off the ideological struggle. Before and after the struggle, something has changed, we must know how to make this live on."[13] Following Mao, moreover, the UCFML sees an urgent task in carrying out investigations not just in the urban working class but also among the poor peasants: "In particular, it is of prime importance to lead militant investigations on the great revolts of poor peasants, especially in West and Central France."[14] To a large extent this last task is taken up in the UCFML's *The Book of the Peasant Poor*, which sums up the organization's militant activity in the countryside in the 1970s in France and which in many ways is the local equivalent of Mao's *Rural Surveys*. Finally, we may also mention the even more recent survey performed in China, in March and April 1989, by Badiou's close friend and collaborator Sylvain Lazarus, together with his Italian comrades Sandro Russo, Claudia Pozzana, and Valerio Romitelli, part of whose joint follow-up discussion was subsequently published in the UCFML's newsletter *Le Perroquet*.[15]

If I have gone into this much detail regarding the question of the investigation, raised anew in the context of *Being and Event*, my reason for doing so is merely to showcase the pivotal role of certain Maoist concepts and principles including in the so-called later works by Badiou. The point is not just to underscore the mere fact that these concepts and principles persist, but also and above all to grasp how, where, and to what purpose they are put to work. In *Being and Event* they tend to come into the picture precisely at the point where truth and knowledge are articulated in what is still called a dialectic—despite the introduction's claim of supposedly having left behind the "stillborn" tradition of dialectical materialism with the turn to mathematics. "This is to say that everything revolves around thinking the truth/knowledge couple," writes Badiou. "What this amounts to, in fact, is thinking the relation [*rapport*]—which is rather a non-relation [*dé-rapport*]—between, on the one hand, a post-evental fidelity, and on the other, a fixed state of knowledge, or what I will call the encyclopaedia of a situation. The key to the problem lies in the way in which a procedure of fidelity *traverses* the existing knowledge, starting from the supernumerary point which is the name of the event."[16] From these statements we can already see at which point in the overall theory concepts such as the investigation operate: there where a truth "traverses" knowledge and subsequently opens the way to "force" the available encyclopedia of a given situation, so as to change the old into the new. Without any explicit mention of its Chinese sources, even for Badiou's later work the investigation is that which ensures the possible connection of certain elements in the existing situation to the break introduced by a rare event.

I would contend that the dialectical rapport between truth and knowledge is precisely the place of inscription of most of Badiou's debts to Maoism. At the same time, the process of fidelity and the sequence of investigations in which such fidelity finds its most basic organized expression also keep the dialectic of truth and knowledge from turning into an inoperative, quasi-mystical or miraculous, duality of the kind that so many critics seem to want to stick on Badiou's own work. This would seem to confirm the fundamental thesis that only an understanding of Badiou's ongoing debts to Maoism can give us insight into his proposed renewal of the materialist dialectic, while, conversely, a miraculous and antidialectical understanding of the relation between truth and knowledge is often the result of an undigested failure to come to terms with the Maoist legacy in Badiou's work.

My aim in fleshing out this thesis regarding Badiou's Maoism, based on the continuing role of notions such as the investigation, is not to reconstruct the facts pertaining to French Maoism, let alone the facts pertaining to Maoist China, but rather to analyze how this double series of events has impacted the work of Badiou in terms of politics and philosophy. Rather than having become a self-confessed post-Marxist, following a career path parallel to that of authors such as Laclau or the early Žižek, Badiou is indeed better described as a post-Maoist. This can be said to be the case, however, only if we are able, in spite of so much backlash in the wake of the postmodernism debate, to retain the active, almost psychoanalytical, meaning of the prefix so as to signal a critical attempt to work through the lasting truths as well as the no less undeniable blind spots of Maoism. "Post-Maoism," in other words, not as that which comes simply after the end of Maoism, or even more simplistically after the death of Mao Zedong and the coming into power of Deng Xiaoping, but as the name for a peculiar historical configuration in which critical thought returns, even if surreptitiously so, to the half-forgotten and half-repressed lessons of Maoism. This configuration is, of course, largely international, with contemporary varieties of post-Maoism existing not only in France but also in Argentina, Chile, the Basque country, or even the United States of America—to name but a few cases beyond the more obvious instances of Peru, Nepal, or the Philippines.

In some ways the current conjuncture in political philosophy can even be said to suffer the consequences of a failed or incomplete passage through Maoism. Indeed, some of the best-known political thinkers of our time, including those who otherwise consider themselves loyal to a certain Marx, become caught in the trappings of a conceptual framework that might have benefited from a more sustained confrontation with some of the Maoist lessons taken up by Badiou. I am thinking, for instance, of the pivotal role attributed to "antagonism" in the writings on radical democracy by Laclau and Mouffe, to whom I will return in chapter 7, or even in the collaborative work by Antonio Negri and Michael Hardt—with the latter duo swearing off any pretense to a dialectical interpretation of the concept of antagonism, and the former showing little or no theoretical appreciation at all for the author of "On Contradiction."[17] As a result, these political philosophers seem to call for recognition of the structural or even ontological fact of antagonism as being constitutive of the social field, rather than working through the peculiar nature of antagonistic contradictions, or the lack thereof, in the global situation today. The irony is that in so doing these political thinkers may very well give themselves an irrefutable air of radicalism while at the same time foreclosing the possibility of actually changing a particular situation—of changing the old into the new, which is precisely what always was to have been done according to Badiou, since for him this ideological struggle between the old and the new, as the effect of lasting contradictions among the people, was precisely one of the more famous universal lessons of the Cultural Revolution.

MAOISM AS POST-LENINISM

Even a quick survey of Badiou's work supports the thesis of an ongoing and sustained debt to Maoism. Not only do his first publications, from *Theory of Contradiction* to *The Rational Kernel of the Hegelian Dialectic*, offer a systematic account of Mao's thought inflected by French theory and philosophy, but his lecture series *The Century* also includes a long lesson, "One Divides into Two," in which Badiou returns to some of the most violent events and debates of the late 1960s in Maoist China, most notably with regard to the formal distinction between antagonistic and nonantagonistic contradictions, in an attempt to think through their possible relevance today. Around the same time, in a separate talk on the Cultural Revolution, Badiou once more confronts Mao's legacy by linking the sequence of events in China between 1966 and 1976 (or, in its most reduced version, between May 1966 and September 1967) to his own concept of a "politics without a party" as practiced by an offshoot of the UCFML, the Organisation Politique. Between these two moments Badiou's relation to Maoism may seem to have been mostly critical, as can be gleaned from his brief remarks, both in talks collected in *Conditions* and in his *Ethics*, about the "disaster" provoked by the Red Guards—until the final turning point in *Logics of Worlds*, a book that, as I have already observed, begins and ends with the example of Mao's China.

The different steps in this evaluation of Maoism immediately raise a series of general questions. A first question concerns the precise extent to which Badiou would have abandoned the principles of his youthful Maoism. After *Theory of the Subject*, which was still strongly overdetermined by his Maoist experience, has he perhaps fallen in line with the contemporary trend that, whether euphoric or melancholy, declares the historical end, if not also the utter doctrinal demise, of Marxism and certainly of the dogma of Marxism-Leninism-Maoism? In a second question, we might want to ask ourselves how innovative and far-reaching Badiou's recent criticisms of the Cultural Revolution and of the disastrous role of the Red Guards really are. In particular, do these criticisms amount to an attempt at self-criticism regarding the excesses in his earlier works? Finally, the question remains to what extent the idea of a politics without a party, which Badiou now finds to be already partially at work in the Cultural Revolution, would undermine his earlier, strongly party-oriented, accounts of Maoism. In other words, how much change has really taken place in Badiou's concept—not to mention the actual practice—of the organization of politics?

"Learn from the masses" and "investigate conditions at the lower levels," Mao had said, and more famously: "Serve the people."[18] For Badiou, once he seems to have abandoned the Maoist vocabulary, the aim is still to learn from truths that are produced outside of philosophy, in the actual conditions of art or politics or science, so as to investigate what would be needed, in terms of conceptual tools, to register and concentrate their effects within philosophy. Though it may be painful to admit that philosophy itself does not produce any truth, the philosopher's task thus consists in serving truths that are produced elsewhere. "A philosophy worthy of the name—that which begins with Parmenides—is in any case antinomical to the service of goods, inasmuch as it endeavours to be at the service of truths, because it is always possible to endeavour to be at the service of something that one does not constitute oneself," concludes Badiou: "Philosophy is thus at the service of art, of science, and of politics. Whether it is also capable of being at the service of love is more doubtful (art, on the other hand, as a mixed procedure, supports the truths of love). In any case, there is no commercial philosophy."[19] The move from "serving the people" to "serving the truths" thus could sum up the trajectory behind Badiou's post-Maoism.

Badiou's openly Maoist years are specifically tied up with the militant (Group for the Foundation of the) Union of Communists of France Marxist-Leninist, or UCFML, sometimes referred to simply as the UCF. The futurity of this small organization, oriented toward a unification of communists that is yet to come, as well as its loyalty to a Mallarméan principle of restricted action, is perhaps not foreign to the ambiguity that surrounds the main political objective of its activists, namely, to found a "party of a new type."[20] The ambiguity lies in the fact that the party of a new type is also already a type of organization that no longer seems to be much of a formal party at all. Maoism, in this sense, is first and foremost the name of an effort to come to terms with the party-form itself as the vanguard of class-consciousness in the strict Leninist sense: "What is called Maoism has developed for our time a deepening of the Leninist conception of the party."[21] Badiou's Maoism, despite its claims to represent the ideological orthodoxy of Marxism-Leninism, is thus already a post-Leninism: both a step away from, and a renewed enquiry into, the party-form of emancipatory politics. In a retrospective statement published in 1981 the UCFML even traces this project back to the group's original founding moment in 1969–

70: "Our conviction that Maoism is a stage of Marxism—its post-Leninist stage—dates back to our foundation. It is rooted in the experience, the universal bearing and the assessment of the Cultural Revolution."[22]

In 1969 Badiou had attempted an innovation from within as a dissident founding member of the Unified Socialist Party (PSU), by coauthoring the pamphlet *Contribution to the Problem of the Construction of a Marxist-Leninist Party of a New Type*, together with Emmanuel Terray, Harry Jancovici, and Denis Ménétrey. This proposal eventually would be rejected by the end of the same year at the PSU's national convention held in Dijon. In the meantime, however, Badiou joined with his fellow-militants Natacha Michel and Sylvain Lazarus, among a few others, to give birth to the UCFML. Despite sharing many ideological interests, not to mention an almost identical name, this group should not be confused with the above-cited UJCML, or UJC(ML), the Union of the Communist Youths (Marxist-Leninist), which likewise drew many members from the student body of the École Normale Supérieure at rue d'Ulm—including numerous fellow-Althusserians such as Rancière and Miller. Formed in February 1966 and led most famously by Robert Linhart, until his personal breakdown two years later, at the exact time when barricades were going up everywhere in the streets of Paris, the UJC(ML) was officially dissolved in the wake of the May 1968 uprising as a result of the group's perceived failure to establish any lasting alliance between the student movement and the struggles of the working class. The UCFML, by contrast, reaches the peak of its activism in the early to mid-1970s precisely as a result of the self-imposed task to continue interrogating the events of May and June 1968, in terms of both their backlash and their belated consequences for the political situation in France and abroad.

As Badiou and Lazarus indicate in the editorial comment included in almost every volume of their "Yénan" series, published in the 1970s by the same editing house owned by François Maspero that also supported Althusser's famous "Théorie" series, there is only one vital question: "What is, here and now, the road to follow so that Marxism and the real workers' movement fuse?"[23] Even several years later, while openly acknowledging the crisis of Marxism, Badiou continues to view Maoism as an unfinished task rather than as a lost cause or a past accomplishment to be savored with historiographic nostalgia: "That which we name 'Maoism' is less a final result than a task, a historical guideline. It is a question of thinking and practising post-Leninism. To measure the old, to clarify the destruction, to recompose politics from the scarcity of its independent anchorings, and all this while history continues to run its course under the darkest of banners."[24] It would be a mistake therefore to identify Badiou's Maoism with a return pure and simple to the orthodoxy of Marxism-Leninism. This orthodoxy is itself rife with contradictions. We can wave no transparent historical banner, nor can we invoke the necessary overarching course of history that would immediately red-flag the political tactics and strategies to be followed. Politics is anchored in its own independent points of reference, which are rare, as well as site-specific, and have a history of their own rather than being subordinated to the direction of a single and unified history beyond or outside of politics.

If there is a shift in this regard in Badiou's ongoing work, it is the slight but significant displacement from the idea of *politicizing history,* which still assumes a relatively external anchoring of politics in history understood at the level of social and economical being, to that of *historicizing politics,* which remits a purely sequential understanding of politics to its own intrinsic historicity. For Badiou it is precisely the Maoist experience that runs up against the impossibility of fully accomplishing the first idea, whereas his recent talk on the Cultural Revolution, together with his talk on the Paris Commune and Natacha Michel's on May '68 from the same cycle, offer good examples of the second: "This cycle of talks, proposed by the Organisation Politique, is meant to clarify the links between history and politics at the start of the new century. Here, in light of this question, we will examine various fundamental episodes in the historicity of politics. For example, the Russian revolution, the Resistance, the Cultural Revolution, May '68, and so on."[25] In other words, it is not just by chance that this debate regarding the historicity of politics happens to serve as a backdrop against which we can reread the Cultural Revolution. Instead, Maoism and the Cultural Revolution, to which the UCFML pledges half of its allegiance in the aftermath of May 1968 in France, also constitute key events in the shifting articulation between politics and history that calls for such readings or investigations in the first place.[26]

POLITICS, CULTURE, AND IDEOLOGY

Accounts of French Maoism, caught up as they are in an effort to explain the contradictory alignment, or lack thereof, with the events of May 1968 and their aftermath, typically draw a clear distinction between ideology

and politics, or between culture and politics, whereby the perceived ineffectiveness of the overall movement as a *political* phenomenon paradoxically receives a positive twist, insofar as it would open up a much wider
space for *cultural* and *ideological* experimentation.

Christophe Bourseiller, in *The Maoists: The Mad History of the French
Red Guards*, completely limits the impact of his subjects to the realm of
culture, where they did, in fact, play the role of an important trigger
for feminist and gay rights struggles in France. Politically, however, the
many French Maoist groups would have entailed little more than a poorly
thought-out combination of left-wing populism and knee-jerk Third-
Worldism, forever oscillating between authoritarianism and anarchy in
terms of their internal organization and bound to disappear for good with
the death of Chairman Mao. "Such is perhaps the ultimate key of Maoism.
As a cultural phenomenon, it provides a comfortable place in which everyone can invest what he or she pleases. That is the reason why it appears in
such heterogeneous fashion from one country to another," Bourseiller concludes, adding brief mentions of Germany, the United States, and Peru as
cases that would prove his point: "How would such diversity be possible, if
Maoism were not, culturally speaking, a gigantic black hole? Maoism does
not exist. It has never existed. Which is no doubt the explanation for its
success."[27] In Bourseiller's eyes, finally, the UCFML appears as little more
than a "sect" caught somewhere in between the spaces of culture, which to
him would seem to be a fantasy screen worthy of further projections, and
that of politics, which according to him ends up having been completely
misguided. Thus, while the group is one of the few Maoist organizations
with a majority of women active in several of its sections, throughout much
of the 1970s it continues to rely on random and seemingly absurd acts of
violence, such as the raiding of supermarkets or the interruption of movie
screenings perceived to be reactionary or fascist, aside from suffering from
what Bourseiller considers to be the cult of personality surrounding a small
number of university intellectuals, first and foremost among them Badiou
himself.

For A. Belden Fields, in his much more scholarly analysis in *Trotskyism
and Maoism: Theory and Practice in France and the United States*, French
Maoism likewise can be divided into two tendencies, which he does not call
"political" and "cultural" but rather "hierarchical" and "anti-hierarchical":
"At least from 1968 to the mid 1970s the major characteristic of French
Maoism was indeed a clear cut dualistic cleavage, with the groups on each

side of the cleavage having virtually nothing to do with one another."[28] At one extreme of the divide we thus find the strict discipline and austerity of the PCMLF, the Marxist-Leninist Communist Party of France, created on December 31, 1967, and forced by de Gaulle's regime to go underground on June 12, 1968, while at the other extreme, a much more favorable light is shed on the spontaneous and slightly anarchistic acts undertaken by the GP, or Gauche Prolétarienne, which arose like a Sphinx out of the ashes of the UJC(ML) in October 1968, only to become the most renowned and media-oriented of all groups of French Maoism. In Fields's account, too, the UCFML appears as a group that somehow sits astride the opposition between "hierarchical" and "anti-hierarchical" Maoism—two adjectives that in the end are little more than code words to describe two opposing attitudes toward the Leninist party. Like the PCMLF, Badiou's organization thus continues to stress the need for an organized form of politics, albeit a future one, while at the same time intervening in the situation of illegal immigrants, for example, with flexible tactics and initiatives comparable to those much more publicized ones used by members and sympathizers of the GP.

Belden Fields in part derives the split in his account of French Maoism from a comparable, this time tripartite, division proposed by Rémi Hess in his much earlier work, *The French Maoists: An Institutional Drift*. Hess— who in an explicit attempt at sociological self-reflexivity explains how he first became interested in Maoism in 1966–67 thanks to Badiou's philosophy course "Marx, Nietzsche, Freud" at the University of Reims—would later become active in the same city in a Maoist splinter-group still strongly inspired by Badiou's thought. Eventually, however, he comes to favor a kind of Maoist cultural politics closely related to the critique of everyday life that was being formulated around the same time by Henri Lefebvre and the Situationist International. Thus, when he draws a line of demarcation between three moments in French Maoism, which he calls "organizational," "ideological," and "libidinal," it should come as no surprise that to the blind discipline and bureaucratic dogmatism of the first, epitomized by the PCMLF, Hess clearly prefers the libertarian spirit of the third, embodied by groups such as those gathered around the journals *Tout* and *Vive la Révolution*, which effectively were among the driving forces behind the MLF, or Movement for the Liberation of Women, and the FHAR, or Homosexual Front of Revolutionary Action. In this overview the UCFML appears, together with the UJC(ML) and its successor the (ex) GP of *La Cause du Peuple*, as an intermediate group, somewhere in between the organizational and the libidinal, on the level of ideological struggles outside the framework of strict party bureaucracy.[29] For Hess, what is particularly interesting and even uncanny about this development of French Maoism, from hard-line party discipline through open ideological struggle all the way to libidinal drift (what Jean-François Lyotard calls a *dérive*, a term already in vogue in the 1960s among Situationists such as Guy Debord), is that it occurs in a chronological order that seems to be the exact opposite of the expected ABC of Leninist party-organization from spontaneity to discipline.

Even from this quick survey of some of the existing literature on French Maoism, two recurrent issues stand out that are more directly relevant for our understanding of the role of Maoism in Badiou's work, namely the loss of autonomy of politics and the status of the party. As for the first issue, few commentators fail to recognize the astonishing expansion to which the political playing field is subject in the late 1960s and early 1970s, with the result that "cultural revolution" becomes a generic term to a large extent cut loose from its concrete moorings in the sequence of events in China. "Now it is a question of investing culture as much as politics," Bourseiller observes: "Maoism, then, becomes more and more fluid, less and less ideological, more and more 'everyday-ist': it is a question of struggling on a day-by-day basis and of opening up new fronts everywhere, even in everyday life."[30] Badiou, however, has always been unwavering in his insistence on the autonomy of politics as a practice that would be irreducible to purely cultural questions. Thus, in his lecture "Politics and Philosophy," included in *Conditions*, he concludes: "In politics, the thing itself is a-cultural, as is every thought and every truth. Comic, purely comic, is the theme of cultural politics, as is the theme of a political culture."[31] Nothing could seem more contradictory, of course, coming from someone with such openly declared loyalty to the events of the Cultural Revolution! Besides, the UCFML insists in the final pages of its founding document: "One of the great lessons of the revolutionary storm of May is that the class struggle is not limited to the factory. Capitalist oppression touches on all domains of social life," and the same text goes on to conclude: "The front of culture and art is also very important. The historical experience of the Great Proletarian Cultural Revolution teaches us that, in certain circumstances, it can even become a decisive front of the class struggle."[32] As a consequence of this decisiveness of culture for politics, the UCFML even formed a special section, the Groupe Foudre starting in 1974 and led primarily by Natacha Michel, to intervene precisely in art and culture at the level of what was considered to be the specificity of contradictions in propaganda—that is, contradictions in forms of consciousness between the old and the new. Ultimately, then, we are not so far removed from the idea of a "revolution of everyday life," as the UCFML's founding document had already suggested: "The revolution is in life and transforms life."[33] In fact, while drawing up a balance sheet, the organization's central journal, *Le Marxiste-Léniniste*, openly rejects the opposition between politics and everyday life that constitutes such a common assumption in most readings of the post-1968 period: "Our politics is new because it refers to the everyday. After 1968, the will to change everyday life is seen in opposition to spectacular and politicist politics. But what the cells [*noyaux*] express through everyday politics in the factory is the affirmation that there is no outcome other than political."[34] Understood in this way, no culture is ever truly apolitical, just as there can be no political truth that somehow would not touch on culture as well.

Admittedly, even at the start of the Cultural Revolution, the "Sixteen Points" were exceedingly vague, even waxing metaphysical, when it came to explaining the significance of the concept translated as "cultural."[35] Parts of this vagueness and ambivalence also carry over into the activities of the UCFML. Following Mao's notion that "there can be no art above the class struggle," for example, the Groupe Foudre by no means accepts "art" or "culture" as sociologically defined spheres or domains that would somehow be separate from politics: "From the beginning, we have criticized the idea of a 'cultural sector' as an objectively defined empty square that the Groupe Foudre would come to occupy."[36] And yet the group also upholds its confidence in the specificity of art: "There is a relative autonomy to art in relation to the social field and to the political forms of the class struggle. Even though it is inscribed in ideological propaganda, art is not transitive to politics. This is because it has its own sedimented history: the history of forms."[37] Badiou himself, finally, in recent years has come to admit that a full understanding of the sequence of events from the late 1960s and early 1970s cannot leave the conditions of politics, art, science, and love completely disjoined, according to a typically modernist bias of their self-declared autonomy. Thus, after seeing how the four conditions of truth are to be separated and unsutured as clear and distinct ideas, most notably in *Manifesto for Philosophy*, we would have to reconsider how, historically speaking, they are nonetheless most often intertwined, forming mixed combinations such as "proletarian art" or "courtly love," as Badiou had originally planned to discuss in *Logics of Worlds*.

When pressured on this topic in the interview reprinted below as appendix 1, Badiou even goes so far as to accept the notion that "culture," rather than merely being a version of "art" emptied out of all truth, as he claims among many other places in the introduction to his *Saint Paul*, might actually be an appropriate name for the "networking" (*réseau*) or "knotting" (*nouage*) among the various truth conditions, which could be newly theorized if "we can consider culture to be the network of various forcings, that is, at a given moment in time, the manner in which the encyclopedic knowledge of the situation is modified under the constraints of various operations of forcing which depend on procedures that are different from one another."[38] What matters in this proposal is the suggestion that once again, with the different operations that force the available knowledge of a given situation after its investigation from the point of view of the event, we are sent back to a dialectic between knowledge and truth—now including a network among multiple truths that eventually might serve to formalize the concept of "culture" itself—through a notion taken from the Maoist legacy and inspired by the Cultural Revolution.

The second issue, regarding the role of the party, is potentially even more polemical. We know that for the openly Maoist Badiou, as late as in his *Theory of the Subject*, "subject" means political subject, and that the party is the only material embodiment of such a subject: "The party is the body of politics, in the strict sense."[39] From this point of view very little seems to have changed since the concept of the party was first reformulated by the UCFML founding document to adapt to our time. We would be wrong, however, to ignore the distance that separates the UCFML itself from the party of the new type. Thus, the opening text is quick to remark: "The UCFML is not, in turn, the Party. It does not pretend to know in advance and to propagate what will be the living reality of the Party. It is the cell or kernel [*noyau*] that promotes and carries the question of the Party into the midst of the masses, it centralizes experiences in light of this project, it formulates directives, it verifies them, and it rectifies them, in the practice of the masses."[40] Badiou's organization considers it unilateral and premature to pretend that there could be an authentic communist party of a new type at this time in France, and, in fact, rejecting the claims of the ex-PCMLF to be this party even after it was forced to become clandestine, the UCFML insists that "at the present moment, it is groupuscular and unproletarian to want to create, purely and simply, the Party."[41] These statements should not be brushed aside as superficial cautionary tales that would hide an unshakeable confidence in the vanguard party. Rather, what is at stake is already to some extent the fate of the Leninist party itself. Clearly, the momentary postponement of the party's actual foundation, as well as the repeated insistence on merely being the harbinger, or *noyau promoteur*, of a future organization that is yet to come, highlight an incipient crisis in the traditional party-form. They are the signs of an unsolved problem—of a question that becomes a problem and an open task precisely as a result of the Cultural Revolution: "An open problem, therefore, in the two senses of the expression: first, as something that is not solved, and second, as something of which the masses must take hold."[42]

Badiou's *Theory of the Subject* could not be clearer in this regard. Marx, Lenin, and Mao appear in the periodization of this book as three stages—three unmistakable episodes according to the intrinsic historicity of politics—in the progressive putting into question of the party as an open task. With the Cultural Revolution the question of the subject of politics eventually is left unanswered under the overwhelming pressure of the masses: "The subjective question (how did the Cultural Revolution, mass uprising against the new bourgeoisie of the state bureaucracy, come up against the rebuilding of the party?) remains in suspense as the key question for all Marxist politics today."[43] We cannot say therefore that the idea of a politics without a party as applied to the Cultural Revolution is only the result of a bold retrospective interpretation in Badiou's so-called later works. Rather, the immanent critique of the party qua form has always been a benchmark of Badiou's Maoism. I would even argue that it is this kind of critical suspension of the party-form of political organization that introduces an irreducible inner distance, or a dialectical scission, into the latter, making it at the same time a form of post-Maoism.

Badiou's brief periodization from *Theory of the Subject* will be reiterated ten years later in a remarkable anonymous text, "The Dialectical Mode," most likely written by Sylvain Lazarus and published in the newsletter of

Organisation Politique, *La Distance Politique*. Whereas Marx would have subordinated politics to the objective course of history as class struggle, and Lenin would propose the party to absorb the widening gap between history and politics, Badiou and Lazarus claim that with Mao the concept of history (or History) as an external referent is absented altogether, in favor of a strictly conjunctural grasp of the laws of politics and their changing situations. "Thinking no longer takes the form of thinking the adequation between politics and History. No hope of fusion is ever present," Lazarus writes, and further on: "The dialectical mode dehistoricizes."[44] With Mao, politics can no longer be transitive to an overarching sense of history, and not even the party can overcome this gap.

To a large extent, in other words, the break with the transitivity of politics, which I previously described in terms of the shift from *politicizing history* to *historicizing politics*, is not a self-critical break *away from* Maoism but the theoretical reflection of a break *internal to* the Maoist mode of politics itself. To use the words from *Theory of the Subject* that apply to the third stage in Badiou's periodization of Marxism, Leninism, and Maoism: "The working class is not able ever to resorb the scission, which gives it its being, between its social immediacy and its political project. Of such a political subject—finally restricted to the action of its place-holder, the party, a body made up of an opaque and multiple soul—we will never say that it constitutes history, not even that it makes history."[45] Clearly, we are several steps removed from an orthodox understanding of the dialectic between history and politics, between social being and consciousness, or between masses and classes, with the party as vanishing mediator or third term between the two. The opposite almost seems to be true: It is only when the rapport between history and politics is definitively broken, or gives way to the rapport of a nonrapport, that Badiou and Lazarus speak of a "dialectical" mode of politics. If dialectical thinking still involves a third term, it is only the process of the scission of the first two that constitutes the tenuous unity of the third.

Finally, on a more empirical note, if we compare the two political organizations in which Badiou principally has been active, one calling for a "party of a new type" and the other for a "politics without a party," should we not conclude by saying that they propose forms of militantism that on the whole and in actual practice are nearly identical? Whether this is then seen as a practical shortcoming of the earlier organization or as a theoretical inconsistency of the later one, the fact of the matter is that the organizational form of politics remains fairly constant for Badiou. In fact, this may very well be a key lesson to be drawn from the suspension of the party-form accomplished during the Cultural Revolution: not the adventurist response of jettisoning all forms of organization but the need for politics to be organized at all—in *noyaux*, committees, communes, or a generically called "political organization."[46] Indeed, if politics is to be more than a short-lived mass uprising or manifestation, what the idea of the party is meant to add, even if its name disappears, is precisely the question of material consistency, embodiment, and durability, that is, the question of organization. "Without organized application, there is no testing ground, no verification, no truth," as we already read in *Theory of Contradiction*: " 'Theory' can then engender only idealist absurdities."[47] Or, as Badiou concludes in *Can Politics Be Thought?*, a book written after the supposed break with his earlier Maoism: "Political organization is necessary in order for the intervention's wager to make a process out of the distance that reaches from an interruption to a fidelity," even if no organized practice will ever be able completely to close the gap torn open by the event in the first place: "In its propagating fidelity, as a stacked-up series of interventions by way of wagers, the organization leaves open the point where the suture of the One fails to seal the Two."[48]

TOWARD A PHILOSOPHICAL CONCEPT
OF DEVIATION

Before interrogating the consequences of Badiou's Maoism for his overall philosophy, let us take a closer look at how the UCFML positions itself within the particular conjuncture of French Maoism. One particularly useful way of doing so involves an analysis of the exact content behind the notion of "leftist" and "rightist" ideological deviations, as they are typically redefined under the influence of Chairman Mao.

From the moment of its foundation onward, the UCFML situates itself polemically in opposition to the two major Maoist organizations that are still in existence in the early 1970s in France: the ex-PCMLF, forced into semiclandestine existence around the journal *L'Humanité Rouge*, and the GP, or Gauche Prolétarienne, led by Benny Lévy (pseudonym Pierre Victor) and most famously organized around *La Cause du Peuple*, the journal that was given a new start in November 1968 under the editorship of Jean-Pierre Le Dantec in collaboration with, among others, the soon-to-become ex-Maoist, if not completely anti-Marxist, New Philosophers André Glucksmann, Guy Lardreau, and Christian Jambet. It is worth considering the tactics that are used in this polemical self-positioning because they consistently follow a logic of twin deviations, overcome by the just middle, which will serve us further as we try to understand the persistent role of the Maoist dialectic in the overall philosophy of Badiou.

In the UCFML's founding document we see the logic of ideological deviations appear from the start: "The national organizations that vindicate Marxism-Leninism and Mao Zedong's thought are irreparably engaged either in a rightist-opportunistic and neo-revisionist political line or in a leftist-opportunistic and putschist line."[49] The militants and sympathizers of the GP of *La Cause du Peuple*, on the one hand, are said to fall prey to a "leftist" deviation, insofar as they combine an overly narrow concept of politics, limited to mere "agitprop," with an almost terrorist appeal to spectacular violence. The noisy vindication of antiauthoritarianism as sheer cop-bashing (*casser du flic*), the physical confrontation with the factory bosses, or the mediatic kidnapping of famous CEOs, together with the journal's purely descriptive retelling of isolated and short-lived episodes in the history of the workers' movement, appear as poor substitutes for the patient work of actual political organization. (According to the UCFML, the narrative style of *La Cause du Peuple* in this sense can even be compared to the later collective project by Rancière and others, in the journal *Les Révoltes Logiques*, which delves into the historical archives of scattered working class and peasant struggles so as to retrieve fleeting moments in the capture of speech.) Without concrete directives, without the cumulative assessment of experience, and without a systematic practice of investigations, the undeniable air of radicalism exuded by *La Cause du Peuple* is often little more than an abstract call to revolt, quickly tilting over into a militarized plea for violence as an end in itself: "Putschism comes in the place of the investigation, of the systematization, and of the directive."[50] An adventurist call to pure activism for its own sake thus forms the "leftist" extreme of the ideological spectrum, represented by the GP.

In a later pamphlet published in 1977, *A Maoist Study: The Situation in China and the So-called Movement of "Critique of the Gang of Four,"* the UCFML would take advantage of the lessons learned from the criticisms against Lin Biao during the latter days of the Cultural Revolution, in order to redefine its own stance in opposition to the GP after the latter's auto-dissolution in November 1973: "When the emphasis was put on the masses, the ex-GP's thinking was purely democratic, and pretended to dissolve itself in spontaneous movement. Just as Lin Biao unilaterally exalted the self-liberation of the masses. But when the ex-GP put the emphasis on organization, it was the complete opposite: the armed, clandestine, and purely putschist nucleus, subtracted from all political control by the people. Just as Lin Biao had wanted excessively to militarize the Revolutionary Committees, and finally attempted a coup."[51] It is against this uncanny proximity, if not the complete reversibility, of massism and putschism among members of the (ex-)GP that the UCFML from the start attempts to define its own ideological and political position.

The ex-PCMLF and the various circles around *L'Humanité Rouge*, in contrast, appear as a "rightist" ideological deviation, insofar as they proclaim to be already the authentic communist party in France, all the while referring the events of the Cultural Revolution to a distant historical "stage" in the edification of socialism, that is, the internal ideological struggle that can only follow the takeover of power, for which the French situation supposedly would not yet be mature. Once again, this leads to a general absence of positive guidelines and directives—matters of organization that in this case are replaced by an unconfessed and purely nostalgic yearning for a return to the long-lost grandeur, back in the 1920s and 1930s, of the old PCF. At the same time, consistent with their denial of the novelty of the Cultural Revolution, the circles that emerge from the ex-PCMLF end up becoming paralyzed by a fearful overestimation of the new repressive apparatuses of the state: "This spirit is particularly evident in their analysis of the alleged '*fascisation*' of the power of the state after May. This analysis has led the militants of *L'Humanité Rouge* to their semi-clandestine existence, their lack of initiative, and their semi-paralysis."[52] Thus, even after greatly boosting its numbers with the addition of disillusioned members from the former UJC(ML) after the defeat of the 1968 revolt, the ex-PCMLF is still unable to invent a concrete political practice that would help overcome this disillusionment, which in any case is but the melancholy flipside of its dogmatic antirepressive stance.

Obviously in keeping with some of Mao's own assertions, most notably in "On Practice" and "On the Correct Handling of Contradictions among the People," about the alternating risks of left-wing adventurism and right-wing dogmatism, the UCFML's argument about twin ideological deviations begins to function as a means to formalize a certain logic of revolt, at a clear distance from the specific cases of the (ex-)GP's antirevisionist violence and the ex-PCMLF's blind defense of established doctrines. Ultimately, the measure of success for avoiding these two extremes depends on the specific links that in any situation tie a given political organization not just to the masses in general but to their most advanced sectors: "Without a mass alliance, there is no mass line. Without a mass line, the only alternative is between practices that are either dogmatic and opportunistic on the right, or else putschist and adventurist."[53] Time and again this is how the argument over deviations from the just line will be reiterated. Beyond the jargon of strictly organizational matters, however, the important point in this context is the way in which this argument at the same time can help us better understand the place and force of Maoism in Badiou's philosophy as a whole.

Here I cannot recount in detail every twist and turn to which the logic of "leftist" and "rightist" ideological deviations becomes subject both in the many publications of the UCFML and in Badiou's own work. Suffice it to track a few representative steps in the forceful conceptual elaboration that turns this logic from a primarily tactical and political question into an issue with profound philosophical consequences.

In *Theory of Contradiction* and *Of Ideology*, two pamphlets to which a third, announced under the title *The Different Types of Contradiction*, unfortunately would never come to be added, Badiou concentrates his critique of ideological deviations on the alternative between Deleuzean anarchism and Althusserian structuralism—with the ex-GP enthusiast André Glucksmann, now turned New Philosopher and anti-Marxist critic of the Gulag, undialectically combining both extremes in living proof of their deep-seated complicity.

Badiou first of all reproaches his former teacher for reducing the logic of Marx's *Capital* to a combinatory of places and instances in the mode of production. Even if the dominant role is allowed to shift from one structural instance to another, there is said to be no place in this overall picture for a contradictory transformation of the structure itself: "The displacement of the terms from one place to another leaves intact the underlying structure of exchange. The mobility of appearances refers to a closed system. The essential conservatism of all structural thinking risks on this point to change dialectics into its opposite: metaphysics."[54] As Balibar would also confirm in a self-critical reflection on his own contribution to *Reading Capital*, this risk of a metaphysical outlook is especially poignant in the use made out of the concept of the mode of production, the radical scientificity of which lies at the core of the original Althusserian project: "The concept of 'mode of production' is an inexhaustible goldmine for deviations of the structuralist type. Taken in isolation, it is only all too easy to give a purely combinatory version of it and to expulse from it the dialectic of forces in favor of the articulation of places."[55] Althusser's scientificist deviation would thus have consisted in limiting the dialectic, which was famously said to be critical and revolutionary in principle, to a conservative and even metaphysical articulation of instances and hierarchies.

Whether or not this is a fair assessment of Althusser's writings in *For Marx* and *Reading Capital* should not concern us here. As I discussed in the first chapter, there are certainly elements in the concepts of over- and underdetermination, if not in structural causality itself, that would bring Althusser much closer to Badiou than the latter in general, except for a few occasions, seems willing to admit. Be that as it may, what should be clear is the need to take the work of his old teacher still one step further in the direction of articulating structure and history, as well as being and existence, from the point of view of loss or destruction that unhinges the structure from within: "The structure has its *being* in a hierarchical combination, but its *existence*, that is to say its history, fuses with that of its destruction. The structure has no other existence beside the movement of its own loss, and each term of the contradiction reflects this transitory mode of existence by its division in its being-for-the-structure and its being-for-the-dissolution-of-the-structure."[56] Later on, of course, this tendency toward loss, impasse, and dissolution inherent in the structure— the dialectic of lack and excess between a structure and its impossible metastructure—will come to mark the site of the immanent break within the structure that is called an event.

If an overemphasis on the structural logic of places marks a "right-wing" or "structuralist" deviation, then, conversely, an exclusive emphasis on the logic of forces will quickly push us into the wide-open arms of a "left-wing" or "anarchist" deviation. At least this is how Badiou in his Maoist years responds to the "anarcho-desirers" who in the early 1970s flock to Deleuze's

courses in Vincennes. What becomes evident in this harsh response, however, is the fact that anarchism and structuralism make for surprisingly
good bedfellows. "In truth, anarchism is merely the flip side of conservative
structuralism. The drift is the shadow of the combinatory," Badiou asserts:
"Structuralism and the ideologies of desire are profoundly coupled to one
another. Far from being opposed, they are confused, in their common
contradiction of the dialectic."[57] The difficult task of a properly materialist
dialectical mode of thinking would thus consist in enacting a split correlation of structure and history, of states and tendencies, of combinatories
and differentials—without allowing either side of the articulation to devi-
ate and relapse into the backlash of a unilateral hypostasis. "The dialectic
brings to life the contradiction of the structural and the qualitative, of the
combinatory and the differential evaluation of forces," Badiou proposes
again and again in a series of variations on the same theme: "The complete
dialectical intelligibility of what is principal must thus apprehend not only
the *state* of things but their *tendency*."[58] Most important, as Marx already
hinted at when he spoke of the essentially revolutionary nature of dialectical reason, it is a question of grasping the tendency, whether toward blockage and loss or toward transformation and change, within the present state
of affairs: "In order to envisage things from the point of view of the future
within the present itself, we must seize hold of this present as tendency, as
increase or decrease, as accumulation of forces, as rupture, and not only as
state, or as figure."[59] This combination, though, cannot take rest in a quiet
complementarity between two symmetrical poles—figure and tendency,
state and movement, place and force. Instead, the resulting articulation
should give way to the divided unity of a process of scission, which is to be
applied to each and every term in the analysis: "Each term, precisely
because it has no existence except as part of a process of scission, is itself
torn apart between its qualitative subordination to the scission taken as
process, that is, as unity, and the movement of transformation of this very
quality itself, the source of which is the uninterrupted struggle between the
two terms and the incessant modification of their rapport."[60]

Using these terms put forth in *Theory of Contradiction* and *Of Ideology*,
we can now theoretically resummarize the logic of leftist and rightist ideological deviations in contrast to the basic elements in Badiou's Maoist
recasting of the materialist dialectic. All deviations, ultimately, slip into a
form of idealism insofar as they disavow what Badiou frequently describes

as the dialecticity of the dialectic: "The dialectic, if I can say so, is itself dialectical, insofar as its conceptual operators, which reflect reality, are all equally split."[61] In their mirroring relationship, the two types of ideological deviation in other words neglect the extent to which structure and tendency, or place and force, must be articulated through the scission of each one of the two terms:

a. In the case of "leftism" it is the structural element inherent in every tendency that is neglected in favor of a viewpoint of pure, unlimited, and affirmative becoming. The typical example of this viewpoint is the adventurist tendencies fostered by May 1968 itself, blown up and revered as an inflated grand event all by itself: "If, indeed, one neglects the structural element, one takes the tendency for an accomplished state of affairs."[62] Everything then fuses into the being of pure becoming.

b. In the case of "rightism" it is the possibility of radical change that is foreclosed in the name of a purely objective analysis of the structure. The typical example of this is still, not surprisingly, the economism of the Second International: "If one neglects the tendential element, one inevitably represses the new in the name of the old, one supports the established order. One becomes installed in an opportunistic attitude of waiting."[63] Everything then is made to depend on the pure state of existing conditions.

In each case, whether by precipitously jumping over one's own shadow or by pusillanimously staying put until the crisis has matured, the unilateral hypostasis of one side of the divided articulation to the exclusion of the other is what prevents the unfolding of a properly dialectical investigation of the two taken together.

It is of course true that every instance or contradiction in society must be seen as part of a structure in dominance, complete with its finally determining instance. In this regard, Badiou argues, reason is certainly on the side of Althusser. "In fact, everything comes down to the following: seized in a given state of things, or all along a particular sequence in its development, every contradiction assigns a determinate *place* to its terms, a place which is itself defined by its relation to the place of the other term," Badiou sums up in *Theory of Contradiction*: "In this sense the dialectic is a logic of places."[64] But it is no less true that every structure of assigned places is constantly being transformed as a result of inner splits, breaks, and changes. In this regard, he holds, reason is also on the side of Deleuze. "Seized in its uninterrupted movement in stages, by contrast, every contradiction confronts *forces* whose nature is differential: what matters in the evaluation of force from the viewpoint of the movement of the contradiction is no longer its transitory state of subordination or domination but its increase or decrease," Badiou continues: "In its tendential or properly historical aspect, the dialectic is a logic of forces."[65] Even if both these views have reason partially on their side, however, each one of them taken in isolation is clearly insufficient. The real difficulty, rather, lies in finding a way to overcome the apparent complementarity between the two, without having recourse to the mediation of a synthesis: "The central dialectical problem is thus the following: how can the logic of places and the logic of forces be articulated—without fusion?"[66]

In Badiou's early reading, the case of Deleuze furthermore gives us an idea of how place and force can even become combined—as, in fact, they usually are—within a "leftist" deviation. In moral terms this traditionally comes down to the presupposition of a stark dualism of necessity and freedom. In "The Party and the Flux," published by the Yénan-Philosophy Group of the UCFML as part of *The Current Situation on the Philosophical Front*, Badiou thus cites an extensive passage from Deleuze's and Guattari's *Anti-Oedipus* in which all the book's well-known dualisms, from the molar versus the molecular all the way to subjugated-groups versus subject-groups, against all expectations seem to find their driving principle in a thinly disguised version of Kant's argument. "Deleuze and Guattari don't hide this much: return to Kant, here's what they came up with to exorcise the Hegelian ghost," Badiou charges: "It is pure, unbound, generic energy, energy as such. That which is law unto itself, or absence of law. The old freedom of autonomy, hastily repainted in the colours of what the youth in revolt legitimately demands: some spit on the bourgeois family."[67] Standing over and against the sheer energy of this unconditional freedom, there is only the blind necessity of a paranoid order that like a vampire feeds on the energy and creativity of freedom, which is then but another name for life itself.

Of this radical dualism of force and place within "leftism" we can also formulate a political variant, in addition to the moral one. This typically comes in the guise of a direct and unmediated opposition between the

masses and the state, or between the plebes and the state—dualities to
which today we should no doubt add the explicitly undialectical or even
antidialectical antagonism between the multitude and empire. Power and
resistance then perennially seem to oppose the same vitally creative masses
to the same deadly repressive system. "In this regard, the 'massist' ideology
that came out of 1968 excels in flattening out the dialectical analysis,"
Badiou remarks: "Always the same exalted masses against the identical
power, the invariable system."[68] Not only does this view of politics fail to
take into account how no movement proceeds concretely as a whole except
by the splits that dislocate and revoke the existing totality: "It is never 'the
masses,' nor the 'movement' that as a whole carry the principle of engen-
derment of the new, but that which in them divides itself from the old."[69]
But, what is more, far from signaling a radically new discovery, the fasci-
nation with "massism" or "movementism"—and again today perhaps we
should add "multitudinism"—was already a prime target of urgent attacks,
more than a century ago, in the eyes of Marx and Engels:

> That the "movement" would be a desiring push, a flowing flux; that
> every institution would be paranoid and in principle heterogeneous to
> the "movement"; that nothing is done *against* the existing order but only
> according to the affirmative schizze that withdraws from this order; that
> therefore it is necessary to replace all organization, all hideous mili-
> tantism, with the self-management—or with the association, there are
> quarrels going on about this in certain cottages—of pure movement: All
> these daring revisions, which are supposed to raise the striking novelty
> of the marginal and dissident masses up against "totalitarian" Marxism-
> Leninism—are word for word that which Marx and Engels, in *The
> German Ideology*, had to tear to pieces—around 1845!—in order to clear
> the terrain for a finally coherent systematization of the revolutionary
> practices of their time.[70]

Cutting across the inoperative dualisms of masses and power, movement and organization, or dissidence and totalitarianism, politics must be
thought through the complete arsenal of concepts implied in the logic of
scission, which is still most succinctly encapsulated in the Maoist formula:
"One divides into two." Badiou explains: "We are in favor of 'One divides
into two.' We are in favor of the increase by scission of the new. We want
neither the sanctified and obscure, inoperative and repetitive, ultraleftist

masses nor the revisionist union, which is but the façade of a sinister dictatorship. What is proletarian, especially today, divides and combats the minute fractures that are internal to the 'movement,' and makes them grow to the point where they become what is principal."[71]

Now, all this may still seem to come down to recovering the notion that there can be no power without the constituent force of resistance, as we are told from Mao to Negri. Someone like Glucksmann, then, might well seem to lead the way. For at the outset of *La cuisinière et le mangeur d'hommes*, the book that, together with *Les Maîtres penseurs*, brought him nationwide fame as a former editor of *La Cause du Peuple* turned New Philosopher, Glucksmann indeed begins by positing a principle worthy of his youthful Maoist years: "In the beginning there was resistance."[72] From this radical, almost ontological, primacy of resistance, however, the attention quickly turns in awe to the overwhelming power of repression displayed by the state. "This is why Glucksmann's political conclusions are properly despairing," Badiou argues in *Of Ideology*: "He tells us 'There where the state ends, the human being begins,' but of the popular combat against the state, he retraces only the morose and repetitive duration, the infinite obstination, while nowhere marking the fact that this continuation accumulates the forces of any accomplishment whatsoever. Upon reading him, it would seem that the human being is not ready to begin."[73] In fact, the antirepressive obsession ultimately contradicts the initial pledge of allegiance to the wildly creative force of popular resistance: "It is inconsistent to read in history the omnipresent contradiction of the masses and the State, to affirm that one is on the side of the plebes, and then to pontificate exclusively about the force and the multiform victorious ruses of the State."[74] Only a short step is then needed, based on the false opposition between masses and the state, to go on to applaud the intrinsically democratic tendencies of the former, even if only by default, this being the only remedy to avoid the totalitarian excesses of the latter, made infamous by the Gulag. This step, as we also know, was swiftly taken by most New Philosophers.

In the collective introduction to *The Current Situation on the Philosophical Front*, as a matter of fact, the Yénan-Philosophy Group charges that *all* revisionist tendencies in French thought of the 1970s, not only on the part of New Philosophers such as Glucksmann but also among Deleuzeans, Althusserians, and Lacanians, can be seen as presupposing categorical oppositions that seek to stamp out any possible diagonal term—whether

class, party, or organization—between the masses and the state. "Everywhere to substitute the couple masses/state for the class struggle: that's all
there is to it," the introduction reads: "The political essence of these 'philosophies' is captured in the following principle, a principle of bitter resentment against the entire history of the twentieth century: 'In order for the
revolt of the masses against the State to be good, it is necessary to reject the
class direction of the proletariat, to stamp out Marxism, to hate the very
idea of the class party.' "[75] The result of such arguments is either the complete denial of antagonistic contradictions altogether or else the jubilatory
recognition of a mere semblance of antagonism. "They dream of a formal
antagonism, of a world broken in two, with no sword other than ideology,"
whereas a complete understanding of emancipatory politics would involve
not just the joy and passion of short-lived revolts but the disciplined labor
of a lasting transformation of the particular situation at hand: "They love
revolt, proclaimed in its universality, but they are secondary in terms of
politics, which is the real transformation of the world in its historical
particularity."[76] One urgent task, therefore, involves precisely the need to
struggle against such revisionist tendencies on the philosophical front.
"*Everyone*, including the Maoists, is after all called upon today, after the
Cultural Revolution and May 68, to take a stance, to discern the new with
regard to the meaning of politics in its complex articulation, its constitutive trilogy: mass movement, class perspective, and State," the introduction continues: "Such is clearly the question of any possible philosophy
today, wherein we can read the primacy of politics (of antagonism) *in its
actuality*."[77]

Finally, it is in the compact series of footnotes to *The Rational Kernel of
the Hegelian Dialectic* that Badiou makes explicit the need for a full-blown
philosophical concept of deviation. Significantly, such a concept cannot be
found in Hegel's idealist dialectic: "Hegel's idealism also manifests itself by
the absence of any positive theory of deviation."[78] Hegel's *Science of Logic*
remains, in fact, caught in the false problematic of an absolute beginning
or, to be more precise—but this is already symptomatic of a disavowed split
that hints at a rational core within the idealist dialectic—in the searching
alternative of two absolute beginnings: Being and Nothing. Badiou, by
contrast, may tacitly seem to agree with Adorno's argument that a truly
materialist dialectic must always start from something, rather than from
either Being or Nothing. " 'Something'—as a cogitatively indispensable

substrate of any concept, including the concept of Being—is the utmost abstraction of the subject-matter that is not identical with thinking, an abstraction not to be abolished by any further thought process," Adorno tells us. "Yet even the minimal trace of nonidentity in the approach to logic, of which the word 'something' reminds us, is unbearable to Hegel."[79] For the Maoist in Badiou, though, as we saw in the discussion of *Theory of the Subject*, every something must always be split—split between itself and something else, as determined by the system in which this something finds its place.

Thus, while the logic of scission borrows heavily from early segments in the *Science of Logic*, especially "Something and Other" and "Determination, Constitution and Limit," Badiou systematically reformulates the basic principles of this logic in his own, now familiar, vocabulary by insisting that every entity be split between that part of it that can be understood according to the logic of places and that part that cannot be accounted for without resorting to a logic of forces. Conversely, determination and limit in their absence or disavowal also allow us to grasp the logic of deviations. "The deviations, the relapses, and so on, are fully thinkable only in dialectical correlation with the determination and the limit of a movement," insofar as both "rightism" and "leftism" merely reconvoke one of the terms of the original contradiction in its isolated purity, that is, "the first one only repeats the dominant term," whereas "the second, by arguing from a state of original purity prior to all determination, will assign to itself the task of finding the other."[80]

Already during his Maoist years, however, Badiou is acutely aware of the fact that the most advanced theoretical and philosophical developments in the late 1960s and 1970s, for instance in Lacanian psychoanalysis, if not already in Althusser and Deleuze as well, cannot be reduced to the caricatures of "structuralist" and "ultraleftist" deviations. We must trace the line of demarcation elsewhere or with greater precision. One way of doing so is by recognizing the extent to which an accomplished form of structuralism—which others may prefer to call poststructuralism, and, technically speaking, this is indeed all there is to the prefix—not only posits the divided nature of both structure and subject but also conceives of their relationship in the uncanny terms of an internal exclusion. This conceptualization therefore entails a complete reworking of the topology of inside and outside—with every inside, every stable identity, and every idealist or humanist interiority being defined in the paradoxical terms of its constitutive outside.

At first, in *The Rational Kernel of the Hegelian Dialectic*, Badiou still seems to reproach "structuralism" as much as "leftism" precisely for ignoring the topology of the constitutive outside. "The root of the failure of all Marxist structuralism, as well as of the 'leftist' current, lies in claiming to organize thought and action from an absolute understanding of oppressive society as System, and then to launch the guideline of dissidence, of exteriority," Badiou writes. "However, there is no exterior, which by no means implies an insurmountable constraint of the interior ('recuperation'), because there is no interior either."[81] In light of this reproach, then, what are we to think of Lacan when, in his later seminars, he becomes a veritable master of these inside/outside topologies? Even more unexpectedly, could we not develop a comparable logic of internal exclusion based on the notion of an absent cause that we find not only in Althusser's canonical writings, as discussed in chapter 1, but also, I might add, in *The Logic of Sense*, no doubt Deleuze's most structuralist book? Would this not satisfy the requirements for a materialist dialectic in Badiou's Maoist version?

One answer to this last question, developed at greater length in *Theory of the Subject*, is anticipated in *The Rational Kernel of the Hegelian Dialectic*. Lacan's psychoanalysis, Badiou states, ultimately reduces the topology of the constitutive outside to the mere recognition of a structural given. This is why the topology of the constitutive outside, as the culminating point of the dialectic of structure and subject, must in turn be divided into a structural and a tendential understanding. "The historical fate of this topology is its inevitable division. We can indeed conceive of this topology in a purely structural fashion: exterior and interior then are discernible on every point, but indiscernible in the Whole, which is supposed as given. This is the path followed by Lacan (but already by Mallarmé) in the way he uses non-orientable surfaces, such as the Moebius ring," Badiou further writes: "But, in fact, we can and we must conceive of the split exterior/interior correlation as a process, whereby the fact that the real is simultaneously at its place and in excess over this place, both inside *and* outside, is due to its unfolding as a qualitative force."[82] In the end, what this criticism confirms is the need for a symptomatic torsion that would not remain on the structural level of the recognition of an outside within but that instead passes over into the disqualification or destruction of the old inside the new.

MAO AS VANISHING MEDIATOR

The role of Maoism for Badiou's overall philosophy in sum consists in allowing him without either separation or fusion to articulate place and force, state and tendency, structure and subject, or being and event. Of course, the diagonal crossing of dualisms that operate in a metaphysical system can be seen as a constant throughout the history of philosophy: "The notion that thought should always establish itself beyond categorical oppositions, thereby delineating an unprecedented diagonal, is constitutive of philosophy itself," so in order to capture the singularity of this or that philosophy, we have to see what specifies the conceptual recourse to one diagonal as opposed to another: "The whole question consists in knowing what value to ascribe to the operators of this diagonal trajectory, and in identifying the unknown resource to which they summon thought."[83] Maoism, in my view, is one such diagonal resource, which even today is still fairly underappreciated in Badiou's own trajectory as a philosopher.

Theory of Contradiction could not be clearer about the philosophical implications of the materialist dialectic as a diagonal traversing of opposites —above all, in this case, the opposites of subject and object. "The problem is to reflect both and at the same time the scission and the reciprocal action of the two categories (subject and object) in the general movement of a process, without excluding that the subjective factor may be the key to this movement," Badiou sums up with a reference to Hegel via Lenin: "For Lenin, it is a question of finding support in Hegel so as to put an end to the *unilateralism* of the categories of subject and object, whether one separates them (metaphysical operation) or one annuls either one of them (absolute idealism or mechanicist materialism)."[84] In a certain sense Badiou only adds that Mao is the spitting image of this materialist Hegel whose praise Lenin sings so loudly on every page of his *Philosophical Notebooks*. But then this suggestion also has profound consequences for Badiou's personal genealogy in relation to the principal philosophical schools at the time in France.

In *Can Politics Be Thought?* Badiou remembers how fiercely the French philosophical scene was divided in the 1960s and 1970s by the last battle of the giants, the polemic between Sartre and Althusser. "When the mediations of politics are clear, it is the philosopher's imperative to subsume them in the direction of a foundation," Badiou writes. "The last debate in

this matter opposed the tenants of liberty, as founding reflective transparency, to the tenants of the structure, as the prescription of a regime of
causality. Sartre against Althusser: this meant, at bottom, the Cause against
the cause."[85] Hegel, whose shadow hangs over this debate at least as much
as Marx's, is then often little more than a code name in this context to
denounce the persistence of humanist and idealist elements in the early
Marx, even if the antihumanist trend according to Badiou is not wholly
incompatible with a return to Hegel of its own, provided that we abandon
the *Phenomenology of Spirit* in favor of the *Science of Logic*.

Sartre, on one hand, found inspiration for his critique of Stalinist dogma
by turning to the arch-Hegelian topics of alienation and the struggle for
self-consciousness whose influence is most strongly felt in the Marx of the
Economic and Philosophic Manuscripts of 1844. For Badiou, however, this
effort, though in many regards heroic, in the end betrays both Hegel and
Marx. "In the *Critique of Dialectical Reason* (but after the young Lukács,
after Korsch), Sartre in a single movement greeted Marxism as the insurmountable horizon of our culture and undertook to dismantle this Marxism by forcing it to realign itself with the original idea that is most foreign
to it: the transparency of the cogito," Badiou writes in *The Rational Kernel
of the Hegelian Dialectic*: "Both this Marx and this Hegel are equally false,
the first for being reduced to the second, and the second for being separated from that part of himself that precisely cleared the path for the first:
the *Great Logic*."[86] Althusser, on the other hand, wanted to reclaim Marx's
radical discovery of a new and unheard-of type of structural causality by
stripping it of all Hegelian elements: "Althusser restituted a kind of brutal
trenchancy to Marxism, isolating it from the subjectivist tradition and
putting it back in the saddle as positive knowledge," yet this project, too, in
the end was a double avoidance: "Marx and Hegel, even though in opposite
terms, found themselves as much foreclosed as in the previous moment:
the materialist Hegel of the *Great Logic* is equally mute for Althusser and
for Sartre."[87]

This grandiose but also debilitating alternative between Sartre and Althusser is what Badiou's dialectic seeks to cross by way of a divided recomposition, all the while remaining loyal to the two major referents of French
Maoism. "What the Cultural Revolution and May 1968 made clear on a
massive scale was the need for something entirely different from an oscillation of national intellectual traditions (between the Descartes of the
cogito, Sartre, and the Descartes of the machines, Althusser), in order to

reinvest Marxism in the real revolutionary movement," Badiou concludes: "The Maoist aim was to break with this alternation, with this avoidance."[88] Finally, as a means to trace a diagonal across the Sartre/Althusser debate, Maoism also implies a return to the conflict of interpretations surrounding Hegel. Hegel's very own division, in fact, seems to be the only remedy against the temptation to submit his work to either a positivist or an idealist reductionism: "Hegel remains the stake of an endless conflict, because the belabored understanding of his division alone is what prohibits, in thinking the relationship Marx/Hegel, both the idealist-romantic deviation and the scientist-academic deviation, as well as, finally, the hatred pure and simple of Marxism."[89]

In all fairness to Sartre and Althusser, though, perhaps we should add that their work also unmistakably contains many of the elements necessary for their division. We have already seen how, in some of Althusser's own formulations, the systematic study of overdetermination under certain conditions, which he also calls "events," reveals the excess of the structure over its immanent resources and how this excess already presupposes the inscription of a subject-effect that is not merely ideological. Conversely, we can also always expect to find remnants of the opacity and counterfinality of the structure, what Sartre calls elements of the "practico-inert," in the midst of the subject's ongoing efforts at reaching the transparency of the cogito as self-consciousness.

One never ceases to divide itself into two. But then the logic of scission and recomposition must likewise be applied to the notions of being and event in Badiou's later work. Otherwise we would miss the singularity of the diagonal operators (site, fidelity, investigation, forcing, and so on) that link a purely mathematical ontology to a theory of the intervening subject. This diagonal, finally, is what Maoism makes possible, both on a philosophical level and on a political level, according to Badiou: "In Maoism, I found something that made it possible for there to be no antinomy between whatever mathematics is capable of transmitting in terms of formal and structural transparency, on the one hand, and on the other, the protocols by which a subject is constituted."[90] Put differently, if Sartre, Althusser, and Lacan name the three masters or teachers behind Badiou's philosophical apprenticeship, then we should add that the Borromean knot between all three, to use a category that was dear to the last in the series, would not have been possible without the unifying thread of the experience of Maoism.

THE BEAUTIFUL SOUL

What I described above as the Maoist-inspired critique of ideological deviations, particularly of the "ultraleftist" variety, in many ways can also be read as a critique of the melodramatic scenarios enacted by the "beautiful soul" in the famous analysis passed on from Hegel to Lacan. Maoism, it would seem, ought in principle to put an end to the notion of a good moral conscience, whose inner beauty is merely inversely proportionate to the sordidness that it projects onto the outside world. In the aftermath of the official Sino-Soviet split, was the whole aim in formalizing the logic of so-called "contradictions among the people" not precisely to avoid opposing the "good" communist subject to the "bad" totalitarian system, so as to displace the split, through the appropriate measures of self-criticism and reeducation, onto the subject's very own interiority—whether this subject is called the people, the masses, the proletariat, the party bureaucracy, or the intelligentsia? But what if Mao and Lin Biao wittingly or unwittingly allowed the widespread flourishing of so many "beautiful souls"? What if the Cultural Revolution contained the scenario for a melodrama of gigantic proportions? Such is, roughly put, one of the guiding questions with which two former militants of the Gauche Prolétarienne in France, Christian Jambet and Guy Lardreau, seek to address and come to terms with their Maoist past.

In *L'Ange* (*The Angel*), the first volume of a projected *Ontology of the Revolution* that would never be completed, Jambet and Lardreau explicitly compare the generic notion of a cultural revolution, which they contrast with an ideological revolution, to the figure of the beautiful soul: "The soul of the cultural revolution is the '*beautiful soul*' in the way in which Lacan describes it after Hegel; insofar as, by assuming what it knows to be its madness in the eyes of this world, it also knows that this is the wisdom of the other world, and that it is this one, in truth, that is mad."[91] Jambet and Lardreau openly seem to want to embrace this melodramatic figure. Any true cultural revolution in its purity thus would have to mark a radical break with the entire corrupt system of work, family, sexuality, and egoism, whereas its ideological perversion always consists in recuperating and subordinating the revolutionary spirit in the name of those very same corrupt values.

Like Nietzsche before them, Jambet and Lardreau want to be the dynamite that breaks the history of the world in two. Or rather, they dream of a revolution that would produce two worlds, by marking a clean break with the existing one. But then, of course, from the perspective of the existing world, the purity of this break cannot fail to disappoint, as no slate can ever prove to be wiped clean enough and no grand exit can sufficiently leave behind the world from which it seeks to escape. Whence the openly angelical appearance of a true cultural revolution, which can never be a kingdom of this world but must rather open the gates to a radically other world. Disappointment and corruption, once more, seem not merely accidental but structural components in the constitution of a cultural revolution's beautiful soul.

Unlike what happens in Badiou's brief account at the start of his *Deleuze*, therefore, in *L'Ange* the Maoist past gives no occasion whatsoever for the use of a narrative present. Lardreau's extensive chapter, "Lin Biao as Will and as Representation," which takes up nearly half of the book, is composed entirely in the past tense—in spite of having been completed in November 1975, barely two years after the dissolution of the Gauche Prolétarienne. Instead, while explicitly refusing an act of apostasy, the proposed solution in dealing with what seem to be unfathomable excesses consists in combining the depiction of a bygone, youthful, and erratic past, with the hope in a future in which the past's rebellious force, after a period of dwelling underground, will reemerge in a madness all the more pure and erratic for having no more links whatsoever that would tie it down to the present moment.

Following Lacan, Lardreau is painfully aware of the law of history by which every rebellion always seems to revert to the search for a master: "Should we admit then that the indisputable maxim: where there is oppression, there is resistance, should be doubled with this one so as to say, is it not?, the truth of the first: where there is revolt, there is submission?"[92] Every cultural revolution is thus bound, as if by an unforgiving inner necessity, to be co-opted by an ideological one. Paradoxically, however, the way out of this blight conundrum for Jambet and Lardreau lies in aggravating the underlying opposition with an even fuller embrace of its Manicheism. What they posit is not a weaker messianic force but an ever stronger will for absolute purity in the struggle between the Master and the Rebel, so as to prepare the latter's return in the form of the Angel. "As for the Rebel himself, we must imagine that he has departed elsewhere, that by taking leave of this history, which he traversed with his fury, he returns to his own, where he does not cease preparing the cultural revolution," Lardreau writes. "One more time in any case we will make the mad wager: the Angel, which we had announced in turn, has always been vanquished—he will end up by triumphing in an unheard-of revolution."[93]

What is fascinating in this context is how the late Daniel Bensaïd, in "Alain Badiou and the Miracle of the Event," seems to replay the scenario staged by Jambet and Lardreau in order this time to attribute its angelical and near-mystical features to the philosophy of Badiou. This proximity is all the more relevant in that Bensaïd's criticisms sum up a viewpoint that over the last few years has become commonplace among a growing number of critics, and even a few admirers, of Badiou's work. Bensaïd opens his critique by giving a fairly typical summary of the entire trajectory of Badiou's thinking:

> Initially, Badiou's thought remained subordinated to the movement of history. But truth has become more fragmentary and discontinuous under the brunt of historical disasters, as though history no longer constituted its basic framework but merely its occasional condition. Truth is no longer a subterranean path manifesting itself in the irruption of the event. Instead, it becomes a post-evental consequence. As "wholly subjective" and a matter of "pure conviction," truth henceforth pertains to the realm of declarations that have neither precedents nor consequences. Although similar to revelation, it still remains a process but one which is entirely contained in the absolute beginning of the event which it faithfully continues.[94]

The price to pay for this radical distancing from history would be exorbitant. In Bensaïd's judgment the result, in fact, is "a philosophy of majestic sovereignty, whose decision seems to be founded upon a nothing that commands a whole," a philosophy haunted by the epistemological cut between event and history, the effect of which would be politically deadening: "The absolute incompatibility between truth and opinion, between philosopher and sophist, between event and history, leads to a practical impasse. The refusal to work within the equivocal contradiction and tension which bind them together ultimately leads to a pure voluntarism, which oscillates between a broadly leftist form of politics and its philosophical circumvention."[95] Leftism, in other words, is now a charge leveled against the only form of politics that can be thought in terms proper to Badiou's philosophy. Because of our constant temptation as mere mortals to give in to the status quo, this philosophy is permanently upset by the guilt of its own sinful impurity. Not unlike in the case of the beautiful soul, any instance of free decision would be threatened by this corruption. "Holy purification is never more than a short step away from voluptuous sin," Bensaïd declares, and again, with reference to some of the more pedestrian proposals of Badiou's Organisation Politique: "This sudden conversion to realism is the profane converse of the heroic thirst for purity."[96]

Now what is particularly striking in Bensaïd's reading is the place attributed to Badiou's Maoism—to be more precise, to Badiou's failure to come to terms with his Maoist past, here quickly equated with Stalinism. "As we hinted earlier, all these contradictions and aporias can be traced back to the refusal of history and to the unsettled score with Stalinism," exclaims Bensaïd, in good Trotskyist fashion: "This failure to clarify his relation to the legacies of Stalinism and Maoism lies at the root of Badiou's inability to clarify his relation to Marx."[97] What I have argued throughout the present chapter, however, might lead to a different conclusion, perhaps even one that is the radical opposite of Bensaïd's. Maoism, for Badiou, involves precisely an ongoing settling of accounts with the kinds of leftist, mystical, or otherwise miraculous definition of the event as an "absolute beginning," marked by an equally "absolute incompatibility" with the realm of worldly being—especially, I might add, when such accusations of "leftism" are used to claim for oneself that one has avoided the wide-open traps of Stalinism. That this settling of accounts in turn involves "the still unresolved difficulty of holding together event and history, act and process, instant and duration" is true enough, but then this is also very much the difficulty tackled by all of Badiou's work.

Plainly put, what happens in Bensaïd's interpretation, as well as in many other critical readings of Badiou, consists in setting up a dogmatic divide between being and event, or between history and event, only then to plead in favor of a more dialectical articulation between the two. On closer consideration Badiou, in other words, seems to stand accused of being not so much a Maoist as a Linbiaoist. Lardreau, from this point of view, still had the virtue of admitting his undying loyalty, which he furthermore confessed was devoid of all concerns for historicity, to Lin Biao. Our contemporary critics, by contrast, can no longer ignore the fact that

Badiou wrote a stunning critique of precisely the kind of mystical politics that, before being attributed to him, was openly embraced by Lardreau's and Jambet's *L'Ange*.

In "Un ange est passé," published under the pseudonym of Georges Peyrol, Badiou had in fact taken issue with the whole idea of cultural revolution as the invariant form of an absolute beginning, or an inviolable break. This criticism offers us another perception of the complete debacle of the Gauche Prolétarienne in the aftermath of the Chinese Cultural Revolution, particularly owing to the encounter of many of its ex-enthusiasts with Lacan: "The turning trick with the Angel consists in the following: to interrogate the Cultural Revolution from the point of its (Lacanian) impossibility, and thus as that which, by raising the question of its existence, leads one to establish this existence in inexistence: another world, a beyond, the kingdom of Angels."[98] The notion of a radical and uncompromising Two, despite the appearance of fidelity to the principle of antagonistic scission, is actually the exact opposite of Mao's lesson that "One divides into two."

L'Ange, by presenting a hyperbolic, properly metaphysical version of two worlds, merely reproduces, according to Badiou's critique, Lin Biao's "ultraleftist" will of absolute purity and genius. "What Lardreau and Jambet, as decided Linbiaoists, call 'cultural revolution' is the absolute and imaginary irruption of the outside-world, the definitive eradication of egoism," Badiou charges: "It means 'breaking the history of the world in two.' It is the ideologism of the remaking of oneself, fascist in its sectarian ambition of absolute purity, of absolute simplicity, of starting anew *from scratch*."[99] Even when the desire for purification is applied with much rhetorical pomp and violence to the spectacle of the intellectual's imaginary self-annihilation, the whole picture remains metaphysical—yet another example of speculative leftism in which the scission of the One is replaced by an eternally Manichean Two. As Badiou concludes: "What to say, except that nothing, especially not the revolt, authorizes the pure Two of metaphysics? The revolt in an exemplary way is that which splits—so not the Two, but the One dividing into Two and thus revealing what the One has always been, the becoming of its own scission."[100] Lardreau and Jambet, postulating the inevitable nature of the One, are obliged to affirm, outside and beyond the first, another One: "Their maxim, against 'one divides into two,' is 'two times one.' "[101]

Similarly, when Badiou invokes the example of the Red Guards in his *Ethics*, as the example of a disaster comparable to Nietzsche's madness, we are still only witnessing the repetition of a criticism already made during the so-called Maoist years. Like Nietzsche, certain Red Guards wished completely to kill and replace, rather than to split, the old by the new. "When Nietzsche proposes to 'break the history of the world in two' by exploding Christian nihilism and generalizing the great Dionysian 'yes' to Life; or when certain Red Guards of the Chinese Cultural Revolution proclaim, in 1967, the complete suppression of self-interest, they are indeed inspired by a vision of a situation in which all interest has disappeared, and in which opinions have been *replaced* by the truth to which Nietzsche and the Red Guards are committed," admits Badiou. "But Nietzsche went mad. The Red Guards, after inflicting immense harm, were imprisoned or shot, or betrayed by their own fidelity."[102] This is not just a remorseful self-criticism. For from his earliest accounts of the logic of scission onward, Badiou has always warned against the perils of seeking a complete break, a total reeducation, or an absolute beginning. "This is because the idea of the simple beginning is a typically metaphysical, that is to say, a conservative presupposition," he writes in *Theory of Contradiction*. "The speculative concept of the Beginning—of which Hegel himself gave an unfinished and divided criticism—serves to suture the dialectic to idealism."[103] All those critics who claim that Badiou over the years has become vulnerable to the charge of leftism, in this sense, are only partially correct at best. Not only do they ignore the explicit treatment of this charge in Badiou's own early writings, but they might also want to consider the numerous passages in the recent work in which an unnuanced and exceedingly binary logic of being and event is rejected in the name of a certain Mao. In the end, we are sent back to a diagonal crossing of "leftism" and "rightism" alike:

> Mao himself—and God knows there was a great deal of violence in the Chinese Revolution—developed a fairly complicated doctrine regarding the difference between contradictions among the people and antagonistic contradictions, and the existence in any process of left, centre, and right wings. He never stopped insisting that in the movement of a process there is always a considerable plurality of nuances, and that if we don't grant some space to this plurality, we are finally driven back to the break-up of the process, more than anything else. It is true that some political sequences did adopt as the internal rule of their development a

very severe bivalent logic, but we need to ask in each case how this bivalence was linked to the singularity of the sequence. It is not a general problem of truth-processes.[104]

Whether or to what extent *Being and Event* and *Logics of Worlds* will be able to account for this plurality of nuances remains to be seen, but the least we can say is that Badiou's work, under the condition of Maoism, has tried to open up a contradictory conceptual space for the articulation—without fusion or deviation—by which an event is linked to a given situation in a process of scission and reciprocal transformation.

FROM DESTRUCTION TO SUBTRACTION?

At this point some readers may wonder whether there is any break at all left in Badiou's work. By resisting the stark opposition between an "early" and a "late" stage that would be marked by the supposed abandonment of the dialectic, have I not forced the interpretation of this philosophy beyond recognition, this time in the direction of a blind continuism? Is there then no need at all to add the slight distance of a prefix to Badiou's Maoism? Or how else should we interpret the gap that warrants the invocation of a *post*-Maoism? Badiou, after all, organizes his talk on the Cultural Revolution around the hypothesis that its series of events marks the end of an era—that is, precisely, the end of the revolutionary era. What are we to make of this hypothesis in light of Badiou's lasting debts to Maoism and, more generally speaking, to Marxism?

In "Communism as Separation" Alberto Toscano provides us with one of the most lucid and sophisticated readings of the immanent break with Marxism-Leninism that would seem to occur in Badiou's work. For Toscano this break becomes definitive around 1985, particularly in *Can Politics Be Thought?*, through a peremptory deconstruction of the metaphysical and classist understanding of politics. Prior to this point, the idea of communism would have involved a politics of transitivity, driven by the motor of antagonism between the dominant structure of representation and the unrepresentable subject who, while being foreclosed, nevertheless can be expected to be an antecedent to itself. As Toscano writes: "What is deserving of the epithet 'metaphysical' in these doctrines is the idea that politics is somehow inscribed in representation, that what is foreclosed by domination is nevertheless endowed with a latent political force; which is to say, that the political subject which emerges out of the labor of the positive, whether this be the appropriation of production or the limitation and destruction of place, is its own obscure precursor."[105] After *Can Politics Be Thought?* Badiou's understanding of politics, in other words, would have shifted from a class-based logic of antagonism, including in its most vehement and terminal version as destruction and terrorizing self-purification, to a logic of subtraction wholly intransitive to any prior social, economical, or otherwise obscurely consistent substance: "What is certain, above all, is that the abandonment of class antagonism as the dialectical support of communist subjectivity affects it with a radical intransitivity to representation as well as with a discontinuity in its manifestations."[106] By abandoning the transitivity of political subjectivity to the structure of antagonism, no matter how tenuous and aleatory the latter is made out to be, Badiou would have definitely abdicated the basic underlying principle of all Marxism-Leninism.

Toscano's careful analysis nonetheless seems to waver somewhat in the attempt to draw a neat conceptual boundary between the operations typical of the transitive mode of politics (reappropriation, destruction, purification) and those that presuppose a certain deconstruction of the metaphysics of transitivity (subtraction, avoidance, distancing). On several points of the description these operations from before and after the break come to resemble one another much more so than the notion of a definitive linear break would seem to justify. At the same time, such resonances do not necessarily signal an inaccuracy in Toscano's account of Badiou's philosophy. In fact, many of the operations that were pivotal before actually do continue to be important today, albeit in different ways or with a different emphasis. Thus, in more recent statements, Badiou's supposedly linear shift from destruction to subtraction, or from purification to the play of minimal difference, gives way to the complex reordering of a simultaneity. Toscano's hesitation bears witness to the possibility of such a combination, which only recently has become a reality for Badiou.

Badiou's Maoism, once again, seems to have a symptomatic function in this context. In fact, what the notion of a deconstruction of the "fiction" of transitivity between the political and the social in Marxism-Leninism seems to omit is the extent to which such a deconstruction was already a lesson learned from Maoism. Badiou's readers all too often seem to infer that what he says of "classical" or "orthodox" Marxism, or Marxism-

Leninism, for instance in *Can Politics Be Thought?* or *Being and Event*, automatically applies, by way of an immanent self-critique, to his own Maoism. This, however, amounts to downplaying the significance not only of Mao's critical notes between 1958 and 1960 on Stalin's *Economical Problems of Socialism in the USSR* and on the official Soviet *Manual of Political Economy* but also of the critique of so-called "workerism," as a prime example of the politics of transitivity, on the part of Badiou and his Maoist comrades in the UCFML.

"Workerism" (*ouvriérisme*), which the UCFML sees as a constitutive ideological defect of the Gauche Prolétarienne, lies in conflating the social being of the working class with its political capacity. In practice the result of such a conflation often entails a limitation of the militant struggle to purely economical demands and their possible convergence, occasionally intensified in a violent upping of the ante as a way to provoke the existing authorities. For the UCFML, however, politics cannot be reduced to a series of economical demands, not even if they are eventually inserted in an expansive chain of equivalences. Nor can the workers be seen, in a falsely populist but otherwise typically moralizing and paternalistic fashion, as being endowed with an innate or automatic political capacity. "It is completely false to think that any social practice of any worker, no matter which one, is revolutionary or proletarian," the UCFML insists in an early circular: "We must firmly combat these orientations which, despite the 'left-wing' air that they may try to put on, are in reality from the right. They indeed reject the mass alliance and the materialist analysis."[107] This also means that the moment of politics cannot be subordinated to purely economical demands, along the lines of typical syndicalist or trade-unionist revindications. In fact, only a clear distinction between the socioeconomical substance of the category of the workers and its organized subjective capacity is capable of preserving the autonomy of politics. "Workerism, the cult of the worker, which did so much damage and which was, much more so than leftism, our infantile disorder, from the point of view of politics means the inability really to handle the question of the party as the leading nucleus [*noyau*] of the people as a whole," another special issue of *Le Marxiste-Léniniste* reads: "Workerism and unionism, as ideologies, the first among certain militants and the second among certain workers, that means the refusal of proletarian political independence."[108] From a Maoist perspective, ultimately, there exist no classes prior to their demarcation in the struggle. To use Badiou's more concentrated philosophical expression of the same principle in *Theory of Contradiction*: "A class does not preexist before the class struggle. To exist means to be opposed. The existence of a term is entirely given in its contradictory correlation with the other term of the scission."[109] For Badiou, then, the real break in terms of the transitivity of politics happens *within* Marxism-Leninism *as a result of* Maoism.

POLITICS AND HISTORICITY

Instead of relying on some version or other of the critique of metaphysics, in which Maoism all too easily risks becoming equated with Marxism-Leninism and the latter in turn becomes a synonym for mere Stalinism, another way of describing the break in Badiou's work revolves around the notion of the intrinsic historicity of politics itself. "To be a Marxist means to be schooled by history," the UCFML posits in a pamphlet distributed after the death of Mao, but then this principle must also be applied to the study of Marxism: "We have to study contemporary history and *practice historical materialism with regard to Marxism itself*."[110] Marxism is not a body of doctrine, whether economical or philosophical, but it is also not simply an ideology and even less a worldview; instead, it is a politics, the politics of communism, the different stages of which form an internal history that can at most be said to be concentrated in the theories of Marx and Engels, Lenin, and Mao.

Thus, when UCFML militants wrote up a balance sheet of their group's trajectory in a 1981 special issue of *Le Marxiste-Léniniste* titled *10 ans de maoïsme* (Ten Years of Maoism), they began by acknowledging the ultimate failure, or the complete depletion of historical power, of what from the start were their two main points of reference, the Cultural Revolution and May 1968: "These referents are today without power of their own. We carry their questions rather than their outcomes."[111] This failure of referentiality does not mean that we are done with the double legacy of Maoism. On the contrary, the questions that are left unresolved in its wake now constitute the stakes for a bold rebeginning of Marxism:

> Against May 68, we know that what is needed is politics, the party, the break; and that the working class as political reality is a task rather than a given.
>
> With regard to the Cultural Revolution, we know that it has failed,

and that the center of Maoism is this failure rather than that which took place.

We who began at the crossover between May 68 and the GPCR, we are conscious that we lasted for other reasons: the political tenacity, and the certitude that communism is a process rather than a result. A process whose material and stakes are the party of the new type, the party of the post-Leninist era, which barely begins, and which is itself caught in the general beginning of this enormous civilization that bears the name of Marxism.

Our fidelity to our origin enjoins us to hold a second beginning. Those who know the period and the risk of their history have the consistency of that which can win and last.[112]

In other pamphlets from the same period the anonymous authors of the UCFML even go so far as to posit that to be a Marxist, one must in a sense become a post-Maoist. Armed with the historical knowledge that the failure of a revolutionary project such as the Paris Commune was perhaps no less instructive for Marx and Lenin than a victory would have been, they call for a sustained enquiry into the obstacles and contradictions that ultimately explain the failure of the Cultural Revolution—a failure symp-tomatically exposed in the trials against the Gang of Four. "The failure of a revolution universally sets the task of specifying what it has stumbled up against; what internal political question kept it, in positive mass condi-tions, from reaching its principal conscious goals," so reads the pamphlet *Questions of Maoism: From the China of the Cultural Revolution to the China of the Beijing Trials*: "Today a Marxist is someone who, within the frame-work of an organized politics, makes an effort to resolve for him or herself the PROBLEMS left hanging by the initial Maoism, the Maoism of Mao Zedong, the Maoism that is contemporary to the Cultural Revolution. There is no other Marxism except this one."[113] Since the fundamental problem left unsolved by the Cultural Revolution is the one of the party, solving this problem at the same time means devising the means to con-stitute a party of a new type, the party of post-Leninism. It is this problem that represents the stumbling block hit upon early on during the Cultural Revolution.

Badiou's central hypothesis in his recent talk on the Cultural Revolution thus reiterates several of the arguments adopted by the UCFML during the late 1970s and early 1980s, when the group was producing a renewed assessment of its militancy in terms of the concept and practice of post-Leninism. The Cultural Revolution would have been unable to resolve the tension between the framework of a single-party state and the massive mobilizations called on to unhinge this whole framework from within. As we read in the UCFML pamphlet published right after Mao's death: "The Cultural Revolution did not radically transform the political thought of the leaders of the Maoist left on questions of organization. It is largely within the context of the Party that, from 1969 until today, political battles have raged regarding the fundamental orientations in the construction of social-ism. Indeed, it seems that a contradiction has subsisted between an overall political orientation that was widely renovated by the Cultural Revolution and an organizational frame the reality and theory of which remained essentially unchanged."[114]

Or, to use the excellent summary by Paul Sandevince (pseudonym for Badiou's fellow militant Sylvain Lazarus), in his *Working Notes on Post-Leninism*:

> Maoism marks a break with regard to Leninism. Or, rather, it opens the necessity of a break, without constituting the conceptual arrangement for this break. There is a relative silence in the Cultural Revolution and from Mao himself on the question of what would be the profile of the party of the new stage. Mao and the GPCR open the era of post-Leninism by clearing new paths on questions of the masses, on the proletariat, but not on proletarian politics, or on the politics of the party. Mao opens post-Leninism in terms of mass politics, but for the moment we cannot say that the principle of unity between mass politics and class (party) politics has been found.[115]

If the Maoism of the Cultural Revolution was a heroic but failed effort to give new organizational shape to a post-Leninist mode of politics, then the task after the failure of the Cultural Revolution is with the aid of a series of militant investigations to prepare a new Maoism, or post-Maoism.

We can thus understand why Badiou, even while acknowledging the closing of an era, would feel neither remorse nor embarrassment before using a narrative present to talk of "the Maoist that I am," in his book on Deleuze, or why he admits, in *Theory of the Subject*, to feeling an "inco-ercible nostalgia" for those years of the Cultural Revolution, even including the "cult of Mao" in which he also participated: "I buy neither the posthumous revenge of Camus over Sartre, nor even the immoderate praise for Raymond Aron, on the grounds that he would have been 'less mistaken,' which indeed is something that is easily achieved when one takes no risks other than to follow the pedagogy of the world as it goes."[116] Maoism and the Cultural Revolution, far from following the pedagogy of the world as we know it, by contrast continue to pose problems for which only a bold and painstaking investigation can begin to formulate possible solutions.

4

THE ONTOLOGICAL IMPASSE

←—————————————————→

THE TURN TO MATHEMATICS

The change between Badiou's two major works from the 1980s may seem proof of an irrevocable shift from dialectics to mathematics—with the former dominating his *Theory of the Subject* together with the slender volume *Can Politics Be Thought?*, which as we saw in fact already anticipates the intervening doctrine of the event, and the latter appearing systematically in *Being and Event*, for which the accompanying *Manifesto for Philosophy* provides a readily accessible context. As Badiou writes about Hegel in *Being and Event*: "Mathematics occurs here as a discontinuity within the dialectic."[1] The same could be said to apply to Badiou's path. Does this trajectory, however, really imply an irredeemable break, or is there an underlying continuity? Are the earlier misgivings, if that is what they are, merely abandoned after the so-called mathematical turn, or do we face a more systematic version of previous insights that in essence remain unchanged or perhaps even become obscured? In what direction, moreover, has this trajectory headed since then?

Being and Event, we now know, is only the first half of a larger project, the second volume of which has finally been published, almost twenty years after the first, under the title *Logics of Worlds*. The ambitious overall aim of this project is to affirm that philosophy, despite repeated declarations of its imminent end, is once more possible. The present times, in other words, are capable of articulating the key philosophical categories of being, truth, and subject in a way that requires neither an inaugural return nor a melancholic traversing of an end but, rather, a decisive step beyond:

"A step within the modern configuration, the one that since Descartes has bound the conditions of philosophy to the three nodal concepts of being, truth, and subject."[2] For Badiou, what is needed at present to link these basic concepts is a philosophy of the event that, despite an irreducible polemical distance, would be compatible both with the critique of metaphysics, as brought to a close by Heidegger, and with the intervening doctrines of the subject, mostly tied to political and clinical experiences, after Marx (as well as Lenin and Mao) and Freud (and Lacan).

In *Being and Event* mathematics provides the master key to articulate—both to join and by way of an impasse to split off—the science of being with the theory of the subject. The book's guiding thesis is deceptively simple: ontology exists, insofar as ever since the Greek origins of philosophy, and as one of its conditions, the science of being has always been mathematics: "It is not a thesis about the world but about discourse. It affirms that mathematics, throughout the entirety of its historical becoming, pronounces what is expressible of being qua being."[3] For Badiou the place where the ontological discourse is developed today, at least if philosophy accepts to take on this decision, is in axiomatic set theory, from Cantor to Cohen. The basic result of his metaontological investigation into set theory holds that everything that presents itself, in any situation whatsoever, is a multiple of multiples, or pure multiple, without One.

The One "is" not, but "there is" One. The latter is only the result of an operation, the count-for-one, applied to the pure multiple, which retroactively must be supposed to be inconsistent. To be means to belong to a multiple, to be counted as one of its elements. A given multiple, or set α, acquires consistency only through the basic operation that counts whatever this multiple presents as so many ones (a, b, c, d, . . .) that belong to this multiple. Prior to this count, though, we must presume that all being paradoxically inconsists, without any Godlike principle or pregiven origin: "There is no God. Which also means: the One is not. The multiple 'without-one'—every multiple being in its turn nothing other than a multiple of multiples—is the law of being. The only stopping point is the void."[4] Badiou's ontology of pure multiplicity agrees in this sense with the critique of the metaphysics of presence so that his deconstruction of the One is another way of declaring the death of God.

Choosing a strict alternative to Heidegger's hermeneutic path, however, Badiou's enquiry does not submit itself to the language of the poets, who

alone would be capable of rescuing the clearing of being. Instead of upend-
ing philosophy in the name of poetry, or art, the critique of metaphysics in
his case is conditioned by the deductive fidelity of pure mathematics.
Badiou thus seeks to avoid the dominant suture of contemporary philosophy in its pious delegation onto poetry. Philosophy today must rather draw
the required consequences from the closure of the age of the poets, which
according to Badiou has run its complete gamut from Hölderlin to Celan.
The axiom, and not the poem, holds the key to a science of being compatible with the theory of the subject, access to which is provided by way of
subtraction, not by interpretive approximation.

All the ontological ideas, axiomatically established in set theory, proceed from the void or empty set, named by the symbol $\emptyset$, which must be
postulated as the only possible proper name of being. The empty set
indeed is universally included in every other set while itself having no
elements that belong to it, and as such it "founds" all mathematical sets. In
a normal situation, however, not only does the void remain invisible or
indiscernible, but the operation of the count, moreover, reduplicates itself
in an attempt to establish the metastructure, or the state of the situation, in
the guise of an uninterrupted totality. This second operation consists in
counting, or representing, as subsets whatever the first count presents as
terms of a given set. The count of the count would then hold for parts just
as the count-for-one holds for elements, with the latter doing for belonging
what the former does for inclusion.

What Badiou calls the state of a situation, in other words, operates by
way of the power-set $p(\alpha)$, which is the set of all the subsets of a given set α.
This can easily be understood if we think of why an operation such as a
recurrent census is a characteristic feature of the modern state. What does
a census produce if not a count of the count—the real question being not
only how many citizens belong to a given nation but also how their numbers are distributed into parts according to variously defined subsets or
groups? The true threat, from the point of view of the state, would be that
in some place, near the borders of the void, there is something that escapes
this counting operation: singular elements belonging to the situation without being documented as part of its state or, the other way around, inexistent parts that are included in the state without having any elements that
are thought to belong to their mass. As Badiou writes: "An inexistent part is
the possible support of the following—which would ruin structure—the

one, somewhere, is not, inconsistency is the law of being, the essence of the structure is the void."[5] The emergence of such uncanny phenomena as inexistent parts or singular elements would fundamentally upset the operation of the redoubled count by which the state seeks to ward off the void that is always the foundation of its precarious consistency. The state of a situation in effect is an imposing defense mechanism set up to guard against the perils of the void.

After the initial guiding decision that mathematics provide the science of being, the fundamental thesis of the whole metaontological enquiry in *Being and Event* affirms that there is an excess of parts over elements, of inclusion over belonging, of representation over presentation. There are always more ways to regroup the elements of a set into parts than there are elements that belong to this set to begin with: $p(\alpha) > \alpha$. The state of a situation, in other words, cannot coincide with this situation itself. The cardinality of the set of all parts or subsets of a set is superior to the cardinality of this set itself, and, in the case of an infinite set, as with most situations in this world, the magnitude of this excess must be assumed to be strictly beyond measure. "There is an irremediable excess of submultiples over terms," an excess which is such that, "however exact the quantitative knowledge of a situation may be, one cannot, other than by an arbitrary decision, estimate by 'how much' its state exceeds it."[6] This is, finally, the ontological impasse—the point of the real in the science of being—around which the entire artifice of *Being and Event* is built: "This gap between α (which counts-as-one the belongings, or elements) and $p(\alpha)$ (which counts-as-one the inclusions, or subsets) is, as we shall see, the point in which the impasse of being resides."[7] With this key formula from *Being and Event*, $p(\alpha) > \alpha$, incidentally, are we not somehow back at the starting point of the materialist dialectic, Ap(AAp), if not its overly structural schema, P vs. A, as formulated in *Theory of the Subject*?

In the second half of *Being and Event* Badiou exploits this point of the real that is proper to the metamathematical analysis of being in order to discern in its deadlock not some originary lack as a cause for pious ecstasy or postmodern respect before the unrepresentable but the closest site where an event, as a contingent and unforeseeable supplement to the situation, raises the void of being in a kind of insurrection and opens a possible space of subjective fidelity. In normal circumstances, as I have noted, the structural impasse that is intrinsic to the state of the situation remains invisible, so that the void that is its foundation appears to be foreclosed. This foreclosure is the very operation that allows the smooth functioning of the established order of things—when everyone does what comes naturally because the state of the situation in effect appears to be second nature. Exceptionally, however, an event can bring the excess out into the open, expose the void as the foundation of all being, and mark the possible onset of a generic procedure of truth. As Badiou observes: "What allows a genuine event to be at the origin of a truth—which is the only thing that can be for all, and can be eternally—is precisely the fact that it relates to the particularity of a situation only from the bias of its void."[8]

An event is always an anomaly for the discourse of pure ontology, insofar as its irruption attests to a breakdown in the count of the count and thus brings out the real of the science of being. And while its chance occurrence uncovers the void that is the foundation of the entire structured situation in which it occurs, the event itself is a multiple that is wholly unfounded, that is to say, defined by the feature of self-belonging that all ontology consists in forbidding. A seemingly natural and well-ordered situation then becomes historical when what is otherwise a structural impasse, proper to the law of representation as such, becomes tangible through the effects of a radically contingent event. As the doctrine of the weakest link implies, all historicity occurs at the point where a deadlock of structural determination is crossed by the irruption of a rare event—an irruption that, as will become clear, cannot be dissociated from the intervention of a subject.

Here I cannot discuss in detail all the categories that mark the intermediate steps on the overall itinerary of *Being and Event*, an itinerary that ranges from the pure multiple of being to the subject, by passing through the situation, the state of the situation, the void, the point of excess, nature and historical situations, the site of the event, the intervention, fidelity, the generic, the indiscernible, and the forcing of truth. What should become evident is how, all along this itinerary, a modern doctrine of the subject as the local configuration of a procedure of truth paradoxically gets anchored in the deconstruction of metaphysics. For the purpose of our discussion regarding politics and the renewal of a materialist dialectic, the most important argument in all of *Being and Event* effectively holds that an event, which brings out the void that is proper to being by revealing the undecidable excess of representation over simple presentation, can only be decided retroactively by way of a subjective intervention. In a concise and, once again, nearly untranslatable formula, a final thesis thus sums up the trajectory of the entire book: "The impasse of being, which causes the quantitative excess of the state to err without measure, is in truth the pass of the Subject."[9] A subject is needed to put a measure on the exorbitant power by which the state of a situation exceeds this situation itself. Through the chance occurrence of an event, the structural fact of the ontological impasse is thus already mediated by subjectivity; without the intervention of a subject faithful to the event, the gap in the structure would not even be visible. The impasse is never purely structural but also at the same time dependent upon a haphazard intervention.

CANTOR'S DIALECTIC

What a marvel of dialectical materialism is this famous diagonal reasoning from Cantor by which that which is left over grounds that which has the value of excess!—BADIOU, *Theory of the Subject*

There are various reasons why this trajectory in *Being and Event,* despite the turn to mathematics, can be seen as dialectical in a new and unexpected sense. Let me point out a few of these reasons before turning to some of the problems involved in this renewed materialist dialectic. First, dialectical thinking, if this is still the appropriate label, continues to be defined in terms of scission and the torsion of scission, not in terms of alienation and the overcoming of alienation. The principle that for dialectics one divides into two, to a large extent, still applies to Badiou's later philosophy following *Being and Event.* Thus, rather than the simple opposition between being and event, what really matters is the split *within* being between presentation and representation. When Žižek presents this prior split as some kind of discovery on his part and a possible blind spot in Badiou's thinking, he is merely repeating the very kernel of the latter's ontology, which is at the same time its immanent deadlock; and, far from presupposing some wild vitality of pure presentation, this impasse of being is nothing but the result of formal counting operations that are impossible to fix. Likewise, an event is not only defined by purely belonging to itself in a manner that could be considered sovereign or absolutist, but it is an event *for* a situation, as indexed by its site. Even the formal matheme of the event inscribes this originary scission. Nothing can take away the fact that an event can occur only at a site that is symptomatic of the situation as a whole. Finally, a truth procedure consists in a *torsion* of the divided situation back on itself, starting from the site of the event and moving in the direction of a generic extension of its truth as applicable to all. These are the concepts that a dialectical reading should reconsider: not just being and event but scission, site, and torsion—the split within being between belonging and inclusion, the site of an event that makes this an event for a specific situation, and the forced return to this situation from the point of view of its generic extension.

Second, dialectical thinking does not consist in establishing a mechanical homology or isomorphism between subject and object but in articulating both through the formal paradox of an impasse, as in the interplay of void and excess. Badiou, in this regard, can be said to participate in a larger trend in post-Marxism (though in his case, as I argued in the previous chapter, it would be better to speak of post-Maoism), which holds not only that the subject is split but also, and more importantly, that a subject is needed to bring out the constitutive impasse of the structure that would have defined objectivity. The immeasurable excess of the state of a situation over this situation itself formalizes the fact that a structure is exceeded by its redoubling in a metastructure. However, this point of the real in ontology, which bars the objective order from achieving a well-ordered closure by causing a measureless excess of the state of the situation over the situation itself, requires at the same time a decision that is nothing if not subjective. The thesis from *Being and Event* that best sums up the book's entire trajectory, in this sense, is also a retrieval of the conclusion from *Theory of the Subject* according to which the real is the *impasse* of formalization but formalization is also the place of the *passe-en-force* of the real.[10] This passage or passing through the impasse is the work of the subject. A subject is called for to put a measure on the exorbitant power of the structure over itself. The structural fact of the impasse of being is already mediated by subjectivity; without the intervention of a subject faithful to the event, the gap in the structure would not even be visible.

Third, the dialectic of substance and subject can be phrased even more explicitly in orthodox terms as the "leap" or "turnabout," the "transformation into the opposite" from quantity to quality. Echoes from Hegel's *Logic* and the "passing over" or *übergehen* into the opposite can also be heard, in other words, in Badiou's idiosyncratic use of the Lacanian *passe*. No objective or quantitative criteria can put an exact measure on the excess of the subsets of the elements, of the state over the situation, or of inclusion over belonging. "It is as though, between the structure in which the immediacy of belonging is delivered and the metastructure which counts as one its parts and regulates the inclusions, a chasm opens that cannot be closed except by a choice without concept," Badiou writes in another key passage from *Being and Event*. "That at this point it is necessary to tolerate the almost complete arbitrariness of a choice, that quantity, the very paradigm of objectivity, leads to pure subjectivity; such is what I would willingly call the Cantor-Gödel-Cohen-Easton symptom. Ontology unveils in its impasse a point in which thought—unconscious that it is being itself which convokes it therein—has always had to divide itself."[11] The mathematics of set theory, far from being incompatible with the dialectic, thus, strangely enough, ends up confirming one of its principal laws. As Hegel himself observed: "It is said, *natura non facit saltum*; and ordinary thinking, when it has to grasp a coming-to-be or a ceasing-to-be, fancies it has done so by representing it as a *gradual* emergence or disappearance," to which the author of the *Logic* responds "that gradualness explains nothing without leaps"—a view enthusiastically endorsed by Lenin in the margins of his *Philosophical Notebooks*: "Leaps! Breaks in gradualness! Leaps! Leaps!"[12] In fact, to grasp how opposites, by leaps and breaks in the gradualness of nature, all of a sudden pass over into one another and come to be identical is one of the most orthodox definitions of the task of the dialectical method: "Dialectics is the doctrine of the *identity of opposites*—how they can be and how they become—under which conditions they become identical, transforming one into the other,—why the human mind must not take these opposites for dead, but for living, conditioned, mobile, transforming one into the other."[13]

Fourth, the break with nature as a gradual and well-ordered structure implies that, for such a break truly to happen, the initial situation will have had to become historical. Badiou's dialectic, if this is indeed the label we want to use, avoids most of the aporias of historicity and structure, of liberty and causality, which still haunted much of the work of Althusser, for instance, in his polemic with Sartre. It was Badiou's Maoism, as we have seen, that enabled him to bring together the doctrine of structural causality with a subject's commitment to a Cause. But this was possible only because overdetermination, upon closer inspection, already signaled that place, similar to the site of an event, where history seizes on a given structure, or where a structural impasse becomes historicized.

Finally, if we decide to continue using the orthodox vocabulary, we might say that this is the point where the materialist dialectic already carries within it the logic of historical materialism. Thus, in *Being and Event* one of the central meditations is devoted to answering the question of what turns a situation into a historical one, and the break between nature and history—between the well-ordered sameness of being and the irruption of a supernumerary event on the edges of the void—is as important in this later book as was the break earlier between structure and history in *Theory of the Subject*. It should also be said, however, that Badiou has only recently begun to supplement his formal definition of what constitutes a historical situation, that is, a situation marked by the site of an event, with the actual study of a few of such sites and situations. *The Century*, in this sense, already provides at least in part a historical counterweight for the more abstract materialist dialectic put forth in *Being and Event*, and the same is true for the case studies devoted to the Cultural Revolution and the Paris Commune, which have been integrated into *Logics of Worlds*. Much more work certainly needs to be done along these lines if we are to grasp how, in the doctrine of being and event, we are not reduced to a stance that is either structural or historicist; rather, we are bound to consider both at the same time in their immanent dialectic.

THE SUBJECT'S PASS: ACT OR EVENT?

In every subject, then, a structural law is tied onto the historically contingent occurrence of an unpredictable wager. Setting out from the void, which prior to the event remains indiscernible in the language of established knowledge, a subjective intervention names the event, which disappears no sooner than it appears; it faithfully connects as many elements of the situation as possible to this name, which is the only trace of the vanished event; and, subsequently, it forces the extended situation from the bias of the new truth *as if* the latter were indeed already generically applicable. "Situated in being, subjective emergence forces the event to decide the true of the situation," Badiou concludes in *Being and Event*, and if we take into account the various conditions or generic procedures of truth, we understand why he could write in the book's introduction that "strictly speaking, there is no subject except the artistic, amorous, scientific, or political."[14]

The pivotal thesis about the impasse of being as pass of the subject is nevertheless open to a fundamental misunderstanding. From a Lacanian point of view, above all, the thesis might as well be inverted so as to reduce the subject's passing to the structural impasse pure and simple. To come to terms with the unbearable kernel of the real, a subject must not only renounce all imaginary ideals and symbolic mandates but also assume the essential inconsistency of the symbolic order itself. This means not just accepting the divided and alienated nature of the subject as one's positive condition but, more importantly, acknowledging that what divides the subject is nothing but the lack that keeps the symbolic order from ever achieving any meaningful closure. If this is still called an event, it would be rather like a symptomatic slippage, which exposes the fact that the symbolic order itself is incomplete—no more able than the subject is to offer any answer to the abysmal question of the other's desire: *Che vuoi?* or "What do you want (from me)?" The subject "is" nothing but the empty place opened up in the structure by the very failure to answer this founding question. Recognition of this ineradicable void in the midst of the structure would then already coincide with the traumatic truth itself—if, that is, there exists such a thing as a truth of the real in psychoanalysis, which in any case would have to be more than its passing acknowledgment.

Žižek, for instance, describes this passage as a kind of ideological anamorphosis, a change of perspective, or, more recently, a parallax view, whereby that which previously served as an unshakable guarantee of meaningfulness all of a sudden appears merely to cover a gaping chasm of nonsense. The task of the subject, then, lies in the purely formal act of conversion, which assumes this immediate speculative identity or short-circuit between absolute power and utter impotence by recognizing the point where the dazzling plenitude of being flips over to reveal its morbid foundation in a thinglike nothingness. Typically, what at first appears to be a purely epistemological obstacle, owing to the subject's limited capacities for knowing as compared to the ungraspable power of some truly infinite entity, from a slightly different perspective—by looking awry at what is usually overlooked—turns out to be an essential ontological feature, inherent to the blocked structure of being itself.

"Where it was, I shall come into being": for a subject the formal act of conversion thus consists in somehow "becoming" what one always already "was" beforehand, namely, the very gap or empty place that impedes the symbolic order to attain full closure. All that happens has already taken place; there is nothing new under the sun, except for the formal gesture by which a subject assumes responsibility for what is happening anyway. "The 'subject' is precisely a name for this 'empty gesture' which changes nothing at the level of positive content (at this level, everything has already happened) but must nevertheless be added for the 'content' itself to achieve its full effectivity," as Žižek concludes in *The Sublime Object of Ideology*: "The only difference lies in a certain change of perspective, in a certain turn through which what was a moment ago experienced as an obstacle, as an impediment, proves itself to be a positive condition."[15] The subject not only posits that what seems to be presupposed as something objectively given is already his or her own doing, but the activity of self-positing must in turn be presupposed as being split from within by an insurmountable deadlock that is not external but immanent to its very essence. In a formal turnabout or instantaneous flip over, devoid of any actual change, the subject's pass would immediately coincide with the recognition of the impasse of the structure of being itself, that is to say, the gap between the real and its impossible symbolization.

The essence of truth, from this psychoanalytical perspective, is not a process so much as a brief traumatic encounter, or illuminating shock, in the midst of everyday reality. It would amount to coming to terms with the real as "a shock of contingent encounter which disrupts the automatic circulation of the symbolic mechanism; a grain of sand preventing its smooth functioning; a traumatic encounter which ruins the balance of the symbolic universe of the subject."[16] This interpretation thus fails to understand the procedure whereby a truth is not something on which we chance in a fleeting change of perspective but something that is actively produced, through a step-by-step intervention, after an event. Žižek, for instance, mistakenly sums up Badiou's philosophy by speaking repeatedly of the miracle of a "Truth-Event."[17] Regardless of the awkward capitals, this syncopated and apocryphal expression collapses into an instantaneous act what is in reality an ongoing and impure procedure, which from a singular event will have led to a generic truth by way of a forced return to the initial situation. We thus become privy to something that resembles "a confusion between event and truth, that is, something that reduces the considerable difficulties involved in maintaining fidelity to an event to a matter of pure insurrection."[18] Whereas for Žižek the appearance of the empty place of the real that is impossible to symbolize is somehow already the act of truth itself, for Badiou a truth comes about only by forcing the real and by

displacing the empty place, so as to make the impossible possible. "A truth
is the infinite result of the wager of a supplementation. Every truth is post-
evental. In particular, there is no 'structural' or objective truth," Badiou
writes in *Manifesto for Philosophy*, so the event that in a sudden flash reveals
the void of a given situation cannot itself already be the truth of this situation. Instead, such a truth requires the labor of a process of fidelity in the
long aftermath of an event—hence the need for a militant or at least organized figure of fidelity, such as the one studied in *Saint Paul*: "Fidelity to the
declaration is crucial, for truth is a process, and not an illumination."[19]

If ultimately psychoanalysis gives preference to the act over and above
the event of philosophy, this is because the act is a pivotal category in all
antiphilosophy. The act is precisely that which serves the purpose of putting down the claims to truth of the philosopher. Conversely, antiphilosophy may always treat the event as though it coincided purely and simply
with its own radical concept of the act. Now, this radicality depends in a
large measure on the punctual, evanescent, and self-referential nature of
the antiphilosophical act—an act that, in the final instance, has no guarantee to offer to us other than the intensity, most often personal and bio-
graphical, with which the antiphilosopher announces its imminence. In
Badiou's vocabulary we might also say that the act, even if it defines itself in
terms of the same historical events in the usual sense of the term, ultimately
derives its authenticity, which it screams from the rooftops, only from the
algebraic side of the real, which sees in it a vanishing cause. If Badiou
occasionally seems to fall prey to the temptation to present the event as
such an absolute break or caesura, as dogmatic in its radicalism as it is
blinding in its instantaneity, then this is because he too does not always
resist the siren's song of antiphilosophy.

FURTHER ELEMENTS OF SELF-CRITICISM

Since the publication of *Being and Event*, and in an implicit return to
Theory of the Subject, Badiou has thus formulated a triple self-criticism, a
more complete answer to which was to take up much of the enormous
conceptual energy spent on *Logics of Worlds*.[20]

1. All the stuff of a given situation cannot be fully accounted for in the
   sole terms of belonging, which is the only verb for the ontological
   discourse. The key to understanding the new work, by contrast, lies in

the greater attention given to the question not only of being but also of appearing, or being-there. This logical and topological emphasis will require a remodeling of the concept of the situation, particularly through the theory of categories or *topoi*, as opposed to the strict ontological purview of axiomatic set theory. Astonishingly, this re-orientation is already announced in the author's very first review article, more than forty years ago, with which I began this study. Badiou indeed concludes his analysis of Althusser by pinpointing the problem of how to define that to which the action of a structure is ap-plied. "There must exist a previous formal discipline, which I would be tempted to call the *theory of historical sets*, which contains *at least* the protocols of donation of the pure multiples onto which the struc-tures are progressively constructed," Badiou writes: "This discipline, which is closely tied in its complete development to the mathematics of set theory, no doubt exceeds the simple donation of a procedure of *belonging*, or of an inaugural system of empty differences."[21] This previous discipline is none other than the theory of categories, which, as an expansion of the set theory of *Being and Event*, forms the basis for *Logics of Worlds*. Situations are then constructed no longer purely on the grounds of a relation of being as belonging and the impasse of inclusion, but in terms of networks, trajectories, and paths, which together give topological coherence to a universe of appearing, that is, a world. This logic of appearing, which occupies the whole first half of *Logics of Worlds*, is anticipated in the small unpublished booklet *Being-There*.

2. The ontological perspective, despite numerous elements that work against this reading, nonetheless risks producing an image of the event exclusively defined in terms of a sovereign and punctual irrup-tion of self-belonging, $E \in E$. Badiou's recent work, however, under-scores ever more clearly the extent to which the truth of an event not only constitutes a vanishing apparition of the void of being but also sets off a regime of consequences to which the belaboring of a truth gives way in a forced return to the situation of departure. In addition to the ontological definition of the event, therefore, we must consider its logical aftermath, following the inferences that are the lasting result of the work of the subject. The event not only is a punctual and self-belonging encounter but also opens up a process of successive implications; it surely emerges in a sudden flash, but its traces must

also be elaborated according to a duration and materiality of its own. Without such a process, by contrast, the event may indeed induce comparisons with the notion of the act in psychoanalysis, as in the most recent works of Žižek or Alenka Zupančič.[22] Since the polemic with Lacan in *Theory of the Subject*, however, Badiou has been quite relentless in his effort to counter this temptation of a typically anti-philosophical act, not by ignoring its insights but by closely examining its most forceful inner mechanisms, as in the unpublished seminar "Lacanian Antiphilosophy."

3. The definition of the subject that corresponds to the ontological perspective of the event is also one-sided. It only includes the effects of fidelity, without considering how any enquiry into the truth of a situation encounters other subjective figures as well, such as those of reaction or denial. It is precisely in this sense that *Being and Event* is more limited than *Theory of the Subject*, where the subject is defined in terms both of the act of subjectivization and of the subjective process in which at least four figures are tied in a knot: anxiety, the superego, courage, and justice. *Logics of Worlds* picks up on this older analysis from the point of view of the different conditions of truth in order to distinguish how for each one of these conditions the act of subjectivization likewise opens up a subjective space configured by the complex interplay between the figure of fidelity and its obscure or reactive counterparts. Part of this investigation could already be appreciated in the unpublished seminar "Axiomatic Theory of the Subject."

FOR A RENEWED THEORY OF THE SUBJECT

In this seminar Badiou initially defines the act of subjectivization as a hysterical figure, capable of detaching an opening statement from the event itself, which as such disappears no sooner than it appears. From the event, ontologically defined in terms of self-belonging, $E \in E$, the hysterical act of subjectivization thus consists no longer just in naming the void but in extracting or detaching an indispensable first statement as true: $E \to p$. A declaration of love is no doubt the simplest example of such an operation of detachment. This first figure would be hysterical insofar as the subject of the statement somehow remains personally implicated in the statement itself, as in the Lacanian formula: "Me, the truth, I speak."[23] Every subject of a truth process, in this sense, would first emerge by being hysterical. To derive a regime of consequences from this initial statement and thus to give consistency to a universalizable truth about the entire situation in which the event took place, a masterly figure is required through which a series of further statements can be inferred from the first one that are no longer tied to the particular person of the speaking subject. This inferential process follows the simple rules of logical implication or *modus ponens*: given p, if p → q, then q. While the point of emergence of a new truth is always caught in a hysterical scheme, the operations of the master name the figure of consequent fidelity. Mastery and hysteria would thus appear to be codependent in their mirroring relationship—with both being required before a truth can come into existence. In fact, if the implicated person of the hysterical act of enunciation is the unconscious to be repressed beneath the bar of the mastery of consequences, then we can also say that, vice versa, the unconscious of the hysterical figure is a regime of mastered inferences. Or perhaps the hysterical figure does not "have" an unconscious but somehow "is" the unconscious. The act of subjectivization is necessary but also strictly speaking inconsequential, yet at the same time the enthralling intensity of the hysterical speech act can always be put forward to denigrate and mock the meager outcome of the master's inferences. This is how the hysteric, like any good antiphilosopher who is never far removed from this figure, can remind the master of the need always to begin anew.

Badiou himself rather quickly abandons the twin names—though not the processes—of the master and the hysteric to avoid any confusion with the theory of four discourses in Lacanian psychoanalysis. The last two figures of reaction and obscurantism in Badiou's new axiomatic theory of the subject also correspond only vaguely to Lacan's university discourse and the discourse of the analyst. A subjective figure, rather, becomes reactive whenever the logical outcome of a truth process in retrospect is considered to be indifferent as compared to the event that caused it. This event might as well not have taken place, and the result would still be exactly the same: no matter if p or not-p → q. In a strangely perverse argument the fact that an event has taken place with unmistakable consequences is thus denied. The subjective support of truth is no longer split by an emergent speech act, as in the hysterical figure, nor barred by the labor of consequences, as in the figure of mastery, but purely and simply obliterated. In a certain sense the reactive figure reenacts the "rightist" extreme of the dialectical process discussed above, whereas the obscure figure is en-

raptured by a "leftist" solution, which turns the event from a singular condition into a radical and unattainable origin or act that from time im-
memorial precedes and overwhelms the search for a specific truth in the
present. Knowledge of this transcendent origin is then simply imposed and
transmitted, instead of being actually detached, which means forever to
obscure the possibility that an unprecedented regime of consequences can
be initiated in the here and now by a rare temporal act of subjectivization.
In this denegation of all present temporality the obscure figure is fundamentally a figure of death. Is it a coincidence, then, that Badiou's unpublished seminar parts ways with the Lacanian theory of four discourses
precisely at this point where the obscure figure is discussed? Should we
not consider the passing acknowledgment of sexual difference, of desire
and of the death drive, or, in a politicized reading, the recognition of
the real kernel of social antagonism, as such a radical and obscene absolutely prior origin, which always already threatens to render impossible—
or merely imaginary and naive—the consequent belaboring of a new and
unheard-of truth?

BETWEEN BEING AND EVENT

The ethical would be to rebegin rather than to continue.
—BADIOU, "Théorie axiomatique du sujet"

For Badiou, in the final instance, everything revolves around the question:
how does true change occur in a given situation? Not only: what is being,
on the one hand, and what is the event, on the other? But: what truly
happens *between* ordinary configurations of the multiple of being and their
supplementation by an unforeseeable event?

Even in *Being and Event* the principal concern in my view is not with a
pristine opposition but with the impure difference of being and event, and
the subject is precisely that which operates in the equivocal space of this in-
between. Critics are mostly one-sided in charging his philosophy with
dogmatism or absolutism for relying on a sovereign divide separating being from event, or with decisionism for defining the event in terms of a
strict self-belonging. Whenever Badiou does seem to establish such a divide as that between truth and knowledge, or between being and event,
these should not be taken as two already separate dimensions or spheres,
which moreover only his critics transcribe with large capitals. Rather, from

the point of a subjective intervention, they stand as the extremes of an ongoing process of detachment and scission.

Despite a recurrent temptation by Mallarmé's wager, Badiou is rarely taken in by the absolute purity of truth as a voluntaristic and self-constituent decision in the radical void of the undecidable. To the contrary, much of his philosophical work is guided by the hypothesis that the opposition between being and event, as is that between structure and subject, far from constituting in turn a structural given that would merely have to be recognized, hinge on the rare contingency of a process, an intervention, a labor. Truth, as an ongoing process, actively destroys the premise of a simple face-off, no matter how heroic or melancholy, between an established order of being and the untainted novelty of an event. Was this not, after all, the harsh lesson in dialectical materialism to be drawn from the events of May '68 according to Badiou himself?

Badiou's philosophy, then, can be read as an untimely recommencement of the materialist dialectic in the sense in which the latter actually would be a philosophy not of pure and absolute beginnings but of painstaking rebeginnings. It is a thought of change situated in whatever can be said of being as pure multiple yet supplemented by the irruption of an event, the truth of which emerges not in a unique and instantaneous vanishing act that would coincide with the event itself but rather after the event, in an ongoing process of fits and starts, of destructions and recompositions, of backlashes and resurrections, of fidelity and the extreme fallout of reaction and obscurantism.

An event is a sudden commencement, but only a recommencement produces the truth of this event. Badiou's philosophy could thus be said to obey not one but two ethical imperatives: "Never give up on one's desire!" and "Always continue!" that is, "Always rebegin!"[24] According to a thoroughly reworked materialist dialectic, always to rebegin means for a subject to keep drawing consequences of events that take place in emancipatory politics, artistic experiments, scientific discoveries, and loving encounters; to force these events in return to come to bear generically on the current situation; and thus to bring a precarious regime of truth, as a small fragment of immortality, out of our finite encyclopedias of available knowledge. Far from being a masterly or dogmatic discourse, philosophy only seeks within its own domain to register the effects of these truths that are produced elsewhere and to invent a conceptual space in which to shelter them.

FORCING THE TRUTH

←————————————————————→

THE FOLLY IN PRAISE: STRONG THOUGHT?

> Shut up or gesticulate: it is all the same. In some place or other they already prepared your condemnation. There is no escape that does not lead to infamy or to the scaffold: your dreams are all too clear; what you need is a strong philosophy.—OCTAVIO PAZ, ¿Aguila o sol?

When the first international conference on Badiou's philosophy was held in 1999 in Bordeaux, the organizers felt the need to publicize the event in the name of "strong thought" (*la pensée forte*), even though for the conference proceedings this reference would later be dropped in favor of the far more modest subtitle "thinking the multiple" (*penser le multiple*). The same expression "strong thought" was also scheduled to serve, but, to my knowledge, never actually appeared, as a subtitle for Jason Barker's introductory guide to Badiou's work. Whatever the reasons for this change of mind in either instance, the fact remains that if this philosophy marks indeed a return or a renewal of "strong" or "forceful" thought, the obvious prior question must ask in what consists the strength or force of this thinking. Such praise, if that is what it is, will remain constrained by opinion as long as we do not take into account the conceptual and philosophical reasons behind it. It cannot be a question of adopting the category of force as a simple positive judgment, nor of reducing it, in a flattened version of the cult of personality, to a charismatic personality trait. These approaches would finally remain external, no doubt useful to the chroniclers of philosophy but without much interest for our understanding of this thinker's work, either in its own right or in relation to its peculiar site in the contemporary philosophical situation. We should analyze, in other words, in what sense a certain passage through force is constitutive of all truth procedures from within the purview of Badiou's own philosophy.

In this chapter, therefore, I want to raise a limited number of questions that bear on the process of the forcing of truth. If our task is not just to explicate but to grasp what singularizes Badiou's work, it is indeed this concept of forcing, together with that of the site, that in my eyes should occupy the center stage inasmuch as it allows us to delimit the intimate distance that, all appearances of proximity notwithstanding, separates this philosopher from the vast majority of his contemporaries, particularly those who work in the neighboring traditions—no doubt among the most important ones in terms of what can be seized of our epoch in thought—of Lacan and Heidegger. A truth, when it is effectuated as a truthful part of the situation, is always forced: such is the insight that will oblige us, first of all, to trace a much more trenchant line of demarcation than usual between Badiou's thinking and the work of philosophers who otherwise may feel close to him, such as Jean-Luc Nancy, Philippe Lacoue-Labarthe, Ernesto Laclau, Chantal Mouffe, Slavoj Žižek, or Alenka Zupančič. This effect of proximity can be explained by various reasons, among which we should certainly count the very notion of the event itself such as it is laid out in *Being and Event*: between the One that is not and the subject of a generic truth. Even while taking their inspiration above all from Heidegger or Lacan, if not from Derrida or Levinas, many of these readers after all may have recognized themselves in Badiou's thinking of the event as a formal defection, or systematic deconstruction, of the One. As François Wahl has observed, "the entire ontological gesture of Badiou can be understood as a deconstruction of the One."[1] In fact, in the long aftermath of the closure of the metaphysical age, the event is precisely that which unites almost all great thinkers on the scene of French philosophy today. This also means, however, that the effective impact of the thought of the event in the current situation remains by and large an obscure affair.

The list would become too long if I were to enumerate all the contemporary philosophers whose entire work revolves around some notion or other of the event. François Zourabichvili's opening remark in his study of Deleuze should in this sense be understood as a warning: "The theme of the event sits today at the center of philosophical preoccupations, it animates the most daring and original attempts. But the spirit of the time does not in and of itself produce a philosophy and it should not mask irreconcilable differences."[2] To affirm about almost any thinker whatsoever that he or she is a thinker of the event thus risks reducing their thought to the spirit of the time, if not to opinion pure and simple. If, on the other hand, we seek to broach the truth by which this thinking of the event is tied to the present of our actuality, we should trace a new set of demarcations. In this regard, perhaps it has never been more urgent to unmask the irreconcilable differences that separate Badiou's thinking from the double tradition marked by the proper names of Heidegger and Lacan.

These differences, I should add at the risk of repeating myself, cannot be easily grasped if the reader ignores all the work prior to *Being and Event*—a book whose utterly classical title tends to hide what happens in the subjective space in between its two terms. What singularizes Badiou's thought is not only the ontological delimitation of the event in terms of a fulgurating cut, or a punctual encounter of the real, but also its logical and topological inscription at the heart of a given situation according to the labor of different subjective figures. According to this reading, what matters the most is not so much the abrupt irruption of a point of the impossible, or of a set that paradoxically belongs only to itself, but the implicative regime of consequences to which an event will have given way in the aftermath of its irruption.

In a first moment, I will clarify the stakes of the debate, even if this means indicating some of the ambiguities that surround the notion of the event as it is put to use in *Being and Event*, both as an alternative to the thinking of being in Heidegger and as an answer to the thinking of the real that anchors the question of the subject in Lacan. Now, if the situation remains potentially obscure as far as the idea of the event is concerned, by contrast all common ground with hermeneutics or psychoanalysis is lost when we take into account the long philosophical trajectory that, from *Theory of the Subject* all the way to the continuation of *Being and Event* in *Conditions* and *Ethics*, is marked first by the idea of torsion, even destruction, and then, by the concept of forcing. In a second step of the argument, I will thus take a shortcut through this conceptual itinerary behind the notion of forcing the truth—the mathematical side must not concern us here—in order to map out in what way it marks a decisive point of bifurcation with regard to large parts of contemporary thinking.

This attempt at a demarcation, I might add, will not borrow the familiar path of separating "strong thinking" from "weak thinking" (*pensiero debole*) in the Italian tradition of Gianni Vattimo and Pier Aldo Rovatti. In France, even more so than in Italy itself, at least for some time, such a rejection constituted almost a ritual—without excluding a certain tone of peremptory or festive derision. The staging of a debate of this kind—against the weakness of a thinking of which no text is ever specifically addressed—holds in my eyes only a limited interest, which is that of operating by way of a symptom. Indeed, what is hidden behind the virulent attacks against Nietzsche's and Heidegger's disciples from the other side of the Alps, if not the judges' own Achilles heel?

Thus, the late Lacoue-Labarthe, who for years devoted himself to the unforgiving interpretation of Heidegger's political mistake, after declaring that one should be "without desire for philosophy," nonetheless feels the need to preempt all possible confusion by adding the following expediting remark in a footnote: "This statement by no means gives support to the complacent notion of *pensiero diebole* [*sic*] introduced by Vattimo and Rovatti a few years ago," given that for the author of this note, "the renunciation of the volontarist *habitus* keeps itself necessarily in the form of a heroism, in the *modern* sense of the term, which is, for example, that of Baudelaire or Benjamin."[3] What is questionable in this line of reasoning, beyond the specific functioning of weak or postmodern thinking, is precisely this other tradition that pretends to be its natural, still modern adversary inasmuch as it renounces all metaphysical will only to ascribe to itself a radicalism that is, after all, more heroic than ever. This is, in all its acuteness, the problematic of which the diatribes against "weak thinking" are only one symptom among others: how does thinking these days manage to be a hero of the renunciation of the desire for philosophy? What is more, how is this tradition, which I will call "radical thinking," capable of attacking the philosophy of Badiou?

Indeed, there is a growing trend in contemporary thought that consists in erecting oneself as an imperious authority, most often following in the steps of Heidegger or Lacan, sometimes together with Derrida or Levinas, in a posture that bars all effective processes of truth by putting itself at once at the service of an implacable lucidity, sometimes melancholy and at other times tragic, with regard to their limits. This condemnation follows a paradoxical temporal logic that ends up being irrefutable, insofar as it finds its reasons in the supposedly violent effects of a process that at the same time and because of this anticipated condemnation is guaranteed never to take place anyhow. The irrefutability of these radical arguments constitutes a decisive issue whose logic is worth formalizing. In any case the overall result of this tendency is clear in that fidelity is blocked even before it can open up any truth procedure whatsoever—either because the latter would appear as yet another avatar of the metaphysical will, or because it falls under the anathema of being of an imaginary or religious nature, or, finally, in a strange combination of both criticisms, because it would be exemplary of a volontarism that is as dogmatic as it is illusory. When this tendency of "radical thinking" does not lead to a kind of aestheticism that would seek merely to *show, expose,* or *render* the real instead of *forcing* it, in terms of politics such a blockage of truth as process most often ends up being a subtle form of Thermidorianism, that is, a subjective figure of cessation whose principal effect is to void the operativity of action, in the sense discussed in *Metapolitics*. (Badiou, in this regard, could certainly have found worthier adversaries among the disciples of Heidegger and Lacan, instead of continuing to interpellate the ex-Maoist renegades who turned almost overnight into the New Philosophers.)

One of the keys in the radical critique of Badiou's thought is precisely the notion of forcing, in the sense that a procedure of truth would in and of itself do violence to the truth—meaning, of course, to an *other* truth, which is also the truth *of the* other, and not the truth as defined by Badiou. It is not only Heidegger or Derrida or Levinas who serve here as reference points for a critique of metaphysical violence, since with a different set of concepts but following a strictly homologous reasoning, as we saw before in the case of Žižek, such a critique can equally well find support in Lacan's antiphilosophy.

Our attempt at demarcation should thus equally address the contemporary trend of "radical" thinking, capable of repudiating not only the "weakness" that would be proper to Vattimo and Rovatti but also the alleged "dogmatism" that this same argument attributes to the philosophy of Badiou. Even if, in principle, it cannot be a question of refuting such forms of radical thinking without completely changing terrain, at least we can offer a reply, no longer by taking as our point of departure the established authority of Heidegger or Lacan but by examining the work of Badiou himself. In a third moment I will thus turn the tables and ask what light the procedure of forcing sheds on this strange polemic, that is, not so much the false debate between "strong" and "weak" thinkers, which to this date remains at best a symptomatic affair, but rather the much more difficult polemic between "radicals" and "dogmatists."[4]

Finally, though, these observations cannot take away the impression that the idea of forcing the truth seems by definition to imply the risk of an abuse, just as the idea of torsion seems almost naturally to evoke that of a wrong, or tort. This will lead us back to the ethical question of the consciousness or conscience of evil. Indeed, from all sides the thought of forcing seems besieged by the risk that would push the process, beyond its proper limits, to the point of disaster. It is moreover this very same risk that justifies the conceptual link established by Badiou's critics between forcing and violence, or between destruction and disaster, whereas the task should really consist in establishing a clear delimitation of the two, in the extent to which such a clear delimitation is even possible. In a fourth and final step, therefore, I will take up the question whether there are indeed intrinsic limits to the process by which a truth passes through a moment of force in one or the other of the generic conditions that define philosophy all along the itinerary of Badiou's work. Is there no stopping point to the process of forcing? And if it were imperative to recognize such a stopping point, would this finally permit us to discern what separates Badiou's thinking from the twin traditions transmitted by Lacan and Heidegger?

LINES OF DEMARCATION

In order to counter the enigma, let us exaggerate it.
—BADIOU, *Theory of the Subject*

With regard to this question, let me start by enumerating some basic facts, beginning with the two books that toward the late 1980s mark an apparent turning point in Badiou's oeuvre: What is, according to *Being and Event* and *Manifesto for Philosophy*, the rapport between Badiou's thinking and that of Heidegger and Lacan?

Heidegger remains, first of all, "the last universally recognizable philosopher,"[5] who will later continue to be interpellated as the one responsible for the renewal of the ontological question: "Our epoch can be said to have been stamped and signed, in philosophy, by the return of the question of Being. This is why it is dominated by Heidegger."[6] In fact, Badiou's generic philosophy of the event is inaugurated by the *refusal* to pursue the themes of the end and the distress according to the hermeneutico-historical path that takes its inspiration from Heidegger's thinking. This refusal, and the accompanying search for an alternative metaontological orientation, that is, the clearing of a path *to the side* of those roads that lead nowhere except to the interpretation of the sense of being, really constitute the founding gesture of Badiou's renewed Platonism. We do well to recall the two motifs that give unity to this inaugural gesture. On the one hand, the aim is to substitute an axiomatic ontology of subtraction for the hermeneutic ontology of presence and the retreat of presence, of the enigma and unconcealment of meaning; on the other, the project consists in interrupting, through the consistent pursuit of the matheme, the suture of philosophy onto the sole poem, by taking one further step in the unfolding of the intrinsic power of each of the four procedures of truth that are science, politics, art, and love.

The treatment of the hermeneutic tradition in *Being and Event* and *Manifesto for Philosophy*, for these same reasons, can nonetheless lead to a number of misunderstandings. It presumes, first of all, that one accepts the description, which is supposed to be consensual, of hermeneutics as a thinking of presence. This description, however, is surprising to an extreme, insofar as it hides the extent to which hermeneutic ontology, too, including in its posthumous avatars in weak thinking, claims to be a thinking of the event. If we simply accept the opposition of subtraction and presence, it thus becomes extremely difficult to grasp in what sense the event of being, for hermeneutics, serves precisely to deconstruct rather than to restore the metaphysics of presence. This potential debate is obscured not only because hermeneutic thinking is voided of its eventlike potential but also, and this is the second reason why there might be a misunderstanding involved, because the ontology of presence is utterly and completely identified with, not to say reduced to, the operation that sutures philosophy to the poem. "What we must recall from Heidegger," Badiou also writes, "is the idea that, in times of distress, thought is foremost on the way to speech,"[7] so that the only possible answer to the hermeneutic tradition necessarily passes through a desuturing of philosophy and the poem: "For this reason, the fundamental criticism of Heidegger can only be the following one: the Age of the Poets is finished, it is necessary *also* to de-suture philosophy from its poetic condition."[8]

This partial and biased reading of hermeneutic ontology explains why, in the wake of the publication of *Being and Event* and *Manifesto for Philosophy*, the debate with the Heideggerian tradition became fixated on the question of the "age of the poets," Badiou's notion that also gives its title to his conference for the seminar organized by Jacques Rancière, *La Politique des poètes: Pourquoi des poètes en temps de détresse?*[9] Witness, for example, the few public exchanges that took place, sometimes hidden a vay in a footnote at the bottom of the page, with Nancy and Lacoue-Labar he. The latter summarizes the debate, or rather reopens it, by stating that the problem cannot be reduced to a suture of philosophy to the sole poem, since the true question at issue is rather some kind of political resuturing of the artistic suture, that is, the aestheticization of politics of which Benjamin already spoke: "There is, if you want, some kind of misunderstanding, which bears on poetry, for sure, but also on politics—or at the very least on a determinate type of politics, even a style, to which the philosophy from which Badiou seeks to demarcate himself is not foreign."[10] At the same time, Lacoue-Labarthe's answer puts into question the link between art, philosophy, and politics, from the point of view not so much of the poem but of the mytheme, in the sense of an immanent putting-to-work of the collective. Of such fictive putting-to-work or self-fashioning we all know only too well what are the disastrous consequences in what Lacoue-Labarthe and Nancy, in *The Nazi Myth*, call "national-aestheticism."[11] To this disastrous outcome we can then barely begin to oppose, on the one hand, the idea of a becoming-prose of poetry, that is, the interruption of myth, and, on the other, the retreat of the political, which is at once a new treatment of that which retreats, or of that which never took place to begin with, for instance, the idea of sovereignty, as the condition both of the possibility and the radical impossibility of politics as such.

By contrast, the clear ontological alternatives between the paths of presence and subtraction, or, in terms of the conditions of philosophy, between the poem and the matheme—these decisions, which are absolutely fundamental to Badiou's philosophy, seem to carry no weight at all for someone like Nancy, who is otherwise ideally placed to judge the questions of art and the event according to Heidegger. In his quite beautiful book *The Sense of the World*, for instance, Nancy comes to a point where he is able to find in the mathematical ontology of substraction what he considers to be "certain formulations that are strictly equivalent to those to which a deconstruction of onto-theology leads," with the difference between the two paths being reduced, by way of "a carefully arranged lexical transcription," to a mere question of styles or modes, whether "a more pathetic mode (Heidegger) or a cooler one (Badiou)."[12] Despite the affir-

mation of a trenchant rupture, some of the subtlest readers of the ontology
of presence thus find nothing if not another endeavor in the general deconstruction of metaphysics when they turn to Badiou.

In sum, *Being and Event*, in spite of an axiomatic elaboration that is in all
regards impeccable, leaves open more than just a few trapdoors in its
monumental edifice.

In the first place, with regard to Heidegger it is not so much a matter of
defining a thought of the event in opposition to the oblique approach of
presence so much as it is a question of opposing two clearly distinct ideas
of the event itself. Besides, in order to elucidate this last opposition, we
might even argue that many of the necessary elements are convoked in
Badiou's *Deleuze*, a book that in this sense talks almost as much of Heidegger as it does of Deleuze.

In the second place, the space for this harsh and often hushed polemic
cannot be reduced to the problems relative to the age of the poets, during
which philosophy ends up being sutured to the enigma of being proffered
by the poetic word. To the contrary, the polemic further extends to other
conditions as well. Thus, an updated confrontation with the path of deconstruction should also bear on the efforts to delimit what the condition
of politics, or of the political, holds for us today, after the critique both of its
immanent presentation by the people or masses and of its external representation by the state. In this regard the reader of *Metapolitics* might have
wished to find a discussion of the collective project surrounding the seminars *Rejouer le politique* and *Le Retrait du politique*, organized several years
ago by Nancy and Lacoue-Labarthe—a project in which Badiou participated with the two conferences that were later published in *Can Politics Be
Thought?*—not to forget the writings of Laclau and Mouffe, especially in
Hegemony and Socialist Strategy, in which the labor of deconstruction is
pursued in search for a new politics of so-called radical democracy.[13] For
sure, such a reading, which I will undertake myself in the next chapter,
would have led to a wholly different outlook, irreducible to the oppositions
of poem and matheme, or presence and subtraction, in order to serve up an
answer to the deconstruction of metaphysics following the steps of Heidegger and Derrida.

The demarcation is equally difficult and thorny, but for entirely different reasons, when we turn our attention to the other major tradition
that serves as an interlocutor for *Being and Event*, namely, the condition of
psychoanalysis after Lacan. Here, too, the effort of a distancing is clearly

announced, but this time it is no longer a question of passing *to the side* so much as of going *beyond* the maligned master. As I mentioned in the previous chapter, however, it seems to me that even in this case, albeit less clearly so than in the case of Heidegger, *Being and Event* is open to a misguided identification. The reader's task is only further complicated by the fact that after this major work, in the conferences from *Conditions* and in a number of interventions still unpublished in France but partially available in Latin America, most notably in Brazil and Argentina, what we see is rather a crossed encounter between philosophy and psychoanalysis, over and above Lacan's own statements on antiphilosophy.[14] In these texts we come to a point where Badiou shows that Lacan says fundamentally the same thing as Plato, all the while inverting the sign of the imaginary with which the psychoanalyst received (or declared nonreceivable) the philosophical lesson of Plato, which Lacan thought needed to be replaced by the discourse of the analyst that he finds in the words of Socrates.

For reasons of circumstance to which a militant form of thought is always bound to respond, this is one of the rare changes of position—the other one being dominated by the progressive and still ambivalent abandonment of the dialectical tradition as discussed in the previous chapters—in Badiou's work. Of course, this body of work contains numerous additions and lengthy amplifications but not really any fundamental break, despite what many have called the mathematical turn.

Reread *Of Ideology* and already you will find all the elements for a critique of the philosophers of desire as "pure force," a critique that would later be reiterated in strictly ontological terms in Badiou's *Deleuze*, with the exception of the slandering adjectives and the insults; open *Theory of Contradiction*, only to come up against the notion that May '68 constituted a blinding event to which the author would not cease to bear witness until tracing its formal trajectory, thirty years later, in his *Saint Paul*; or, again, take *Theory of the Subject*, and already you will find, though still sutured to politics, the four generic procedures of truth, as well as the ideas of the event and its site, here called the "outplace" of the " 'splace'," or the ethical work of fidelity in the name of "courage" and "justice" over and beyond "anxiety" and the "superego," following the process that would reappear in *Ethics* and, in a truly remarkable manner, in the seminars devoted to a new *Axiomatic Theory of the Subject* in preparation for *Logics of Worlds*. By contrast, if we read only "Antiphilosophy: Lacan and Plato," Badiou's talk at the famous conference "Lacan with the Philosophers" that is taken up in

Conditions, we will experience grave difficulties to understand what can well have been the cause for the brutal split, ten or fifteen years earlier, introduced in the first version of *Theory of the Subject*.

We thus must go back in time in order to be able to ground the desire, still latent today but in somewhat muted terms, to move beyond Lacan. What is, first of all, the heart of the polemic with psychoanalysis in *Being and Event* and *Conditions*? Just as in the case of the debate with hermeneutic ontology, this struggle too can be summarized by two motifs. Badiou proposes, on one hand, a reaffirmation of philosophy by way of its clarifying separation, through Platonism, from the statements of antiphilosophy; on the other, he insists on reinforcing the mathematical paradigm in order to resist the temptation to let oneself be seduced by the themes of finitude, the untranscendable horizon of language, or even the projection of the real of enjoyment into a properly religious or mystical beyond, insofar as it resists all symbolization—themes that were borrowed, either by the master himself or by some of his disciples, from the hermeneutic and neoexistentialist traditions. These two operations summarize quite aptly the rapport of inner distancing, or crossed approaching, between Lacanian psychoanalysis and Badiou's philosophy.

Where, then, lies the exact place of the division? According to the final meditations in *Being and Event*, as we saw in the previous chapter, this distance not only depends on the location of the void, whether as lack or as empty or void-set, on the side of being or on the side of the subject: "Yes or no," Badiou asks, "is the void-set the proper name of being qua being? Or is it necessary to think that it is the subject for which such a name is appropriate?"[15] On closer inspection, however, it turns out that it is perhaps equally important to distinguish what happens at the place of the void and, thus, to qualify the nature of the latter, rather than merely to alternate its location. For Lacan, as I said before, the thinking of truth remains constrained by a logic of the impasse, or even by the *passe* as a pure impasse of the structure, whereas for Badiou, the whole point is to anchor in the impasse the forced passage of a subject who would no longer be directly transitive to the structure of being and to the inner excess of its representation but who, in the aftermath of an event's taking place, can be said to be rare, local, and yet immortal: "The choice here is between a structural recurrence, which thinks the subject-effect as void-set, thus as identifiable within the uniform networks of experience, and a hypothesis of the rarity of the subject, which suspends its occurrence from the event, from the intervention, and from the generic paths of fidelity, both returning the void to, and reinsuring it within, a function of suture to being, the knowledge of which is deployed by mathematics alone."[16]

This is precisely the point where the polemic with Lacan finally rejoins the debate with the hermeneutic tradition in the wake of Heidegger. As François Wahl explains in his introductory essay in *Conditions*: "According to Lacan, only an empty subject can be sutured to the discourse of science; whereas, according to Badiou, the void is rather what sutures the subject to being. In other words: Lacan still makes being come to presence in language, whereas Badiou grants a 'little' being to the—rare—subject, but being is thought only by subtraction."[17] The trajectory behind this further disagreement, though, may not be so easily mapped out when we follow the final section of *Being and Event* or the conferences on philosophy and psychoanalysis from *Conditions*, whereas it is precisely what defines the central stakes behind Badiou's entire *Theory of the Subject*.

Clarifying this division, which in my eyes is pivotal for the polemic not only with Lacan but also with Heidegger, both being considered as commonplaces of contemporary thinking, also allows us to situate the misunderstanding that has already formed around Badiou's work, not only in the United States and the United Kingdom but also in France. I have already alluded to certain thinkers, like Nancy, who seem to experience no difficulty whatsoever in ignoring the distance that, according to Badiou's work itself, should separate it from Heideggerian thinking. More recently, with regard to the legacy of Lacan, Žižek has taken on Badiou's *Saint Paul*, first of all, and, then, *Being and Event*, in order to reveal in them what he considers a dogmatic form of thinking that, especially with regard to the death drive, runs even the risk of denial and pure nonthought: "When Badiou adamantly opposes the 'morbid obsession with death,' when he opposes the Truth-Event to the death drive, and so on, he is at his weakest, succumbing to the *temptation of the non-thought*."[18] Žižek himself seeks to avoid this temptation, not without some speculative haste, thanks to a mode of thinking that would be more recognizing of the radical negativity that is still always that of repetition and the death drive.

What a curious chiasmus, on the part of these readers, between their sense of proximity there where the author himself posits the need for an absolute choice, in one way or the other, and their postulate of an insurmountable distance there where the author hints at the possibility of a progressive rapprochement! Clearly, we are in need of new lines of demarcation, or at the very least the recall of old partitions now fallen into oblivion. On the one hand, we must undo the evidence of an all-too-superficial refusal of the ontology of presence by remarking the place of the true disagreement, as far as Heidegger's legacy is concerned, and, on the other, we must put into context the more recent essays in rapprochement so as to reaffirm, in all its original force, the previous dislocation with regard to the legacy of Lacan. Such is the double purpose of this chapter, which I hope will foster the polemic with further interventions by way of a reply or a rejoinder.

In this missed encounter, finally, the reader will have noticed that it is the notion of the event itself that lends itself to misunderstandings. This is either because one recognizes in it the only question worthy of thought, namely, the coming to presence of being itself, with all this implies in terms of the defeat of the metaphysics of presence; or because one sees in it a transcription of the kernel of the real, as a point of the impossible in the midst of the symbolic order—an alternative that can then always be turned back, in a supposedly ever more radical way, against the philosophy of the event in Badiou himself.

Donation of being or act of the real: because of the general homonymy that surrounds the idea of the event today, a large part of contemporary thought, precisely that part that roughly follows either a deconstructive-hermeneutic or a psychoanalytic orientation, will have been able to recognize itself, as in a deforming mirror, in what is certainly a master concept of Badiou's entire oeuvre. By contrast, that which, perhaps more than any other concept, separates the generic philosophy of the event both from the interpretation of the meaning of being and from the science of the real and its formalization, is the notion of forcing, which together with veridicity and the unnameable is part of what we might call the doctrine of the passage through the impasse.

THE PASSAGE THROUGH THE IMPASSE

Forcing? Who said forcing? Who, even in a language that cannot be heard, speaking to himself, would have committed the imprudence of saying "forcing"?—NATHALIE SARRAUTE, *Vous les entendez?*

In order to get to the heart of the disagreement, I thus propose to go back in time. Indeed, even if "forcing" names a concept whose ontologico-mathematical scaffolding is not completed until the final meditations of *Being and Event*, it is already fully operative, from a logico-dialectical point of view, in the seminar from some twenty years before, in *Theory of the Subject*.

In this first approach, as I discussed in chapter 2, the idea of forcing serves above all to mark the intimate distance that separates the materialist dialectic from the structural one found in Lacan. The latter, in fact, remains on the idealist side of the dialectic insofar as it proposes a thinking of the place and its lack, following a logic that opposes the set of assigned places vis-à-vis that which has an impact on this ensemble only by vanishing into it, reabsorbing and annulling its very excess. According to Badiou, the only way to be loyal to the materialist dialectic is by pursuing the division of the place by that rare force that exceptionally interrupts the established order in a strange torsion back onto that which excludes it. It is this reflective torsion, which is symptomatic at the start and destructive in the end, that is called "forcing," including in its strict mathematical sense, in *Being and Event* or *Conditions*.

Roughly speaking, it is a question of passing from a relation of internal exclusion, which is still too structurally complementary, between places and forces, to the spiraling torsion of the former by the latter. As Badiou affirms: "Force is that which, on the bases of the repeatable, and by dividing itself from it, occurs as non-repeatable," in a logic of torsion that alone makes the truth of the event: "From this point of view, just as there is only one subject, there is also only one force, whose existence always surfaces as an event."[19] The event, therefore, does not depend solely on the coming into being of a lack of being nor on the showing of a being in retreat. A truth does not coincide with the gap or impasse in the structure, nor should we identify the void, on the edges of which an event occurs, purely and simply with the truth of the situation of which this gap would be the symptom. What is more, an empty place cannot even be located as such if it were not for the upsurge of an event, of which a subject will have constituted a local instance.

Take the example of the political procedure. Badiou writes: "It is not an empty place, not even that of power, that triggers the emergence, in the disorder of the political, of the subject of its occupation."[20] On the contrary, by taking one further step that is absolutely essential, it is also necessary to exceed this unoccupyable empty place. We can conclude from this that the true is always forced, submitted as it is to a torsion of force onto the very place that divides it. "Therein lies the subjective essence of the true: that it is twisted," as Badiou further writes: "The torsion of the true designates a circularity without unity of plan, a discontinuous curve."[21] It is only at the cost of such a torsion, dislocation, or breakdown of the rule, which corresponds to the forcing of the situation, that finally the effect will be broken by which the impossible would remain bound by the law of structure. For this to happen, the intervening trajectory of a subject will have been necessary—that is to say, a loyal trajectory of finite investigations and forced anticipations, suspended from the infinity of a generic truth, which itself is convoked by an event at the edges of the void.

In sum, just as in *Theory of the Subject* it is necessary to divide the rule of lack from the process of its torsion, which alone is capable of producing something new, so also in *Being and Event* it is necessary to supplement the dialectic of void and excess with a subject's labor of forcing.

A second reminder of the differend between Badiou and Lacan will also allow us to refine the arguments that are at play in the polemic with Heideggerianism. In this case it is no longer the opposition between lack and torsion that is at stake but the opposition, which cuts diagonally across the first, between cause and consistency, or between algebra and topology.

As we saw in chapter 1, much of Badiou's work represents an extended critique of the doctrine of absent causality that, toward the end of the 1960s, was supposed to lay the groundwork for a renewal of dialectical materialism. According to this doctrine every structure is overdetermined by a cause whose effects vanish in the whole of which it guarantees the conditions of existence. For Badiou this doctrine—once the real is circumscribed as cause of the totality on the basis of the latter's symptomatic inconsistencies—nonetheless is unable to think the real as that which gives way to a new consistency. It is thus unable to deliver anything but the repetition of the law and the lack that overdetermines it. By contrast, in order fully to become materialist, the dialectic will have to think not only the cause but also consistency—just as psychoanalysis, after giving primacy to the structure or to the symbolic order, barely begins to think the consistency of the real: "There is no more imperious demand than to keep the distance between cause and consistency as the dialectical division of the-effects-of-the-real. What is thereby at stake is the subject."[22]

Algebra or topology? Cause or consistency? At first sight these two questions would seem to suffice to discern the respective influences on contemporary thinking of Lacan and Heidegger. Thus, the former aims to situate the point of the real in order to answer, by means of the efficacy of a vanishing cause, the theological question of the supreme being, whereas the latter proposes to deconstruct the metaphysical tradition by opening the algebra of the cause to the topological unlimitation of consistency, poetically evoked in the name of the open. In fact, in a remarkable interview with Natacha Michel, published in the newsletter *Le Perroquet* on the occasion of the publication of *Theory of the Subject*, Badiou breaks with this strict alternative by including even Heidegger's thought in the doctrine of structural causality that takes its inspiration, after Spinoza and Freud, from Lacan and Althusser. Even hermeneutic ontology, through the idea of the retreat of being, would depend on a doctrine of the vanishing term: "In Heidegger you find in fact a speculative formalism of the causality of lack because being is active in its oblivion, which makes of Heidegger a contemporary thinker. All the more so in that what he prophesies is that the rediscovery of the consistent proximity of being is reached precisely by depunctuating the cause."[23] Whether being is defined as the event of the open or as a point of the real, whether one gains access to it by way of interpreting the poem or by formalizing the signifier, in order for a new truth to occur in the situation, we must supplement the thought of the causal efficacy of lack with the consistent recomposition of the being of this lack.

Ultimately, this is how *Theory of the Subject* allows us to reaccentuate the doctrine of the forcing of truth in *Being and Event*:

1. It is a question not only of locating the void or of depunctuating the open but also of articulating, in a single subjective mesh, the lack and the destruction, the void and the forcing, the impasse and the pass.
2. It is a question not only of opposing nature to history, or structure to history, but also of articulating a structural impasse with its event-related subjectivization, all the while sidestepping the conventional redoubling of the objective and the subjective, of the transcendental and the empirical.

Truth, in order to become effective in the situation, must be forced. That this is always the case should not be understood in the sense of a structural invariant. Forcing is, on the contrary, that which in principle breaks, through a symptomatic and reflective torsion, with all structural or transcendental points of view—even with those cases in which, as happens so often today, the structure is supposed to include what we might call its point of internal excess, its constitutive outside. Furthermore, this break with the point of view of structure, or of nature, far from being necessary, is in turn aleatory, risky, and fragile to an extreme. I would even say, remembering one of the most striking pages from Badiou's *Saint Paul*, that forcing is a tenacious process that gives way to the experience of an extreme weakness: "Whoever is the subject of a truth (of love, of art, or science, or politics) knows that, in effect, he bears a treasure, that he is traversed by an infinite capacity. Whether or not this truth, so precarious, continues to deploy itself depends solely on his subjective weakness."[24] It would thus be utterly misguided to flaunt the force or strength of this philosopher's thinking by mocking the so-called weak thinking of his contemporaries.

WHAT IS RADICAL THINKING?

La faim qui d'aucun fruit ici ne se régale
Trouve en leur docte manque une saveur égale.
—STÉPHANE MALLARMÉ, *Œuvres*

We are now in a better position to return to the question of radical thinking, whose adversary is considered not too weak but too dogmatic. It is clear wherein lies the guarantee of radicalism in the case of hermeneutic or psychoanalytic thinking, namely, in the presence in retreat, or even the apparition, subtracted from all language games, of a vanishing term—either the event of being that gives itself only by withdrawing itself, or the real as the cause that resists absolutely to be symbolized. Such a point, which interrupts the thinking of representation by bearing witness to an intractable caesura, by this very fact opens up the properly perverse or obscurantist possibility of canceling out all generic procedures by taking away everything they might eventually carry in terms of immanent truth.

The problem, therefore, is not only the suture to the poem, or the primacy of the signifier; there is also a new way of thinking politics, or of thinking the political, that in this manner finds the means to recover itself in a typically melancholy fashion. It can do so, however, only by finding support in a bottomless foundation that itself remains off-limits or off-site. And it is precisely this capacity to open up the perspective to a constitutive outside that guarantees to this mode of thinking an insurmountable degree of radicalism with regard to all those other philosophies that will then always appear to be metaphysical or imaginary or dogmatic, because they are based on a fidelity to an active process of intervention in the situation.

Let me try to turn the tables and provide a diagnostic of this radical thinking from the point of view of Badiou's own philosophy. Nearly all contemporary forms of thinking that could be called radical in this sense ultimately revolve around two operations, the general effect of which in my eyes is the simultaneous evacuation of the event, of truth, and of the subject:

1. Radical thinking reduces the event to the site of its possibility, that is, to the point of excess that is unrepresentable according to the language of the situation itself. This point of excess, however, can nevertheless allow the radical thinkers to rejoin the philosophy of generic truths, most notably through the doctrine of the unnameable.
2. The point of excess is identified with that which always already causes a deadlock in the order of representation, that is, with a gap, or a ground in retreat, which from the outset marks the donation or emergence of being, as well as the identity or splitting of the subject.

In this double treatment, not only is the event reduced to its mere site, but this site does not even really open a historical situation, since it rather leads back to the order of nature, or to the structure, regardless of whether nature and structure are in immanent excess over and above themselves.

The gift of being opens the path to its vanishing, but it is the oscillation of this vanishing being that, once it is annulled or foreclosed, constitutes the bottomless ground, for instance, of what defines the political today— once it is accepted that the political can no longer be defined in terms of the identification of a social bond but rather by the retreat of all bonds and all identities.

In the perspective proper to radical thinking, the event itself ultimately comes to coincide with being and with truth. This means both to ontologize the event and to eventalize being. But this means at the same time the suspension of all truth as an effective process. Indeed, what is evacuated from the horizon of the thinkable in radical thought is precisely the idea of a situation that is historical and not purely structural or statelike; furthermore, what is also lacking is a process of torsion or forcing of the situation in which the historical site of the event will have opened the hole of a specific impossibility.

By contrast, in order for a generic truth to take place in the situation, we must posit that there will have been an event and not only the site of its foreclosed possibility; there will have been an active intervention in the situation, which thus becomes historical, and not only a lack of being of the structure; there will have been fidelity to the processes of truth, which produce the passage of a subject, and not only the interminable analysis of the impasses of the real; and finally, there will have been a forcing of the truthfulness of the situation depending on its generic extension, and not only the recognition of the excess, or of the void, in a gap that is always already immanent to the structure.

In sum, is it a question of avoiding misrecognition by finding sustenance in the bottomless ground of the real, this point of little or no being that is both the obstacle and the vanishing cause of the order of thinking? Or should we move beyond recognition, even beyond respect for the other, bypassing all these good intentions that without knowing it may hide the desire not so much to recognize or respect the other but to be recognized and found respectable oneself? And this further step, like the step beyond Lacan or the step to the side of Heidegger that Badiou so stubbornly seeks out in *Being and Event*, if it dares to ignore the desire of respectability, should it not also risk the forcing of truth?

Is forcing, finally, an essential feature of every process of truth, or does it rather constitute an excess with regard to the generic procedures themselves? If fidelity is the name of the sustained enquiry, from the point of view of a chance event, into a given situation, shall we say that forcing marks a breakdown in this fidelity in the direction of evil, or is a certain breakdown of the rule inseparable from this process? In other words, is truth always forced, or does this happen only when, instead of being loyal to the true, violence is done to it?

In the end the difficulty with the notion of forcing consists in thinking at the same time the event in the situation, without falling into pure immanence, and the event outside the situation, without invoking an absolute transcendence. This comes down to following a kind of spiraling trajectory through the oppositions of inside and outside, of immanence and transcendence, of constructivism and mysticism—all the while avoiding the radical answer, which today has become somewhat of a commonplace and which consists in reducing this relation of internal exclusion to a purely structural given. For a true production of new knowledges to happen, in any case, a breakdown of the rule, a passage by force, or a symptomatic torsion will have been necessary, marking a series of intervening ruptures that can then always be interpreted as being too violent from the point of view that nowadays combines the deconstruction of metaphysics with the psychoanalytical critique of the subject. However, it is precisely in such terms that Badiou defines the process of forcing in his *L'Éthique*: "We shall say that the truth *forces* knowledges. The verb *to force* indicates that since the power of a truth is that of a break, it is by violating established and circulating knowledges that a truth returns to the immediacy of the situation, or reworks that sort of portable encyclopaedia from which opinions, communications and sociality draw their meaning."[25] Without the violent return of a truth to the situation all there ultimately will have been are established facts or consensual opinions, significations, and interpretations. Is it not surprising and paradoxical, then, to notice that such a reshuffling of opinions under the influence of a subject-language might be most effectively foreclosed by radical thinking, which situates itself always prior to all actual processes of verification, in the name of a more originary truth that is also always more absolutely other?

NO STOPPING POINT: THE MOMENT TO CONTINUE

> That is why you must be vigilant and look over the empty place so as to preserve it, whereas I must look over it so as to change it.
> —MAURICE BLANCHOT, *Le Dernier homme*

Even if the process of forcing is inherent in every truth that is effective within a given situation, we still run the risk of falling in the traps of a simulacrum, terror, or disaster. The forcing of truth is inseparable from these themes, which concern the general appearance of evil. It would seem that nothing protects the purity of the process of forcing from metaphysical violence, or from absolute wrong, even though the forcing of truth is inscribed precisely in an egalitarian direction of nondomination. Is there no limit, then, to the process of forcing?

In two conferences, "Truth: Forcing and the Unnameable" and "Subtraction," both published in *Conditions*, as well as in the final part of *Ethics*, Badiou posits the need for a stopping point. However, this is by no means the view presented in *Theory of the Subject*, nor even in the final meditations from *Being and Event*. In his seminar, for instance, in order to go against the foreclosed terms of the Mallarméan dialectic that are the master, death, and language—a trinity whose foreclosure shows in straightforward manner that there is such a thing as a nonconceptualizable element— Badiou quotes approvingly the following sentence from Mao: "We will come to know everything that we did not know before."[26] The process of the torsion of the knowable, of which the book goes on to elaborate the various ethical figures, would not know any limits; there would only be the risk, or the temptation, to fall back into the eternal repetition of lack and law, of anxiety and the superego.

We have to wait for the two conferences in *Conditions* and then *Ethics* in order to register the stopping point in the process of forcing. Badiou's *Ethics* is categorical in this regard: "At least one real element must exist, one multiple existing in the situation, which remains inaccessible to truthful nominations, and is exclusively reserved to opinion, to the language of the situation. At least one point that the truth cannot force. I shall call this element the unnameable of a truth."[27] In fact, in a footnote from *Conditions* there is already discussion of an unnameable typical of each of the four conditions of truth: "Every type of generic procedure admits a specific unnameable. Thus, the unnameable specific to love is sexual enjoyment; that of politics is the collective; that of the poem is language; that of mathematics is consistency."[28]

With regard to this change in position on the power or powerlessness of truth, I would like to ask a simple and perhaps naive question to conclude this chapter: Why is there a need for an unnameable?

Will Badiou finally be included among the witnesses—whether they call themselves modern or postmodern, melancholy or enthusiastic—of the unpresentable, now reinterpreted as the unnameable? If it is true that one should have confidence, or at least show a wise belief in the process of fidelity in order to anticipate the completion of its generic extension, what can be the part of the subject when facing the unnameable? What? Perhaps suspicion, or an updated version of learned ignorance, following once again the example of Mallarmé's overly structural dialectic? The absence or the subtraction that receives no gift of truth whatsoever, would thus find in its lack a taste that is always more radical than hitherto imagined.

My question is not: given that there is an unnameable, how should we bear witness to it? But rather: why should we stand up to the test of an unnameable point to begin with? Why should thinking, in each of its generic procedures, recognize its impotence before this empty symbol of the pure real, bare life without truths, which is not unlike the *ptyx* for Mallarmé?

Badiou, of course, is obliged to have recourse to the notion of an unforceable point at the very moment when he makes his plea for an ethics of truths in the plural, more specifically, when he must find a means to distinguish the process of fidelity to an event from the simulacrum or deformation of such a process. The unnameable, then, would be the guarantee of the impotence of truth as well as the safeguard against its transfiguration into disaster, terror, or simulation. However, in the current philosophical situation Badiou's return to the notion of a necessary impasse risks falling short of his own thinking all the while aligning himself, without knowing it, with this radical thought that takes its inspiration from Heidegger and Lacan, including the recuperation of such themes by certain hermeneutic and psychoanalytical currents.

A second risk is that the unnameable operates only as a kind of point in reserve, from which perspective any subjective procedure of truth could be read as always already involving a disaster. However, such radicalism would become resolutely obscurantist, since the unnameable, instead of mapping an internal limit of an effective procedure of truth, would then block the very possibility of a regime of fidelity to any event whatsoever. Thus, the postulate of the unnameable can always lead back to the transcendent presentation of a measure beyond measure, or of a ground without any bottom. Indeed, does assuming the unnameable in order to stop evil not mean proposing an insuperable limit to all generic thinking of truth? Will radical truth, then, consist exclusively in passing the test of the stopping point, rather than exceeding its empty placement? To make the real appear, or render it, as such, rather than to derive from it a new regime of appearance?

In my eyes, there can be no doubt that it is in this direction that the doctrine of the unnameable risks being appropriated. "Ne pas céder sur son désir" (not to give up on one's desire) for instance, would then come to mean not to stop assuming the finitude of the human being, his or her tragic or comical nothingness. In other words, we should look to it to make sure that the notion of the unnameable does not become the supporting base for a new nihilist definition of ethics, that is to say, a definition that would start from the avoidance of disaster as the sole reference point of truth. In this regard, let us recall another maxim of Badiou's ethics of truths in the plural: "A disaster (*désastre*) is worth more than an unbeing (*dés-être*)."[29] Or, to put it in inverted or negative terms: "Worse than misrecognition is recognition."[30]

Finally, it must be possible to sustain the intrinsic forcing of all processes of truth, unless one is content to fall back on the side of a thinking of lack and finitude, of the indecency of sense and the death drive. This requires that we know how to avoid, with regard to the unnameable, both the foreclosure of all militant intervening processes and the recourse to a philosophy of recognition and sheer negativity. Then, and only then, will thought stop being constrained in this double role, which is always a stubborn one, that makes of thinking either the interpreter of the enigma of being, or else the analyst of the eclipse of the signifier. By contrast, in a symptomatic torsion of meaning and enigma, thought will also by force involve the production of new knowledges. With regard to the legacy of Lacan and Heidegger, indeed, we will never be done with drawing all the necessary consequences out of this one principle, apparently so simple, that Badiou formulates toward the end of *Being and Event*: "There are not only significations, or interpretations. There are truths, also."[31]

6

LOGICS OF CHANGE

←————————————————→

CONTINUITIES AND DISCONTINUITIES

> It is necessary to think discontinuity *as such*, a discontinuity that can-
> not be reduced to any creative univocity, as indistinct or chaotic as the
> concept of such a univocity may be.—BADIOU, *Logics of Worlds*

> A subject is a sequence involving continuities and discontinuities,
> openings and points. The "and" incarnates itself as subject.—BADIOU,
> *Logics of Worlds*

Badiou's decision to give *Logics of Worlds* the subtitle of *Being and Event 2* would seem to leave no doubt as to his intention for the new work to be read as a straightforward continuation, if not also the ultimate completion, of the first volume. In fact, very early on in the book the author boasts about being one of the rare thinkers actually to have finished such a projected second and final tome—as opposed to, say, Heidegger or Sartre, who for a variety of reasons at once personal, theoretical, and ideological were unable to accomplish the same feat respectively for *Being and Time* and the *Critique of Dialectical Reason*. It is true that the author may soon find himself forced to backtrack a little from this ambitious claim, insofar as he has recently begun announcing a third volume to the series, tentatively titled *The Immanence of Truths*, which may very well take several years more to be completed. Still, none of this would seem to diminish the dominant role of *Being and Event* in terms of how the reader is expected to understand the works from the last two decades; on the contrary, this role only seems to become stronger and clearer—with the new tome being announced as bearing the subtitle *Being and Event 3*.

The general trend behind the continuation of Badiou's project would also seem to be equally clear and explicit. Thus, the shift from the first to the second volume of *Being and Event* is defined as the passage from ontology to logic, or from the science of being qua being to the science of appearing. At least, the latter sense is how we must understand *logic* for Badiou, that is to say, as the formal study not of the coherence or meaningfulness of language and of propositions *about* the world (which would be logic only in the "smaller" or "restricted" sense, which has become dominant in philosophy since the so-called linguistic turn) but of the appearance and consistency *of* a world qua world (which is what Badiou calls the "greater" logic, following in this the example of Hegel). "What the book of 1988 did on the level of pure being—to determine the ontological type of truths and the abstract form of the subject that activates them—the present book seeks to do on the level of being-there, or appearing, or worlds," Badiou explains. "In this regard, *Logics of Worlds* is to *Being and Event* what Hegel's *Phenomenology of Spirit* is to his *Science of Logic*, even if the chronological order is the inverse: an immanent capture of the givens of being-there, a local trajectory of the figures of the truth and the subject, and not a deductive analytic of the forms of being."[1] From the abstract forms of being we thus move to the local figures of appearing, just as the method changes from a strictly deductive (mathematical) analytic to an immanent (phenomenological) dialectic. As a result the very status of formalization also undergoes significant changes. Thus, for instance, whereas *Being and Event*, with its claim that mathematics *is* ontology, uses axiomatic formalization as a wholly intrinsic apparatus, notwithstanding some of the problems that immediately beset this treatment as I discussed in the introduction, *Logics of Worlds* treats the question of formalization in a much softer and murkier way, ranging from the strictly deductive to the seemingly illustrative capture of a wealth of examples or cases. "Objective phenomenology and written transparency," writes Badiou about the new book's double movement of thought, that is, the constant going back and forth between worldly variants and formal or transcendental invariance: "As infinitely diversified figures of being-there, worlds effectively absorb the infinite nuances of qualitative intensities into a transcendental framework whose operations are invariant. We can fully account for these nuances of appearing only through the mediation of examples drawn from varied worlds, and from the invariance of transcendental operations; that is, by contrasting the coherence of the examples and the transparency of forms."[2] But this difference in the degree of formalization does not take away any strength from the symmetrical claim made for the use of mathematical and logical forms in both *Being and Event* and *Logics of Worlds*, insofar as set theory is to ontology for the first volume what category theory is to logic for the second.

The symmetry becomes even stronger if we look for a moment beyond the actual books and take into account the fact that, just as *Being and Event* is accompanied by a *Manifesto for Philosophy*, which didactically conveys its message to a broader audience, so too do we find that *Logics of Worlds* is supplemented by a *Second Manifesto for Philosophy*. Badiou evidently is inspired in this regard by the example of André Breton's first and second surrealist manifestos. "Let us simplify and hope: twenty years ago, writing a Manifesto meant saying: 'Philosophy is something completely different from what they tell you that it is. So try and see that which you do not see,'" Badiou explains. "Today, writing a second Manifesto is rather like saying: 'Yes! Philosophy can be what you desire it to be. Try really to see that which you see.'"[3] Everything thus seems to be set in place to foster a reading of Badiou's overall philosophical project in terms of the grand synthesis of *Being and Event*, divided for now into two symmetrical volumes but possibly to be expanded in the future with the additional volume of *The Immanence of Truths*.

The real purport of *Logics of Worlds*, however, is perhaps not limited to being an extension, no matter how ambitious, of the first volume of *Being and Event*. As a matter of fact, to understand the relation between these two volumes, I propose to reiterate my working hypothesis according to which Badiou is the author of three, and not just of two, major works. He himself talks of "the dialectic of my two 'great' books, the old and the new—that is the dialectic of *onto*-logy and onto-*logy*, or of being and appearing."[4] For my part, in a summary of the entire trajectory traced in the preceding chapters, I would add that *Theory of the Subject* serves as a kind of vanishing mediator between the two volumes of *Being and Event*. To phrase this idea in the syntax that defines the so-called materialist dialectic in the preface to *Logics of Worlds*, we could posit that, in effect, there is only being and event, except that there is also the subject. In fact, it is precisely the subject that incarnates the syntax of the exception that distinguishes the materialist dialectic from what Badiou in the same preface dubs "democratic materialism," since for the latter there is in the final instance no subject, or—in a heavy ethical injunction—there should not be any subject of universal truths. Thus, truth and subject, two concepts that, furthermore, from this

point of view are inseparable, allow us to move beyond the general consensus of our time. Indeed, if democratic materialism says: "There are only
bodies and languages," or, in an anthropological variation on the same
principle: "There are only individuals and communities," then "the materialist dialectic says: 'There are only bodies and languages, except that
there are truths.' The 'except that' *exists* qua subject. In other words, if
a body avers itself capable of producing effects that exceed the bodies-
languages system (and such effects are called truths), this body will be said
to be subjectivized."[5] The importance of this supplementation by the subject and, thus, by the book that most extensively treats of its theory should
have become clear throughout the preceding pages. Suffice it to underscore
here that, in *Logics of Worlds*, the subject explicitly marks the space of the
formal operations that take place, under certain rare and occasional conditions, between the normal regime of a world of appearing and its evental
exception. "Every subjective formula suspends the subject between event
and truth. The subject is the labor of this in-between, the effectuation of
the subjective space itself. The event, for its part, has disappeared, and the
truth will not appear," says Badiou in his seminar on the new axiomatic
theory of the subject, in preparation for Book I of *Logics of Worlds*: "In-
between of a disappearing and an inappearing. Suspension between an
unassignable origin and an improbable accomplishment, for which a finite
substitute will be given. This is what is present in any project to exist qua
subject."[6]

     As a consequence of this constitutive in-betweenness the space of the
subject is never pure or univocal. To the contrary, as Badiou suggest in
one of the many summaries of the overarching structure behind *Logics of
Worlds*, the subject is always a kind of compromise formation on the way
from a given world, which is composed of bodies and languages, to an
eternally available truth, which nonetheless will have to be embodied and
put back into language as well—unless, of course, it is left as some unattainable, otherworldly, or transcendent ideal, as in the common caricatures of
the very notion of a Platonic Idea:

> We begin directly with the underlying ontological components: world
> and event—the latter breaking with the presentational logic of the for-
> mer. The subjective form is then assigned to a localization in being
> which is ambiguous. On the one hand, the subject is only a set of
> the world's elements, and therefore an object in the scene on which

the world presents multiplicities; on the other, the subject orients this object—in terms of the effects it is capable of producing—in a direction that stems from an event. The subject can therefore be said to be the only known form of a conceivable "compromise" between the phenomenal persistence of a world and its evental rearrangement.[7]

The subject appears as the only "compromise" or "ambiguity" possible in the relation between a given world and the truth that follows from an event's having taken place in this world. Unless we take seriously the place of the subject between being and truth, we will never understand the nature of this relation between world and event. In that case we may very well move in the direction of a miraculous reading of the event, whether to praise it for its radicalism or to blame it for its dogmatism, but we would still miss out on what in my eyes constitutes the pivotal contribution of all of Badiou's philosophical work. To come to terms with this contribution requires that we grasp the sense of the recommencement, not only of materialism but also of the dialectic—previously defined as a logic of internal division, including the division of materialism itself—which is also at work in *Logics of Worlds*.

My goal in the present chapter, therefore, by no means amounts to a well-nigh impossible effort to summarize the entire project behind *Logics of Worlds*. Instead, I will limit myself to foregrounding some of its major points, both in terms of what is conceptually innovative and in terms of what appears to have been abandoned, all the while underscoring some of the tensions that persist within the project of the book in general.

Another way of formulating the working hypothesis behind this reading would involve taking up an observation from fellow ex-Althusserian, Yves Duroux, who mentions that the new book can be read as the rewriting of *Theory of the Subject* under the condition of *Being and Event*. By contrast, I would argue that, as far as the continuities and discontinuities are concerned between Badiou's three major books, *Logics of Worlds* can also be read as a rewriting of *Being and Event* under the condition of *Theory of the Subject*. This becomes visible particularly through the dialectic of algebra and topology or of the vanishing cause and the new consistency. In the pages that follow, I will thus begin by recalling the stakes of this dialectic as it is adopted from *Theory of the Subject*, before discussing the innovations, reformulations, and abandonments that took place between *Being and Event* and *Logics of Worlds*.

If we consider the presence of a polemical trajectory that runs the gamut from *Theory of the Subject*, via the penultimate meditation in *Being and Event* (also titled "Theory of the Subject"), all the way to the "Formal Theory (Meta-physics) of the Subject," in *Logics of Worlds*, it is evident that what persists is precisely the question of the subject: "This goes to show that in the long-run, the theme of the subject unifies my intellectual under-taking, against those [who] would define (post)modernity by the de-construction of this concept."[8] Among those who might wish to decon-struct the subject, we could of course cite the example of Derrida himself, who, in *Politics of Friendship*, actually seems to serve up a direct and explicit response to the title of Badiou's first major book, if not also, implicitly, to the decisionism that is commonly attributed to *Being and Event*. Derrida thus separates the twin notions of the (singular) event and of the (genu-ine) decision from any founding reference to the subject:

> *A theory of the subject is incapable of accounting for the slightest decision.* But this must be said *a fortiori* of the event, and of the event with regard to the decision. For if nothing ever happens to a subject, nothing deserv-ing the name "event," the schema of decision tends regularly—at least, in its ordinary and hegemonic sense (that which seems dominant still in Schmittian decisionism, in his theory of exception and of sovereignty) —to imply the instance of the subject, a classic, free, and wilful subject, therefore a subject to whom nothing can happen, not even the singular event for which he believes to have taken and kept the initiative: for example, in an exceptional situation.[9]

From the point of view of deconstruction, not only is there no subject of the event, but more strictly speaking there should not be any either. For no sooner is there a subject than there can no longer be any genuine event. As Badiou also writes in *Logics of Worlds*:

> That is the directly ideological meaning of the post-Heideggerian de-construction, under the accusation "metaphysical," of the category of subject: to prepare a democracy without a (political) subject, to deliver individuals over to the serial organization of identities or to the face-to-face confrontation with the desolation of their enjoyment. In the France of the sixties only Sartre (in a reactive mode) and Lacan (in an inventive mode) refused to play a part in this drama. Consequently, both found themselves faced with the dialectic between subject (as structure) and

subjectivization (as act). What does the subject subjectivize? As we've said, the subject comes to the place of the "except that."[10]

Badiou's overall response to this accusation in a sense amounts to pleading guilty as charged. He thus openly defines his project not just as a new physics (a new theory of bodies and objects) but even as a new metaphysics (a new theory of the subject)—with the metaphysics in *Logics of Worlds* appearing right from the start, in Book I, long before the physics concerning the question of incorporation, or the question of the embodiment of truth, is elaborated in Book VII.

My reading of *Logics of Worlds* in light of *Theory of the Subject*, then, aims to shed light on the continuing relevance of the materialist dialectic articulated around the subject of an exceptional truth, and, in so doing, it should further help unravel the dualism suggested in the title *Being and Event*. It should show not only how the two volumes of this project, *Being and Event* and *Logics of Worlds*, hang together in terms of the dialectic between algebra and topology, or between structure and act, but also how each volume in itself, when seen in light of its older precedent, *Theory of the Subject*, is internally divided according to precisely such a dialectic. Finally, it might even provide us with a number of anticipated criticisms of the treatment given to this dialectic in the later works. Indeed, whereas *Being and Event*, despite the concepts and practices that tend to work against this tendency, can be said to remain by and large structural or algebraic, in the sense that the ontological orientation almost by default presents the event as a punctual evanescence, or a kind of disappearing act, by contrast *Logics of Worlds* opens out onto a topological and sequential orientation, focused on the consequences of the event after the latter itself has all but vanished or disappeared.

Incidentally, we could adduce further textual indices that would be proof of the rebeginning of *Theory of the Subject* in *Logics of Worlds*: the return to the thematic of destruction, and even of the necessary part of death, in any truth procedure; the return of the four affects of courage, justice, anxiety, and the superego, with the latter now having been rebaptized as terror; the reprise of the concept of the inexistent, which anchors the logic of change in that which "in-exists," or that which exists only minimally, in the situation or world that is subject to change; and, in general, the return to the familiar references to Mao and Hegel—especially, as far as the latter is concerned, through the opening segments on determination and limit in the *Science of Logic*. Not only does Badiou note that "Hegel thinks with an altogether unique incisiveness the correlation between, on one hand, the local externalization of being (being-there) and, on the other, the logic of determination, understood as the coherent figure of the situation of being," but with the new work it also becomes clear to what extent Hegel's *Science of Logic*, especially through the early moments of the argument before they undergo the totalizing effects of speculative idealism, is actually one of the most constant references in all of Badiou's work: "I have never ceased measuring myself up to this magnificent book, almost as unreadable as Joyce's *Finnegans Wake*."[11] Of course, this reprise or this recommencement does not exclude a considerable amount of self-criticisms. Thus, according to Badiou's own judgment in *Logics of Worlds*, the older *Theory of the Subject* would have fallen short of its goal by cutting straight to the dialectic, without passing through the materialism of a "greater logic," a judgment not unlike the way in which *Being and Event*, as I commented above, criticizes *Theory of the Subject* for having assumed that "there is" subjectivization, without giving this presupposition a systematic ontological "substructure."[12] Each of these retrospective self-criticisms, though, could be refuted on the basis of the targeted work itself. Thus, *Theory of the Subject* actually does *not* jump straight to the dialectic but devotes a central part of its argument to the materialist redefinition of materialism, just as it does *not* ignore the ontological anchorage of subjectivity but actually already situates it in the excess of inclusion over belonging, of parts over elements, as defined in set theory.

This peculiar reading of *Logics of Worlds*, finally, gives much more weight to what I would call the "logics of change," encapsulated in Books I and V through VII, than to the "greater logic," or to the theory of appearing per se, which takes up Books II through IV. This slanted view is in my eyes justified by the fact that ultimately the avowed goal even of this massive follow-up to *Being and Event* is not the doctrine of how a world appears, complete with its transcendental regime, its objects, and its relations among objects, but rather the doctrine of how a world can become transformed as the result of a subjective intervention. Badiou, in other words, still positions himself somewhere in the lineage of the eleventh of Marx's "Theses on Feuerbach," not so much in the sense that he would claim for philosophy itself the capacity to change the world rather than variously to interpret it, nor in the antiphilosophical sense that such a transformation would have to be the result of a practice of and in the real as opposed to the limited activity of purely speculative reason, but in the sense that he assigns to philosophy—in the ideological context of a new materialist dialectic—the task of formulating a systematic interpretation of the very possibility of transforming the world to begin with. Besides, further confirmation of this reading can be found in the fact that Badiou's ongoing seminar for the academic year 2010–11 is devoted to the topic "What does 'changing the world' mean?"

ALGEBRA AND TOPOLOGY

Let us briefly recall the argument from *Theory of the Subject* regarding the dialectic of algebra and topology. Badiou, referring in particular to Lacan, posits that the real is not only a point that stands in a position of being the vanishing cause, or of the empty place, for desire as lack of being, but also a knot or node for the subjective forcing of a new consistency that would stand in excess over this empty place and thus would destroy its law. Algebraic is the side of the real as vanishing cause; topological is the side of the real as emergent consistency. The materialist dialectic, which at the time of *Theory of the Subject* still goes by the orthodox name of dialectical materialism without inverting the noun and the predicate, requires that we conceive of its unity as divided into an algebra and a topology.

Now, could we not propose the hypothesis according to which Badiou in *Being and Event* would have accomplished only the first half of this programmatic statement, that is to say, the algebraic deduction of the universe of pure multiplicity starting from the vanishing term of the void, or of the empty set, following the axioms of post-Cantorian set theory? Moreover, should we not conclude that the outcome of this first elaboration is an overly punctual, if not heavily self-sufficient, definition of the event? And, to avoid the otherwise justifiable misunderstanding that sees in the event merely a secularization of the miracle of grace, would this first definition not have to be tied to its second aspect, on the side of topology, starting for instance from the notion of the evental site, which, already in *Being and Event* itself, marks the self-belonging with an index of symptomatic specificity? Finally, is not such a topological elaboration, precisely through the theory of categories or *topoi*, what we find in *Logics of Worlds* of which *Theory of the Subject*, with the division of the real into cause and consistency, or into algebra and topology, would have announced the necessity a long time ago, over and against the risk of a dogmatic reading of *Being and Event*? To be sure, this would already present us with a picture of the unity of these works that is rather different from the otherwise frequent but also terminologically somewhat confusing comparison with Hegel's *Science of Logic* and *Phenomenology of Spirit*.

To be sure, I do not wish to claim that *Theory of the Subject* is the preemptive synthesis of *Being and Event* and *Logics of Worlds*. In the wake of the exhaustion of orthodox dialectical thought, it probably can never be a question of synthesis but at best of a split articulation, a disjunction, or a difference in the strong sense of the term: "Let's agree that by 'dialectic,' following Hegel, we are to understand that the essence of all difference is the third term that marks the gap between the two others."[13] This is also, I would argue, what we can find retroactively in *Theory of the Subject*, namely: the third term that marks the gap between *Being and Event* and *Logics of Worlds*. But then a gap, as any Hegelian would be quick to add, is also at the same time a linkage, just as a limit, once it is thought, becomes a boundary to be crossed.

In fact, just as there are already several concepts and operations in *Being and Event*, most notably "evental site" and "forcing" as discussed above, that add a topological orientation to the algebraic core, so, too, can we find the dialectic of cause and consistency at work within *Logics of Worlds*. Even here, in other words, the seeming predominance of the topological orientation is at the same time counteracted by an overly structural tendency. *Theory of the Subject* thus allows one to perceive the internal scission of each of the subsequent two volumes. On the one hand, for example, that which in the new book is called "site" is defined once again by its punctual and evanescent character, which like a lightning strike disappears no sooner than it appears. The site according to *Logics of Worlds* is to be read ontologically as a case of self-belonging: "In what concerns the thinking of its pure being, a site is simply a multiple to which it happens that it is an element of itself."[14] More technically, Badiou gives the following definition: "Take any world whatever. *A multiple which is an object of this world—whose elements are indexed on the transcendental of the world—is a 'site' if it happens to count itself in the referential field of its own indexing*."[15] There is a truth to this disappearing, however, thanks only to the elaboration of a series of consequences, that is to say, thanks to a new regime of consistency, which as a result profoundly changes and reshuffles the coordinates of the situation of departure. The purely ontological description must thus be supplemented with a topological elaboration of the intensity of the changes that follow from the vanishing site: "Self-belonging annuls itself as soon as it is forced, as soon as it happens. A site is a vanishing term: it appears only in order to disappear. The problem is to register its consequences in appearing."[16] If we look at the site from the standpoint of self-belonging or reflexivity, then the emphasis will be on the upsurge of the new as such, as a pure breaking point. But the price to be paid for such an absolute discontinuity would be a radicalism that is as intense as it is devoid of veritable consequences. By contrast, if we have ears only for that which can be organized in terms of the consistent effects after the event, then we may well lose track of the radical novelty introduced by the event in an existing world.

Both aspects—discontinuity and continuity, the site and its consequences, absolute novelty and minimal duration—are separable only at the level of the exposition. In reality, at least if and when there occurs an event or a singular change in the strong sense, one cannot exist without the other. Badiou shows us this dilemma in the case of the Paris Commune, discussed at length in Book V of *Logics of Worlds*: "For what counts is not only the exceptional intensity of its surging up—the fact that we are dealing with a violent episode that creates appearing—but the glorious and uncertain consequences that this upsurge, despite its vanishing, sets out."[17] The full and adequate evaluation of an event will thus depend entirely on this dialectic between the site and its consequences, or between the algebra of the cause and the topology of its consistency: "To judge if an aleatory adjunction to the world deserves to be taken, not just as a singularity beyond modifications and facts, but as an event, we must look to that portion of it which endures in the concentration, beyond itself, of its intensity."[18] This is because an event, in order to be lived as the genuine occasion for a new truth, supposes that one is not simply seduced by the pure glow of the real without at the same time drawing the necessary consequences from this point for a new situation or a new world. This is also how Badiou concludes "What Is It to Live?," the final section of *Logics of Worlds*: "It is not enough to identify a trace. One must incorporate oneself into what the trace authorizes in terms of consequences." Or again: "It is necessary to enter into its composition, to become an active element of this body. The only relation to the present is that of incorporation: the incorporation into this immanent cohesion of the world which springs from the becoming-existent of the eventual trace, as a new birth beyond all the facts and markers of time."[19] Otherwise, in the absence of incorporation, it will always be possible to turn the abruptness of the pure real, as a sudden flash, against the so-called dogmatism or decisionism inherent in any lasting and consequent elaboration of a singular yet universal truth. In fact, it is precisely in this sense that a certain psychoanalysis, with the theme of the real as impossible, no less than a certain deconstruction, with the theme of the originary trace, can become the skeptical, if not openly antiphilosophical, opponents with regard to the traditional love of truth of the philosopher.

FINITUDE AND MYSTICISM

> To break with empiricism is to think the event as the advent of what subtracts itself from all experience: the ontologically un-founded and the transcendentally discontinuous. To break with dogmatism is to remove the event from the ascendancy of the One.—BADIOU, *Logics of Worlds*

If now we look at some of the changes and reformulations to which Badiou subjects his thinking in the passage from *Being and Event* to *Logics of Worlds*, aside from the overarching shift from ontology to logic, or from pure being to its appearing in a world, we can distinguish two major series of changes. First, the new formal (metaphysical) theory of the subject recoups the richness of various figures, affects, and destinations, as opposed to the unique figure of fidelity as the positive connector to the name of the event, which is all that we find in the strictly ontological definition of the subject. In addition to the figure of fidelity we thus obtain the figures of reaction and obscurantism, as well as the possibility of reactivating a past fidelity in the present. To these figures there correspond different operations and destinations, ranging from the (faithful) production of a present to its (reactive) denial or (obscure) occultation all the way to its (eventual) resurrection. In fact, making explicit what seems to be the guiding hypothesis behind Badiou's presentation, I would suggest that we envision fidelity, reaction, and obscurantism not so much as autonomous subjects but rather as so many figures within a larger subjective space, which as a result would be riven with tensions, the internal strife within the subject that marks its historical scansion. "The theory of the subject thus contains three distinct formal arrangements. Of course, the general subjective field is necessarily inaugurated by a faithful subject, so that the point-by-point work of consequences may be visible as pure present," Badiou himself concludes. "But generally, from the first signs that we have been accorded the gift of a present, the reactive and obscure subjects are already at work, as rivals and accomplices in weakening the substance of this present or occulting its appearance."[20] Second, the theory of change in a parallel fashion is enriched not only with the new doctrines of points and of the body of truth but also with a much wider scale of types of change, from simple modification all the way to the maximal transformation that would be the event proper. "As we shall see, I am now able fundamentally to equate 'site' and 'evental multiplicity'—thus avoiding all the banal aporias of the dialectic between structure and historicity—and that I do so without any recourse to a mysterious naming," Badiou explains at the start of Book V of *Logics of Worlds*, which is entirely devoted to the typology of change: "Moreover, in place of the rigid opposition between situation and event, I unfold the nuances of transformation, from mobile-immobile modification all the way to the event properly so-called, by way of the neutrality of fact."[21] The typology of change is one of ascending intensity and radical-ism: *modification* refers to the immanent dynamic of change that is always possible within a situation or world, without for this reason disrupting its regularity; a *fact* includes a site but without the maximal intensity that would make it a singularity; and an *event* properly speaking is a strong singularity whose value of appearance is maximal and whose consequences are likewise maximal, in the sense that they give existence to the inexis-tent that is proper to the world in which the event takes place. "In brief, we can say that existing maximally for the duration of its appearance/disappearance confers on the site the power of a singularity—but that the force of a singularity lies in making its consequences, and not just itself, exist maximally. We reserve the name 'event' for a strong singularity."[22] This is precisely what is illustrated through the didactic example of the Paris Commune.

Even more remarkable are the abandonments pure and simple, that is, those concepts from *Being and Event*, or even from *Conditions* and *Ethics*, for which the reader will search in vain in *Logics of Worlds*. Among the latter I will limit myself to mentioning the most flagrant abandonments, which are furthermore intimately related: first, the doctrine of names, or the problem of the naming of the event as being the initial form of a faithful intervention; and, second, the doctrine of the unnameable as the halting point for the process of forcing of truth, a point meant to serve as a guarantee against the temptation of disaster according to the ethics of truth.

If indeed there is a common orientation behind these innovations, reshufflings, and abandonments, I would argue that there is a double argument at stake here: against finitude, on one hand, and against the mysticism of the event, on the other. This double argument, aside from highlighting two fundamental ways in which Badiou's work as a whole has been received thus far, can also be read as a self-criticism on the part of the philosopher himself. In short, it would be a question of staying clear of all absolutizations of the event, whether from the bottom or from the top. We should neither skeptically fall back on yet another reiteration of our finite "human condition" as sheer mortals nor dogmatically raise ourselves up to a "mystical element" that would escape the laws of this human, all too human, world of ours.

Badiou directs the blade of his criticism in the first place against the theme of finitude, which, following Heidegger's reading of Kant, can be said to sum up the common denominator of all modern philosophy, all the way to its popularization in the ideological atmosphere of so-called democratic materialism: "In a general sense, the materialist dialectic opposes the real infinity of truths to the principle of finitude which is deducible from democratic maxims."[23] We might even say that with his return to Hegel's dialectic after and in light of Cantor's "actual infinity," Badiou's philosophy truly marks the beginning of the twenty-first century, whereas the previous century, with its ongoing variations on the "analytic of finitude," to use an expression that Foucault in *The Order of Things* borrows from Heidegger, remains entirely dominated by the professorial figure of Kant. "Finitude, the constant harping on of our mortal being, in brief, the fear of death as the only passion—these are the bitter ingredients of democratic materialism."[24] But a truth is precisely that which transcends the limits of finitude, without for this reason presupposing an older—religious or merely potential as opposed to actual—infinity: "A truth procedure has nothing to do with the limits of the human species, our 'consciousness,' our 'finitude,' our 'faculties' and other determinations of democratic materialism."[25] This is why to the latter's ideological atmosphere, marked by finitude, the materialist dialectic opposes the ingredients of the knowable infinite. "To think existence *without finitude*—that is the liberatory imperative, which extricates existence from the ultimate signifier of its submission, death," Badiou posits: "So it is important that by 'materialist dialectic' we understand the deployment of a critique of every critique. To have done, if possible, with the watered-down Kant of limits, rights and unknowables. To affirm, with Mao Tse-tung (why not?): 'We will come to know everything that we did not know before.' "[26]

And yet, as I pointed out in the previous chapter, under the heading of the unnameable such as it is developed between *Being and Event* and *Ethics* and such as it is occasionally still deployed by Žižek in his critical rejoinders, it is certainly possible to read Badiou's thought as an argument of respect toward the finitude of our condition as mere mortals, human beings obliged to accept a transcendent limit beyond which we should not push the process of forcing the truth. As Badiou himself admits in his interview with Peter Hallward and myself: "Basically, by recognizing the quasi-ontological category of the unnameable, I made concessions to the pervasive moralism of the 1980s and 1990s. I made concessions to the obsessive omnipresence of the problem of Evil."[27] Given the renewed diatribe against finitude, it would therefore appear to be wholly consistent to see that the notion of the unnameable, together with the doctrine of naming in general as the first form of fidelity toward an event, is purely and simply abandoned in *Logics of Worlds*. "It's quite possible that the category of the unnameable may prove irrelevant," Badiou announces in the same interview, which was taped shortly before the new book's publication: "The general idea is to substitute, for the overly moralizing idea of a totality marked by an unnameable point, the idea (which is far more closely linked to the concrete practices of truth) of a field of consequences whose logic must be both reconstructed and respected"; and, more generally speaking: "We are no longer in the logic of *names*, but in a logic of *consequences*. We will simply say that there are some things that are inconsequential, that some things do not enter into the field of consequences."[28] In order to be done with the analytic of finitude as it lingers on in parts of *Being and Event* and especially in *Ethics*, Badiou thus sees himself forced in *Logics of Worlds* purely and completely to abandon the combined problematic of naming and the unnameable.

The other changes and abandonments, by contrast, seem at least partly inspired by a growing effort to avoid the hypostatization of the event as pure discontinuity, shining break, or glorious instant of self-belonging. In this case it is a matter of going against the mysticism of the event as a miracle cut loose of all links to the situation or to the world as we know it. As Badiou writes most succinctly in his *Second Manifesto for Philosophy*: "A truth is a disappeared event of which the world little by little makes appear, in the disparate materials of appearing, the unpredictable body."[29] Such is precisely one of the wagers behind the renewal of materialism, namely, to situate the process of truth within the given immanence of the world, and not somewhere outside of this world.

The fact remains that aside from a few "problems of connection and continuity" mentioned by the author himself, *Logics of Worlds* also seems to leave "for another time, or for others to solve," the elaboration of certain doctrines that already had been promised for this second tome of *Being and Event*. I am thinking, in particular, of the aforementioned promise of a more systematic account of the "networks" or "knottings" among two or more truth procedures that would produce, for example, a "political art" or an "amorous politics," not to mention complex events such as May '68 and its aftermath, which tie together art, politics, and love—perhaps even science. Finally, I am also thinking of the precise links between the concept of the "evental site" in *Being and Event* and "site" according to *Logics of Worlds*. For these two concepts certainly should not be conflated.

Indeed, whereas "evental site" in the first volume of *Being and Event* registers the limit of the event's self-belonging by inscribing a crucial scission at the very heart of the matheme of the event, without which the latter would not be an event *for* a specific situation, it seems to me that "site" in the doctrine of change of *Logics of Worlds* risks being read once again in terms of pure reflexivity or self-belonging. This would bring us back to a structural, algebraic, or idealist dialectic. Badiou certainly warns his readers against such an interpretation, especially by insisting that the logic of the site, aside from the traits of reflexivity, revelation of the void, and instantaneity, must also unfold a system of consequences within the world in which the site appears in the first place: "The site must in fact be thought, not only in terms of the three ontological particularities that we have just accorded it, but also in the logical (or intra-worldly) deployment of its consequences. Since the site is a figure of the instant, since it only appears to disappear, true duration can only be that of consequences."[30] However, even or especially in the example of the Paris Commune discussed in Book V of *Logics of Worlds*, there is a lingering temptation to privilege the moment of the upsurge as such, that is, the sudden and well-nigh miraculous turnabout, the instant of sheer formal conversion by which "we are nothing" flips over and becomes "let us be all."

We could also say that the treatment of the "site" in *Logics of Worlds*, instead of pursuing the topological effort already begun with "evental site" in *Being and Event*, exemplifies the two approaches to Badiou's thought and the thinking of the event in general. There is first of all the perspective of self-belonging. "The site is the appearing/disappearing of a multiple whose paradox is self-belonging. The logic of the site concerns the distribution of intensities around this disappeared point which is the site," writes Badiou, before quoting a favorite expression of his father's: "We must therefore begin by the beginning: what is the value of existence of the site itself? We will then proceed by dealing with what this allows us to infer about consequences."[31] This first approach thus dreams of beginning from the pure beginning—even at the risk of staying at the level of a miraculous conception of the event. The second, on the other hand, seeks to circumvent the specter of leftism that is barely hidden behind the dream of an absolute beginning, by placing the emphasis on the slow work of returning to the situation of departure. Now, in other words, the whole key lies in the rebeginning or the recommencement: "Commencements are to be measured by the re-commencements they enable."[32] In this second case, though, contrary to the temptations that surround the radical dream of speculative leftism, the opposite risk consists in falling into a flattened form of historicism pure and simple, whereas perhaps the real task before us requires a renewal not just of dialectical materialism, or of the materialist dialectic, but of historical materialism as well.

THE (RE)COMMENCEMENT OF
HISTORICAL MATERIALISM?

After having read *Logics of Worlds* in manuscript form, in fact, I sent a slightly malicious note to Badiou in which I asked him whether, now that he had given proof of wanting to return to the long-standing tradition of dialectical materialism, the old Stalin might not have asked him about his credentials in terms of historical materialism. I do not think that Badiou has ever again responded so quickly, in a matter of minutes at best, in order to remind me not only that *The Century* already presents a series of lessons in historical materialism but also that the same could be said about large parts of *Logics of Worlds*:

> As far as the crucial destiny of historical materialism is concerned, which quite simply is political materialism, I do not think I am falling short. I believe that you can read the long Scholium on Mao at the end of Book VII in *Logics of Worlds*: you will see that *Logics of Worlds* contains, directly, a very strong dosage of historical materialism. And why is this? Because *Logics of Worlds* is a theory of the subjectivizable body and not only, or not principally, a theory of the "laws" of the dialectic, or of the consistency of appearance (even though this question is quantitatively important, because it is also difficult, a bit like the critique of empirio-criticism for Lenin). This being said, Stalin is not a good master, not at all. As I recall in the Preface to *Logics of Worlds*, the political hero of the century, after Lenin, is Mao, and Mao explicitly *against* Stalin (even though not in the sense of the petit-bourgeois democrats or the Trotskyists). To understand this point is key to historical materialism as applied to the twentieth century.[33]

Imagine, then, my surprise when I read the following passage from the conclusion of the published version of *Logics of Worlds*: "Democratic materialism has a passion for history: it is truly the only authentic historical materialism," which is why Badiou now proposes to stay clear of the other—historical—half of the Stalinist legacy altogether so as to stick only to an inverted formulation of dialectical materialism as materialist dialectic: "Contrary to what transpires in the Stalinist version of Marxism—a version that Althusser inherited, though he disrupted it from within—it is crucial to disjoin the materialist dialectic, the philosophy of emancipation through truths, from historical materialism, the philosophy of alienation by language-bodies. To break with the cult of genealogies and narratives means restoring the past as the amplitude of the present."[34]

It seems to me that on this point, at least, it is possible to extend Badiou's philosophical work. Precisely as a philosopher, the latter tends for the most part to reabsorb the historical base of the event into an immanent conceptualization of the event's essence, so that the condition—the event that happens outside of philosophy—paradoxically comes to be appropriated by the conditioned—by the philosophy of the event. In this sense the promise of a renewal of historical materialism as an accompanying piece, if not also a correction, of the materialist dialectic hits upon the obstacle of an exclusively philosophical treatment of the event. This makes it extremely difficult to follow the philosopher's advice and begin thinking *with* Badiou. That is to say, it makes it difficult to go beyond the exegetical commentary on Badiou's own thinking by actually putting his thought to work so to think the events of our time or of previous times.

In the preface to *Being and Event* Badiou insists that he wants his philosophy to serve as a toolbox to think events in any or all of the four conditions of truth that for him are science, politics, love, and art: "The categories that this book deploys, from the pure multiple to the subject, constitute the general order of a thought which is such that it can be *practised* across the entirety of the contemporary system of reference. These categories are available for the service of scientific procedures just as they are for those of politics or analysis. They attempt to organize an abstract vision of the requirements of the epoch."[35] While seemingly self-effacing, however, this suggestion of practical availability also presents us with a number of problems. Perhaps these problems even amount to authentic aporias— otherwise not a very common term in this thinker's personal vocabulary— which somehow would be inherent in Badiou's philosophy: not necessarily shortcomings but inevitable side-effects of the enormous gravitational pull of his thinking. Allow me to illustrate this with two examples, one for each of the two volumes of *Being and Event*.

Let us first of all take the case of the reading of Mallarmé in Meditation 17 of the first volume of *Being and Event*. Here we do not obtain an analysis of Mallarmé as an event in French symbolist or post-Hugolian poetry so much as a commentary on Mallarmé as the poet-thinker of the eventfulness or eventality of the event. "A poem by Mallarmé always fixes the place of an aleatory event; an event to be interpreted on the basis of the traces it leaves behind," Badiou posits at the opening of this pivotal meditation, and again, immediately afterward on the same page, he adds: "Mallarmé is a thinker of the event-drama, in the double sense of the staging of its appearance-disappearance ('. . . we do not have an idea of it, solely in the state of a glimmer, for it is immediately resolved . . .') and of its interpretation which gives it the status of an 'acquisition for ever.' "[36] Mallarmé's *A Cast of Dice . . .* , for example, is read along these lines as an emblem of the pure event as such: "The event in question in *A Cast of Dice . . .* is therefore that of the production of an absolute symbol of the event. The stakes of casting dice 'from the bottom of a shipwreck' are those of making an event out of the thought of the event."[37]

Of course, it is one thing to read Mallarmé as the poet-thinker of the event of the event and quite another to read his work as an event in nineteenth-century French poetry. It is almost, though, as if Badiou's meditation, by a strange inward necessity, were unable to preserve the poet's radical innovation in the history of poetry, which would be addressed by the second approach, except by replacing it with, or displacing it onto, the concentrated rigor and self-contained formalization of the first approach.

Something similar happens in the case of the sections devoted to Paul Valéry in Book VII of *Logics of Worlds*. Here too, the poem is read as a subtle disposition of the different elements and processes involved in the transformative change produced by an event. "In our terms, this poem is the story of an event," Badiou writes of *Marine Cemetery* (*Le Cimetière marin*), and in a footnote he adds that Valéry matches Mallarmé's extraordinary skills in this regard: "It is indeed the question of the 'pure event' that connects the Mallarmé of *A Cast of Dice* with the Valéry of *Marine Cemetery*: under what conditions can the poem capture what lies beyond what is, what purely happens? And, what then is the status of thought, if it is true that such a happening jolts its corporeal support in a lightning strike?"[38] In both of these cases, poetry is not read *as an event* so much as in terms of a poetic *theory* of the event qua event.

The issue at stake is not exactly the same as the one involved in the event's difficult or impossible exemplification, about which Derrida has spoken in illuminating ways. When asked by Giovanna Borradori whether 9/11 was what she calls a "major event," for instance, Derrida at first seems to hesitate in ways similar to when, in an interview from *Without Alibi*, Peggy Kamuf asks him to name the events that for him would have marked the history of the twentieth century after World War II. But there is more than hesitation in the answer given to Borradori. Derrida actually goes so far as to outline an inescapable predicament. Indeed, if an event in principle must be unforeseeable, then how could we know, by what kind of prior knowledge, whether or not x or y, which did happen, really constitute an event? If we have a prior concept of what constitutes an event, if we know what the conditions are without which it is impossible to speak of an event in the "true" or "proper" sense of the term: if indeed we have such a philosophical concept or transcendental understanding of the conditions of possibility of an event, then by necessity any case that serves as an example of such an event no longer would be an event, since it would be predictable, foreseeable, exemplifiable in advance. If there is a horizon of expectation, in other words, there can be no event. Or, to put it the other way around, there is an event only when there is no horizon of expectation, or only when there is a horizon of nonknowledge—of a faltering knowledge, or a powerlessness to know, to comprehend, to foresee, to expect.

In his answer to Borradori, Derrida is both admirably genuine and rigorous when it comes to defining this difficulty as an intrinsic paradox of the notion of the event: "A major event should be so unforeseeable and irruptive that it disturbs even the horizon of the concept or essence on the basis of which we believe we recognize an event *as such*. That is why all the 'philosophical' questions remain open, perhaps even beyond philosophy itself, as soon as it is a matter of thinking the event."[39] This structure of impossible possibility overdetermines every occurrence of the event in deconstruction. Thus, in "A Certain Impossible Possibility of Saying the Event," which transcribes a seminar in Montréal from a few years ago, Derrida exemplifies this logic with the confession, the gift, forgiveness, and hospitality. In each case, what enables the saying of the event is also necessarily what disables it. The singularity of the event as such always in principle exceeds the capacity of thought to instantiate its operation. Thinking, by definition, falls short of the singularity of the event: "One of the traits of the event is not only that it comes as something which is unpredictable and which tears apart the ordinary course of history but also that it is absolutely singular. However, the stating of the event, the stating of knowledge as to the event misses in a way *a priori*, from the start, the singularity of the event by the simple fact that it comes afterward and loses singularity in a generality."[40] No saying or showing of the event is thus ever on a par with the singularity of the event. Instead, the act of thinking the event according to a deconstructivist orientation must accept the challenge of plunging itself into the night of its own impossibility. "Every time that the *saying-the-event* exceeds this dimension of information, of knowledge, of cognition, it engages itself," according to Derrida, "in the night of a non-knowledge, of something which is not purely ignorance but which is of an order that no longer belongs to the order of knowledge."[41]

Badiou's readings of Mallarmé or Valéry bring up an aporia that is altogether different from Derrida's. Whereas the latter insists on how the singularity of the event in principle exceeds its concept or essence, to the point where he seems to flirt with a certain version of wise ignorance, the former instead seems completely undeterred and demonstrates an almost boundless confidence in the powers of thought to think the event, except that, in the process of this demonstration, most events that are supposed to give rise to the various truths that condition philosophy from the outside become transposed into so many theories of the event, of truth, of the body, or of the subject, and so on. In other words, it is as if Badiou's philosophy, instead of serving the truths that are produced outside of it in the four conditions or generic procedures, could not avoid looping these instances back upon themselves before tying them in with a strictly intra-philosophical apparatus—namely, his own. If Mallarmé and Valéry are part of a new artistic configuration, as a result of the symbolist innovation, we learn but little about what these radical commencements authorize in terms of recommencements within modern French poetry. Rather, the intraphilosophical apparatus seems to lead to a hypostasis of the pure event or commencement as such, thanks to the philosopheme of self-theorization—with poetry providing the theory of its own eventality.

When I asked Badiou about this in the interview from a few years ago reproduced in the appendix, he admitted that this was indeed a real problem, one "which obviously entails a rather large amount of philosophical appropriation of the condition." In fact, he added, it might be the only plausible way to argue that his philosophy carries a dogmatic streak in it, insofar as "I submit the condition to the conditioned."[42] Yet in the same interview Badiou insists on the specificity of the philosophical act, which is neither that of the poet nor that of the critic. In this sense the operations of displacement or conceptual condensation to which the philosopher subjects the poets should not be confused with his personal tastes (other writers may be his preferred authors) or even with the events that would have conditioned his philosophy the most (as in the case of Wagner, who until recently was almost entirely absent from Badiou's published work and who was never presented as the "musician-thinker" of the eventality of the event in the way that Mallarmé or Valéry appear as "poet-thinkers" of the event). This response then appears to be developed, this time in relation to political rather than literary events, in a long endnote—in fact by far the longest note—in the section "Notes, Commentaries and Digressions" at the end of *Logics of Worlds*. At stake in this note are not only the relationships between the work of the philosopher and his commitments as a militant, most notably within the Organisation Politique, but also the relationships between, on one hand, the eternity of truths, including political truths, and, on the other, the historicity of different "modes" of doing politics. Badiou more specifically draws a distinction between the operations of thought that are proper to philosophy and the conditions that constitute its outside. "That which has been thought and invoked as a condition by a philosophy is reconceived in such a way that it becomes another thought, even though it may be the only other (philosophical) thought *compatible* with the initial conditioning thought," Badiou writes. "In short, the relation of philosophy to other kinds of thought cannot be evaluated in terms of identity or contradiction, neither from its own point of view nor from that of these other kinds of thought. Rather, it is a matter of knowing what it is that—as an effect of conceptual sublimations (or speculative formalizations)—remains essentially compatible with the philosophy in question, and what is instead organically alien to it."[43] Other than "sublimation" and "formalization," this note also describes the operations of philosophy in terms of "(re)nomination" or "projection," adding terminological variety and nuance to the rather more limited play on the "seizing" of truths in philosophy and vice versa, philosophy's being "seized" by some nonphilosophical truths, in Badiou's *Manifesto for Philosophy* or *Conditions*. Finally, thanks to these operations, it would seem that the philosophical act can and must be distinguished from politics, without for this reason contradicting the latter, insofar as it is this act that turns the truths of politics, with the nominalist discontinuity of their different "modes," toward the subjective "invariants" that remain constant throughout history.

If these strategies may seem justifiable on behalf of a philosopher whose thought operations are by definition unique to philosophy even though they are conditioned by events outside of it, there comes a point where such selective appropriations and speculative displacements of the condition back onto the conditioned, or of the events back onto the philosophy of the event, can become real obstacles to that philosophy's application. Indeed, it is not difficult to imagine how the available options for such an application are reduced to two mirroring extremes. Either we could privilege the systematicity of the philosopher's conceptual apparatus, in which case the events studied by application actually risk becoming nothing more than illustrations of concepts, the rigorous definition of which would be extrinsic to the events themselves, or we could privilege the radical break introduced by the events in question at the expense of the philosopher's systematization, in which case the events risk becoming the occasion for a typically antiphilosophical appeal to the ineffable singularity of experience, over and above its impoverished conceptualization.

In response to this I would propose that we also consider a recommencement of historical materialism. To do so may require that we renew the task of theory, as distinct from both philosophy and the truth procedures that condition it, in order to trace a diagonal across these two extremes so as to produce an effective thinking of the event. I would argue that theory has a role of its own to play in this context—one perhaps comparable to the role of psychoanalysis for the condition of love, or to the role of "inaesthetics" for art and "metapolitics" for politics, when they are not yet equated with philosophy as such. But, as I suggested earlier, it seems to me that the texts in *Metapolitics* and *Handbook of Inaesthetics* do not yet quite accomplish the program they announce in their respective epigraphs. *Metapolitics*, for instance, sticks for the most part to a programmatic enunciation of the principles for a metapolitics, compared to the treatment of politics by thinkers such as Althusser, Lazarus, or Rancière. Aside from the chapters on the concepts of "justice" or "democracy," the real examples of a metapolitical reading, through which philosophy thinks politics in its immanent historicity, can be found in Badiou's lectures on the Cultural Revolution, on the Paris Commune, and on May '68, variously reworked in *Polemics* and *Logics of Worlds*. To continue this line of work would demand that we trace a diagonal across the two extremes of exemplifying conceptualization and anticonceptual ecstasy. Unless we fall into insipid mimeticism, albeit with an eye on killing the master, it is a question of finding a way to be neither a mere disciple of the philosopher nor an antiphilosophical adversary.

PHILOSOPHY, POLITICS, HISTORY:
MARX IN REVERSE

Badiou's requirements for philosophy are perhaps overly demanding if it is our aim to take him up on his offer of applying the conceptual apparatus of *Being and Event*. In his *Manifesto* he even goes so far as to suggest that, in the absence of a strict compossibility among the truths produced in all four of these conditions, philosophy also ceases to exist. "We shall thus posit that there are four conditions of philosophy, and that the lack of a single one gives rise to its dissipation, just as the emergence of all four conditioned its apparition."[44] But, I would argue, perhaps we need not follow the philosopher in these exorbitant demands. My proposal is rather to work more closely on the conditions, as it were at the grassroots level, all the while trying to stay clear of the pull by which the philosopher almost inevitably seems to tie the conditions back into the conditioned. This task, by which I would redefine the field of critical theory as a unique and specific contribution to historical materialism, involves a precarious balancing act between, on the one hand, the quasi-transcendental if not outright transcendent repetition of the essence of the event and, on the other, the empiricist dissolving of the event into the prior conditions or prerequisites that explain away the chance surprise of its emergence.

In any case the underlying problem regarding the relation between art or politics and the historicity of their concepts and practices is certainly not unique to Badiou's work, and it seems to me at least an equally burning issue for someone like Rancière. This also means that in their mutual attacks, the one by Badiou in *Metapolitics* against Rancière's "apoliticism," and the one by Rancière in *Aesthetics and Its Discontents* against Badiou's modernist "aestheticism," what remains hidden or unsaid concerns precisely the other pole—art or the aesthetic regime for Rancière and politics for Badiou—being those conditions of truth, or regimes of thinking, for which each has proven himself capable of setting up a new configuration of historicity, otherwise absent or at least insufficiently elaborated in the polemical chasm between the two.

To illustrate this last point, let me return one more time to the case of Mallarmé. The principal task for the work of theory of the historical materialist consists in coming to an understanding about the double valence of Mallarmé's case, not only as a poet-thinker of the event in and of itself but at the same time as an innovator within French postromantic poetry. For Badiou, as we saw, the first half of this reading seems to take away most interest from the second. By contrast, it is the second half of the question that receives much greater attention in Rancière's short book on Mallarmé. The latter remains without a doubt the great poet of the eventlike nature of the event, emblematized by the sirens: "Mallarmé transforms them into emblems of the poem itself, power of a song that is capable both of making itself heard and of transforming itself into silence."[45] But we should also add immediately that according to this reading, the eventlike nature of the poem is inseparable from the equally singular relation it establishes with the place and time of its appearance: "The poem escapes the abyss that awaits it because it modifies the very mode of fiction, substituting the song of a vanishing siren for the great epic of Ulysses. What the siren metaphorizes, what the poem renders effective, then, is precisely the event and the calculated risk of the poem in an era and a 'mental environment' that are not yet ready to welcome it."[46] Rancière understands these two aspects—the event and its relation to an era and an environment not yet ready for it—as part of one and the same question.

Based on indications such as these, we can begin to see the consequences of an important philosophical decision: the value of affirming the "there is" of Mallarméan poetry, like that of any "there is," is inseparably structural *and* evental, transcendental *and* historical. Each time there is an event, in politics perhaps no less than in poetry, we witness a breakdown of principle that at the same time allows a reconstruction of its links with history. One thing does not exclude but rather presupposes the other. Otherwise, in the absence of such an articulation, which seems to me key to a reinvigoration of historical materialism, we would fall into a leftist scheme or an overly structural fixation on the materialist dialectic alone.

On the other hand, when it comes to politics, it is Badiou who in his recent work on the Paris Commune or the Cultural Revolution may have contributed more elements to reconstitute the link between history and politics than Rancière. Such a history of different "modes" of doing politics would evidently be hard to come by if we started from a book such as Rancière's *Disagreement*. In this last book there certainly are "ages" or "eras" such as "the Marxist age" or "the nihilist age," just as in an article written with Danielle Rancière for *Les Révoltes Logiques* there is talk of "the post-leftist age," but in the last instance history only seems to determine the successive eras of the covering-up of an invariant form of politics, to which the book seeks to restitute its "improper property" that is also "the ultimate secret of any social order," namely, "the pure and simple equality of anyone and everyone," which serves as "the basis and original gulf of the community order."[47]

To overcome the chasm of this missed encounter between Badiou and

Rancière, it seems to me that the question of the historicity of thought imposes itself as a question that can no longer be postponed. Thus, we must come to understand what it means to think under the condition of certain transformations in art or in politics. Not only: what does it mean to think in the present? But also and above all: what does it mean to think in the present under the condition of certain events from the past, whether in the long or in the short run? The risk involved in giving too quick an answer to these questions should be clear enough: the historicity of art or politics would be reduced to mere historicism, the event would be re-aligned with the system of constraints that made it possible, and the radicalism of the disruption would end up getting diluted in the proverbial water under the bridge. Yet it is possible that the price to be paid for not taking into account these questions is even higher: a radicalism pivoting on its own emptiness, a thinking of the pure "there is" of art and politics cut off from any inscription in a place and according to specific historical modes, and finally the falling-back in the false appeal of a certain speculative leftism that our age, the nihilist age of the ethical turn and postpolitics, had flattered itself for having been able to do without. Unless we grab hold of individual events only as so many illustrations in yet another rehashing of a philosopher's basic conceptual apparatus, however, we can and perhaps must try to think events in such a way as to transform philosophy itself. This would be a formidable task, if not the only task, for theory.

Let us say that the task before us is the exact inverse of the one confronting the reader of Marx. If the author of *Capital* does in fact present a philosophy, which Engels will label dialectical materialism, we have no access to this philosophy except by reading between the lines of Marx's explicit work as the founder of a materialist science of history. The two, though different in nature, are nonetheless inseparable. "It is impossible to oppose a theoretical concept of history to a real history defined by its empirical complexity-impurity. In the Marxist epistemology, complexity itself is constructed according to the concepts of the theory," as Badiou also wrote several decades ago in personal correspondence with Emmanuel Terray: "To account for the constitution of real societies is the very task of the theory of history."[48] Symmetrically, it is just as impossible to separate the theoretical concepts of the materialist dialectician, as formal arrangement, from their adherences at the level of historical experience. It would then be a question of reconstructing, for Badiou's recent works, what remains more unified at the level of the exposition in a seminar such as *Theory of the Subject.* If the author of the two volumes of *Being and Event* can now boast about his having initiated a new philosophical stage in the systematization of the materialist dialectic, what remains to be explained would be this genealogy implied within the formal theory, that is, the new historical materialism about which he fears, for reasons that are consistent with his own philosophy, that it will for the most part have reactionary consequences.

In the end this plea for renewing the task of theory as part of the recommencement of historical materialism, though firmly anchored in the general atmosphere of the materialist dialectic, comes down to writing a kind of Borgesian "history of eternity." In *Logics of Worlds*, because of the book's polemic against the cultural-historical relativism typical of so-called democratic materialism, Badiou undoubtedly insists much more on the eternal and invariant character of truth, just as he demands, in *Manifesto for Philosophy*, that philosophy separates itself from the sense of guilt imparted by the belief that it must be judged in the tribunal of history of the past century, universally considered to have been criminal. Against the disastrous effects of this generalized historicism, therefore, it is only logical that the eternal and invariant aspect would be given priority, insofar as history, contrary to what happens in the nineteenth century, no longer has any intrinsically critical or revolutionary value, as is still the case for Hegel or Marx. And yet even for Badiou there is a historical unfolding of eternal truths, of truths that are addressed to all and for all times. Thus, he wonders whether it is even justified to separate the conceptual formalisms from their genealogical anchorage. It is precisely in order to answer this question that Badiou asks us not only "to bring historicism to a close and dispel all the myths engendered by temporalizing the concept" but also to consider the possibility of presenting the appearing of a truth—for example the truth of mathematics, but the same could be said of the truth of politics— as a "history of truth" that is at the same time "the human history of eternity," that is to say, "an empirical historicization of the eternity of truths."[49]

The underlying challenge, then, is actually to think under the condition of certain historical events, the truths of which are nonetheless eternal and available for all times. This also means to restitute the historicity of past and present events, without dissolving the singularity of their transformative power into the sum total of their prior conditionings. In other words, there might well be a need to supplement the philosophy of the event with a balanced combination of criticism and theory. This form of thinking would be critical, insofar as it is also historical and genealogical, while risking to become merely empiricist or positivistic; and it would be theoretical, insofar as it is conceptual and transcendental, while risking to become purely dogmatic if not downright mystical. Now, it is certainly true that for this inveterate Platonist not much seems to have changed since the beginnings of philosophy in ancient Greece. "There have been few, very few, crucial changes in the nature of the problems of thought since Plato, for instance. But, on the basis of some truth-procedures that unfold subjectivizable bodies, point by point, one reconstitutes a different past, a history of achievements, discoveries, breakthroughs, which is by no means a cultural monumentality but a legible succession of fragments of eternity."[50] It is this history of eternity, not only in principle but also in the thickness of actual bodies and situations, that remains almost entirely to be written. And yet, perhaps this history is no longer the task of the philosopher, who instead prefers to devote himself body and soul to his new translation, which he calls a "hypertranslation," of Plato's *Republic*, announced under the new title *Du Commun(isme)* (*Of the Common* or *Of Communism*).[51]

FROM POTENTIALITY TO INEXISTENCE

←————————————————————→

THE DREAMWORK DOES THINK

> They have no ideals to realize, but to set free the elements of the
> new society with which the old collapsing bourgeois society itself is
> pregnant.—MARX, *The Civil War in France*

If Badiou himself does not take up the work of the historical materialist, we can nevertheless draw several principles from his philosophical work that significantly reshuffle the ways in which historical change has been envisaged over the past century and a half. In fact, the philosophy of the event also presupposes a new understanding of the relation of the event to the historical conditions that precede and surround it. Traditionally, this relation has been described in terms of a potential with which human history would supposedly already be pregnant. Thus, Marx, in one of his most fascinating letters to Arnold Ruge from 1843, published the following year in the short-lived *Deutsch-Französische Jahrbücher*, writes about the task ahead for the communist movement if a revolutionary change is to follow from criticism of the current state of affairs: "It will then become evident that the world has long possessed the dream of something of which it has only to be conscious in order to possess it in reality. It will become evident that it is not a question of drawing a great mental dividing line between past and future, but of *realising* the thoughts of the past. Lastly, it will become evident that humanity is not beginning a *new* work, but is consciously carrying into effect its old work."[1] In a nutshell these lines concentrate the force of a long-standing tradition of thinking about potentiality—in this case referring to the field of politics but similar arguments could be made for art and aesthetics—preparing the way for Lenin's famous notion that politics itself is an art rather than a spontaneous happening or a scientific fact. The tradition in question holds that radical change is the realization or fulfillment of dreams, ideals, or hopes that lie already dormant in the situation of departure, even if we are not yet fully conscious of them. The new, accordingly, consists in bringing the old to fruition, so that all change presupposes the existence of a situation complete with the potential for upheaval, which is just waiting to be put into actual practice through conscious action. Political change, more specifically, is the conscious actualization of historical potentiality.

Marx proffered similar statements elsewhere in his writings, including in the well-known 1859 preface to his *Contribution to the Critique of Political Economy*: "No social order ever perishes before all the productive forces for which there is room in it have developed; and new, higher relations of production never appear before the material conditions of their existence have matured in the womb of the old society itself. Therefore mankind always sets itself only such tasks as it can solve; since, looking at the matter more closely, it will always be found that the task itself arises only when the material conditions of its solution already exist or are at least in the process of formation."[2] Here, as Althusser would later insist in his posthumous notes on "Marx in His Limits," the presupposition is that the dialectic of history proceeds without a hitch from a problem to its solution as a result of the fulfillment—the filling and the exceeding—of prior material conditions at the level of society or of the productive forces. In a commentary on the 1859 preface, Althusser writes: "Let us also note that, in any case, *it is the productive forces which are the motor of the upheaval*: they need only develop until they have not only 'filled' the capacities of the relations of production, but exceed them, causing the carapace to split open and new relations of production, ready and waiting in the old society, to take their place."[3] Even if we follow the late Althusser in asserting that, except in very few passages such as these, Marx actually never upheld the primacy of the productive forces over the relations of production, we would still have to come to terms with the persistence of an underlying paradigm of potentiality according to which the new—in this case communism—emerges and develops from within the bosom of the old—from within the existing antagonisms of bourgeois society. As Marx and Engels also write in *The German Ideology*: "We call communism the *real* movement which abolishes the present state of things. The conditions of this movement result from the now existing premise."[4]

Thus, in politics, the paradigm of potentiality articulates three basic terms: (1) the now existing premise of a given situation or world; (2) the dream or thought of something that is already present in this world but that escapes its rational grip precisely insofar as it can be said to be only a dream; and (3) the conscious action, or the act of becoming conscious, that is the necessary and perhaps even sufficient condition for this dream to become actual. Revolutions, from this point of view, appear as so many sleeping beauties of history, lying in wait for the kiss of political conscious-ness in order for them to wake up and actually live their dream.

Many thinkers in the tradition of Western Marxism, from Georg Lukács to Walter Benjamin to Guy Debord, have taken up this idea from Marx, often with a direct reference to the passage quoted above from the letter to Ruge. Benjamin, for example, famously compares the task of dialectical thinking for the historical materialist to the awakening of dream-images from the past, as if to produce a surrealist flash of recognizability. "The realization of dream elements in the course of waking up is the canon of dialectics. It is paradigmatic for the thinker and binding for the historian," Benjamin writes in one of his notebooks for *The Arcades Project*, in which he also wonders: "Is awakening perhaps the synthesis of dream conscious-ness (as thesis) and waking consciousness (as antithesis)? Then the mo-ment of awakening would be identical with the 'now of recognizability,' in which things put on their true—surrealist—face."[5] Each in his own unique way, to be sure, seems to embrace the underlying presupposition that the possibility of the new as such is transitive to a potential held out by the old, so that the future is not separate from but immanent to the present as an untapped resource handed down to us from the past.

WHAT IS TO BE DREAMED?

> Of course, this is all by way of example, only to *illustrate* the fact that at the present moment, *without treating insurrection as an art*, it is impossi-ble to remain loyal to Marxism.—LENIN, "Marxism and Insurrection"

Even Lenin appears to repeat a similar idea, albeit with an added twist. Thus, the notion that revolutionary politics lies in concentrating already existing social and economical contradictions, which I discussed in my introduction, can still be considered a rephrasing in different terms of the model of the actualization of potentiality. In fact, the whole paradigm for thinking of potentiality in politics enters into a crisis with the split between the view of politics as the concentrated expression of already existing economical contradictions and the view that politics must take precedence over economics. Some of these tensions can also be perceived in Lenin's own recourse to the image of a dream in need of achievement. "It is necessary to dream!" he writes, not without a certain alarm or embarrassment, in *What Is to Be Done?* And imagining—or dreaming of—the possible criticisms of his comrades who might ask "whether a Marxist has any right at all to dream, knowing that according to Marx mankind always sets itself tasks it can solve," he goes on seeking a place to hide behind a long quote from Dimitri Pisarev:

> "There are rifts and rifts," wrote Pisarev of the rift between dreams and reality. "My dream may run ahead of the natural march of events or may fly off at a tangent in a direction in which no natural march of events will ever proceed. In the first case my dream will not cause any harm; it may even support and augment the energy of a person at work. . . . There is nothing in such dreams that would distort or paralyse labour-power. On the contrary, if man were completely deprived of the ability to dream in this way, if he could not from time to time run ahead and mentally conceive, in an entire and completed picture, the product to which his hands are only just beginning to lend shape, then I cannot at all imagine what stimulus there would be to induce man to undertake and complete extensive and strenuous work in the sphere of art, science, and practical life. . . . The rift between dreams and reality causes no harm if only the individual dreaming believes seriously in his dream, if he attentively observes life, compares his observations with his castles in the air, and if, generally speaking, he works conscientiously for the achievement of his fantasies. When there is some connection between dreams and life then all is well."[6]

On one hand, Lenin's measuring stick—as Jacques Derrida also points out in a short text titled "What Is to Be Done with the Question 'What Is to Be Done?'?"—still consists in knowing how to overcome the rift between fantasy and life by conscientiously "achieving" the dream.[7] On the other, however, there now also appears to be a virtue to the rift as such. It is what enables one to "run ahead" of one's proper time and place, so as to act according to an anticipated completion, or a fictitious extension, of the task at hand. Transposed into political terms, the act of consciousness then no longer simply fulfills the potential of a dream nor provides the solution to a problem that humankind already possesses without knowing it; instead, it is the dream that opens up a gap or rift between being and consciousness in the first place. Only the dream, or what I would describe more generally as a certain degree of fiction, enables the separation between knowledge and truth, for instance, between the knowledge accumulated in the science of history through the critique of political economy and the truth of emancipatory politics.

My point is obviously not to rehearse these worn-out distinctions in the history of Marxism and Leninism. Nor do I merely want to dress them up in the fashionable terms of contemporary post-Marxism. Instead, what I am proposing is that we extract from them some of the categories that together constitute a solid conceptual apparatus, the validity of which is now increasingly being put into question together with most other tenets of Marx and Marxism.

Regardless of the periodization, indeed, there can be no doubt that the crisis of Marxism—both in its Soviet and its Western version, with Maoism admittedly presenting a unique case that depending on one's perspective can be seen as both an exception to and a final confirmation of the crisis of Marxism and Leninism—is inseparable from a radical critique of this articulation between potentiality and actuality with which an older tradition explained the emergence of radical political change. To understand this in greater detail, we must come to terms with the relation between the concepts of history, politics, and truth—the latter being the name with which from now on I will refer to the dreamwork mentioned by Marx and Lenin, arguing with Jacques Lacan in *The Ethics of Psychoanalysis* that "every truth has the structure of fiction" in a sense that is no longer purely pejorative: "The fictive, in effect, is not essentially what is misleading but, properly speaking, what I call the symbolic."[8] The point is not to oppose the truth of the real, not even in terms of the class struggle, to the fictions of ideology or of the imaginary. To the contrary, without the symbolic efficacy of a certain fictive work there would be no real in the first place. "The real is always the object of a fiction, that is to say of a construction of the space in which the visible, the sayable and the feasible are tied together," as Jacques Rancière also writes: "The work of politics that invents new subjects and introduces new objects is also a fictive work. Thus the relation of art to politics is not a passage from fiction to the real but a relation between two ways of producing fictions."[9] In my eyes, it is precisely a thorough reconfiguration of the space outlined by history, politics, and truth as inscribed in the structure of a dreamlike fiction that is responsible for the different approaches to potentiality that can be found in theory and philosophy today. Badiou's work can be usefully contrasted on this very question of potentiality with that of thinkers such as Deleuze or Derrida, as well as with more recent proposals from Agamben to Žižek.

"Politics is in a structure of fiction," asserts Badiou in his *Theory of the Subject*, finding inspiration not only in Lacan but also in Mallarmé, when the latter writes that "the social relation and its momentary measure, condensed or expanded to allow for government, is a fiction. It belongs to the domain of Letters."[10] In *Can Politics Be Thought?* Badiou returns to this same passage from Mallarmé, but now he introduces a slight distance by adopting the fashionable distinction between politics and the political: "*The political* is never anything but the fiction in which *a politics* makes the hole of the event."[11] It is this displacement in the relation of truth to fiction that we must come to understand in terms of its effects for the articulation between history and politics. What has changed in this articulation? "What takes a salutary leave along with the political, at the same time as the narrative and linear figure of the novel, is the fiction of a measure: the idea that the social bond is measurable in thought according to the philosophical norm of the good State, or even of the good Revolution, which amounts to the same thing," explains Badiou: "It is this object, now State and now Revolution, fictively evoked as the active foundation of the political philosopheme, which turns out to be doubtful today in its pretense to be a concept of political experience."[12] As we will see, these doubts also apply to the conceptual paradigm that traditionally is put in place to think of change as the actualization of a potential inherent in the existing social bond.

HISTORY DOES NOT EXIST: TIME'S BROKEN ARROW

Badiou, in the first of two interviews reprinted below in the appendices, claims that his entire philosophy—like Marx's, perhaps, if indeed he has one and if he is not rather an antiphilosopher—aims at thinking the new in the situation. Paraphrasing Marx's letter to Ruge, we might even say that Badiou's aim in his principal work, *Being and Event*, is also not to insert a great mental dividing line separating being from the event according to some rigid binary, even though this reading in recent years has become canonical as I explained in my introduction, but neither can we say that the truth of an event is merely the *fulfillment* of the thought of being. For an event to occur there must be a rupture or discontinuity. Consequently, the new—the emergent truth of an event—does not already lie dormant as a hidden potential within the old—within the existing situation of being. The difficult task consists rather in articulating the emergence of an event onto a rift or scission at the heart of the normal representation of being itself. How, then, can we relate the break of the new to the situation at hand if we cannot rely on the fulfillment of a hidden potential nor opt for the opposite extreme of cutting the link between being and event altogether? Three concepts will guide us along this twisted path in the articulation of knowledge and truth, being and event, and history and politics, namely: the concepts of the impossible, the site, and the inexistent.

For Badiou, in any case, the articulation of being and event does not, or no longer, require that the new be present as a potential within the bosom of the old. In fact, he may seem to have shifted his position somewhat in this regard. In chapter 3 I described this shift as a move from the *politicization of history* to the *historicization of politics*. Even the image of this shift is potentially misleading, however, if we want to understand the overall project of Badiou's philosophy. Such a shift takes place only apparently at the moment of the crisis or saturation of Badiou's Maoism, somewhere in between *Theory of the Subject* and *Can Politics Be Thought?* In reality it would be better to say that what may seem to be a historical shift is itself rather a necessary oscillation that is present from beginning to end throughout Badiou's work. Like the tension between the two definitions of politics contained in Lenin's statement, this oscillation is due to the fact that there are no longer (if ever there were) any structural or historical guarantees for politics. Such guarantees are not *given* but must be *produced*. This is why politics takes precedence over the class analysis of the critique of political economy.

Political conflict, in other words, cannot be derived from prior data that would be given at the level of society or the economy. As Badiou writes in *Manifesto for Philosophy*: "What is being sought after today is a thinking of politics that, while dealing with strife, having the structural Two in its field of intervention, does not have this Two as an objective essence."[13] This insight, which many readers will have interpreted as a self-criticism coming from the later Badiou, is already fully at work in earlier texts. Thus, in *Theory of the Subject*, referring to Mao's portrayal of the uncertain future of communism, we can read "the following, which is crucial for Marxism: history does not exist (it would be a figure of the whole). Only historical periods or historicizations (figures of the One-of-the-two) exist."[14] Precisely because of this reason, politics is an art and not a science, namely, because there is no objective guarantee, in the sense of existing class contradictions, for the emergence of political antagonisms; instead, all such antagonisms are themselves the product of an artful intervention, with which a subject responds to the unpredictability of an event. If the event no longer depends on scientific or historical *knowledge*, though, this is only because it is a question of political *truth*. The necessary nonknowledge should not serve as an alibi for voluntaristic adventurism nor as an excuse for self-righteous inaction; rather, it is part of the very structure of undecidability of the event in the relation between politics and history.

The paradigm of potentiality, however, may well be inadequate for understanding the undecidable nature of the event. Indeed, at least in the way this paradigm has been handed down to us as part of the history of metaphysics, say from Aristotle to Hegel, there seems to be an arrow that necessarily leads out of potentiality into the bull's eye of actuality. It is this teleological necessity that is variously questioned, interrupted, or purely and simply abandoned in contemporary postmetaphysical thinking. Badiou's philosophy, even while proclaiming to be both a physics and a metaphysics, is in this sense part of a wider range of options in the putting into crisis of the paradigm of potentiality and its actualization.

Among the different options available for the deconstruction or overcoming of the metaphysical couple potentiality/actuality, I will briefly mention three alternative approaches, before returning in more detail to Badiou's formulations. In any case, the following options are not mutually exclusive and certain thinkers share features from two or all three of them:

1. *Potentiality without actuality, or spectrality without presence.* Common to Agamben or Derrida and their followers, this approach in a certain sense interrupts the arrow's flight, or refuses to let go of it, so as to hold on to the bow's innermost tension as a moment of pure potentiality without actuality. If in fact we can still speak in terms of potentiality in this case, it is only on the absolute condition that it be kept separate from the

illusions of self-presence and actuality. "It must therefore exceed any presence as presence to itself," as Derrida writes in *Specters of Marx*. "At least it has to make this presence possible only on the basis of the movement of some disjointing, disjunction, or disproportion: in the inadequation to self."[15] This also means that rather than following the direction of time's arrow, as a certain reading of Marx would purport based on texts such as the 1859 preface, true politics—even or especially a politics of justice for which communism might still serve as a proper name—is untimely and disjointed from history. "To be just: beyond the living present in general—and beyond its simple negative reversal. A spectral moment, a moment that no longer belongs to time, if one understands by this word the linking of modalized presents (past present, actual present: 'now,' future present)."[16]

We could also say that, for Derrida, the doctrinaire image of the historical materialist, who already with Benjamin begins to show his or her true "surrealist" face, must be replaced by that of another "scholar," perhaps that of the post-Marxist. "*Thou art a Scholler: speake to it Horatio,*" Derrida quotes Marcellus's words to Horatio in *Hamlet*. "Marcellus was perhaps anticipating the coming, one day, one night, several centuries later, of another 'scholar.' The latter would finally be capable, beyond the opposition between presence and non-presence, actuality and inactuality, life and non-life, of thinking the possibility of the specter, the specter as possibility."[17] Marx's limit as a "scholar" of political economy or a "scientist" of history according to Derrida consists precisely in the thought that the dividing line between the dream potential and its realization ought to pass into actuality. This is the same line that Marx in his letter to Ruge sought not so much to insert between the past and the future but rather to think in terms of the fulfillment of a contradictory present. "Marx thought, to be sure, on his side, from the other side, that the dividing line between the ghost and actuality ought to be crossed, like utopia itself, by a realization, that is, by a revolution; but *he too* will have continued to believe, to try to believe in the existence of this dividing line as real limit and conceptual distinction. He too? No, someone in him. Who? The 'Marxist' who will engender what for a long time is going to prevail under the name of 'Marxism.' "[18] For Derrida, in contrast, because there is never or there must never be any actualization into the living present of ontology, much less a certain or necessary one, a spectral possibility or potentiality is also always

a form of inactuality or impotentiality. Without feeding into virile anxi-
eties, pure potentiality as impotentiality should be seen as a source of
critical force. "It is a potentiality that is not simply the potential to do this
or that thing but potential to not-do, potential not to pass into actuality," as
Agamben writes: "Contrary to the traditional idea of potentiality that is
annulled in actuality, here we are confronted with a potentiality that con-
serves itself and saves itself in actuality. Here potentiality, so to speak,
survives actuality and, in this way, *gives itself to itself*."[19] Potentiality without
actuality, in other words, is the very root of freedom and justice, so that a
new thinking of pure potentiality might well be the condition for a re-
politicization, or for another concept of the political.

2. Real virtuality, or the actualization of virtuality and the virtualization of the actual.

Common to Deleuze and, strangely enough, via Benjamin, to certain recent writings of Žižek, this approach forgoes the conceptual opposition of
the real and the possible, and perhaps even that of the potential and the
actual, in favor of a model of virtuality. "The only danger in all this is that
the virtual could be confused with the possible," Deleuze warns in *Difference and Repetition*: "The possible is opposed to the real; the process
undergone by the possible is therefore a 'realization.' By contrast, the
virtual is not opposed to the real; it possesses a full reality by itself. The
process it undergoes is that of actualization."[20] If we can still use the notion
of "potential" to describe this process, it can only be on the condition that
we avoid reducing the logic of change to one of "realization," meaning
either the "limitation" imposed by possibles upon each other or the "opposition" of the merely possible to the reality of the real. Potentiality, in other
words, should not be reduced to the possibility of an existent that, while
nonexistent for the time being, nevertheless is already possible before its
birth at the level of its concept. "What difference can there be between the
existent and the non-existent if the non-existent is already possible, already
included in the concept and having all the characteristics that the concept
confers upon it as a possibility," Deleuze also writes, arguing instead for
an idea of the actualization of the virtual as producing genuine difference
in repetition without resemblance to a pregiven possible. Here, in fact,
Deleuze indirectly seems to be alluding to some of Marx's formulations
quoted earlier: "For a potential or virtual object, to be actualized is to

create divergent lines which correspond to—without resembling—a virtual multiplicity. The virtual possesses the reality of a task to be performed or a problem to be solved: it is the problem which orientates, conditions and engenders solutions, but these do not resemble the conditions of the problem."[21]

To continue using the same metaphor, we could say that in this second scenario the arrow coming out of the bow shuttles back and forth between the virtual and the actual, without ever having to pass through the merely possible. The virtual becomes actual by effectuating itself, but everything actual can also be countereffectuated so as to signal an instance of virtuality: "In going from A to B and then B to A, we do not arrive back at the point of departure as in a bare repetition; rather, the repetition between A and B and B and A is the progressive trajectory or description of the whole of a problematic field."[22] Such would be for example the task of repetition in history from the point of view of politics. "What repetition repeats is not the way the past 'effectively was,' but the virtuality inherent to the past and betrayed by its past actualization," writes Žižek, expanding on Deleuze's basic insight with additional clues taken from Benjamin: "In this precise sense, the emergence of the New changes the past itself, that is, it retroactively changes (not the actual past—we are not in science fiction—but) the balance between actuality and virtuality in the past" so that its inner excess "is not simply abolished, dismissed as irrelevant, but, as it were, transposed into the virtual state, continuing to haunt the emancipatory imaginary as a dream waiting to be realized."[23]

3. Actual impossibility, or the possibility of the impossible.

This is how I would describe Badiou's approach, strongly influenced by certain ideas from Lacan that he also shares with Žižek. Here, as in certain cartoon scenes, the arrow suddenly loops back in midair—but not so as to return to the shooter unchanged but rather so as to set into motion a spiraling movement that marks the periodization of history. Politics, thus, is the art of making the impossible possible, which is one reason why it always entails a form of aesthetics as well. "Let me add in passing that a maxim that is very much in vogue among parliamentary politicians, especially 'from the left,' is the one that declares: 'Politics is the art of the possible,'" Badiou writes in *Theory of the Subject*, referring to this debate as a clear example if ever there was one of the class struggle in theory: "As far as I am concerned, I posit explicitly that *politics is the art of the impossible.*"[24] If politics is the *art* and not the *science* of the impossible, which would be mathematics, this is because of the hurried and unpredictable nature of its interventions, none of which are guaranteed by the objective course of history. As Badiou suggests in *Can Politics Be Thought?*: "Politics often boils down to having to ask the right question, the one that makes a break so as to deliver that of which the table, the unity of the hypothesis, continued to guarantee the impossible possibility. Therein lies the whole hurried aesthetic of the intervention."[25]

POLITICS AS THE ART OF THE IMPOSSIBLE

> Today there is much ado about communication. And yet it is clear that it is incommunication that, by making the impossible a possibility, puts truth into circulation in politics.—BADIOU, *Peut-on penser la politique?*

Here I should immediately reiterate that the category of the impossible is not the same as the forbidden. Badiou thus refuses to see any political value in the twin processes of interdiction and transgression. What is forbidden designates an effect of the structure. Within the constraints of a given logical structure, for example, certain statements are prohibited insofar as the slot for them within the table of available options is purely and simply crossed out. This slot is what Deleuze would call the empty square in the structure. Like the impossible, the prohibition of this option may very well mark a point of the real, insofar as it is the absent cause that holds the structure itself in place. As such, however, it cannot become the target of a genuine political intervention:

> This real, however, is only structural. It is the lack proper to all possible statements. It has nothing to do with any situation whatsoever, since every situation, that is to say, every complex order of propositions, whether true or false, realizes a possibility that stands under the condition of this lack. I will posit that such a structural lack is a *forbidden* of the place. The forbidden, in my eyes, is not a political category, because it is unrealizable in any situation whatsoever. It is a category of the very being of the Law. In this I also posit that the classical notion of the transgression of a prohibition, if it has some erotic virtue as is often pretended, has zero political virtue.[26]

What is forbidden as a structural point of the real, therefore, must be distinguished from what is here called historically impossible. "To the forbidden, I will oppose the historicity of the *impossible*," Badiou adds: "The impossible is a category of the subject, not of the place; of the event, and not of the structure. It is what gives politics its very being."[27] Or, to use the terms from Badiou's *Metapolitics*: "Prohibition is always a regime of the State; impossibility is a regime of the Real."[28]

The logic of change that emerges from these brief reflections on interdiction and impossibility in *Can Politics Be Thought?* no longer corresponds to the romantic or surrealist imagery of a dream destined to a rude awakening and/or its fulfillment. Nor are we talking of the hidden potential that is already present within the existing world, ready to become actual. Rather, the task of a political intervention is twofold: (1) to turn a deaf ear to the noisy declarations about the impossibility of what is not, so as to enable oneself to hear what happens; and (2) based on an event as such a happening, to put into circulation a supplementary statement or proposition that forces the possibility of that which the dominant structure stubbornly confines to the realm of the impossible.

If we can speak of a "prepolitical" situation in this context, it is not in the sense that social or economical contradictions would be waiting to become properly "political" through their concentrated expression but rather in the sense that the "normal" regime of things all of a sudden is interrupted by an "absurd" or "abnormal" fact, so that now a prior impossibility becomes visible through the retroactive effect of an intervention that at the same time turns this impossible into an unheard-of possibility:

> The essence of the impossible, which is historically assigned, amounts to being deaf to the voice of the time. Thus is created a prepolitical situation whose principle, as you see, is the interruption: interruption of the ordinary social hearing, putting aside of all the facts. This is also why the police arrives, which is always the fact police, the police against the deaf: "Are you deaf?" says the cop. He is right. The police is never anything other than the amplifier of already established facts, their maximum noise, destined to all whose actions and words attest, since it is historically impossible, that they are hard of hearing.[29]

Nothing guarantees this passage of the impossible into the possible. No linear accumulation of elements in the original situation will ever produce the leap from quantity to quality that happens as the result of an event or aleatory encounter. "This means that no determination of the being which issues from the 'taking-hold' of the encounter is prefigured, even in outline, in the being of the elements that converge in the encounter," as Badiou's former teacher Althusser also writes in his own later musings on the aleatory logic of change with which he seeks to overcome the crisis of Marxism. "Quite the contrary: no determination of these elements can be assigned, except by *working backwards* from the result to its becoming."[30] Not only is the becoming-possible of an impossibility entirely contingent, falling outside of the realm of scientific objectivity, but it also requires the unpredictable wager of an intervening subject. "That is, instead of thinking contingency as a modality of necessity, or an exception to it, we must think necessity as the becoming-necessary of the encounter of contingencies."[31] The new, in other words, is never simply the teleological fulfillment or realization of a tendency already present within the old but, what is more, a tendency appears as such only as the retroactive effect of a subjective intervention: "*Without this 'intervention,' the tendency will never be automatically realized.*"[32]

Here we come upon the most crucial argument against the older model of change as the actualization of an already existing potentiality. For Badiou, in order to enable a genuine thinking of the event, not only should we replace the category of potentiality with that of impossibility but, in a given situation, the latter is not even apparent except as the backwards effect of a subject. "The subjective effect here is that we must supplement the situation for the event which it contains, perhaps, to become manifest to begin with," Badiou writes and, parodying Lacan in half-serious, half-mocking fashion, he adds: "A subject, hence a politics, is the in-between of an event to be elucidated and an event that elucidates. It is that which an event represents for another event."[33] Without a subjective intervention there is no historical impossibility either—only the ordinary structure of things with its inherent prohibitions or interdictions. Only a subject can unblock the impossible and, based on this interruption, trigger the circulation of a new truth for the situation as a whole: "It is here that the logic of intervention begins which is the point of supplementation by which, previously blocked in the situation, the truth circulates in the figure of the event."[34] This means that, in the end, a truth not only will have created entirely new possibilities, instead of merely realizing the situation's hidden potential, but it also is responsible for the emergence of impossibility itself as the subject's very own retroactive effect. "In order to grasp this reversal of contingency into necessity, one should leave behind the standard linear historical time structured as the realization of possibilities (at the temporal moment X, there are multiple possible directions history can take, and what actually takes place is the realization of one of the possibilities)," Žižek also argues in his book *In Defense of Lost Causes*. Indeed, "what this linear time is unable to grasp is the paradox of a contingent actual emergency which retroactively creates its own possibility: only when the thing takes place can we 'see' how it was possible."[35]

Badiou summarizes and illustrates this understanding of politics as the art of the impossible in an eloquent passage from his essay on Wittgenstein's antiphilosophy. "As for politics, it has value only insofar as it prescribes a 'possibility' for a situation that the immanent norm of this situation defines precisely as impossible—impossibility which, moreover, is actually required for the situation to be consistent," he writes, before giving specific examples: "This is evident when we think of the execution of the King in 1793 (which Kant, by the way, considered explicitly to be unthinkable), or of the directive 'all the power to the soviets' in 1917, or of Mao's maxim, which is intrinsically impossible, or even absurd, that the weaker can vanquish the stronger."[36] In a paradoxical sense, *both* the newly prescribed possibility *and* the impossibility within the existing situation are the simultaneous result of the political intervention of a subject.

We should not lose sight of this double effect of the subject's retroaction back upon the structure of its own situation, even if elsewhere the emphasis seems to fall almost exclusively on the production of new possibilities, to the point where we might seem to revert to the paradigm of a hidden potentiality. In *Metapolitics*, for example, responding to the tradition of political philosophy in a series of rhetorical questions that seem to encapsulate his own view of politics, Badiou writes: "If politics is not a truth procedure touching the being of the collective in question, or even the construction and the animation of a new and singular collective, aiming for the control or transformation of what is, what can it be? I mean: what can it be *for philosophy*? Neither a determinant factor as far as the objectivity of situations is concerned, nor a militant agent in the seizure of their latent possibles, what does politics consist in?"[37] Are we not back here in the older model of politics as the seizure and realization of possibilities already latent in the situation of departure?

   Alternately, if we ignore the link with the existing situation altogether, do we not fall prey to the opposite risk, that of a certain speculative leftism, which would define politics purely in terms of a self-authorizing prescription? This would seem to be the case in a later definition from *Metapolitics*: "A politics is a hazardous, militant and always partially undivided fidelity to evental singularity under a solely self-authorizing prescription. The universality of political truth that results from such a fidelity is itself legible, like all truth, only retroactively, in the form of a knowledge."[38] This view of politics as a strictly self-constituting prescription, or as a sovereign decision, is one of the results of a strong antidialectical impulse that runs through all of the writings collected in *Metapolitics*. This impulse is antidialectical precisely in the sense of refusing to think of politics in terms of a cobelonging of being and consciousness—regardless of whether this cobelonging is already inscribed within history or else requires the intervention of a party vanguard or hegemonic movement. For Badiou and Lazarus, politics is wholly subjective; it takes place in the realm of thought, without depending on the historical determination of so-called objective factors: "In any case, politics is only thinkable through itself."[39] And yet, a political intervention is never merely blind adventurism; it takes its inception from a singular event, which in turn is anchored in the present situation by way of a symptomatic link: "A contemporary politics is always *politics-there* [*politique-là*]. Its 'doing,' which is the same thing as its thought, prescribes the place."[40] Thus, even in *Metapolitics*, and despite a heightened emphasis on the self-authorizing prescription of new possibles, politics as the art of the impossible is still understood in terms of a symptomatic link to the situation in which it takes place.

   In order to conceive of a logic of change without falling back on the paradigm of potential and act inherited from Aristotle's metaphysics, therefore, we must think together the following principles: (1) a contemporary politics is the prescription of previously unheard-of and seemingly absurd possibilities; (2) a politics is not an objective given but the doing of an intervening subject; (3) political interventions are tied to the existing situation by virtue of the condensation of impossibilities that are symptomatic of this situation as a whole; and (4) the impossibility that gives a politics its singular place is legible only as the retroactive effect of that very same subjective intervention, for which this impossibility provides the minimal anchorage that keeps it from veering off into blind adventurism. These last two principles, in particular, provide a necessary corrective against the danger of subjectivism that lurks behind the first two. For Badiou's canonical work this can be summarized through a discussion of the combined role of the subject's intervention and of its site in *Being and Event* and *Logics of Worlds*, which I discussed in chapters 4 and 6.

FROM SUBJECTIVE INTERVENTION
TO EVENTAL SITE

Philosophy has no other legitimate aim except to help find the new names that will bring into existence the unknown world that is only waiting for us because we are waiting for it.—BADIOU, "The Caesura of Nihilism"

Thus, a key development for the theory of the event that recurs from *Can Politics Be Thought?* all the way to *Being and Event* can be said to lie in the notion that the impasse of the structure becomes visible only as a result of the retroactive effect of a subject's intervention. This intervention, though, should not be seen as a purely self-authorizing act or a sovereign decision, which would mark the possibility of an absolute beginning as a kind of primordial or grand event; nor can the event be reduced to the paradoxical effect of self-belonging, forbidden in set theory. As I repeatedly mentioned above, an event is always an event *for* a specific situation, as defined by the evental site that is symptomatic of this situation as a whole. It is not an absolute ex nihilo creation but a production that starts out from the edges of the concrete void that is proper to this situation and to this situation alone: "There are events uniquely in situations which present at least one site. The event is attached, in its very definition, to the place, to the point, in which the historicity of the situation is concentrated. Every event has a site which can be singularized in a historical situation."[41] This does not mean that the event already lies hidden as a sleeping potential within the situation at hand, ready to be actualized, for only an intervention loyal to the event retroactively defines the site of this event as such in the first place. "The confusion of the existence of the site (for example, the working class, or a given state of artistic tendencies, or a scientific impasse) with the necessity of the event itself is the cross of determinist or globalizing thought. The site is only ever a *condition of being* for the event," Badiou adds in an important reminder of the mutually determining role of the intervention and the site: "It is always possible that no event actually occur. Strictly speaking, a site is only 'evental' insofar as it is retroactively qualified by the occurrence of an event."[42] Specifically, this intervention takes the form of a looping or bootstrapping mechanism by which a subject comes to open up a minimal gap within its own conditions of existence. This is the moment of determining the determination by which the logic of change exceeds the conundrum of traditional debates over determinism and freedom.

The theory of the evental site thus appears to sit at the core of the articulation of being and event, in which the immanent deadlock of objectivity simultaneously enables and presupposes a subjective intervention. As Deleuze was one of the first to tell Badiou on reading the manuscript of *Being and Event*, the evental site—together with the related operation of forcing—may well be the book's most original conceptual creation: "It was Deleuze who, very early on, even before our correspondence, at the time when *Being and Event* had just appeared, told me that the heart of my philosophy was the theory of the site of the event. It was this theory, he told me, that explained why one is not in immanence, which he regretted a lot, but neither is one in transcendence. . . . The site is that which would diagonally cross the opposition of immanence and transcendence."[43] It is precisely because an event is always anchored in a specific situation by way of its symptomatic site that it is neither transcendent (it is not "beyond" the situation at hand) nor immanent (it is not "already" lying dormant, virtually or potentially, within the situation as we know it).

Badiou describes the site in highly metaphorical language as laying *aux bords du vide*, or on the edges of the void. More specifically, he defines the site as follows: "I will term *evental site* an entirely abnormal multiple: that is, a multiple such that none of its elements are presented in the situation," and he goes on to explain his own use of such highly poetic language:

> It becomes clearer why an evental site can be said to be "on the edge of the void" when we remember that from the perspective of the situation this multiple is made up exclusively of non-presented multiples. Just "beneath" this multiple—if we consider the multiples from which it is composed—there is *nothing*, because none of its terms are themselves counted-as-one. A site is therefore the *minimal* effect of structure which can be conceived; it is such that it belongs to the situation, whilst what belongs to it in turn does not.[44]

"Site" in *Logics of Worlds*, though, would seem to put us back in a more traditional understanding of the event in terms of self-reflexivity, without the symptomatic tie to the existing situation and the bootstrap mechanism of subjective intervention that brings out such a tie in the first place. Could we not say, then, that from "evental site" in *Being and Event* to "site" in *Logics of Worlds*, the theory of the event loses the historical anchorage provided by the earlier concept? This question cannot be addressed properly, however, without taking into consideration another concept, namely, that of the inexistent—a concept that may seem to be an entirely new creation in *Logics of Worlds* when in actual fact it is one of the many notions from the latter that hearken back to Badiou's *Theory of the Subject*. At the same time, we will see that the earlier treatment of the inexistent provides us with an anticipated critique of the way in which this concept may appear to function in the more recent work.

LOGICS OF THE INEXISTENT

The concept of the inexistent performs two related functions in *Logics of Worlds*. On one hand, at the level of what the book calls the transcendental logic of appearing, the inexistent serves as an index of the strict contingency of everything that appears. "Every object, considered in its being as a pure multiple, is inexorably marked by the fact that in appearing in this world it could have also not appeared," and the inexistent, as a "reserve of being" withdrawn from appearance, is precisely that which points to this necessity of contingency for every existence: "We can also say that a real point of inexistence is traced in existence—which measures the degree of appearance of an object in the world—in which we can read the fact that the object as a whole could have not existed."[45]

As a matter of fact, this argument in favor of inexistence as the sign or trace of contingency is already anticipated by Althusser in some of his unpublished work from the 1970s, most notably in the manuscript for his *Book on Communism*. What Althusser describes in terms of "nonexistence" is indeed strictly comparable to the role of the inexistent in *Logics of Worlds*. "The secret of the historical existence of existent modes of production," for example, "is to be sought less in the accomplished fact of the conditions of their existence than in the annulled, because non-accomplished fact of the conditions of non-existence of the same modes of production (for these conditions have sometimes been the death of them)."[46] Even Marxist historical materialism, far from reducing the analysis of modes of production to an enumeration of the iron laws of development, can be reconceptualized through the notion of nonexistence as the concrete analysis of historical contingency.

What Badiou adds to this idea is the fact that, in every existing object, grasped as pure multiple in its being, the law of the necessity of contingency is marked, in the order of appearing, by a specific element, which is called the object's inexistent: "We can conclude the following: given an object in a world, there exists a single element of this object which inexists in that world. It is this element that we call the proper inexistent of the object. It testifies, in the sphere of appearance, for the contingency of being-there. In this sense, its (ontological) being has (logical) non-being as its being-there."[47] Technically, the inexistent is not simply a mark of inexistence *in general*, which one would be tempted to write $\varnothing$, but the inexistent of a specific object A and of this object alone, which therefore should be written $\varnothing_A$. By way of example, Badiou briefly discusses the "Indians" as the inexistent proper to the world of "Quebec-between-1918-and-1950." They are the "without-rights" who reveal the contingency of the objective order of "civic and political rights" reserved for the Quebecois, just as the workers' political capacity, in a later example from *Logics of Worlds*, marks the inexistent proper to the situation in France for the "uncertain world of this Spring 1871" right before the Paris Commune. In the extent to which the historicity of situations such as Quebec or France lies condensed therein, we could also say that the first function of the inexistent is not altogether so different from the role of the evental site in *Being and Event*. For *Logics of Worlds*, too, an event is tied to the situation or world for which it is an event, but now the nodal point where this tying together of world and event occurs is depicted as the inexistent proper to this world.

The function of the inexistent in *Logics of Worlds*, however, is not limited to that of revealing, testifying, or bearing witness to the contingency of all objects that appear in a given world. At the level of real change, as opposed to the logical structure of appearance of a given world, the inexistent also serves to differentiate a "weak" from a "strong" singularity, which is what the book theorizes under the name of the event properly speaking, insofar as the latter alone is capable of "lifting" or "sublating" (Badiou uses *relever* and *relève*, which in the wake of Derrida's work have become the quasi-official French translations of Hegel's *aufheben* and *Aufhebung*) the inexistent to maximal existence. Indeed, "the 'sublation' of this nothingness, that is the tipping-over of a nil intensity of existence into a maximal intensity, characterises real change. Among the numerous consequences of a jolt affecting an object of the world, such a sublation is in effect the signature of what we call an event."[48] In the case of the Paris Commune this means bringing to "(a provisionally maximal) political existence the workers who were inexistent on its eve," Badiou posits, before drawing a general principle from this case: "The strong singularity can thus be recognized by the fact that its consequence in the world is to make exist within it the proper inexistent of the object-site."[49]

Real change, as the effect of a strong singularity or event, is inherently violent. It never simply amounts to bringing the old to fruition but carries a considerable amount of destruction. Here, as a matter of fact, Badiou returns to another one of his old Maoist convictions: "Thus, through an inevitable death under the injunction of the event, is inaugurated the destruction of what linked the multiple A to the transcendental of the world. The opening of a space of creation requires destruction."[50] In the case of the Paris Commune, despite the eventual defeat of the uprising, this means that—for a brief moment at least—the order that legitimates the workers' political inexistence is destroyed. "Though crushed and convulsive, the absolutization of the workers' political capacity—the existence of the inexistent—nonetheless destroyed an essential form of subjection, that of proletarian political possibility to bourgeois political manoeuvring," Badiou concludes, before paraphrasing Freud's famous maxim *Wo es war, soll Ich werden*: "What we can say is that there where an inexistent lay, the destruction of what legitimated this inexistence came to be."[51]

However, even with the reinjection of a significant dose of destruction, which Badiou had tried to avoid identifying with the new in an attempt at self-criticism in *Being and Event*, the discussion of the inexistent in *Logics of Worlds* nonetheless opens itself up to an anticipated critique from the point of view of Badiou's *Theory of the Subject*. In this earlier work, in fact, the inexistent already receives an extensive treatment that, in keeping with the book's Maoist understanding of the dialectic as a logic of scission, introduces an important split or division into the very heart of this concept as well.

There are thus two distinct sides or slopes from which we can approach the inexistent according to *Theory of the Subject*. The first orientation, which can be called structural or algebraic and which is treated in the seminar session of May 8, 1978, titled "The Inexistent," posits that no structure is complete without including-excluding some element, which as a consequence is marked with the stamp of nothingness: "Lacan and Milner are very clear about this. All totality requires that there in-exists at least one term which is not of the Whole, which does not belong to it. This impossible belonging sets the empty frontier of the Whole. It inexists with regard to the Whole, but it also in-exists, in the extent that it is designated as the impossibility from which the possibility of every being of the Whole derives its rule."[52] The example discussed at some length in this case concerns the *sans-papiers* or "illegal" immigrant workers whose exclusion is guaranteed by the regulations regarding nationality of the French state. "The immigrant proletarians are the inexistent proper to the national totality"; that is, they constitute the element that must be "included out," as Žižek would say, in order for this totality to gain consistency at all: "Among us, this is taken care of by the laws and practices of expulsion against immigrants, which remind the latter at all times of the prohibition of interiority within the national multiple, and thus of the impossibility, with regards to the whole, of a multinational composition of the nation."[53] Understood in this way, the inexistent is the inherent limit point of any given totality.

The reach of this structural concept of the inexistent, though, is overly restricted inasmuch as it remains bound by the existing constraints of the totality that is already in place. The most that a political intervention can hope to accomplish from this point of view is to give existence to the inexistent, as ironically seems to be the case in *Logics of Worlds*. "Here we have the first concept of the inexistent as the subjective polarity for the interruption of the law and the destruction of the whole," Badiou writes in *Theory of the Subject*: "It is the *forced* occupation of the unoccupyable place."[54] In the example under consideration, this would mean giving equal rights to those immigrant workers who are the without-rights of the French nation-state. But such an understanding of the inexistent, though certainly not negligible by any means, is immediately criticized for its feeble political effects, reduced to the support for the protest struggles of a given social force. It is here that certain conclusions from *Logics of Worlds* can be said to have been found wanting in advance, based on the division of the concept of the inexistent proposed in *Theory of the Subject*.

"Is this all?" Badiou asks in the next session of his seminar, dated May 15, 1978: "In matters of the subject, is the inexistent all that exists?"[55] If this were all there is to the matter, then the excess of the event would squarely fall back into the empty place that marks the internal limit of the existing structure. "In this universe, the excess of the multiple is ultimately reduced to whatever the algebra of it tolerates: it fits *just* under the concept of the inexistent that delimits the whole," for example, in the case of the illegal immigrant workers: "Those who want to *limit* the revolt of the immigrants to the subjective element of trade unionism declare that the equality of rights, that is, the occupation of the unoccupyable place, is all that the action is about."[56] For Badiou, however, there is another side to the role of the inexistent in the logic of change, an orientation that is no longer just algebraic or structural but also topological and historical. "The political construction of a multinational class unity defines a topology that exceeds from within the law of imperialist society and that by no means can be reduced to the forcing of the empty place," he warns against those who would limit politics to showing solidarity and demanding full legal existence for the immigrant workers as the proper inexistent of the world of the French: "There exists a recourse of excess which is immanent to the whole, and of which the occupation of the unoccupyable place is only the structural constraint, or the prescribed occasion."[57] From this second point of view the inexistent no longer merely signals the internal exclusion or constitutive outside of a given world. Nor should a political intervention be limited to naming or filling the inexistent's empty place. By contrast, the structure as a whole undergoes the transformative effects of an unmeasurable, properly free-floating excess over the empty place.

In sum, if the inexistent marks a kind of negative potential latent within the situation at hand, then from the point of view of the first perspective a subject's intervention does no more than positivize this negative potential of the inexistent by giving it full existence, whereas the second perspective presupposes the power of a qualitative break by which the subject, in a forceful backward torsion, escapes the local measure of what is possible and impossible. "Political force, once it is let loose, no longer distinguishes as before," adds Badiou. "It teaches us to say 'no' differently," in a logical revolt that completely reshuffles the old problem of determinism: "The 'No!' of the revolt is not implied by the local conditions. It is forced by the inexistence of an absolute constraint that would force submission in such a way that it transcends the immediate conditions."[58] Thus, from Marx's potentiality, captured in the fiction of a dream image waiting to become realized, to Badiou's inexistence, forced both to reveal the contingency of the existing world and to exceed its laws of impossibility, the logic of change will finally have come full circle along its polemical trajectory.

In *L'Hypothèse communiste* (*The Communist Hypothesis*), the fifth installment of his series *Circonstances*, Badiou sums this up by playing off both the element of (new) possibility and the element of (real) impossibility:

> What is important to note here is that an event is not the realization of a possibility that resides within the situation or that is dependent on the transcendental laws of the world. An event is the creation of new possibilities. It is located not simply at the level of objective possibilities but at the level of the possibility of possibilities. Another way of putting this is: with respect to a situation or a world, an event paves the way for the possibility of what—from the limited perspective of the make-up of this situation or the legality of this world—is strictly impossible. If we keep in mind here that, for Lacan, the real = impossible, the intrinsically real aspect of the event will be readily seen. We might also say that an event is the occurrence of the real as its own future possibility.[59]

Instead of a deterministic line of continuity between potential and act, we obtain a dialectical break between a given situation, complete with its inherently excluded empty place, and the unlimited excess over this very same empty place. Instead of falling prey to the illusions of heroic grandeur of a purely self-authorizing act, the subject's intervention in a given situation is always bound to the site where this situation's historicity is concentrated. And, finally, instead of fulfilling objective conditions already in place or at least in the process of formation in the existing world, a subject is capable of introducing a minimal gap, or the dreamlike fiction of a generic extension, within its own determination, the force of which may very well be impossible to limit. Is this whole new logic of change perhaps not the secret truth-content even of Marx's original dream?

8

FOR LACK OF POLITICS

←—————————————→

DEMOCRATIC MATERIALISM OR
RADICAL DEMOCRACY?

We saw earlier how Badiou opens *Logics of Worlds* with an ardent plea in favor of the materialist dialectic, over and against what he calls democratic materialism. Proponents of the latter, he claims, typically hold on to the materialist dogma according to which "there are only bodies and languages," whereas materialism becomes dialectical rather than purely democratic by adding the possibility of a rare exception: "Yes, there are only bodies and languages—except that there are also truths."[1] The exact nature of this opposition, though, is not always sufficiently highlighted even in the full version of the argument of *Logics of Worlds*. Badiou briefly quotes Antonio Negri, for example, in the discussion of democratic materialism, but from the content of Negri's letter it would seem that both thinkers actually reject the notion that all is but body and language. Conversely, to the extent that psychoanalysis is in fact concerned with enjoyment and discourse, particularly in light of the radical finitude of our human condition, it would appear to sit squarely on the side of democratic materialism. Yet even in *Logics of Worlds* Badiou never stops praising the dialectical virtues of someone like Lacan.

Perhaps, then, democratic materialism as the name for the adversary of the materialist dialectic is badly chosen, or at least ill-defined. In fact, several of the most original political thinkers from recent years have tried to radicalize the promise of democracy for our late-modern or postmodern times in ways that are not easily subsumed under the label of democratic materialism as defined by Badiou. Thus, it is to the promise of such a politics of "radical democracy" that I propose to turn in what follows by actively putting to work the polemical undercurrent of previous chapters. My aim is thus further to move beyond the discussion of Badiou's own thought in order ever more actively to think *with* some of his concepts, more particularly regarding the current political debate over the status and idea of democracy. In other words, rather than remaining at the level of exegesis, which always means somewhat desperately trying to stabilize the correct reading of a thinker, it is a question of taking up a transformative and critical sort of reading by way of a separate and localized—theoretical—intervention in the present that attempts to think of our actuality in the terms provided by Badiou.

Over the last few decades the description of the state of political philosophy, like that of so many other domains of thought, has become inseparable from a certain critique of modernity. The idea of modernity, of course, had been linked for more than two centuries to the tumultuous destiny of the so-called democratic revolution. It would seem logical, then, to expect that the concept of democracy would have suffered a slow process of decline as well, at least in the thought of those philosophers for whom modernity has finally exhausted its conceptual resources to think our time in all its conflicting aspects. And yet, today, we see that the idea of democracy, even if it has not come out totally unscathed from the process, has been curiously strengthened by the critique of modernity. From the point of view of postmodern philosophy, understood in a broad sense to encompass deconstruction as well as the most recent forms of hermeneutics, a new consensus, or a new common sense, effectively surrounds the radical promise of democracy. There thus arises the idea of a radical, or postmodern, democracy.

According to one of its more famous Heideggerian definitions, modernity would be the age of the image of the world. Modern would be that time when humanity slowly managed to represent to itself the totality of beings as a calculable image in the mirror of reason. Through science and technique, the subject of modern times increasingly reduces the always-open question of being to the category of a mere object—or a clear and distinct idea—only to arrive, by the end of the nineteenth century, at the nihilist moment when "there 'is' nothing to Being as such."[2] Modernity appears, then, as the age dominated by the transparency of the subject, master of itself and sovereign proprietor of truth, as well as by the presence of the world as a set of objects always closely at hand, or immediately present to the mind. Heidegger says as well: "The fact itself that man becomes subject and the world object is nothing but a consequence of the imposition of the essence of technique."[3] Modern would be that period in which nothing "is" if it does not fall under the domain of consciousness, that is, under the control of the representational system that always seeks to oppose the world to the mirror of human reason. Finally, if the idea of forcefully dominating reality, according to this way of thinking, is what defines the essence of the metaphysical project, then the modern age of technique and science will also have been the nihilist age of the fulfillment of metaphysics, which at one and the same time is its exhaustion and its end.

Postmodern thought hovers around a relentless critique of modernity as the age of the image of the world. This age seems both "finished" and "finite" in the sense of being achieved, fulfilled, and mortal all at once. In the last decades, though, this critique of finite modernity has strangely come closer again to the idea of democracy. Particularly from a Heideggerian or Lacanian perspective, the thought of the political draws on a new concept of "radical" or "postmodern" democracy, paradoxically anchored in the essential unfulfillment of both subject and object as the founding poles of modernity. As Gianni Vattimo writes: "Even if it seems paradoxical, it is precisely the adoption of a nihilist perspective that can give democratic politics the ability to face the phantasmagoria of the postmodern world in a way that is not simply defensive or reactive."[4] On one hand this idea of democracy must take into account the different efforts in the deconstruction of the metaphysics of presence, according to which being is reducible to an object, a mere entity among others; on the other hand the new political philosophy of democracy must also make its own the psychoanalytic criticism of the ideology of the subject, which postulates that the subject is a stable, transparent, and undivided entity. To the objectivity of the technical and scientific gaze, Heidegger's philosophy opposes the task of rethinking the true question of being, the emergence of being as a singular event, following the unique gift of temporality that alone is worthy of thought, while Lacan's teachings unmask the imaginary presupposition of an immediateness to one's self by contrasting it with the law of the other, following the traumatic kernel of the real as the principle of the symbolic order. If it does not want to fall back into the traps of metaphysical dogmatism and authoritarianism, the discussion of the concept of democracy must respond to these two tendencies in the critique of modernity.

The political philosophy of radical democracy thus implies a mutual deconstruction of the subject and object of political representation. The supposed freedom of the autonomous subject and the alleged objectivity of the social structure are only articulated in the space opened up by a gap that is constitutive of both poles: "There is a subject because the substance —objectivity—does not succeed in constituting itself completely."[5] Here, then, emerges the concept of a radical democracy whose representational system would be traversed, both on the side of the representing subject and on the side of the represented object, by a central emptiness, a necessary want-to-be, or an unsurpassable lack.

In a deliberately ambiguous sense we might rephrase this by saying that the political philosophy of radical democracy is the irrefutable argument for a lack of politics. Radical democracy itself presupposes the logic of lack, insofar as that which marks a democratic society is precisely its central absence, which is also its absent center. The new philosophy of democracy presupposes always the impossibility of constituting society as a closed, totalized, self-sufficient entity. The organizing principle of this constitutive lack is that unavoidable kernel of antagonism, the fundamental differend or disagreement for which there exists no possible litigation and whose sinister presence inevitably blocks the meaningful completion of the social into a totality that will always only have been illusory to begin with. "The social only exists in the vain attempt to institute that impossible object: society," concludes Laclau in his own *New Reflections on the Revolution of Our Time*: "Society, then, in the end is irrepresentable," but "this unfulfillment of the social is our main source of political hope in the modern world: only it can ensure the conditions of a radical democracy."[6] The persistence of antagonism, which always already imposes the structure of lack at the very core of society itself, is what makes democracy at the same time possible and impossible. The political, then, is the hegemonic battlefield opened up by this structural lack. Such an argument, though, also speaks ambiguously for a lack of politics, insofar as what is lacking in the philosophy of "*the political*" that surrounds the argument for a radical democracy is precisely the process of "*a politics*."[7] For the key thinkers in this tradition, however, this absence is not a defect, or an accidental deformation of politics, insofar as the emptiness, gap, or lack at the heart of the social constitutes the paradoxical condition of possibility of radical democracy itself.

For the criticism of modernity to allow a radical reevaluation of democracy, the thought of the political must first go through the prolonged stages

of crisis and then the absolute exhaustion of the various revolutionary
sequences of the socialist and communist left, from Marx to Lenin to
Stalin, and from Mao to Che Guevara to Castro, so as finally to assume—if
not in principle then at least in actual fact—the fatal collapse of really
existing socialism. It is then that the new democratic alternative emerges:
instead of opposing the praise of socialism to the barbarism of capitalism,
political philosophy over the last decades has mainly, if not solely, formulated itself on the basis of a rejection of the terror of totalitarianism in the
name of a radical, plural, and literally anarchic democracy. From the opposition "socialism or barbarism" we move—who knows if this is really a
step forward—to "democracy or totalitarianism," or even more recently, to
"democracy or terrorism." If it is difficult to judge whether this signals
progress, it is because in both cases the verdict, whether for condemnation
or for liberty, befalls an excluded third. Moreover, the displacement, beginning in the late 1960s, from revolutionary fervor to the topics of govern-
ability and the transition to democracy obviously hides a radical change in
relation to the value of the tradition inaugurated by Marx. Besides continuing the criticism of modernity, today's philosophy of democracy in effect
implies the interminable analysis or deconstruction of the entire Marxist
legacy, itself to be divided, according to some of its belated critics, into a
critical and a metaphysical part. As Derrida writes in *Specters of Marx*: "It is
an ontology of presence—critical but predeconstructive—as effective reality and objectivity."[8] Marxism would then mean fidelity to the extreme
contingency of political processes, as reflected in *The Communist Manifesto*, but also faith in the unbreakable scientificity of history as a unitary
process dominated by labor, as analyzed in *Capital*. The philosophers of
radical democracy will always seek to gain a foothold in the first tendency
so as to deconstruct the essentialism of the second. Thus, aside from
appearing to be postmodern, the political philosophy of radical democracy, in one way or another, must also be considered post-Marxist.

Of course, neither Heidegger nor Lacan supports democracy; on the
contrary, both question in principle the worthiness of any initiative or
subjective decision to really transform the order of things. Any attempt
to "overcome" metaphysics, according to Heidegger, will only lock itself
deeper into the quagmire of the history of metaphysics, just as it is not
possible either, according to Lacan, to "subvert" the order of desire, much
less "liberate" humanity from the chains of capitalism, without falling into

the trap of an imaginary wish, easily reversible into its dogmatic opposite. "Nietzsche's countermovement against metaphysics is, as the mere turning upside down of metaphysics, an inextricable entanglement in metaphysics," warns Heidegger in *The Question Concerning Technology*, while Lacan, talking about the possibility of denouncing the capitalist's discourse, says in *Television*: "I only remark that I cannot seriously do it, because in denouncing it I reinforce it, I normalize it, that is, I perfect it."[9] In neither of these two fundamental bodies of thought will the reader find an easy or immediate answer to the question "What is to be done?" beyond continuing the rigorous and properly interminable labor of analyzing, criticizing, and deconstructing modernity's fundamental assumptions.

Both Lacan and Heidegger have at their disposal an extraordinary lucidity—part tragic and part melancholy—to reveal the naivety, if not the utter uselessness, of any project for real change. Heidegger, for example, rejects the emancipatory idea of the taking of power because it does not question the principle of domination itself but simply pretends to exchange one power for the other: "The struggle between those who are in power and those who want to come to power: On every side there is the struggle for power. Everywhere power itself is what is determinative. Through this struggle for power, the being of power is posited in the being of its unconditional dominance by both sides."[10] For this reason the German thinker must, in the last instance, maintain himself in a kind of necessary ignorance as to the political consequences of his philosophical thought. He in no way defends democracy's regime: "A decisive question for me today is: how can a political system accommodate itself to the technological age, and which political system would this be? I have no answer to this question. I am not convinced that it is democracy."[11] To the extent it still supposes the subject as a stable foundation, the project to overcome technical alienation, particularly by force, only worsens the mastery of the technical-scientific view of the world. Lacan responds in a similar way when asked what the political implications of psychoanalysis are: "In any case, there is no progress. All that is gained on one side is lost on the other. As one does not know what has been lost, one thinks one has won."[12] The underlying principle of this compromising entanglement had already been formulated in Lacan's *Écrits*: "In the movement that progressively leads man to adequate self-conscience, his freedom becomes inseparable from the development of his servitude."[13] This extreme lucidity regarding the imminent reversibility of any emancipatory project leads both thinkers in their final years to a profound disillusionment, wrapped in abrupt silences, that is completely foreign to the derivation of a political praxis from theoretico-philosophical reflections. The "case" of the Nazi sympathy of the young Heidegger might even be considered the result of a still hegemonic wish of philosophy over politics. This is Lacoue-Labarthe's hypothesis, for example, about Heidegger's politics. The German thinker would have perceived in Nazism, for a moment perhaps not so short, the possibility of resolving one's mind in favor of the decisive ideas of fundamental ontology so as to exit, finally, from the desert of the age of modern technique in which only inauthenticity reigns.[14] Strictly speaking, this hope is unjustifiable from within Heidegger's thought, particularly in the later years. There remains, then, only art, especially poetry, to rescue some traces of the originary event of being, free from all its metaphysical moorings. In a much less scandalous but no less provocative fashion, as I discussed in chapter 2, the rebellious students of France's May revolt also do not get the expected support from their teacher but only the acidity of his criticism, his usual provocations and even his open mockery when after 1968 they once again obediently start attending Lacan's seminar. "If you had a bit of patience, and if you really wanted our impromptus to continue, I would tell you that, always, the revolutionary aspiration has only a single possible outcome—of ending up as the master's discourse. This is what experience has proved," he concludes before his students in the newly formed university of Paris VIII at Vincennes (where Badiou would soon begin setting up the Philosophy Department together with Foucault), a year after the revolt: "What you aspire to as revolutionaries is a master. You will get one."[15] There remains, then, only the rigor of analysis, as science of the real, to traverse the exorbitant processes of the impossible, far from the ideals of human liberation.

Heidegger's and Lacan's most faithful commentators, philologically speaking, also deny the possibility of drawing a specific politics, even less the defense of a political regime such as democracy, whether liberal or otherwise, from the thought of these two authors. Instead, they question the very idea of anchoring, as always, practice in theory—just as politics used to be derived, in antiquity, from first philosophy, that is, from ontology as the science of being or, in modern times, from a special branch of metaphysics, for example, epistemology as the theory of knowledge. The deconstructive criticism of modernity targets precisely this process of deriving politics from a founding term or an essential point of origin. As Reiner Schürmann writes: "Deconstructing metaphysics means to interrupt—literally to unhinge—the speculative shift from theory to practice."[16] One should not expect any political prescription either from the works themselves or from the most faithful commentaries of Heidegger or Lacan. Of the latter, for example, Jean-Claude Milner writes: "Just as science and politics have nothing to do with each other—except committing crimes—because they do not belong to the same world nor even to the same universe, so too psychoanalysis has nothing to do with politics—except telling stupidities."[17] Again, in terms of the first thinker, Schürmann observes: "In no stage of his work is Heidegger interested in praxis as a topic of the 'practical' disciplines, ethics and politics"; on the contrary, "With the turn taken by Heideggerian phenomenology after the publishing of *Being and Time*, the question 'What is to be done?' remains as if suspended in a void."[18] Or, as Dominique Janicaud warns us: "Let us not deceive ourselves: we will not find in Heidegger an answer to the Leninist question 'What is to be done?'"[19]

We must wait for the work of seemingly less faithful, or in another sense more original, followers of Heidegger and Lacan, if we want to articulate the critique of modernity with a new—radical or postmodern—approach to the idea of democracy. It is an intriguing spectacle to see how these two thinkers, whose work in many ways seems so adverse to the desire for progress, have been vindicated by some of the most radical strands of contemporary political and philosophical thinking, to the point where many '68ers find profound echoes between Maoism and Lacanian psychoanalysis, while certain interpreters of Heidegger draw a distinction between a leftist and a rightist reading, in a way akin to what happened with the legacy of Hegel. Among those who over the past years have approached the idea of democracy from the thinking of Heidegger, I am referring above all to figures such as Derrida, Nancy, Lacoue-Labarthe, Vattimo, and even Schürmann. As for the tradition to think about democracy inspired by Lacan, we can refer in part to the work of Claude Lefort, as well as to the early work of Žižek, while the combined result of these two tendencies—Lacan and Heidegger articulated by way of Derrida—comes through most clearly in the work of Laclau and Mouffe, starting with *Hegemony and Socialist Strategy*. Finally, a summary of the presuppositions behind the new idea of democracy, though now it is not called radical but democracy

pure and simple, can also be found in the political philosophy of Roberto
Esposito. Democracy is radical, then, when it constitutes a symbolic order
in the Lacanian sense of the term, which can also be said to be anarchic,
this time in line with the thinking of Heidegger. From this perspective
democracy appears articulated as a precarious social totality, hegemonic
yet never fully accomplished, on the basis of a vanishing term whose
function in this whole is similar to that of being for Heidegger or of the
real for Lacan.

The event of being, in the deconstruction of ontology, gives its origin to
the history of metaphysics; this origin, however, only offers itself by withdrawing itself at the same time and, as such, is itself irreducible to the
continuous unfolding of history. The real, in the doctrine of psychoanalysis, is the point of the impossible that structures the symbolic order of
desire; the real itself, however, is that which absolutely resists symbolization. It is in a similar way that the place of power appears in the political
philosophy of radical democracy. Whether it is called lack, difference, or
antagonism, the founding term around which the social order is constructed is an empty term; better yet, it is an absent cause that completely
vanishes into its effects. With respect to the order of democracy it is
perhaps worth recalling Lefort's well-known thesis: "Empty, unoccupyable,
in such a way that no individual can be consubstantial to it, the place of
power reveals itself as impossible to figure."[20] This thesis seems ready-made
to retrofit the concept of radical democracy into the critique of the subject after Lacan. As Žižek writes: "The Lacanian definition of democracy
would then be: a sociopolitical order in which the People do not exist—do
not exist as a unity, embodied in their unique representative. That is why
the basic feature of the democratic order is that the place of Power is, by
the necessity of its structure, an empty place."[21] Only by remaining empty
does the place of power in radical democracy make possible the regime of
democratic representation; this place itself is a nonplace or blank space
that is impossible to represent, much less to embody in a particular historical subject—whether the proletariat, the party, or the charismatic leader. In
an extreme reading even civil society or the multitude no longer offer a
valid alternative, insofar as they would do no more than reiterate the
illusion of a unique and indivisible bond in eternal opposition to the
apparatuses of the state or of empire.

The structure of radical democracy paradoxically displays its greatest force at the point of its greatest weakness, when it endlessly exposes the fragility of its Achilles' heel. It articulates the field of the social following the principle of a lack of foundation, which is both and at the same time the condition of possibility of democracy and the condition of its rigorous impossibility. It is here that contemporary political philosophy uncovers the promise of a new concept of democracy insofar as the incomplete nature of the project of modernity, far from threatening the democratic regime with extinction, is in fact its only chance for survival. As Mouffe states: "Indeed, if one sees the democratic revolution as Lefort portrays it, as the distinctive feature of modernity, it then becomes clear that what one means when one refers to postmodernity in philosophy is a recognition of the impossibility of any ultimate foundation or final legitimation that is constitutive of the very advent of the democratic form of society and thus of modernity itself."[22] This idea of democracy is "radical" not because it inaugurates a return to the "root" of the human essence or to the basis of some ultimate truth but, to the contrary, because it abandons any pretension to found politics on a principle of substantive power, whether objectively or subjectively.

THE PRINCIPLE OF ANARCHY

If *arkhê*, in Greek, has the double meaning of a principle both as foundation and as beginning of a process of cause and effect, then radical democracy has no principle; it lacks an *arkhê*. Radical democracy, in this etymological sense, would also be anarchic. As Schürmann explains: "The anarchy that will be at issue here is the name of a history affecting the ground or foundation of action, a history where the bedrock yields and where it becomes obvious that the principle of cohesion, be it authoritarian or 'rational,' is no longer anything more than a blank space deprived of legislative, normative power."[23] Or in the words of Rancière: "Politics is not the actualization of a principle, of the law or of the 'proper' of a community. Politics has no *arkhê*. It is, in the strict sense, anarchic. As Plato has marked, democracy has no *arkhê*, no measure."[24] Based on this paradoxical principle of anarchy, democracy constitutes a complex structure without a center, an indeterminate regime of plurality, the foundation of which coincides neither with a substance nor with an essence but rather opens itself up, as if in an abyss, onto the bottomless ground of a vanishing term.

The power of radical-anarchic democracy is always already out of place, or beside itself. Hence the attraction of the idea that our times are out of joint, following Hamlet's well-worn phrase that has been much celebrated by Derrida and Laclau: "The time is out of joint. O cursed spite, / That ever I was born to set it right!"[25] As opposed to its literary and communist precursors, however, the specter that nowadays haunts the world precisely no longer seeks to right the wrongs of our time; on the contrary, the very desire of such a rectitude, as in the famous just or correct line of Marxism-Leninism, would be the mark of a metaphysical pretense, transposed to the field of politics according to the age-old habit of deriving a practice from a foundation previously established in theory. With the specter it is rather a question of keeping forever open the messianic promise of disjunction as the very condition of true democracy, instead of incarnating this promise in some concrete messianism, to keep open the principle of anarchy, without confusing the latter with any particular historical form of anarchism. Radical democracy, in other words, forms a symbolic order the radicality of which consists in never being accomplished or self-present, being rather essentially improper, divided, separated from itself. It founds, on the basis of a bottomless foundation, a politics of the "improper," the "impolitical" or "unpolitical" against all politics "proper," that is, above all, against totalitarian politics, supposed to be metaphysical in the attempt to achieve what is "proper" precisely by "reappropriating" history through the subject of politics—whether as proletariat, as the people, or even, in an extreme deconstruction of communism and socialism, as generic humanity.[26]

Radical democracy, as opposed to its commonly known versions from liberalism to really existing socialism, does not pretend to represent the power of the social but rather to recognize the constitutive unbinding of the idea of society as such. "Society doesn't exist," or "There is no such thing as society," is the first watchword of the thinkers of radical democracy, a slogan obviously inspired by the Lacanian axiom: "There is no such thing as a sexual relationship."[27] The new idea of democracy is not based on the plenitude of the social bond but on its essential lack, due to the unbinding, or the dislocation, of the social whole by an intrinsic exteriority. It does not rely on a previously established identity but on the constitutive alterity of any society. As Esposito writes: "Democracy is that which guards alterity, which does not give illusions or consolations, which does not dream terrible conclusions: the one, immanence, transparency."[28] Above all, radical democracy is not grounded in the sovereignty of the people, whether direct or delegated by other means, but robs the ground from beneath any pretension to derive a politics from the immediate, organic, or substantial self-presence of a given community. Such self-presence is nothing but the eternal referent of myth, from the German romantics to the totalitarian-isms of the twentieth century. "Community is neither the value, nor the finality, nor the content of democracy. The latter is literally *emptied* of community: imprisoned in its finite limits, in its pure definition," Esposito concludes: "This alone is democracy without myths: the full subtraction from any presumed community."[29]

Grounded in the inherent lack of the field of the political, radical de-mocracy always seeks to avoid the imminent threat of totalitarianism that lies at the core of democracy itself. If totalitarianism, according to much twentieth-century political thinking, cannot be explained except in antago-nistic relation to democracy, then the same thesis can also be put the other way around. Radical democracy always lives in the shadow of Hitler and Stalin. Without the negative reference to totalitarianism this idea of de-mocracy loses all its radicalism. Today, moreover, the opponent may even be completely mistaken. The most urgent political problem, at the start of this new millennium perhaps no less than a century and a half ago, is not so much the otherwise undeniable terror of totalitarianism so much as the savagery of capitalism. We have to ask ourselves if totalitarianism really still constitutes "the most important fact of our time" or "the sociopolitical experience that defines our time," as stated in the 1980s and 1990s by fol-lowers of Lefort—faithful inheritors, also in this sense, of Hannah Arendt's work. But we also have to ask ourselves whether the war against terrorism today does not replay a similar debate on the other end of the political spectrum—similar, that is, to the way in which democracy found itself only in opposition to totalitarianism.

To the threats of bureaucratic totalitarianism, which would represent the culmination of the desire for plenitude according to which the meta-physics of presence ends with the brutal dominion of calculating reason, the political philosophy of democracy opposes the principles of difference, plurality, contingency, and alterity. In a world controlled by market logic, however, these principles not only lose a large part of their radical appeal but if these principles do not serve to register the anchoring point of a true emancipatory political sequence, they even run the risk of turning into so many supplements for the soul in today's capitalo-parliamentarism. Finally, we have to ask ourselves if the market really functions according to the totalitarian or fundamentalist myth of self-presence, of incarnated power, or if, on the contrary, capitalism itself is perfectly capable of hosting in its midst the plurality of differences, since this is precisely how the law of generalized equivalence circulates among us.

Perhaps what the philosophers of radical democracy manage to introduce into the debate about modernity is only the point of departure of a political sequence: the other, or difference, in this sense, alludes above all to a notion of liberty, which is certainly a name worth recuperating to refer to the multiple without one. In and of itself, however, the multiple does not yet prescribe any particular politics, whether emancipatory or reactionary. On the contrary, even if it efficiently sums up the principle of anarchy, the multiple without one also risks becoming a precious metaphor, in an ontological key, to describe the essence of global capital. Behind the idea of radical democracy, speaking of the social as of a pure multiple without essence nor transcendence, there would thus lurk a deep unity, that is, the structure of the market itself.[30]

Radical democracy is accomplished and threatened at the same time during what seems to be its only momentary "realization," that is, either the interminable discussion of parliamentarism or the cyclical process of elections: the vote and the public debate. While the representational posts are declared vacant for a brief time, the empty place of power is "rendered" but only formally, not really, since to exhibit the empty place of power as real would surely provoke a form of "terror," as when a revolution "forces" the imperative according to which the place of power in a democracy must always be kept symbolically vacated. "At the moment of elections, the whole hierarchic network of social relations is in a way suspended, put in parentheses; 'society' as an organic unity ceases to exist, it changes into a contingent collection of atomized individuals, of abstract units," writes Žižek in *The Sublime Object of Ideology*, when he is still a fervent supporter of the idea of radical democracy. "Only the acceptance of such a risk, only such a readiness to hand over one's fate to 'irrational' hazard, renders 'democracy' possible: it is in this sense that we should read the dictum of Winston Churchill which I have already mentioned: 'democracy is the worst of all possible political systems, the only problem is that none of the others is better.' "[31]

Here, again, we can see which idea of politics is excluded from the alternative between democracy and totalitarianism, namely, so-called revolutionary politics, or in a more generic sense, the emancipatory overturning of the social structure itself, previously vindicated by the militant left. For lack of a true political sequence, by contrast, radical democracy limits itself to assuming, as in a kind of death drive, the inherent impossibility of the symbolic order of any given society. The project seems to formulate itself only in terms of a categorical imperative that obliges us to recognize the intrinsic negativity of the social, as though the task consisted merely in learning to live with the impasse. As Žižek clearly states, at least in his early work, adopting a viewpoint of which he himself later on would become one of the staunchest critics: "In this perspective, the 'death drive,' this dimension of radical negativity, cannot be reduced to an expression of alienated social conditions, it defines *la condition humaine* as such: there is no solution, no escape from it; the thing to do is not to 'overcome,' to 'abolish' it, but to come to terms with it, to learn to recognize it in its terrifying dimension and then, on the basis of this fundamental recognition, to try to articulate a *modus vivendi* with it."[32] In this mode of recognizing the constitutive deadlock of any society, in order to learn how to live with it, consists the experience of radical democracy.

ARCHIAESTHETICS AND ARCHIPOLITICS

In the order of a radical democracy, anarchically founded on the lack of society as on a community without origin nor mythical ground, philosophy runs the risk of doing no more than exhibiting without end the empty, unthinkable, and unrepresentable place of alterity, different from any essential presence or substance. Esposito affirms: "Only when incomplete can democracy remain as such. In this case, it is not its potentialization that saves it, but its renunciation. Or its limit, an absence of substance, of essence, of value. In other words, precisely the fact of being a technique that suppresses within itself any ambition to represent that which *cannot* be represented."[33] If it does not want to become a new transcendental structure, which would be the structure of the unrepresentable lack, radical democracy needs a new "ethos" or "experience" to be lived by all citizens as an adventure proper to each and every one. In a commentary on Lefort's thinking, Marc De Kesel writes: "Whatever the formal power of its structure is, a democracy would benefit a great deal from a democratic ethos, from a realization that the proper of community is to be a symbolical order, and that for this reason, it can never achieve the plenitude of itself."[34] In order not to remain on the level of the purely categorical, the constitutive void of the order of radical democracy, in some way, must be presented as such, that is, as empty, lacking, evanescent. There must be a way to render the vertigo of a radical, anarchic, and plural democracy—without any accomplishment or fulfillment whatsoever. Democracy requires a way of imposing itself not only on the purely structural plane but also, as a form of subjective experience, on the level of everyday life.

At the same time, it is clear that the proponents of the idea of radical democracy, as they themselves wish to underscore by using this adjective, are not satisfied with really existing democracies. In the media, during elections, in parliamentarism, what is presented to the citizens is actually an ideal image of democracy as the principle of the power of the people in terms of an undivided totality. Sooner or later all politicians talk of "the people" as if in the mirror of society they found direct access to the proper origin of public opinion and political decision making. This is an imaginary way of representing the empty place of power as though it were fully occupied by the people themselves. But we also know that it is in the yearning for plenitude that the totalitarian temptation resides according to the philosophy of radical democracy. The truly democratic adventure, by contrast, requires a capacity to recognize not only the finitude of every political actor but also the constitutive alterity of the entire social field. As De Kesel adds: "A democracy can only support itself with a mentality that moderates every idealism with a notion of finitude, that has ceased to expect 'everything' from life and from living-together (whether in the future or not) and that has reconciled itself with the insuperable lack that is the ground of our existence."[35] This principle of finitude is opposed to the dialectic of the finite and the infinite, mortality and the immortal. As a principle of alterity, it is also opposed to the vision of society as an objective totality, the description of which would be the task of political scientists, economists, or sociologists. The democratic ethos consists in assuming the inevitable lack of all necessarily plural subjects of politics, without making this antagonism in turn depend on the objects and interests that are tied to a predetermined subset, or class, of society.

Radical democracy, according to some of its proponents, must nevertheless transgress the imperative according to which nothing can occupy or represent the empty place of power. The search is then on for some efficacious form of presenting this symbolic whole itself, without falling into imaginary illusions. This presentation does not belong to the discussion of democratic politics itself. It exceeds it toward a disastrous exterior, where the threats always lurk of the terror of a real void and the illusion of an imaginary plenitude. To avoid these two extremes, without being satisfied with the electoral-parliamentary game, proponents of the idea of radical democracy sometimes seek to present the alterity of its order as an Idea, in the Kantian sense, which means that it would be aesthetically imaginable but really unpresentable—an unspeakable Idea that nevertheless, in some way, is indirectly discernible, as a guide or guiding thread, in the events of history itself. Among such equivocal signs of democracy in terms of a politics of difference, we could count the sublime, the uncanny, the saintly, and the tragic.

Since there are no proofs that democracy is on the road to improvement, the idea of universal progress can only be presented by the common sense in a sublime manner. "It results from this that the universality invoked by the beautiful and the sublime is merely an Idea of community, for which no proof, that is, no direct presentation, will ever be found, but only indirect presentation," Lyotard affirms. "The ideal is not presentable to the sensibility; the free society is no more demonstrable than the free act. And in the same way, there will always be a profound tension between what one ought to be and what one is. Only one thing is certain: right cannot be de facto; real society draws legitimacy not from itself but from a community that is not properly nameable, merely required."[36] Since there can be no object that would correspond to the intuition of the community in question, the respect for democracy invites us to the enthusiasm worthy of a saintly idea. De Kesel writes: "Precisely by presenting this idea as 'saintly' one would recognize its imaginary character and avoid the pretension of believing oneself capable of really accomplishing it. To affirm the finitude of the political would mean in this sense to sacralize an idea of politics."[37] Since there can be no coincidence between the right and the fact of democracy without falling into a metaphysical or transcendental illusion, the democratic adventure is always traversed by a breach as by a sinister, uncanny experience. Thus affirms Derrida: "At stake here is the very concept of democracy as concept of a promise that can only arise in such a *diastema* (failure, inadequation, disjunction, disadjustment, being 'out of joint'). That is why we always propose to speak of a democracy *to come*, not of a *future* democracy in the future present, not even of a regulating idea, in the Kantian sense, or of a utopia—at least to the extent that their inaccessibility would still retain the temporal form of a *future present*, of a future modality of the *living present*."[38] Finally, since there can be no identity either at the origin or in the end, the excess of alterity haunts the core of radical democracy with a tragic destiny. "The tragic image that must accompany democracy shows, therefore, the terror against which it has erected itself as a dike," De Kesel concludes: "In this image of the unacceptable, the necessarily imaginary tendency of democracy hits as it were upon itself as its own limit and fatally the destiny is revealed whereby it cannot install itself by *necessity* but only in a *finite* manner."[39]

The political philosophy of radical democracy thus calls forth a certain aesthetic. It opens the search for an aesthetic analogon of the political, not in the intuition of the suprasensible infinite but through a finite presentation of finitude itself. This quest offers a first way to avoid the reduction of the democratic adventure to the formal structure of the parliamentarian-electoral play. The aesthetic presentation of the place of power reveals, above all, the inevitable alterity of the void at the center of democracy itself. This lack is the always-unfinished destiny of democracy. Partially rendered visible, if not actually forgotten, during the electoral cycles or in the public debate, the structure of lack cannot be presented as such except through an aesthetic experience. "What we cannot speak about we must pass over in silence," Wittgenstein had written in his *Tractatus Logico-Philosophicus*: "There are, indeed, things that cannot be put into words. They *make themselves manifest*. They are what is mystical."[40] Similarly, the task of political philosophy, in the eyes of some, would be to make manifest this unspeakable, properly mystical or aesthetic, part of democratic society. On the other hand, to exceed the strict framework of existing parliamentarism, the philosophy of radical democracy sometimes also takes on the radically anarchic or messianic search, beyond or beneath any concrete situation, of the groundless ground of politics itself—no longer in the plenitude of human nature but in the abyss of liberty, if this name is still appropriate, anterior to any specific individual or collective project. This search offers a second way to avoid remaining within the limits of philosophy either on a purely transcendental plane or merely on the level of really existing representative democracies. Rather than finding a ground for politics, the philosophy of radical democracy in this case proposes to interrupt history in a violent mimetic repetition of the revolutionary act itself. "The awareness that they are about to make the continuum of history explode is characteristic of the revolutionary classes at the moment of their action," writes Walter Benjamin famously in his "Theses on the Philosophy of History": "The historical materialist leaves it to others to be drained by the whore called 'Once upon a time' in historicism's bordello. He remains in control of his powers, man enough to blast open the continuum of history."[41] In a similar vein certain philosophers of radical democracy appeal mimetically to the unforeseeable irruption, outside of any horizon of expectation, of the revolutionary act as an event that, even if it has never really taken place nor perhaps will ever take place in a future present, nonetheless is always already on the verge of exploding.

All political philosophies, as Badiou repeatedly insists, stand under the condition of a specific mode of doing politics. The only effective politics behind the concept of radical democracy, however, still seems to reside in the double parliamentary-electoral game, in the properly interminable conversation achieved by means of the vote and the public debate. In order not to identify itself with the glaring limits of really existing democracy, the political philosophy of radical democracy sometimes has recourse to the quest for an aesthetic analogy in a paradoxical and necessarily violent presentation of the void of power in the midst of democracy itself. By way of such aesthetic presentation, political philosophy transcends in some way the framework of what can be thought in history or in the social sciences. This alternative could be called archiaesthetic, if we accept Badiou's explanation about Wittgenstein: "I say archi-aesthetic, because it is not a question of substituting art for philosophy. It is rather a question of posing *within* the scientific or propositional activity the principle of a clarity the (mystical) element of which is beyond this activity, and the real paradigm of which is art. It is a question therefore of firmly establishing the laws of the sayable (the thinkable), in such a way that the unsayable (the unthinkable, which in the final instance is given only in the form of art) be *situated* as 'upper limit' of the sayable itself."[42] Aside from this archiaesthetic alternative, there remains the desire to repeat the power of an absolutely radical event in an imitation, within philosophy, of the revolutionary act, as when Benjamin seeks to blast open the continuum of history or when Nietzsche, calling himself dynamite, pretends to break history in two. In this way political philosophy promises to be able to transcend the mere administration of the existing order of things. This desire for a radical act can be called archipolitical, if once again we take into account the explanations given by Badiou: "The philosophical act is *archipolitical* in the sense that it seeks to revolutionize humanity at a more radical level than the calculations of politics," as in the case of Nietzsche: "He proposes to make formally equivalent the philosophical act as an act of thinking with the explosive potentiality that is apparent in the politico-historical revolution."[43] This is also the sense in which we could understand a certain function of the "act" in Žižek, even though in Žižek's recent work, as I suggested in the previous chapter, this notion is brought much closer to the secular miracle of an "event" that makes the impossible possible.

If we set aside the archiaesthetic and archipolitical alternatives, there exists not exactly a complicity but certainly a disconcerting compatibility between the essential incompletion of radical democracy and the eternal promises of a democracy that is forever to come for the majority of countries, particularly in the Third World. "Contingency is the presupposition of democratic freedom," I read some years ago in the flyer for a conference on democracy in Mexico: "Democracy, like the rule of law that shelters it, is always unsatisfied, subject as it is to the vertigo of a 'development' that is never absolutely accomplished."[44] To compare the philosophy of radical democracy to any existing political regime may seem to entail an act of bad faith, but this is precisely the problem: the philosophico-ontological framework surrounding the new concept of democracy transforms the question about actual situations into a rhetorical question or into an act of bad faith with respect to the radicality of the idea itself. To think through the effective political processes of the recent past, a different theoretical framework is needed, one in which democracy would no longer appear as endlessly adrift between form and content, between the state of principle and the state of fact, between the empirical and the transcendental, or between the imaginary, the real, and the symbolic. This is not to say that politics, following the metaphysical scheme, should be derived once more from philosophy, nor that only philosophers are capable of truly conceiving of the essence of the political. Instead there may be a specific role reserved for theory to register the effects of the political sequences of the last decades, especially since the closure of the revolutionary sequence, the specter of which still haunted the world until the end of the 1960s and the early 1970s.

FUTURE TASKS FOR THINKING POLITICS

To register the various sequences of emancipatory politics over the last decades, what I defined as theory rather than as philosophy in the strict sense must first traverse and then exceed the frame of deconstruction that uncovers a principle of difference or lack underlying the representational scheme of the political. The point of departure to rethink politics today cannot just be the structural gap that always already determines the democratic order; it must also lead to an excess over this empty place itself. Such an excess coincides, no doubt, with the forced truths, even the terror, that are so often invoked in order to threaten democracy with the immanent dangers of totalitarianism or fundamentalism. To think through the transformation of a situation without reducing it either to yet another form of totalitarianism or to the violence of metaphysics, theory then might have to undergo a double displacement.

In the first place, the aim would be to oppose an ontology of actuality, in the sense defined by Michel Foucault, to the deconstruction of metaphysics initiated by Heidegger.[45] This would allow us to view the event not as a unique phenomenon, nor as the equivocal origin of the destiny of metaphysics, always given and withdrawn at once. What takes place is not only the singular event of being, the opening of which, by giving origin to the history of metaphysics, is in itself nonhistorical, being perhaps only aesthetically or poetically presentable. It is clear that in comparison with such a radical, or arch-originary origin, any change of the actually existing situation must inevitably appear to be a form of terror. There is, however, not only the event of the gift of freedom but a variety of events in the plural, the haphazard irruption of which has a specific site as their point of departure in history. If we accept these new parameters, according to which being is thinkable in a situation without falling into the millenarian forgetfulness of the ontological difference, the task of theory would be historically and conceptually to map out the specific events—political and otherwise—whose configuration mark what we call our present.

In the second place, it would also be necessary to define the subject of truth not only on the basis of a fundamental lack but based on the displacement and transformation of this empty space itself. To supplement the categories of lack or void with the forcing or torsion of the point of the impossible, as I discussed at length above, is the principal aim in Badiou's *Theory of the Subject*, with which he seeks to respond mainly to Lacan.

Instead of merely recognizing how a subject is tragically split by the structure of lack, what is at stake is to sustain, by means of this process of splitting, a process that would actually elaborate new truths in a series of consequences derived from the events that take place, for example, in art or in politics.

To think the actuality of the present and to historicize the processes of subjectivization—this double proposal can perhaps inspire new ways of thinking politics so as to articulate the critique of modernity in a direction different from the idea of radical democracy that is based on the doctrines of Heidegger and Lacan—without abandoning the requirements of deconstruction the latter two have imposed inescapably on all future theoretical work. By contrast, the philosophy of radical democracy rarely exceeds the frame of traditional political philosophy, inasmuch as it is still a question of deliberating the uses and disadvantages of different modes of organizing society. In other words, it judges politics from outside, in exteriority, starting from a necessary comparison of various types of symbolic ordering—basically, democracy and totalitarianism—as so many regimes of the state.

From the point of view of Badiou's thinking, democracy does not constitute a regime of representation, but neither does it coincide purely and simply with a form of social or everyday life. Rather, democracy is an immanent aspect of politics only if politics exceeds the frame of representationalism in order to designate a process of truth initiated from that which precisely cannot be represented. If the unrepresentable is the point of departure of a particular politics, in a sense that is otherwise compatible with the theory of radical democracy, then it is now no longer a question of recognizing in this void the tragic or messianic condition of possibility of the democratic regime but of extending and exceeding it in a wager that would be loyal to the specific events that force the situation there where such a void reveals the site of a specific impossibility. Democracy, then, would name the process that defines a sequence of emancipatory politics, in which the impossible is displaced onto the possibility, in the future anterior of a wager, of that which was considered impossible in the current state of this situation itself.[46]

The difference between these two concepts of democracy could be rephrased in terms of the great principles of the French Revolution. As Badiou indicates: "It turns out that the capacity of seizing inherent to the terms liberty, equality and fraternity remains intact, and that, in a recurrent fashion, philosophical polemic circulates between them."⁴⁷ It would be an illuminating exercise to trace the contours of the theoretical distribution of these terms today. The common ground would be the place of *liberty*. What the argument for a lack of politics introduces into the debate on democracy is the idea of liberty as a privileged name to refer to the multiple without one. Through the concept of *difference*, for example, the political philosophy of radical democracy has the virtue of registering the possible point of inception of a true political sequence. We might also say that the common sense of today's political philosophy consists in deconstructing the concept of *fraternity*, by translating it in terms of a *community* destined to remain forever improper, unnameable, or inoperative precisely because of the dissolving effects of liberty as an affirmation of difference.⁴⁸ However, by remaining enclosed within the debate about various forms of ordering a society, this philosophy can do little more than register the void as the structural lack in democracy—the empty place of power—as a regime of the state.

In the best of all cases, what political philosophy seeks to measure under the name of liberty is the aberrant excess of representation of the state of a situation over the presentation of this situation itself. This is how the place of civil society, or of the masses, tends to be discussed in relation to that of the state, and perhaps a similar operation lurks behind the opposition between the multitude and empire. This remains, however, a way of thinking about politics in exteriority. Badiou's metapolitical orientation, on the other hand, also starts out from the point of the real as impossible for which the name of liberty is worth keeping, but it opposes itself to political philosophy so as to think through a sequence of politics as a form of thinking in interiority. What is needed, in other words, is a revised principle of *equality* in action. Starting from the impossible of a specific situation, an emancipatory politics elaborates the prescriptive statements that are indispensable to transform the impossibility of this starting point by way of a universal law. More precisely, this process first assigns a measure to the excess of representation; that is, it sets a limit to the power of the state; second, it belabors the particulars of the situation to render impossible any inegalitarian statement and make equality possible in this fixed distance, the just measure of which could be called liberty; finally, it seeks to anticipate the generic applicability of the egalitarian statement to the whole situation itself. From this point of view, democracy names the intrinsic efficacy of the process of an emancipatory politics. A thinking of political sequences such as this one certainly is not excluded from the political philosophy of radical democracy, but thus far it has not become visible in this tradition except in an ambiguous argument for a lack of politics.

More recently, however, Badiou has placed great doubts before any attempt—his own included—to salvage democracy by seeing in it not a regime of the state but an intrinsic aspect of all emancipatory politics. Referring to Rancière's defense of the word in *Hatred of Democracy*, he wonders in *The Communist Hypothesis*: "I am not sure that the word can so easily be salvaged, or, at any rate, I think that making a detour through the idea of communism is unavoidable."[49] In my conclusion I will follow Badiou on this detour, particularly by inquiring into the link between this idea of communism and the tradition of Marxism.

Conclusion

THE SPECULATIVE LEFT

COMMUNISM WITHOUT MARXISM?

Communism is for us not a *state of affairs* which is to be established, an *ideal* to which reality [will] have to adjust itself. We call communism the *real* movement which abolishes the present state of things.
—MARX AND ENGELS, *The German Ideology*

I am tempted to conclude this book by quoting a friend of mine who once provocatively described Badiou as a philosopher who is first and foremost a communist before being, or perhaps even without being, a Marxist. Long before recent texts such as *The Communist Hypothesis* were to leave not even a shred of doubt in this regard, a passage from *Of an Obscure Disaster: On the End of the Truth of the State*, Badiou's take on the collapse of the Soviet Union, would seem to confirm this bold assessment. Thus, in an otherwise unsurprising rebuttal against all nostalgic or posthistorical judgments regarding the "death" of communism, Badiou all of a sudden affirms the invariant and seemingly eternal nature of a certain communist subjectivity: "From Spartacus to Mao (not the Mao of the state, who also exists, but the rebellious extreme, complicated Mao), from the Greek democratic insurrections to the worldwide decade 1966–1976, it is and has been, in this sense, a question of communism. It will always be a question of communism, even if the word, soiled, is replaced by some other designation of the concept that it covers, the philosophical and thus eternal concept of rebellious subjectivity."[1]

In the chapter "Must the Communist Hypothesis Be Abandoned?" from *The Meaning of Sarkozy*, Badiou restates this principled belief in communism in almost identical terms:

Since the French Revolution and its gradually universal echo, since the most radically egalitarian developments of that Revolution, the decrees of Robespierre's Committee of Public Safety on the "maximum" and Babeuf's theorizations, we know (when I say "we," I mean humanity in the abstract, and the knowledge in question is universally available on the paths of emancipation) that *communism is the right hypothesis.* Indeed, there is no other, or at least I am not aware of one. All those who abandon this hypothesis immediately resign themselves to the market economy, to parliamentary democracy—the form of state suited to capitalism—and to the inevitable and "natural" character of the most monstrous inequalities.[2]

Badiou's affirmation of an invariant form of communism in need of an audacious resurrection puts him in the company of a small but significant number of radical thinkers in the late 1980s and early 1990s who likewise seek to salvage a certain communist notion from the simultaneous collapse of so-called totalitarianism and of the revolutionary project that the various state regimes of "really existing socialism" had long ceased to stand for. "The project: to rescue 'communism' from its own disrepute," Félix Guattari and Toni Negri write in the opening lines of *Communists like Us*, before explaining what they mean by such an operation: "We need to save the glorious dream of communism from Jacobin mystifications and Stalinist nightmares alike; let's give it back this power of articulation: an alliance, between the liberation of work and the liberation of subjectivity."[3] Guattari and Negri even seem to anticipate Badiou's very own style when they juxtapose the dream of "communism" with a notion of "democracy" that similarly would have to be saved from its disrepute. "At this juncture the word 'democracy' begs redefinition," they write: "The word 'communism' has clearly been defaced, but the word democracy itself has been trashed and mutilated. From the Greek *polis* to the popular uprisings of the Renaissance and Reformation, from the proletarian rebellions that coexisted with the great liberal revolutions, democracy has always been synonymous with the legitimation of power through the people."[4] Like democracy when properly understood, communism would name this invariant process whereby (the) people constitute themselves as (the) people, in a movement of immanent self-legitimation.

Despite a strong preference for the notion of democracy, we can also find a defense of communism in an otherwise very different philosophical tradition, one more indebted to Derrida and Heidegger than to Deleuze or Spinoza. "*Communism,* without doubt, is the archaic name of a thinking which is still entirely to come," Jean-Luc Nancy suggests in *The Compearance*: "When it will have come, it will not carry this name—in fact, it will not be 'thought' in the sense that this is understood. It will be a *thing*. And this thing, perhaps, is already here and does not let us go. But perhaps it is here in a manner that we are unable to recognize."[5] Earlier, in *The Inoperative Community*, Nancy had already ventured out into the vast expanses of this unpredictable future: "The community of the interrupted myth, that is, the community that in a sense is without community, or communism without community, is our destination. In other words, it is that toward which we are called, or remitted, as to our ownmost future."[6] In this case, to be sure, the future of communism will not be given over to the pure self-immanence of the people as people; instead, it belongs to the core of all future politics, according to the temporality of what is yet to come, to be marked by the radical finitude of each and every community. Communism, in other words, not as the exposure of sheer immanence but as the tracing of a groundless being-in-common, torn away from the nightmarish dreams of immanence and transcendence alike, and incommensurate to all known attributes and properties, whether of substance or of the subject. "We have no model, no matrices for this tracing or for this writing. I even think that the unprecedented and the unheard-of can no longer come about," concludes Nancy. "But perhaps it is precisely when all signs are missing that the unheard-of becomes again not only possible but, in a sense, certain. Here the historicity of our history comes in, as does the future-to-come of the suspended meaning of the old word 'communism.'"[7] Despite the shift from absolute immanence to radical finitude, in this orientation, too, we are witness to a project to salvage an idea or practice of communism from the agonizing history of its own defacement.

In a long footnote Nancy even goes on to cite Badiou himself as someone who would be "better placed" to speak of the "paleonymy" (in Derrida's sense) that would affect the word and concept of "communism," quoting the following words from Badiou's *Theory of the Subject*:

> The word "communism" has contracted some mould, that's for sure. But the roses and the gladioluses, the hairdresses, the sirens and the consoles, were also eaten by moths in that fin-de-siècle poetry which was given the name of "symbolism" and which all in all was a catastrophe. Let us try to be no more communist in the sense of Brezhnev or

Marchais than Mallarmé was a symbolist in the manner of Vielé-Griffin. If symbolism has held up so gloriously well with the swans and the stars, let us see if we can do as much with the revolution and communism. It is because we take the exact measure of their power, and thus of their sharing, that words may be innocent.[8]

If we were to continue along the lines of this shared genealogy, to which we could no doubt add several other proper names, we might indeed have to conclude that Badiou participates in a wider trend to salvage communism, as an unheard-of type of rebellious subjectivity or an unprecedented form of being-in-common, both from its actual fate in the collapsed socialist states and perhaps even from its place throughout the history of Marxism. Nothing could be more misleading, however, than to accept the premise behind this genealogy, namely, that communism may be understood apart from Marxism, just as conversely few tasks could be more urgent than to specify what are the exact relations between communism and Marxism in Badiou's view.

For Badiou there emerges a speculative type of leftism whenever communism is disjoined, and nowadays supposedly set free, from the historicity intrinsic to the various stages of Marxism. The critique of speculative leftism in this sense is actually a constant throughout Badiou's work. At the same time, a common objection among readers of this work holds that Badiou himself, by sovereignly setting apart the fidelity to an event from any concrete genealogical inscription of the event in the existing situation of being, over the years increasingly would have painted himself into a similarly narrow corner as a dogmatic, absolutist, or even mystical thinker. According to this objection, Badiou himself in other words would be yet another example of "left-wing communism" as the "infantile disorder" of a mature and fully developed communism, to use Lenin's well-known words, even if we might have to turn these words around today, following the example set not so long ago by Gabriel and Daniel Cohn-Bendit, in terms of communism as the "senile disorder" of an eternally youthful and invariant "leftism."[9] Once we grasp the logic behind Badiou's critique of speculative leftism, however, we will also be better equipped to address this objection according to which he himself, if not before then at least ever more clearly so in recent years, falls prey to precisely such a leftist temptation of wanting to be a communist without also being a Marxist.

THE COMMUNIST INVARIANTS

> In what historical conditions does the universal ideological resis-
> tance of the exploited take the form of a radical vindication, which
> bears on the very existence of class contradictions and of the state,
> and which envisions the process of their annihilation? Key ques-
> tion of universal ideological history: who then is communist? —
> BADIOU AND BALMÈS, *De l'idéologie*

The first task consists in refining our understanding of the invariant nature
of communist subjectivity briefly recapitulated in *Of an Obscure Disaster*.
Badiou originally proposed the idea of invariant communism, or of com-
munist invariants, more than thirty years ago in his Maoist booklet *Of
Ideology* written in collaboration with the Lacanian psychoanalyst François
Balmès. Based in large part on *The Peasant War in Germany* by Friedrich
Engels, particularly as seen through the intriguing case of Thomas Münzer,
Badiou and Balmès propose the hypothesis that all mass revolutionary
uprisings throughout history aspire to realize a limited set of communist
principles: "Our hypothesis holds that all the great mass revolts of the
successive exploited classes (slaves, peasants, proletarians) find their ideological expression in egalitarian, anti-property and anti-state formulations
that outline the basic features for a communist program."[10] Such spontaneous rebellion of the exploited masses typically leads to a war of insurrection, in which communism comes to define a general ideological position
against the state: "The elements of this general positioning of the insurgent
producers are what we call the *communist invariants*: ideological invariants
of communist type that are constantly regenerated in the process of unification of the great popular revolts of all times."[11] We thus can begin to
understand at least superficially why the later Badiou, when faced with the
many purported "deaths" of Marxism, would want to retrieve this invariant
communism as an eternal form of rebellious subjectivity.

We should not forget, though, that the communist invariants are the
work of the masses in a broad sense. There is as yet no specific class
determination to the logic of revolt in which slaves, plebeians, serfs, peasants, or workers rise up against the powers that be: "The communist
invariants have no defined class character: they synthesize the universal
aspiration of the exploited to topple every principle of exploitation and
oppression. They emerge on the terrain of the contradiction between
masses and the state."[12] In this broad-based resistance against the state

apparatuses lies the unlimited power and energy of the masses; in fact, the authors see no other reason why communists should have infinite confidence in the people as such. Badiou and Balmès, however, also argue that this massive ideological communism remains deficient without the historical means for its realization. As a rule, they even posit a certain counter-finality at the root of history. That is to say, most often the spontaneous revolt of the masses is appropriated and diverted by those historical forces that are in the process of becoming dominant precisely as an unintended effect of the revolt itself. This is the argument, so frequently used for the sake of a reactionary disavowal, about how history always seems to proceed behind the back of the masses. Engels himself is forced to admit at the end of his study that the princes were the only ones to profit from the Peasant War. Similarly, the Jacobins are often said merely to have paved the road for the bourgeoisie, just as the rebellious spirit of the students and workers who took to the streets in the late sixties, unbeknownst to themselves, would have worked to the benefit of the newly emergent technocrats.

Within any ideological struggle, we can thus distinguish a minimum of three factors. First, we find the relatively *old form* of the revolt, that is, the ideology of the old dominant classes, as when the religious ideology of Protestantism is used heretically to organize the peasants in Münzer's Germany. Second, we have the *unchanged content* of the communist program, that is, the immediate popular substance of all great revolts, from Spartacus to Mao. Finally, true *historical novelty* is the work no longer of the masses in general but of that specific fraction or class which, under the given circumstances, is able to take hold of the moment for its own long-term benefit: "Ideology, seized as a conflictual process, always puts into play a triple determination: two class determinations (old and new, counter-revolutionary and revolutionary), and one mass determination (the communist invariants)."[13] The real key in the discussion over the historicity of communism, as opposed to its spontaneous eternity, lies in this difficult dialectic of masses and classes, in which both are caught at cross-purposes in the uneven struggle between the old and the new.

With the revolt of the proletariat, however, there supposedly would come an end to the rule of historical counterfinality. Instead of seeing their egalitarian demands co-opted and drained for the benefit of the newly emergent dominant classes, the workers who after the massive revolts of 1848 in Europe organized themselves as proletariat would be the first historical force actually to take control of the basic communist program: "With the proletariat, ideological resistance becomes not only the *repetition* of the invariant but also the mastery of its *realization*."[14] This unique moment coincides with the birth of Marxism. The latter, in fact, is nothing but the accumulation of all the knowledge conveyed by the millenarian ideological struggle around the communist invariants—including many of the failed revolts from past centuries, whose broken and repressed memory is never lost forever but rather haunts the present as its uncanny and shadowy double: "Marxism-Leninism is that which avers that the proletariat, heir to a secular ideological struggle surrounding the communist program, is also the realizer of this heritage. Marxism-Leninism not only accumulates the ideological resistance but also transforms it into knowledge and project."[15] Marxism and communism thus rely on one another in a paradoxical history of eternity—that is, the historical unfolding of an eternal revolt. Let us say: Marxism without communism is empty, but communism without Marxism is blind.

Only under the direction of the proletariat would the complete dialectic of masses, classes, and the state become adequate to its historical task. As for the materialist question regarding the specific conditions that make this adequation possible, suffice it to say that it is capitalism itself that first brings into existence and then organizes the proletarian revolutionary capacity. The proletariat is even said to acquire an unprecedented logical and epistemological capacity. Perhaps we are not so far removed after all from the central idea in Georg Lukács's *History and Class Consciousness*. "The proletariat is the producer of the first logic of the revolution," Badiou and Balmès solemnly claim: "In this sense, the proletarian ideology, in its concrete form of Marxism-Leninism, stops being the resistance displayed on the basis of the radical but historically utopian critique of class society in general, so as to become the revolutionary knowledge of this society and, consequently, the organizing principle of its effective destruction."[16] This also means that, in the absence of an organized accumulation of critique, the spontaneous and immediate antagonism of masses against the state runs the risk of quickly being reversed. As Badiou and Balmès warn while reflecting back on May 1968 in France: "This purely ideological radicality inevitably changes over into its opposite: once the mass festivals of democracy and discourse are over, things make place for the modernist restoration of order among workers and bosses."[17] The regeneration of the invariant communist program, in other words, is a powerful but insufficient weapon: "We say that, left to its own devices, abandoned to the unilateral exaltation of libertarian tendencies, this regeneration does not outlive the movement itself of which it is the reflection, and it ineluctably reverses into capitulation, into ideological servilism."[18] Unless of course it is to remain an ideal that will be always yet to come, communism names the real movement that abolishes the present state of injustice only when it is historically tied to the various stages of Marxism.

MARXIST POLITICS

> We must conceive of Marxism as the accumulated wisdom of popular revolutions, the reason they engender, and the fixation and precision of their target.—BADIOU, *Théorie de la contradiction*

We might also ask somewhat bluntly: What do Badiou's critics mean when they deplore the fact that he would not (or not sufficiently) be a Marxist? "Marxism" in this context seems to stand alternatively for a philosophy, a science of history, or, above all, a critique of political economy. Badiou, according to these accounts, would not be able to give us an updated critique of global capitalism or of the new world order dominated by an unprecedented explosion of immaterial labor caught in the meshes of new and ever more flexible regimes of control. No matter how sophisticated they may well turn out to be in their own right, such readings nonetheless fail to grasp the strictly political significance of Marxism. Paul Sandevince sums up this significance with his usual concision: "Marxism is not a doctrine, whether philosophical or economical. Marxism is the politics of the proletariat in its actuality." And later: "Marxism is the politics of communism."[19] "Science of history?" Badiou also wonders in disbelief about the nature of Marxism in *Theory of the Subject,* only to serve up a firm rebuttal of his own: "*Marxism is the discourse with which the proletariat sustains itself as subject.* We must never let go of this idea."[20] Marxism, as incapable as any other form of knowledge at making an objective, let alone scientific, totality out of the constitutive dispersion of history, nevertheless cannot be grasped outside the framework of periodized referentiality in which communism becomes part of a real historical movement.

There are two perspectives, or two directions, from which we might read the problem of historical referentiality, which alone organizes the communist invariants and thereby gives structure to the body of accumulated knowledge that is Marxism. If we start mainly from within this corpus itself, the question becomes one of periodizing the systematizations to which the substance of mass revolts becomes subject in the writings of Marx, Engels, Lenin, Mao, and so on. Rather than concentrating on the discovery of a new, structural type of causality in *Capital* or even, for that matter, on the *Grundrisse* as the dynamic center of Marxian thought, Badiou and his cohorts thus always favor the more historical and interventionist writings such as Engels's *The Peasant War in Germany*, Lenin's *What Is to Be Done?*, or Mao's *Problems of Strategy in China's Revolutionary War*, in addition to the all too obvious choice of *The Communist Manifesto*. Marxism, Leninism, and Maoism are thereby tied to the principal episodes in an otherwise orthodox periodization of revolutionary activity: "The great stages of Marxism are punctuated by the proletarian revolutions and, precisely, the great Marxists are those who have directed and synthesized the findings of the theory, ideology, and politics of the proletariat in the light of these same revolutions: Marx and Engels for the Paris Commune, Lenin and Stalin for the October Revolution, Mao Zedong for the Cultural Revolution."[21]

As we have seen, much of Badiou's *Theory of the Subject* and several of his recent investigations and talks taken up in *Logics of Worlds* deal extensively with this periodization, most notably through a new appraisal of the rapport between history and politics in the Paris Commune and the Cultural Revolution in China. These texts actually form a strong component of historical materialism that is necessarily contained within the materialist dialectic according to Badiou.

This first historical perspective does not pretend foolishly to ignore the crisis that affects every piece of knowledge associated with Marxism. To the contrary, as Badiou declares in a seminar from *Theory of the Subject*, dated November 7, 1977, that is to say, at the height of fame and media-coverage of the New Philosophers: "Yes, let us admit it without detours: Marxism is in crisis; Marxism is atomized. Past the impulse and creative scission of the 1960s, after the national liberation struggles and the cultural revolution, what we inherit in times of crisis and the imminent threat of war is a narrow and fragmentary assemblage of thought and action, caught in a labyrinth of ruins and survivals."[22] However, this unabashed admission of the sense of an ending does not foreclose the possibility, and perhaps even the obligation, to give a new beginning to Marxism. "To defend Marxism today means to defend a weakness," Badiou may well state in the same seminar from *Theory of the Subject* but only to add: "We must *practise* Marxism."[23] For Badiou and his friends this means first and foremost to take cognizance not of the solutions so much as of the problems left unsolved during the last revolutionary sequence from the twentieth century, the one that between 1966 and 1976 was marked by the name of Mao Zedong. One thus necessarily must remain a Marxist even, or especially, when it comes to understanding the crisis and unresolved problems of Marxism.

Another perspective from which to read the problem of historical referentiality would move in the opposite direction by starting from the emancipatory events of the past two centuries themselves so as to study when and where they rely for support on the discourse of Marxism. Once again following the arguments of his friend Sandevince, Badiou outlines three such moments or referents in *Can Politics Be Thought?* These correspond to the workers' movement, the victorious formation of socialist state regimes, and the national liberation struggles. From this perspective, to be sure, the sense of an ending is no less painfully obvious than from the first one. Indeed, nothing seems to be left standing in terms of Marxism's capacity to lay claims on history after the collapse of the Soviet Union, after the revealed capacity for military expansion of liberated countries such as Vietnam, and especially after the appearance of workers' movements such as Solidarity in Poland that are openly anti-Marxist: "The great historical mass pulsations no longer refer to Marxism since—at least—the end of the Cultural Revolution: Look at Poland, or at Iran. Because of this we see an expatriation of politics. Its historical territoriality is no longer transitive to it. The age of auto-referentiality is closed. Politics no longer has a historical homeland."[24]

However, from this point of view, too, there is space for a possible recomposition, even a second birth, of Marxism. Badiou proposes in particular not just to repeat but to reinvent Marx's founding gesture in *The Communist Manifesto*, which consists in listening to the social hysterias of the 1840s in order to answer them with the hypothesis of a hitherto inexistent political capacity. "If Marxism today is indefensible, it is because we have to start it," Badiou claims: "We must redo the *Manifesto*."[25] Even in Marxism's irredeemable loss of referents, part of the emphasis should fall on the question of referentiality more so than on the melancholic experience of loss alone. This also means that one should be the subject, rather than the cynical object, of the crisis and destruction of Marxism. "What does it mean to be a Marxist today?" Badiou asks before venturing an answer of his own: "To stand for Marxism means to occupy a place that is destroyed and, thus, uninhabitable. I posit that there exists a Marxist subjectivity that inhabits the uninhabitable."[26] In the end the important point remains that, without the consistency of a previously invisible political subjectivity, without the hypothesis of an unwarranted capacity of non-domination, or without the ability to give organizational form to the wager of an invariant communism, there is not a breath of life left to be found in the whole doctrinal body of Marxism.

CRITIQUE OF PURE LEFTISM

> It is never "the masses," nor the "movement" that as a whole carry
> the principle of engenderment of the new, but that which in them
> divides itself from the old.— BADIOU, *Théorie de la contradiction*

Where do we stand today with regard to the dialectics between masses, classes, and the state, between the people and the proletariat, or between the dispersed elements of an invariant and generic communism and the organized forms of knowledge concentrated in the writings of Marxism?

Everything would seem to indicate that, in an era marked by the end of referentiality, all that is left in the eyes of our most radical contemporary thinkers is the unlimited and spontaneous affirmative energy of pure communism, purged of all its historically compromising and saturated ties to the parties, groups, organizations, or state regimes that once invoked the now infamous names of Marx, Lenin, or Mao. Conceptually, this leads many thinkers to postulate a direct and unmediated opposition—without diagonal terms such as class, party, or organization—between the masses and the state, or between the plebes and the state.

Today, a similar opposition may still be at work not only in Hardt and Negri's argument over multitude and empire but also among other thinkers who still are variously influenced by an opposition emblematized in Pierre Clastres's *Society against the State*: from the relation of exteriority between war machine and state apparatus, as posited by Deleuze and Guattari in their *Nomadology*, all the way to the recent repetition of a similar scheme in Miguel Abensour's *Democracy against the State*. In all these cases leftism involves an external opposition that is as radical as it is politically inoperative, along the lines of the spontaneous and unmediated antagonism between masses and the state discussed by Badiou and Balmès in *Of Ideology*. This is left-wing communism, or communism without Marxism, as if all that remains were nothing but the communist invariants outside their determination in terms of a specific historical class, fraction, party, or other, guided by the knowledge referred to in Marxism.

Badiou, however, has always argued against the leftist operation that radically unties the dialectical knot between masses, classes, and state, or between communism and Marxism. Thus, in the preceding chapters we have come across a number of variations on this theme, a detailed overview of which would produce what we might call a critique of pure leftist reason:

1. There is first of all the philosophical variation that opposes *place* and *force*, or *structure* and *tendency*, as discussed in *Theory of Contradiction* and *Of Ideology*. Leftism ignores the fact that every force is necessarily determined by a system of assigned places in which it finds its space. This structural element inherent in every tendency is neglected in favor of a viewpoint of pure, unlimited, and affirmative becoming, as in many a "movementist" tendency fostered by May 1968.

2. In the moral variation, we have the familiar dualism of *freedom* and *necessity*, or of *autonomy* and *determinism*, which Badiou in *The Current Situation on the Philosophical Front* attributes to the hidden Kantianism of the authors of *Anti-Oedipus*. Badiou moreover finds that this moral dualism also underlies the oppositions between *subject-groups* and *subjugated groups*, as well as between the *molecular* and the *molar*.

3. In the political variation, we find the dualisms of *plebes* and *state*, or of *students* and *cops*, especially during and after May 1968. These, too, receive a harsh rebuttal on Badiou's part. Critics of the necessarily repressive or totalitarian nature of the state, he holds, can then pontificate endlessly about the virtues of the masses, or of civil society, without even for a moment taking their eyes off the fascinating omnipotence of the state's coercive and hegemonic machinery.

4. Finally, we also obtain a psychoanalytical variation on the same theme in terms of the dualism of *tuchè* and *automaton* that roughly corresponds to the encounter with the real and the automatism of the reality principle. In *Can Politics Be Thought?* Badiou not only draws on this Aristotelian dyad by way of Lacan, but he also applies it to the

deconstructively inspired arguments of Nancy and Lacoue-Labarthe regarding the retreat of the political: "The thought of the essence of the political as retreat slips into the distance, which is almost nil and which our time makes into its misfortune, between fortune and repetition, between *tuchè* and *automaton*."[27] In this case the anticipation of the transcendental conditions of possibility of an unforeseeable event, a radical act, or a genuine encounter with the real, which are also always its conditions of impossibility, is substituted for the actual interruption of the automatism of capital.

Given this ongoing critique of the speculative left in all its variations, to what extent can we say that Badiou himself is capable of resisting the leftist temptation? Have not most of his critics, including Slavoj Žižek, Peter Hallward, Françoise Proust, Eustache Kouvélakis, and Daniel Bensaïd, suggested in one way or another that Badiou is actually one of the most formidably dogmatic leftists of our time? This harsh judgment, however, refuses to absorb the long-standing critique of leftism that we find throughout Badiou's writings. Even *Being and Event*, a book that at every turn of the page seems pushed in the direction of dogmatism and hyperbole by the sheer power of mathematical abstraction, seeks to avoid the traps of a relation of pure exteriority between its two founding terms. As a matter of fact, it is precisely at the heart of this book that we find an acute definition of the speculative left as the temptation to turn the notion of a political intervention, for example, into the blind voluntaristic or miraculous event of an ultra-one, or an absolute beginning, utterly cut off from the structure of the situation at hand. "We can call *speculative leftism* every thinking of being supported by the theme of an absolute beginning. Speculative leftism imagines that the intervention is authorized only by itself, and breaks with the situation with no other support than its own negative will," Badiou writes: "Speculative leftism is fascinated by the ultra-one of the event, and thinks it is possible in its name to deny all immanence to the structured regime of the count-for-one."[28] Badiou's own philosophy, as I have argued throughout this book, does not pretend to save the purity of the event by haughtily withdrawing from all immanence and situatedness. The point is to study the consequences of an event within the situation, not to elevate the event into a wholly other dimension beyond being.

Even so, what is perhaps most intriguing in this respect is the way in which speculative leftism nevertheless constitutes a permanent temptation inherent in Badiou's thinking. Not only have we seen significant strokes, or *coups de barre*, to the left or to the right—for example, after *Being and Event* Badiou himself corrects the dangerously leftist notion of the pure event as absolute beginning by inscribing the event within the domain of appearing in a world—but now it turns out that even the extended argument in *Logics of Worlds* is in need of further elaboration, announced for the third volume in the series, titled *The Immanence of Truths*. Instead of attacking this work on the grounds that it offers at best a sectarian and mystical form of leftism, it would be more productive to continue studying in detail these internal shifts and self-criticisms on the part of a philosopher who in spite of his self-assured appearance never ceases to put into doubt the conclusions of his own work.

More importantly, I wonder why all those critics mentioned above, in their implicit or explicit quest for a more historically or dialectically grounded mediation of being and event, cannot find a meeting place somewhere in between, whereby they might find an accomplice rather than an adversary in Badiou. I admit that such a renewed understanding of the common project to think an emancipatory politics would entail a radical overhaul of some of our most deeply ingrained intellectual habits—such as the habit of polemicizing among factions within the left, always positioning oneself in terms of a neither/nor response to other thinkers, rather than in the inclusive terms of a both/and stance, or the habit of preferring the self-destructive radicalism of an ever more vigilant deconstruction over and above the collective project of making a common front. Without in turn wishing to speculate about this, in these times of near-global political reaction few tasks seem to me more urgent than actively and historically to reconstruct the positive elements, beyond the polemics, that many of these thinkers share not just in their common rejection of speculative leftism but also in their desire to put an end to the hegemony of the right.

IN DIALOGUE WITH ALAIN BADIOU

Appendix 1

CAN CHANGE BE THOUGHT?

An Interview with Alain Badiou Conducted by Bruno Bosteels
(Paris, June 10, 1999)

Bruno Bosteels. I would like to begin by situating your work in the context of May '68 in France. In *Theory of Contradiction* you mention that the events of that year mark, both in philosophical terms and in every other regard, your "Road to Damascus." This statement seems almost to be a direct anticipation by some thirty years of your recent book, *Saint Paul: The Foundation of Universalism,* as if to suggest that all this time was needed in order to come to grips with the effects of the student movement and the encounter between students and workers. What has always impressed me in this regard is the force of continuity between your thought and the events of May '68 and its aftermath. There are few philosophers who have been able to continue in that line of thinking without falling into either melancholy or resentment. How do you see this situation today? Could we not say that your two most important books to date, *Theory of the Subject* and *Being and Event,* even if we put aside for a moment the profound change that occurred between them, are still in some way the answer after the fact to this event that struck you on your road to Damascus?

Alain Badiou. Indeed, I think that, to use my own terminology, my fidelity to what happened in that period is unquestionable, but it is also profound, because I think that a large part of my philosophy at bottom is an attempt fully to come to terms, including from my own experience, with what happened then, while at the same time explaining the reasons for remaining loyal to those events. I am always surprised, in fact, by the many cases of disloyalty, backlash, and abandonment. I cannot see any justification for this, other than a certain form of historicism, namely, the argument that, ultimately, you should always keep up with the times at all cost, and since times are changing and, as is only normal, the counterrevolution comes after the revolution, so then to be modern means always that you should somehow fall in line with the sequence of events of your time.

I am very surprised to see, for instance, that today everything that does not amount to surrender pure and simple to generalized capitalism (let us call it this) is considered to be archaic or old-fashioned, as though in a way there existed no other definition of what it means to be modern than, quite simply, to be at all times caught in the dominant forms of the moment. I ask myself if behind all this there does not lurk still a difficult settling of accounts with historicism and with the conviction that you must always be in tune with what I would call the average of our time, and that, otherwise, you are marginalized, belated, lagging behind, or archaic.

For me, I would add that this loyalty to the sequence initiated by May '68 has never posed any real difficulties, except for the fact that such loyalty has become rare nowadays—and, of course, there lies the real problem. Subjectively, not only does this loyalty not present any problem, but also I continue to think that the complete elucidation of what took place there, together with the invention of ways of remaining loyal to those events, is the real task of contemporary thinking. I, for one, cannot see any other task. That being said, I also would not like to make a virtue, or a heroic exception, out of this fidelity. For me, in any case, it is probably abandonment that would be difficult, and not fidelity.

THE MOTIF OF THE END

BB. On several occasions in your work, particularly in *Metapolitics* but already in *Theory of the Subject*, you have addressed a particular way of responding, or of failing to respond, to the events of 1968. One case in point would be the New Philosopher who, according to your thesis in "What Is a Thermidorean?," can be defined as someone who makes it impossible even to think of this sequence of events. Today, however, I see only little interest in replying to the New Philosophers. There is a much more daunting challenge put forth by other thinkers, some of them being among the most subtle and lucid interpreters in the tradition of Heidegger and Derrida. I am thinking for example of Philippe Lacoue-Labarthe and Jean-Luc Nancy, who from a rather melancholy point of view, including in the psychoanalytical sense of the term, attempt to transform this very impossibility and retreat of the revolution, of sovereignty, or even more generally, of all politics as hitherto conceived, into the argument for a new beginning, or a retreatment, of the political as such. In your case, even though there are evidently breaks and reformulations in your work, I see no reticence, and thus almost no melancholy, no desire to explain the past as if it were an effect of youthful fervor, a misguided dream, or even the expression of an unfounded hope in another order beyond the law of capital and market administration. To anticipate a bit, what is your position with regard to this other tendency, which clearly is not that of the New Philosophers, being more akin to the critique of metaphysics in the wake of Heidegger?

AB. Of course, I see what you mean. And I should say, by the way, that for quite a long time now I have been traveling in friendship alongside Philippe Lacoue-Labarthe and Jean-Luc Nancy. I hold them in the highest esteem and love them very much. We met in the early 1980s, precisely at a time which for me, no doubt, was the period of maximum isolation, because the New Philosophy had been installed, everybody had rallied more or less to the socialist Left and to Mitterrand, and truth be told, if you consider my own politico-philosophical position, precisely at the time of *Theory of the Subject*, you will find that it went completely against the grain and was worked out in absolute isolation. I really should thank Lacoue-Labarthe and Nancy for not having participated in this isolation and for having invited me to the political seminar, which they directed at the time in rue d'Ulm. For this reason I absolutely distinguish what you call their "tendency" from that of denegation pure and simple. At the same time, it is true that we do not share the same subjectivity and, as a result, we do not think in the same terms about those events, because they nonetheless confirm a certain paradigm of the end, which, I think, comes from the crossing between their Heideggerianism, after all, and their evaluation of the twentieth century. This authorizes them, by the way, to present themselves—truthfully I believe—as left-Heideggerians. I mean, in an allusion to Hegel, we could speak of "young" Heideggerians, in comparison to the "old" Heideggerians: Heideggerians of the Left.

Nevertheless, the motif of the end is there, and something in the thesis

of the retreat of the political, which is their own nostalgic thesis, is in tune
with, or can be fully understood only from within, the space of the closure
of metaphysics. I am convinced of this. It is indeed one of the modalities of
the closure of metaphysics. In terms of their account of the twentieth
century, this means that they accept to say that what has been blindly
attempted in the past century is now effectively closed, and this statement
will then converge with, or will be tied to, a much vaster historical framework of which the question of politics is only one modality among others.
Hence probably also the need, in their vocabulary, to desublimate politics,
to consent to a politics without the sublime. This can also be phrased as
follows: to pass from the poem into prose, or to conceive of the poem itself
as prose. I understand this politically too: to conceive of the poem as prose
means, really, that the heroic form of politics is effectively finished and over
with, and that we should seek out or reopen another figure for the labor of
thought that is politics. For this reason, I think, they need to traverse the
end, or the figure of the end, in order to reopen the question of the political
or of politics, in a modality that I am afraid remains by and large prophetic.
I am afraid that this is no less but also no more than the promise of the
return of the gods as in Heidegger. I am afraid that whenever a notion of
the end has this kind of historical importance or density, the announcement of the resurrection remains always at bottom the natural regime of
thought. Thinking, then, remains installed in a certain linkage between the
lack and the announcement, from which it can find no escape.

My own position is different. I am convinced that at all times the politics
of emancipation have been essential, that in any case there has not been,
properly speaking, one unique experience in the twentieth century but a
diversity of experiences that surely presented certain common traits but
that were nevertheless essentially multiple and heterogeneous, and that
these sequences are saturated. The questions posed by this saturation are
extremely complex but not more so than at other times. I mean, at bottom,
what were the questions posed to the thinkers and militants from the
beginning of the nineteenth century by the fact that the sequence of the
French Revolution was in all evidence closed? These questions are somehow replayed today. Besides, the various tendencies that we can discern
today already existed, metaphorically or analogically speaking, at that time.
The nostalgic-melancholy tendency can easily be found among writers of
the early nineteenth century, and so can the prophetic-idealist tendency as

well. And then Marx proposes an entirely different angle, because if you consider things in terms of capital, you are somewhere else absolutely than where the French Revolution was.

In this regard my loyalty cannot be any less: I can perfectly well admit that a whole series of internal features of politics from the past century, let us say of revolutionary politics, its avatars and its sequences, is saturated and, at the same time, admit that we still have considerable difficulties, both in thought and in practice, to go beyond this saturation. A large part of the current disposition in this matter is purely experimental, trying out new possibilities that go neither in the eschatological sense of the end or the retreat of the political, nor in the sense of a renunciation, which is only another figure of the end, namely, the end of illusions.

The ambiguity of the motif of the end comes from the fact that this question can receive two possible treatments. When an end is declared, whether it is the end of metaphysics, the end of politics, or eventually the end of philosophy itself, two approaches are possible. The first is to say: it was only an illusion, and we have been awakened; our eyes have been opened, and we have ceased being duped. And then the second treatment is: it was much more than an illusion; it was an historical disposition, something of the nature of a figure, but this figure has perished, and we should move on to another. With regard to this motif of the end, in other words, you basically have a critical figure, that of disillusion, and then a prophetic one, which consists in passing from one figure to another. Both, in my eyes, render politics practically impossible. The first because, after all, it amounts to the acceptance of the established order. This has been true ever since the modern bildungsroman, ever since *Les Illusions perdues*, by Balzac: when all illusions are lost, this means that one is finally part of the world as it is, and thus the world will be administered, but there will be no politics as I understand it. But the second treatment offers no solution either, because in this case what replaces politics is the announcement of the conditions of possibility of its resurrection, while politics itself is paralyzed.

I really believe that the motif of the end is politically intractable. It is of course true that things come to an end, but then a sufficiently elaborated ontology of multiplicity is needed in order to be able to admit that what comes to an end is always only *one* figure among others of the politics of emancipation, and that the latter has always existed in such multiplicity.

IN THE SHADOW OF MAO

BB. In order to understand how your current work responds to, or avoids, both these positions, particularly with regard to the motif of the end, and so as to sidestep the debate about metaphysics or the overcoming of metaphysics, I would like to go back in time, to the period right before and after May '68. Philosophically speaking, this moment is dominated by the well-known debates regarding structure and history, or structure and subject. Let us say: Althusser against Sartre, or Lacan against Debord and the Situationists. Once we admit that it is at this time that the question of the event as such begins to be formulated, particularly from the point of view of politics, your work appears to sit between these two positions, by articulating the later philosophy of Sartre with that of Althusser, or by reformulating Lacanian psychoanalysis in terms of the Marxist doctrine, in *Theory of the Subject.* I would argue that it is in this in-between of the traditions of Sartre and Althusser that you make it possible to think of the event *in* a situation. The articulation of these two apparently heterogeneous traditions, though, in large part becomes possible only thanks to the input of Maoism. More so than in the trends of post-Marxism, as is the case for other members of your generation, it seems to me that your work should be resituated in a certain post-Maoism.

AB. Yes, yes, absolutely.

BB. Now, in this debate regarding the event as situated between history and structure, how do you see the place of your own work, particularly at the time of your texts on Maoism, from *Theory of Contradiction* all the way to *Theory of the Subject?*

AB. I would like to say first of all that your question seems to me absolutely pertinent, because for a long time now I've been thinking that I had had the chance, in a sense, of being just a little bit older than the rest of my generation, if I can use a slightly absurd expression (*laughs*). If I think of those who have been Althusserians, Lacanians, and Maoists—which was the normal itinerary for the militant intelligentsia from 1968 to 1972—they were all a bit younger than me. So what did this mean, to be a bit younger than me? It meant that, in a way, they had not had the time to be Sartreans. They had not really been Sartreans, and they also had not known any political situation in which they would have had to think in the categories proper to Sartre. As for me, I had known a very powerful political situation, the Algerian War, and I believe that it makes a major difference to have known this situation, in which progressive positions could be taken up from within the philosophical categories that were Sartre's own. These were the categories of commitment, of anticolonialism, and the kind of Sartrean thesis that held that colonialism is a system, which can be found in his texts of that period.

I found in Sartre's theory of practical freedom, and particularly in the subjectivized Marxism that he was already trying to produce, something with which to engage myself politically, in spite of everything, in the situation. This did not keep me from taking my distance from Sartre, nor from participating in that generation that, indeed, started to take a major interest in the question of the structure. But in the end I entered into this debate from the point of view of Sartre, whereas for most others in my generation this question of the structure has been their immediate philosophical education, so that they really entered the debate *against* Sartre and not *from* Sartre. And in general, one should say, against phenomenology.

So there was a small temporal discrepancy, which in effect put me in a position in between, I think we can put it that way. This meant that, despite everything, I have always been concerned in a privileged way by the question of how something could still be called "subject" within the most rigorous conditions possible of the investigation of structures. This question echoed for me with an even older question, which I had raised at the time when I was fully Sartrean, namely, the question of how to make Sartre compatible with the intelligibility of mathematics. Of course, this is not at all a Sartrean question, but at bottom I had always been a secret Platonist for love of mathematics and their regime of intelligibility. I remember very clearly having formed the project of one day constructing something like a Sartrean thought of mathematics, or of science in general, which Sartre had left aside for the most part. This particular circumstance explains why I nevertheless have always been interested in the question of structural formalism all the while maintaining the category of the subject.

This really meant that in the end I was more Lacanian than Althusserian, even though I was close to Althusser. But I have never been a member of the group of Althusserians from the first generation. I was always an Althusserian free agent, always a bit marginal. Besides, I was not a member of the Communist Party: politically and philosophically, there was always something that did not quite click. Althusserians, by the way, always reproached me for continuing to be a Sartrean after all. That debate was always present. And Maoism has tied all this together.

Maoism has played an absolutely essential role. I mean the flamboyant kind of Maoism from the period of the Cultural Revolution: Maoism presenting itself as an alternative to revisionism, that is to say, after all, as an alternative to the fate of the USSR, and in the final instance, but this is now completely obscured even though it is most important, as an alternative to Stalinism. This was a conscious effort on the part of Mao. Everything then becomes very complicated because at one point the Chinese seem to have defended Stalin against Khrushchev, while the truth of the matter is that, particularly at the time of the Cultural Revolution, Mao thought of himself as attempting or proposing an alternative to the path in the construction of socialism on which Stalin had taken Leninism. So why was this so important? Because in Maoism, a very special place seemed to have been reserved for the question of subjectivity in politics—for a properly political subjectivity. In other words, there is the novelty of a break with the theory according to which consciousness is never anything more than consciousness of the objective conditions. Of course, Maoism also inherited much of the analyses of Marx, of Leninism, and the categories of the situation, of knowing the situation, and so on, are very important, but clearly there is a movement—how should we put this?—that tends toward the subjective heroism of thought and of the capacity for thinking, which struck an entirely new tone and which for me was tied to the events of '68, opening up a space from where to read those events, and thus constituting the road to Damascus that we discussed a moment ago.

I would like to say that Maoism, in the end, has been the proof for me that in the actual space of effective politics, and not just in political philosophy, a close knot could be tied between the most uncompromising formalism and the most radical subjectivism. That was the whole point. In Maoism, I found something that made it possible for there to be no antinomy between whatever mathematics is capable of transmitting in terms of formal and structural transparency, on the one hand, and on the other, the protocols by which a subject is constituted. These two questions were no longer incompatible. And I would add that I remain very sensitive in this regard, even though this also goes completely against the grain but that's fine with me, to the Chinese political style. This is something that always struck me, namely, its extraordinary formulaic quality, in an almost mathematical sense of the word.

BB. The capacity to present mathemes, so to speak?

AB. Exactly, to present the matheme of the situation, using sentences that possess at the same time an absolute transparency and an exceptional complexity or density, because they take charge of the situation in its entirety. This formulaic political style, which you very legitimately connect with the matheme, and which I myself have always connected with the matheme in the Lacanian sense of the word, has also contributed to the fact that Maoism has been for me a considerable school from the point of view of my personal history, in politics but also in philosophy. Moreover, and to conclude on this point, it was also manifest that for Mao and for the Chinese there existed a system of statements regarding the respective places of philosophy, politics, and economy, which completely upset the traditional disposition of these grand registers. That is absolutely obvious, and it is not by chance that at the heart of Mao's work you find *Five Philosophical Essays*. It is not simply out of coquetry that they are called this way, but the disposition of philosophy with regard to politics in my eyes is not at all the same for Mao and in Stalinism, nor even for Mao and for Lenin.

BB. Probably for this same reason Maoism also constitutes a crucial point of reference for Althusser in his theory of overdetermination, as the inner limit of structuralism?

AB. Exactly. I think that Althusser has found the Maoist theory of contradiction at the exact moment when he was trying, with considerable difficulties I should add, to determine the point where the structure is in excess over itself, that's right, the point which he sought in the Leninist theory of the weakest link, in the question of overdetermination, and, finally, in the theory of the principal aspect of the contradiction according to Mao. All this means pinning down the structural point that is also at the same time the point of breakdown of the structure.

BB. Maoism, in sum, enables a certain combination, or no longer finds an incompatibility, between an extremely rigorous, almost mathematical, form of structuralism and a kind of subjectivism that would no longer be humanist in the strict sense of Sartre?

AB. Yes, yes.

BB. It is at this very point where we find ourselves in the company of another tradition of contemporary thought, for example, in the work of Ernesto Laclau—whose trajectory in Argentina, and later in Great Britain, is to some extent parallel to yours. To use your later terminology, this tradition concentrates on the void, on the point of excess, or on what you also call the "outsite" of the structure, on the one hand, and, on the other, on a subject that would no longer be the humanistic subject of plenitude but a subject that is "split" from within. It is at the point of articulation between the two that you, as a Sartrean-Althusserian-Lacanian, can propose a thought of the event combined with a rigorous analysis of the situation.

AB. Yes, definitely, that is absolutely evident. There are many of us who finally have worked with different means in that breach in our heritage. And I think that it was indispensable to do so, in the conditions that were specifically ours, by going through the experience of Maoism. Besides, but here we are moving a bit in another direction, this is a question about which I am quite passionate at this moment. I mean, when I am listening to you, my question is: What of all this can be effectively transmitted? At bottom, what is the internal link between the traversing of the Maoist experience in all its dimensions and the arrangement of thought, the matrix or the kernel of which you have just recalled? And is this link of such a nature as to enable us truly and persuasively to isolate it, in the way I have attempted to do, starting in *Being and Event*, so as to reconstruct all the elements while separating them from their political genealogy? In a way, we can say that *Theory of the Subject* is a book in which the essential elements are already absolutely present while remaining in close proximity to their genealogy. That is why I have often said that this book is rather more like Hegel's *Phenomenology of Spirit* than like his *Logic*. It is rather something that remains caught in the movement itself of the figures, very close to the experience of Maoism; it integrates this experience and thinks through the philosophical disposition in close proximity to its genealogy. Afterward, in *Being and Event*, I have attempted a separation, but sometimes I wonder whether this is justified, I mean: in the end should a true transmission not also be capable of transmitting this genealogy and this experience themselves?

Transmitting an experience is always of a slightly different order than transmitting the formal arrangement in which this experience is reflected or thought out. That is a question that intrigues me in terms of my job as a teacher. After all, I would very much like that all this were transmitted to the young people. We must corrupt the youth; after all, that is the job of the philosopher (*laughter*). I wouldn't mind corrupting the youth, who are in dire need of a bit of corruption, or else they are completely corrupted but in the wrong sense. And I observe, since that is a bit the topic of our conversation, that they end up demanding the transmission not only of the intellectual or theoretical or philosophical framework but also of that which enabled us to think in such a way, and not otherwise, in the first place. Thus, we find ourselves again talking about the 1960s, not only in the architecture of their thought but as a site, to use my own vocabulary: as the site of an event. What has this site been? I am currently looking for protocols of transmission that would enable us to think that too. That is why, in my lectures at the Collège International de Philosophie, I began to talk about the twentieth century and about the figures of the present, and so on.

This is not a question of history, or of historical facts. It is a matter of transmitting the experimental adherences of the very concept itself and how the concept is a result, in the sense of being a result of experiences. All this goes to confirm absolutely your thesis according to which Maoism has been decisive in this context.

DEVIATIONS LEFT AND RIGHT

BB. For this reason I always insist that your early Maoist works, *Of Ideology* or *Theory of Contradiction*, should not be forgotten. Besides, I am convinced that even *Being and Event* should be read with the concepts of *Theory of the Subject* in mind, rather than only the other way around. Precisely because the articulation with the historical situation, as in the case of the aftermath of May '68, can then be mapped out dialectically. What is more, in the way in which this sequence of events is later reinterpreted, we can already perceive the beginnings of a backlash, which you describe in detail in *Theory of the Subject*. In fact, you distinguish two types of backlash. On the one hand, there are those who would say that the movement was absolutely pure, untainted by the situation, so that ultimately nothing really new took place in terms of the consequences of the event for the situation

itself; on the other, there are those who would deny that there even was a
movement to begin with, so that all that really took place was the placement
of pure being as such. These two extremes, in a sense, could also serve to
define the reception of your work as a whole with regard to the thought of
the event. The two perspectives, which your philosophy aims to articulate
by avoiding precisely their extremism, could still be said to correspond to
pure subjectivism and pure structuralism. In Maoist terms we might call
these the two types of deviation, respectively, on the Left and on the Right:
adventurism and opportunism, or anarchism and determinism, the delir-
ium of spontaneity and the iron laws of history. In the context of contemporary philosophy, finally, the same alternative seems to repeat itself between,
on the one hand, a prophetic, or messianic, philosophy of the event, which
remains absolutely outside the situation, and, on the other, the purely
structural analysis of what is objectively given, which remains on the level of
what you label the state of the situation. In this last case the analysis can
even pinpoint the void or the excess of the structure over itself, but finally it
does nothing more than to recognize that inner limit itself. The event, then,
would merely consist in an instantaneous apparition of the void as such, to
be recognized by the political philosopher, without actually processing the
consequences of any fidelity to the event. This question of the void and of
the point of excess seems to me to be essential. For this reason, I would add,
the pivot of your work could very well be said to be the concepts, first, of the
"outsite," in *Theory of the Subject*, and later, of the "evental site," in *Being and
Event*. These concepts alone keep us from losing sight of the specificity of
the event, while at the same time avoiding the two extreme interpretations,
which would reaffirm either that "nothing will have taken place but the
place" or that what has taken place is a force or an event so pure, or so
sovereign, reminiscent of the "beautiful soul," so as to have no connection
whatsoever to the situation in which it finds its place.

AB. Yes, absolutely, I agree with your interpretation. This is indeed the
whole battle that is raging quietly on the question of the event. Let us say
that everything in philosophy that is somewhat progressive and that does
not inherit a completely rotten view of politics somehow hovers around
the notion of the event. We can all agree on that. However, there are
considerable divergences within the space of this agreement. And I believe
that you have perfectly mapped out the terrain. Thus, on the one hand, the
event will itself be conflated with something that in fact pertains to its

structural condition of possibility. It is not at all the same thing to say that there is a site of an event and to say that there is an event. It is not at all the same thing to say that every situation contains a point of excess, a blank space, a blind spot, or an unpresented point, and to say that this already amounts to the event's effectuation properly speaking. In that case the event becomes structuralized, and it is shown simply to be the intimate point of breakage of the situation, that is, in fact, something like its being, or its point of the real. But then there is no politics, no fidelity, only a kind of blockage. All this in the end produces conceptions that in terms of politics are inevitably pessimist, in a Lacanian sense. There is always a blindness because one is always mistaken about the unchangeable nature of this intimate fracture, or of this sovereign excess that is constitutive of the situation. And on the other hand, indeed, the event can appear in its pure form, which we can find in Christian Jambet, because he directly gives it a theological framework, but also in the work of many others. In this case the event ultimately seems to be transhistorical.

BB. Without horizon, the event is being itself?

AB. At that moment, the event is being, absolutely, but being in its specific historicality, which is finally inappropriate for being in the situation. I think that this is a correct way of marking out the field. And it is true that my effort has always been one of articulation, in the sense that one can at the same time push to the end the properly structural theory of lack and excess, as well as their dialectical correlation, but in the renewed sense of the dialectic as used in *Theory of the Subject*, and consider the arrival of the event, which evidently would not be readable without such structural formalism but which can neither be reduced to it nor is indifferent to it. And it is from there that everything will be exploited in the system of consequences. That is indeed my position, absolutely. Of course, one could say that it is still a measure of my original fidelity to the events of 1968, because my position sustains that there are always consequences. Especially because I think that the regime of consequences is intrinsically infinite. Thus, there are always consequences; we are not reduced to waiting until the promise is kept, which is after all the prophetic position, nor are we obliged to say that there is nothing left and to make do with this nothing. Subjectively, that is the alternative to which I do not want to limit myself. That's for sure.

LACK OR DESTRUCTION

BB. I think that, for this very same reason, even before *Being and Event*, where you polemicize mostly with the ontologies of presence, that is, ultimately, with Heidegger, it is in *Theory of the Subject* that the passage from lack to destruction, in your polemic with Lacan, is really pivotal, even if later on you seem to want to abandon, or correct, the concept of destruction. In any case, it is the torsion by which something passes through at the site of the event.

AB. The concept of torsion is fundamental.

BB. To avoid conflating the site of the event, or the void of the situation, with the event itself, a passage is needed through the impasse. It is not enough to recognize the impasse of the structure, but it is also necessary, in a sense, to pass through it.

AB. I come back to this question of lack and destruction in subsequent elaborations. In *Theory of the Subject* I was strictly Mallarméan: "Destruction was my Beatrice," and the passage from lack to destruction is the exemplary torsion. I am more reserved on this topic in *Being and Event*, because in some way I think that there is something in "destruction," even in the signifier itself, that is a bit one-sided, in relation to the properly creative dimension of that which occurs or takes place. I now plan completely to rework this matter, since what I am doing right now is once again closer to *Theory of the Subject* than to *Being and Event*. In some regards it is once again more dialectically worked out. I think that I will end up by saying that in any case there has to be a *dérèglement*: a deregulation, or a breakdown of the rules.

BB. In an active sense?

AB. That's it. One cannot pretend simply to recognize the place of the void; let us keep this name for the moment. It is absolutely indispensable that there be a breakdown of the rule, because otherwise there is nothing more than a recognition. But recognition is equivalent to misrecognition; in my eyes it has no virtue in and of itself. So then, there has to be a breakdown of the rule; that is to say, there must be something that, including in the order of appearing itself, in the way in which the situation is simply given, no longer remains within the bounds of the analysis, not even in terms of its immanent excess, something that no longer is of the same order as before. You call this traversing the impasse, and I totally agree with the formulation. In any case I would say deregulation of the excess itself, and not just identification of its position or of its law. In fact, the consequences are always those of a breakdown of the rule; they are not the consequences of the structural position of the excess. They are the results of the upsetting and breaking down of the rule. If we suppose, as I do in *Being and Event*, that there is something supernumerary, then we must understand how this is not simply supernumerary but an intrinsic factor in the deregulation of the previous situation as given. Consequently, in my upcoming work I will combine supernumerary and destruction, instead of opposing them as I did in *Being and Event*. I will say: Let us not underestimate the fact that there is something that appears as such and that in a way was not there before, so that there is a supplementation, or a creation, a positive dimension, and that remains the point around which everything hangs together. But, at the same time, we would not understand what is at issue if we did not see that this supernumerary element has a completely deregulating function in the regime of appearance of the situation itself, and, thus, in a certain sense, it does destroy something after all; namely, it destroys a regime of existence, if I can say so, which was previously given. Indeed, something that was not entirely present in *Being and Event*, and that I will now redeploy, finally going back to my oldest sources, is the real distinction between being and existence. In fact, I will combine a certain generic stability of being, an uncovering of being in truth, with something that nevertheless profoundly changes the regime of existence. Finally, and to wrap up this discussion, which is extremely important, politically speaking, but also very abstract, I believe that I will assert that, whenever an event occurs, there is supplementation of being and destruction of existence.

EVENT OR ENCOUNTER

BB. I have a bit of a side-question about the genealogy of your work, which concerns your relation to Althusser. In your analyses you mostly concentrate on those canonical texts by Althusser in which he speaks of history as a process with neither subject nor end. However, I am thinking more now of Althusser's posthumous texts, published in the two volumes of *Écrits philosophiques et politiques*. Here Althusser seems to extend his analysis of the structure of overdetermination by trying to pinpoint the weakest link for the events of May '68, for example, even though he is ultimately unable to recognize the subjective forces capable of shaking up the structure at this very point. My question refers to this attempt on Althusser's part, perhaps in answer to his earlier blindness, to reconstitute what he calls a "subterranean" tradition, namely, the tradition of a materialism of the encounter, or a materialism of the aleatory, which seems to be his quest for a philosophy of the event, now called the encounter.

AB. Yes, absolutely.

BB. At that point, though (we are speaking of the early 1980s), could we not say that the master finally has become the disciple to one of his own disciples? What is your relation to this part in the final, posthumous work of Althusser?

AB. Listen, I have the impression that what you say tells the essence. I believe that in his final research Althusser realized, first of all, that an ontological framework was needed and that materialism finally could not simply be an epistemological category, that it was necessary to go further, that an ontological framework was unavoidable; and in the end he saw that this ontology needed to include the aleatory, in what he then called an aleatory materialism, and, like everyone else, he went to look for this on the side of atoms, clinamen, Lucretius, etc. That's unavoidable. Besides, in *Theory of the Subject* that is also very much present. For my part I think that Althusser, indeed, has remained our contemporary because he saw very clearly that something of the order of the event, of chance, of the aleatory had to be inscribed and understood ontologically in the framework of intelligibility that finally led to revolutionary politics itself. At the same time, I believe that he did not say his final word on the issue. All that remains a transitional clue, and it would have been necessary to see how in the final analysis, having grasped, reworked, and redeployed this, he would have rearticulated it to the ensemble of his previous framings. I have the feeling that he did not submit his intuitions in this regard to the ultimate test, that he had neither the time nor perhaps the desire or the subjective possibility of doing so. This goes to show to what extent Althusser remained a fundamental contemporary for us, which is what I claim today even after having attacked him most vigorously for political reasons.

RADICALS AND DOGMATISTS:
REPLYING TO THE CRITICS

BB. Let us turn now to the question of radical philosophy that I anticipated a moment ago. I think that we could address some of the responses to your work, taking as our reference point not only *Being and Event* but also *Theory of the Subject* or even your Maoism. Often continuing in the vein of Althusserianism and Lacanianism, various authors have criticized your work, in the name of a certain philosophical radicalism, for being dogmatic, or absolutist, in the way you would oppose being and event, or the situation and an unbounded beyond that would be so pure and so transcendent so as to seem almost religious. It might be possible, however, to answer this charge of dogmatism from within your very own categories. First, we might say that in several of these readings the event is conflated with the site of its possibility. Second, and more important, we might also say that the two deviations that you discuss in your work from the 1970s and early 1980s—let us call them anarchism or voluntarism, on the one hand, and, on the other, structuralism or determinism—strangely enough are being articulated, I wouldn't say in a dialectical resolution but rather by virtue of their inherent antinomian character. I am thinking, in particular, of the work of Ernesto Laclau and Slavoj Žižek. From the point of the structure, or the state of the situation, they may very well pinpoint the void, or the term of excess or lack in the Lacanian sense, a term that, as a vanishing cause, sustains the entire symbolical or social order, even while being itself in retreat—and here there would be an interesting parallel with the event for Heidegger.

AB. Yes, totally.

BB. But this term, which you call a vanishing term in *Theory of the Subject*, also allows the critic to adopt an ever more radical point of view, from which any concrete event or specific fidelity to the event will inevitably appear to be either naive or dogmatic, or both at once—not unlike the sense in which Maoism was accused of being a strange mixture of anarchic and totalitarian voluntarism. What I found in your work, however, is precisely a set of concepts and categories that allowed me to understand the logic of such radical arguments. Finally, this logic seems to remain on the level of the state, or of structural representation. Or rather, insofar as it is a matter of the void or gap that sustains this totality, we should perhaps speak of poststructural representation. Thus, we have the endlessly re-peated argument about the subject divided by the gap in the structure, about the structure split by the void, and in the end, the void circulates a bit everywhere, mainly between subject and structure. But this circulating void, whether as the real or as the kernel of antagonism and so on, can then be turned back against any trajectory of fidelity, no matter how precari-ous, with regard to a concrete event. Today, radical philosophy seems to amount to a strange and paradoxical kind of structural, or poststructural, anarchism: an ideal combination of adventurism that allows one to be radical, and of a structuralism that allows one to be rigorous.

AB (*laughing very hard*). Yes, absolutely. You describe the situation very well. And in this regard I would like to insist that, even in the title *Being and Event*, the "and" is fundamental.

BB. The conjunction or disjunction?

AB. The "and" is fundamental. At bottom what I want to say is this: It is not the opposition between the event and the situation that interests me first and foremost. That is not the focus of my interest. Besides, from this point of view I have always complained about being read in a way that is askew, or about being read only for the first chapters and then nobody reads the core of the proposal. Because, in my eyes, the principal contribution of my work does not consist in opposing the situation to the event. In a certain sense, that is something that everybody does these days. The principal contribu-tion consists in posing the following question: What can we derive or infer from this from the point of view of the situation itself? Ultimately, it is the situation that interests me. I don't think that we can grasp completely what a trajectory of truth is in a situation without the hypothesis of the absolute, or radical, arrival of an event. I agree. But in the end what interests me is the situational unfolding of the event, not the transcendence or the entrench-ment of the event itself. Thus, in my eyes, the fundamental categories are those of genericity and of forcing. Genericity can be understood as the trajectory of aleatory consequences, which are all suspended from what-ever the trace of the event is in the situation; and forcing consists in the equally extremely complex and hypothetical way in which truths, including political truths, influence and displace the general system of our encyclo-pedias, and thus, of knowledge.

In the end, therefore, I would like to be evaluated or judged on this part of my project, because in my opinion that is where the heart of the matter lies, as well as its novelty, even as far as the attempt is concerned to illuminate the militant dimension of a procedure of truth. However, I am very surprised to see that, in general, for reasons of their own interests, the commentators jump on the event to qualify it as transcendence, and then they tackle the category of truth as being inadequate, or as dogmatizing the figure of intimate excess. But I do not see how it can be dogmatized, given that we are in a register of consequences.

Truth, for me, is not the name of the event, even though that is how it is often interpreted. Truth is what unfolds as a system of consequences, secured by an unheard-of figure of the subject as consequence of the rupture of the event. It is so little dogmatic that it is rather always declared in the figure of an aleatory wager, which is kept up without having anything dogmatic about it, and without any guarantees from the event's transcendence in and of itself.

Thus, finally, what I try to develop is indeed a series of conceptions that adopt neither a statelike or structuralized figure of immanent excess nor a figure that would remit the event to some ineffective archetypal promise. Really, in the end, I have only one question: What is the new in a situation? My unique philosophical question, I would say, is the following: Can we think that there is something new in the situation, not the new outside the situation nor the new somewhere else, but can we really think of novelty and treat it in the situation? The system of philosophical answers that I elaborate, whatever its complexity may be, is subordinated to that question and to no other. Even when there is event, structure, formalization, mathematics, multiplicity, and so on, this is exclusively destined, in my eyes, to think through the new in terms of the situation. But, of course, to think the new in situation, we also have to think the situation, and thus we have to think what is repetition, what is the old, what is not new, and after that we have to think the new. At least in this regard I remain more profoundly Hegelian. That is, I am convinced that the new can only be thought as process. There certainly is novelty in the event's upsurge, but this novelty is always evanescent. That is not where we can pinpoint the new in its materiality. But that is precisely the point that interests me: the materiality of the new.

THE SOVEREIGN EVENT?

BB. In a way you have already started answering some of the charges of dogmatism or absolutism that are frequently leveled against your work. I would like to tease out more specifically the reasons behind these charges. The first reason, which you have just answered, concerns the rigid oppositions such as between being and event. In your work, however, the point is not simply to oppose them but to know what happens between the two in terms of transformation, disordering, or forcing. Thus, with regard to all the other oppositions as well—opinion and truth, history and politics, the animal and the immortal in us, interests and eternity—is it always a question of studying how these oppositions themselves are subject to torsion?

AB. Absolutely.

BB. A second motif behind the allegation of dogmatism holds that the event is presented as absolutely sovereign, in the sense of being self-referential. The event would refer to nothing outside itself. It is a multiple with the property of belonging to itself. To this reading we should first of all reply that the event is clearly *not only* a self-referential multiple.

AB. Not at all, precisely.

BB. In that case we would indeed fall into the trap of an absolute purity.

AB. The event is self-referential *and*, in addition, it is nothing else than the set of elements of its site. Here, the same principle applies: if you isolate self-referentiality and the set of elements of the site, you cannot adequately think through what I propose as the event's figure. Because as multiple, the event's figure mobilizes the elements of the site, delivered from the axiom of foundation. Subtracted from this axiom, and thus unfounded, the multiple of the elements of the site is going to act in a peculiar manner, namely, by immanentizing its own multiplicity. But you cannot isolate this point of the event's material singularity as such, since the event is tied to the situation by way of its site, and the theory of the site is fairly complex. It was Deleuze who, very early on, even before our correspondence, at the time when *Being and Event* had just appeared, told me that the heart of my philosophy was the theory of the site of the event. It was this theory, he told me, that explained why one is not in immanence, which he regretted a lot, but neither is one in transcendence. That's what he told me. The site is that which would diagonally cross the opposition of immanence and transcendence.

BB. Deleuze also offered another reading, perhaps prior to your correspondence, in *What Is Philosophy?* This other reading, which signals a third reason for our debate, concerns the position of philosophy itself in relation to its conditions. Here, too, it is often said that in your work, philosophy appears to occupy a position that is transcendent to its conditions. However, in response to this last objection, the opposite could also be said, since for you philosophy produces no truths of its own, being rather always under condition, and thus by no means is philosophy put on a pedestal.

AB. Not at all. In this aspect, too, I think that I am fairly Hegelian. In certain regards philosophy would rather have a tendency always to arrive too late. Ultimately, the owl of Minerva only takes flight at dusk. I understand this fairly well, even though obviously not for the same reasons as Hegel. I understand that the major problem for the philosopher is to arrive early enough. I really believe this is the case. This is why philosophers must constantly engage with the experiences of their time, have an ear for what happens, and listen to the antiphilosopher, because the antiphilosopher is always busy saying to him: "But what you, the philosopher, are talking about no longer exists, or it doesn't really exist, and then there is this, which you don't talk about and which is essential," and so on. That is a real convocation to one's time. It is truly a race against time. Indeed, I am convinced that the procedures of truth do not wait for philosophy. Thus, to speak of transcendence when it is really a matter of designating as quickly as possible whatever is proceeding, of saying "yes, that is where it proceeds," frankly I think that is an unfair trial, unfair because it often dissimulates its very opposite, that is, the refusal to place philosophy really under the system of its conditions. In fact, I am surprised to see in this regard how the majority of philosophers of our time are content with very little. That is, after all, they isolate very few things in our actual experience that they would consider sufficient to assure the contemporariness of philosophy.

THE DENIAL OF HISTORY

BB. Someone who seems to have had the intention to think his time is certainly Michel Foucault. In one of the earliest interviews with Foucault, an interview in which you participated along with Georges Canguilhem,

you already try to define philosophy as the thought of one's time—what
you would later describe as providing a space of compossibility for the
conditions of truth. In *Metapolitics* you recognize in Foucault someone
who, despite seeking to think through the singularity of his time, finally
would have lost sight of the event itself, having reduced it to sheer history
in the heterogeneous articulation of knowledge and power, the discursive
and the nondiscursive. My question concerns the topics of history and
historicism, which you mentioned before. In your earlier work, in *Theory of
the Subject*, for instance, you oppose structure and history by privileging
the latter without wanting to ignore the former; and in *Being and Event*,
similarly, you oppose nature and history. In more recent texts such as
Metapolitics, though, you seem to follow the position of your friend and
colleague Sylvain Lazarus by rejecting time as a category to think through
politics, just as you seem rather forcefully to reject history. If we think of
the work of Foucault, however, could we not say that his lifelong effort has
also been to reflect on the four conditions of art, or literature; of science,
particularly the threshold of the human sciences in most of his writings; of
love, for instance in *History of Sexuality*; and finally, of the question of
politics, which is also patent in his active militantism. Even if Foucault's
terms would seem to fall on the side of those categories that, in *Saint Paul*,
you oppose to the conditions of truth properly speaking, that is, even if he
prefers knowledge over truth, sexuality over love, and so on, should we not
recognize in him this gigantic effort to reflect on the events of our time in
what he called an "ontology of actuality" or a "critical ontology of the
present"? Even this expression itself has lost nothing of its provocative
power. Indeed, if we were to follow the dominant line of ontological enquiry in the wake of Heidegger, how could we even think of such a project as an "ontology of actuality"? From the point of view of the destruction of the metaphysics of presence, this would seem to be sheer nonsense.
And yet this project is in line with your own attempt to find an alternative ontological path to the tradition of Heidegger. Should we not consider Foucault, then, as someone who has similarly recast the ontological
situation, by mapping out his time according to the four conditions of
truth?

AB. But of course, what you suggest about Foucault is very illuminating and
seems quite right. In Foucault, besides, I have always felt, rather than
understood, this vivaciousness or this tension to make thought contempo-

rary with its time. You could sense this in his very character. When he died, I wrote that for me he had always been like a streetwalker: someone whom you could perfectly well imagine as a man of the archives and the libraries, but in reality he was very much the opposite: he only did all that in order to walk in the city. I think that's true. But what always struck me in him is the way in which he almost systematically took one step to the side in comparison to what I considered to be the conditioning center of philosophy. I don't know how to say this, except by suggesting that, in effect, instead of love, you have sexuality. That would be the major case. But, to be more detailed, consider for example Foucault's eighteenth century: that seems to be almost the photographic negative of my view. If someone asks me about the eighteenth century, I would say Rousseau, about whom Foucault says almost nothing; I would say the set of developments in mathematics up until and including Gauss; I would say the emergence of critical revolutionary theory and the destitution of religion. But he says something else entirely. It almost seems as if, in some way, the discursive truth of a time comes at the price of stripping this time of its generic procedures. Finally, the situation for him draws the contours of an episteme insofar as one first of all subtracts that which made an exception to it.

Come to think of it, as I am listening to you, that is what I would call history. It is the attempt to write the history of everything, to grasp a situation outside the belaboring of this situation by the generic procedures properly speaking. That is only normal, because history must treat of time without eternity, at least that is one way of putting it. When I deny history, or when I polemicize against history, that is what I am opposed to. I am not against the relation to our past, even less so against the presence of the past, because, on the contrary, I think that the past can convoke you with an enormous liveliness as present. But I am against this figure that apprehends situations in their time by first subtracting any hypothesis concerning the way in which this time has been treated by something other than itself, that is, ultimately, by subtracting the procedures of truth of which this time occasionally has been the site. It is in this sense that I would say that there is a certain complacency toward history on the part of Foucault. Not in the sense in which he would have opposed history to what after him you call an ontology of actuality. Thus, I have always understood that the full comprehension of the epistemes ultimately was destined for him to provide a thought of the singularity of the present. I really believe so. But his understanding of history is methodical and at bottom consists in deposing the singularity of a time in a subtraction of its genericity, while I would proceed the other way around, I would pick up a given time from the point of its genericity.

CONDITIONS FOR PHILOSOPHY

BB. Moving on to a possible objection of my own, I sometimes have the impression that there is, if not exactly a problem, at least a complementary risk in your way of reading the actuality of our time. Let us take the condition of art or literature, for instance, your readings of Mallarmé or Beckett. As a literary critic I get the impression that the events you study are converted, and I don't know if this is inevitable, into theoreticians of the event itself. Thus, when I read your analysis of Beckett, I find a very subtle and at the same time systematic account of the trajectory of the event itself. Likewise with Mallarmé. In these readings I find Mallarmé or Beckett not so much as events in the field of the literature of their time but rather as thinkers in their own right of the event as event.

AB. Yes, but you are totally right in making me this reproach, which obviously entails a rather large amount of philosophical appropriation of the condition. If one were to make the objection that I submit the condition to the conditioned, it is rather in the way you've just done that one should proceed, instead of in terms of transcendence. Because it is evident that, first of all, the selection of examples is oriented for me by the fact that the conceptual means that are needed strategically in order to allow for philosophical compossibility push me to choose certain writers or authors in whom precisely there is already present something like an internal disposition toward the event and its consequences. Besides, I would add that the writers whom I discuss in terms of philosophy are not necessarily the ones I prefer. So there you can see that if I were to remain, so to speak, in my literary innocence, that is, if I were to receive the evental imprint of a writer from within the question of writing itself, from within literature, then my choices would be entirely different, because it is true that the evental mode of existence of a writer in the very field of literature is not exactly the same as his or her existence as a conditional figure for a determinate philosophical framework. This much at least should be accepted. Thus, I think that literary events are indeed operative for philosophy, but when philosophy puts them as conditions for its own development, it nonetheless proceeds through operations of selection, change, or transformation. In my eyes these operations are not exactly falsifications, but they are, after all, displacements. The most intense subjective feeling I have about this is that there are artists, even whole artistic fields such as painting, or specific artists for whom I have a strong appreciation and who have contributed decisively to my intimate education, if I can say so, but about whom I have never said a word in my philosophy. That is because we have to take very seriously the fact that what operates as a condition for a certain philosophical disposition is indeed the evental value of literature, but not at all in and of itself, and because we are not obliged in philosophy to speak about everything. We are not in a relation to the totality; we stand rather in a relation to whatever has come, or to that which we have allowed to come in a position of condition. Of course, at any given moment, this condition can be thought dialectically, or interactively, as we would say today. Thus, there can be no doubt that Mallarmé, above all, but also Beckett have been instructive for me on the question of the event, but if, in return, I do justice to this instruction from within philosophy, it is evident that I will make them out to be, more so than they actually are, theoreticians of themselves —which they are, by the way, more so than others, and that is the reason why they have functioned as a condition for my philosophy. So, yes, the network of interactions is very complicated, but I don't think that in the end it is a transcendent subsumption but rather a practical interaction— which, it is true, I don't perform on just about anything.

ON THE QUESTION OF CULTURE

BB. Still in relation to the conditions of philosophy, I would like to raise another question, which might signal a final motif for polemics. I am referring no longer to philosophy's subsumption of its conditions but rather to the purity of the conditions themselves and to the eventual relations between them. In *Saint Paul* you clearly distinguish "true" art and "mere" culture, just as you oppose love and sexuality, politics and administration, truth and knowledge. Similarly, in *Conditions* you write against the confusion between various of these conditions: "Politics itself is a-cultural as is all thought and all truth. Comical, purely comical, is the theme of a cultural politics, as is that of political culture." I found this rather surprising, coming

from someone who has been so profoundly marked by the sequence of the
so-called Cultural Revolution!

AB (*laughs*). Well yes.

BB. I am thinking of your works written under the influence of this particular sequence, leading up to the major synthesis in *Theory of the Subject*.
Even if, in this last text, you write, "there only is a political subject, which
explains why the subject is rare and sequential," you nonetheless offer
many analyses of the other conditions as well: not only love, or science and
mathematics, but also the poetry of Mallarmé and the tragedies of Aeschylus and Sophocles. The four conditions are already fully present. This
seems to contradict the rejection of the kind of combination that would
constitute, for example, a politics of art. Why, then, this later need not only
to preserve their purity but also to avoid their interaction? Furthermore, in
response to your recent text "The Age of the Poets," Lacoue-Labarthe
points out that the real problem, even in your own terms, is not so much
the need to desuture philosophy from poetry alone but rather the far more
complicated problem of undoing the political resuturing of the suture
between philosophy and art, that is, undoing the "aestheticization of politics" already denounced by Walter Benjamin—whose general argument
Lacoue-Labarthe and Nancy adopt in *The Nazi Myth*. In this context it
does seem necessary indeed to desuture the conditions of philosophy.
However, if we go back to the sequence of the Cultural Revolution, or to
the events of May '68 and to so much that went on in the 1960s, is it not
equally important to understand the peculiar articulation of art, politics,
love, and science? Can we really understand this era if we separate and
purify these conditions? I know that you are working on this very question,
by studying the possible "networks" between various procedures of truth.
And I believe that Deleuze and Guattari, in *What Is Philosophy?*, are faced
with the same problem. Thus, after distinguishing art, science, and philosophy, they too end by discussing the issue of what they call the possible
"interferences" between them.

AB. Yes, it is evident that we must conceive of a theory of the network of
conditions and, thus, we must come back to the question of culture, which
in *Saint Paul* had an essentially polemical function. I did not want to enter a
culturalist approach for this series of questions because then everything
necessarily gets lost completely. But that does not mean that we could in

effect maintain a doctrine of the absolute purity of the conditions with regard to one another. The point is simply to know what exactly is a crossing, or a linkage, between various truth procedures. The privileged field of exercise for this type of question indeed has always been that of art and politics. The attempts to do the same for science and politics have been more adventurous, even though I always found that it was extremely interesting to see, for example, if it made sense to oppose proletarian science and bourgeois science. Such attempts were extremely radical, and they go back a long time. Already I am thinking of the intervention made at the trial of Lavoisier: "The Republic has no need for scientists." This is not exactly the issue of culture, but it does point to the crossover between science and politics. And then there is also the question of the expert: how the expert must first be a communist and only then an expert, or how one should be expert *and* communist. These questions in the end are fundamental. Of course, in philosophy one always proceeds first by separation, but now I am indeed convinced that we have to study the knots or networks. By doing so, you have to realize that we enter a complex investigation about the historicity of the situation, because in fact, the linkages are the way in which the historicity of a situation causes the active truth procedures to follow trajectories that will no longer remain entirely independent from one another.

We need a theory of what I call the networking or the tying together of truth procedures. Eventually, I see no reason why this could not be called "culture," provided that we completely reconstruct a formalized concept of culture. Indeed, we can consider culture to be the network of various forcings, that is, at a given moment in time, the manner in which the encyclopedic knowledge of the situation is modified under the constraints of various operations of forcing which depend on procedures that are different from one another. On the one hand there is indeed the tying together of various procedures, but on the other hand there is also the fact that knowledge is changed under the blind or unperceived pressure of these truth procedures. Thus, I will have to pick up this question of the binding, or knotting, both on the level of forcing and on the level of the procedures themselves. This might signal my path toward a reconstruction of the concept of culture. We must proceed with caution in this matter, however, because the history of philosophy shows that, just as the moments of separation can be radical and foundational, so too the moments of binding are always traps for the imaginary and for historicism.

Let us take the example of Kant. Nobody has divided more radically, but beginning with the *Critique of Judgment*, we realize that he is obsessed with tying together everything that previously had been divided. Besides, this is the principal interest of most contemporary Kantians: not so much the divisions but rather questions such as the reflective judgment, the harmony of faculties, and the resonance among things. I have the impression that this puts us immediately on a terrain that is infinitely less stable and more complex, but that is exactly where we have to go.

BB. You also asked me once about the status of cultural studies in the United States. Following the explanations you have just given, this is perhaps how we might define a valid project for cultural studies, provided that we pass through a reflection on what constitutes an event: to study the interactions among the conditions of art, politics, and so on. This is not where cultural studies is at the moment, because they may seem to present more of a mixture instead of a rigorous articulation, mostly between art and politics, or between art, politics, and sexuality. And the great model, of course, is most often Foucault, who has always been the thinker of such links.

AB. Of course, absolutely, that was entirely his purpose. What is more, I am convinced that in order to think through the linkages or interferences among the various conditions, I will be once more coming in close proximity to Foucault. You are right in saying that he is the great thinker of such linkages. For him, that was the principal motif. An episteme, for example, is a knot or an interweaving.

RETURN TO THE VOID

BB. I have one last question, which concerns the place of the void in your latest work. In the conclusion to your book on *Ethics* you distinguish the event from its doubles, or its simulacra: terror, betrayal, and disaster. I have the impression, though, that in order to be able to sustain the truth of the events, without conceding anything to the temptation of their simulacra, you have recourse to an axiomatic argument that is once more based on respect for, or recognition of, the void that would be inherent in everything that happens in the aftermath of an event. I wonder whether this does not put us back in a doctrine of lack, and ultimately, in a statelike prescription, even negatively formulated, of the being of the event, which would be tied to the permanence of a gap, or a void, which one cannot fill or substantialize without falling into Evil. Do you foresee other perspectives to distinguish an event that is true, not to say authentic, from its doubles?

AB. Sure. The answer in *Ethics* is insufficient even in my own eyes. It is always possible to object to it that we are thus sent back to a kind of arch-conscience, or arch-consciousness, to some faculty of discernment between the pure void and the filled void. In the end, then, we are still in the theory according to which there is an arch-perception of Evil. I expect to respond to this question in a different way in my upcoming work. This will require some considerable detours, which in fact are caught up in the revision that I am currently undertaking of the theory of the event, on the one hand, and of the theory of the subject, on the other. I am now coming back to a theory of the subject that arranges for a plurality of figures, as in *Theory of the Subject*, whereas in *Being and Event*, I went back in a sense to a unique figure of the subject. The quadruple construction (courage, anxiety, superego, and justice) in *Theory of the Subject* allowed for a broader configuration, and I am going to return to this theory of configurations in my forthcoming *Logics of Worlds*. From within this theory I should be able to treat in a completely different way the question regarding the distinction between the event and its simulacrum.

Translated by Bruno Bosteels

Appendix 2

BEYOND FORMALIZATION

An Interview with Alain Badiou Conducted by Peter Hallward
and Bruno Bosteels (Paris, July 2, 2002)

THINKING THE CENTURY

Peter Hallward. We'd like to start with some questions about the book you've just finished on the twentieth century, then talk about your current lecture series on aspects of the present historical moment, before finishing with a few points relating to your major work in progress, *Logics of Worlds.*

Starting then with *The Century*: what is your basic thesis in this book? In particular, can you explain the relationship between the "passion for the real" [*passion du réel*] you describe as characteristic of the truly inventive or innovative sequences of the last century, and the various programs of radical formalization this passion inspired?

Alain Badiou. I should begin by saying that my lectures on the twentieth century were devised in reaction to the mass of prevailing opinion against various media campaigns regarding the meaning of the last century. In France the question of the twentieth century has been dominated—in the official record—by the ideas of totalitarianism, of the great massacres, of communism as crime, and the equation of communism with fascism. The twentieth century has been designated as the century of horror and mass crime. My lectures on the twentieth century sought to propose a different version of what happened—different, though not necessarily contrary as regards the facts. It is not a question of opposing facts with other facts but of finding another path or a way of thinking, so as to approach the century. This path had to be constructed. To do so, I sought out certain theses that the twentieth century proposed in the realm of thought—theses that would be compatible with the unfolding of the major political, artistic, and scientific experiments that took place in that century.

In the end I identified as the possible center of the century's experience something I've called the passion for the real. What is this passion? It is the will to arrive—at all costs—at a real validation of one's hypotheses or programs. This passion for the real is a voluntarism. It marks a break with the idea that history carries with it, in its own movement, the realization of a certain number of promises, prophecies, or programs. Rather, a real will is needed to *arrive* at the realization of this promise or that program. The nineteenth century was by and large the century of progress, of an idea of progress tied to a certain idea of history. The twentieth century was fundamentally a century of the real, of the will to the real [*la volonté du réel*]. A century in which it was necessary to have precise and practicable projects concerning the transformation of the world.

I then saw that this passion of the real—the idea that things had to take place, here and now, that they had to *come about*, to *realize* themselves—implied a whole series of other notions. For instance, the notion of the appearing of a new humanity, or that of a total revolutionary overthrow of existing societies, or the creation of a new world, etc. And I saw that these consequences were themselves conditioned by a process of uninterrupted purification of the real. In order to arrive at the real, to produce it, a method was needed to eliminate the old world, to eliminate all the habits and things of old. In my view, a large part of the violence of the century, the extreme political cruelty that dominated its first sixty years or so, was rooted in the conviction that ultimately no price is too high for an absolute beginning. If it is really a matter of founding a new world, then the price paid by the old world, even in the number of deaths or the quantity of suffering, becomes a relatively secondary question.

In this sense the relation to the real is not a matter of realism but is instead expressed through a powerful will to formalization. Indeed, it is a matter of attaining a radical simplification that would allow one to extract the kernel of the opposition between the new and the old in its purest form. One can only extract this kernel by proceeding through a series of extrications or disentanglements, through a series of axiomatic, formalizing, and often brutal simplifications that allow one to operate this distinction without too many nuances or complications because if one reestablishes nuance or complexity, the pure idea of creation and novelty is in turn enfeebled.

The major consequence of my hypothesis is that there is no contradiction, but rather complementarity, between, on the one hand, the idea that the twentieth century was the century of the passion of the real, and, on the other, the obvious fact that the century's avant-gardes were fundamentally formal ones. The idea that the avant-gardes were concerned with creation in the domain of forms is evident in the case of art, but if you think about it it's no less clear in politics. What took the name of Marxism-Leninism, for instance, when you look at it closely, is nothing but an extremely formalized view of Marxism itself. Today this type of stance is said to be "dogmatic," but in reality it was not lived or practiced as a dogma or a belief. Rather, it was lived and practiced as an effective process of formalization. Needless to say, with regard to a large number of issues Leninism proceeded by way of extremely stark simplifications. But these simplifications should not be understood in terms of a stupid dogmatism. In the final analysis, they bear a great affinity to the paintings of Mondrian or Malevich, which are themselves projects that pursue radical simplifications of the project of painting.

You see, I tried to get a sense of the profound unity of the century's aesthetic adventure (understood as an adventure governed by formal abstraction and all its consequences, by defiguration [*défiguration*] and its consequences) and the century's political adventure, which was that of a radical and revolutionary simplification guided by the idea of an absolute beginning. We could add that the movement of radical formalization is equally dominant in the history of mathematics. The creation of modern algebra and general topology is situated in this selfsame space of thought, and was inspired by the effort to begin the whole of mathematics all over again, by way of a complete formalization.

PH. How then are we to understand the opacity, so to speak, introduced by the state apparatus (the police, the army) into this political project to formalize or simplify society, to make it transparent? Can this be dismissed as a merely contingent perversion of the communist project?

AB. One day, someone should write a new history of the state in the twentieth century, a history that would not entirely subordinate the question to the opposition between democracy and totalitarianism, or between parliamentarism and bureaucracy. I believe that the twentieth century has indeed been the century of state power. But I also believe that the state itself really embodied, in the most extreme instances, something like the omnipotence of creation. We must understand where the *possibility* of these figures of the state comes from—for example, of states of the Stalinist type. It is obviously absurd to reduce these states to their extraordinary police function, which they certainly exerted. But we must inquire about the conditions of possibility of these functions. We know very well that a link must be found between the policing and dictatorial pressures, on the one hand, and, on the other, the general system of the subjective factors that made them possible. Everyone knows that in Russia, as well as in the rest of the world, the Stalinist state was endowed with a real aura. It was not merely the sinister figure that we otherwise can and should associate with it. Where did this aura come from? I think that the state itself was experienced as the formalization of absolute novelty, that it was itself an instance of formalization and thereby also a violently simplified state in regards to its operational capacity. Think of the general directives of these states, the five-year plans, the "great leaps forward," the powerful ideological campaigns. This formalizing function, which was also one of purification [*épuration*, signifying both purification and purging] and simplification, is also perfectly evident in what was called the cult of personality, the extraordinary devotion accorded to the supreme leader. This is because this cult is nothing but another formal conviction. It comes down to the idea that the state should be able to present itself in the *simple* figure of a single will. To reduce the state to the figure of a charismatic leader is ultimately an effort related to the dialectic of singularity and universality: if the objectives of the state are formally universal, if they embody universal emancipation, then the state must itself be absolutely singular. In the end this absolute singularity is simply the singularity of a single body, a single will, and a single leader. Thus, the dialectic between singularity and universality, considered with respect to an absolutely formal agency [*instance*], ends up—in a way that is consistent and not at all paradoxical—in such Stalinist or otherwise despotic figures of the state.

The problem is that there is obviously something mistaken in this line of reasoning. The truth is that there can never be any genuinely absolute beginning. Everything is ultimately a matter of procedure and labor; truths are always plural and never single or unique [*uniques*], even in their own particular domain, and so on. Consequently, state formalization (and this will be true of the other formalizations as well) is prey to the real in a way that always partially differs from how it pretends to be. In other words, it differs from what it presents as its own absolute capacity without reserve; it differs from the absolutist character it attributes to its own inauguration, to the unhindered pursuit of its project; it differs, in short, from the entire thematic of the resolute march toward socialism. This "march," in fact, doesn't exist. There is always only a localized becoming, irreducible to all totalization, which in turn is to be thought only as a singular point within this local becoming.

To my mind this last remark is of great importance. The formalization organized by the passion for the real leads to a kind of crushing of the local under the weight of the global. Each and every localization of the procedure is immediately thought as an instance of the totality.

Such a relation to the real cannot be sustained indefinitely. Hence the massive inversion that progressively takes place, which shifts the terrain onto the side of nontransparency, secrecy, and hidden operations. Those who know what's really going on, those who have knowledge of the singularity of the situation, are supposed to keep quiet, and all the rest of it. Thus, little by little, a sort of general corrosion of the situation occurs that, while announcing the absolute formal transparency of a grandiose project, is turned into an extremely defensive procedure. Everything that is locally produced seems at all times to threaten the aim of global transparency. Thus (and this is something very striking when you read the serious studies on Stalinism, which are generally written by British scholars, or scholars from the United States, who have a less ideological relation to Stalinism than do the French or the Italians), the conviction held by the leaders of these revolutionary states is in fact nothing but the awareness of an absolute discrepancy between the situation and the means at their disposal. They themselves have the impression of being absolutely precarious figures. Any circumstance whatsoever gives them the impression that their own overthrow is imminent. On top of the police violence and the reciprocal surveillance of everyone by everyone, this subjectivity generates as its own guiding rule the circulation of lies and secrets, together with the nonrevelation of what's really going on. But this rule can in turn be explained from the vantage point of the relation between the real and the formal, as well as of the relation between singularity and universality. That is to say, a universality that should remain local and prudent (as is always the case of true universality) is forced instead to bear an absolutely formal globality, and one is immediately obliged to refer this to an all-powerful singularity, to a will as inscrutable as God's—to take up a comparison that you [Peter] often draw between the event's absolutism and the theory of sovereignty.

I wanted to clarify this entire matter by showing that in the political, aesthetic, and scientific adventures of the century we are not dealing with pathologies of gratuitous cruelty, or with some kind of historical sadism—a ridiculous hypothesis—but rather with significant intellectual operators [opérateurs]. That is why I adopted the method of always restricting myself as closely as possible to that which the century itself said about the century, so as to avoid being caught in retrospection, in the tribunals of history or judgment. The twentieth century interrogated itself with particular intensity regarding its own nature, its own singularity. I wanted to remain very close to this interrogation, as well as to the intimate reasons of that which remains cloaked in shadow from the point of view of retrospective judgment—I mean the remarkable enthusiasm that surrounded all these developments. The widespread popular enthusiasm for communist politics, the creative enthusiasm of the artistic avant-gardes, the Promethean enthusiasm of the scientists. . . . To reduce this enthusiasm to the domain of the imaginary, to mere illusions, to misleading utopias, is to engage in a completely vacuous argument.

I find this argument just as weak and false, by the way, when it is used with reference to religion. Even today, it is an aberration to explain the subjective power of religion, at its highest moments, in terms of the logic of imaginary alienation. It is infinitely easier and more truthful to understand that there really is a genuine subjective dimension present in that which ultimately, in my own jargon, resembles a confusion between event and truth, that is, something that reduces the considerable difficulties involved in maintaining fidelity to an event to a matter of pure insurrection. These difficulties require an infinite series of local inventions. It is always tempting (and moreover it is partially correct) to claim that these local inventions are anticipated by the primordial figure of the sequence, by the pure power of the pure event—for instance, the figure of the revolution, in politics, and I think that we could prove the same holds in art and in the sciences. It is beyond doubt, for example, that the project of a complete formalization of mathematics by Bourbaki in France, which in one respect led to something grandiose, at the same time also failed (if one must really speak of failure) as dramatically as did the construction of socialism in the USSR. It was something grandiose, which generated true enthusiasm and renovated mathematical thinking, but nevertheless it never proved possible to show that the actual development of mathematics was really *anticipated* by a stable axiomatic foundation. All the evidence points to the fact that the movement of mathematics also includes the need to modify the axioms, to transform them, to introduce new ones, and sometimes even to accept that the general position to which one adhered had to be abandoned. No formalization can claim to encompass the totality of the consequences of the event that it draws upon. However, the idea that it could be otherwise is not simply an illusion or an alienation. It is a powerful and creative subjective disposition, which brings to light new strata of the real.

I think the same is true of art. The various manifestos and new orientations proposed during the century sought to lead art back to the expression of its own conditions. The end of art was declared on the basis of an integral formalization of art's own possibility. Everything that had to do with art's relation to empirical reality, to the contingency of representations, to imitation, was proclaimed to be nothing but a form of retardation [*arriération mentale*]. This whole movement was formidable, enlightening, and creative. By and large, it has defined the century—but it could not anticipate the development of art for an indefinitely long time. In fact, the question today instead concerns the identification of formal conditions for a new realism.

THE CULTURAL REVOLUTION

Bruno Bosteels. To what extent does your own itinerary reflect a growing critical distance from this effort of the century? I am thinking in particular about your continuing debts to Maoism. At the height of the Cultural Revolution the passion for the real was indeed exceptionally strong and often included an extremely violent tendency to purify the revolutionary attitude from all remnants of so-called revisionism—the tendency to annihilate the old and to develop the new. Does your current work on the twentieth century amount to some kind of self-criticism in this regard? After all, you devote a central lecture in *The Century* to the sequence of the Cultural Revolution and you seem to want to reevaluate the significance of the famous idea that "One divides into two." To what extent does your conception of "subtraction," as opposed to what you used to call "destruction," offer a genuinely alternative conception of radical innovation, subjective sacrifice, purification, and so on?

AB. If I felt that I needed to make a self-criticism I would make one, but I don't think it's the case. Maoism really was an epic attempt, as Mao himself would have said, to relaunch the subjective process of the revolution. But this relaunching took place within the framework of categories inherited from Leninism and Stalinism, that is, at base, within a figure of the party-state conceived as the only *formal* figure of power. The idea of the Cultural Revolution was that the mass dynamics of the revolution were to be relaunched as a process of renovation, reform, and transformation of the party-state. Mao himself, however, observed that this was impossible. There are some texts of Mao's in which he accepts unequivocally that something in the Cultural Revolution did not work. The mobilization of the masses, among the youth and the workers, was huge. But it destroyed itself through divisions, factions and anarchic violence. The desperate preservation of the party-state framework in the midst of this storm finally led to its restoration in completely reactive conditions (the ubiquitous reintroduction of capitalist methods, etc.). This is why we can define the Cultural Revolution as a saturation. It saturates the form of the party-state inherited from Lenin and from the Russian Revolution. The Cultural Revolution was an experiment at the farthest reaches of the truth procedure that had been initiated by the October revolution.

Perhaps the issue needs to be considered on an even larger scale. The Cultural Revolution was perhaps also the last revolution. Between the October revolution and the Cultural Revolution, or even between the French Revolution and the Cultural Revolution, there takes place a saturation of the category of revolution as a singular form of the relationship between mass movement and state power.

The word *revolution* designates a historical form of the relation between politics and the state. This term first of all sets the relation politics / state— or politics / power—in a logic of antagonism, contradiction, or civil war. In the second place it sets this relation in a logic of sublation [*relève*]; that is, it aligns it with the project of a new state that would be entirely different: a revolutionary, republican state, the dictatorship of the proletariat, etc. It is this figure of the sublation of the state by another state under the decisive pressure of the—popular, mass, or class—historical actor that the word

revolution designates. We could say that the Cultural Revolution constitutes the extreme limit of the age of revolutions.

PH. And the turn to subtraction, as opposed to destruction, is part of this
new, postrevolutionary orientation?

AB. For the time being I don't want to accord a metaphysical privilege to
subtraction. I call "subtraction" that which, from within the previous sequence itself, as early as the start of the twentieth century, presents itself as
a possible path that differs from the dominant one. It is not just an idea that
comes "after" antagonism and revolution. It is an idea that is dialectically
articulated with those of antagonism, the simplifying formalization, the
absolute advent of the new, etc. Malevich's painting, for example, can be
interpreted in two different ways. We can say that it expresses a destructive
radicalism: starting out from a destruction of all figuration, Malevich allows the purely pictorial to arise in the form of an absolute beginning. But
we might also say that in fact, this painting finds its point of departure
in what I've called the minimal difference, the minimal gap—for instance
the gap between white and white—and that it draws considerable consequences from the capture of this minimal difference. These two interpretations do not contradict one another. There is something like an ideological
decision involved here, one that gives priority to subtraction (or minimal
difference) rather than to destruction (or antagonistic contradiction).

   Is it really productive, today, to fix the determination of politics within
the framework of a global antagonism? Can we, except in a completely
abstract way, call on a massive Two, a Two capable of structuring all
situations: bourgeoisie against proletariat, or even republicans against aris-
tocrats? Once again, I do not repudiate any of this, but it seems to me that
we are obliged, at least for the moment (I also don't wish to anticipate the
course of things), to consider the consequences of that which is given as a
local difference, that is, to think and to act on *one* point or, at most, a few.
For instance, in terms of the organization of workers without official residency papers [*prolétaires sans papiers*]; or on the question of Palestine; or
on the "Western" and American aggressions against Serbia, against Afghan-
istan, or against Iraq. And we must construct, on the basis of these points,
an adequate political logic, without a preliminary formal guarantee that
something like a contradiction within the totality necessarily structures
this local differentiation. We can only rely on principles and we can only
treat, on the basis of these principles, local situations in such a way as to

pursue singular political processes within them. Based on this minimal, local, or punctual differentiation (or as the Lacanians would say, based on this point of the real), you will begin experiments to ascertain if the general system of consequences (that is, the political logic thought in terms of its results), is homogeneous or heterogeneous to the disposition of the state of your situation. Let's call "state logic" that which pretends to carry the meaning of the totality and that therefore includes governments and ordinary "political" apparatuses, as well as the economy or legal system.

In Maoism itself there are elements of a subtractive type, if only because the revolutionary history of the liberated zones is different from the history of insurrections. Insurrectionism is the concentration in one point of a global deliberation; it is a certain relationship of the local and the global where you globally force the issue on one point. But, in the history of the Chinese revolution, insurrectionism failed. The uprisings in Canton or in Shanghai were drowned in blood. The alternative logic proposed by Mao sets out a wholly different relationship between local confrontation and the situation as a whole. This is what Sylvain Lazarus has called the "dialectical" mode of politics. When you find yourself in Yenan for years, with a popular army and an independent administration, you do not stand in a metonymic relation to the global state of things. Yenan does not present the punctual test of strength in which the fate of global confrontation will be decided. You are somewhere, a place in which you have managed to remain, perhaps a place to which you were eventually to retreat, as in the case of the Long March. You were somewhere else; then you came here, and you have tried to preserve your strength by moving from one point to another. The temporality involved in this movement is not at all that of insurrection. The whole problem is that of endurance. This is what Mao calls "the prolonged war." So the Maoist experiment was different, and I'd say that something in the liberated zones was already rather more "subtractive" than antagonistic in the traditional sense of the latter term. In particular, I'm thinking of the idea of holding out on one point in such a way as to have the capacity to preserve your forces, without necessarily engaging them immediately in a global confrontation. Much the same could be said regarding Mao's quite remarkable idea of limiting an antagonism [*économiser l'antagonisme*]. Mao often repeated that it is better to treat all contradictions as if they were secondary ones, contradictions in the midst of the people, rather than between the people and their enemy.

Now I think it's clear that these general ideas continue to exercise a real influence. Every interesting political experience today takes place along these lines. This is also the reason why the "planetary" demonstrations against globalization, such as the one in Genoa, demonstrations whose model is clearly insurrectional (even if in them the insurrectional schema is considerably weakened), are absolutely archaic and sterile. All the more so to the extent that they congregate around the meetings of their adversary. What's the point of concentrating one's forces, not in the place decided according to the needs of a long-term and independent political strategy but rather in precisely those places where the governments and global banking institutions hold their economico-political ceremonies? Here is another subtractive imperative: never appear where you are most expected. Make sure that your own action is not undertaken on terrain decided by the adversary. It's also the case that the "anti-globalization" movements dedicate themselves to a systemic and economicist identification of the adversary, which is already utterly misguided.

PH. I certainly see the strategic value in such a "guerrilla" approach to politics, one that asks what can be done here and now, with these particular people, these particular resources, etc. But how can we think such an approach together with Marx's basic insight, that each of these individual "points," as you describe them, are indeed structured by global, systematic processes of exploitation or domination?

AB. I'm not saying that we cannot think of each point as being determined by the global situation. But when we think of them that way, we do nothing to enhance the strategic capacity of the point in question. We need to distinguish here the analytical view of the situation and its political view. This distinction is of considerable importance. In approaching a singular point, one must always begin with its singularity. This does not mean that singularity is incompatible with a general analysis. However, it's not the general analysis that gives this singular point its political value but rather the political deployment, experienced as a possibility, of its singularity. Today, for instance, we can always state that the world is polarized, that we should analyze the various manifestations of U.S. sovereignty, the question of wars, the renewed forms of capital, etc. But all this does not determine anything effective in the field of politics. In my own philosophical vocabulary I would say that these analyses are truthful [*véridiques*] but not true [*vraies*]. Consider the example of Chiapas. It's clear that, from the moment when it was constituted, this new arena of political activity could not be derived from any general analysis. If we stick to the general analysis, we can immediately and quite reasonably conclude that this attempt is destined to fail, in exactly the same way that here in France those who devote themselves to global analysis conclude that it's necessary to participate in elections, that representative democracy must be upheld, because that is what the consensus deems to be the only acceptable space in which to negotiate the political relations of force. The conclusion will thus be that any truly independent politics is impossible. *L'Organisation politique*, for example, is impossible.

Objective Marxist analysis is an excellent, even indispensable practice, but it's impossible to construct a politics of emancipation as a consequence of this analysis. Those who do so find themselves on the side of the totality and of its movement, hence on the side of the actually dominant power. To my mind, the "anti-globalization" movements, or the Italian autonomists who follow the analyses of Toni Negri, for example, are only the spectacular face of the adaptations to domination. Their undifferentiated "move-mentism" integrates smoothly with the necessary adjustments of capital and in my view does not constitute any really independent political space. In order to treat a local situation in its political terms, that is, in its subjective terms, something more is needed than an understanding of the local derived from the general analysis. The subjectivization of a singular situation cannot be reduced to the idea that this situation is expressive of the totality.

This issue already sets Mao apart from Lenin—or at least from what Lenin could still believe in abstract terms. When Lenin says that consciousness comes from outside, what he means is that the scientific knowledge of the inclusion of a particular situation in the general situation—in the situation of imperialism as the superior stage of capitalism—*creates* revolutionary consciousness. Today, I don't think (and already Mao and a few others had some insights into this matter) that a reflexive and systematic Marxist analysis of the general distribution of capitalist and imperialist phenomena in the contemporary world constitutes a consciousness that is sufficiently subtracted, precisely, from this distribution.

PH. But is there a danger, then, that you simply presuppose, in a less explicit way, the criteria that define a political situation, or the circumstances in which political subjectivization can take place? That you effectively treat each such singular point as if shaped by less precise (because less explicit) patterns of domination or inequality, and each mobilization as inspired by a prescription that in each case is relatively predictable: the militant refusal of domination or the subjective assertion of political equality? That despite your professed interest in the singularity of a situation, you affirm a conception of political truth that is always formally, fundamentally, the same?

AB. For a philosopher political thinking is always the same and always different. On the one hand, it's always the same because it's based on principles. Politics, like all active thought, is axiomatic. It's true that, in my conception of them, these axioms are relatively stable. They are always egalitarian axioms. Notwithstanding this axiomatic stability, in politics you have what we might call directives [*mots d'ordre*], which are singular inventions. The distinction between principles and directives is as essential in politics as the distinction in mathematics between the great axioms of a theory and its particular theorems. The directives express the way in which the principles, which are largely invariant, might become active in a situation. And their activity in the situation is also their transformation; they never simply stay the same. Just as we cannot maintain that the determination of political singularity is transitive to the global analysis, it isn't simply transitive to axioms of the will or to strictly egalitarian maxims. I'm neither objectivist nor subjectivist with respect to these questions. In the end what happens is the constitution of the situation *into a political situation* by the emergence of directives. When these emerge, they also provide some indication of the political capacity of the people in the situation.

Take the Palestinian situation, for example. We can say that this situation today is clearly defined: it is a colonial situation, perhaps even the last colonial situation. In this sense it has a particular status: it figures as a sort of summary or consummation of a much larger sequence, the sequence of colonial occupations and the wars of liberation. This is also why the situation is so violent and so exemplary. From the point of view of subjective principles the situation is not especially complex. The axiom in question, in the end, is "a country and a state for the Palestinians." On the other hand, as things stand today, what are the exact directives for this situation? To my mind this question is far more complicated, and this is one of the reasons for the relative weakness of the Palestinians. This isn't a criticism (which would be ridiculous), it's an observation. Today, the actual directives that might be capable of really attracting a universal sympathy to the

Palestinian cause, are precarious or badly formulated. It's in this sense that the situation in Palestine is both a situation that is objectively and subjectively eminent and well-defined [*éminente et constituée*], and at the same time, politically speaking, it is a rather confused and weak situation.

THE DIALECTIC OF THE DIALECTICAL
AND THE NONDIALECTICAL

BB. Now that we are talking in terms of objective and subjective conditions, I'd like to ask you about your current understanding of dialectics. It's clear that in *Theory of the Subject* (1982) you maintained a broadly dialectical position, and as late as *Can Politics Be Thought?* (1985) you suggest that terms such as *situation, intervention, fidelity,* and so on, can lead to a renewal of dialectical thought. *Being and Event* (1988), however, seems to abandon or sidestep this tradition in favor of a strictly mathematical approach, even though you continue to speak of a "dialectic" of void and excess. Then again, in what I've had a chance to read of the first chapters of *Logics of Worlds*, you continue to measure your approach alongside, and against, Hegel's *Science of Logic*, in particular against Hegel's understanding of the negative. Through much of *The Century*, finally, your analysis is indebted to what Deleuze called "disjunctive synthesis." Much of the inventive force of the twentieth century would have privileged a type of nondialectical solution: disjunctive resolutions of the relation, for example, between politics and history, between the subjective and the objective, between beginnings and ends, or between the real and its appearances. So where do you stand vis-à-vis the dialectic now? Would you say that the last century's penchant for disjunctive synthesis indicates a lasting exhaustion of dialectical thought? Or do the failures of the last century suggest that the dialectic is perhaps incomplete, or still unfulfilled, but not in principle finished and over with?

AB. That is a major question. You could almost say that my entire enterprise is one giant confrontation [*démêlé*] with the dialectic. That is why sometimes I declare myself a dialectician and write in defense of the great dialecticians (but I mean the French dialecticians,[1] which is not exactly the same as the Hegelian dialectic), while at other times I declare myself an antidialectician. You are absolutely right to perceive a certain confusion in this whole business.

First of all, I'd like to say that the nineteenth century was the great century of dialectics, in the ordinary sense of the term. Fundamentally, dialectics means the dialectics of progress. This is already the case with Hegel. In the end we go toward the Absolute, however long it may take before we get there. And if the negation does not exhaust itself, if negativity is creative and is not absorbed into itself, it is because it is pregnant with finality. The question of the labor of the negative is not simply the question of the efficacy of the negative; it is also the question of its *work*, in the sense of an artisan of History. This great nineteenth-century dialectical tradition of thought allows us to think a sort of fusion between politics and history. Political subjectivity can feed on historical certainty. We might say—and in any case this has always been my conviction—that *The Communist Manifesto* is the great political text of the nineteenth century. It is the great text of that fundamental historical optimism that foresees, under the name of "communism," the triumph of generic humanity. It's well known that for Marx "proletariat" is the name for the historical agent of this triumph. And I remind you that in my own speculations, "generic" is the property of the True.

What happens at the beginning of the twentieth century? We go from the promise of a reconciliation or emancipation borne by history (which is the Marxist thesis) to the will, animated by the passion of the real, to force the issue, to accelerate the proletarian victory. We move to the Leninist idea according to which everything is still carried by history, of course, but where in the end what is fundamental is precisely the decision, the organization, and the force of political will. As my friend Sylvain Lazarus has shown, we move from a consciousness organized by history to a consciousness organized by the party.

In the nineteenth century both historicism and dialectical thinking (in the Hegelian sense) share a common destiny. Hegel's principal thesis was that "truth is the same as the history of truth," and this thesis endures through any number of materialist reversals and elaborations.

But what are the consequences for dialectics, when we arrive at the moment that recognizes the supremacy of the political principle of organization, the moment that celebrates the party as the source of political truth (a moment that is fully reached only with Stalin)? Which aspects of the dialectic are retained? Which aspects are dropped? I think that what is retained is certainly the antagonism, and hence the negativity, but in a purely disjunctive sense: there is conflict, there is violence. What is preserved from history, and from its metaphor, is the figure of war. I'm perfectly prepared to say that Marxism in the twentieth century was, deep down, a Marxism of war, of class warfare. In nineteenth-century Marxist thinking this conception of class warfare was supported by the *general* figure of history. In the twentieth century, what is preserved and stressed is war as such. So what is retained from Hegelian finality, from the Absolute, in war? It is the idea of the ultimate war, the idea of a final war, a war that in a sense would itself be the Absolute. What happens, in the end, is that the Absolute no longer figures as the outcome of conflict. The Absolute as "goal": nobody has any experience of this; nobody seriously announces that this will come to pass. The Absolute is rather the idea of the final conflict, of the final struggle, very literally. The idea of a decisive war. The twentieth century presented itself to people's minds as a century that would bring the decisive war, the war to end all wars. It's in this sense that I speak of disjunctive synthesis. Instead of a figure of reconciliation, that is, a figure of the Absolute as synthesis, as that which absorbs all previous determinations, we have the presentation of the Absolute itself in the guise of war.

From this point of view I would like to reply to an objection that Bruno has often made to me. Don't I now have too pacified a view of things? Was I right to give up the central place of destruction? I would answer as follows: I think that the idea that war is the absolute of subjectivity is now saturated; it is an idea that no longer has any political intensity. That's all I'm saying. I don't think that implacable conflict is a thing of the past or that there will be no more wars. It's the idea of the war to end all wars that I criticize, because in the end, in the field of politics, this idea was the last figure of the One. This idea, that of the "final struggle," indicates an inadequate acknowledgment of multiplicity. The ultimate war is the moment when the One takes possession of war, including war within the domain of the state. The Stalinist state was evidently a state of war, a militarized state, and this was also true at its very heart. It is one of the very few states that coldly decided to liquidate half of its military hierarchy. This is the war against oneself. Why? Because here, in the end, the only instance of the absolute that one can take hold of is war. Such is the outcome, within dialectical thinking, of the passage from the historicist dialectic to the voluntaristic, partisan, or party dialectic: a self-immolation in the absolute of destruction.

This tendency, which is related to the intellectual transformations that took place at the beginning of the twentieth century, is not limited to so-called totalitarian politics. We could observe how, in the arts or sciences, there was also a passage from a constructive dialectic, one tied to the history of progress, to a dialectic of experimental immolation [*brûlure expérimentale*], of disjunction and destruction. This is why, in the end, the outcome of the experiment becomes indifferent. There is something in the century's thinking that says: "The process is more important than the product." In politics, this means that war is really more important than its result, that the class struggle is more important than its product, that the terrorist socialist state is more important than communism (which never arrives). The transition is itself interminable, and as a warlike transition, it is all that matters. We should recall Stalin's thesis, according to which the class struggle intensifies and becomes even more violent under socialism. This means that socialism, which was once anticipated as a peaceful outcome of the violent revolution, becomes in reality only one of several stages of conflict and an even more violent stage than the previous one.

I think that today we must learn what politics means in times of peace, even if this politics is a politics of war. We need to invert the way we think about these questions. We must find a way to subordinate the politics of war to a subtractive understanding of politics—a politics that has no guarantee either in history or in the state. How can we understand emancipatory politics in terms other than those of the absolute of war? Mao, more than any other political thinker, was a military leader. Nevertheless Mao already sought to subordinate the absolute of war to something else. He considered that the principal tasks of the people's army were political. We too are experimenting with a politics that would not be completely implicated with the question of power. Because it is the struggle for power that ends up leading revolutionaries to the absolutization of war. What does it mean to construct, preserve, and deploy one's force, to hold firm on one point, in the domain of peace? This is our main question, so long as no one forgets that when it's necessary to fight, we will fight. You don't always have the choice.

PH. To what extent does your distance from dialectics, your determination to pursue a wholly affirmative conception of truth, push you toward an ultimately abstract conception of truth, or at least one whose subjective integrity is largely detached from the objective or concrete circumstances of its situation? In other words, just how radical is the process of subtraction? A thinker like Foucault (himself hardly a disciple of Hegel) works insistently toward an evacuation of all the things that fix or determine or specify the way people think or act in a situation, precisely by paying close attention to what he called the "microscopic" processes of its regulation or specification. By comparison, your conception of politics seems to leave very little scope for a dialectical relation with the historical or the social dimension.

AB. Abstraction is the foundation of all thought. However, the procedures of truth should not be reduced to abstraction. Yes, we start with the affirmation of a principle, with an axiomatic proposition. But the whole question is to know how and at what moment the axiom becomes the directive of a situation. It can do so only if something from the situation itself passes into it. It's obvious that a demand, for example for the "unconditional regularization of all workers without residency papers [*ouvriers sans-papiers*]," implies the existence of workers without papers, the pertinence of the question of their papers, the effect of certain governmental policies, etc. Above all, it's necessary that the *sans-papiers* themselves speak out about the situation, that they speak about it politically and not just by bearing witness to their own misery or misfortune. (It's time we recognized, by the way, that in politics misfortune does not exist.)

As for Foucault, I think that he completely underestimates the importance of separation [*la séparation*]. Among his disciples this tendency only gets worse. If there is now a convergence between "Foucauldianism" and "Negrism," if Agamben relies on Foucault, etc., it's because they all share the philosophical axiom that resistance is only the obverse of power. Resistance is coextensive with power itself. In particular, you begin thinking politics through consideration of the forms of power. I think that this is completely wrong. If you enter politics by thinking the forms of power then you will always end up with the state (in the general sense of the word) as your referent. Even the famous "multitudes," which is only a pedantic word for mass movements (and in particular petit-bourgeois mass movements) are thought of as "constituent" *with regard* to domination. All this is only a historicism painted in fashionable hues. It's striking, moreover, that, besides Foucault, the philosophical sources for the "Negrist" current are to be found on the side of Spinoza and Deleuze. Both these thinkers are hostile to any form of the Two; they propose a metaphysical politics, in the guise of a politics of the One, or what for me is a politics of the One. This is an antidialectical politics in the precise sense that it excludes negativity and, thus, in the end, the domain of the subject, or what for me is the subject. I am entirely opposed to the thesis according to which it is presumed possible, merely by isolating (within the orbit of domination and control) that which has a constituent value, to create a space of liberty cut from the same cloth as that of the existing powers themselves. That which goes by the name "resistance," in this instance, is only a component of the progress of power itself. In its current form, the anti-globalization movement is nothing other than a somewhat wild operator (not even that wild, after all) of capitalist globalization itself. In any case, it's not at all heterogeneous to it. It seeks to sketch out, for the imminent future, the new forms of comfort to be enjoyed by our planet's idle [*désœuvrée*] petite bourgeoisie

POWER AND RESISTANCE

BB. We were talking about some themes in Michael Hardt's and Toni Negri's *Empire* a few days ago. The most important of these is the reversibility between power and resistance, or between Empire and multitude— both appearing as a bloc, in a global, and no doubt much too structural way, in a relation of immanent and thus antidialectical reciprocity. However, this relation of immanence explains that, in some way, Empire also always already means the power of the multitude. This imposes, then, merely a certain reading strategy, and perhaps it doesn't even allow for anything else. We remain, therefore, in spite of everything, in an interpretive, even hermeneutic, approach. You've already analyzed this in your book on Deleuze, in terms of the doctrine of the "double signature": every thing, for Deleuze, can be read both as an entity and in some sense as signaling being itself. With Negri and Hardt this double signature is deployed in political terms. In an extremely seductive manner, especially for our times, dominated as they are by the homogeneity with no escape of the laws of the market and of war, it then becomes possible to read even a most brutal instance of domination by way of a sign of the very thing it represses, that is, the creativity and effervescence of the pure multitude, which for them in the end is nothing but the political, or politico-ontological name for Life. Is this how you would reply to the theses expounded in *Empire* by Hardt and Negri? Aren't there more profound affinities, for example, with your *Metapolitics*?

AB. In *The Communist Manifesto* Marx already praised capitalism in an ambivalent way, based on a double reading. On the one hand, capitalism destroys all the moth-eaten figures of the old world, all the old feudal and sacred bonds. In this sense it is the violent creator of a new leverage point for generic humanity. On the other hand, the bourgeoisie is already organized in such a way as to maintain its domination; in this sense it is the designated enemy of a new creative cycle, whose agent is the proletariat. Negri and his friends are desperately looking to reestablish this inaugural vision, in which the "multitudes" are both the result of capitalist atomization and the new creative initiator of a "horizontal" modernity (networks, transversalities, "nonorganizations," etc.). But all this amounts only to dreamy hallucination [*une rêverie hallucinée*]. Where is this "creative" capacity of the multitudes? All we've seen are very ordinary performances from the well-worn repertoire of petit-bourgeois mass movements, noisily laying claim to the right to enjoy without doing anything, while taking special care to avoid any form of discipline, whereas we know that discipline, in all fields, is the key to truths. Without the least hesitation Marx would have recognized in Negri a backward romantic. I believe that deep down, what truly fascinates these "movementists" is capitalist activity itself, its flexibility and also its violence. They designate by "multitude" flexibility of a comparable sort, a predicate which their fictions attribute to "social movements." But today, there is nothing to be gained from the category of movement. This is because this category is itself coupled to the logic of the state. It is the task of politics to construct new forms of discipline to replace the discipline of political parties, which are now saturated.

PH. Nevertheless, one of Foucault's fundamental ideas was precisely that the localization of a possible break is always ramified, that it cannot be concentrated in a singular and exclusive point. To adequately think one such point (injustice in prisons, for example), you need to treat it precisely as an overdetermined instance within a wider network. In this specific case it's obviously a matter of understanding that the operation of punitive or disciplinary power is located not only in this point, which is the instance of the prison as such (itself a point that, as you well know, Foucault treated for some time in as "punctual," as focused, and as militant a fashion as you could wish for), but also in the general configuration of power at issue in the organization of work, the education of children, the surveillance of public health, sexuality, etc. And he says this is not so as to lose himself in the complexity of the network but, on the contrary, to analyze it in detail, to understand its effects, the better to clarify and undo it—and therefore very much in order to keep himself, to borrow from your vocabulary, *at a distance* from the normalizing effects of power (since, unlike Deleuze, Foucault did not believe that you could ever escape absolutely from the networks of power). For example, I think that when you treat the question of the *sans-papiers* by considering the question of immigration along *with* the question of the organization of work, you are in fact being quite faithful to Foucault.

AB. But the actual content of the political statements made by those who claim to be following in Foucault's footsteps does not localize this break [*la coupure*] anywhere. Of course, a given situation must be envisaged within an open space. There is a topology of situations, to which Foucault himself made important contributions. But in the end you need to find a way to crystallize the political break into differentiated statements. And these statements must concentrate the political rupture on a single point. It is these statements that are the bearers of discipline, in the sense that politics is nothing other than the constitution of the power of statements and the public exploration of their consequences. Now, "power" and "consequences" mean organization, perseverance, unity, and discipline—in politics, and likewise in art and in the sciences. It seems to me that the people I'm criticizing here—let us call them the third generation of Foucauldians —abhor every crystallization and retreat to the idea that creative power will be "expressed" in the free unfolding of the multitudes. On this point the organized logic of power is opposed to the expressive logic of power. Or perhaps you might say that axiomatic thought is opposed to descriptive thought. Plato against Aristotle.

IMAGES OF THE PRESENT TIME

PH. Can we move on now to look more closely at the way you propose to understand the "Images of the Present Time," to borrow the title of your current lecture series at the Collège International de Philosophie? Has this new three-year series picked up where the previous series on the twentieth century left off?

AB. The lessons on the twentieth century aroused considerable interest. I decided that it was worth continuing the project by angling it toward the present time. Can we think the *present* philosophically? Can we reply to Hegel, who argued that philosophy always comes after the fact, that it recapitulates in the concept what has already taken place?

For the moment I'm guided by two main ideas. The first is that in order to think the contemporary world in any fundamental way, it's necessary to take as your point of departure not the critique of capitalism but the critique of democracy. To separate thought from the dominant forms of ideology has always been one of philosophy's crucial tasks. Philosophy is useless if it doesn't allow us to criticize consensual and falsely self-evident ideas. Today it's easy to see that the consensual category is not at all that of liberal economics. In fact, lots of people are perfectly happy to criticize what Viviane Forrester, in a superficial and successful book, referred to as "the economic horror." We are constantly being reminded of the cynicism of stock markets, the devastation of the planet, the famine in Africa, and so on. At the same time, this denunciation is in my view completely ineffective, precisely because it is an economico-objectivist one. The denunciation of objective mechanisms leads at best to reformist proposals of an entirely illusory nature. By contrast, no one is ready to criticize democracy. This is a real taboo, a genuine consensual fetish. Everywhere in the world democracy is the true subjective principle—the rallying point—of liberal capitalism. So my first idea was to think about the role of the word *democracy* in the framework of a functional analysis: what exactly is its function, where is it situated, how does it operate as subjective fetish, etc. I've incorporated within this aspect a careful rereading of Plato's critique of democracy.

The second idea is the obverse of the first. It's a matter of identifying what I call contemporary nihilism; in other words, today's ordinary regime of subjectivity. I say that an ordinary subject, today, is nothing but a body facing the market. Who is the citizen of the market? This is a necessarily nihilistic figure, but it's a singular nihilism, a nihilism of enjoyment.

In the end the goal is to clarify the coupling of nihilism and democracy as a politico-subjective configuration of the present time. Speaking in the terms of *Being and Event*, you could say that this coupling constitutes the "encyclopedia" of the present time. It's what organizes its regime of production, its institutions, its system of judgment and naming, its validations and countervalidations. Today, truth procedures involve finding a passage —which is always local, difficult, but creative—through the encyclopedic coupling of democracy and nihilism.

Today's truth procedures will figure as "authoritarian" (because they must exceed democratic consensus) and affirmative (because they must exceed nihilistic subjectivity). This correlation of affirmation and authority is a particular characteristic of the present moment, because the encyclopedia of this present is democratico-nihilistic. There have been times when things were different, of course, for example times in which nihilism figured as part of the cross to be borne by those who sought to proclaim a truth. This was the case, for example, during the end of the nineteenth century.

PH. Could you give us some examples of today's truth procedures?

AB. This is my project for next year: to identify the sequences that escape from the democratico-nihilistic encyclopedia. For example, it's from this angle that I read your work on postcolonial literature.[2] I read it and ask myself: isn't there something here that anticipates, as a result of the postcolonial situation, something pertaining to affirmation and authority? And I think that other artistic examples can be found, in a certain return to musical constructivism, in the tentative experiments of contemporary writers trying to move past postmodernism, in the way some painters are now abandoning the formalism of the nonfigurative, etc. I'm also very struck by the great debate in today's physics that sets those pursuing the axiomatic renewal of physics on the basis of a generalized doctrine of scalar transformations (and therefore an even more generalized relativity than the currently available version) against those who defend a configuration cobbled together from developments in quantum mechanics (a configuration that is extraordinarily sophisticated but nonetheless trapped in a hopeless empiricism).

BB. Did your work on antiphilosophy—your lectures on Nietzsche, Wittgenstein, Lacan, and Saint Paul, among others—prepare the ground for this analysis of our contemporary nihilism? Are antiphilosophy and nihilism part of the same configuration? What precise role does antiphilosophy play in the organization of today's nihilism, as you describe it?

AB. The analysis of what I called antiphilosophy offered a sort of genealogy of this nihilism's dominant operators. Although you couldn't say that Lacan was a nihilist, and still less a democrat (in fact, you couldn't call Wittgenstein a democrat either, to say nothing of Nietzsche, who was an overt

antidemocrat), I nevertheless think that these antiphilosophers anticipated a fundamental trait of contemporary nihilism, namely the thesis that
in the last instance there is nothing but bodies and language. I equate
contemporary nihilism with a certain position of the body; in this sense
our nihilism is all the more important insofar as it presents itself in the
guise of a materialism. Such would be the materialism of democratic multiplicity, which is nothing but the multiplicity of bodies. Spinoza already
proposed systematic arguments that work along these lines, which you still
find among the theoreticians of the multitude—even in Balibar. Everyone
believes that the starting point is the multiplicity of bodies. We might say
that this idea—that there is nothing but bodies and language—traverses all
of contemporary antiphilosophy. Ever since Nietzsche, contemporary antiphilosophy wishes to have done with Platonism. But what is Platonism?
Fundamentally, and this is why I always declare myself a Platonist, Platonism says that there is something other than bodies and language. There
are truths, and a truth is neither a singular body (since it is generic) nor a
phrase (since it punches a hole in the encyclopedia of the situation).

The critical examination of antiphilosophy is already the examination of
those who maintain that there is nothing but language and bodies. What I
want to show is that, beneath its materialist surface, this thesis does nothing but prepare the contemporary consensus, the democratico-nihilistic
consensus. This is why in my seminar I presented a reading of Pierre
Guyotat, in particular of the *Tombeau pour cinq cent mille soldats*. Guyotat is
the most radical writer of an atomistic vision of bodies. In the real [*réel*] of
colonial war there is nothing but bodies, and between these bodies there is
only sexual attraction, which operates like a deathly consumption. The
only relief to be found in this universe is in linguistic sublimation. Let's say
that for Guyotat, all there is are the sexed body and the poem. Incidentally,
this is precisely Lucretius's position, at least in the version that Jean-Claude
Milner and Guy Lardreau are today trying to revitalize, the first explicitly
against Plato (and against me) and the other by cobbling together a "materialist" Plato (precisely in the sense of our nihilistic materialism).

Now, it is indeed absolutely necessary to maintain that there is nothing
but language and bodies if one wants subjects to be subjects of the market.
Such a subject is someone who identifies him- or herself as a consumer,
someone exposed to the market. The consumer can be rich or poor, accomplished or clumsy—it doesn't matter. The essential thing is that every-

body stands before the market, whether one resents it or assents to it. But you can only reach this point and hold this position insofar as you are essentially a desiring body summoned by the general language of advertisement. The consumer is a body of (nihilistic) enjoyment submitted to a (democratic) linguistic injunction. The only obstacle to this injunction is the Idea, the intractable element of a truth. This is why the only truth of the pseudo-materialist thesis "there is nothing but bodies and language" lies in the presumption that every idea is useless. When all is said and done, the democratic imperative becomes: "Live without any Idea." Or if you prefer: "Buy your enjoyment."

FROM *BEING AND EVENT* TO *LOGICS OF WORLDS*

PH. I'd like to conclude with some questions about the changes to your general system proposed in your forthcoming *Logics of Worlds*. *Being and Event* obviously dealt with the question of being; with *Logics of Worlds* you are moving on to the question of appearing and appearance. What is the relation between the one and the other? What is the relationship between being and what you present in terms of being-there?

AB. We should start from the way *Being and Event* sets out its most basic category, the category of situation. In *Being and Event* there are two fundamental theses regarding being-as-being. First thesis: being is pure multiplicity, and so the science of being is mathematics, mathematics as they have developed over the course of history. Second thesis: a multiplicity is always presented in a situation. The concept of situation is designed to think being-as-being not only in its internal composition as pure multiplicity but also as having to be presented as the element of a multiplicity. The fundamental operator in the ontology of the multiple is *belonging*—A ∈ B, which reads "A belongs to B." Obviously this operator cannot be symmetrical (it does not have the same sense for A as it does for B). Multiplicity can be thought either as a constitutive element of another multiplicity or as a collecting together of other multiplicities (as its elements). This distinction does not have any great philosophical importance in *Being and Event* because that book remains on a very formal level. The only thing that needed to be axiomatized, via the axiom of foundation, was the rule which ensures that the situation can never be an element of itself.

The question, then, of how we should think this particular dimension of being-as-being—the fact that being-as-being can be deployed as truth only to the extent that it belongs to a situation—remains absolutely open. It's this obligation to belong to a situation, the fact that every multiple-being must be localized, that I have decided to call "being-there." By treating such localizations as "worlds," what I'm trying to propose is a way of thinking being-there.

So—and now I'm getting to your question—it's clear that you cannot pass directly from being-as-being to being-there. Were I to pass from the one to the other by rational deduction, I would simply be engaged in a reconstruction of Hegelianism. I would be drawing a figure of being-there from the being of multiplicity. Against this Hegelian inspiration I assume the contingency of being-there. But, at the same time, I defend a variant of the thesis according to which it is of the essence of being to be-there. The two statements must be asserted together: being-there (or belonging to a world) pertains to the essence of being, but being-there cannot be drawn out or inferred from the essence of being. Every being is presented in a world, but no singular world can be drawn out from the system of multiplicities of which it is composed. It remains impossible to deduce the singularity of a world. But we can and must examine the conditions of possibility of being-there, the logic of worlds. The approach is more phenomenological, or critical, than that of pure ontology. I'm trying to describe the laws under which appearance can be thought.

PH. If it's not possible to move smoothly from the one to the other, are there then two irreducibly distinct operations at work here? First, a being (or a multiplicity) *is* insofar as it belongs to another multiplicity, i.e., insofar as it is presented in a situation or set. And second, this same being then *appears* insofar as it appears as part of a world (which is obviously a much larger notion than a set). Or do these two actions, belonging and appearing, overlap in some other sense?

AB. With Hegel I assume that it's of the essence of being to be there and therefore that there is an intrinsic dimension of being that is engaged within appearance; but at the same time there is a contingency to this appearance, to this being-there-in-a-world. Our only access to being is in the form of being-there. Even when we think being-as-being in the field of mathematics, we must recall that historically constituted mathematics is itself a world and therefore a dimension of being-there. I hold absolutely to the thesis that figures expressly in *Being and Event,* that ontology is a situation. We can therefore say the following: *there are only worlds* [*il n'y a que des mondes*]. So what is a world? This is the question with which the book is concerned, at least in its first movement.

PH. One of the arguments that can be made against *Being and Event* is that you simplify the actual mechanics of domination and specification—the mechanics conceived, for instance, in terms of hegemony by Gramsci, and in terms of power by Foucault—by referring them back to a single operation, the re-presentation performed by the state. Might a comparable argument be made against *Logics of Worlds,* that you now refer everything back to what you call the transcendental regime [*le transcendental*] of a world, which determines the relative intensity with which different things appear in a world? Isn't the whole question one of distinguishing and analyzing the various processes that shape this transcendental regime? I can easily see the descriptive value of such an operator, but its explanatory value is less obvious.

AB. Strictly speaking, the transcendental cannot be reduced to the degrees of intensity of appearance, even if these degrees constitute the basis for the ordering of appearance. The transcendental regime includes singular operations, like the conjunction or the envelope, along with immanent topologies, like the theory of points, etc. The transcendental regime will account for two things that are formally essential. First, what does it mean to say that two entities appearing in a given world have something in common? Second, how does it happen that a region of the world possesses a certain consistency? And what is this consistency? I answer these questions by means of what I believe to be a quite original theory of objects. This theory is not exclusively descriptive; it also accounts for *why* there is an object. That is, it accounts for why and how the One comes to be in the domain of appearance [*pourquoi et comment y-a-t-il de l'Un dans l'apparaître*]. This is why, in this book, I equate the laws of appearance with a logic. What is at stake is thinking consistency in general, the consistency of all that appears.

PH. What is the precise role that relation plays in your new conception of things? In *Being and Event* you effectively exclude relations from the domain of being, or presentation, and tend to consider them exclusively from the perspective of the state, or of re-presentation.

AB. Relation is defined very precisely in *Logics of Worlds*. In pure being there is only the multiple, and therefore relation is not [*la relation n'est pas*]. In the domain of appearing, on the contrary, there is relation, precisely in the sense that there is existence. I make a distinction between being and existence, inasmuch as existence is being in its specific intensity of appearance, being such as it appears "there," in *a* world. Relation is not between two beings, but relation exists between two existents. It is a fact of the world and not a fact of being.

PH. And what happens then when an event takes place? Does an event suspend the prevailing rules that govern the way things appear in a world?

AB. This is precisely the question I'm working on at the moment. I would like the theory of the event to be at once logical and ontological. I would like to maintain, if at all possible, the essential aspects of the ontological definition of the event. The essence of this definition is that the event is an unfounded multiplicity: it does not obey the axiom of foundation, because it is its own element; it belongs to itself. This is why, in *Being and Event*, I said that the event is an "ultra-One." I would also like to retain the theory of the event-site [*site événementiel*]: the event in some sense is always a surging forth of the site, or an insurrection of the site, which for a moment comes to belong to itself. But I would also like to introduce the idea that the event is a deregulation of the logic of the world, a transcendental dysfunction. An event modifies the rules of appearance. How? This is empirically attested by every genuine event: something whose value within the world was null or very weak attains, all of a sudden, in the event, a strong or even maximal intensity of existence. Within appearance the core of the question of the event is really summed up by the idea that "we are nothing, let us be everything" (in the words of the *Internationale*). An element that prior to the event was indifferent, or even nonexistent, which did not appear, comes to appear. An existence—the political existence of the workers, for example—that the transcendental regime had measured as minimal, that was null from the vantage point of the world, all of a sudden turns out to have a maximal intensity. Therefore the event will conserve its ontological character as a surging forth of the site in a moment of self-belonging [*auto-appartenance*] and, at the same time, it will produce a brutal transformation of the regime of intensity, so as to allow that which was inexistent to come into existence.

PH. Will an event figure as maximally intense within the existing limits of its world, or will it appear above and beyond the preestablished maximum level of intensity?

AB. These are complicated technical details that to my mind do not really have important consequences. If an element finds itself absolutely modified in its transcendental degree of existence, then slowly but surely the transcendental regime in its entirety will no longer be able to maintain its rules. Everything will change: the comparisons of intensity in appearance, the existences involved, the possibility of relations, etc. There will be a rearrangement of the transcendental regime and, therefore, strictly speaking, a change of world.

The truth procedure itself will also receive a double status. I certainly aim to conserve its status as a generic production, its horizon of genericity. But, on the other hand, it will proceed to reconstruct—locally, to begin with—the whole set of rules by which things appear in keeping with the fact that something that previously did not appear now must appear. Something that was invisible must now become visible. Therefore, a truth procedure will also consist in a rearrangement of transcendental correlations, around this passage from inexistence to existence. In particular, given that every object possesses its own inexistent [*un inexistant propre*], if this inexistent acquires a maximal value, then another element will have to take its place. All of a sudden the question of destruction reappears, ineluctably. It's in this sense that I hope to satisfy our friend Bruno with a synthesis of *Theory of the Subject* and *Being and Event*. I am obliged here to reintroduce the theme of destruction, whereas in *Being and Event* I thought I could make do with supplementation alone. In order for that which does not appear in a world to suddenly appear within it (and appear, most often, with the maximal value of appearance), there is a price to pay. Something must disappear. In other words, something must die, or at least die to the world in question.

For example, the moment that something like the proletariat comes to exist within politics, it is indeed necessary to accept the fact that something which prior to this irruption possessed prestige and intensity finds itself annulled or denied—for example, aristocratic values, bourgeois authority, the family, private property, etc. And by the same token, it's this element of new existential intensity—the proletariat—that will now mark all possible political subjectivities, at least for the duration of a certain sequence. Proletarian politics will be defined as that form of politics that assumes, or even produces, the consequences of this modification of intensity. Reactive politics, on the other hand, will be that which acts as if the old transcendental circumstances had themselves produced the consequences in question, as if the existential upsurge of the proletariat was of no consequence whatsoever.

In order to think through all this, I will need a general theory of change in the domain of appearing. You will see that I distinguish between four types of change: modifications (which are consistent with the transcendental regime), weak singularities (or novelties with no strong existential consequences), strong singularities (which imply an important existential change but whose consequences remain measurable), and, finally, events (strong singularities whose consequences are virtually infinite).

BB. In your seminar "The Axiomatic Theory of the Subject" you also anticipate a whole segment of *Logics of Worlds* that will present a typology of various subjective figures, adding the reactive and obscure figures to that of fidelity, which was the only one considered in *Being and Event*. Concretely, what will be the consequences of this new configuration of things for your theory of the subject?

AB. In *Being and Event* the theory of the subject is reduced to its name; in other words the subject is absolutely nothing more than the local dimension of a truth, a point of truth. Inasmuch as there is an active element to the subject, it is to be found entirely in the process of forcing, as you yourself demonstrated in your contribution to the Bordeaux conference.[3] In *Logics of Worlds* the fundamental notion of *consequence* is introduced; since we are in the realm of the transcendental, or of logic, we can give a rigorous meaning to the operator of consequence. But it will be necessary to locate differentially the subject within a wider virtuality, which I call the subjective space. It's not at all as it was in *Being and Event*, where all that's described is the truth procedure, where the subject is nothing but a finite fragment of this procedure. It was, I must admit, a compromise with the modern notions concerning the finitude of human subjects, notions that I nevertheless try to oppose whenever I get the chance. Bruno made this objection, to which I am quite sensitive, very early on. All in all, in *Being and Event* the subject is defined as a finite instance of the infinity of the True. What this means, in the end, is that one can only enter into the space of the subject as finite, under axioms of finitude, which is by no means a satisfactory solution.

Hegel's position has some advantages here. He maintains the possibility that the subject dialecticizes the infinite in an immanent way; this constitutes the genuine theme of absolute knowledge. Leaving the anecdote about the end of history to one side, what's true in absolute knowledge is the idea that the finite can hold the infinite, that it's possible for the finite and the infinite not to figure as essentially disconnected. This was not exactly the case in *Being and Event*, where it's said rather that the infinite carries or bears the finite, that a truth carries the subject. We come back here to the question of dialectics: I'd like to develop a new dialectic, one that accepts that the distribution of truth and subject need not coincide with the distribution of infinite and finite.

My argument therefore is as follows: I demonstrate that the subject is identified by a type of marking, a postevental effect, whose system of operations is infinite. In other words, subjective capacity really is infinite, once the subject is constituted under the mark of the event. Why? Because subjective capacity amounts to drawing the consequences of a change, of a new situation, and if this change is evental, then its consequences are infinite.

In *Being and Event* subjectivization ultimately fades away no less than does the event. Its status remains somewhat indeterminate, outside the thematics of the name of the event. But, as Lyotard suggested to me from the beginning: isn't the naming of the event itself already fundamentally a form of subjectivization? And isn't there then a second subjectivization that is under the condition of the name fixed by the first subjectivization? Isn't the subject, as is often the case in philosophy, thereby presupposed by its very constitution?

I think that in my new arrangement the infinite capacity of subjects can be maintained in an immanent fashion because the notion of consequence will be constantly bound to the subject itself: this subject will need to have been specifically marked by the event in order really to participate in the labor of consequences.

THE UNNAMEABLE

PH. What will the consequences of this be for your somewhat problematic theory of the unnameable?

AB. It's quite possible that the category of the unnameable may prove irrelevant. The theory of appearance provides all by itself the guarantee that every object of a world is marked (in its multiple composition) by an inexistent term. Since an event produces the intensification of an inexistence, at the cost of an inevitable price to be paid in terms of destruction, there is no need to limit the effects of this intensification. Once a price has been paid in the domain of the inexistent, one cannot act as if this price had not indeed been paid. Disaster will no longer consist in wanting to name the unnameable at all costs but rather in claiming that one can make something pass from inexistence to existence, in a given world, without paying any price. Ethics will consist instead in the assumption and evaluation of this price. In sum, I'm coming back to the maxim of the Chinese communists during the Cultural Revolution: "No construction without destruction." Ethics consists in applying this maxim with clarity and with moderation. Of everything that comes into existence or comes to be constructed, we must ask: does it possess a universal value that might justify the particular destruction that its coming into existence demands?

PH. Can you describe how this might work more precisely? In the case of love, for instance, whose unnameable aspect was sexual pleasure: in what sense is such pleasure now directly accessible to the subject of love? At what price?

AB. I'm not saying that the inexistent will take the place of the unnameable. I'm not saying that sexual desire will become inexistent. The perspective is a different one. The unnameable testified to a point, within the general field in question, that remained inaccessible to the positivity of the true. These points of opacity, these resistances to the forcing of forms of knowledge, will always exist. But *unnameable* is not the right word. I've already done away with the moment of the naming of the event. In the procedure of love it may happen that one is unable to draw all the consequences implied by an encounter (in such a way that the sexual factor might be entirely absorbed in these consequences). This does not mean that the sexual is unnameable. We are no longer in the logic of *names* but in a logic of *consequences*. I will simply say that there are some things that are inconsequential, that some things do not enter into the field of consequences.

PH. Does a subject no longer run the risk, then, of perverting or totalizing a truth, as you suggest in *Ethics*?

AB. The risk does not disappear. But it's no longer of the order of a forced nomination. Basically, by recognizing the quasi-ontological category of the unnameable, I made concessions to the pervasive moralism of the 1980s and 1990s. I made concessions to the obsessive omnipresence of the problem of Evil. I no longer feel obliged to make such concessions. But neither do I wish to give up on the general idea of an ethic of truths. What corrupts a subject is the process of treating as a possible consequence of an event something that is not in fact a consequence. In brief, it's a matter of logical arrogance. For there's no reason why the possible consequences of a new intensity of existence should be identical to the totality of the world. To be honest, I have yet to work out these ethical questions in detail. The general idea is to substitute, for the overly moralizing idea of a totality marked by an unnameable point, the idea (which is far more closely linked to the concrete practices of truth) of a field of consequences whose logic must be both reconstructed and respected. I'll be taking up these difficult questions in the final chapter of *Logics of Worlds*.

Translated by Bruno Bosteels and Alberto Toscano

INTRODUCTION

1 Alain Badiou, "L'Investigation transcendantale," in *Alain Badiou: Penser le multiple*, edited by Charles Ramond (Paris: L'Harmattan, 2002), 7. Unless indicated otherwise, all translations are my own.

2 Ibid., 7–8.

3 Peter Hallward, *Badiou: A Subject to Truth* (Minneapolis: University of Minnesota Press, 2003), 174. Hallward here cleverly attributes a criticism of Badiou's Kantianism to other readers who, perhaps like myself, would argue for a more Hegelian reading. However, he is quick to add: "Although Badiou's truths are too emphatically situated in a particular situation to be vulnerable to the sort of arguments Hegel marshals against Kant, still the subtractive configuration of these truths is unlikely to seduce Badiou's more conventionally dialectical or materialist critics" (174).

4 Slavoj Žižek, "The Politics of Truth, or, Alain Badiou as a Reader of St Paul," in *The Ticklish Subject: The Absent Centre of Political Ontology* (London: Verso, 1999), 163. This chapter also appears in an earlier version as "Psychoanalysis in Post-Marxism: The Case of Alain Badiou," *South Atlantic Quarterly* 97, no. 2 (1998): 235–61. After I responded to this Žižekian reading of Badiou, in "Alain Badiou's Theory of the Subject: The Re-commencement of Dialectical Materialism?," published in two parts in *Pli: The Warwick Journal of Philosophy* 12 (2001): 200–229; and 13 (2002): 173–208, Žižek responded in turn with equal vehemence in a section titled "Lacan and Badiou," which is part of the introduction to the second edition of *For They Know Not What They Do: Enjoyment as a Political Factor* (London: Verso, 2002), lxxxi–lxxxviii. See also Žižek's contribution "From Purification to Subtraction: Badiou and the Real," in *Think Again: Alain Badiou and the Future of Philosophy*, edited by Peter Hallward (London: Continuum, 2004), 165–81. Here Žižek reiterates the charge of a hidden Kantianism: "Again, the hidden Kantian reference is crucial here: the gap which separates the pure multiplicity of the Real from the appearing of a 'world' whose coordinates are given in a set of categories which predetermine its horizon is the very gap which, in Kant, separates the Thing-in-itself from our phenomenal reality, i.e. from the way things appear to us as objects of our experience" (174). I

answer this new series of articles in "Badiou without Žižek," in "The Philosophy of Alain Badiou," edited by Matthew Wilkens, a special issue of *Polygraph: An International Journal of Culture & Politics* 17 (2005): 223–46. Finally, the polemic continues in a more muted tone in Žižek's "On Alain Badiou and *Logiques des mondes*," online at www.lacan.com/zizbadman.htm. For an initial treatment of this last text from Žižek, see below, chapters 3 and 7.

5 Alain Badiou, *Le Siècle* (Paris: Seuil, 2005), 231; *The Century*, translated by Alberto Toscano (Cambridge: Polity, 2007), 164.

6 Alain Badiou, *Logiques des mondes: L'Être et l'événement, 2* (Paris: Seuil, 2006), 561; *Logics of Worlds: Being and Event, 2*, translated by Alberto Toscano (London: Continuum, 2009), 537.

7 Vladimir I. Lenin, "Once Again on the Trade Unions, the Current Situation, and the Mistakes of Trotsky and Bukharin," in vol. 32 of his *Collected Works* (Moscow: Progress Publishers, 1965), 93.

8 Alain Badiou, *Théorie du sujet* (Paris: Seuil, 1982), 21; *Theory of the Subject*, translated by Bruno Bosteels (London: Continuum, 2009), 3.

9 As Badiou explains, "the epithet 'neo-Kantian' was the crushing accusation that Deleuze most often tried to pin on me" (Alain Badiou, *Deleuze: "La clameur de l'être"* [Paris: Hachette, 1997], 147; *Deleuze: The Clamor of Being*, translated by Louise Burchill [Minneapolis: University of Minnesota Press, 2000], 99). For Badiou's own ways of pinning the same epithet on Deleuze and Guattari see, among others, the following scathing remark:

> For quite a while, I wondered what this "desire" of theirs was, wedged as I was between the sexual connotations and all the machinic, industrial brass they covered it over with to look materialist. Well, it is the Freedom of Kantian critique, no more, no less. It is the unconditional: a subjective impulse that invisibly escapes the whole sensible order of ends, the whole rational fabric of causes. It is pure, unbound, generic energy, energy as such. That which is law unto itself, or absence of law. The old freedom of autonomy, hastily repainted in the colors of what the youth in revolt legitimately demands: some spit on the bourgeois family.

Or again, more narrowly targeting Deleuze:

> The rule of the Good, with Deleuze, is the categorical imperative stood on its feet, by means of the amusing substitution of the particular for the universal: always act so that the maxim of your actions be rigorously particular. Deleuze would like to be to Kant what Marx is to Hegel, Deleuze flips Kant upside down: the categorical imperative, but a desiring one, the unconditional, but materialist, the autonomy of the subject, but like a running flow. Sadly, turn Kant, and you will find Hume, which is the same thing—and Deleuze's first academic crushes.

See Alain Badiou, "Le Flux et le parti (dans les marges de l'*Anti-Œdipe*)," in *La Situation actuelle sur le front de la philosophie* (Paris: François Maspero, 1977), 31–32; in English: "The Flux and the Party: In the Margins of Anti-Oedipus," translated by Laura Balladur and Simon Krysl, in "Immanence, Transcendence, and Utopia," edited by Marta Hernández Salván and Juan Carlos Rodríguez, special issue of *Polygraph: An International Journal of Culture & Politics* 15–16 (2004): 75–92. See also my commentary on and extension of this argument in "Logics of Antagonism: In the Margins of Alain Badiou's 'The Flux and the Party,'" in the same issue of *Polygraph* 15–16 (2004): 93–107.

10 See appendix 1, 307.

11 Ibid.

12 Vladimir I. Lenin, *Philosophical Notebooks*, translated by Clemens Dutt, edited by Stewart Smith, vol. 38 of Lenin's *Collected Works* (Moscow: Progress Publishers, 1961), 360, also available online at www.marxists.org.

13 Mao Zedong, "On Contradiction," in *On Practice and Contradiction* (London: Verso, 2007), 88.

14 See appendix 1, 306. Badiou would later repeat this claim about the importance of the "and" in the title of *Being and Event*. See the brief section "A propos du 'et' entre être et événement," in *Écrits autour de la pensée d'Alain Badiou*, edited by Bruno Besana and Olivier Feltham (Paris: L'Harmattan, 2007), 103–4. Here, Badiou confirms that the most important concepts needed to think this link between being and event are the "evental" site (in *Being and Event*) and the inexistent raised up to maximal existence (in *Logics of Worlds*). For more on the role of these concepts see below, chapters 4 and 7.

15 Alain Badiou, *Peut-on penser la politique?* (Paris: Seuil, 1985), 84; *Can Politics Be Thought?*, translated by Bruno Bosteels (Durham: Duke University Press, forthcoming).

16 Badiou, *Logiques des mondes*, 11; *Logics of Worlds*, 3 (translation slightly modified). The preface to this book has also been translated separately as "Democratic Materialism and the Materialist Dialectic," translated by Alberto Toscano, *Radical Philosophy* 130 (2005): 20–24, 21.

17 Hallward, *Badiou*, 49–50; see also later in the same text, where Hallward repeats his claim that "since his explicitly Maoist days, Badiou has in some ways moved to a more rather than a less 'absolutist' position. He has moved further from any approach mediated by the activity of interpretation, broadly understood. In place of a partisan truth carried to some extent by a dialectical process of historical change, Badiou's work now affirms a subject whose very existence is 'maintained only by his own prescription'" (290–91). If this is indeed the case, and if Hallward's critique of absolutism is meant as a call for a more dialectical articulation, then should we not devote more time to Badiou's so-called early works?

One of Badiou's French interpreters adopts a similar chronological point of view:

At bottom the whole affair is defined, on a grand scale, by the place of the dialectical question in this author's work. The dialectic at first seems to be Badiou's big thing, starting with *Theory of Contradiction*, in conformity with a

Marxist and Maoist orientation. In this context, *Theory of the Subject* pushes this dialectical analysis of the real to the limit by assigning it to its artistic, mathematical, and political registers. But afterwards everything seems to suggest that the dialectic had to be progressively abandoned by Badiou in favor of a discourse on the multiple, which indeed expresses an approach that is different from the dialectical angle. *Being and Event* does not say a word about the dialectic and Badiou himself has been heard announcing that the time of the dialectic had been consumed.

See Fabien Tarby, *La Philosophie d'Alain Badiou* (Paris: L'Harmattan, 2005), 27. The notion (which other critics have hurled back against my reading of Badiou) that *Being and Event* does not say a word about the dialectic is in any case thoroughly mistaken, both in the literal sense (on my last count the term appears at least twenty-five times in the book) and for broader interpretive reasons (with the dialectics of void and excess, of the one and the many, of presentation and representation, of event and intervention, and of truth and knowledge, after all, constituting pivotal moments in the book's overall architecture). For a first dialectical reading of this work in particular and Badiou's philosophy in general see Bosteels, "On the Subject of the Dialectic." Parts of this article have been revised and incorporated here.

Needless to say, Badiou's open adoption of the name *materialist dialectic* for the ideological framework of his entire philosophical undertaking, in *Logics of Worlds*, complicates even further the notion of a break between his "early" and his "late" works. In fact, I would argue that it underscores the risk of a common bias among his readers and among readers of philosophy generally, according to which a philosopher's work progresses, as if in a bildungsroman, from early mistakes and lost illusions (Balzac's *Les Illusions perdues*) to ever more perfected versions of the same fundamental insight (the "one central thought" that Heidegger ascribes to all great thinkers as their fundamental "unthought"). In literature, interestingly, this bias is far from being so dominant; on the contrary, many literary writers are considered epigones of the unattainable heights of their own earlier work. And while I am not suggesting that this is the case with Badiou, we do well to be wary of such a bias.

18 Lenin, "Once Again on the Trade Unions, the Current Situation, and the Mistakes of Trotsky and Bukharin," 83.

19 On the primacy of politics in Maoism see, among others, the following classical formulation in "On Contradiction": "When the superstructure (politics, culture, etc.) obstructs the development of the economic base, political and cultural changes become principal and decisive" (Mao, *On Practice and Contradiction*, 92). Mao's only words spoken directly to the public below the Rostrum of the Tiananmen Square during the process of the Cultural Revolution also refer to this same principle: "You must let politics take command, go to the masses, and be with the masses. You must conduct the great proletarian Cultural Revolution even better." See Mao Zedong, "Directives Regarding Cultural Revolution (1966–1969)," in *Selected Works*, vol. 9, www.marxists.org.

20 On the notion of historical modes of politics and their saturation see in particular Sylvain Lazarus, "Singularité et modes historiques de la politique," in *L'Anthropologie du nom* (Paris: Seuil, 1997), 88–94. This book is discussed in Badiou, *Abrégé de métapolitique* (Paris: Seuil, 1998), 35–66; *Metapolitics*, translated by Jason Barker (London: Verso, 2005), 26–57.

21 In Lazarus's work this refusal of relationality and intentionality depends in no small measure on an idiosyncratic definition of thought as *rapport de*, an expression that Jason Barker renders in the English translation of *Metapolitics* as "relation of," as opposed to "relation to" (*rapport à*). See also Badiou's commentary: "That which is thought in thought must be thinkable apart from the (positivist) form of the object. One will thus say that thought, inasmuch as it is thinkable, is a 'relation' of that which is thought in it, and which has no objectal status. 'Relation of' is clearly opposed to 'relation to.' Thought is not a relation *to* the object, it is an *internal* relation of its Real, which taken 'in itself' remains indistinct, since it is presented only through the identification of a singular thought" (Badiou, *Abrégé de métapolitique*, 36–37; *Metapolitics*, 27–28). Perhaps it is worth recalling that *rapport* in French can also mean "ratio" and especially "report." In this last regard an interesting link could be established with a comparable meaning of the Spanish *relación*, as "report," "account," "narrative," or "story," with the genre of the conquistador's *relación* to His Majesty, according to some critics, lying at the origin, via the picaresque, of the modern novel. All thinking, to return to Lazarus and Badiou's frame, would then be a report of its real, except now this report is no longer addressed to some higher authority but only refers to its own inner logic and consistency.

22 See also the anonymous text, almost certainly written by Sylvain Lazarus, "Le mode dialectique," *La Distance Politique* 3 (May 1992): 4–6. This text has been translated into English as "The Dialectical Mode," translated by Bruno Bosteels, in "Alain Badiou and Cultural Revolution," a special issue of *positions: east asia cultures critique* 13, no. 3 (2005): 663–68. For further commentary see below, chapter 3.

23 Jacques Rancière, *Aux bords du politique*, 2nd exp. edn. (Paris: La Fabrique, 1998), 42–43; *On the Shores of Politics*, translated by Liz Heron (London: Verso, 1995), 25.

24 Badiou, *Abrégé de métapolitique*, 58; *Metapolitics*, 48 (translation modified).

25 Ibid., 60; 51.

26 Badiou, *Théorie du sujet*, 22; *Theory of the Subject*, 3–4.

27 Alain Badiou, Joël Bellassen, and Louis Mossot, "Hegel en France," in *Le Noyau rationnel de la dialectique hégélienne: Traductions, introductions et commentaires autour d'un texte de Zhang Shiying, Pékin, 1972* (Paris: François Maspero, 1978), 11–17. This work is currently being translated by Tzuchien Tho. For further discussion see also Bruno Bosteels, "Hegel," in *Alain Badiou: Key Concepts*, edited by Justin Clemens and A. J. Bartlett (London: Acumen, 2010), 137–45.

28 See appendix 1, 307.

29 Badiou, *Le Siècle*, 91; *The Century*, 59 (translation slightly modified).

30 Ibid., 30; 15. It is no doubt for this very reason that Badiou repeatedly speaks of "Freud's courage" and "audacity" in these lectures: "Freud approaches the question of his own audacity with regard to the real of sex, or to the mental genealogy of sexuality; or again, . . . of a face-to-face confrontation between thought and sex" (*Le Siècle*, 105; *The Century*, 69 [translation modified to retain the *face-à-face*]). Beneath the obvious tone of admiration, I read in these and other comments an underlying strain of criticism—the symptom of a problem for which the century did not provide a satisfactory dialectical answer, with violence standing in for what does not fail to be missed.

31 Ibid., 52–53; 31–32 (translation modified).

32 Alain Badiou, *L'Être et l'événement* (Paris: Seuil, 1988), 11; *Being and Event*, translated by Oliver Feltham (London: Continuum, 2005), 4 (translation modified).

33 Badiou, *Peut-on penser la politique?* 84.

34 Ibid., 86.

35 Ibid., 89.

36 Alain Badiou, "L'Entretien de Bruxelles," *Les Temps Modernes* 526 (1990): 1–26, 15.

37 Alain Badiou, *Manifeste pour la philosophie* (Paris: Seuil, 1989), 72; *Manifesto for Philosophy*, translated by Norman Madarasz (Albany: State University of New York Press, 1999), 90–91 (translation modified so as to use "politics" instead of "the political" for *la politique*, in keeping with the arguments formulated below [see note 45]).

38 Alain Badiou and François Balmès, *De l'idéologie* (Paris: François Maspero, 1976), 100.

39 Badiou, *Abrégé de métapolitique*, 56; *Metapolitics*, 46.

40 Badiou, *Théorie du sujet*, 143–44; *Theory of the Subject*, 126. See also Badiou, *Peut-on penser la politique?*: "Political organization is required for the intervention by way of the wager to make a process out of the gap between an interruption and a fidelity. In this sense, organization is nothing other than the consistency of politics" (112).

41 Badiou, *Abrégé de métapolitique*, 33; *Metapolitics*, 23.

42 Ibid., 19; 10 (translation modified).

43 See, for instance, Jacques Rancière, *La Mésentente: Politique et philosophie* (Paris: Galilée, 1995), 99; *Disagreement: Politics and Philosophy*, translated by Julie Rose (Minneapolis: University of Minnesota Press, 1999), 63–64. Rancière discusses three forms or types of such an encounter, or missed encounter, between politics and (political) philosophy, which he names "archipolitics" (Plato), "parapolitics" (Aristotle to Hobbes to Tocqueville), and "metapolitics" (Marx). I will return below to the difficult question of deciding whether Badiou's metapolitics also falls under the same concept designated by this term for Rancière.

44 Badiou, *Abrégé de métapolitique*, 98; *Metapolitics*, 86.

45 Ibid., 7; xlix (translation modified). The distinction between "politics" (*la politique* in French, *die Politik* in German) and "the political" (*le politique* or *das*

Politische) has a long history in political theory, from Carl Schmitt to Claude Lefort to Ernesto Laclau and Chantal Mouffe. Several authors have recently tried to transform this difference, now called the political difference, into the equivalent of Heidegger's ontological difference between beings and being. For a didactic overview of this trend, which would define the core of "Left Heideggerianism" in analogy with "Left Hegelianism," see Oliver Marchart, *Postfoundational Political Thought: Political Difference in Nancy, Lefort, Badiou, and Laclau* (Edinburgh: Edinburgh University Press, 2007). I discuss this use of the distinction of politics and the political in "Afterword: Being, Thinking, Acting, or, On the Uses and Disadvantages of Ontology for Politics," in *A Leftist Ontology: Beyond Relativism and Identity Politics*, edited by Carsten Strathausen (Minneapolis: University of Minnesota Press, 2009), 235–51. In this same volume see also the articles by Roland Végsö and Sorin Radu Cucu, both of whom remind us that, after Derrida's reading of Heidegger, especially, there can be no absolute or pure separation between the ontological and the ontic. Badiou, for his part, adopts the distinction of *le politique* and *la politique* in *Peut-on penser la politique?* but only to invert the evaluation of both terms in comparison with the way in which Jean-Luc Nancy and Philippe Lacoue-Labarthe, in the proposal for the seminar on "the retreat of the political" in which Badiou first presented the materials of *Peut-on penser la politique?*, had favored *le politique* over *la politique* as usual. In *Metapolitics*, by contrast, Badiou proposes more radically to "reject the expression '*the* political,' which precisely suggests a specific faculty, a common sense. There are only plural instances of politics, irreducible to one another, and which do not comprise any homogeneous history," in *Abrégé de métapolitique*, 25, 33; *Metapolitics*, 16, 23. I should add that this terminological debate is rendered even more opaque as a result of Norman Madarasz's rather strange decision, in his English version of Badiou's *Manifesto for Philosophy*, to translate *la politique* as "the political" and *le politique* as "politics." The only way to explain this decision is to suppose that the translator, by thus putting the opposition the other way around again in English, wishes to make Badiou homogeneous with a diffuse form of Heideggerianism, whether leftist or rightist.

46 Joseph de Maistre, *Essai sur le principe générateur des constitutions politiques et des autres institutions humaines* (Paris: Société Typographique, 1814), iii.

47 On the use of *metapolitics* in Alain de Benoist's New Right see Michael Torigian, "The Philosophical Foundations of the French New Right," *Telos* 117 (1999): 6–42. A broader overview of the metapolitical program among the European New Right can be found in Tamir Bar-On, *Where Have All the Fascists Gone?* (Aldershot, UK: Ashgate, 2007). See also the work of the Italian thinker Silvano Panunzio, *Metapolitica: La Roma eterna e la nuova Gerusalemme* (Roma: Babuino, 1979); and his follower, now residing in Chile, Primo Siena, *La Espada de Perseo: Itinerarios metapolíticos* (Santiago: Universidad Gabriela Mistral / Instituto de Cultura Italiana de Chile, 2007). In Argentina there is also the similar work of Alberto Buela, *Ensayos de disenso (sobre metapolítica)* (Bar-

celona: Nueva República, 1999) and *Metapolítica y filosofía* (Buenos Aires: Theoría, 2002).

48 Strangely enough, this expression of "the nonpolitical ground of politics," which defines the object of metapolitics according to Alberto Buela, can also be found in Rancière's *Disagreement*, where it defines the paradoxical play of equality that lies at the root of politics as such, presumably untainted by all forms of political philosophizing, whether metapolitical or otherwise. See Rancière, *La Mésentente*, 95; *Disagreement*, 61. A move from militant politics to the nonpolitical ground of politics also informs two other terminological proposals: that of the "impolitical," or "unpolitical," as defined by Roberto Esposito in *Categorie dell'impolitico* (Bologna: Il Mulino, 1988); and that of "infrapolitics," as portrayed by Alberto Moreiras in *Línea de sombra: El no-sujeto de lo político* (Santiago de Chile: Palinodia, 2006). For further discussion of these two related projects see Bosteels, "Politics, Infrapolitics, and the Impolitical: Notes on the Thought of Roberto Esposito and Alberto Moreiras," *CR: The New Centennial Review* 10, no. 2 (2010): 205–38.

49 Giacomo Marramao, "Metapolitica," *Laboratorio Politico* 1 (1983): 99. See also Benedetto Croce, "In qual senso la libertà sia un concetto metapolitico" (1938), in *Pagine sparse* (Naples: Ricciardi, 1941), 2:411–13; Antonio Negri, "La Concezione metapolitica della storia di B. Croce," *Giornale Critico della Filosofia Italiana* 20 (1966): 485–540; and Manfred Riedel, *Metaphysik und Metapolitik: Studien zu Aristoteles und zur politischen Sprache der neuzeitlichen Philosophie* (Frankfurt am Main: Suhrkamp, 1975). In the Netherlands Mgr. A. H. van Luyn, the Bishop of Rotterdam, defends liberty, equality, and solidarity as "metapolitical" values that precede and transcend all cultural, ideological, and religious differences, in *Politiek en metapolitiek: Gewetensvol in de Randstad* (Kampen: Kok, 2008).

50 Alain Badiou, *D'un désastre obscur (Droit, Etat, Politique)* (La Tour d'Aigues: Éditions de l'Aube, 1991), 12; in English: "Philosophy and the 'death of communism,'" in Alain Badiou, *Infinite Thought: Truth and the Return of Philosophy*, translated by and edited by Oliver Feltham and Justin Clemens (London: Continuum, 2003), 130. A complete version of this text has been translated by Barbara P. Fulks as "Of an Obscure Disaster: On the End of the Truth of the State," in *Lacanian Ink* 22 (2003): 58–89.

51 Badiou, *Abrégé de métapolitique*, 112–13; *Metapolitics*, 99.

52 Rancière, *La Mésentente*, 99; *Disagreement*, 65. For further discussion of this part of Rancière's work see Bosteels, "Archipolitics, Parapolitics, Metapolitics," in *Jacques Rancière: Key Concepts*, edited by Jean-Philippe Deranty (London: Acumen, 2010), 80–92.

53 Rancière, *La Mésentente*, 123; *Disagreement*, 85. The double use of the concept of class as described by Rancière corresponds quite neatly to what Lazarus and Badiou discuss as a "circulating term" between the objective and the subjective, the historical and the political.

54 Badiou, *Théorie du sujet*, 46; *Theory of the Subject*, 28. As for the first, scientific
    suture of Badiou's thinking, see especially "Philosophie et vérité," the televised
    interview for the series *L'enseignement de la philosophie*, broadcast on March 27,
    1965. This is the last in a series of six interviews that Badiou conducted between
    January and March 1965 on, respectively, the themes of "Philosophy and Its
    History" (with Jean Hyppolite), "Philosophy and Science" (with Georges Can-
    guilhem), "Philosophy and Sociology" (with Raymond Aron), "Philosophy and
    Psychology" (with Michel Foucault), "Philosophy and Language" (with Paul
    Ricoeur), and "Philosophy and Truth" (with all of the above, as well as the
    program's organizer, Dina Dreyfus). To my knowledge the interview with Fou-
    cault is the only one to have been published separately. See Michel Foucault,
    "Philosophie et psychologie," *Dits et écrits, 1954–1988*, edited by Daniel Defert
    and François Ewald (Paris: Gallimard,1994), 1:438–48; in English: "Philosophy
    and Psychology," in *The Essential Works of Foucault, 1954–1984*, vol. 2, *Aesthetics,
    Method, and Epistemology*, edited by James D. Faubion (New York: New Press,
    1998), 249–60. In many ways these interviews in which a chain-smoking Badiou
    is visibly entertained while provoking and seducing his mentors and some of
    France's most illustrious philosophers at the time, marks his true entrance onto
    the philosophical stage. For an excellent study, based on the author's doctoral
    dissertation, see Tamara Chaplin Matheson, "Embodying the Mind, Producing
    the Nation: Philosophy on French Television," *Journal of the History of Ideas* 67,
    no. 2 (2006): 315–41.

55 Alain Badiou, *Conditions* (Paris: Seuil, 1992), 234n41; *Conditions*, translated by
    Steven Corcoran (London: Continuum, 2009), 305n12 (translation modified).

56 Badiou, *Manifeste pour la philosophie*, 91; *Manifesto for Philosophy*, 108 (transla-
    tion modified).

57 Badiou, *Abrégé de métapolitique*, 12; *Metapolitics*, 4 (translation modified).

58 Ibid., 15; 6–7 (translation modified). For another example of the role of mathe-
    matics as a paradigmatic discipline of thought, in this case for the solving of a
    political problem, see also one of the final paragraphs from Badiou's public
    journal on the war in Iraq: "As restricted as it may be, action here makes itself
    infinite by the detour through thought that solves, in an organized way, a precise
    political problem, where an unexpected possible is extracted from an impossible
    matter. On this point, too, the mathematical paradigm can be of use: the emer-
    gence of an entirely new, far-reaching theory comes about when thought con-
    centrates on a problem whose formulation may seem entirely singular, not to
    say extraordinarily narrow." See Badiou, "Fragments d'un journal public sur la
    guerre américaine contre l'Irak," *Circonstances, 2: Irak, foulard, Allemagne/France*
    (Paris: Éditions Lignes et Manifestes, 2004), 48–49; in English: "Fragments of a
    Public Journal on the American War against Iraq," in *Polemics*, translated by
    Steve Corcoran (London: Verso, 2006), 57 (translation modified).

59 Badiou, *Abrégé de métapolitique*, 56; *Metapolitics*, 46. In French the sentence
    "Peut-on penser la politique comme pensée?" obviously contains the title of

Badiou's earlier book *Peut-on penser la politique?* while highlighting the double meaning that is perhaps even better captured in English, *Can Politics Be Thought?*, which is to say, both "Can we think politics?" and "Can politics be a form of thought in its own right?"

60 Peter Hallward, "Politics: Equality and Justice," in *Badiou*, 223–42. In chapter 3, below, I propose to do for Badiou's militantism in the Maoist or post-Maoist UCFML what Hallward did with great detail for the politics without a party of Organisation Politique. The latter group, OP, founded in 1985, gathers members of the UCFML, which in turn emerged in 1970 amid the worldwide revolutionary sequence of 1966 to 1976. For more information see the theses or guidelines of the group in *Qu'est ce que l'Organisation politique?* (Paris: Le Perroquet, 2001). Badiou also discusses some of the recent activities of this group in his interview with Hallward, reprinted as an "Appendix: Politics and Philosophy," in *Ethics*, 95–144. The OP has now officially ceased to exist, with several subgroups vying for the claim of being the true and rightful inheritor.

61 Recently this second approach, which in many ways brings us back to a more traditional form of political theory, appears to have taken off so that we now have at our disposal a whole series of comparisons of Badiou with Rancière, Balibar, Derrida, Nancy, Marion, and Žižek. See, e.g., Nick Hewlett, *Badiou, Balibar, Rancière: Rethinking Emancipation* (London: Continuum, 2007); Antonio Calcagno, *Badiou and Derrida: Politics, Events and Their Time* (London: Continuum, 2007); Adam Miller, *Badiou, Marion and St Paul: Immanent Grace* (London: Continuum, 2008); Adrian Johnston, *Badiou, Žižek, and Political Transformations: The Cadence of Change* (Evanston: Northwestern University Press, 2009). Since all these studies came out after the bulk of the present book had been written, I have not been able to incorporate their findings as much as I would have liked to.

62 Badiou, *Abrégé de métapolitique*, 141, 142; *Metapolitics*, 126, 127. Here, again, we witness the antidialectical rage at work in Badiou's work from the 1990s, as opposed to his earlier, allegedly conventional, view of periodization in Hegel's dialectic. Indeed, did he not argue in *Theory of the Subject* for precisely such a dialectical periodization of politics in terms of its result and its belated thinkability? Already in Badiou's most Hegelian book, however, we can observe certain hesitations in this regard, anticipated in the ironic touches of the following statement: "The Hegelian absolute, which is the name of the procedure of looping back the dialectical process, turns out to be the fusion of the process as concept and the process as effectuation. When in any active reality the reflection upon its own history comes to the surface, it is because this reality has run its course. There is nothing left but to absolve it: the absolute gives it its blessing. This is the reason why Minerva's bird, the owl of patient knowledge, only takes flight at dusk, with its silent wing saluting the contrary light of the Truth" (*Théorie du sujet*, 37; *Theory of the Subject*, 19). To this circular and idealist looping back of history upon the absolute, a properly materialist dialectic opposes a spiraling periodization.

63 Badiou, *Abrégé de métapolitique*, 155; *Metapolitics*, 141.

64 Karl Marx, "On the Jewish Question," in *The Portable Karl Marx*, edited by Eugene Kamenka (New York: Penguin, 1983), 114. Daniel Bensaïd has recently written an extraordinary presentation and commentary on this polemical text, in his edition of Marx, *Sur la question juive* (Paris: La Fabrique, 2008).

65 Sam Gillespie, *The Mathematics of Novelty: Badiou's Minimalist Metaphysics* (Melbourne: re.press, 2008), 72. Badiou's main work in mathematics, which the author considers his strongest theoretical statement, is *Le Nombre et les nombres* (Paris: Seuil, 1990); *Number and Numbers*, translated by Robin Mackay (Cambridge: Polity, 2008). This work is reviewed by Gilles Châtelet in *Annuaire philosophique, 1989–1990* (Paris: Seuil, 1991), 200–229. For general discussions of the import of mathematics, especially Cantorian set theory, for Badiou's philosophy see Jean-Michel Salanskis, "Les Mathématiques chez x avec x = Alain Badiou," in Ramond, *Alain Badiou: Penser le multiple*, 81–106; Jean-Jacques Sczeciniarz, "L'Être ou la structure (faire l'ontologie, est-ce dire les mathématiques sans l'opératoire qui les fait exister? Est-ce produire la contemplation des objets?)," in Ramond, *Alain Badiou: Penser le multiple*, 107–47; Hallward, "Mathematics and Science" and "Appendix: On the Development of Transfinite Set Theory," in *Badiou*, 209–21, 323–48; and B. Madison Mount, "The Cantorian Revolution: Alain Badiou on the Philosophy of Set Theory," *Polygraph: An International Journal of Culture & Politics* 17 (2005): 41–91. The most accessible introduction to axiomatic set theory for mathematically challenged readers of Badiou like myself can be found in Oliver Feltham and Justin Clemens, "An Introduction to Alain Badiou's Philosophy," in Badiou, *Infinite Thought*, 1–38. On the role of category theory, which is to *Logics of Worlds* what set theory is to *Being and Event*, see Norman Madarasz, "On Alain Badiou's Treatment of Category Theory in View of a Transitory Ontology," in *Alain Badiou: Philosophy and Its Conditions*, 23–43; and Justin Clemens, "Had we but worlds enough, and time, this absolute, philosopher . . . !," in *The Praxis of Alain Badiou*, edited by Paul Ashton, A. J. Bartlett, and Justin Clemens (Melbourne: re.press, 2007), 102–43.

66 Badiou, *L'Être et l'événement*, 15; *Being and Event*, 8.

67 Badiou, *Manifeste pour la philosophie*, 76–77; *Manifesto for Philosophy*, 95.

68 Zachary Fraser, at the end of a painstaking and highly specialized account of Badiou's use of mathematics, refers briefly to this double inscription: "The paradox here, is that throughout *Being and Event*, mathematics is charged with a double task. It is repeatedly summoned not only to provide the ontological lineaments of the world, but also to stand as an exemplary truth procedure—indeed, as the paradigm for an entire species of truth procedures (the scientific)" (Fraser, "The Law of the Subject: Alain Badiou, Luitzen Brouwer and the Kripkean Analyses of Forcing and the Heyting Calculus," in Ashton, Bartlett, and Clemens, *The Praxis of Alain Badiou*, 67). Fraser's solution for this paradox consists in proposing that mathematical intuitionism, as defined by Brouwer, is actually more appropriate to account for the process of subjectivization than

Badiou with his axiomatic and anti-intuitionist definition of mathematics is willing to accept. In other words, the answer to bridge the gap between mathematics as ontology and mathematics as a truth procedure would require a change in the type of mathematics adopted! Brian Anthony Smith comes closer to my argument when he draws a clear line of demarcation between ontology and the theory of the subject based in truth procedures. Such a distinction, he argues astutely, requires a thorough temporalization of mathematics: "This is a recurrent theme in *Being and Event*: Badiou makes significant philosophical distinctions by dissecting mathematical proofs and procedures, which are taken mathematically to occur all at once, and imposing a temporal structure on them." Smith continues: "The entire theory of the event rests fundamentally on this situated and temporal appropriation of set theory. This is Badiou's philosophical use of ontology, the concepts of the individual inhabitant of a situation, and therefore the subject are *not* mathematical/ontological concepts" (Smith, "The Limits of the Subject in Badiou's *Being and Event*," in Ashton, Bartlett, and Clemens, *The Praxis of Alain Badiou*, 87, 89). With this introduction of temporality and historicity into the axiomatic space of mathematics we are clearly embarking on an understanding of the event in general, for example in politics, which would not have to be the slave to mathematics. See also B. Madison Mount's observations about Badiou's fundamental orientation with regard to the impasse of mathematics, which transversally cuts across the other three (constructivist, generic, and transcendent) orientations: "Rather, the transversal orientation seeks to reckon with the plural *truths* of the mathematical aporia as processes of truth-production in the conjuncture of ontology and metaontology. It rehistoricizes the decisions of the other three orientations, and, in so doing, brings the discursive system engendered by the Cantorian revolution into conversation with the post-Galilean but pre-revolutionary moment of modern philosophy" (Madison Mount, "The Cantorian Revolution," 53). Perhaps Fraser's plea for a reevaluation of intuitionism, if I understand him correctly, is meant in part to answer the same problem as Smith's or Madison Mount's appeal to temporality and historicity. None of these commentators goes so far as to accept a limited role of mathematics for the treatment of truth procedures such as politics, about which for the most part they remain silent. On the contrary, their contagious enthusiasm for the Cantorian revolution frequently pushes them to the point of what we would have to call a complete suture of philosophy onto mathematics.

69 Alain Badiou, *Theoretical Writings*, edited and translated by Ray Brassier and Alberto Toscano (London: Continuum, 2006), 10, 32.

70 Ibid., 19.

71 Ibid., 16.

72 Badiou, *L'Être et l'événement*, 111; *Being and Event*, 95. Interestingly, the use of Hegel's One-One (*das eine Eins*) in *Being and Event*, designating the unity of the count-for-one as state, is diametrically opposed to its use in *Theory of the Subject*, where this unifying function is ascribed to the political party and aimed *against* the state. See Badiou, *Théorie du sujet*, 229–30; *Theory of the Subject*, 213–14.

73 Badiou, *L'Être et l'événement*, 9–10; *Being and Event*, 3–4. The fact that in *Meta-politics*, using another expression from Lazarus, Badiou sees most circulating terms as being ideological also raises the question whether philosophy, insofar as it can be said to circulate among ontology, theories of the subject, and its own history, does not have a fundamental ideological function.

74 Badiou, *L'Être et l'événement*, 121; *Being and Event*, 104.

75 Badiou, *Théorie du sujet*, 33; *Theory of the Subject*, 15. Still referring to his formal-mathematical reading of Hegel's dialectic, Badiou adds a second response, claiming that the objection of an ill-formed use of mathematics overdetermined by politics simply is not true, insofar as Hegel himself actually finds the model for his dialectic in Christianity. So far from being a misuse on Badiou's part, the ex-emplifying utilization of logical and mathematical forms would already be at work in Hegel. For a different problematization of the issue of translation in Badiou's thinking in general, with regard to mathematics as much as to poetry, see Charles Ramond, "Système et traduction chez Alain Badiou," in Ramond, *Alain Badiou: Penser le multiple*, 525–40.

76 Badiou, *Théorie du sujet*, 165; *Theory of the Subject*, 148. Significantly, in this section, called "On a certain dialectical use of the mathematical text," part of the chapter "Torsion," Badiou proposes to discuss "a certain use of mathematics that is properly my own, without seeming proper to anyone else: neither to mathe-maticians, who find it metaphorical, nor to others, who are intimidated by it" (ibid.). Some readers no doubt will object that this symptomatic use of mathe-matics as displayed in *Theory of the Subject* no longer applies to *Being and Event*, where mathematics *is* ontology, intrinsically, without the detours of a symp-tomatology. To this I would reply that mathematics displays an intrinsic ra-tionality only as the discourse of being qua being, and even here, as we will see, a retroactive analysis displays the nonrandom nature of many of the conceptual operators put into place by the philosopher. For a slightly different criticism of the limitations of Badiou's intrinsic ontology see Jean-Toussaint Desanti, "Some Remarks on the Intrinsic Ontology of Alain Badiou," translated by Ray Brassier, in Hallward, *Think Again*, 59–66. Finally, I might add that politics is not the only truth procedure that actively conditions some of the signifiers used in Badiou's metaontology. An entire metaphorical apparatus, including the "errant" or "wan-dering" nature of the excess of the power set of an infinite set, the "event" as "advent" or "adventure," not to mention the depiction of the "site" as being "on the edges of the void," in fact recalls the modern novel's origins in the chivalric imagination. This opening of Badiou's metaontology onto the theory of fiction, in particular the chivalric romance, is beautifully suggested by Simone Pinet in the conclusion of her essay "On the Subject of Fiction: Islands and the Emer-gence of the Novel," in "New Coordinates: Spatial Mappings, National Trajec-tories," edited by Robert A. Davidson and Joan Ramon Resina, special issue of *diacritics* 33, nos. 3–4 (2003): 173–87.

77 In the interview reproduced in the first of two appendices, Badiou promises to include a treatment of the *réseaux* or "networks" and *nouages* or "knottings"

among two or more of the truth procedures in *Logics of Worlds*, which at the time of the interview had not yet appeared. In the published version of this sequel to *Being and Event*, however, no such theory is to be found. Instead, we may safely assume that this is one of the topics that the author leaves for later, perhaps for the new volume announced under the title *L'Immanence des vérités*, or to others to elaborate. The reader interested in pursuing this thread will find promising suggestions in *Écrits autour de la pensée d'Alain Badiou*, edited by Bruno Besana and Olivier Feltham especially in the editors' preface (9–19) and in the section "Badiou et la pensée contemporaine du multiple" (55–100). For an explicit treatment of the "interferences" between art, science, and philosophy, from within a different framework that is worth contrasting with Badiou's, see Gilles Deleuze and Félix Guattari, *What Is Philosophy?* 201–18.

78 Vladimir I. Lenin, *The State and Revolution*, in vol. 25 of his *Collected Works* (see esp. "Chapter III, Experience of the Paris Commune of 1871: Marx's Analysis").

79 Badiou, *L'Être et l'événement*, 125; *Being and Event*, 108.

80 Alain Badiou, "Ontology and Politics. An Interview with Alain Badiou," in Badiou, *Infinite Thought*, 182. Within the strictly mathematical discourse, too, infinity of course requires a primary axiomatic decision: "Now, just like the empty set, or zero, *the infinite will not be deduced*: we have to *decide* its existence axiomatically, which comes down to admitting that one takes this existence, not for a construction of thought, but for a fact of Being," as Badiou states in *Le Nombre et les nombres*, 60–61; *Number and Numbers*, 44. The point I am trying to make, however, concerns the fact that in the case of non-ontological situations this decision for infinity, without which the theorem of excess simply cannot be imported from mathematics into historical or political situations, seems to boil down to deciding what is more interesting—a notion that one would expect more easily coming from Deleuze than from Badiou: "It is more interesting and more attuned to the necessity of the times than declaring that we are finite and all is finite, we are mortal beings, being for death and so on. We are being-for-the-infinite," Badiou also states in "Ontology and Politics," 183.

81 Lenin, *Philosophical Notebooks*, 180, 196. To the theory of reflection, however, we should add the notion of an asymptotic approach to the real: "Cognition is the eternal, infinite approach of thought to the object. The reflection of nature in the thought of man must be understood not in a 'dead,' not in an 'abstract' manner, *not without movement, not without contradictions, but in an eternal process of movement, emergence* of contradictions and their solution" (ibid., 195). In the words of Badiou: "Materialist knowledge is both and at the same time reflection of the real movement and tendential approximation of this movement. It both redoubles it and, without ever managing to do so, tends to identify itself with it. Knowledge is an image in movement. Considered as a material process, it is divided according to its exactitude (reflection, absolute character of knowledge) and according to its inexactitude (tendency, relative character of knowledge). The internal, asymptotic law of this division consists in reabsorbing itself in unity. But two never fuse into one, the image in movement remains divided from

its object" (Alain Badiou, *Théorie de la contradiction* [Paris: François Maspero, 1975], 40). For a detailed discussion of the necessary distinction and combination of the reflection theory of knowledge and the asymptotic approach of the real see also *Théorie du sujet*, 206–16; *Theory of the Subject*, 191–200.

82　Theodor W. Adorno, "Skoteinos, or How to Read Hegel," in *Hegel: Three Studies*, translated by Shierry Weber Nicholson (Cambridge: MIT Press, 1993), 139.

CHAPTER 1. THE ABSENT CAUSE

1　Thus, for example, in German—not to forget the biblical "beginning" (in the sense of the Hebrew *bereshith* that gives its name to the book of Genesis, or in the sense of the Latin *principium* that begins the Gospel according to John)—a distinction is frequently drawn in philosophy between *Anfang, Beginn, Prinzip, Entstehung, Herkunft*, and *Ursprung*. On the different, often almost diametrically opposed, valorizations of these terms in the work of Nietzsche, Heidegger, Walter Benjamin, or Hannah Arendt see, among others, Michel Foucault, "Nietzsche, Genealogy, History," in *Language, Counter-memory, Practice: Selected Essays and Interviews*, edited by Donald F. Bouchard (Ithaca: Cornell University Press, 1977), 139–64; or the chapters "Principium e initium" and "Beginn, Anfang, Ursprung," in Roberto Esposito, *L'Origine della politica: Hannah Arendt o Simone Weil?* (Rome: Donzelli, 1996), 25–50. With regard to the beginning in Hegel see the footnotes in Badiou, Bellassen, and Mossot, *Le Noyau rationnel de la dialectique hégélienne*, esp. note "(a) On Being, Nothingness, Becoming": "Idealism in this beginning of the logic stems from the fact that there is a beginning, and if we want to be rigorous we will not say that the one (Being) transforms itself into the other (Nothingness) but that there is a problematic of the beginning" (29).

2　Rancière, *La Mésentente*, 96; *Disagreement*, 61.

3　Badiou, *Peut-on penser la politique?*, 12.

4　Badiou, *Théorie du sujet*, 202; *Theory of the Subject*, 186.

5　See Louis Althusser, "Tendances en philosophie," in *Éléments d'autocritique* (Paris: Hachette, 1974), 85–101; "Tendencies in Philosophy," in *Essays in Self-Criticism*, translated by Grahame Lock (New York: NLB, 1976), 142–50.

6　Louis Althusser, *Lénine et la philosophie* (Paris: François Maspero, 1969), 11, 57; "Lenin and Philosophy," in *Lenin and Philosophy and Other Essays*, translated by Ben Brewster (New York: Monthly Review Press, 1971), 27, 68.

7　Althusser, *Éléments d'autocritique*, 91; *Essays in Self-Criticism*, 145–46; and *Filosofía y marxismo*, 47; this part of the interview with Navarro is not translated in "Philosophy and Marxism," in Althusser, *Philosophy of the Encounter*.

8　Althusser, *Filosofía y marxismo*, 56–57; "Philosophy and Marxism," 275. Where the English says "grownups," the Spanish has *personas ilustres* and the French *grandes personnes*. Thus, as the Spanish original suggests, aside from grownups (or adults), this expression could also allude to great or famous people, which is how I have translated it into English. We should no doubt connect these notions of the "outside" or the "back" of philosophy to Gilles Deleuze's affirmations, most notably with regard to the "thought of the outside" in Foucault and, in his "Letter to a Severe Critic," with regard to the task of the philosopher to take predecessors "from behind" in an act of "buggery" so as to "make a bastard child behind their back" (*leur faire un enfant dans le dos*). See Gilles Deleuze, *Foucault* (Paris: Minuit, 1986), 77–99; and Gilles Deleuze, *Pourparlers, 1972–1990* (Paris: Minuit, 1990), 15. In English: *Foucault*, translated by Seán Handt (Minneapolis: University of Minnesota Press, 1988), 70–93; and *Negotiations*, translated by Martin Joughin (New York: Columbia University Press, 1995), 6. In fact, it is Foucault himself who first speaks of a "thought of the outside," in his homage to Maurice Blanchot, "La pensée du dehors," *Critique* 229 (1966): 523–46; in English: *Maurice Blanchot: The Thought from Outside*, translated by Brian Massumi (New York: Zone Books, 1987).

9   Althusser, *Filosofía y marxismo*, 73, 62; "Philosophy and Marxism," 287, 280 (translation modified).

10 Alain Badiou, "Qu'est-ce que Louis Althusser entend par 'philosophie'?" in *Politique et philosophie dans l'œuvre de Louis Althusser*, edited by Sylvain Lazarus (Paris: PUF, 1993), 29–45. This piece has been reissued as a central part of Alain Badiou, *Petit panthéon portatif* (Paris: La Fabrique, 2008), 57–87; *Pocket Pantheon: Figures of Postwar Philosophy*, translated by David Macey (London: Verso, 2009), 54–89, 79, 89. Badiou here objects in particular to the lingering idealism of Althusser's definition of the labor of philosophy as one of ideological "mediation" or "representation" of other practices, principally politics and science, for the realm of theory. This has not, however, kept Badiou himself, years later, from speaking in terms of "representation," as when he writes: "In the context of a becoming-subject, the event (whose entire being lies in disappearing) is represented by a trace: the world (which as such does not allow for any subject) is represented by a body" (*Logiques des mondes*, 90; *Logics of Worlds*, 80).

11 Alain Badiou, "Le (Re)commencement du matérialisme dialectique," *Critique* 240 (1967): 438–67. In addition to *For Marx* and *Reading Capital*, this review deals with a short article by Althusser, "Matérialisme historique et matérialisme dialectique," *Cahiers Marxistes-Léninistes* 11 (1966). In the likely absence of an original copy of this article, the reader may want to consult the Spanish translation, which appeared in Mexico together with Badiou's review of Althusser in a well-known and often reprinted booklet, *Materialismo histórico y materialismo dialéctico*, translated by Nora Rosenfeld de Pasternac, José Arico, and Santiago Funes (Mexico: Pasado y Presente, 1969). For many readers in Latin America this booklet was their main point of entry to the work of Badiou. *Cahiers Marxistes-Léninistes*, on the other hand, was the important publication of the section of the Union des étudiants communistes, or UEC, at the École Normale Supérieure, and subsequently it became the theoretical and political organ of the Maoist group Union des jeunesses communistes (marxiste-léniniste), or UJC (ml). On the importance of this publication and the role of Althusserians in

French Maoism in general, the reader may consult the slightly sensationalist study by Christophe Bourseiller, *Les Maoïstes: La Folle histoire des gardes rouges français* (Paris: Plon, 1996). Finally, the theme of the "recommencement" or "rebeginning" truly is a constant in Badiou's oeuvre. See, e.g., the interview with Natacha Michel about *Théorie du sujet*, "Re-naissance de la philosophie," published in two parts in *Le Perroquet* 6 (1982): 1, 8–10; and 13–14 (1982): 1, 10–13; or the article on the crisis and the renewal of Marxism, which anticipates many of the arguments from *Peut-on penser la politique?*, "La figure du (re)commencement," *Le Perroquet* 42 (1984): 1, 8–9. We should no doubt compare and contrast this theme in Badiou, on one hand, with Althusser's discussion of the necessity and contingency of the beginning of any philosopher, including Marx, in *Pour Marx* (Paris: Maspéro, 1965; La Découverte, 1986), 60, 71 (quotations are from the 1986 edition); *For Marx*, translated by Ben Brewster (London: Verso, 1969), 63–64, 74; and, on the other hand, with the element of return and thus of constant rebeginning introduced by Althusser's "self-critical" rapport to his own earlier works, as discussed by Balibar: "Tabula rasa, or radical rebeginning? Or definitive stumbling block for all connections to new statements?," in Étienne Balibar, *Écrits pour Althusser* (Paris: La Découverte, 1991), 67. For Badiou, in any case, the theme dominates the entire twentieth century: "What is the new? The century is obsessed with this question, because ever since its inception the century has summoned itself as a figure of commencement. And first of all as the (re)commencement of Man: the new man" (*Le Siècle*, 99; *The Century*, 65).

12 Althusser, *Pour Marx*, 25; *For Marx*, 33 (translation modified). For a succinct discussion see Gregory Elliott, "A Recommencement of Dialectical Materialism," in *Althusser: The Detour of Theory* (London: Verso, 1987), 70–114. In the chapter in question, despite the use of the same title, Elliott only incidentally refers to Badiou's review article and completely ignores all of the later work by Althusser's onetime student.

13 Althusser, *Pour Marx*, 25; *For Marx*, 33 (translation modified).

14 Badiou, "Sutures," in *Manifeste pour la philosophie*, 41–48; *Manifesto for Philosophy*, 61–67. With regard to Althusser's obligatory lesson about politics as a condition for philosophy, see "Althusser: Le Subjectif sans sujet," in Badiou, *Abrégé de métapolitique*, 67–76; "Althusser: Subjectivity without a Subject," in *Metapolitics*, 58–67. For Althusser's own description of his double suturing of philosophy see *Éléments d'autocritique*, 100–101; *Essays in Self-Criticism*, 148–50.

15 Badiou, "Le (Re)commencement du matérialisme dialectique," 449.

16 Althusser, *Pour Marx*, 169; *For Marx*, 168 (translation modified). Admittedly, this attempt to distinguish *theory*, "theory," and Theory was to be short-lived.

17 Badiou, "Le (Re)commencement du matérialisme dialectique," 450.

18 Ibid.

19 Althusser, *Pour Marx*, 171; *For Marx*, 170–71. Peter Hallward, in a personal note to me, insists that for Badiou mathematics *is* such a pure theoretical practice, in fact the *only* science that is axiomatically set free, once and for all, from the

ongoing struggle against ideology mentioned by Althusser. To answer this objection would require that we take up the enormous task of investigating the double status of mathematical science, both as the discourse of ontology and as one subjective condition of truth among others, in Badiou's philosophy. For an initial discussion of this issue see the section "Whither Mathematics?" in my introduction above. The history of mathematics, in any case, is also marked by a never-ending struggle against the force of ideological intuition. "The historicity of mathematics is nothing but the labour of the infinite, its ongoing and unpredictable re-exposition," so that there is never any final or definitive break in this case either: "One must begin again, because mathematics is always beginning again and transforming its abstract panoply of concepts. One has to begin studying, writing and understanding again that which is in fact the hardest thing in the world to understand and whose abstraction is the most insolent, because the philosophical struggle against the alliance of finitude and obscurantism will only be rekindled through this recommencement" (Alain Badiou, "Mathématiques et philosophie," *Failles* 2 [2006]: 60–61; in English: "Mathematics and Philosophy," *Theoretical Writings*, 19).

20 Badiou, "Le (Re)commencement du matérialisme dialectique," 452. On the question of the purity and impurity of all conceptual distinctions in Althusser see also the important text by François Matheron, "Louis Althusser ou l'impure pureté du concept," in *Dictionnaire Marx contemporain*, edited by Jacques Bidet and Stathis Kouvélakis (Paris: PUF, 2001); in English: "Louis Althusser, or the Impure Purity of the Concept," in *Critical Companion to Contemporary Marxism*, edited by Jacques Bidet and Stathis Kouvélakis (Leiden: Brill, 2008), 503–27.

21 Badiou, "Le (Re)commencement du matérialisme dialectique," 455.

22 Ibid., 457.

23 See, e.g., the criticisms in Henri Lefebvre, *L'Idéologie structuraliste* (Paris: Anthropos, 1971); as well as several articles in Denise Avenas, et al., *Contre Althusser, pour Marx*, exp. edn. (Paris: Passion, 1999).

24 Badiou, *Théorie du sujet*, 138; *Theory of the Subject*, 120. See also Althusser's discussion of the universal and the specific in *Pour Marx*, 186–87; *For Marx*, 183: "If the universal has to be this specificity," he writes, "we have no right to invoke a universal which is not the universal of this specificity."

25 Althusser, *Pour Marx*, 215; *For Marx*, 209 (translation modified).

26 Ibid., 113; 113 (translation modified).

27 Badiou, *Abrégé de métapolitique*, 75; *Metapolitics*, 65 (translation slightly modified).

28 Ibid., 155; 141 (translation slightly modified).

29 Althusser, *Pour Marx*, 126; *For Marx*, 127 (translation modified).

30 Badiou, "Le (Re)commencement du matérialisme dialectique," 458.

31 Étienne Balibar, "Avant-propos pour la réédition de 1996," in Althusser, *Pour Marx* (Paris: Découverte, 1996), ix.

32 Alain Badiou, "L'Autonomie du processus esthétique," *Cahiers Marxistes-*

Léninistes 12–13 (1966): 77–89. This article (frequently misquoted in existing bibliographies as "L'autonomie du processus historique") was supposed to become a book-length study on *l'effet romanesque*, "the novelistic effect," for Althusser's series Théorie at Maspero. See Althusser's allusion to this project in Louis Althusser, *Lettres à Franca (1961–1973)* (Paris: Stock/IMEC, 1998), 691. A book that actually was published in this series the same year, and the most systematic investigation of literature along the lines of Althusser's theory of four discourses, remains Pierre Macherey's *Pour une théorie de la production littéraire* (Paris: Maspero, 1966); in English: *A Theory of Literary Production*, translated by Geoffrey Wall (London: Routledge, 1978).

33 See Alain Badiou, "Théorie axiomatique du sujet (Notes du cours 1996–1998)" (author's unpublished typescript). For a succinct exposition of Lacan's theory of four discourses, with clear hints of the influence of Badiou's thought, see Bruce Fink, "The Status of Psychoanalytic Discourse," in *The Lacanian Subject: Between Language and Jouissance* (Princeton: Princeton University Press, 1995), 127–46.

34 Louis Althusser, "Ideology and Ideological State Apparatuses (Notes Towards an Investigation)," in *Lenin and Philosophy and Other Essays*, 127–88. It is no doubt the overwhelming influence of this essay by Althusser in critical discourses over the last few decades that has given rise to such a strong attempt to debunk its presuppositions—an anticanonical project that in recent years has started to form something of a canon in its own right. Along with the texts by Žižek discussed below see Mladen Dolar, "Beyond Interpellation," *Qui Parle* 6, no. 2 (1993): 73–96; and Judith Butler, *The Psychic Life of Power: Theories in Subjection* (Stanford: Stanford University Press, 1997), 106–31.

35 Althusser to Gudrun Werner-Hervieu, quoted in Louis Althusser, *Ecrits sur la psychanalyse*, edited by Olivier Corpet and François Matheron (Paris: Stock/IMEC, 1993), 12. Unfortunately, this letter, which is quoted by the editors in their presentation of the French edition, is not included in the English version, Louis Althusser, *Writings on Psychoanalysis: Freud and Lacan*, edited by Olivier Corpet and François Matheron, translated by Jeffrey Mehlman (New York: Columbia University Press, 1996), nor in Louis Althusser, *The Humanist Controversy and Other Writings*, edited by François Matheron, translated by G. M. Goshgarian (London: Verso, 2006).

36 Badiou, *Abrégé de métapolitique*, 68–69; *Metapolitics*, 59 (translation modified).

37 Badiou, *Le Siècle*, 76n1; *The Century*, 209.

38 For Lacan's note and Miller's personal recollection of the effect this caused in him see the correspondence quoted in Althusser, *Ecrits sur la psychanalyse*, 304; in English: Althusser, "Correspondence with Jacques Lacan," in *Writings on Psychoanalysis*, 144–45.

39 See especially Elisabeth Roudinesco, "Dialogue with Louis Althusser," in *Jacques Lacan: Outline of Life, History of a Thought* (New York: Columbia University Press, 1997), 293–308.

40 Jacques-Alain Miller, "Action de la structure," *Cahiers pour l'analyse* 9 (1966): 93–105, 103. The journal *Cahiers pour l'analyse*, with ten thematic issues between 1966 and 1969, was the remarkable organon of the Cercle d'Épistémologie at the École Normale Supérieure. Badiou started participating in the journal precisely with this special issue, devoted to the *Généalogie des sciences*, in which Michel Foucault also formulates his own archaeological theory of discourse and event in response to a questionnaire by members from the Cercle. See Foucault, "Réponse au Cercle d'Épistémologie," *Cahiers pour l'analyse* 9 (1968): 9–40; in English: "On the Archaeology of the Human Sciences: Response to the Epistemology Circle," in *The Essential Works of Foucault*, 2:279–96. Parts of this interview also appear in slightly reworked and fictionalized form in the conclusion to Foucault's *L'Archéologie du savoir* (Paris: Gallimard, 1969), 259–75; *The Archaeology of Knowledge and the Discourse on Language* (New York: Pantheon, 1972), 199–211. At the Center for Research in Modern European Philosophy, under the title "Concept and Form: The *Cahiers pour l'analyse* and Contemporary French Thought," Peter Hallward currently heads the ambitious and long-overdue project of translating and editing the most important contributions from this journal to French theory, philosophy, science, and psychoanalysis.

41 Jacques-Alain Miller, "La Suture (Éléments de la logique du signifiant)," *Cahiers pour l'analyse* 1 (1966): 37–49; and Jacques-Alain Miller, "Matrice," *Ornicar?* 4 (1975). Badiou will rely on this second article in his *Théorie du sujet* and more recently still refers to both texts as canonical in another footnote to *The Century*: "Two articles by Jacques-Alain Miller remain canonical in terms of what happens to the concept of the subject when the latter is determined by a logic of which it is not the centre but rather the lateral effect" (*Le Siècle*, 143n1; *The Century*, 211). About Miller's "La Suture" Badiou also writes: "His text founds a certain regime of compatibility between structuralism and the Lacanian theory of the subject. I am myself periodically brought back to this foundation, albeit only on condition of disrupting it somewhat. Twenty-five years later, 'I am here; I am still here' " (Badiou, "Note complémentaire sur un usage contemporain de Frege," *Le Nombre et les nombres*, 36; "Additional Note on a Contemporary Usage of Frege," *Number and Numbers*, 24). An earlier translation of this chapter from *Number and Numbers* can be found in *Umbr(a)*, with a commentary by Sam Gillespie, "Hegel Unsutured (An Addendum to Badiou)," *Umbr(a)* 1 (1996): 57–69. Miller recently reissued most of his juvenilia in *Un Début dans la vie* (Paris: Gallimard, 2002). In English see "Suture (Elements of the Logic of the Signifier)," translated by Jacqueline Rose, *Screen* 18, no. 4 (1978): 24–34; "Matrix," translated by Daniel G. Collins, *Lacanian Ink* 12 (1997): 45–51; and "Action of the Structure," translated by Peter Bradley, *The Symptom* 10 (spring 2009), www.lacan.com.

42 See Slavoj Žižek, *Le Plus sublime des hystériques: Hegel passe* (Paris: Point Hors Ligne, 1988); and Slavoj Žižek, *Ils ne savent pas ce qu'ils font: Le Sinthome idéologique* (Paris: Point Hors Ligne, 1990). Translations of this two-volume work

can be found, with numerous changes and additions, in *The Sublime Object of Ideology* (London: Verso, 1989); *For They Know Not What They Do: Enjoyment as Political Factor* (London: Verso, 1991); and *The Metastases of Enjoyment: Six Essays on Woman and Causality* (London: Verso, 1994). It should be noted that similar titles in English and French by no means cover identical tables of content. Žižek, furthermore, only seems to stick to the same basic Lacanian concepts, but in fact these terms often receive dramatically different interpretations. His dialogue with contemporary thinkers, finally, offers a superb example of the Machiavellian art of war in philosophy—often implicitly presenting an opponent's positions as being entirely his own before explicitly attacking them for reasons that in fact apply only to an earlier position of his. Many criticisms in Žižek's books can and must thus be read as self-criticisms, so that a coherent overall interpretation of this vast body of work is quickly becoming a fascinating impossibility. For a practical refutation of this impossibility, informed by a thorough knowledge of Badiou's philosophy as well, see the outstanding work of Adrian Johnston, *Žižek's Ontology: A Transcendental Materialist Theory of Subjectivity* (Evanston: Northwestern University Press, 2008).

43 Slavoj Žižek, *In Defense of Lost Causes* (London: Verso, 2008), 3.

44 Slavoj Žižek, "The Politics of Truth, or, Alain Badiou as a Reader of St. Paul," in *The Ticklish Subject: The Absent Centre of Political Ontology* (London: Verso, 1999), 127–70; and Alain Badiou, *Ethics: An Essay on the Understanding of Evil*, translated by Peter Hallward (London: Verso, 2001). The latter work also contains a useful bibliography and translator's introduction in which Hallward anticipates some of the criticisms from his *Badiou: A Subject to Truth*. See also Peter Hallward, "Generic Sovereignty: The Philosophy of Alain Badiou," *Angelaki: Journal of the Theoretical Humanities* 3, no. 3 (1998): 87–111. Hallward's criticisms, which target above all the sovereign, absolutist, and nonrelational tendencies in Badiou's thought, coincide to some extent with the argument against dogmatism made by Žižek. In his introduction to Badiou's *Ethics*, however, Hallward already seems to have tempered these criticisms quite a bit and pays more attention to the situated and impure specificity of all truth processes, along the lines of the materialist reading I present here.

45 Ernesto Laclau and Chantal Mouffe, *Hegemony and Socialist Strategy: Towards a Radical Democratic Politics* (London: Verso, 1985). For a useful didactic overview of the common doctrine of Laclau, Mouffe, and Žižek see Yannis Stavrakakis, *Lacan and the Political* (London: Routledge, 1999). Jason Barker discusses Badiou's work in the context of post-Marxism in "De l'État au maître: Badiou et le post-marxisme," in *Écrits autour de la pensée d'Alain Badiou*, 187–93. By contrast, for a Badiou-inspired critique of the political philosophy of radical democracy, which is tied to the doctrine of structural causality, see chapter 8 below.

46 Laclau and Mouffe, *Hegemony and Socialist Strategy*, 111.

47 Ibid., 88n1.

48 Badiou, "Le (Re)commencement du matérialisme dialectique," 457n23. For fur-

ther explanations Badiou refers to Miller's "La Suture" and to Claude Lévi-Strauss's classic "Introduction à l'œuvre de Mauss," in Marcel Mauss, *Sociologie et anthropologie* (Paris: PUF, 1950). Compare also Gilles Deleuze's explanations about the role of the "empty place" in the structure, in "A Quoi reconnaît-on le structuralisme?" in *La Philosophie au XXe siècle*, edited by François Châtelet (Paris: Hachette, 1973; Bruxelles: Marabout, 1979), 292–329; available in English as "How Do We Recognize Structuralism?" in *Desert Islands and Other Texts, 1953–1974*, edited by David Lapoujade, translated by Michael Taormina (New York: Semiotext(e), 2004), 175–92, and what I take to be Badiou's implicit reading of this text in his *Deleuze*, 57–63; 36–39. For Žižek, however, "the basic gesture of 'structuralism' is to reduce the imaginary richness to a formal network of symbolic relations: what escapes the structuralist perspective is that this formal structure is itself tied by an umbilical cord to some radically contingent material element which, in its pure particularity, 'is' the structure, embodies it. Why? Because the big Other, the symbolic order, is always *barré*, failed, crossed-out, mutilated, and the contingent material element embodies this internal blockage, limit, of the symbolic structure" (Žižek, *The Sublime Object of Ideology*, 183). For a discussion of the role of the "empty place" or "nonplace" in the transition from structuralism to poststructuralism see my "Nonplaces: An Anecdoted Topography of Contemporary French Theory," in "New Coordinates: Spatial Mappings, National Trajectories," edited by Bob Davidson and Joan Ramon Resina, a special issue of *diacritics* 33, nos. 3–4 (2003): 117–39.

49 Žižek, *The Sublime Object of Ideology*, 163.

50 Ibid., 209; and Ernesto Laclau, preface to *The Sublime Object of Ideology*, xiv–xv. Žižek usually rejects any proximity to deconstruction, except in phrasings such as these about conditions of impossibility being at the same time positive conditions of possibility, while Derrida has always remained a constant reference for Laclau.

51 Ernesto Laclau, *New Reflections on the Revolution of Our Time* (London: Verso, 1990), 92.

52 Žižek, *The Sublime Object of Ideology*, 5. At the end of *Theory of the Subject*, faced with the tiresome question of ideology, Badiou asks: "What more is there to add, except the evident viscosity of their entwining, to the different formulations of the 'human condition,' dogmatically exalted in its power as absolute (art and religion) or sceptically reduced to its deficiency and to the inexorability of death? To show that all this sticks to our skin in the form of a transcendent denial of the class struggle goes no further than the certified report of some materialist bailiff" (*Théorie du sujet*, 317–18; *Theory of the Subject*, 302).

53 Žižek, *The Sublime Object of Ideology*, 44. On the level of theoretical anecdotes I am tempted to counter this objection by recalling how Althusser explains his absence from Lacan's seminar, which he himself had invited to the École at rue d'Ulm: "I don't attend: which is the climax of enjoyment. Absence. A funny absence. There are funny absences, good absences" (Althusser, *Ecrits sur la psychanalyse*, 11). This thought should no doubt be tied to Althusser's general

reflection, in a letter to his analyst, about the efficacy of determinate absence. From a more theoretical perspective, moreover, Althusser himself ends these last texts on psychoanalysis by questioning the instability of Freud's two founding notions of fantasy and drive. Finally, the reader will find an exemplary analysis of fantasy as the ultimate support of ideology and identity in Althusser's vitriolic intervention during and after the meeting in which Lacan announced the dissolution of his School.

54 Žižek, *The Metastases of Enjoyment*, 62. The fact that there is always a subject *par excellence* (the subject of lack) as well as the real *par excellence* (the real as enjoyment, or surplus-enjoyment) is symptomatic of the mechanism by which Žižek produces the irrefutable radicalism of his antiphilosophical act—an act that should *not* be confused with Badiou's notion of the event. For a more detailed account of the difference between the philosophical treatment of the event and the antiphilosophical preference for the act see Bruno Bosteels, "Radical Antiphilosophy," *Filozofski Vestnik* 29, no. 2 (2009): 155–87, esp. 177–78.

55 Žižek, *The Metastases of Enjoyment*, 61; Žižek, *The Sublime Object of Ideology*, 124.

56 Žižek, *The Metastases of Enjoyment*, 135–36n18.

57 Žižek, *In Defense of Lost Causes*, 288–89. See also Badiou's conclusion about the structural dialectic: "The cause is lost. The loss is lost" (*Théorie du sujet*, 246; *Theory of the Subject*, 230).

58 Badiou, "Le (Re)commencement du matérialisme dialectique," 445.

59 Badiou, *Deleuze*, 8; 2; and *Théorie du sujet*, 13; *Theory of the Subject*, xl.

CHAPTER 2. LACK AND DESTRUCTION

1 These texts are taken up posthumously, under the apt subheadings of "Textes de crise" and "Louis Althusser après Althusser," in *Écrits philosophiques et politiques*, edited by François Matheron (Paris: Stock/IMEC, 1994), 1:367–537, 553–94; in English: "Marx in His Limits" and "The Underground Current of the Materialism of the Encounter" can be found in Louis Althusser, *Philosophy of the Encounter: Later Writings, 1978–1987*, edited by François Matheron and Oliver Corpet, translated by G. M. Goshgarian (London: Verso, 2006), 7–207. For the importance of these texts see, among others, Gregory Elliott, "Ghostlier Demarcations: On the Posthumous Edition of Althusser's Writings," *Radical Philosophy* 90 (1998): 20–32.

2 Althusser, "Le Courant souterrain du matérialisme de la rencontre," in *Écrits philosophiques et politiques*, 1:584; "The Underground Current of the Materialism of the Encounter," in *Philosophy of the Encounter*, 196. For a short, slightly bitter, criticism of this unfinished text see Pierre Ramond, "Le Matérialisme d'Althusser," in *Althusser philosophe*, edited by Pierre Ramond (Paris: PUF, 1997), 167–79. A positive evaluation can be found in Antonio Negri, "Notes on the Evolution of the Thought of the Later Althusser," in *Postmodern Materialism and the Future of Marxist Theory: Essays in the Althusserian Tradition*, edited by Antonio Callari and David F. Ruccio (Hanover: University Press of New

England / Wesleyan University Press, 1996), 51–68; see also Miguel E. Vatter, "Machiavelli after Marx: The Self-Overcoming of Marxism in the Late Althusser," *Theory & Event* 7, no. 4 (2005). Althusser's official opinion about the
university crisis, which is obviously one of the immediate causes of May 1968,
can be appreciated in "Problèmes étudiants," *La Nouvelle Critique* 152 (Jan.
1964): 80–111; and, after the events, in "À propos de l'article de Michel Verret sur
Mai étudiant," *La Pensée* 145 (June 1969); and in a letter to Maria Antonia
Macciocchi reproduced in *Lettere dall'interno del PCI a Louis Althusser*. Here
Althusser posits: "An encounter may occur or not occur. It can be a 'brief
encounter,' relatively accidental, in which case it will not lead to any *fusion* of
forces. This was the case in May, where the meeting workers / employees on the
one hand and students and young intellectuals on the other was a brief encounter which did not lead, for a whole series of reasons I will mention very briefly
and very generally, to any kind of *fusion*" (letter of March 15, 1969, quoted in
M. A. Macciocchi, *Letters from inside the Italian Communist Party to Louis Althusser* (London: NLB, 1973), 306–7. Rancière speaks in this regard about a
double play on Althusser's part, "militant communist on the side of the court-
yard, antirevisionist Maoist theoretician on the side of the garden," and he
concludes: "Althusser has no more chances to catch the revolution than Achilles
the tortoise" (Jacques Rancière, *La Leçon d'Althusser* [Paris: Gallimard, 1974],
50, 137n1). It is worthwhile to contrast these Althusserian statements with Badiou's almost instantaneous analysis in "Brouillon d'un commencement," first
published toward the end of 1968 in the Belgian journal *Textures* and recently
reissued as part of *L'Hypothèse communiste: Circonstances, 5* (Paris: Nouvelles
Éditions Lignes, 2009), 59–73; in English, "Outline of a Beginning," in *The
Communist Hypothesis*, translated by David Macey and Steve Corcoran (London: Verso, 2010), 68–90. This last volume also contains an analysis on the
occasion of the most recent anniversary of the events in which Badiou, without
being blind to the weaknesses of the revolt at the level of new forms of political
organization, interprets the "linkage" or "fusion" between the workers' movement and the student movement, by passing through the libertarian or cultural
component. See "Mai 68 revisité, quarante ans après," *L'Hypothèse communiste*,
39–57; "May '68 Revisited, 40 Years On," in *The Communist Hypothesis*, 43–
67. This analysis, in many ways, is diametrically opposed to Althusser's with
regard to the nonencounter: "All the initiatives that allowed us to circulate
between these three heterogeneous movements, and especially between the
student movement and the workers' movement, were our treasure-trove" (50;
57–58). For Badiou, in any case, we should not exaggerate the importance of
May 1968 per se according to the mysticism of some "grand" event, which would
be to the detriment of the consequences of this event, not fully realized until the
1970s, in French Maoism: "May '68 is an ambiguous episode, situated between
the dismal festive and sexual ideology that still encumbers us and the far more
original levy of a direct alliance between students and young workers. It is in the

period between Autumn 1968 and Autumn 1979—from the creation of Maoist factory cells to the strikes of Sonacotra—that the truly creative consequences of the second aspect of May '68 work themselves out. As happens in practically all the becomings of a subject of truth, this set of consequences—which we can call 'Maoist politics'—strongly prevails, in terms of both interest for thinking and universality, over the event 'May '68,' which lends it its subjective possibility" (Badiou, *Logiques des mondes*, 589; *Logics of Worlds*, 566 [translation slightly modified]).

3 Badiou, *Théorie de la contradiction*, 9; and Badiou with Balmès, *De l'idéologie*, 7. I will return to these two booklets to consider them in greater detail in my conclusion. In any case it would be interesting to compare Badiou and Balmès's critique of the Althusserian theory of ideology with that formulated by Rancière in "Sur la théorie de l'idéologie," a text written in 1969 and taken up in his *La Leçon d'Althusser*, 227–77.

4 Badiou and Balmès, *De l'idéologie*, 19. A summary of this early phase of Badiou's writings can be found in Jason Barker, "Maoist Beginnings," in *Alain Badiou: A Critical Introduction* (London: Pluto, 2002), 12–38. See chapter 3 below for a more detailed analysis.

5 For a discussion of Badiou's response to André Glucksmann and to the duo of Christian Jambet and Guy Lardreau see chapter 3. Badiou defines the subjectivity of these ex-Maoist apostasies and renegacies in "Qu'est-ce qu'un Thermidorien?" in *Abrégé de métapolitique*, 139–54; "What Is a Thermidorean?" *Metapolitics*, 124–40. See also Badiou, "Roads to Renegacy: Interview by Eric Hazan," translated by David Fernbach, *New Left Review* 53 (Sept.–Oct. 2008): 125–33.

6 See the appendix in Jacques Lacan, *Le Séminaire de Jacques Lacan*, edited by Jacques-Alain Miller, *Livre XVII: L'Envers de la psychanalyse* (Paris: Seuil, 1991), 239; *The Seminar of Jacques Lacan*, edited by Jacques-Alain Miller, *Book XVII: The Other Side of Psychoanalysis*, translated by Russell Grigg (New York: W. W. Norton, 2007), 207. I refer the reader in particular to the commentaries in the special volume *Jacques Lacan and the Other Side of Psychoanalysis*, edited by Justin Clemens and Russell Grigg (Durham: Duke University Press, 2006); and more recently to Jean-Michel Rabaté, "68 + 1: Lacan's *année érotique*," *Parrhesia* 6 (2009): 28–45.

7 In recent texts, admittedly, Žižek also frequently turns to Badiou for positive support while continuing to criticize Rancière's celebrations of short-lived outbursts of aestheticized revolt: "Peter Hallward is right to point out that, in today's 'society of the spectacle' such an aesthetic reconfiguration has lost its subversive dimension: it can easily be appropriated into the existing order. The true task lies not in momentary democratic explosions which undermine the established 'police' order, but in the dimension designated by Badiou as that of 'fidelity' to the Event: translating/inscribing the democratic explosion into the positive 'police' order, imposing on social reality a *new* lasting order" (Žižek, *In Defense of Lost Causes*, 418–19).

8 Badiou, *Théorie du sujet*, 24; *Theory of the Subject*, 6.

9 Ibid., 32, 40; 14, 22. Badiou devotes an entire chapter of *The Century* to the particularly violent episode of the struggle in the ideological history of the Chinese Cultural Revolution, between the defendants of the idea that "Two fuse into One" and the adherents of "One divides into Two." See *Le Siècle*, 89–101; *The Century*, 58–67. See also Badiou's earlier commentary in *Le Noyau rationnel de la dialectique hégélienne*.

10 Badiou, *Théorie du sujet*, 29–30; *Theory of the Subject*, 12. One of Althusser's most breathtaking texts, "Le 'Piccolo,' Bertolazzi et Brecht," in *Pour Marx*, is the closest he comes to Badiou's philosophy and theory of the subject, including the false dialectic of melodrama, which opposes the Hegelian beautiful soul to the corrupt outside world, and the following, extremely condensed version of dialectical time in the process of torsion: "A time in which some history must take place. A time moved from within by an irresistible force, producing its own content. It is a dialectical time *par excellence*. A time that abolishes the other one," that is, the empty time without history, together with "the structure of its spatial figuration" (*Pour Marx*, 137; *For Marx*, 137).

11 Badiou, *Théorie du sujet*, 30; *Theory of the Subject*, 12. Badiou illustrates this dialectic with a lengthy excursion into the ancient history of the Christian Church, with its twin heresies: "rightist" Arianism, for whom Christ is wholly mortal, pure P; and "leftist" Gnosticism, for whom God is inhumanely divine, pure A. Given this crucial rereading of Hegel's dialectic and the history of Christianity, it is quite surprising to see that Badiou's *Théorie du sujet* is not even so much as mentioned in Judith Butler's *Subjects of Desire: Hegelian Reflections in Twentieth-Century France* (New York: Columbia University Press, 1999).

12 I discuss the risk of a speculative-leftist scheme in Rancière's own *Disagreement* in my contribution to the international conference on Rancière's work, held at Cérisy-la-Salle in May 2005. See Bruno Bosteels, "La Leçon de Rancière: Malaise dans la politique ou on a raison de se mésentendre," in *La Philosophie déplacée: Autour de Jacques Rancière*, edited by Laurence Cornu and Patrice Vermeren (Lyon: Horlieu, 2006), 49–70; in English: "Rancière's Leftism, or, Politics and Its Discontents," in *Jacques Rancière: History, Politics, Aesthetics*, edited by Gabriel Rockhill and Philip Watts (Durham: Duke University Press, 2009), 158–75.

13 Badiou, *Théorie du sujet*, 60, 30; *Theory of the Subject*, 42, 12.

14 Lacan, *Écrits* (Paris: Seuil, 1966), 861.

15 Badiou, *Théorie du sujet*, 81; *Theory of the Subject*, 63.

16 Ibid., 89; 71.

17 Ibid., 151–52; 133–34. Later on, Badiou will adopt and rephrase this Lacanian definition of the subject, as that which one signifier S_1 represents to another signifier S_2, so as to define a subject as that which an event E_1 represents to another event E_2: "A subject, thus a politics, is the in-between of an event to be elucidated and an event that elucidates. It is that which an event represents to another event" (Badiou, *Peut-on penser la politique?*, 101). This goes to show

the potentially misleading, overly structural-ontological, orientation of Badiou's later work up to and including *Being and Event*, the inevitable one-sidedness of which should be supplemented with the topological orientation of a (new) theory of the subject. This will be accomplished in *Logics of Worlds*, which in this regard stands as an implicit self-criticism of the point of view presented in *Can Politics Be Thought?* and *Being and Event*, all the while taking up again certain arguments from *Theory of the Subject*. Badiou mentions these self-criticisms in the preface to the English translation of his *Ethics*: "This idea presumed, in effect, that there were two events rather than one (the event-event and the event-naming), and likewise two subjects rather than one (the subject who names the event, and the subject who is faithful to this naming)" (Alain Badiou, *L'Éthique: Essai sur la conscience du mal* [Paris: NOUS, 2003], 12–13 [this is the second edition of *L'Éthique*; the first, which is the edition I use elsewhere in this book, was published by Hatier in 1993]; *Ethics: An Essay on the Understanding of Evil* [London: Verso, 2001], lvi). See also the preface to the Spanish translation of *Being and Event*, "Prólogo a la edición castellana," in *El ser y el acontecimiento*, translated by Raúl J. Cerdeiras, Alejandro A. Cerletti, and Nilda Prados (Buenos Aires: Manantial, 1999), 5–8.

18 Badiou, *Théorie du sujet*, 52, 115; *Theory of the Subject*, 96, 34.

19 Ibid., 126; 113. See also Lacan, *Le Séminaire de Jacques Lacan*, edited by Jacques-Alain Miller, *Livre XX: Encore* (Paris: Seuil, 1975), 79; *The Seminar of Jacques Lacan*, edited by Jacques-Alain Miller, *Book XX: Encore, 1972–1973*, translated by Bruce Fink (New York: W. W. Norton, 1998), 86 (translation modified). Lacan's original sentence is nearly untranslatable: "Quand un fait deux, il n'y a jamais de retour. Ça ne revient pas à faire de nouveau un, même un nouveau." Fink translates: "When one gives rise to two, there is never a return. They don't revert to making one again, even if it is a new one."

20 Badiou, *Théorie du sujet*, 200; *Theory of the Subject*, 184.

21 Ibid., 202; 185–86. An entire segment of this work is thus devoted to a "Retournement matérialiste du matérialisme" (*Théorie du sujet*, 193–255; "A Materialist Reversal of Materialism," *Theory of the Subject*, 177–239).

22 Ibid., 204; 188.

23 Ibid., 150–51; 133. Elsewhere Badiou also writes: "Lacan's last effort, after having unfolded [reading *déployé* for the obvious typo of *déploré*, unfortunately left standing in the existing English translation] the theory of the subject's subservience to the signifying rule, was meant to push as far as possible the investigation of its relation to the real. The signifying rules were no longer sufficient for this purpose. What was needed in a way was a geometry of the unconscious, a new figuration of the three instances in which the subject-effect unfolds itself (symbolic, imaginary, real). Lacan's recourse to topology was an internal requirement born of this new stage of his thinking, which evinces his deep-seated materialism" (*Petit panthéon portatif*, 13–14; *Pocket Pantheon*, 3 [translation corrected]). Žižek sums this up even more concisely: "Therein resides the shift in

Lacan's work announced by his *Seminar VII* on the ethics of psychoanalysis: the shift from the axis I-S to the axis S-R" (Žižek, *In Defense of Lost Causes*, 396).

24 Badiou, *Théorie du sujet*, 145; *Theory of the Subject*, 127.

25 Ibid., 243–44; 227–28.

26 Ibid., 149; 131.

27 Ibid., 41; 23. In the Lacanian École freudienne de Paris the procedure of *la passe* instated in 1967 describes the end of a training analysis when the position of the analysand gives way to that of the analyst, that is, the end of analysis testified by the *passant* to a committee of *passeurs* or "passers" who in turn relay the account to a jury that decides whether or not to award the "pass." Badiou's use of the concept in *Theory of the Subject* and *Being and Event* is clearly inspired by this definition, but it is not restricted to the therapeutic situation. In *Theory of the Subject* Badiou refers to the heated debates provoked by this procedure up to ten years after its introduction by Lacan (who, upon listening in silence to the formal complaints raised at a meeting in 1978, went so far as to call it a "complete failure"). In addition, Badiou systematically plays on the dialectic between *passe* and *impasse* (sometimes spelled *im-passe*, with a hyphen, so as to highlight the pun), in a key argument that will reappear in *Being and Event*. For Lacan's original proposition see "Proposition du 9 octobre 1967 sur le psychanalyste de l'École," *Scilicet* 1 (1968): 14–30; repr. in Jacques Lacan, *Autres écrits* (Paris: Seuil, 2001), 243–59. Among the numerous discussions of this analytical procedure I want to mention the testimonies in the collective volume *La Passe et le réel: Témoignages imprévus sur la fin de l'analyse* (Paris: Agalma, 1998).

28 Badiou, *Théorie du sujet*, 27, 59; *Theory of the Subject*, 8, 41. The two sentences are nearly untranslatable: "Tout ça qui est se rapporte à ça dans une distance de ça qui tient au lieu où ça est" and "Il arrive, disons, que '*ça fasse je,*'" whereby the emphasis falls on the "doing" or "making," *faire*, of a process, which is not just a *werden*, a "becoming" or "coming-into-being" as in Freud's original formulation: *Wo es war, soll Ich werden.*

29 Ibid., 307; 291.

30 Lacan, *Le Séminaire de Jacques Lacan*, edited by Jacques-Alain Miller, *Livre I: Les Écrits techniques de Freud* (Paris: Seuil, 1975), 119; *The Seminar of Jacques Lacan*, edited by Jacques-Alain Miller, *Book I: Freud's Papers on Technique, 1953–1954*, translated by John Forrester (New York: W. W. Norton, 1988), 102.

31 Badiou, *Théorie du sujet*, 309; *Theory of the Subject*, 157.

32 Ibid., 176–77, 310; 160, 294.

33 Ibid., 176–77; 159.

34 Ibid., 277; 261. For a further discussion of this alternative, between the empty place of power and the excess over this empty place, with reference to the sinister future of the Left in the aftermath of 1968, not only in France but also and especially in Mexico, see Bruno Bosteels, "Travesías del fantasma: Pequeña metapolítica del 68 en México," *Metapolítica* 12 (1999): 733–68; in English: "The Melancholy Left: Specters of 1968 in Mexico and Beyond," in *(1968) Episodes of*

Culture in Contest, edited by Cathy Crane and Nicholas Muellner (Cambridge: Cambridge Scholars Publishing, 2008), 74–90.

35 Judith Butler, *Antigone's Claim: Kinship between Life and Death* (New York: Columbia University Press, 2000), 57.

36 See Jacques Derrida, *Force de loi* (Paris: Galilée, 1994), 121; in English: "Force of Law: The 'Mystical Foundation of Authority,'" translated by Mary Quaintance, in *Acts of Religion,* edited by Gil Anidjar (New York: Routledge, 2002), 286.

37 Badiou, *Théorie du sujet,* 178; *Theory of the Subject,* 161. In the final theses of his *Rhapsodie pour le théâtre* (Paris: Imprimerie Nationale, 1990) Badiou implicitly raises an even more wide-ranging question: Why should tragedy be the model for our theory of the subject? Why not comedy? His answer is that the social taboo on stereotypes makes a contemporary comedy nearly impossible: "Today, the tiniest Aristophanes would be dragged into court for defamation, and the play would be prohibited in a summary judgment, to be enforced immediately. There can be no comedy, in the classical sense, where corporations and private owners hold the right over their public image" ("Rhapsody for the Theatre: A Short Philosophical Treatise," translated by Bruno Bosteels, *Theatre Survey* 49, no. 2 [2008]: 187–238, 233). This brief treatise, with its play on the analytic and the dialectic in the prolonged analogy between theater and politics, is in many ways the closest relative of *Theory of the Subject* among Badiou's later works.

38 Badiou, *Théorie du sujet,* 182; *Theory of the Subject,* 165.

39 Ibid., 179; 162.

40 Butler, *Antigone's Claim,* 10, 28.

41 Badiou, *Théorie du sujet,* 163; *Theory of the Subject,* 145.

42 Ibid.

43 Ibid., 164; 146. Badiou is referring to a brief passage in Lacan, *Le Séminaire,* edited by Jacques-Alain Miller, *Livre XI: Les Quatre concepts fondamentaux de la psychanalyse* (Paris: Seuil, 1973; Points, 1990), 49–50; *The Four Fundamental Concepts of Psycho-Analysis,* translated by Alan Sheridan (New York: W. W. Norton, 1981), 51. Here Lacan himself, in answer to a question from Pierre Kaufman, refers back to his seminar from the previous year (1962–63), devoted entirely to the topic of anxiety but published only recently and, thus, not available to Badiou at the time of writing *Theory of the Subject.* See Jacques Lacan, *Le Séminaire de Jacques Lacan,* edited by Jacques-Alain Miller, *Livre X: L'Angoisse* (Paris: Seuil, 2004). More recently, Badiou has written a brief review of this edition, "Angoisse chez Lacan," in *Agenda de la pensée contemporaine: Printemps 2005* (Paris: PUF, 2005), 27–29; available in English as Badiou, "Lacan. Seminar, Book X: Anxiety," *Lacanian Ink* 26 (2005): 70–71. For more detailed accounts of Lacan's understanding of anxiety see Bernard Baas, "L'Angoisse et la vérité," *Le Désir pur* (Louvain: Peeters, 1992), 83–119; as well as Renata Salecl, *On Anxiety* (New York: Routledge, 2004). I should add that Badiou also does not (or again, given the dates of publication, could not) discuss Lacan's own interpretation of Antigone, in *Le Séminaire de Jacques Lacan,* edited by Jacques-Alain Miller, *Livre*

VII: *L'Éthique de la psychanalyse* (Paris: Seuil, 1986); *The Seminar of Jacques Lacan*, edited by Jacques-Alain Miller, *Book VII: The Ethics of Psychoanalysis, 1959–1960*, translated by Dennis Porter (New York: W. W. Norton, 1997). Within the vast bibliography on Antigone and psychoanalysis, or on tragedy and psychoanalysis in general, a superb example remains Zupančič's "Ethics and Tragedy in Psychoanalysis," in Alenka Zupančič, *Ethics of the Real*, 170–248. For a commentary on Lacan's seminar *The Ethics of Psychoanalysis*, see Marc de Kesel, *Eros & Ethiek: Een lectuur van Jacques Lacans Séminaire VII* (Leuven: Acco, 2002); and, on Antigone in particular, see Philippe Lacoue-Labarthe, "De l'éthique: À propos d'*Antigone*," *Lacan avec les philosophes* (Paris: Albin Michel, 1991), 19–36.

44 Badiou, *Théorie du sujet*, 164, 173; *Theory of the Subject*, 146, 156.

45 Ibid., 183; 166. I will not discuss the extent to which this reading of return and exile is meant as a corrective to Hölderlin's reading of Sophocles. See Friedrich Hölderlin, *Essays and Letters on Theory*, edited and translated by Thomas Pfau (Albany: State University of New York Press, 1988), 101–16. Nor will I go into further details regarding either Badiou's overall relation to Hölderlin or the latter's role, including in a direct criticism of Badiou, for someone like the late Philippe Lacoue-Labarthe. A good starting point to address this polemic would be to compare Badiou's meditation on Hölderlin in *Being and Event* with Lacoue-Labarthe's answers to the notion of the "age of the poets" that Badiou proposes in his "L'Âge des poètes," part of a seminar edited by Jacques Rancière, *La Politique des poètes: Pourquoi des poètes en temps de détresse* (Paris: Albin Michel, 1992), 21–63. As part of the cycle of conferences of Le Perroquet organized by Badiou, Lacoue-Labarthe also presented his talk "Le Courage du poète" on Hölderlin. Several texts in this polemic have been compiled and translated in Philippe Lacoue-Labarthe, *Heidegger and the Politics of Poetry*, translated by Jeff Port (Urbana: University of Illinois Press, 2007). See also, in the same volume, the translator's introduction, titled "The Courage of Thought" (ix–xviii). For Lacoue-Labarthe's own independent approach to Hölderlin's theater in general and Antigone in particular see *Métaphrase, suivi de Le théâtre de Hölderlin* (Paris: PUF, 1998).

46 Badiou, *Théorie du sujet*, 183; *Theory of the Subject*, 166.

47 Ibid., 176; 159.

48 Ibid., 174; 157.

49 For Walter Benjamin's original text see *Zur Kritik der Gewalt und andere Aufsätze*, edited by Herbert Marcuse (Frankfurt am Main: Suhrkamp, 1965); in English: "Critique of Violence," *Reflections: Essays, Aphorisms, Autobiographical Writings*, edited by Peter Demetz (New York: Schocken, 1978), 277–300.

50 Badiou, *Théorie du sujet*, 180; *Theory of the Subject*, 163. Of course, Badiou also discusses issues of law, right, and justice in other places of his work; see, e.g., "Paul contre la loi," in *Saint Paul: La fondation de l'universalisme* (Paris: PUF, 1997), 79–89; "Paul against the Law," in *Saint Paul: The Foundation of Universal-*

ism, translated by Ray Brassier (Stanford: Stanford University Press, 2003), 75–85; in *D'un désastre obscur (Droit, État, Politique)* (La Tour d'Aigues: Éditions de l'Aube, 1991; new edition with the subtitle *Sur la fin de la vérité d'État*, 1998); in English: "Of an Obscure Disaster: On the End of the Truth of the State," translated by Barbara P. Fulks, *Lacanian Ink* 22 (2003): 58–89; and in *L'Éthique*, 10–12; *Ethics*, 8–10. However, these discussions are all too brief and rather minor in scope when compared to the pivotal reflections on law and nonlaw in *Theory of the Subject.*

51 Žižek, *For They Know Not What They Do*, lxxxiii. I answer some of these objections, which Žižek raised against my earlier reading of Badiou's *Theory of the Subject*, in "Badiou without Žižek."

52 Žižek, "On Alain Badiou and *Logiques des mondes*," www.lacan.com/zizbadman .htm. See also Žižek, *In Defense of Lost Causes*, 394–96.

53 Derrida, *Force de loi*, 93–94; "Force of Law," 272.

54 Ibid., 46; 248–49. It is intriguing to note how Lacan, contrary to Derrida, insists that with regard to anxiety the fundamental question is *always* one of economizing, canalizing or administering it in measured amounts: "In experience, it is necessary to canalize it and, if I may say so, to take it in small doses, so that one is not overcome by it. This is a difficulty similar to that of bringing the subject into contact with the real" (*Le Séminaire de Jacques Lacan*, edited by Jacques-Alain Miller, *Livre XI: Les Quatre concepts fondamentaux de la psychanalyse*, 49–50; *The Four Fundamental Concepts of Psycho-Analysis*, 50).

55 Derrida, *Force de loi*, 87; "Force of Law," 269.

56 Ibid., 39–40; 245. To this rhetorical question, "Est-il jamais possible de dire: je sais que je suis juste" (Is it ever possible to say: I know that I am just?), which Derrida himself does not hesitate to answer in the negative, I am tempted to oppose Beckett's affirmation from *Comment c'est*, which Badiou often quotes and according to which "en tout cas on est dans la justice je n'ai jamais entendu dire le contraire" (in any case we have our being in justice I have never heard anything to the contrary). See Alain Badiou, *Beckett: L'Increvable désir* (Paris: Hachette, 1995), 53; *On Beckett*, edited by Alberto Toscano and Nina Power (London: Clinamen, 2003), 64. Again, Badiou's point in *Logics of Worlds* and *The Century* is quite the opposite of Derrida's: all fidelity (of love, politics, and so on) worth the name is to a present and not to ruins from the past or to the future of what is to-come: "Besides, I'm convinced that the subjective capacities of action, courage or even resignation are always in the present tense. Who has ever done anything in the name of an undetermined future?" (*Le Siècle*, 36; *The Century*, 20). Contrast this with Derrida's proposal to draw "a short treatise on the love of ruins" from Benjamin's work: "What else is there to love, anyway? One cannot love a monument, a work of architecture, an institution as such except in an experience itself precarious in its fragility: it has not always been there, it will not always be there, it is finite. . . . How can one love otherwise than in this finitude?" (*Force de loi*, 105; "Force of Law," 278).

57 Derrida, *Force de loi*, 89; "Force of Law," 269–70.

58 Badiou, *Théorie du sujet*, 173; *Theory of the Subject*, 156.

59 Ibid., 158; 140.

60 Ibid., 159–60; 142.

61 Ibid., 160; 142.

62 Butler, *Antigone's Claim*, 21. Not surprisingly, these are also the kinds of criticism —defending pure voluntarism or radical anarchy—most commonly hurled at Badiou as well.

63 Alain Badiou, *De quoi Sarkozy est-il le nom? Circonstances, 4* (Paris: Lignes, 2007), 151, 130; *The Meaning of Sarkozy*, translated by David Fernbach (London: Verso, 2008), 97 (translation slightly modified). The English word *basis* here translates Badiou's *fond*, which we could also render as *bedrock*, *ground*, or *background*. By using *fond* instead of *base* (as in the International when *le monde change de base*), Badiou, I am arguing here, is hearkening back to the problematic of form and formless ground, *forme* and *fond*. On the reevaluation of Marx's problematic rapport to the Asiatic mode of production and primitive communism see Roger Bartra, ed., *El modo de producción asiático: Problemas de la historia de los países coloniales* (Mexico City: Era, 1969); and Qhananchiri [a.k.a. Álvaro García Linera], *De Demonios escondidos y momentos de revolución: Marx y la revolución social en las extremidades del cuerpo capitalista* (La Paz: Ofensiva Roja, 1991). Gayatri Chakravorty Spivak also obliquely hints at the role of the Asiatic mode of production as the name for an unsolved problem in Marx; see Gayatri Chakravorty Spivak, *A Critique of Postcolonial Reason: Toward a History of the Vanishing Present* (Cambridge: Harvard University Press, 1999), 67–111.

64 Badiou, *Manifeste pour la philosophie*, 48; *Manifesto for Philosophy*, 67.

65 Alenka Zupančič, "The Fifth Condition," in Hallward, *Think Again*, 191.

66 Badiou, *Théorie du sujet*, 109, 259; *Theory of the Subject*, 91, 243.

67 Anonymous, "Sur le XXe siècle et la politique," in *La Distance Politique* 35 (2001): 3–4. None of the articles in this newsletter bears an individual signature.

68 Badiou, *Saint Paul*, 2; *Saint Paul*, 2 (translation modified). Much more careful attention should be paid to this recent rebirth of interest in saintly figures among thinkers of the Left—from Saint Augustine for Jean-François Lyotard and León Rozitchner to Saint Paul for Badiou and Žižek all the way to Saint Francis for Michael Hardt and Toni Negri. For an initial problematization of this trend see Bruno Bosteels, "Are There Any Saints Left? León Rozitchner as a Reader of Saint Augustine," in "Cities of Men, Cities of God: Augustine and Late Secularism," edited by Leo Russ, special issue of *Polygraph: An International Journal of Culture & Politics* 19–20 (2008): 7–22.

69 Badiou, *D'un désastre obscur*, 57; "Of an Obscure Disaster," 87 (translation modified).

70 Badiou, *Abrégé de métapolitique*, 83–84; *Metapolitics*, 74–75.

71 Marx, letter to Ferdinand Freiligrath, Feb. 29, 1860, quoted in Álvaro García Linera, *La potencia plebeya: Acción colectiva e identidades indígenas, obreras y populares en Bolivia*, edited by Pablo Stefanoni (Buenos Aires: Prometeo/

CLACSO, 2008), 82. García Linera repeatedly comes back to what he considers, based on this letter, a dialectic between the party in the ephemeral sense and in the grand historical sense. For further discussion see my "The Leftist Hypothesis: Communism in the Age of Terror," in *The Idea of Communism*, edited by Costas Douzinas and Slavoj Žižek (London: Verso, 2010), 60–61.

72 Badiou, *L'Être et l'événement*, 10; *Being and Event*, 4 (translation modified).

73 Badiou, *Théorie de la contradiction*, 27, 86. For a ferocious attack on these and other comparable statements from Badiou's early Maoist work see Jean-Marie Brohm, "La Réception d'Althusser: Histoire politique d'une imposture," in Denise Avenas et al., *Contre Althusser, pour Marx* (Paris: Passion, 1999), 278–87. Just to give the reader an idea of the fierceness of this attack: Brohm describes Badiou as a "Maoist pit bull" (279n25).

74 Badiou, *L'Être et l'événement*, 446; *Being and Event*, 407 (translation modified).

75 Badiou, *L'Éthique*, 76; *Ethics*, 86.

76 Quoted and commented on at length by Althusser, *Pour Marx*, 87–88; *For Marx*, 89.

77 See the interviews reproduced in the appendices, "Can Change Be Thought?" and "Beyond Formalization."

78 Badiou, *Logiques des mondes*, 400; *Logics of Worlds*, 379–80.

79 Cf. ibid., 417; 395; and Badiou, *Théorie de la contradiction*, 86.

80 Badiou, *Logiques des mondes*, 418; *Logics of Worlds*, 396.

CHAPTER 3. ONE DIVIDES INTO TWO

1 Badiou, *Deleuze: The Clamor of Being*, 2.

2 Badiou, *Deleuze: "La clameur de l'être,"* 8.

3 Rimbaud's poem, which Badiou also uses with reference to his recollection of the structuralist years of the late 1960s and of Jacques-Alain Miller's work on structural causality in particular (see note 40 of chapter 1 above), would be worth studying in detail in this context, if for no other reason than to reproduce the tone of the era right after the Paris Commune, which also seems to fit the period of Badiou's Maoism after May 1968.

4 Badiou, *Théorie de la contradiction*, 50–51.

5 Alain Badiou, "Les 4 dialecticiens français: Pascal, Rousseau, Mallarmé, Lacan," *Le Perroquet: Quinzomadaire d'opinion* 22 (March–April 1983): 11. Much of this text, but not the passage quoted here, is integrated in Badiou, "Généalogie de la dialectique," in *Peut-on penser la politique?* 84–91. It seems to me that *"il y a des critères . . ."* in the French original should read *"il y va des critères . . . ,"* which is how I have translated the sentence, but the first option, of course, would only further confirm my thesis.

6 Badiou, *Ethics*, 42. See also "Les Deux sources du maoïsme en France," in UCFML, *Le Maoïsme, marxisme de notre temps* (Marseille: Potemkine, 1976), 7–8. Incidentally, this double allegiance brings up the problem of how two events can become entangled in one and the same situation in the first place, when Badiou

does not even entertain this as a possibility in *Being and Event*. Mao's legacy
thus time and again will bring us face to face with problems of articulation
as entanglement, encroachment, scission and mixture, in stark contrast to the
more miraculous and absolutist tendencies (or their interpretation as such) of
Badiou's major concepts.

7   Barker, *Alain Badiou*, 25. Later on, this same author admits: "Badiou's avowed
aim in *Being and the Event* is to leave behind the 'still-born' legacy of dialectical
materialism. However, the traces of Marxism—and Maoism—arguably persist,
here and there, despite the introduction of this radical, 'post-Cantorian' variety
of what Badiou names 'subtractive ontology' " (84).

8   Hallward, *Badiou*, 30. While I am in agreement with the thesis of continuity, my
own reading of Badiou's philosophy throughout this book stresses other concepts as being more properly decisive for understanding this continuity: concepts such as scission, or the process of purification, rather than the pure as such;
situatedness, or the symptomatic site of an event, rather than the singular in and
of itself; and forcing, or the reapplication of a generic extension onto the situation of departure, rather than the affirmation of generic universality as such.

9   Badiou, *L'Être et l'événement*, 365; *Being and Event*, 331 (translation modified).

10 See Mao, *Quotations from Chairman Mao Tsetung* (Beijing: Foreign Languages
Press, 1972), 230–36.

11 Ibid., 230. In French the word used for "investigation" is precisely *enquête*. Barker
translates the term as "inquest" and Hallward as "investigation." For Badiou's
own definition of the concept see *L'Être et l'événement*, 363–72; *Being and Event*,
327–43. See also François Marmor, "Les Livres et les enquêtes: Pour un 'marxisme concret,' " in *Le Maoïsme: Philosophie et politique* (Paris: PUF, 1976), 47–51.

12 Serge July, quoted in Christophe Bourseiller, *Les Maoïstes: La Folle histoire des
gardes rouges français* (Paris: Plon, 1996), 161. Bourseiller himself also explains:
"The investigation is another idea from the Chinese. Its concept is luminous: in
order to know the working class and peasantry well, one must proceed with a
systematic and objective investigation by going on location. It is a matter of
leaving behind the universities in order to go there where exploitation is most
ravaging. Of practicing concrete analysis. This foregrounding of the investigation will be one of the principal features of the Maoist movement" (80).

13 UCFML, *Première année d'existence d'une organisation maoïste, printemps 1970/
printemps 1971* (Paris: François Maspero, 1972), 100, 169.

14 UCFML, *La Révolution prolétarienne en France et comment construire le parti de
l'époque de la pensée de Mao Tsé-toung* (Paris: François Maspero, 1970), 46.

15 See "Dialogue autour de Tien An Men," a special issue of *Le Perroquet: Quinzomadaire d'opinion* 86–87 (March 1990). Parts of the survey in Guanzhou have
also been published in Lazarus, *L'Anthropologie du nom*, 233–49; and Sylvain
Lazarus, *Chercher ailleurs et autrement: Sur la doctrine des lieux, l'économie, l'effondrement du socialisme* (Paris: Les Conférences du Perroquet, 1992).

16 Badiou, *L'Être et l'événement*, 361; *Being and Event*, 327 (translation modified).

17 See, e.g., Laclau and Mouffe, *Hegemony and Socialist Strategy*, 95; and Michael Hardt and Antonio Negri, *Empire* (Cambridge: Harvard University Press, 2000), 63–64.

18 Mao, *Quotations from Chairman Mao Tsetung*, 170–74.

19 Badiou, *L'Être et l'événement*, 375–76; *Being and Event*, 341 (translation modified).

20 See UCFML, *La Révolution prolétarienne en France*, passim.

21 "Maoïsme et question du parti," in "Le Maoïsme," special issue of *Le Marxiste-Léniniste: Journal Central du Groupe pour la Fondation de l'Union des Communistes de France Marxistes Léninistes* 12 (fall 1976): 20.

22 "Le Maoïsme: Une étape du marxisme," in "10 ans de maoïsme: Une histoire, un bilan, une politique," special double issue of *Le Marxiste-Léniniste* 50–51 (spring 1981): 7. See also Paul Sandevince (pseudonym for Sylvain Lazarus), *Notes de travail sur le post-léninisme* (Paris: Potemkine, 1980). Even if retrospectively the UCFML claims to have been post-Leninist from the beginning, it also distinguishes various stages along the way. See the dossier translated in "Alain Badiou and Cultural Revolution," a special issue of *positions: east asia cultures critique* 13, no. 3 (2005): 515–33.

23 See also the introduction to *La Révolution prolétarienne en France*: "If we commit ourselves to fusing the universal truth of Marxism-Leninism, the highest and entirely new stage of which is Mao Zedong's thought, into the concrete practice of the revolution in France, the latter for sure will be victorious. This fusion requires that Mao Zedong's thought really be considered a guide for action" (9–10).

24 Badiou, *Théorie du sujet*, 198; *Theory of the Subject*, 182.

25 Alain Badiou, *La Révolution Culturelle: La Dernière révolution?* (Paris: Les Conférences du Rouge-Gorge, 2002), 31. Other talks in this series include Sylvain Lazarus's "Les Trois régimes du siècle" (2001), Natacha Michel's "Ô jeunesse! Ô Vieillesse! Mai 68, le mai mao" (2002), Badiou's "La Commune de Paris" (2003), Judith Balso's "Politiques et figures du travail dans le Portugal des années 1974/1979" (2003), and Martine Leruch's "Qu'en est-il de la pensée du nazisme aujourd'hui?" (2004). The programmatic statement for the series lays out a form of metapolitics as historical materialism, namely, "to clarify, at the start of the new century, the links between history and politics. In light of this question, we will study various fundamental episodes in the historicity of politics: for instance, the Russian revolution, the Resistance, the Cultural Revolution, May '68.... It will be a matter in each case of doing justice to the singularity of the events, all the while retaining, for thinking, whatever they illuminate about politics, the history of its forms, of its creations and thus of what is to be done and thought now" (inside blurb). For further examples of what I consider to be a metapolitical reading in this sense see Peter Hallward, *Damning the Flood: Haiti, Aristide, and the Politics of Containment* (London: Verso, 2008); and Bruno Bosteels, "Travesías del fantasma: Pequeña metapolítica del 68 en México," *Metapolítica: Revista Trimestral*

de Teoría y Ciencia de la Política 12 (1999): 733–68; partially translated as "The Melancholy Left: Specters of 1968 in Mexico and Beyond," in *(1968) Episodes of Culture in Contest*, edited by Cathy Crane and Nicholas Muellner.

26 See Alessandro Russo, "The Conclusive Scene: Mao and the Red Guards in July 1968," in "Alain Badiou and Cultural Revolution," a special issue of *positions: east asia cultures critique* 13, no. 3 (2005): 535–74.

27 Bourseiller, *Les Maoïstes*, 300. In the end, and despite the wealth of documents and anecdotes, Bourseiller's interpretation boils down to the familiar picture of Maoism and of the Cultural Revolution as a sinister struggle for power. See also, more recently, Richard Wolin, "Excursus: On the Sectarian Maoism of Alain Badiou," in *The Wind from the East: French Intellectuals, the Cultural Revolution, and the Legacy of the 1960s* (Princeton: Princeton University Press, 2010), 155–76.

28 A. Belden Fields, *Trotskyism and Maoism: Theory and Practice in France and the United States* (New York: Praeger, 1988), 87.

29 Rémi Hess, *Les Maoïstes français: Une dérive institutionnelle* (Paris: Anthropos, 1974), 207–12.

30 Bourseiller, *Les Maoïstes*, 130, 150.

31 Badiou, *Conditions*, 250; 175.

32 UCFML, *La Révolution prolétarienne en France*, 126. As in the case of Mao on determination respectively by the infrastructure, practice, or politics over and above the superstructure, theory, or ideology, here too this question of priority is a conjunctural one: "There is no absolute priority of the struggle in the factories over the struggle in the housing projects, but the inverse is not true either" (126). Though without absolute priority, nevertheless, in modern historical circumstances the factory retains a symptomatic function with regard to other sites. Those readers who would consider this argument, too, a leftover of Badiou's bygone dialectical period would do well to consider an extraordinary text, "L'Usine comme site événementiel," which was originally meant for inclusion in *Being and Event* but appeared only in *Le Perroquet* 62–63 (April 22–May 10, 1986): 1, 4–6.

33 UCFML, *La Révolution prolétarienne en France*, 119.

34 *Le Marxiste-Léniniste* 50–51 (1981): 17.

35 Badiou, *La Révolution Culturelle*, 11. See also Alessandro Russo, "How to Translate 'Cultural Revolution'?," *Inter-Asia Cultural Studies* 7, no. 4 (2006): 673–82.

36 "L'Art et la culture: Un groupe maoïste, le groupe FOUDRE," *Le Marxiste-Léniniste* 50–51 (1981): 20.

37 Ibid., 21.

38 See appendix 1.

39 Badiou, *Théorie du sujet*, 46, 306; *Theory of the Subject*, 28, 290.

40 UCFML, *La Révolution prolétarienne en France*, 5.

41 Ibid., 65. See also the earlier statement, which dates from the start of 1970: "In May 1968 (and the situation is the same today), there exists neither a party nor a group that is authentically Marxist-Leninist" (13). As A. Belden Fields observes, in chapter 3 of his *Trotskyism and Maoism in France and the United States*: "The

UCFML has made no claim to be a party, as have the other two organizations [Parti Communiste Marxiste-Léniniste de France, PCMLF, and Parti Communiste Révolutionnaire (marxiste-léniniste), PCR(m-l)]. In fact, it has not even claimed to be a 'union' yet, but a 'group' for the formation of a 'union.' It has readily admitted that it does not yet have a mass base which would entitle it legitimately to refer to itself as a party. It also questions the legitimacy of the PCMLF and the PCR(m-l) for so doing."

42   UCFML, "Commentaire préliminaire," in Sandevince, Notes de travail sur le post-léninisme, 4.

43   Badiou, Théorie du sujet, 65; Theory of the Subject, 47.

44   Anonymous, "Le Mode dialectique," La Distance Politique 5.

45   Badiou, Théorie du sujet, 205; Theory of the Subject, 188.

46   For an overview of the different forms of organization associated with the UCFML see Le Marxiste-Léniniste 50–51 (spring 1981).

47   Badiou, Théorie de la contradiction, 20.

48   Badiou, Peut-on penser la politique? 112.

49   UCFML, La Révolution prolétarienne en France, 4. See also later on: "If one asks, in general and abstract terms, without analyzing the concrete situation from the point of view of the people's revolutionary unity, which aspect is principal: exploitation or oppression, one falls by force either in the economism and opportunism of the right or else in the putschism and the purely military point of view of the left" (83). Here, again, L'Humanité Rouge and La Cause du Peuple are discussed as representative of these respective deviations.

50   UCFML, La Révolution prolétarienne en France, 56.

51   UCFML, Une Étude maoïste: La Situation en Chine et le mouvement dit de "critique de la bande des Quatre" (Marseille: Potemkine, 1977), 9.

52   UCFML, La Révolution prolétarienne en France, 68. Insofar as the GP, too, will increasingly become obsessed with the "fascist" turn of the state apparatus in France, the militants of this organization are also sometimes described in the writings of the UCFML in terms of a "rightist" deviation, similar to that of the ex-PCMLF.

53   Ibid., 108.

54   Badiou, Théorie de la contradiction, 71.

55   Badiou and Balmès, De l'idéologie, 29n20.

56   Badiou, Théorie de la contradiction, 80.

57   Ibid., 75.

58   Ibid., 76, 78–79.

59   Ibid., 79.

60   Ibid., 80.

61   Ibid., 81.

62   Ibid.

63   Ibid., 81–82.

64   Ibid., 82.

65 Ibid.

66 Ibid.

67 Badiou, "Le Flux et le parti (dans les marges de l'*Anti-Œdipe*)," 31–32.

68 Badiou, *Théorie de la contradiction*, 69.

69 Ibid.

70 Ibid., 72.

71 Ibid., 69.

72 André Glucksmann, *La Cuisinière et le mangeur d'hommes* (Paris: Seuil, 1975), 21.

73 Badiou and Balmès, *De l'idéologie*, 52–53.

74 Ibid., 53.

75 Groupe Yénan-Philosophie, "État de front," *La Situation actuelle sur le front de la philosophie*, 12. In addition to Deleuze, Lacan, and Althusser, a fourth interlocutor—Michel Foucault—is mentioned in a footnote as the subject to be addressed in a future discussion, but this polemic never took place. This lacuna can still be felt in Badiou's current work, in which certain readers might want to see a more sustained confrontation not only with Foucault's final seminars, on biopolitics and the hermeneutics of the subject, at the Collège de France, but already with his own definition of the event, as announced in the interview with members of the Cercle d'Épistémologie in *Cahiers pour l'analyse* mentioned above.

76 Ibid., 10. The mention of Nietzsche's archipolitical attempt "to break the history of the world in two" anticipates a future version of this same polemic, in which Badiou will once again reject the radical-anarchic figure of antagonism, or the two as such, as part of Nietzsche's problematic legacy. See Alain Badiou, *Casser en deux l'histoire du monde?* (Paris: Les Conférences du Perroquet, 1992). This and other texts will be translated and taken up in Alain Badiou, *What Is Antiphilosophy? Writings on Kierkegaard, Nietzsche, and Lacan*, edited and translated by Bruno Bosteels (Durham: Duke University Press, forthcoming). Compare also with Alenka Zupančič's book, deeply inspired by Badiou's thinking, *The Shortest Shadow: Nietzsche's Philosophy of the Two* (Cambridge: MIT Press, 2003).

77 Groupe Yénan-Philosophie, "État de front," 12–13.

78 Badiou, Bellassen, and Mossot, *Le Noyau rationnel de la dialectique hégélienne*, 73, esp. note "(k) Le concept philosophique de déviation."

79 Theodor W. Adorno, *Negative Dialectics*, translated by E. B. Ashton (New York: Continuum, 1990), 135.

80 Badiou, Bellassen, and Mossot, *Le Noyau rationnel de la dialectique hégélienne*, 73–74.

81 Ibid., 40.

82 Ibid., 39.

83 Badiou, *Theoretical Writings*, 69.

84 Badiou, *Théorie de la contradiction*, 56.

85 Badiou, *Peut-on penser la politique?* 10. Insofar as Lacanian psychoanalysis now prospers officially in the *École de la Cause*, just as Sartre's Cause echoes *La Cause du Peuple*, we might also add Lacan to the polemic between Sartre and Althusser.

The question is, of course, on which side? Or perhaps we should ask ourselves whether a Lacanian logic of the cause (as *Chose* or Thing, *das Ding*) does not interrupt the possibility of being loyal to a political Cause, just as Althusser's structural causality may have kept the author of *For Marx* from joining Sartre's Cause on the side of the Maoists. Žižek has recently tried to reconcile both meanings of the cause: "The standard political trope 'the cause of freedom' should be taken more literally than is usually intended, including *both* main meanings of the term 'cause,' a cause which produces effects and a political cause that mobilizes us. Perhaps, the two meanings are not as disparate as they may appear: the Cause that mobilizes us (the 'cause of freedom') acts as the absent Cause which disturbs the network of causality" (Žižek, *In Defense of Lost Causes*, 289). As Badiou also writes: "Lacan in effect established that the cause of desire is an object that has been lost, that is lacking, and that, being articulated under the symbolic law, desire has no substance and no nature. It only has a truth" (Badiou, *Petit panthéon portatif*, 12–13; *Pocket Pantheon*, 2).

86 Badiou, Bellassen, and Mossot, *Le Noyau rationnel de la dialectique hégélienne*, 13–14.

87 Ibid.

88 Ibid., 15.

89 Ibid., 17.

90 See appendix 1 herein.

91 Guy Lardreau and Christian Jambet, *L'Ange: Ontologie de la révolution 1. Pour une cynégétique du semblant* (Paris: Bernard Grasset, 1976), 96.

92 Ibid., 167.

93 Ibid., 168.

94 Daniel Bensaïd, "Alain Badiou and the Miracle of the Event," in Hallward, *Think Again*, 95.

95 Ibid., 101, 105.

96 Ibid., 103.

97 Ibid., 103–4.

98 Georges Peyrol (pseudonym for Alain Badiou), "Un Ange est passé," in *La Situation actuelle sur le front de la philosophie*, 69.

99 Ibid., 72.

100 Ibid., 73.

101 Ibid.

102 Badiou, *L'Éthique*, 74–75; *Ethics*, 84.

103 Badiou, *Théorie de la contradiction*, 53, 55.

104 Badiou, *Ethics*, 118–19.

105 Alberto Toscano, "Communism as Separation," in Hallward, *Think Again*, 143.

106 Ibid., 145.

107 "Circulaire sur quelques problèmes idéologiques" (Sept. 1970), repr. in UCFML, *Première année d'existence d'une organisation maoïste, printemps 1970/printemps 1971*, 20.

108 *Le Marxiste-Léniniste* 12 (fall 1976): 21.

109 Badiou, *Théorie de la contradiction*, 70.

110 UCFML, *Sur le maoïsme et la situation en Chine après la mort de Mao Tsé-Toung* (Marseille: Potemkine, 1976), 1–2.

111 Anonymous, "Introduction," *Le Marxiste-Léniniste* 50–51 (1981): 1.

112 Ibid.

113 UCFML, *Questions du maoïsme: De la Chine de la Révolution Culturelle à la Chine des Procès de Pékin* (Marseille: Potemkine, 1981), 10.

114 UCFML, *Sur le maoïsme et la situation en Chine après la mort de Mao Tsé-Toung*, 16–17.

115 Sandevince, *Notes de travail sur le post-léninisme*, 9.

116 Badiou, *Théorie du sujet*, 318; *Theory of the Subject*, 302.

CHAPTER 4. THE ONTOLOGICAL IMPASSE

1 Badiou, *L'Être et l'événement*, 189; *Being and Event*, 169.

2 Badiou, *Manifeste pour la philosophie*, 12; *Manifesto for Philosophy*, 32 (translation modified).

3 Badiou, *L'Être et l'événement*, 14; *Being and Event*, 8.

4 Badiou, *L'Éthique*, 25; *Ethics*, 25.

5 Badiou, *L'Être et l'événement*, 113; *Being and Event*, 97.

6 Ibid., 113, 307; 97, 278.

7 Ibid., 97; 83.

8 Badiou, *L'Éthique*, 65; *Ethics*, 73.

9 Badiou, *L'Être et l'événement*, 469; *Being and Event*, 429.

10 Badiou, *Théorie du sujet*, 40; *Theory of the Subject*, 23. For further discussion see chapter 2 above.

11 Badiou, *L'Être et l'événement*, 309; *Being and Event*, 280 (translation modified).

12 Lenin, *Philosophical Notebooks*, 123.

13 Ibid., 109.

14 Badiou, *L'Être et l'événement*, 469, 24; *Being and Event*, 430, 18 (translation modified).

15 Žižek, *The Sublime Object of Ideology*, 221, 176.

16 Ibid., 171.

17 Žižek, "The Politics of Truth," in *The Ticklish Subject*, passim.

18 See 323.

19 Badiou, *Manifeste pour la philosophie*, 89; *Manifesto for Philosophy*, 106–7 (translation modified); and Badiou, *Saint Paul*, 16; 15. In recent books Žižek also redefines the Lacanian notion of the act by placing greater emphasis on the problematic of the morning after and by insisting that, far from involving a merely structural recognition of the real as impossible, the act makes the impossible possible. For a more detailed discussion of this change see Bruno Bosteels, "In Search of the Act," in *The Actuality of Communism* (London: Verso, 2011).

20 For a good summary of this recent self-criticism see Badiou's preface to the

Spanish edition of *L'Être et l'événement* in *El Ser y el acontecimiento*, translated by Raúl J. Cerdeiras, Alejandro A. Cerletti, and Nilda Prados (Buenos Aires: Manantial, 1999), 5–8. Similar self-criticisms appear in Badiou's preface to the English translation of his *Ethics* and in the interview "Beyond Formalization," appended above.

21 Badiou, "Le (Re)commencement du matérialisme dialectique," 461. See also Barker, *Alain Badiou*, 17. It is inaccurate, though, to read this early text as an anticipation of the subsequent turn to axiomatic set theory alone. In his critique of Althusser, Badiou is rather already announcing, with forty years of anticipation, the need to move beyond the ontology of belonging (the "algebra" according to *Theory of the Subject*, based on axiomatic set theory) toward a logic of appearing (a "topology," based on the theory of categories, or *topoi*)—a move that is actually not accomplished until the sequel to *Being and Event*, in *Logics of Worlds*. In his review of Althusser, Badiou announces this shift: "The theory of categories is perhaps the most significant epistemological event of these last years, due to the radical effort of abstraction to which it bears witness. Mathematical structures are not properly speaking constructed in it according to operational links between elements of a pure multiplicity (set); but they rather appear as 'summits' of a network of trajectories in which the structural correspondences (the morphisms) are primary" (Badiou, "Le (Re)commencement du matérialisme dialectique," 464).

22 Lacan, incidentally, began to develop his own understanding of the act in his seminar for 1967–68, *L'Acte psychanalytique*, a seminar that—like Badiou's contribution *Le Concept de modèle* to Althusser's *Cours de philosophie pour scientifiques*—was interrupted by the events of May '68 in France. A comparison between Žižek's and Badiou's theory of the subject, I should add, is seriously hindered by terminological matters—with Žižek calling "subject" (of lack) and "subjectivation" (as interpellation) what for Badiou would be more akin, respectively, to (evanescent, hysterical) "act of subjectivization" and (consistent, masterly) "subjective process." Invoking opposite reasons yet using the same terms, each thinker could thus accuse the other of remaining at the level of mere subjectivization! On notions of the act in relation to Lacan, Žižek, and Badiou see Ed Pluth, *Signifiers and Acts: Freedom in Lacan's Theory of the Subject* (Albany: State University of New York Press, 2007), 115–38.

23 Badiou, "Théorie axiomatique du sujet" (author's unpublished typescript), seminars of Dec. 4, 1996, and Jan. 9, 1997.

24 See also Badiou, *L'Éthique*, esp. 70–78; *Ethics*, 79–91.

CHAPTER 5. FORCING THE TRUTH

1 François Wahl, *Une Soirée philosophique* (Paris: Potemkine, 1988), 7. See also the conclusion of Meditation 1 in *Being and Event*: "Ontology, axiom system of the particular inconsistency of multiplicities, seizes the in-itself of the multiple by forming into consistency all inconsistency and forming into inconsistency all

consistency. It thereby deconstructs any one-effect" (Badiou, *L'Être et l'événement*, 39; *Being and Event*, 30).

2 François Zourabichvili, *Deleuze: Une Philosophie de l'événement* (Paris: PUF, 1994), 21.

3 Philippe Lacoue-Labarthe, *La Fiction du politique* (Paris: Christian Bourgois, 1987), 19n1. Lacoue-Labarthe refers to (but then misspells the title-concept of) the collection of essays *Il Pensiero debole*, edited by Gianni Vattimo and Pier Aldo Rovatti (Milan: Feltrinelli, 1983). Lacoue-Labarthe himself, incidentally, affirms only a few pages further down in this same book, after having rejected the possibility of formulating a properly Heideggerian philosophy: "There are, as is inevitable, certain Heideggerian theses to which one can or cannot subscribe. But these theses are not organized into a philosophy, except in the weak sense of philosophy" (25). As for Baudelaire or Benjamin, what should we make of this somewhat mysterious reference to heroism? Perhaps the image Benjamin uses in his "Theses on the History of Philosophy," when he writes that "the historical materialist leaves it to the historian to let himself be drained by the whore called 'once upon a time,' where he is man enough to blast out of history"? Even to this typically Nietzschean and misogynist image of the antiphilosophical act—"blast open history" here being the strict equivalent of Nietzsche's "breaking the history of the world in two"—we might oppose the "weak messianic force" of which the last of Benjamin's "Theses" speaks. For many of these unsolved questions see also the excellent study by Françoise Proust, *L'Histoire à contretemps: Le Temps historique chez Walter Benjamin* (Paris: Cerf, 1994). As for the symptomatic value of violence in the responses to weak thought see the commentaries by Alessandro dal Lago and Pier Aldo Rovatti in *Elogio del pudore: Per un pensiero debole* (Milan: Feltrinelli, 1989).

4 How curious to see Badiou stand accused of being a dogmatic thinker, when he himself devotes some of his most brilliant pages to this question, by opposing his thinking to the logic of dogmatism in *Théorie du sujet* and *Peut-on penser la politique?* See, particularly, in this last text, the section titled "Qu'est-ce que le dogmatisme?" (*Peut-on penser le politique?*, 109–12); and, in the first, "Diagonales de l'imaginaire" (*Théorie du sujet*, 313–19; *Theory of the Subject*, 297–303).

5 Badiou, *L'Être et l'événement*, 7; *Being and Event*, 1.

6 Badiou, *Deleuze*, 31; 19.

7 Alain Badiou, *Court traité d'ontologie transitoire* (Paris: Seuil, 1998), 121; *Briefings on Existence: A Short Treatise on Transitory Ontology*, translated by Norman Madarasz (Albany: State University of New York Press, 2006), 108.

8 Badiou, *Manifeste pour la philosophie*, 55; *Manifesto for Philosophy*, 74 (translation modified).

9 Badiou, "L'Âge des poètes," 21–38.

10 Lacoue-Labarthe, "Poésie, philosophie, politique," 47.

11 Philippe Lacoue-Labarthe and Jean-Luc Nancy, *Le Mythe nazi* (La Tour d'Aigues: Éditions de l'Aube, 1991).

12 Jean-Luc Nancy, *Le Sens du monde* (Paris: Galilée, 1993), 114n1, 33n1; *The Sense of the World*, translated by Jeffrey S. Librett (Minneapolis: University of Minnesota Press, 1997), 175n19. With regard to the subject who decides in the face of the event according to Badiou, Nancy explains: "One is, at bottom, on a Heideggerian register, that of '*Das Ereignis trägt die Wahrheit = die Wahrheit durchragt das Ereignis*' (the event carries truth = truths juts out through the event), where the verb *durchragen* would call for a long gloss. It is 'jutting across,' and thus also 'piercing' and almost 'tearing' ('incising' in Badiou's vocabulary). Any thought that privileges truth, that takes on *the style of truth*, dedicates itself to the tension of an internal tornness, whether it does so in a more pathos-laden mode (Heidegger) or in a cooler mode (Badiou)" (ibid.). The line from Heidegger about the event and truth is also used in Nancy's short intervention at the roundtable on "Lacan avec Heidegger" during the conference *Lacan avec les philosophes*.

13 See the two collections of papers produced during the seminar on the political organized at the École Normale Supérieure in rue d'Ulm by Lacoue-Labarthe and Nancy: *Rejouer le politique* (Paris: Galilée, 1981) and *Le Retrait du politique* (Paris: Galilée, 1983); in English: a selection can be found in Philippe Lacoue-Labarthe and Jean-Luc Nancy, *Retreating the Political*, edited and translated by Simon Sparks (New York: Routledge, 1997). See also below, chapter 8, where I discuss the theory of radical democracy.

14 See, e.g., Badiou, "Philosophie et psychanalyse," in *Conditions*, 275–326; *Conditions*, 201–10; *Para uma nova teoria do sujeito: Conferências brasileiras*, translated by Emerson Xavier da Silva and Gilda Sodré, edited by Ari Roitman and Paulo Becker (Rio de Janeiro: Relume-Dumará, 1994); and "Ciclo de Conferencias en Buenos Aires, Abril-Mayo 2000," a special issue of the journal *Acontecimiento: Revista para pensar la política* 19–20 (2000).

15 Badiou, *L'Être et l'événement*, 472; *Being and Event*, 433.

16 Ibid.

17 Wahl, "Le Soustractif," in Badiou, *Conditions*, 38; in English, "The Subtractive," in *Conditions*, xxxi (translation modified).

18 Žižek, *The Ticklish Subject*, 145.

19 Badiou, *Théorie du sujet*, 160; *Theory of the Subject*, 142.

20 Ibid., 149; 131.

21 Ibid., 139, 141; 121, 123.

22 Ibid., 251; 235.

23 Natacha Michel, "Re-naissance de la philosophie: Entretien avec Alain Badiou: *Théorie du sujet*," *Le Perroquet: Quinzomadaire d'opinion* 13–14 (1982): 11–12.

24 Badiou, *Saint Paul*, 57; 54.

25 Badiou, *L'Éthique*, 62; *Ethics*, 70.

26 Badiou, *Théorie du sujet*, 123; *Theory of the Subject*, 106.

27 Badiou, *L'Éthique*, 76; *Ethics*, 85–86.

28 Badiou, *Conditions*, 224n38; 305n8. See also *L'Éthique*, 77; *Ethics*, 86–87.

29 Badiou, *Conditions*, 230; 159. For Lacan, by contrast, the *passe* of the subject

always involves a certain *désêtre* or "unbeing." See, e.g., "Proposition du 9 octobre 1967 sur le psychanalyste de l'École" (*Scilicet* 1 [1968]: 25), where Lacan writes: "Dans ce virage où le sujet voit chavirer l'assurance qu'il prenait de ce fantasme où se constitue pour chacun sa fenêtre sur le réel, ce qui s'aperçoit, c'est que la prise du désir n'est rien que celle d'un désêtre" (In this turnabout in which the subject witnesses the capsizing of the guarantee it drew from the fantasy through which everyone constitutes a window onto the real, what can be perceived is that the hold of desire is nothing else than that of an unbeing) (repr. in Lacan, *Autres écrits*, 254).

30 Badiou, *Peut-on penser la politique?* 16.

31 Badiou, *L'Être et l'événement*, 469; *Being and Event*, 430.

CHAPTER 6. LOGICS OF CHANGE

1   Badiou, *Logiques des mondes*, 16; *Logics of Worlds*, 8 (translation modified).

2   Ibid., 47–48, 50; 38, 41.

3   Alain Badiou, *Second manifeste pour la philosophie* (Paris: Fayard, 2009), 13.

4   Badiou, *Logiques des mondes*, 553; *Logics of Worlds*, 529.

5   Ibid., 53; 45 (translation modified).

6   Badiou, "Théorie axiomatique du sujet," seminar of Jan. 14, 1998.

7   Badiou, *Logiques des mondes*, 89; *Logics of Worlds*, 79.

8   Ibid., 548; 524.

9   Jacques Derrida, *Politiques de l'amitié* (Paris: Galilée, 1994), 87; *Politics of Friendship*, translated by George Collins (London: Verso, 1997), 68.

10 Badiou, *Logiques des mondes*, 58–59; *Logics of Worlds*, 50–51 (translation modified). This passage is more ambiguous than it would seem at first glance. Badiou, indeed, seems to equate the outcome of (a certain use of) psychoanalysis, namely, the "face-to-face" confrontation with one's idiotic enjoyment, with the conclusion of the post-Heideggerian deconstruction of ontology, leading to the need of what some would call a philosophy of the nonsubject. More generally speaking, it is not always clear from this and other passages in *Logics of Worlds* whether Lacan's version of psychoanalysis, contrary to what is affirmed here, really escapes the thematics of finitude and jouissance that Badiou associates with democratic materialism, or whether it does not actually counteract the inventive fidelity to a notion of the subject qua exception, which would follow along the lines of the materialist dialectic. On the question of the unifying category of the subject, retained only by Sartre and Lacan in the midst of right-wing (Heidegger) and left-wing (Althusser) criticisms of this category as either metaphysical or ideological, see also *Logiques des mondes*, 548; *Logics of Worlds*, 524–25. I discuss Althusser's case in chapter 1; for a detailed discussion and critique of the proposal of a (radical) democracy without a (political) subject, see chapter 8.

11 Badiou, *Logiques des mondes*, 156, 555; *Logics of Worlds*, 144, 549 (translation modified). For further discussion see my "Hegel."

12 Badiou, *Logiques des mondes*, 53–54; *Logics of Worlds*, 45–46. See chapter 4 above.

13 Ibid., 12; 4.

14 Ibid., 386; 366.

15 Ibid., 383; 363.

16 Ibid., 413; 391.

17 Ibid., 396; 375.

18 Ibid., 397; 376.

19 Ibid., 529; 508.

20 Ibid., 70; 61–62. There is some oscillation at work in this part of *Logics of Worlds*, insofar as Badiou sometimes uses expressions such as "reactive subject" or "obscure subject" while at other times he seems to prefer speaking of so many "figures," from the faithful to the obscure, within a dynamic "subjective field." Anyone familiar with the polemics surrounding Badiou's Maoism, discussed in chapter 3, will be able to appreciate the advantages of the latter formulation over the former.

21 Ibid., 381; 361.

22 Ibid., 394–95; 374.

23 Ibid., 15; 7.

24 Ibid., 536; 514. Badiou speaks here, as elsewhere, of "democratic materialism" and "materialist dialectic" as two antagonistic "ideological atmospheres," and it would be a mistake on our part to associate these too quickly with the philosophies that may or may not inspire them. Nevertheless, the fact remains that, even when they are not read in detail, Heidegger's interpretation of finitude in *Kant and the Problem of Metaphysics* and its reprise in the final section of Foucault's *The Order of Things* have put their mark on the intellectual constellation of the past century. "Where there had formerly been a correlation between a *metaphysics* of representation and of the infinite and an *analysis* of living beings, of man's desires, and of the words of his language, we find being constituted an *analytic* of finitude and human existence, and in opposition to it (though in correlative opposition) a perpetual tendency to constitute a *metaphysics* of life, labour, and language," writes Foucault. "But, more fundamentally, our culture crossed the threshold beyond which we recognize our modernity when finitude was conceived in an interminable cross-reference with itself." See Michel Foucault, "L'Homme et ses doubles," in *Les Mots et les choses: Une archéologie des sciences humaines* (Paris: Gallimard, 1966), 328–29; in English: *The Order of Things: An Archaeology of the Human Sciences* (New York: Vintage, 1973), 317–18; and Martin Heidegger, *Kant and the Problem of Metaphysics*, translated by Richard Taft (Bloomington: Indiana University Press, 1997). I address the prevalence of the finitist argument (which we can find in the work of nearly all contemporary "continental" thinkers from Jean-Luc Nancy to Avital Ronell and from Françoise Dastur to Simon Critchley, the latter incidentally in an eclectic mixture of Levinas and Badiou), in Bruno Bosteels, "The Jargon of Finitude, or Materialism Today," *Radical Philosophy* 155 (April 2009): 41–47.

25 Badiou, *Logiques des mondes*, 79–80; *Logics of Worlds*, 71.

26 Ibid., 284, 16; 268, 8. All of this could be summed up by saying that Badiou is opposed to Kant as a shorthand notation for the argument in favor of finitude with which the whole twentieth century waged war against any lingering Platonism: "To render impracticable all of Plato's shining promises—this was the task of the obsessive from Königsberg, our first *professor*" (*Logiques des mondes*, 561; *Logics of Worlds*, 537).

27 See 350.

28 Ibid.

29 Badiou, *Second manifeste pour la philosophie*, 104.

30 Badiou, *Logiques des mondes*, 388; *Logics of Worlds*, 369.

31 Ibid., 391; 371.

32 Ibid., 396; 375.

33 Personal correspondence with the author, March 1, 2005. I've already suggested, in chapter 1, that this scholium to Book VII of *Logics of Worlds*, "A Political Variant of the Physics of the Subject-of-Truth," which treats of the conditions of existence of the Maoist "red power" in China from 1927 to 1929, should be juxtaposed and compared to Lenin's well-known analysis of the conditions of the October 1917 revolution and their reprise in terms of "overdetermination" and "underdetermination" in the work of Althusser.

34 Badiou, *Logiques des mondes*, 531; *Logics of Worlds*, 509.

35 Badiou, *L'Être et l'événement*, 10; *Being and Event*, 4 (translation corrected). See also, less modestly, the end of the author's preface to the English translation: "I would like this publication to mark an obvious fact: the nullity of the opposition between analytic thought and continental thought. And I would like this book to be read, appreciated, staked out, and contested as much by the inheritors of the formal and experimental grandeur of the sciences or of the law, as it is by the aesthetes of contemporary nihilism, the refined amateurs of literary deconstruction, the wild militants of a de-alienated world, and by those who are deliciously isolated by amorous constructions" (*Being and Event*, xv).

36 Badiou, *L'Être et l'événement*, 213; *Being and Event*, 191.

37 Ibid., 215; 193.

38 Badiou, *Logiques des mondes*, 477, 541; *Logics of Worlds*, 455, 518 (translation modified).

39 Derrida in Giovanna Borradori, *Philosophy in a Time of Terror: Dialogues with Jürgen Habermas and Jacques Derrida* (Chicago: University of Chicago Press, 2003), 90.

40 Ibid., 89. See also Jacques Derrida, "A Certain Impossible Possibility of Saying the Event," in *The Late Derrida*, edited by W. J. T. Mitchell and Arnold I. Davidson (Chicago: University of Chicago Press, 2007), 223–43.

41 Derrida in Borradori, *Philosophy in a Time of Terror*, 92. Picking up on this last point, we might also want to ask whether an event, as studied in terms of its subjective induction through historical materialism, in the way Badiou claims to

do in his final scholium on Mao in *Logics of Worlds*, should not perhaps also disturb the tranquility of the materialist dialectic. Should we not say that events, which historicize a structure, also have the power of exceeding the structure of historicity? For Badiou, however, events in politics, for instance, while no longer subject to the "laws" of the dialectic in their Stalinist version, nonetheless retain an unchanged structure, also called the condition's numericity.

42 See 312. I cannot agree, in this regard, with Alberto Toscano's vote of confidence in Badiou's "inaesthetics," in the Translator's Note to *Handbook of Inaesthetics*, when he writes: "Rather than seeking to welcome (that is, to absorb) the poem into the realm of speculative thinking in a hermeneutic vein, Badiou's approach is committed both to declaring the autonomy of artistic procedures (poetic or literary, cinematic or theatrical) and to registering what he calls their 'intra-philosophical effects' " (Badiou, *Handbook of Inaesthetics*, x). While this may very well be Badiou's commitment, it is far more doubtful whether Badiou himself lives up to this promise in his writings on the likes of Mallarmé, Valéry, or Beckett. See also Badiou's explanations about the selectiveness of the poets that are said to condition contemporary philosophy in the "age of the poets" according to *Manifesto for Philosophy*:

> Yet, the poetry and poets we are speaking of are neither all the poetry nor all the poets, but rather those whose work is immediately recognizable as a work of thought and for whom the poem is, at the very locus where philosophy falters, a locus of language wherein a proposition about being and about time is enacted. These poets did not *decide* to take the place of philosophers; they did not write with the clarified awareness of having assumed these functions. Instead one must imagine that they were submitted to a kind of intellectual pressure, induced by the absence of free play in philosophy, the need to constitute, from within their art, that general space of reception for thought and the generic procedures that philosophy, sutured as it was, could no longer establish. (*Manifeste pour la philosophie*, 49; *Manifesto for Philosophy*, 69)

43 Badiou, *Logiques des mondes*, 544–45; *Logics of Worlds*, 520.

44 Badiou, *Manifeste pour la philosophie*, 15; *Manifesto for Philosophy*, 35.

45 Jacques Rancière, *Mallarmé: La Politique de la sirène* (Paris: Hachette, 1996), 24.

46 Ibid., 25.

47 Rancière, *La Mésentente*, 116, and passim; *Disagreement*, 79. For a more detailed analysis of Rancière's restricted nominalism and the singularity of politics as treated in *Disagreement* see my "Rancière's Leftism, or, Politics and Its Discontents."

48 Badiou, quoted in Emmanuel Terray, *Le Marxisme devant les sociétés "primitives": Deux études* (Paris: François Maspero, 1972), 43.

49 Badiou, "Philosophie et mathématique," in *Conditions*, 178; *Conditions*, 112; and *Logiques des mondes*, 76; *Logics of Worlds*, 67. On the question of truth and the history of truth in Badiou see also the long essay by Étienne Balibar, " 'Histoire de la vérité': Alain Badiou dans la philosophie française," in *Alain Badiou: Penser*

le multiple, 497–523; in English: "The History of Truth: Alain Badiou in French Philosophy," in Hallward, *Think Again*, 21–38.

50 Badiou, *Logiques des mondes*, 532; *Logics of Worlds*, 510.

51 Badiou, *L'Hypothèse communiste*, 182; *The Communist Hypothesis*, 230.

CHAPTER 7. FROM POTENTIALITY TO INEXISTENCE

1 Karl Marx to Arnold Ruge (Kreuznach, Sept. 1843), included in "Letters from the *Deutsch-Französische Jahrbücher*," in vol. 3 of *Marx/Engels Collected Works* (Moscow: Progress Publishers, 1975), 133–45, 144 (translation modified).

2 See Marx, preface to *A Contribution to the Critique of Political Economy*, in vol. 29 of *Marx/Engels Collected Works* (Moscow: Progress Publishers, 1977), 261–65.

3 Althusser, "Marx dans ses limites," 424; *Philosophy of the Encounter*, 58.

4 Karl Marx and Friedrich Engels, *The German Ideology*, translated by Clemens Dutt et al., vol. 5 of *Marx/Engels Collected Works* (Moscow: Progress Publishers, 1975), 49.

5 Walter Benjamin, *The Arcades Project*, translated by Howard Eiland and Kevin McLaughlin, edited by Rolf Tiedemann (Cambridge: Belknap, 1999), 464, 364. See also Georg Lukács, *History and Class-Consciousness: Studies in Marxist Dialectics*, translated by Rodney Livingstone (Cambridge: MIT Press, 1972), 270; and Guy Debord, *The Society of the Spectacle*, translated by Donald Nicholson-Smith (Cambridge: MIT Press, 1995), thesis 164: "The world already possesses the dream of a time, of which it must now possess the consciousness so as to really live it."

6 Lenin, *What Is to Be Done?* in vol. 1 of *Collected Works*, 110.

7 Derrida, with Alain Minc, "Penser ce qui vient," *Le Nouveau Monde* 92 (1994): 91–110, reissued as part of *Derrida pour les temps à venir*, edited by René Major (Paris: Stock, 2007), 17–62; also available in Spanish as "¿Qué hacer de la pregunta '¿Qué hacer?'?," translated by Bruno Mazzoldi, in *El tiempo de una tesis: Deconstrucción e implicaciones conceptuales* (Barcelona: Anthropos, 1997), 29–39.

8 Jacques Lacan, *Le Séminaire de Jacques Lacan*, edited by Jacques-Alain Miller, *Livre VII: L'Éthique de la psychanalyse*, 21, 22–23; *The Seminar of Jacques Lacan*, edited by Jacques-Alain Miller, *Book VII: The Ethics of Psychoanalysis*, translated by Dennis Porter, 12 (translation modified). On the use of fiction as a passage through nonbeing from which a truth may emerge see also the discussion of reasoning via the absurd as an operator of mathematical fidelity in Meditation 24 of *Being and Event*.

9 Jacques Rancière, *Le Spectateur émancipé* (Paris: La Fabrique, 2008), 84. This passage is drawn from a chapter, "Les paradoxes de l'art politique," that does not appear in the English translation of *The Emancipated Spectator*, translated by Gregory Elliott (London: Verso, 2009). A very different version of this chapter can be found in English as "The Paradoxes of Political Art," in Jacques Rancière, *Dissensus: On Politics and Aesthetics*, translated by Steven Corcoran (London: Continuum, 2010), 134–51.

10 Badiou, *Théorie du sujet*, 103; *Theory of the Subject*, 85.

11 Badiou, *Peut-on penser la politique?* 12.

12 Ibid., 12.

13 Badiou, *Manifeste pour la philosophie*, 72; *Manifesto for Philosophy*, 90 (translation modified). See also my explanation of this point in my introduction.

14 Badiou, *Théorie du sujet*, 110; *Theory of the Subject*, 92.

15 Jacques Derrida, *Spectres de Marx. L'État de la dette, le travail du deuil et la nouvelle Internationale* (Paris: Galilée, 1993), 16; *Specters of Marx: The State of the Debt, the Work of Mourning, and the New International*, translated by Peggy Kamuf (New York: Routledge, 1994), xix.

16 Ibid., 17; xx.

17 Ibid., 34; 12.

18 Ibid., 70–71; 38–39.

19 Giorgio Agamben, *Potentialities: Collected Essays in Philosophy*, translated by Daniel Heller-Roazen (Stanford: Stanford University Press, 1999), 179–80, 184.

20 Gilles Deleuze, *Différence et répétition* (Paris: Presses Universitaires de France, 1968), 272–73; *Difference and Repetition*, translated by Paul Patton (New York: Columbia University Press, 1994), 211; quoted in Badiou, *Deleuze*, 161; *Deleuze*, 112.

21 Quoted in Badiou, *Deleuze*, 162–63; *Deleuze*, 112–13. Aside from referring to Marx's letter to Ruge and the 1859 preface, Deleuze is also alluding to the famous formulation that can be found in Henri Bergson's *The Creative Mind*: "The stating and solving of the problem are here very close to being equivalent: The truly great problems are set forth only when they are solved," a formulation that Deleuze himself relates to Marx's formulation in the 1859 preface. See Gilles Deleuze, *Le Bergsonisme* (Paris: Presses Universitaires de France, 1997), 4; in English, *Bergsonism*, translated by Hugh Tomlinson and Barbara Habberjam (New York: Zone Books, 1988), 16.

22 Quoted in Badiou, *Deleuze*, 160; 111.

23 Žižek, "On Alain Badiou and *Logiques des mondes*," www.lacan.com/zizbadman .htm. See also the near-identical passages in Žižek, *Organs without Bodies: On Deleuze and Consequences* (New York: Routledge, 2004), 31; and *In Defense of Lost Causes* (London: Verso, 2008), 394–96.

24 Badiou, *Théorie du sujet*, 333; *Theory of the Subject*, 317. Žižek, in his discussion of Badiou, Balibar, and Rancière, states exactly the same principle, perhaps drawing on Badiou: "One can also put it in terms of the well-known definition of politics as the 'art of the possible': authentic politics is, rather, the exact opposite, that is, the art of the *impossible*—it changes the very parameters of what is considered 'possible' in the existing constellation" (*The Ticklish Subject*, 199).

25 Badiou, *Peut-on penser la politique?* 101.

26 Ibid., 93–94. If we are to believe Lacan, perhaps the transgression of a prohibition does not have much erotic value either. More radically, perhaps there is no such thing as transgression at all. "What analysis shows, if it shows anything at all . . . is very precisely the fact that we don't ever transgress. Sneaking around is

not transgressing. Seeing a door half-open is not the same as going through it." See Lacan, *Le Séminaire de Jacques Lacan*, edited by Jacques-Alain Miller, *Livre XVII: L'Envers de la psychanalyse*, 19; *The Seminar of Jacques Lacan, Book XVII: The Other Side of Psychoanalysis*, translated by Russell Grigg, 19.

27 Badiou, *Peut-on penser la politique?* 95.

28 Badiou, *Abrégé de métapolitique*, 106; *Metapolitics*, 93.

29 Badiou, *Peut-on penser la politique?*, 96.

30 Althusser, "Le courant souterrain du matérialisme de la rencontre," 581; "The Underground Current of the Materialism of the Encounter," in *Philosophy of the Encounter*, 193.

31 Ibid., 581; 193–94.

32 Althusser, "Marx dans ses limites," 463; "Marx in His Limits," in *Philosophy of the Encounter*, 94.

33 Badiou, *Peut-on penser la politique?*, 101.

34 Ibid.

35 Žižek, *In Defense of Lost Causes*, 180. In the end, far from signaling progress of the current era over the metaphysical illusions of our predecessors, is this way of thinking politics as the art of the impossible perhaps just another way of reading Marx's legacy? Stathis Kouvelakis, in his impressive reading of Marx's early work, seems to think so. "Marx's revolutionary political position is not the fruit of a free choice among several 'positive' possibilities, for it proceeds, literally, from an impossibility: it is the production of a new possibility," concludes Kouvelakis. "Rather, it surges up out of a contradiction and a struggle that divide even individuals from themselves . . . confronting them with possibilities that pre-existed their consciousness; this is so even if the typical task of revolutionary politics consists precisely in re-elaborating these possibilities by playing on their internal contradictions in order to generate new possibilities." See Stathis Kouvelakis, *Philosophy and Revolution: From Kant to Marx*, translated by G. M. Goshgarian (London: Verso, 2003), 278.

36 Alain Badiou, *L'Antiphilosophie de Wittgenstein* (Caen: NOUS, 2009), 48.

37 Badiou, *Abrégé de métapolitique*, 20–21; *Metapolitics*, 11. See also a later statement from *Metapolitics*, once more negatively formulated as a rebuttal against the Thermidorean definition of politics: "First, note here how political subjectivity is referred back to order, rather than to the possibility of bringing about that which is latent in a situation, under some maxim or other" (*Metapolitics*, 132). Admittedly, the original French does not mention latency, only *ce dont une situation est porteuse* for "that which is latent in a situation" (*Abrégé de métapolitique*, 148).

38 Ibid., 33; 23.

39 Ibid., 58; 49.

40 Ibid., 57; 47.

41 Badiou, *L'Être et l'événement*, 199; *Being and Event*, 178–79.

42 Ibid., 200; 179.

43 See 308–9. It is somewhat surprising, to say the least, that this evaluation of the significance of the eventual site for Badiou's overall philosophical project does not

make it into the actual note dedicated to *Being and Event* in *What Is Philosophy?*, translated by Hugh Tomlinson and Graham Burchell (New York: Columbia University Press, 1994), 152–53. After all, did not Deleuze and Guattari also devote a long opening section of this book to what they call "geophilosophy," arguing for an understanding of the philosophical concept not in terms of the representation of objects by subjects but rather in terms of the relation of thought to territory and to the earth? And did they not quote the text "What Is a Site?" by Marcel Détienne, the historian of ancient Greece, as a major point of reference for their geophilosophy?

44 Badiou, *L'Être et l'événement*, 195; *Being and Event*, 175.

45 Badiou, *Logiques des mondes*, 339; *Logics of Worlds*, 322.

46 Althusser, quoted in the Translator's Introduction, *Philosophy of the Encounter*, xlvi–xlvii.

47 Badiou, *Logiques des mondes*, 338; *Logics of Worlds*, 324.

48 Ibid., 362; 343.

49 Ibid., 398; 377.

50 Ibid., 418; 396.

51 Ibid., 400; 379.

52 Badiou, *Théorie du sujet*, 279; *Theory of the Subject*, 263. Badiou is referring to the treatment of the logic of the not-all in Lacan's seminar "L'Étourdit," originally published in *Scilicet* 4 (1973): 5–52; and included in Lacan, *Autres écrits*, 449–95; and Jean-Claude Milner's commentary in *L'Amour de la langue* (Paris: Seuil, 1978).

53 Badiou, *Théorie du sujet*, 279; *Theory of the Subject*, 263.

54 Ibid.

55 Ibid., 281; 265.

56 Ibid., 282; 266.

57 Ibid.

58 Ibid., 288–89; 272–73.

59 Badiou, *L'Hypothèse communiste*, 191; *The Communist Hypothesis*, 243.

CHAPTER 8. FOR LACK OF POLITICS

1 Badiou, *Logiques des mondes*, 9, 12; *Logics of Worlds*, 1, 4.

2 Martin Heidegger, *Nietzsche*, translated by David Farell Krell (San Francisco: Harper and Row, 1991), 4:201.

3 Quoted in Badiou, "Heidegger envisagé comme lieu commun," in *Manifeste pour la philosophie*, 27; *Manifesto for Philosophy*, 47. The quote is from "What Are Poets For?" in Heidegger, *Poetry, Language, Thought*, translated by Albert Hofstadter (New York: Harper and Row, 1971), 112.

4 Gianni Vattimo, "Hermenéutica, democracia y emancipación," in *Filosofía, política, religión: Más allá del "pensamiento débil,"* edited by Lluis Alvarez (Oviedo: Nobel, 1996), 67.

5 Ernesto Laclau, preface to Žižek, *The Sublime Object of Ideology*, xv.

6   Laclau, *New Reflections on the Revolution of Our Time* (London: Verso, 1990), 92, 82.

7   For this use of the opposition between the political (*le politique*) and politics (*la politique*) see my discussion in the introduction above.

8   Derrida, *Specters of Marx*, 170.

9   Heidegger, "The Word of Nietzsche," in *The Question Concerning Technology and Other Essays*, translated by William Lovitt (New York: Harper and Row, 1977), 61; Jacques Lacan, *Télévision* (Paris: Seuil, 1974), 26; in English: *Television: A Challenge to the Psychoanalytic Establishment*, translated by Denis Hollier, Rosalind Krauss, and Annette Michelson (New York: W. W. Norton, 1990), 16.

10 Martin Heidegger, "The Overcoming of Metaphysics," in *The End of Philosophy*, translated by Joan Stambaugh (New York: Harper and Row, 1973), 102.

11 Martin Heidegger, "Only a God Can Save Us," in *The Heidegger Controversy*, edited by Richard Wolin (Cambridge: MIT Press, 1993), 104. Despite commenting on this and other comparable passages, in which the destruction of metaphysics bespeaks a necessary ignorance as to its political consequences, Reiner Schürmann nonetheless puts forth the hypothesis that direct democracy would come closest to the postmetaphysical notion of being as presencing. See Schürmann, *Heidegger on Being and Acting: From Principles to Anarchy*, translated by Christine Marie-Gros (Bloomington: Indiana University Press, 1990), 290.

12 Jacques Lacan, "Conférences et entretiens dans les universités nord-américaines," *Scilicet* 6–7 (1975): 37.

13 Lacan, *Écrits*, 182. For an excellent analysis of this and some of the following statements by Lacan see Peter Starr's "The Tragic Ear of the Intellectual: Lacan," in Peter Starr, *Logics of Failed Revolt: French Theory after May '68* (Stanford: Stanford University Press, 1995), 37–76.

14 See Philippe Lacoue-Labarthe, "La Transcendance finit dans la politique," in Lacoue-Labarthe and Nancy, *Rejouer le politique*, 171–214; in English: "Transcendence Ends in Politics," in Philippe Lacoue-Labarthe, *Typography*, translated by Christopher Fynsk (Palo Alto: Stanford University Press, 1989), 267–300.

15 Jacques Lacan, "Analyticon," in *Le Séminaire de Jacques Lacan*, edited by Jacques Alain Miller, *Livre XVII: L'Envers de la psychanalyse*, 239; *The Seminar of Jacques Lacan*, edited by Jacques-Alain Miller, *Book XVII: The Other Side of Psychoanalysis*, translated by Russell Grigg, 207.

16 Reiner Schürmann, "Que faire à la fin de la métaphysique?" in *Cahier de l'Herne Heidegger* (Paris: L'Herne, 1983), 452.

17 Jean-Claude Milner, *L'Œuvre claire: Lacan, la science, la philosophie* (Paris: Seuil, 1995), 150–51.

18 Schürmann, "Que faire à la fin de la métaphysique?", 453.

19 Dominique Janicaud, "Face à la domination: Heidegger, le marxisme et l'écologie," in *Cahier de l'Herne Heidegger*, 478.

20 Claude Lefort, "La question de la démocratie," in Lacoue-Labarthe and Nancy, *Le Retrait du politique*, 80.

21 Žižek, *The Sublime Object of Ideology*, 147; see also Stavrakakis, *Lacan and the Political*. In more recent books of his, frequently in a frontal, if not *ad hominem*, attack on Laclau and Stavrakakis, Žižek turns completely against this argument in favor of radical democracy, for example by disinviting "the usual gang of democracy-to-come-deconstructionist-postsecular-Levinasian-respect-for-Otherness suspects" (*The Parallax View*, 12).

22 Chantal Mouffe, "Radical Democracy: Modern or Postmodern?" in *The Return of the Political* (London: Verso, 1993), 11–12.

23 Schürmann, *Heidegger on Being and Acting*, 6.

24 Rancière, *Aux bords du politique*, 84.

25 See Derrida, *Specters of Marx*, passim; and Ernesto Laclau, "The Time Is Out of Joint," in *Emancipation(s)* (London: Verso, 1996), 67–83.

26 For the politics of the improper and the impolitical or unpolitical see especially Esposito, *Categorie dell'impolitico*; and Roberto Esposito, ed., *Oltre la politica: Antologia del pensiero "impolitico"* (Milan: Mondadori, 1996). I discuss this argument in Bosteels, "Politics, Infrapolitics, and the Impolitical."

27 See my discussion in chapter 2.

28 Roberto Esposito, "Democrazia," in *Nove pensieri sulla politica* (Bologna: Il Mulino, 1993), 58.

29 Ibid., 53, 49.

30 For this argument see also Badiou, *Saint Paul*, 5–16; 8–15.

31 Žižek, *The Sublime Object of Ideology*, 148.

32 Ibid., 5.

33 Esposito, *Nove pensieri sulla politica*, 43.

34 Marc De Kesel, "De schil van de democratie (Over Claude Leforts democratiebegrip)," in *Wij, modernen: Essays over subject & moderniteit* (Leuven: Peeters, 1998), 72.

35 Ibid., 81–82.

36 Jean-François Lyotard, *L'Enthousiasme: La Critique kantienne de l'histoire* (Paris: Galilée, 1986), 70; *Enthusiasm: The Kantian Critique of History*, translated by Georges Van Den Abbeele (Minneapolis: University of Minnesota Press, 2009), 36; and Jean-François Lyotard, *Le Postmoderne expliqué aux enfants* (Paris: Galilée, 1988), 72; *The Postmodern Explained: Correspondence, 1982–1985*, edited by Julian Pefanis and Morgan Thomas (Minneapolis: University of Minnesota Press, 1993), 50–51.

37 De Kesel, "De schil van de democratie (Over Claude Leforts democratiebegrip)," 80.

38 Derrida, *Specters of Marx*, 64–65.

39 De Kesel, "De schil van de democratie (Over Claude Leforts democratiebegrip)," 81.

40 Ludwig Wittgenstein, *Tractatus Logico-Philosophicus*, translated by D. F. Pears and B. F. McGuinness (London: Routledge, 2001), 89 (6.522, 7).

41 Walter Benjamin, "Theses on the Philosophy of History," in *Illuminations: Essays*

and Reflections, translated by Harry Zohn (New York: Schocken, 1968), 261–62 (theses XV and XVI).

42 Alain Badiou, "Silence, solipsisme, sainteté: L'Antiphilosophie de Wittgenstein," *Barca! Poésie, Politique, Psychanalyse* 3 (1994): 17. This text has been revised and published as the first essay in Alain Badiou, *L'Antiphilosophie de Wittgenstein* (Paris: NOUS, 2009).

43 Alain Badiou, *Casser en deux l'histoire du monde?* (Paris: Les Conférences du Perroquet, 1992), 11.

44 These words, quoted from the Spanish political thinker Agapito Maestre, stood as a motto for the conference "El vértigo de la democracia" (The Vertigo of Democracy), where the present chapter was first read in public, in Puebla, Mexico (March 1999).

45 Michel Foucault, "What Is Enlightenment?" translated by Catherine Porter, in *The Foucault Reader* (New York: Vintage, 1984), 47. See also the attempts directly or indirectly to take up part of this task by Gianni Vattimo, "Ontologia dell'attualità," in *Filosofia '87* (Rome: Laterza, 1988), 201–23; and by Fredric Jameson in *A Singular Modernity: Essay on the Ontology of the Present* (London: Verso, 2002).

46 See, in particular, Alain Badiou, "Raisonnement hautement spéculatif sur le concept de démocratie," in *Abrégé de métapolitique,* 89–108; in English: "A Speculative Disquisition on the Concept of Democracy," in *Metapolitics,* 78–95.

47 Badiou, *Conditions,* 247; 173.

48 Jean-Luc Nancy, *La Communauté désœuvrée* (Paris: Christian Bourgois, 1990); in English: *The Inoperative Community,* edited by Peter Connor (Minneapolis: University of Minnesota Press, 1991); Maurice Blanchot, *La Communauté inavouable* (Paris: Minuit, 1984); in English: *The Unavowable Community,* translated by Pierre Joris (Barrytown, N.Y.: Station Hill Press, 1988); Giorgio Agamben, *La comunità che viene* (Turin: Einaudi, 1990); in English: *The Coming Community,* translated by Michael Hardt (Minneapolis: University of Minnesota Press, 1993); Roberto Esposito, *Communitas: Origine e destino della comunità* (Turin: Einaudi, 1998); in English: *Communitas: The Origin and Destiny of Community,* translated by Timothy C. Campbell (Palo Alto: Stanford University Press, 2009). Badiou tackles this rebirth of political philosophy from the notion of "community" in "L'Outrepassement politique du philosophème de la communauté," in *Politique et modernité* (Paris: Osiris, 1992), 55–67.

49 Badiou, *L'Hypothèse communiste,* 196n1; *The Communist Hypothesis,* 249n10.

CONCLUSION

1 Badiou, *D'un désastre obscur: Sur la fin de la vérité d'État* (La Tour d'Aigues: Éditions de l'Aube, 1998), 14; in English: "Philosophy and the 'Death of Communism,'" in Badiou, *Infinite Thought,* 131. Though partial, this English translation is certainly preferable to the complete translation prepared by Barbara P. Fulks for *Lacanian Ink.*

2 Badiou, *De quoi Sarkozy est-il le nom?* 129–30; *The Meaning of Sarkozy*, 97–98.

3 Félix Guattari and Toni Negri, *Communists like Us: New Spaces of Liberty, New Lines of Alliance*, translated by Michael Ryan (New York: Semiotext(e), 1990), 7, 19. Here I should add that the basic argument for this conclusion was formulated and published in *South Atlantic Quarterly* before Badiou published his new books on Sarkozy and *The Communist Hypothesis* for his *Circonstances* series, confirming my underlying argument, and long before he actually gathered many of the thinkers mentioned here—including Toni Negri and Jean-Luc Nancy—for the March 2009 conference "On the Idea of Communism" co-organized with Slavoj Žižek and Costas Douzinas at Birkbeck College. See the proceedings published in French as *L'Idée du communisme*, edited by Alain Badiou and Slavoj Žižek (Paris: Lignes, 2010); and in English as *The Idea of Communism*, edited by Costas Douzinas and Slavoj Žižek (London: Verso, 2010). I develop some of the consequences of the dialectic between speculative leftism and communism in Bosteels, *The Actuality of Communism*.

4 Guattari and Negri, *Communists like Us*, 55.

5 Jean-Luc Nancy and Jean-Christophe Bailly, *La Comparution (politique à venir)* (Paris: Christian Bourgois, 1991), 62; in English: "*La Comparution*/The Compearance: From the Existence of 'Communism' to the Community of 'Existence,'" translated by Tracy B. Strong, *Political Theory* 20, no. 3 (1992): 377.

6 Nancy, *La Communauté désœuvrée*, 177; *The Inoperative Community*, 71 (translation modified).

7 Nancy, *La Comparution*, 100; 393 (translation modified).

8 Badiou, *Théorie du sujet*, 115 (quoted in *La Comparution*, 63n5; 394n5 [translation corrected]).

9 Compare Daniel Cohn-Bendit and Gabriel Cohn-Bendit, *Le Gauchisme, remède à la maladie sénile du communisme* (Paris: Seuil, 1968); in English: *Obsolete Communism: The Left-Wing Alternative*, translated by Arnold Pomerans (New York: McGraw-Hill, 1968); and Lenin's classic *Left-Wing Communism, an Infantile Disorder*, translated by Julius Katzer, in vol. 31 of Lenin's *Collected Works* (Moscow: Progress Publishers, 1964), 17–118.

10 Badiou and Balmès, *De l'idéologie*, 66. Ernesto Laclau early on in his career discusses the hypothesis of communist invariants, which according to him are actually neither communist nor invariant; see Ernesto Laclau, *Politics and Ideology in Marxist Theory: Capitalism, Fascism, Populism* (London: New Left Books, 1977), 167–72. If Laclau finds Badiou and Balmès's argument wanting, though, this can also be explained at least in part by the fact that he seeks to produce an opposition similar to the masses/state opposition, this time in the Gramscian terms of people/power bloc—an opposition that is precisely the target of Badiou and Balmès's criticism of the limits of left-wing communism.

11 Badiou and Balmès, *De l'idéologie*, 67.

12 Ibid.

13 Ibid., 69. Gilles Deleuze and Félix Guattari salute the originality of this dialectic of masses and classes in *A Thousand Plateaus: Capitalism and Schizophrenia*,

translation and foreword by Brian Massumi (Minneapolis: University of Minnesota Press, 1987). Like Laclau, however, they have serious reservations: "But it is difficult to see, first of all, why masses are not themselves historical variables, and second, why the word is applied only to the exploited (the 'peasant-plebeian' mass), when it is also suitable for seigneurial, bourgeois masses, or even monetary masses" (537n20).

14 Badiou and Balmès, *De l'idéologie*, 74.

15 Ibid., 75.

16 Ibid., 96, 79.

17 Ibid., 83.

18 Ibid., 84.

19 Paul Sandevince (pseudonym for Sylvain Lazarus), *Qu'est-ce qu'une politique marxiste?* (Marseille: Potemkine, 1978), 6. This pamphlet was published by the Maoist UCFML, in which both Lazarus and Badiou were active until the early 1980s. See chapter 3 above for more details.

20 Badiou, *Théorie du sujet*, 62; *Theory of the Subject*, 44.

21 UCFML, *Sur le maoïsme et la situation en Chine après la mort de Mao Tsé-Toung*, 3.

22 Badiou, *Théorie du sujet*, 198; *Theory of the Subject*, 182.

23 Ibid.

24 Badiou, *Peut-on penser la politique?*, 56. See also Alberto Toscano, "Marxism Expatriated: Alain Badiou's Turn," in *Critical Companion to Contemporary Marxism*, edited by Jacques Bidet and Stathis Kouvelakis (Leiden: Brill, 2008), 529–48.

25 Badiou, *Peut-on penser la politique?*, 56, 60.

26 Ibid., 55.

27 Ibid., 11.

28 Badiou, *L'Être et l'événement*, 232–33; *Being and Event*, 210. A much earlier use of the expression "speculative leftism" can be found in Rancière, *La Leçon d'Althusser*: "The double Althusserian truth after May 1968 finds itself shattered between two poles: the speculative leftism of the all-powerful ideological apparatuses and the speculative zdanovism of the class struggle in theory, which interrogates each word in order to make it confess its class" (146, see also 110n1, regarding the search for an "absolute beginning" as the sign of an ultraleftist interpretation of the link between Althusserianism and Maoism).

APPENDIX 2: BEYOND FORMALIZATION

1 Badiou is referring here to a singular pantheon composed of Pascal, Rousseau, Mallarmé, and Lacan. See "Généalogie de la dialectique," in *Peut-on penser la politique?*, 84–91.

2 Peter Hallward, *Absolutely Postcolonial: Writing between the Singular and the Specific* (Manchester: Manchester University Press, 2001).

3 Bruno Bosteels, "Vérité et forçage: Badiou avec Heidegger et Lacan," in *Alain Badiou: Penser le multiple*, edited by Charles Ramond (Paris: L'Harmattan, 2002), 259–93. This article has been reworked into chapter 5 above.

SELECTED BIBLIOGRAPHY

Adorno, Theodor W. *Hegel: Three Studies*. Translated by Shierry Weber Nicholson. Cambridge: MIT Press, 1993.

———. *Negative Dialectics*. Translated by E. B. Ashton. New York: Continuum, 1990.

Agamben, Giorgio. *La comunità che viene*. Turin: Einaudi, 1990. Translated by Michael Hardt as *The Coming Community* (Minneapolis: University of Minnesota Press, 1993).

———. *Potentialities: Collected Essays in Philosophy*. Translated by Daniel Heller-Roazen. Stanford: Stanford University Press, 1999.

Althusser, Louis. "À propos de l'article de Michel Verret sur *Mai étudiant*." *La Pensée* 145 (June 1969): 3–14.

———. *Écrits philosophiques et politiques*. 2 vols. Edited by François Matheron. Paris: Stock/IMEC, 1994.

———. *Écrits sur la psychanalyse*. Edited by Olivier Corpet and François Matheron. Paris: Stock/IMEC, 1993. *Writings on Psychoanalysis: Freud and Lacan*. Edited by Olivier Corpet and François Matheron. Translated by Jeffrey Mehlman. New York: Columbia University Press, 1996.

———. *Éléments d'autocritique*. Paris: Hachette, 1974. Translated by Grahame Lock as *Essays in Self-Criticism* (New York: NLB, 1976).

———. *Filosofía y marxismo: Entrevista por Fernanda Navarro*. Mexico: Siglo Veintiuno, 1988.

———. *The Humanist Controversy and Other Writings*. Edited by François Matheron. Translated by G. M. Goshgarian. London: Verso, 2006.

———. *Lénine et la philosophie*. Paris: François Maspero, 1969. Translated by Ben Brewster as *Lenin and Philosophy and Other Essays* (New York: Monthly Review Press, 1971).

———. *Lettres à Franca (1961–1973)*. Paris: Stock/IMEC, 1998.

———. *Philosophy of the Encounter: Later Writings, 1978–1987*. Edited by François Matheron and Oliver Corpet. Translated by G. M. Goshgarian. London: Verso, 2006.

———. *Pour Marx*. Paris: Maspero, 1965; Paris: La Découverte, 1986. Translated by Ben Brewster as *For Marx* (London: Verso, 1969).

——. "Problèmes étudiants." *La Nouvelle Critique* 152 (Jan. 1964): 80–111.

Althusser, Louis, and Alain Badiou. *Materialismo histórico y materialismo dialéctico.* Translated by Nora Rosenfeld de Pasternac, José Arico, and Santiago Funes. Mexico: Pasado y Presente, 1969.

Anonymous. "Le Mode dialectique." *La Distance Politique* 3 (May 1992): 4–6. Translated by Bruno Bosteels as "The Dialectical mode," in "Alain Badiou and Cultural Revolution." Special issue, *positions: east asia cultures critique* 13, no. 3 (2005): 663–68.

Avenas, Denise, et al. *Contre Althusser, pour Marx.* Exp. edn. Paris: Passion, 1999.

Badiou, Alain. *Abrégé de métapolitique.* Paris: Seuil, 1998. Translated by Jason Barker as *Metapolitics* (London: Verso, 2005).

——. "Angoisse chez Lacan." In *Agenda de la pensée contemporaine: Printemps 2005,* 27–29. Paris: PUF, 2005. Translated by Barbara P. Fulks as "Lacan. Seminar, Book X: Anxiety." *Lacanian Ink* 26 (2005): 70–71.

——."A propos du 'et' entre être et événement." In *Écrits autour de la pensée d'Alain Badiou,* edited by Bruno Besana and Olivier Feltham, 103–4. Paris: L'Harmattan, 2007.

——. *Beckett: L'Increvable désir.* Paris: Hachette, 1995. Translated by Alberto Toscano as *On Beckett.* Edited by Alberto Toscano and Nina Power (London: Clinamen, 2003).

——. "Beyond Formalisation: An Interview." By Bruno Bosteels and Peter Hallward. *Angelaki: Journal of the Theoretical Humanities* 8, no. 2 (Aug. 2003): 111–36.

——. *Casser en deux l'histoire du monde?* Paris: Les Conférences du Perroquet, 1992.

——. "Ciclo de Conferencias en Buenos Aires, Abril-Mayo 2000." Special issue, *Acontecimiento: Revista para pensar la política* 19–20 (2000).

——. *Circonstances, 2: Irak, foulard, Allemagne/France.* Paris: Éditions Lignes et Manifestes, 2004.

——. *Conditions.* Paris: Seuil, 1992. Translated by Steven Corcoran as *Conditions* (London: Continuum, 2009).

——. *Court traité d'ontologie transitoire.* Paris: Seuil, 1998. Translated by Norman Madarasz as *Briefings on Existence: A Short Treatise on Transitory Ontology* (Albany: State University of New York Press, 2006).

——. *Deleuze: "La Clameur de l'être."* Paris: Hachette, 1997. Translated by Louise Burchill as *Deleuze: The Clamor of Being* (Minneapolis: University of Minnesota Press, 2000).

——. "Democratic Materialism and the Materialist Dialectic." Translated by Alberto Toscano. *Radical Philosophy* 130 (2005): 20–24.

——. *De quoi Sarkozy est-il le nom? Circonstances, 4.* Paris: Lignes, 2007. Translated by David Fernbach as *The Meaning of Sarkozy* (London: Verso, 2008).

——. *D'un désastre obscur (Droit, État, Politique).* La Tour d'Aigues: Éditions de l'Aube, 1991; new edition with the subtitle *Sur la fin de la vérité d'État* (La Tour d'Aigues: Éditions de l'Aube, 1998). Translated by Barbara P. Fulks as "Of an Obscure Disaster: On the End of the Truth of the State." *Lacanian Ink* 22 (2003): 58–89.

——. *El ser y el acontecimiento*. Translated by Raúl J. Cerdeiras, Alejandro A. Cerletti, and Nilda Prados. Buenos Aires: Manantial, 1999.

——. *Infinite Thought: Truth and the Return of Philosophy*. Translated and edited by Oliver Feltham and Justin Clemens. London: Continuum, 2003.

——. "La Figure du (re)commencement." *Le Perroquet* 42 (1984): 1, 8–9.

——. "L'Âge des poètes." In Rancière, *La Politique des poètes*, 21–63.

——. *L'Antiphilosophie de Wittgenstein*. Paris: NOUS, 2009.

——. *La Révolution Culturelle: La Dernière révolution?* Paris: Les Conférences du Rouge-Gorge, 2002.

——. "L'Autonomie du processus esthétique." *Cahiers Marxistes-Léninistes* 12–13 (1966): 77–89.

——. "Le Flux et le parti (dans les marges de l'*Anti-Œdipe*)." In *La Situation actuelle sur le front de la philosophie*, 31–32. Paris: François Maspero, 1977. Translated by Laura Balladur and Simon Krysl as "The Flux and the Party: In the Margins of Anti-Oedipus." In "Immanence, Transcendence, and Utopia," edited by Marta Hernández Salván and Juan Carlos Rodríguez. Special issue, *Polygraph: An International Journal of Culture & Politics* 15–16 (2004): 75–92.

——. *Le Nombre et les nombres*. Paris: Seuil, 1990. Translated by Robin Mackay as *Number and Numbers* (Cambridge: Polity, 2008).

——. "L'Entretien de Bruxelles." *Les Temps Modernes* 526 (1990): 1–26.

——. "Le (Re)commencement du matérialisme dialectique." *Critique* 240 (1967): 438–67.

——. *Le Siècle*. Paris: Seuil, 2005. Translated by Alberto Toscano as *The Century* (Cambridge: Polity, 2007).

——. *L'Éthique: Essai sur la conscience du mal* (Paris: Hatier, 1993). Translated by Peter Hallward as *Ethics: An Essay on the Understanding of Evil* (London: Verso, 2001).

——. *L'Être et l'événement*. Paris: Seuil, 1988. Translated by Oliver Feltham as *Being and Event* (London: Continuum, 2005).

——. *L'Hypothèse communiste: Circonstances, 5*. Paris: Nouvelles Éditions Lignes, 2009. Translated by David Macey and Steve Corcoran as *The Communist Hypothesis* (London: Verso, 2010).

——. "L'Investigation transcendantale." In Charles Ramond, *Alain Badiou: Penser le multiple*, 7–18.

——. *Logiques des mondes: L'Être et l'événement, 2*. Paris: Seuil, 2006. Translated by Alberto Toscano as *Logics of Worlds: Being and Event, 2*. (London: Continuum, 2009).

——. "L'Outrepassement politique du philosophème de la communauté." *Politique et modernité*. Paris: Osiris, 1992.

——. "L'Usine comme site événementiel." *Le Perroquet* 62–63 (April 22–May 10, 1986): 1, 4–6.

——. *Manifeste pour la philosophie*. Paris: Seuil, 1989. Translated by Norman Madarasz as *Manifesto for Philosophy* (Albany: State University of New York Press, 1999).

———. "Mathématiques et philosophie." *Failles* 2 (2006): 42–61. Translated by Ray Brassier and Alberto Toscano as "Mathematics and Philosophy," in Badiou, *Theoretical Writings*, 3–20.

———. *Para uma nova teoria do sujeito: Conferências brasileiras.* Translated by Emerson Xavier da Silva and Gilda Sodré. Edited by Ari Roitman and Paulo Becker. Rio de Janeiro: Relume-Dumará, 1994.

———. *Petit panthéon portatif.* Paris: La Fabrique, 2008. Translated by David Macey as *Pocket Pantheon: Figures of Postwar Philosophy* (London: Verso, 2009).

———. *Peut-on penser la politique?* Paris: Seuil, 1985.

———. *Polemics.* Translated by Steve Corcoran. London: Verso, 2006.

———. "Qu'est-ce que Louis Althusser entend par 'philosophie'?" In *Politique et philosophie dans l'œuvre de Louis Althusser*, edited by Sylvain Lazarus, 29–45. Paris: PUF, 1993.

———. *Rhapsodie pour le théâtre.* Paris: Imprimerie Nationale, 1990. Translated by Bruno Bosteels as "Rhapsody for the Theatre: A Short Philosophical Treatise," in *Theatre Survey* 49, no. 2 (2008): 187–238.

———. "Roads to Renegacy: Interview by Eric Hazan." Translated by David Fernbach. *New Left Review* 53 (Sept.–Oct. 2008): 125–33.

———. *Saint Paul: La fondation de l'universalisme.* Paris: PUF, 1997. Translated by Ray Brassier as *Saint Paul: The Foundation of Universalism* (Stanford: Stanford University Press, 2003).

———. *Second manifeste pour la philosophie.* Paris: Fayard, 2009.

———. "Silence, solipsisme, sainteté: L'Antiphilosophie de Wittgenstein." *Barca! Poésie, Politique, Psychanalyse* 3 (1994): 13–53.

———. *Theoretical Writings.* Edited and translated by Ray Brassier and Alberto Toscano. London: Continuum, 2006.

———. "Théorie axiomatique du sujet (Notes du cours 1996–1998)." Typescript.

———. *Théorie de la contradiction.* Paris: François Maspero, 1975.

———. *Théorie du sujet.* Paris: Seuil, 1982. Translated by Bruno Bosteels as *Theory of the Subject* (London: Continuum, 2009).

Badiou, Alain, and François Balmès. *De l'idéologie.* Paris: François Maspero, 1976.

Badiou, Alain, Joël Bellassen, and Louis Mossot. *Le Noyau rationnel de la dialectique hégélienne: Traductions, introductions et commentaires autour d'un texte de Zhang Shiying, Pékin, 1972.* Paris: François Maspero, 1978.

Balibar, Étienne. "Avant-propos pour la réédition de 1996." In Althusser, *Pour Marx*, i–xiv. Paris: La Découverte, 1996.

———. *Écrits pour Althusser.* Paris: La Découverte, 1991.

———. " 'Histoire de la vérité': Alain Badiou dans la philosophie française." In Charles Ramond, *Alain Badiou: Penser le multiple*, 497–523. Translated by David Macey as "The History of Truth: Alain Badiou in French Philosophy." In Hallward, *Think Again*, 21–38.

Barker, Jason. *Alain Badiou: A Critical Introduction.* London: Pluto, 2002.

———. "De l'État au maître: Badiou et le post-marxisme." In *Écrits autour de la pensée d'Alain Badiou*, edited by Bruno Besana and Olivier Feltham, 187–93. Paris: L'Harmattan,2007.

Bar-On, Tamir. *Where Have All the Fascists Gone?* Aldershot, UK: Ashgate, 2007.

Belden Fields, A. *Trotskyism and Maoism: Theory and Practice in France and the United States.* New York: Praeger, 1988.

Benjamin, Walter. *The Arcades Project.* Translated by Howard Eiland and Kevin McLaughlin. Edited by Rolf Tiedemann. Cambridge: Belknap, 1999.

——. *Illuminations: Essays and Reflections.* Translated by Harry Zohn. New York: Schocken, 1968.

Benoist, Alain de. *Vu de droite: Anthologie des idées contemporaines.* Paris: Copernic, 1978.

Bensaïd, Daniel. "Alain Badiou and the Miracle of the Event." In Hallward, *Think Again*, 94–105.

Blanchot, Maurice. *La Communauté inavouable.* Paris: Minuit, 1984. Translated by Pierre Joris as *The Unavowable Community* (Barrytown, N.Y.: Station Hill Press, 1988).

Borradori, Giovanna. *Philosophy in a Time of Terror: Dialogues with Jürgen Habermas and Jacques Derrida.* Chicago: University of Chicago Press, 2003.

Bosteels, Bruno. "Afterword: Being, Thinking, Acting, or, On the Uses and Disadvantages of Ontology for Politics." In *A Leftist Ontology: Beyond Relativism and Identity Politics*, edited by Carsten Strathausen, 235–51. Minneapolis: University of Minnesota Press, 2009.

——. "Alain Badiou's Theory of the Subject: The Re-commencement of Dialectical Materialism?" *Pli: The Warwick Journal of Philosophy* 12 (2001): 200–229; and 13 (2002): 173–208.

——. "Archipolitics, Parapolitics, Metapolitics." In *Jacques Rancière: Key Concepts*, edited by Jean-Philippe Deranty, 80–92. London: Acumen, 2010.

——. "Badiou without Žižek." In "The Philosophy of Alain Badiou," edited by Matthew Wilkens. Special issue of *Polygraph: An International Journal of Culture & Politics* 17 (2005): 223–46.

——. "Can Change Be Thought? A Dialogue with Alain Badiou." In *Alain Badiou: Philosophy and Its Conditions*, edited by Gabriel Riera, 237–61. Albany: State University of New York Press, 2005.

——. "Hegel." In *Alain Badiou: Key Concepts*, edited by Justin Clemens and A. J. Bartlett, 137–45. London: Acumen, 2010.

——. "The Jargon of Finitude, or Materialism Today." *Radical Philosophy* 155 (April 2009): 41–47.

——. "La Leçon de Rancière: Malaise dans la politique ou on a raison de se mésentendre." In *La Philosophie déplacée: Autour de Jacques Rancière*, edited by Laurence Cornu and Patrice Vermeren, 49–70. Lyon: Horlieu, 2006.

——. "The Leftist Hypothesis: Communism in the Age of Terror." In *The Idea of Communism*, edited by Costas Douzinas and Slavoj Žižek, 33–66. London: Verso, 2010.

——. "Logics of Antagonism: In the Margins of Alain Badiou's 'The Flux and the

Party.'" In "Immanence, Transcendence, and Utopia," edited by Marta Hernández Salván and Juan Carlos Rodríguez. Special issue, *Polygraph: An International Journal of Culture & Politics* 15–16 (2004): 93–107.

——. "Nonplaces: An Anecdoted Topography of Contemporary French Theory." In "New Coordinates: Spatial Mappings, National Trajectories," edited by Bob Davidson and Joan Ramon Resina. Special issue, *diacritics* 33, nos. 3–4 (2003): 117–39.

——. "On the Subject of the Dialectic." In Hallward, *Think Again*, 150–64.

——. "Politics, Infrapolitics, and the Impolitical: Notes on the Thought of Roberto Esposito and Alberto Moreiras." *CR: The New Centennial Review* 10, no. 2 (2010): 205–38.

——. "Radical Antiphilosophy." *Filozofski Vestnik* 29, no. 2 (2009): 155–87.

——. "Rancière's Leftism, or, Politics and Its Discontents." In *Jacques Rancière: History, Politics, Aesthetics*, edited by Gabriel Rockhill and Philip Watts, 158–75. Durham: Duke University Press, 2009.

——. "Travesías del fantasma: Pequeña metapolítica del 68 en México." *Metapolítica* 12 (1999): 733–68. Translated as "The Melancholy Left: Specters of 1968 in Mexico and Beyond." In *(1968) Episodes of Culture in Contest*, edited by Cathy Crane and Nicholas Muellner, 74–90. Cambridge: Cambridge Scholars Publishing, 2008.

——. "Vérité et forçage: Badiou avec Heidegger et Lacan." In Charles Ramond, *Alain Badiou: Penser le multiple*, 259–93.

Bourseiller, Christophe. *Les Maoïstes: La Folle histoire des gardes rouges français.* Paris: Plon, 1996.

Brohm, Jean-Marie. "La Réception d'Althusser: Histoire politique d'une imposture." In Denise Avenas et al., *Contre Althusser, pour Marx*, 278–87.

Buela, Alberto. *Ensayos de disenso (sobre metapolítica).* Barcelona: Nueva República, 1999.

——. *Metapolítica y filosofía.* Buenos Aires: Theoría, 2002.

Butler, Judith. *Antigone's Claim: Kinship between Life and Death.* New York: Columbia University Press, 2000.

——. *The Psychic Life of Power: Theories in Subjection.* Stanford: Stanford University Press, 1997.

——. *Subjects of Desire: Hegelian Reflections in Twentieth-Century France.* New York: Columbia University Press, 1999.

Calcagno, Antonio. *Badiou and Derrida: Politics, Events and Their Time.* London: Continuum, 2007.

Chaplin Matheson, Tamara. "Embodying the Mind, Producing the Nation: Philosophy on French Television." *Journal of the History of Ideas* 67, no. 2 (2006): 315–41.

Châtelet, Gilles. Review of *Le Nombre et les nombres*, by Alain Badiou. In *Annuaire philosophique, 1989–1990*, edited by François Wahl, 200–229. Paris: Seuil, 1991.

Clemens, Justin. "Had we but worlds enough, and time, this absolute, philosopher . . . !" In *The Praxis of Alain Badiou*, edited by Paul Ashton, A. J. Bartlett, and Justin Clemens, 102–43. Melbourne: re.press, 2007.

Cohn-Bendit, Daniel, and Gabriel Cohn-Bendit. *Le Gauchisme, remède à la maladie sénile du communisme*. Paris: Seuil, 1968. Translated by Arnold Pomerans as *Obsolete Communism: The Left-Wing Alternative* (New York: McGraw-Hill, 1968).

Croce, Benedetto. "In qual senso la libertà sia un concetto metapolitico." *Pagine sparse*. Vol. 2, 411–13. Naples: Ricciardi, 1941.

dal Lago, Alessandro, and Pier Aldo Rovatti. *Elogio del pudore: Per un pensiero debole*. Milan: Feltrinelli, 1989.

Debord, Guy. *The Society of the Spectacle*. Translated by Donald Nicholson-Smith. Cambridge: MIT Press, 1995.

De Kesel, Marc. *Eros & Ethiek: Een lectuur van Jacques Lacans Séminaire VII*. Leuven: Acco, 2002.

———. *Wij, modernen: Essays over subject & moderniteit*. Leuven: Peeters, 1998.

Deleuze, Gilles. "Á quoi reconnaît-on le structuralisme?" In *La Philosophie au XXe siècle*, edited by François Châtelet. Paris: Hachette, 1973; repr., Bruxelles: Marabout, 1979. 292–329. Translated by Michael Taormina as "How Do We Recognize Structuralism?" In *Desert Islands and Other Texts, 1953–1974*, edited by David Lapoujade, 175–92 (New York: Semiotext(e), 2004).

———. *Foucault*. Paris: Minuit, 1986. Translated by Seán Handt as *Foucault* (Minneapolis: University of Minnesota Press, 1988).

———. *Pourparlers, 1972–1990*. Paris: Minuit, 1990. Translated by Martin Joughin as *Negotiations* (New York: Columbia University Press, 1995).

Deleuze, Gilles, and Félix Guattari. *A Thousand Plateaus: Capitalism and Schizophrenia*. Translated by Brian Massumi. Minneapolis: University of Minnesota Press, 1987.

———. *What Is Philosophy?* Translated by Hugh Tomlinson and Graham Burchell. New York: Columbia University Press, 1994.

Derrida, Jacques. "A Certain Impossible Possibility of Saying the Event." In *The Late Derrida*, edited by W. J. T. Mitchell and Arnold I. Davidson, 223–43. Chicago: University of Chicago Press, 2007.

———. *Force de loi*. Paris: Galilée, 1994. Translated by Mary Quaintance as "Force of Law: The 'Mystical Foundation of Authority.'" In *Acts of Religion*, edited by Gil Anidjar, 230–98 (New York: Routledge, 2002).

———. *Politiques de l'amitié*. Paris: Galilée, 1994. Translated by George Collins as *Politics of Friendship* (London: Verso, 1997).

———. *Spectres de Marx. L'État de la dette, le travail du deuil et la nouvelle Internationale*. Paris: Galilée, 1993. Translated by Peggy Kamuf as *Specters of Marx: The State of the Debt, the Work of Mourning, and the New International* (New York: Routledge, 1994).

Derrida, Jacques, and Alain Minc. "Penser ce qui vient." *Le Nouveau Monde* 92 (1994): 91–110. Reprinted in *Derrida pour les temps à venir*, edited by René Major, 17–62. Paris: Stock, 2007.

Desanti, Jean-Toussaint. "Some Remarks on the Intrinsic Ontology of Alain Badiou." Translated by Ray Brassier. In Hallward, *Think Again*, 59–66.

Dolar, Mladen. "Beyond Interpellation." *Qui Parle* 6, no. 2 (1993): 73–96.

Elliott, Gregory. *Althusser: The Detour of Theory*. London: Verso, 1987.
——. "Ghostlier Demarcations: On the Posthumous Edition of Althusser's Writings." *Radical Philosophy* 90 (1998): 20–32.
Esposito, Roberto. *Categorie dell'impolitico*. 2nd edn. Bologna: Il Mulino, 1999.
——. *Communitas: Origine e destino della comunità*. Turin: Einaudi, 1998. Translated by Timothy C. Campbell as *Communitas: The Origin and Destiny of Community* (Palo Alto: Stanford University Press, 2009).
——. *L'Origine della politica: Hannah Arendt o Simone Weil?* Rome: Donzelli, 1996.
——. *Nove pensieri sulla politica*. Bologna: Il Mulino, 1993.
——, ed. *Oltre la politica: Antologia del pensiero "impolitico."* Milan: Mondadori, 1996.
Fink, Bruce. *The Lacanian Subject: Between Language and Jouissance*. Princeton: Princeton University Press, 1995.
Foucault, Michel. "La Pensée du dehors." *Critique* 229 (1966): 523–46. Translated by Brian Massumi as *Maurice Blanchot: The Thought from Outside* (New York: Zone Books, 1987).
——. *L'Archéologie du savoir*. Paris: Gallimard, 1969. Translated by A. M. Sheridan Smith as *The Archaeology of Knowledge and The Discourse on Language* (New York: Pantheon, 1972).
——. *Les Mots et les choses: Une archéologie des sciences humaines*. Paris: Gallimard, 1966. Translated as *The Order of Things: An Archaeology of the Human Sciences* (New York: Vintage, 1973).
——. "Nietzsche, Genealogy, History." In *Language, Counter-memory, Practice: Selected Essays and Interviews*, edited by Donald F. Bouchard, 139–64. Ithaca: Cornell University Press, 1977.
——. "Philosophie et psychologie." In *Dits et écrits, 1954–1988*, edited by Daniel Defert and François Ewald. Vol. 1, 438–48. Paris: Gallimard, 1994. Translated by Robert Hurley as "Philosophy and Psychology." In *The Essential Works of Foucault, 1954–1984*. Vol. 2, *Aesthetics, Method, and Epistemology*, edited by James D. Faubion, 249–60 (New York: New Press, 1998).
——. "Réponse au Cercle d'Épistémologie." *Cahiers pour l'analyse* 9 (1968): 9–40. Translated as "On the Archaeology of the Human Sciences: Response to the Epistemology Circle." In *The Essential Works of Foucault, 1954–1984*. Vol. 2, *Aesthetics, Method, and Epistemology*, edited by James D. Faubion, 279–96 (New York: New Press, 1998).
Fraser, Zachary. "The Law of the Subject: Alain Badiou, Luitzen Brouwer and the Kripkean Analyses of Forcing and the Heyting Calculus." In *The Praxis of Alain Badiou*, edited by Paul Ashton, A. J. Bartlett, and Justin Clemens, 23–70. Melbourne: re.press, 2007.
Gillespie, Sam. "Hegel Unsutured (An Addendum to Badiou)." *Umbr(a)* 1 (1996): 57–69.
——. *The Mathematics of Novelty: Badiou's Minimalist Metaphysics*. Melbourne: re.press, 2008.
Glucksmann, André. *La Cuisinière et le mangeur d'hommes*. Paris: Seuil, 1975.

Guattari, Félix, and Antonio Negri. *Communists like Us: New Spaces of Liberty, New Lines of Alliance*. Translated by Michael Ryan. New York: Semiotext(e), 1990.

Hallward, Peter. *Absolutely Postcolonial: Writing between the Singular and the Specific*. Manchester: Manchester University Press, 2001.

———. *Badiou: A Subject to Truth*. Minneapolis: University of Minnesota Press, 2003.

———. "Generic Sovereignty: The Philosophy of Alain Badiou." *Angelaki: Journal of the Theoretical Humanities* 3, no. 3 (1998): 87–111.

———, ed. *Think Again: Alain Badiou and the Future of Philosophy*. London: Continuum, 2004.

Hardt, Michael, and Antonio Negri. *Empire*. Cambridge: Harvard University Press, 2000.

Heidegger, Martin. *The End of Philosophy*. Translated by Joan Stambaugh. New York: Harper and Row, 1973.

———. *Kant and the Problem of Metaphysics*. Translated by Richard Taft. Bloomington: Indiana University Press, 1997.

———. *Nietzsche*. 4 vols. Translated by David Farell Krell. San Francisco: Harper and Row, 1991.

———. "Only a God Can Save Us." In *The Heidegger Controversy*, edited by Richard Wolin, 91–116. Cambridge: MIT Press, 1993.

———. *Poetry, Language, Thought*. Translated by Albert Hofstadter. New York: Harper and Row, 1971.

———. *The Question Concerning Technology and Other Essays*. Translated by William Lovitt. New York: Harper and Row, 1977.

Hess, Rémi. *Les Maoïstes français: Une dérive institutionnelle*. Paris: Anthropos, 1974.

Hewlett, Nick. *Badiou, Balibar, Rancière: Rethinking Emancipation*. London: Continuum, 2007.

Hölderlin, Friedrich. *Essays and Letters on Theory*. Edited and translated by Thomas Pfau. Albany: State University of New York Press, 1988.

Jameson, Fredric. *A Singular Modernity: Essay on the Ontology of the Present*. London: Verso, 2002.

Janicaud, Dominique. "Face à la domination: Heidegger, le marxisme et l'écologie." In *Cahier de l'Herne Heidegger*. Paris: L'Herne, 1983.

Johnston, Adrian. *Badiou, Žižek, and Political Transformations: The Cadence of Change*. Evanston: Northwestern University Press, 2009.

———. *Žižek's Ontology: A Transcendental Materialist Theory of Subjectivity*. Evanston: Northwestern University Press, 2008.

Kouvelakis, Stathis. *Philosophy and Revolution: From Kant to Marx*. Translated by G. M. Goshgarian. London: Verso, 2003.

Lacan, Jacques. *Autres écrits*. Paris: Seuil, 2001.

———. *Écrits*. Paris: Seuil, 1966.

———. *Le Séminaire de Jacques Lacan*. Edited by Jacques-Alain Miller. *Livre I: Les Écrits techniques de Freud*. Paris: Seuil, 1975. Translated by John Forrester as *The*

Seminar of Jacques Lacan. Edited by Jacques-Alain Miller. *Book I: Freud's Papers on Technique, 1953–1954* (New York: W. W. Norton, 1988).

———. *Le Séminaire de Jacques Lacan.* Edited by Jacques-Alain Miller. *Livre VII: L'Éthique de la psychanalyse.* Paris: Seuil, 1986. Translated by Dennis Porter as *The Seminar of Jacques Lacan.* Edited by Jacques-Alain Miller. *Book VII: The Ethics of Psychoanalysis* (New York: W. W. Norton, 1992).

———. *Le Séminaire de Jacques Lacan.* Edited by Jacques-Alain Miller. *Livre X: L'Angoisse.* Paris: Seuil, 2004.

———. *Le Séminaire de Jacques Lacan.* Edited by Jacques-Alain Miller. *Livre XI: Les Quatre concepts fondamentaux de la psychanalyse.* Paris: Seuil 1973; Points 1990. Translated by Alan Sheridan as *The Seminar of Jacques Lacan.* Edited by Jacques-Alain Miller. *Book XI: The Four Fundamental Concepts of Psycho-Analysis* (New York: W. W. Norton, 1981).

———. *Le Séminaire de Jacques Lacan.* Edited by Jacques-Alain Miller. *Livre XVII: L'Envers de la psychanalyse.* Paris: Seuil, 1991. Translated by Russell Grigg as *The Seminar of Jacques Lacan.* Edited by Jacques-Alain Miller. *Book XVII: The Other Side of Psychoanalysis* (New York: W. W. Norton, 2007).

———. *Le Séminaire de Jacques Lacan.* Edited by Jacques-Alain Miller. *Livre XX: Encore.* Paris: Seuil, 1975. Translated by Bruce Fink as *The Seminar of Jacques Lacan.* Edited by Jacques-Alain Miller. *Book XX: Encore, 1972–1973* (New York: W. W. Norton, 1998).

———. *Télévision.* Paris: Seuil, 1974. Translated by Denis Hollier, Rosalind Krauss, and Annette Michelson as *Television: A Challenge to the Psychoanalytic Establishment* (New York: W. W. Norton, 1990).

Laclau, Ernesto. *Emancipation(s).* London: Verso, 1996.

———. *New Reflections on the Revolution of Our Time.* London: Verso, 1990.

———. *Politics and Ideology in Marxist Theory: Capitalism, Fascism, Populism.* London: New Left Books, 1977.

Laclau, Ernesto, and Chantal Mouffe. *Hegemony and Socialist Strategy: Towards a Radical Democratic Politics.* London: Verso, 1985.

Lacoue-Labarthe, Philippe. "De l'éthique: À propos d'*Antigone*." In *Lacan avec les philosophes,* 19–36. Paris: Albin Michel, 1991.

———. *Heidegger and the Politics of Poetry.* Translated by Jeff Port. Urbana: University of Illinois Press, 2007.

———. *La Fiction du politique.* Paris: Christian Bourgois, 1987.

———. *Métaphrase, suivi de Le théâtre de Hölderlin.* Paris: PUF, 1998.

———. "Poésie, philosophie, politique." In Rancière, *La Politique des poètes,* 39–64.

———. *Typography.* Translated by Christopher Fynsk. Palo Alto: Stanford University Press, 1989.

Lacoue-Labarthe, Philippe, and Jean-Luc Nancy. *Le Mythe nazi.* La Tour d'Aigues: Éditions de l'Aube, 1991.

———. *Le Retrait du politique.* Paris: Galilée, 1983.

———. *Rejouer le politique.* Paris: Galilée, 1981.

———. *Retreating the Political*. Edited and translated by Simon Sparks. New York: Routledge, 1997.

Lardreau, Guy, and Christian Jambet. *L'Ange: Ontologie de la révolution 1. Pour une cynégétique du semblant*. Paris: Bernard Grasset, 1976.

Lazarus, Sylvain. *L'Anthropologie du nom*. Paris: Seuil, 1997.

———. *Chercher ailleurs et autrement: Sur la doctrine des lieux, l'économie, l'effondrement du socialisme*. Paris: Les Conférences du Perroquet, 1992.

Lefebvre, Henri. *L'Idéologie structuraliste*. Paris: Anthropos, 1971.

Lefort, Claude. "La Question de la démocratie." In Lacoue-Labarthe and Nancy, *Le Retrait du politique*, 71–88.

Lenin, Vladimir I. *Collected Works*. 45 Vols. Moscow: Foreign Language Press and Progress Publishers, 1960–70.

———. *Left-Wing Communism, an Infantile Disorder*. Translated by Julius Katzer. *Collected Works*. Vol. 31, 17–118. Moscow: Progress Publishers, 1964.

———. "Once Again on the Trade Unions, the Current Situation, and the Mistakes of Trotsky and Bukharin." *Collected Works*. Vol. 32, 70–107. Moscow: Progress Publishers, 1965.

———. *Philosophical Notebooks*. Translated by Clemens Dutt. Edited by Stewart Smith. *Collected Works*. Vol. 38. Moscow: Progress Publishers, 1961.

———. *The State and Revolution*. *Collected Works*. Vol. 25, 381–492. Moscow: Progress Publishers, 1969.

Lukács, Georg. *History and Class-Consciousness: Studies in Marxist Dialectics*. Translated by Rodney Livingstone. Cambridge: MIT Press, 1972.

Luyn, A. H. van. *Politiek en metapolitiek: Gewetensvol in de Randstad*. Kampen: Kok, 2008.

Lyotard, Jean-François. *L'Enthousiasme: La Critique kantienne de l'histoire*. Paris: Galilée, 1986. Translated by Georges Van Den Abbeele as *Enthusiasm: The Kantian Critique of History* (Minneapolis: University of Minnesota Press, 2009).

———. *Le Postmoderne expliqué aux enfants*. Paris: Galilée, 1988. Translated by Julian Pefanis and Morgan Thomas as *The Postmodern Explained: Correspondence, 1982– 1985* (Minneapolis: University of Minnesota Press, 1993).

Macciocchi, Maria Antonia. *Letters from inside the Italian Communist Party to Louis Althusser*. London: NLB, 1973.

Macherey, Pierre. *Pour une théorie de la production littéraire*. Paris: Maspero, 1966. Translated by Geoffrey Wall as *A Theory of Literary Production* (London: Routledge, 1978).

Madarasz, Norman. "On Alain Badiou's Treatment of Category Theory in View of a Transitory Ontology." In *Alain Badiou: Philosophy and Its Conditions*, edited by Gabriel Riera, 23–43. Albany: State University of New York Press, 2005.

Madison Mount, B. "The Cantorian Revolution: Alain Badiou on the Philosophy of Set Theory." *Polygraph: An International Journal of Culture & Politics* 17 (2005): 41–91.

Maistre, Joseph de. *Essai sur le principe générateur des constitutions politiques et des autres institutions humaines.* Paris: Société Typographique, 1814.

Mao, Zedong. *On Practice and Contradiction.* London: Verso, 2007.

———. *Quotations from Chairman Mao Tsetung.* Beijing: Foreign Languages Press, 1972.

Marchart, Oliver. *Post-foundational Political Thought: Political Difference in Nancy, Lefort, Badiou, and Laclau.* Edinburgh: Edinburgh University Press, 2007.

Marmor, François. *Le Maoïsme: Philosophie et politique.* Paris: PUF, 1976.

Marramao, Giacomo. "Metapolitica." *Laboratorio Politico* 1 (1983): 95–121.

Marx, Karl. "Letters from the *Deutsch-Französische Jahrbücher.*" *Marx/Engels Collected Works.* Vol. 3, 133–45. Moscow: Progress Publishers, 1975.

———. "On the Jewish Question." In *The Portable Karl Marx,* edited by Eugene Kamenka, 96–114. New York: Penguin, 1983.

Marx, Karl, and Friedrich Engels. *The German Ideology.* Edited by C. J. Arthur. New York: International Publishers, 1991.

Matheron, François. "Louis Althusser, or the Impure Purity of the Concept." In *Critical Companion to Contemporary Marxism,* edited by Jacques Bidet and Stathis Kouvélakis, 503–27. Leiden: Brill, 2008.

Mauss, Marcel. *Sociologie et anthropologie.* Paris: PUF, 1950.

Michel, Natacha. "Re-naissance de la philosophie: Entretien avec Alain Badiou: *Théorie du sujet.*" *Le Perroquet: Quinzomadaire d'opinion* 6 (1982): 1, 8–10; and 13–14 (1982): 1, 10–13.

Miller, Adam. *Badiou, Marion and St Paul: Immanent Grace.* London: Continuum, 2008.

Miller, Jacques-Alain. "Action de la structure." *Cahiers pour l'analyse* 9 (1966): 93–105. Translated by Peter Bradley as "Action of the Structure." *The Symptom* 10 (spring 2009).

———. "La Suture (Éléments de la logique du signifiant)." *Cahiers pour l'analyse* 1 (1966): 37–49. Translated by Jacqueline Rose as "Suture (Elements of the Logic of the Signifier)." *Screen* 18, no. 4 (1978): 24–34.

———. "Matrice." *Ornicar?* 4 (1975). Translated by Daniel G. Collins as "Matrix." *Lacanian Ink* 12 (1997): 45–51.

———. *Un Début dans la vie.* Paris: Gallimard, 2002.

Milner, Jean-Claude. *L'Œuvre claire: Lacan, la science, la philosophie.* Paris: Seuil, 1995.

Moreiras, Alberto. *Línea de sombra: El no-sujeto de lo político.* Santiago de Chile: Palinodia, 2006.

Mouffe, Chantal. *The Return of the Political.* London: Verso, 1993.

Nancy, Jean-Luc. *La Communauté désœuvrée.* Paris: Christian Bourgois, 1990. Translated by Peter Connor, Lisa Garbus, Michael Holland, and Simona Sawhney as *The Inoperative Community.* Edited by Peter Connor (Minneapolis: University of Minnesota Press, 1991).

———. *Le Sens du monde.* Paris: Galilée, 1993. Translated by Jeffrey S. Librett as *The Sense of the World* (Minneapolis: University of Minnesota Press, 1997).

Nancy, Jean-Luc, and Jean-Christophe Bailly. *La Comparution (politique à venir)*. Paris: Christian Bourgois, 1991. Translated by Tracy B. Strong as *"La comparution/* The Compearance: From the Existence of 'Communism' to the Community of 'Existence.'"* Political Theory* 20, no. 3 (1992): 371–98.

Negri, Antonio. "La Concezione metapolitica della storia di B. Croce." *Giornale Critico della Filosofia Italiana* 20 (1966): 485–540.

———. "Notes on the Evolution of the Thought of the Later Althusser." In *Postmodern Materialism and the Future of Marxist Theory: Essays in the Althusserian Tradition*, edited by Antonio Callari and David F. Ruccio, 51–68. Hanover: University Press of New England/Wesleyan University Press, 1996.

Panunzio, Silvano. *Metapolitica: La Roma eterna e la nuova Gerusalemme*. Roma: Babuino, 1979.

Peyrol, Georges. "Un Ange est passé." *La Situation actuelle sur le front de la philosophie*. Paris: François Maspero, 1977.

Pluth, Ed. *Signifiers and Acts: Freedom in Lacan's Theory of the Subject*. Albany: State University of New York Press, 2007.

Rabaté, Jean-Michel. "68 + 1: Lacan's *année érotique*." *Parrhesia* 6 (2009): 28–45.

Ramond, Charles, ed. *Alain Badiou: Penser le multiple*. Paris: L'Harmattan, 2002.

———. "Système et traduction chez Alain Badiou." In Charles Ramond, *Alain Badiou: Penser le multiple*, 525–40.

Ramond, Pierre. "Le Matérialisme d'Althusser." In *Althusser philosophe*, edited by Pierre Ramond, 167–79. Paris: PUF, 1997.

Rancière, Jacques. *Aux bords du politique*. Paris: La Fabrique, 1998. Translated by Liz Heron as *On the Shores of Politics* (London: Verso, 1995).

———. *Dissensus: On Politics and Aesthetics*. Translated by Steven Corcoran. London: Continuum, 2010.

———. *La Leçon d'Althusser*. Paris: Gallimard, 1974.

———. *La Mésentente: Politique et philosophie*. Paris: Galilée, 1995. Translated by Julie Rose as *Disagreement: Politics and Philosophy* (Minneapolis: University of Minnesota Press, 1999).

———, ed. *La Politique des poètes: Pourquoi des poètes en temps de détresse?* Paris: Albin Michel, 1992.

———. *Le Philosophe et ses pauvres*. Paris: Fayard, 1983. Translated by John Drury, Corinne Oster, and Andrew Parker as *The Philosopher and His Poor*. Edited by Andrew Parker. Durham: Duke University Press, 2004.

———. *Le Spectateur émancipé*. Paris: La Fabrique, 2008. Translated by Gregory Elliott as *The Emancipated Spectator* (London: Verso, 2009).

———. *Les Scènes du peuple (Les Révoltes Logiques, 1975/1985)*. Lyon: Horlieu, 2003.

———. *Mallarmé: La Politique de la sirène*. Paris: Hachette, 1996.

Riedel, Manfred. *Metaphysik und Metapolitik: Studien zu Aristoteles und zur politischen Sprache der neuzeitlichen Philosophie*. Frankfurt am Main: Suhrkamp, 1975.

Roudinesco, Elisabeth. *Jacques Lacan: Outline of Life, History of a Thought*. New York: Columbia University Press, 1997.

Russo, Alessandro. "The Conclusive Scene: Mao and the Red Guards in July 1968."

In "Alain Badiou and Cultural Revolution." Special issue, *positions: east asia cultures critique* 13, no. 3 (2005): 535–74.

———. "How to Translate 'Cultural Revolution'?" *Inter-Asia Cultural Studies* 7, no. 4 (2006): 673–82.

Salanskis, Jean-Michel. "Les Mathématiques chez x avec x = Alain Badiou." In Charles Ramond, *Alain Badiou: Penser le multiple*, 81–106.

Sandevince, Paul. *Notes de travail sur le post-léninisme*. Paris: Potemkine, 1980.

———. *Qu'est-ce qu'une politique marxiste?* Marseille: Potemkine, 1978.

Schürmann, Reiner. *Heidegger on Being and Acting: From Principles to Anarchy*. Translated by Christine Marie-Gros. Bloomington: Indiana University Press, 1990.

———. "Que faire à la fin de la métaphysique?" In *Cahier de l'Herne Heidegger*. Paris: L'Herne, 1983.

Scceciniarz, Jean-Jacques. "L'Être ou la structure (faire l'ontologie, est-ce dire les mathématiques sans l'opératoire qui les fait exister? Est-ce produire la contemplation des objets?)." In Charles Ramond, *Alain Badiou: Penser le multiple*, 107–47.

Siena, Primo. *La espada de Perseo: Itinerarios metapolíticos*. Santiago: Universidad Gabriela Mistral–Instituto de Cultura Italiana de Chile, 2007.

Smith, Brian Anthony. "The Limits of the Subject in Badiou's *Being and Event*." In *The Praxis of Alain Badiou*, edited by Paul Ashton, A. J. Bartlett, and Justin Clemens, 71–101. Melbourne: re.press, 2007.

Starr, Peter. *Logics of Failed Revolt: French Theory after May '68*. Stanford: Stanford University Press, 1995.

Stavrakakis, Yannis. *Lacan and the Political*. London: Routledge, 1999.

Tarby, Fabien. *La Philosophie d'Alain Badiou*. Paris: L'Harmattan, 2005.

Terray, Emmanuel. *Le Marxisme devant les sociétés "primitives": Deux études*. Paris: François Maspero, 1972.

Torigian, Michael. "The Philosophical Foundations of the French New Right." *Telos* 117 (1999): 6–42.

Toscano, Alberto. "Communism as Separation." In Hallward, *Think Again*, 138–49.

———."Marxism Expatriated: Alain Badiou's Turn." In *Critical Companion to Contemporary Marxism*, edited by Jacques Bidet and Stathis Kouvelakis, 529–48. Leiden: Brill, 2008.

UCFML [Groupe pour la fondation de l'Union des Communistes Français (marxiste-léniniste)]. *La Révolution prolétarienne en France et comment construire le parti de l'époque de la pensée de Mao Tsé-toung*. Paris: François Maspero, 1970.

———. *Le Maoïsme, marxisme de notre temps*. Marseille: Potemkine, 1976.

———. *Première année d'existence d'une organisation maoïste, printemps 1970/printemps 1971*. Paris: François Maspero, 1972.

———. *Questions du maoïsme: De la Chine de la Révolution Culturelle à la Chine des Procès de Pékin*. Marseille: Potemkine, 1981.

———. *Sur le maoïsme et la situation en Chine après la mort de Mao Tsé-Toung*. Marseille: Potemkine, 1976.

——. *Une Étude maoïste: La Situation en Chine et le mouvement dit de "critique de la bande des Quatre."* Marseille: Potemkine, 1977.

Vatter, Miguel E. "Machiavelli after Marx: The Self-Overcoming of Marxism in the Late Althusser." *Theory & Event* 7, no. 4 (2005).

Vattimo, Gianni. *Filosofía, política, religión: Más allá del "pensamiento débil."* Edited by Lluis Alvarez. Oviedo: Nobel, 1996.

——. "Ontologia dell'attualità." *Filosofia '87.* Rome: Laterza, 1988. 201–23.

Vattimo, Gianni, and Pier Aldo Rovatti, eds. *Il pensiero debole.* Milan: Feltrinelli, 1983.

Wittgenstein, Ludwig. *Tractatus Logico-Philosophicus.* Translated by D. F. Pears and B. F. McGuinness. London: Routledge, 2001.

Wolin, Richard. *The Wind from the East: French Intellectuals, the Cultural Revolution, and the Legacy of the 1960s.* Princeton: Princeton University Press, 2010.

Žižek, Slavoj. *For They Know Not What They Do: Enjoyment as a Political Factor.* 2nd edn. London: Verso, 2002.

——. "From Purification to Subtraction: Badiou and the Real." In Hallward, *Think Again*, 165–81.

——. *Ils ne savent pas ce qu'ils font: Le Sinthome idéologique.* Paris: Point Hors Ligne, 1990.

——. *In Defense of Lost Causes.* London: Verso, 2008.

——. *Le Plus sublime des hystériques: Hegel passe.* Paris: Point Hors Ligne, 1988.

——. *The Metastases of Enjoyment: Six Essays on Woman and Causality.* London: Verso, 1994.

——. *Organs without Bodies: On Deleuze and Consequences.* New York: Routledge, 2004.

——. "Psychoanalysis in Post-Marxism: The Case of Alain Badiou." *South Atlantic Quarterly* 97, no. 2 (1998): 235–61.

——. *The Sublime Object of Ideology.* London: Verso, 1989.

——. *The Ticklish Subject: The Absent Centre of Political Ontology.* London: Verso, 1999.

Zourabichvili, François. *Deleuze: Une Philosophie de l'événement.* Paris: PUF, 1994.

Zupančič, Alenka. *Ethics of the Real: Kant, Lacan.* London: Verso, 2000.

——. *The Shortest Shadow: Nietzsche's Philosophy of the Two.* Cambridge: MIT Press, 2003.

INDEX

BRUNO BOSTEELS is a professor of Romance studies at Cornell University. He is the author of several books, including *Alain Badiou, une trajectoire polémique* (2009) and *The Actuality of Communism* (2011). He is the translator of *Theory of the Subject* (2009) and *Wittgenstein's Antiphilosophy* (2011), both by Alain Badiou.

Library of Congress Cataloging-in-Publication Data
Bosteels, Bruno.
Badiou and politics / Bruno Bosteels.
p. cm.—(Post-contemporary interventions)
ISBN 978-0-8223-5058-3 (cloth : alk. paper)
ISBN 978-0-8223-5076-7 (pbk. : alk. paper)
1. Badiou, Alain—Criticism and interpretation.
2. Badiou, Alain—Political and social views.
3. Philosophy, French—20th century.
I. Title.
II. Series: Post-contemporary interventions.
B2430.B274B678   2011
320.092—dc22   2011006308